Christmas 2013

To James

with love

From Mater x

CW01667013

L.S.LOWRY
THE ART AND THE ARTIST

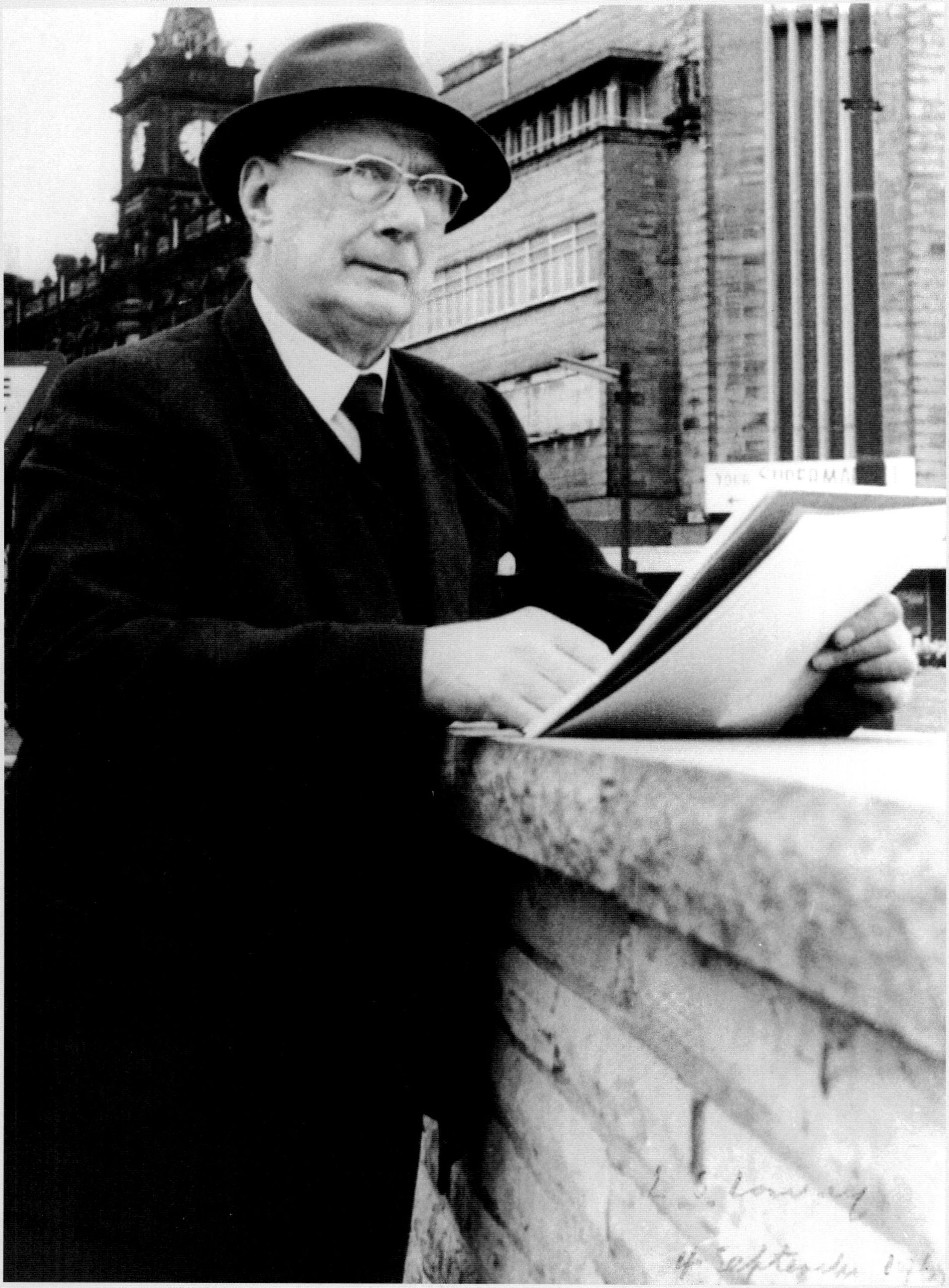

L.S.LOWRY
THE ART AND THE ARTIST

T.G.ROSENTHAL

With 265 illustrations, 205 in colour

Unicorn Press

Publisher's Note
All works of art and quotations from the interviews, letters and other words by L. S. Lowry © the Estate of L. S. Lowry 2010 unless otherwise stated

Measurements are given in centimetres, height before width.

First published in the United Kingdom in 2010
by Unicorn Press, 47 Earlham Road,
Norwich NR2 3AD in association with Bridgewater Press

www.unicornpress.org

British Library Cataloguing in Publication Data
A catalogue record for this book is available from the British Library

ISBN 978 1 906509 06 4 (hardback)
ISBN 978 1 906509 14 9 (paperback)

Designed by Nick Newton

Printed and bound in China for Latitude Press Limited

Frontispiece: Photograph by unknown photographer of Lowry sketching, 1965.

Page 6: Self Portrait, 1925, oil on board, 57.2 × 47.2 cm.

THIS BOOK IS DEDICATED
IN MEMORIAM

LAWRENCE FANE

10 September 1933 – 28 November 2008
Great friend and sculptor

IN FORTUNAM

My grandson Arne who already has a good eye

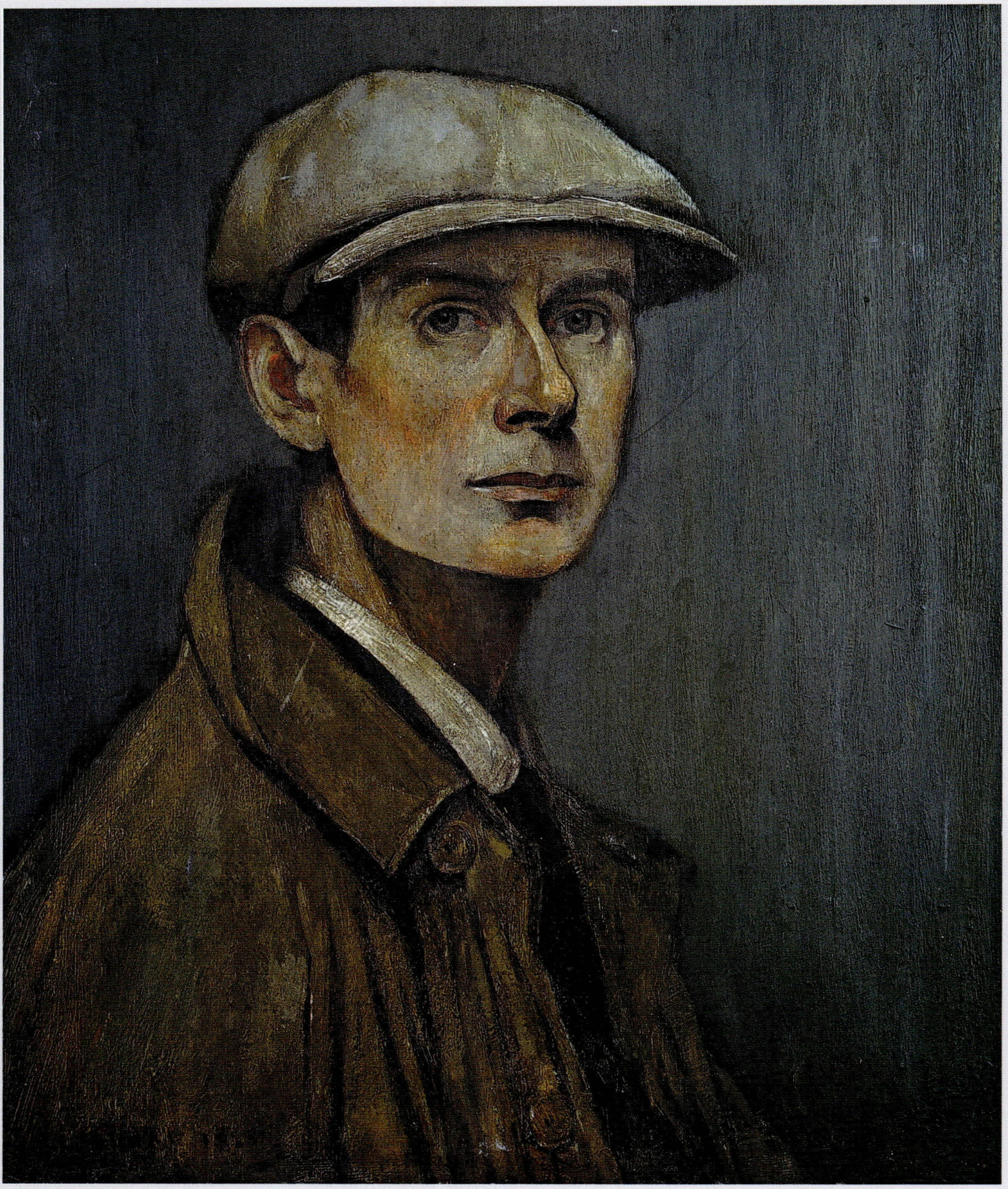

CONTENTS

PREFACE

An author's involvement with a particular artist can take many forms and can be sparked off by any number of circumstances. It might be an eye-opening retrospective; a close friendship; a long academic study; an enthusiasm triggered by an individual teacher. In the case of this book on L. S. Lowry it was – and remains – a more or less osmotic process begun in my childhood more than sixty years ago. My formative years were spent in the so-called Greater Manchester area as it then was. I lived in Manchester but spent many hours exploring on my bicycle not only that city but also Salford, Stockport and many other towns and suburbs which Lowry painted and drew so obsessively. This being largely in wartime, family holidays, sparse as they were, were taken in Lytham St Anne's, and other north-western seaside resorts which were also frequently recorded by Lowry. After my family moved to London I returned frequently to Manchester and its environs to catch up with relations and friends. I remained fascinated by Salford in particular as it had changed beyond recognition, was "urbanly renewed" with largely characterless, merely imposing, office blocks, council estates, little box-like "executive homes" and had put up towering blocks of "luxury flats". Thus, as I became an adult and discovered in my study of art the characteristic paintings of L. S. Lowry, they spoke to me not so much of a vanished world but of an instantly recognisable terrain which gradually disappeared; yet which continued to haunt my imagination.

It was, of course, only as an adult that I began to perceive Lowry's particular genius and, by an odd mixture of coincidence and my profession, that I was lucky enough to meet and spend time with him. These modest encounters are not themselves of any art-historical importance but they are, I believe, of considerable value to those who are interested in Lowry's life and work. They are recorded in this book as part of an enthusiasm that has lasted a lifetime without, I hope, descending into hagiography.

Perhaps this study of Lowry's work needs explaining. It is not written or presented in the form normally used for this kind of book, which begins with the artist's juvenilia and then proceeds chronologically through the entire *œuvre,* or at least that proportion of it for which there is space in a manageable form, until the book ends with the artist's death and an analysis of his last pictures.

For Lowry this method would not be appropriate. If one excludes the juvenilia, which, for a man who had a full-time day job and attended several art schools and had various teachers, extended for at least twenty years, Lowry had only one basic style and only two classic themes: the industrial scenes and, when he grew tired of them, the "grotesques", the studies of individuals or small groups of individuals, who, to put it crudely, were in many ways the inhabitants, the populace of the cityscapes writ large instead of being mere faces in the crowds which so obsessed Lowry. There are many twentieth-century artists of note who regularly changed their themes and styles to cope with changed circumstances, whether personal, financial, marital or their domicile and/or nationality. Lowry was not among them. Once he had discovered the allure and beauty of the industrial landscape he knew so well, he stayed with it and did not even alter his style when he switched from the broad canvases of the city to the more closely-focused studies of the city's inhabitants for the grotesques.

Thus, when he did deviate from this chosen, highly-regulated path to do the occasional portrait, or to express his love of non-industrial landscapes or his fascination with water, be it sea, lake, river, canal or beach, to deal with those subjects as they occurred chronologically within the two big subjects would be, at best, to hold up the narrative and any thesis it might contain and, at worst, to cause confusion for the reader. Which is why there are separate chapters specifically for the sea and for the (mostly) rural landscapes. There are other chapters which do not fit into any conventional pattern because I wanted to illuminate Lowry's character in such a way as to throw more light onto his art and its method and therefore to help explain the sometimes seemingly inexplicable aspects of his personal and artistic character such as 'Lowry and Women', the 'Interlude' and the relationship with the now almost forgotten and certainly underrated artist friend, David Carr, and the remarkable re-creation by Paul Driver of Lowry's last days. There is also a rebuttal of the insidious and wrong-headed charge that Lowry suffered from Asperger's Syndrome. The discussion of each of these topics if taken individually, may sound superfluous but I believe that cumulatively they add to our knowledge and, above all, our understanding of a much misunderstood and much underrated English eccentric and genius.

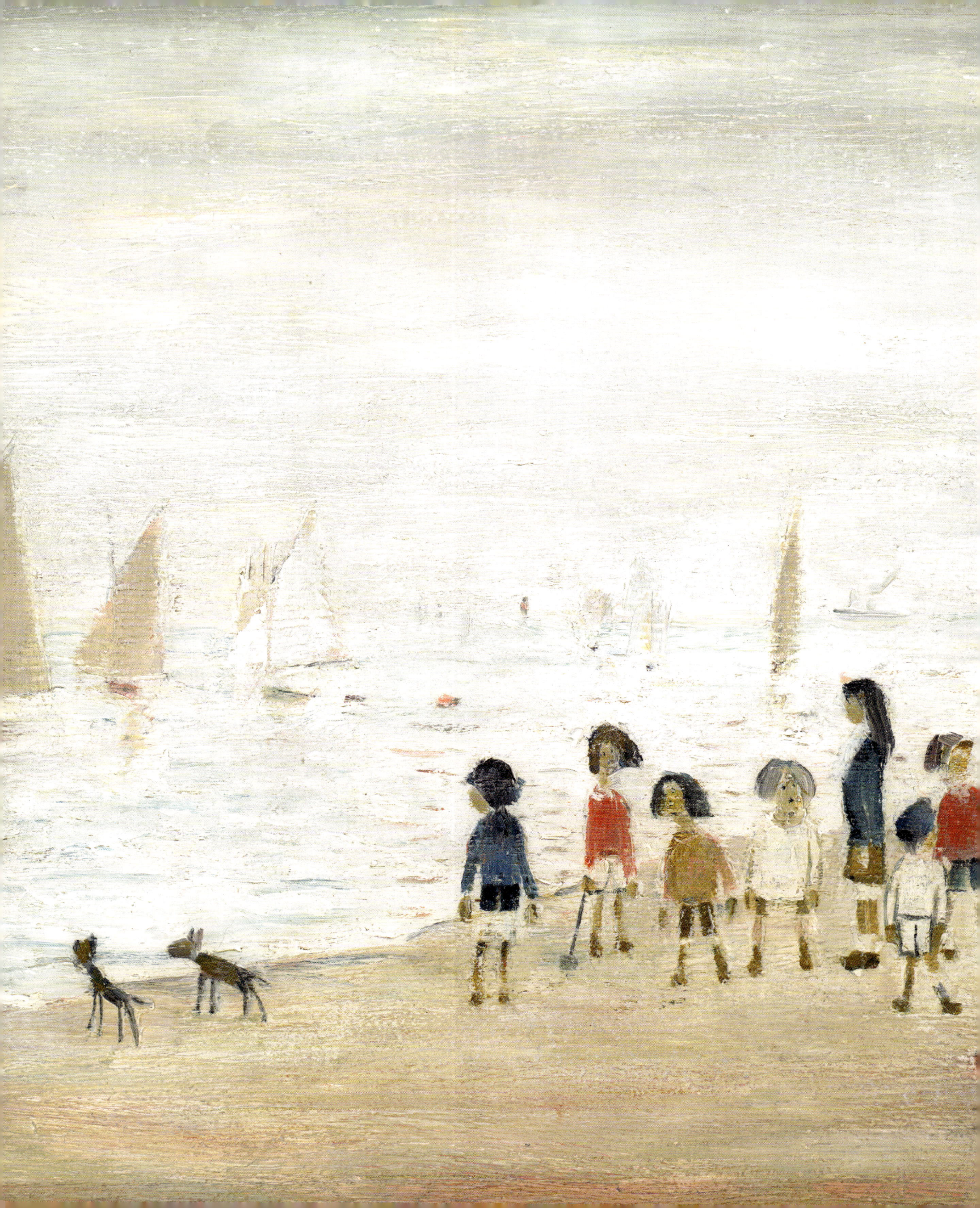

CHAPTER 1

LOWRY IN PERSON

Solitude is the school of genius
Edward Gibbon

Just as those ignorant concerning Lowry's art use the phase "matchstick men" so those who know little of his life refer to him as a recluse on the grounds that he lived alone in a small house in a remote village. The recluse cliché is just as absurdly wide of the mark as the matchstick men label. Recluses don't on the whole travel all over Britain, take holidays by the seaside, carry on correspondences with punctilious correctness nor, above all, do several broadcasts and countless interviews. The several editions of Shelley Rohde's biography of Lowry and various reminiscences of him by people like his sometime dealers, Tilly Marshall or Andras Kalman, are full of non-reclusive information about him, some of it interesting, some of it, as in the case of Tilly Marshall's book, unpleasantly revealing about Lowry's personal habits as if the author were revenging herself on his frequent sponging off her and her husband's art gallery which had, admittedly, done so much for the artist in the North East. In fact her husband, the guiding spirit of the Stone Gallery in Newcastle, Ronald Marshall, showed and promoted Lowry's work with great skill and enthusiasm. He managed, without denting the success of Lowry's London dealers, to enhance Lowry's country-wide reputation and acceptance.

Shelley Rohde was not really a biographer although, as a working journalist, she was a dedicated truffle-hound and her definitive identification of Lowry's mythical female *belle idéal* (see Chapter 13) is quite compelling. Because the books are, ultimately, fascinating collections of anecdotes and the reminiscences and correspondence of Lowry's carefully maintained, but always separated, friends they are, even if somewhat artlessly written, full of vital information; but Lowry still awaits a biographer who fully understands the nature of the subject's art and the narrative skill to interweave the art with the life and thus makes sense of it as Hilary Spurling has done with Matisse, David Cairns did with Berlioz and as John Richardson (at time of writing at least) is so heroically doing with Picasso.

Nonetheless the most casual reading of Rohde makes it clear that Lowry was, although a lifelong bachelor, the least reclusive of men who had long friendships with fellow artists, distinguished academics, a handful of key patrons and a succession of young women (see Chapter 13).

Lowry was not a recluse but a *solitary* and, in Gibbon's lapidary phrase, solitude is the school of genius. After a lifetime of work and friendship with living artists I have not known a single great painter or sculptor who was not totally ruthless about his work which always came before everything else. The principal advantage of being a bachelor and celibate artist

Detail from *People at the Beach*, 1955, (p.233).

is the obvious one of the lack of family ties and therefore a responsibility to no one except oneself in organising one's hours. Thus his single-mindedness about his art – which in other circumstances one could term artistic ruthlessness – was easy to satisfy while not being too obvious to alienate friends. Once his control-freak, bedfast mother died he was a free man at last; free to paint all night if he chose to; free to live where and how he liked; free to be, albeit gregarious, a solitary.

My first encounter with Lowry was in 1960 when I visited Manchester on business. I was the assistant sales manager of an art-book publishers and I was calling on the local booksellers to try to boost trade. Having spent my childhood in the city, it was a welcome return to old haunts, so I stayed over for the weekend and arranged to lunch with an old Cambridge friend. Lunch was at his parents' house in Mottram-in-Longdendale just over the Cheshire border. My friend's father was, among other things, the Treasurer for the annual Mottram Show and, as such, was a friend of the village's most celebrated citizen, L. S. Lowry. I persuaded my friend to take me round for a visit.

The door was opened slowly and reluctantly by the artist. He greeted David with just enough friendliness not to offend and regarded me with considerable and doubtless justified suspicion – a stranger arriving unannounced on a Sunday afternoon. At that time Lowry was 73, about six feet tall, heavily, solidly built but not overweight, with a lot of short grey hair, heavy spectacles and oddly imposing in a paint-spattered, dark three-piece suit and one of those thickly textured striped shirts with neither collar nor tie.

Far from looking like an artist, he was every inch the retired rent collector he was, the kind of man you'd see nursing a pint of mild, sitting by himself in the snug of a thousand pubs in the North West.

Lowry grumbled at us for not having warned him of our arrival, complained that we had caught him unawares in his painting clothes, and generally made us, me in particular, feel like unwelcome intruders. While Lowry made us some tea, I prowled around the front room of the modest two-up two-down stone house. It was a chilly day and the room, despite a small, two-bar electric fire, was cold and David and I kept our coats on while I scanned the walls for examples of the artist's work.

There were none; just some nondescript pieces of Victoriana, but there was one quite staggeringly beautiful drawing of a woman's head. I don't know where it is now, but I have still got a clear impression, after nearly fifty years, of a luminous, clear-eyed face, a mass of hair and the powerful blackness of the line. It was large, probably about 20 inches high by 16 inches wide, and dominated the wall by the sheer force of a significant work of art surrounded by dross. When Lowry brought in the tea I ventured to say that I admired the drawing.

"Oh, do you like it?"

"Yes", I lamely replied.

"Do you *really* like it?" he persisted.

"Yes, really, it's magnificent."

His somewhat closed and wary face relaxed a little and he offered the smallest hint of a smile.

"Do you know who did it?" he asked in the tones of a pedagogue who knew that his floundering pupil would *not* know the answer.

"Well, Mr Lowry, I can't be sure" – the drawing was unsigned – "but it could be a Rossetti."

"A Rossetti, eh?" and he looked wickedly in my friend's direction with the unspoken subject of 'how could you bring this idiot to spoil my Sunday afternoon when I'm busy painting?'

He then looked at me and said, "Well, you're quite right. It *is* a Rossetti and I love it more than any other drawing I've ever seen," and what the Sovietologists used to call a thaw began to set in.

After some desultory chat, about not very much, I dared to compliment him on a magnificent, long-case clock in the corner, the only piece of furniture in the room that you wouldn't have to pay someone else to cart away. The inquisition proceeded on similar lines to the earlier one.

After swearing that I *really* admired it, Lowry, of course, asked me to identify its maker. Now, while I do know a little about art, antiques are, for me, mostly *terra incognita*. But I was extraordinarily lucky. The only great English clockmaker whose name had impinged on my brain was that of Tompion. So it was double or quits time and I named him as tentatively as I could.

"Right. Yes. It is. A Tompion, yes." He looked wonderfully gleeful, which seemed a little excessive as a reaction to my mini-quiz. But the glee was not for me. It was for himself. "Do you know where I got it? A Tompion. Yes?"

He paused to let me give the obvious negative response and then, marvellously animated and sounding like that old north-country radio comic, Al Read, he told us that he'd found it "in a junk shop in Rochdale. The owner didn't know what it was. It didn't work and it was all covered in dust and muck and he wanted ten bob for it. Ten shillings for a Tompion. He were blind. Blind and daft with it. So I offered seven and six and he took it. Of course it cost me a few bob to have it restored, but just you listen to it when it strikes." Which, ten minutes later, it did, and when the sound had faded away he chuckled again. "A Tompion, oh yes. He didn't know, that fella in Rochdale. A Tompion."

Al Read was born in Salford on 3 March, 1909. He began his career as a comedian only in his forties, having been appointed as a director, at 23, of the family meat packing business. This had been founded by his grandfather, the first man to produce tinned meat. He did his first broadcast on 10 March, 1950 and was given his first "Al Read Show" in September 1951, but no matter how successful would not do more than one show a month. Like Kenneth Horne of "Much Binding in the Marsh" fame, who was chairman of a paper manufacturing business, he would not give up the day job. But, following a Christmas performance for the Royal Family at Windsor, he recognized his talent and his ensuing celebrity and, in 1956, sold his business and became a full-time performer with his perennial catchphrases "Right monkey" and "You'll be lucky". Physically he was the antithesis of Lowry, conventionally good-looking, immaculately groomed and smartly dressed with a light, attractive voice, whereas Lowry was, doubtless deliberately, scruffy, indeed shambolically turned out, with a much deeper voice. But their accents were identical and they shared a genuinely sardonic sense of humour, at once sly and dry and, while Lowry would have died rather than perform on a public stage, whenever I was in his company and listening to him talk, complain or mock some pretentious critic or would-be patron, I always heard the vocal tones and spirit of Read. Read died, aged 78, in 1987 but some of his radio programmes were still being repeated at the beginning of this century and are still available on recordings.

By this time Lowry was beaming and his somewhat mournful countenance was transformed so that I at last felt able to ask whether it would be possible to see some of his work.

"Well you'd better come into the back room, then. It's very dirty, mind. You'd better watch that fancy coat of yours. Don't want to get paint on it."

It was the invitation I had not dared to hope for – and yet finally I was entering the studio of L. S. Lowry. It was indeed dirty, chaotic, apparently disorganised. Paintings, both finished and unfinished, leaning against the walls, facing outwards or with the backs of the canvases and boards turned towards us. On the easel was a barely begun townscape. I was, after years of schoolboy and undergraduate enthusiasm, in my own private heaven.

After another lengthy catechism, I was led in. It was, particularly to someone who had played in the streets that he depicted so vividly, had attended a primary school of the kind he painted, who had seen the factory gates and the football crowds that so fascinated him – an overwhelming experience that many visits over the years to the old Salford City Art Gallery, with its great Lowry collection – since transferred to the Lowry arts centre, which opened in April 2000 – have never eradicated.

Against the serried and carefully curated ranks of a formal gallery, the higgledy-piggledy randomness of a messy artist's studio will always win in terms of both physical experience and aesthetic appreciation. Without glamorous framing and ultra-sophisticated spotlighting, and with only a couple of unshaded 100-watt bulbs for illumination, one's perceptions become both immediate and stark, with little opportunity for careful reflection, so that the magic of that exposure to his art was as deep as it was unforgettable.

At 24, and without the benefit of Shelley Rohde's 1979 biography, or the relentless cascade of confessional and gossip-ridden journalism of the past twenty years, I did not dare ask him about the identity of the girl with huge eyes and centre-parted glossy black hair who stared at us from a particularly powerful canvas. Which is just as well, since she never existed, being an amalgam of several young women of a certain physical type whom he befriended but never touched.

What was so striking, apart from the obvious impact of the townscapes, teeming with what the ignorant call his "matchstick men", was the extraordinary individuality and scrupulous differentiation of the hundreds of human beings then all within a few feet of my gaze.

I made what stumbling conversation I could, offering my jejune opinions on art in general and of his own work in particular and, by sheer luck, managed not to dispel his cheerful mood. Lowry, often wrongly described as a recluse and a loner, was in fact not only gregarious but an acute, drily witty talker. Just as his paintings, far from being naïve, are immensely sophisticated in both their composition and their humour, in private speech he himself was simple, direct, yet perceptive about his art – as I was to discover not only on that bleak winter afternoon but in later, more formal encounters when I was armed with a tape recorder.

As it got dark outside I felt that we should not outstay what had turned into a genuinely warm welcome, but the incipient collector in me would not be still, so I asked if it would be possible at least to consider acquiring one of his pictures. Another catechism about liking his work came and went and he then asked me which picture I fancied. Unerringly, having no idea as to his prices, apart from knowing that they would be far beyond my means, I pointed at the smallest one.

Done in oil on board, it measures only 6.5 inches high by 5.6 inches and contains a group of three people, a girl with her back to us, another, older girl facing us, a small boy in a red sweater and half a dog. In the classic Lowry white background there are some barely visible vertical black streaks, indicating the possibility of some factory chimneys in the distance; at the bottom, a black strip that simultaneously represents the kerb and unifies the structure of the picture.

"Oh, do you really like that one?"

"Very much, but of course I don't know if I can afford it."

"Well, what do you *want* to pay for it?"

As a tyro publishing executive who had not yet paid off all his student debts and whose take-home pay was £11 and fifteen shillings a week, this seemed an insoluble problem. I knew nothing of prices and values.

So I told Lowry that I would happily give him all the money I had on me. This was in the days when "unless prior arrangements have been made with the management", hotels did not take cheques and there were, of course, no credit cards. I had therefore drawn from my employers a cash advance of £15 to cover the expenses of my trip.

I reckoned that I could borrow some cash from my friend who would take my cheque, so that I need not spend the next week washing dishes at the Midland Hotel, and extracted the three five-pound notes and nervously proferred them to the great man. Being an exceptionally kind man, he took them and said that that price was fine by him if it was fine by me, and how would I get home? I assured him of my return ticket and decided not to mention the hotel.

"But do you *really* like it?"

I again swore my undying love for the picture, whereupon the old devil, which, to some extent he really was, said: "But it's not finished. I tell you what, I'll finish it and send it on to you. David will have your address."

I offered some mild platitudes about being unable to bear being parted from this great treasure.

"All right then. I'll finish it for you now."

I muttered my gratitude and wondered how so small a panel could perch on his easel. It didn't. He had vast hands and he held it comfortably in his left while spending the next thirty minutes with a series of small brushes in his right.

It was only many years later that I discovered that there were senior Royal Academicians who considered him an amateur, a "Sunday painter". They'd clearly never seen him at work. He was right. It wasn't finished but at the end of that half hour it certainly was. A highlight here, a black line there, a deepening of the red, a thickening of his heavy, greyish white and it was an unmistakable finished Lowry work of art. I examined it more closely and saw that it had in fact already been signed and this picture, "finished" in 1960, was actually dated 1957.

Then the old tease put it on the easel and proclaimed that while it was indeed now finished it was still wet and would have to remain with him for a few more days to dry and then he would dispatch it to me.

Somehow I managed not to gibber but persuaded him to let me pack it up in some silver foil he had in his kitchen and gave him an assurance that I would keep it upright and free of all harmful contact until I got it back to London.

After that there was occasional correspondence but I wasn't to meet Lowry again until the autumn of the following year, 1961. Again it was at his little stone house and I was accompanied by the poet and, at that time, senior BBC Third Programme talks producer Anthony Thwaite. I interviewed Lowry for a radio arts programme called New Comment. It was not my skills as broadcaster but Lowry's spellbinding talk that made the transmission get the highest "Appreciation Index" of any item broadcast on New Comment that year. We spent hours with the tape running because neither Anthony nor I could bear the thought of cutting off his flow of reminiscences, his views on art and on his own work.

Unfortunately no copy still exists of the sound tape but what follows is an edited transcript of the actual broadcast transmitted on the BBC Third Programme (now known as Radio 3) on Wednesday 8 November, 1961:

ROSENTHAL: I think one thing which most people would agree about Mr Lowry is that your work is the most natural and, in a better sense of that word, uninhibited. Have you had a great deal of formal training in your painting?

LOWRY: I went to the Manchester School of Art but did nothing but the antique, preparatory antique, and laughed for a long time but did no painting at all at the School of Art. I went to a private portrait painter William Fitz for painting lessons. He guided you also: you used your own colour: you did what you liked but he simply guided you.

ROSENTHAL: There is in fact absolutely nothing academic in your work. This is because presumably you picked up what you wanted to pick up and that was all. Is that a fair thing to say?

LOWRY: Well I did things in my own way, as I see them, without regard to anybody or anything else all my life really. I've seen these industrial scenes for a long time. Since 1919 to be quite exact. And I've just done them as I saw them without regard to anything else.

ROSENTHAL: Talking of those industrial scenes, an awful lot of people first of all, they don't understand your work. I think because they immediately say that your work is depressing. But those I think are the kind of people who would say that the scenery is depressing simply because they can't see it. I was brought up as a child in Manchester, I've seen the things you've painted, for many, many, years. I can see their beauty – I love them. A few others do too but not very many. Can you explain why it is that the beauty of those things are not immediately apparent yet you yourself have managed to put over the beauty of this landscape with, I think, outstanding success.

LOWRY: Well I suppose it's the way I looked at it. We went to live in Pendlebury in 1909 on the other side of Manchester ... At first I disliked the scenery very much indeed, and then I got used to it, and then I got interested in it, and then I got to like it somewhat, and then after quite a while I got obsessed by it.

ROSENTHAL: I'm glad you used the word 'obsessed' yourself because I wanted to use it and often I think it is an impertinence to suggest the word. But I couldn't help feeling that, for example, in your last show, there are two paintings there which are not from this area as it were; there is a large painting of London's Piccadilly Circus and a very large one of Ebbw Vale. And yet it seems to me that the obsession which you mentioned with the landscape had carried you along, as it were, to Piccadilly and to Ebbw Vale.

LOWRY: Yes.

ROSENTHAL: So that Piccadilly and Ebbw Vale in many ways look rather like ... Mottram-in-Longdendale and the area round it. Do you think this is too far fetched?

LOWRY: No I quite think it must be so because I've painted industrial scenes for very, very many years – about thirty years I should think really – and I got it into my system and I go off to a place like Ebbw Vale and I see Ebbw Vale something like this part. I don't think it is very different. Piccadilly to me looks well rather like any other place. It's not like parts of London which are very distinctive. I think Piccadilly Circus looking from the angle I took it from looks rather like anywhere else except for the statue of Eros in the middle.

ROSENTHAL: And this has come out in the painting of course.

LOWRY: Yes.

ROSENTHAL: It's immediately recognisable as Piccadilly Circus; Eros is there; the red buses are there.

LOWRY: Yes. But the figures.

ROSENTHAL: But the figures. And the whole atmosphere is in fact, for want of a better word obsessive.

LOWRY: Yes, I'm afraid so.

ROSENTHAL: But to sort of go away for a moment from these standard landscapes you've painted I think a lot of very wonderful seascapes. Do you in fact cover very much of our coast. You've picked up the sea and the lakes which you do very well and yet which you don't show as much as the paintings for which you're rather better known.

LOWRY: Well I travel about a lot. In fact you may almost say I spend my time now in just travelling in this country – I don't go abroad. I spend my time in painting and going round seeing my friends ... my friends are all scattered in the places I paint and I'm very fond of these places and now ... ah well there's not much to memorise in a seascape – you just do a seascape. You see it as it's been a long time. I know the sea pretty well. I'm very fond of it. And the lakes the same angle. The lakes quite a lot. And the lakes not far from here you know, the reservoirs; woodland reservoirs, Manchester Corporation Waterworks. Now they're very fine, pictorially, you know.

ROSENTHAL: Which aspect of the Lake District fascinates you more? The water or the mountains?

LOWRY: Oh the lake, the blackish sort of lake, like Buttermere, I'd say. It's the lake really which ... I would never think of painting the mountains without the lake.

ROSENTHAL: You seem, Mr Lowry, to be an artist who is very self-aware. Henry Moore once said when he was asked if he for example read all the Jungian psychoanalytical studies of his work and whether he thought it was a good thing to do so. He said 'No', he thought this was a very bad thing because if you become too much self-aware, too much aware, of the mental processes which go into your art eventually you will kill the spark which creates the art. Do you agree with this?

LOWRY: Well I don't know really. I never have. I just work on my own, apart from what's said about it. I don't think I could go in any other way if I wanted to really now. At my time of life I just work as I work. Put it this way: That you start a picture and it takes its own course and you follow like a man in a dream – I don't really know – yes, you start the picture without knowing where it will end ... It always does finish up all right you know ... but you don't know.

ROSENTHAL: I see that around the studio where we're sitting now there must be forty or fifty paintings the majority of which are not complete. Do you like to start on one thing and see it all the way through or do you prefer to hop from one canvas to another as the mood takes you?

LOWRY: I have to hop from one canvas 'cos I can't finish them right off. I've tried to finish them right off and can't. They all take a long time. And the strange thing about it is when I think I've almost done one right away in the end that takes the longest time to finish. It's queer that, I've often wondered about it.

ROSENTHAL: In other words you don't like your work to come easily to you.

LOWRY: It doesn't. It won't because I want it to. It certainly won't. It's very perverse – it won't do it.

ROSENTHAL: Actually I used the word canvas. This in fact is rather a misnomer because I suppose, looking round, there's only one in twenty on canvas. Do you prefer boards?

LOWRY: Well I use canvases for fair sized pictures but for little pictures I like wood. I like wood very much. Or there's good … excellent substitute for wood now which – these are what we call beaver …

ROSENTHAL: Hardboard.

LOWRY: Hardboard.

ROSENTHAL: … board and hardboard and things like that.

LOWRY: Very good. For small pictures only. I wouldn't start a 24 × 20 on a board like that: I'd do it on a canvas – all my larger pictures.

ROSENTHAL: There's also an enormous predominance of white on your paintings. Why is that?

LOWRY: Can't help it, it just is.

ROSENTHAL: It does enable you though to show I think very remarkable skill which is basically an economical one I think. You know you can by means of one or two lines suggest an entire atmosphere, almost an entire human scene. I have a small painting of yours which consists of three small child figures on a dead white background and there's just one very tiny black line which is just pavement and another smaller shadowy one, vertical one, which gives the effect of a lamp-post, and there you have a complete thing. Can you explain this economy at all?

LOWRY: Well I can tell you how it started. At first when I first did these industrial scenes I did them rather low tone, low key, and they got very low after a short time. And I spent a lot of time on these pictures and I didn't like it you see. And so I went lighter. I was advised once to go … paint them very light indeed and I did and I find after a few years they've become just right.

ROSENTHAL: Yes.

LOWRY: You see the white drops away – it's bound to drop. I was advised to do that many, many years ago. 'That's no use' a man said. He was a very knowledgeable gentleman too. He said 'It's too dark, look at it, it's much too dark against the cream wall'. He said 'You'll have to paint that lighter'. So I thought there's a lot in it you see but I was cross with him for a while naturally but afterwards I thought, 'Well he's quite right' and I painted them white. But I noticed the white was mellow you know. It drops to just right.

ROSENTHAL: Some people have said – and I can't help thinking they're right – that your work has an atmosphere of the 1920s – the figures seem to be twenty-ish – when you do go into paintings that are genuinely depressing in that they show the grim aspects of this depression in the period of the twenties and perhaps of the early thirties you seem somehow to have stuck with this: there's no sign in your work of what is usually called today 'the affluent society'; your industrial people still have the sombreness of the people of the twenties. Where in fact today in the industrial North the workers are showing almost as many signs of the affluent society as the workers in the Midlands or the South …

LOWRY: Well of course you won't see a large number of people coming away from a factory … I don't think they look much better than they used to in the old days. Individually yes – perhaps – but not as a crowd … I think the crowds look just the same. But I just do them as I see them I suppose. I started doing these things in the 1920s well my mind still sticks in the 1920s because I do them nearly all from memory. I just do the figures as I saw them, and the houses as I see those too. Some people say they're less like houses, they're like little boxes.

ROSENTHAL: Some people like living in little boxes.

LOWRY: That's right. That's what I told them but they don't agree.

ROSENTHAL: But one thing that struck me is that very rarely it seems that you paint people as people. You don't often try to show in any way detailed studies of individuals. Is this because you are not interested in people as individuals; you are much more interested in people in the mass, as a whole, is this a reflection of the basic interest in humanity or what? How would you ...

LOWRY: Well I don't care for portraits: I am not interested in painting a portrait at all. I've tried ... I've only done one person in the last – oh – call it thirty years ago. I like to imagine people, build them up, create my own ... well, individuals if you like.

ROSENTHAL: And yet despite this apparent lack of interest in individuals as such your people come extremely alive.

LOWRY: ... yes, I'm glad to hear you say that. I think they do sometimes but what I think is nothing: it's what the other side thinks. Isn't it really? Do you think?

ROSENTHAL: Are you sensitive to the opinions of others and do they ever affect your own work?

LOWRY: Oh I listen ... you get a lot of advice from people, particularly people who don't paint. Oh very often. Indeed I've got a lot of help from young people mostly who don't paint but are interested. Oh I always listen to what anybody says. I ... oh ... a young lady, a friend of mine, came in one day and said 'Look here' she said 'this is all very well you paint in two dimensions all the time'. So when she'd gone I put in ... I altered it of course.

ROSENTHAL: But did you really alter the picture for the better?

LOWRY: Oh yes. The party was quite right: it was flat. I hadn't noticed it. She was quite right – I told her so: 'I'll alter it completely' I said.

ROSENTHAL: How interested are you in fact in three dimensional effect in your painting?

LOWRY: Oh not very much.

ROSENTHAL: You just find yourself an instinctive painter rather than an intellectual?

LOWRY: I think so, yes. I think so, yes. Yes. Definitely.

ROSENTHAL: Are you very much occupied or preoccupied with the problem of loneliness?

LOWRY: No, I am lonely, I live by myself, I've got good friends but I'm lonely when I'm by myself, as far as I know. I simply paint as I feel. I suppose I've painted a lot of pictures people say are lonely, such as the sea, an odd figure at the sea I paint, I never seem to paint anything *on* the sea when I paint the sea. And ... erh ... I either put a lot of people on a landscape or none, people, say.

ROSENTHAL: Do you feel that the figures that you put into your more crowded scenes have any relationship with each other?

LOWRY: People say not and I'm inclined to agree with them. Isolated figures yes.

ROSENTHAL: Well they are. But I think they're only isolated in the terribly crowded ones like for example the football match where they have a very obvious cohesion simply because there are so many of them crammed together. But in fact looking round here your small wood panels there, for example when you have the children playing, the children seem very much together and belong to each other. Is this done deliberately?

LOWRY: Oh no it just comes. I'm very glad that you say that. Just comes. Just paint the picture and it comes.

ROSENTHAL: Do you think that it's interesting that a painter should be so obsessed with this as you yourself are?

LOWRY: I see no reason why a man shouldn't keep on painting the same thing all his life if he wants to. Because if when he doesn't want to he'll change and he probably won't be able to go back to it.

ROSENTHAL: A great number of painters, composers, writers, have achieved their greatest work in their seventies even in their eighties and sometimes, even in their late seventies they've completely changed to something new. Do you think there's any chance of you doing that?

LOWRY: I've not noticed it. I ... [laughter] ... I'm leaving it rather late aren't I now because I'm in my seventy-fourth year. I've changed a little I think but not a lot. What I shall always feel I think is that the industrial scene is my best work.

ROSENTHAL: Yes. That's ... that's very true.

LOWRY: Is it true do you think?

ROSENTHAL: Oh completely true.

LOWRY: Yes completely.

(end of broadcast transcription)

. . . .

Lowry serious, as opposed to mischievous, could be wonderfully terse, all part, no doubt, of his quite elaborately constructed public persona. I'm sure that those who think his pictures simple would also characterise his personality in the same way.

That would be foolish. This was an endlessly patient and subtle man who always knew what he was doing, whether personally or in paint. He once (as is fully described later on in this chapter by Edwin Mullins),famously applied seven coats of white paint to a piece of cardboard, put it away in a drawer without any light for seven years and, at the end of that time, gave another piece of card its multiple ration of white so that he could compare the effects of time on his favourite colour.

When I asked him about his feeling for the halt, the lame, the down-and-out who so fill his pictures, he said: "I feel very interested in them. I have a sympathy for them even if I know there's nothing I can do for them. I listen to them." One of the few discerning critics to admire him in his lifetime, Edwin Mullins, speculated that Lowry was intrigued by these outcasts because he felt himself to be an isolated person.

As for his passion for Rossetti, he said: "I'm fascinated by the paintings of his ladies. Nothing else."

Lowry was much more self-aware than most acquaintances realised and once observed of those much admired pre-Raphaelite ladies, "They are not real women, they are dreams."

In response to the obvious question about his industrial landscapes, he was both frank and cagey. "I see them. I'm interested in them. They're not beautiful, I know that. I just do them, that's all. I got obsessed by it, I can't say why. It just happened."

His industrial scenes are, in fact, an almost uncannily accurate rendering of something that has no corporeal existence in that form, but is a paradigm of an almost vanished segment of North-West England. While wholly imaginary in both concept and composition, the individual components are real, based on his endless perambulations through the area as a rent collector and minor functionary in an estate agent's office, when he invariably made pencil sketches of buildings and characters who appealed to him.

The last time we met was in September 1966 when I made a long radio feature about him for the Third Programme. It was part re-interview of him and part symposium of the views of various art world dignitaries and fellow painters. My wife and I drove up to a seaside hotel near Sunderland where he was staying (and often used as his North-East base), for which the word modest would be a considerable overstatement.

We had lunch together – a vile meal, even by the standards of the time – and, not too seriously, Lowry maintained that he was a poor man and had been one for forty years. I would have used more than a pinch of salt had I known then what I know now; that via his dealers he had, in 1964, bought at a Christies' auction Rossetti's oil portrait of Jane Morris, known as *Proserpine*, for 5,000 guineas (probably a million pounds today)

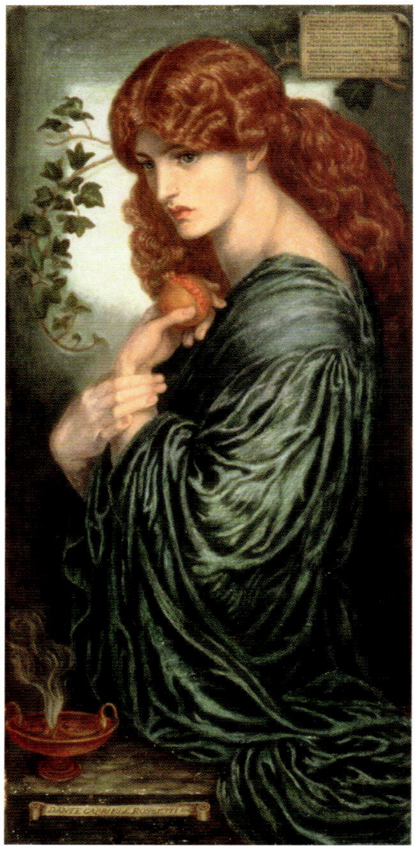

Proserpine, by D. G. Rossetti, 1882, oil on canvas, 78.7 × 39.2 cm.

It became his favourite picture and he bought other pre-Raphaelites – sometimes exchanging them for his own paintings – as well as works by Daumier and the two near-contemporaries he most admired, Lucian Freud and Jacob Epstein. His simple living was no pose. It was part of his character and never conflicted with his massive generosity to others.

I set out below the BBC transcription from the actual broadcast of the symposium transmitted on the BBC's Third Programme on Saturday 26 November, 1966. This 45 minute programme was compiled and introduced, with appropriate linking passages, by me and was broadcast under the title *Every Day in the Week*.

ROSENTHAL: L. S. Lowry is now nearly eighty years old, and while no one could ever have accused him of being an *enfant terrible*, he is now respectable enough to receive the accolade of an Arts Council retrospective exhibition. Yet he is, in his way, one of the most paradoxical artists England has ever produced. One can look at his paintings for a few seconds and instantly understand them while at the same time they are highly complex works of art. His painting technique also looks, at first glance, crude and unfinished yet is immensely subtle. His choice of subject matter, the industrial North of England and the stunted factory workers and derelicts whom one still finds there, inspire instant gloom in those who feel that their cocooned home counties existence will be threatened, if not actually sullied, by a trip north of the Trent for anything other than grouse shooting, yet Lowry is in fact a lyrical and poetical recorder of a landscape which has as much intricate visual beauty as the Sussex Downs if one only opens one's eyes to it. To many who have only seen his occasional excursions onto the television screen and have not come to grips with his paintings, he is a comical old buffer from up north, yet his reluctance to intellectualise about his own work conceals, as usual, with the best visual artists, an acute and perceptive mind. In other words, Lowry isn't half so simple as he appears, and sometimes sounds. For instance, it takes a man of more than average perception to give up painting effective if conventional portraits and competent, but derivative Barbizon-type landscapes. Why did Lowry suddenly change the subject matter of his work?

LOWRY: ... I lived up to 21 years of age on the residential side, and we went to live on the other side for business reasons – a very industrial town called Pendlebury, between Manchester and Bolton. And at first I disliked it intensely ... then after quite a year or two I got used to it, and then interested in it and then, and then I got obsessed by it and practically did nothing else for 25 to 30 years.

ROSENTHAL: Before you moved, had you in fact been painting non-industrial subjects?

LOWRY: Painting portraits and landscapes. Just the ordinary portraits and just ordinary landscapes. And that's all. Little sea pieces and just the ordinary things that most people do. And after going to Pendlebury I did nothing after getting used to the subject matter in Pendlebury. I did nothing else for 25 or 30 years.

ROSENTHAL: What made you become obsessed with it?

LOWRY: Can't say. Just happened. It just happened.

ROSENTHAL: Was it the visual appearance of the factory chimneys and of the factory crowds, or was it in fact what these things meant to you and to other people?

LOWRY: No, it was purely pictorial. I looked upon the people as the main feature and the background to the whole thing – the setting.

ROSENTHAL: I asked Lowry if he thought his landscapes were beautiful.

LOWRY: Well, I wouldn't say beautiful. I'd use ... I see them and I'm interested and I just do them. That's all. I don't ... I just see them, do them there, the attraction – something, I quite can't see what. I do them. It's really the same way as somebody driving outside and seeing a landscape as I would see, and he draws it and thinks it's interesting, and that's what it is.

ROSENTHAL: Interesting, yes. But, I think, something more than that, and also significant by the mere fact of its being done at all. This is what Herbert Read had to say when I asked him to amplify what he had once said about Lowry's being a revolutionary.

READ: Perhaps the word revolutionary was rather strong. But he is original in the sense that he has seen the possibilities for painting that exist in the industrial landscape in this country. It's really quite extraordinary that in an industrial country like this no-one ... no painter of any significance has ever taken the industrial landscape as a subject, and what you might call industrial art just does not exist. But Lowry had the ... well, yes, it's revolutionary in the sense that he had the new vision of the artistic value of this subject. No-one else had seen the industrial landscape as potentially an artistic subject ... but naturally there may be behind it some preference of an ideological nature; some preference for the working-class as such, for the life of the people as such. That may have guided him towards selection of this particular subject-matter. I don't know Lowry well enough to know whether that is ... has been a determining influence in his life.

ROSENTHAL: But he paints, you know, what they call the dark Satanic mills; do you think that he sees them with the same sort of vision as, let us say, Blake?

READ: Well, I don't think the vision is Satanic in Blake's sense. Blake was romantic and opposed, I suppose, to the industrial development of England as such. Whereas Lowry, I think, accepts it. To Lowry it is a natural background to his life and thought. I think there is that difference. Therefore I would say that his vision is not Satanic. He accepts the Industrial Revolution and makes the most of it.

ROSENTHAL: I think that sentence about accepting the Industrial Revolution is a key one, since in many ways it exemplifies the differences between North and South in this country, which in turn are reflected in the different attitudes to Lowry. There are those who, quite simply, find Lowry's paintings ugly; others find beauty in them. Beauty is still of course very much a matter of the eye of the beholder, and this applies as much to the industrial North itself as to the paintings of it. This is how John Rothenstein reconciles the paradox.

ROTHENSTEIN: I think he's done one very important thing historically. I think the whole history of modern art ... has been the history of expansion with the concept of beauty, that is to say in times of Classical Greece very few things were thought beautiful and in modern times artists have taken more and more things and beautified them, presented them to the world in terms of poetic beauty, and Lowry has taken, if the inhabitants will forgive my saying so, one of the dreariest regions, visually speaking, of the whole civilised world, and presented it in terms of an extremely moving poetry, and therefore by doing so he's expanded our whole conception of what is beautiful and what may be beautiful.

ROSENTHAL: In its triumph over what ought, in theory, to be bleak and grim, the beauty that Lowry imposes is, almost literally, transcendental, although Herbert Read finds that the relative beauty of subject and treatment are somehow integral and intrinsic.

READ: Well, anyone who has had any experience of this industrial landscape does feel its poetry. I myself – in my youth – was familiar with the industrial landscape round Leeds, and very much moved by its subtleties of form and colour. The outlines of the West Yorkshire mills and their chimneys and so on often have very great formal beauty. And then there is this atmosphere which is created by the smoke and fog and so on, but can be a great beauty from an atmospheric point of view, from a colour point of view. If one learns to see things, as it were to disassociate the form and atmosphere from the function, then one sees that it has beauty and that this beauty can be conveyed in painting. That industrial landscape, as it were, becomes an equivalent to the romantic landscapes of, shall we say, Corot?

ROSENTHAL: You've also observed Lowry's fidelity to this Northern industrial landscape. Do you think that Lowry could in fact have been as good a painter as he is if he had not been born in this environment and if he had not in fact devoted the majority of his painting career to that environment?

READ: No, I doubt if he would have developed in the same way or become the same kind of artist in a different environment. I think that the industrial landscape found its poet as it were, its artist, in Lowry, and that he had a particular kind of sensibility which saw the possibilities in that landscape. He has, of course, formal qualities which are universal. He has not only a sense of form and composition, but a personal colour sense, personal feeling for harmony of various kinds, which might have been transposed into other subject matter. [My guess is that he would not have been inspired by different kinds of landscape.]

ROSENTHAL: As a matter of fact Lowry has also done a large number of seascapes, some of which are entirely successful as paintings, but I can't help seeing some significance both in Herbert Read's last remark and in the fact that Lowry has turned more to the sea in the last few years when he has, at least partly, abandoned the industrial scene in order to paint a lot of seascapes recently.

LOWRY: I like to do seascapes. I'm very fond, now and then, of doing beach scenes. But the fact is that after getting used to the industrial scene, I never painted ... and a friend of mine thinks I might have started painting the sea later on in life and it probably would have happened, I should say.

ROSENTHAL: Well, you have in fact painted a lot of seascapes?

LOWRY: Quite a number, but not what you'd call a lot. Every so often I like to do them, and what interests me here is of course the shipping on the sea and the rivers and the sea itself.

ROSENTHAL: What is it about the sea that attracts you as a painter?

LOWRY: The vastness of it and the wonderful different conditions on it. It's changing all the time. Anything's possible ... you can hear it strumming over the promenade. It was a wonderful sight, but it was very fearsome to my way of thinking, particularly the east coast far more than the west.

ROSENTHAL: In a sense the sea has been an escape for Lowry from the industrialism that has haunted him, but it's not a very far-reaching escape; Lowry has now adopted the sea at Roker on the coast by Sunderland, a move which John Rothenstein saw as being eminently logical.

ROTHENSTEIN: Well, he happened to be lunching with me one day, and he was talking about the north east coast and he said, I'm thinking of settling there, so I said to him, I suppose you think you've discovered a place that's even more forbidding than Salford, and there was a long silence and he said, I think that's just about it.

ROSENTHAL: Actually, however forbidding the town of Sunderland may be, the sea at Roker can be magnificent, and indeed was just that when I visited Lowry and recorded these conversations with him in his regular first floor room in a hotel overlooking the water.

LOWRY: The sea, well I like the sea for its own sake. I'm very fond of the sea ... oh yes, I'm very fond of the sea.

ROSENTHAL: But while he's fond of it, he also finds it terrible, and I asked him why.

LOWRY: Well, it comes in, comes in and comes in. There it is, this vast expanse, and I often wonder and often say to friends, I wonder wouldn't it be dreadful ... what would happen if the sea suddenly didn't ... the tide didn't turn and the sea came on and on and on and on and on. What would it be like? Wouldn't it be wonderful just to see it? Just fancy ... on and on and on ... didn't stop at all. Went on for ever. Awful, isn't it? And I often think too that these people reckon that the tide will come in and are waiting outside with the ships that are going to come in with the tide in Newcastle on the Tyne, and I often wonder what would happen if the tide didn't come in and went somewhere else. If the tide did come in ... I don't know what it is that keeps it so ... but it's a dreadful thing, it can be dreadful ... at times, you know. Have you been on the sea ... do you feel the same thing? It's all around you ...

ROSENTHAL: I think that some of this obsessional attitude towards the sea is reflected in the paintings themselves. His seas are neither conventionally placid or typically tempestuous. Instead they are simultaneously both the subject and the object of a quiet intensity which is reflected in the concentration on a virtually monochromatic scale of grey and white. In this they become more concentrated versions of his industrial skies, and I think it's worth looking at his handling of paint from the point of view of other painters ... Josef Herman, who has a high regard for Lowry, has shared an exhibition with him. I asked him whether he didn't find Lowry's technique to a certain extent uninteresting and unsensual.

HERMAN: I don't agree that the technique is uninteresting, but what I do agree with is there are no sensual qualities to it. But this was to my mind a deliberate choice in technique. The paste-like quality of his whites, or the blacks, they achieve a certain plasticity without going into the research of itself ... Lowry does not explore but what he uses are colours which struck him as true to life, and because he lived in an industrial area and because the subject matter is of this area, naturally the restricted palette, is a truer expression of this.

ROSENTHAL: And what about when he moves away from the industrial area? When he does his seascapes, some of which are very beautiful indeed?

HERMAN: Yes, this is perfectly true, but in painting, if once you acquire a technique, and once you acquire a style, you use it in whatever subject you will tackle, you see, and therefore between his seascapes and his cityscapes there exists no difference either in technique or style.

Michael Ayrton also approves of Lowry's technique:

AYRTON: I think it was inspired in him to limit his range to the extent that he has done. As a technician I would have thought he was comparatively rudimentary, but needs to be nothing else.

ROSENTHAL: Inevitably, I suppose, when you talk about Lowry's technique you come up against the question of whether or not he is a naïve or primitive painter. The borderline between a painter like Lowry and the obvious primitives like Bauchant or Bombois is probably just as clear as that between Lowry and the obviously bad Sunday painters like Grandma Moses. But having said that, it's far harder clearly to define where Lowry stands in relationship to them and primitive art in general. This is what Herbert Read says:

READ: I don't think he is naïve in the strict sense of the word. I mean, I've met Mr Lowry and talked to him. I've seen the film that my son made of him, where he spoke a great deal about his life and ideals.[1] I don't think he is naïve in the proper sense of the word. But, well, I search for the right kind of word to describe him, I think he is a simple man in a certain sense of that word. He lives a simple life, and although that in itself might be pose, I don't think it is. I think he has a genuine preference for the simple life, and that this is part of his character which determines the nature of his painting.

ROSENTHAL: Professor E. H. Gombrich also fails to see anything of the primitive in Lowry:

GOMBRICH: From the point of view of his very subtle gradation of tone and his very great awareness of tonal values, he is certainly not a primitive painter in the same sense in which, let us say, Grandma Moses is a primitive painter.

ROSENTHAL: And this is how Edwin Mullins, who did the catalogue for the retrospective exhibition, sees him:

MULLINS: In terms of the way he paints, he is anything but naïve; a lot of people think of Lowry as a very simple, almost primitive painter, I think it very important to stress that in the way he actually applies his paint, in the interest he has in the texture and colour of paint, he has an entirely professional approach. There's that story which he has often told of how be became interested in the colour white. How he painted one board, one piece of card, with several coats of white paint, and then locked this card away so that air couldn't get to it, just as though it were in fact under glass, for seven years, and then before he took it out he painted another card with exactly the same white, and then unlocked the other one, and compared the two, and as a result of comparing the two he realised what he wanted to obtain from the texture of white. Now, this is immensely scientific and sophisticated and very much the reverse of a naïve approach to painting. And Lowry to me is a master of his particular way of using paint, particularly, of course, monochrome painting. He's not, to my mind, a colourist as such. His colours emerge from colourlessness, from black, from grey, from white, from slight tints of white; he's a master at being able to produce eight or nine different colours out of white, another eight or nine out of black, and give the appearance of a multicoloured canvas, where in fact colour does not exist. This I think is an important contribution that he's made, even if it isn't a contribution which other painters may learn from. But don't get the impression – I hope no one does get the impression – that he is a simpleton. He's very far from that.

ROSENTHAL: Indeed he is. You only have to look at his human figures to see that. Next to factory chimneys and dark streets the images conjured up by the name Lowry are most often those of people, either eccentric individuals or crowds of rushing homunculi, faintly Chaplinesque, slightly pathetic, sometimes compassionately observed, sometimes seen and depicted with a slightly sardonic humour. Lowry is fascinated by society's rejects and accepts his fascination as a matter of course.

LOWRY: I just do them for the same reason as some people paint a still-life or a landscape or anything else. But these last years, I've been doing quite a number of down-and-outs, you call them. I really feel very interested in them. And I feel a sort of, well, I have a sympathy for them. You can't do anything for them, you know. There they are, looking into space, you've done all this scene, they'll be standing there suffering, might be standing ... as far as I know. And you can't do anything about it. It's too late. I might want to chat with some of them. Got a lot to say – you know, very nice people. And until you get onto their private life. One man I remember quite well – be was very, very nice, and he was in a park, and he said, "Can you spare tuppence for me, guvnor, for a cup of tea? I haven't had anything to eat or drink for ooh, two days". I said, I'll give you two pence with pleasure, but when you've told me you've had nothing for two days, I don't believe you ... what the dickens you like. And he laughed heartily and we got talking, got in conversation. Well, and then I saw him by strange chance in another park about a fortnight after and we like ... started chattering again, you know. And he talked a great deal about himself. So much so as to encourage me to ask him what had happened to him, of course – he said, and he dried up, and he didn't say a word. Ten minutes went by, and I said good afternoon to him and he didn't say a word. He closed up just like that.

ROSENTHAL: One can see why these people fascinate him from a visual point of view, and Edwin Mullins has this explanation for their actual fascination:

MULLINS: This contrast between extreme loneliness and a concern with a bustling, teeming human life, like an ant-hill, gives you I think the two opposite poles of his way of looking at the world, and they are very much part of his own particular feelings perhaps about the society in which he lives. I think it's very important that Lowry is a man who has never felt himself to belong in any way to the world around him. He has an entirely detached attitude to life as it is lived, and the way he paints is almost like someone looking at our world from another world. I think that the figures he draws, these caricatures that he's done increasingly with old age, have a frightening detachment which, at the same time, as he presents his figures, in a detached way, they manage to reflect his own personal mood, his own loneliness, his own feelings that life has rather passed him by. This is a very curious combination of subjectivity and feelings of really having no pity, no love, no hate, no concern at all for the wellbeing of other people, he looks upon people with a kind of fascinated curiosity. He's interested in outcasts, partly because he himself feels himself to be an isolated person, but also because he thinks they're so very funny. Now only a man with this frightening degree of detachment could present the grotesque in other people with this almost coldness. I find this aspect of Lowry very frightening and very, very powerful. I can't imagine a committed human being, a human being who loved others, was involved in others, who had lived, one is tempted to say lived a normal married life, Lowry has never married, he has very few friends, one can't imagine a person, other than Lowry, being able to present people in quite this ruthless way.

ROSENTHAL: Is Lowry detached and ruthless and lonely? Perhaps he's all these things, and they are reflected in his figures. Yet all these qualities are at variance with the gentleness of his personality, which, as Herbert Read said, isn't a pose. He is generous to other artists and buys their work, notably that of Sheila Fell, but I wonder whether it isn't significant that among earlier artists he really only likes the Victorians, whose painting, for all its sentimentality, remained curiously unemotional. Lowry has several Rossetti drawings in his house, and I asked him why he liked Rossetti:

LOWRY: … fascinated by the paintings of his ladies. Nothing else. Not his subject pictures. Do you ever … what it is that attracts me, I don't know. That's all it is. He's the only man who I've ever really seriously … I shall keep on collecting Rossettis. I like some of the others. I'm very fond, you know, very interested in Victorian art. I don't mean it's very great art, particularly nowadays, I think so … I like it more than ever. I like all of them. I like the place. I like the lot. In a sense. Rossetti is the only one I ever wanted to possess, and I've got some very good ones, I think, and I'd like to have some more some time.

ROSENTHAL: Yet there could be few painters more different from Lowry than the precise, almost clinical Rossetti. Lowry's art is much more diffuse, much more the result of imagination given a forward push by a couple of pinches of reality. As Edwin Mullins says:

MULLINS: Lowry, in fact, very rarely records literally what he has seen. A great number of his compositions, I should say probably the majority of his compositions, are made up from a host of different impressions that his memory has stored up. He will build up a canvas starting from, he doesn't know what. He's told me that he's often started with a seascape and, in the course of working through the night very often, it has become a mill-scene, or a mill-scene has become a landscape, or an empty landscape with lakes has become a composition full of little bustling figures … the point of this is, I think, that he's to a very great extent a subjective painter. He's not an objective recorder of something seen. And to me the impact of a Lowry is very largely that one is made aware of the personal feelings of Lowry. He's recording as it were the scene from within him, not just what the eyes see.

ROSENTHAL: I think that that in many ways is the key to Lowry's art. Neither wholly imaginative nor wholly recording, it's an interpretation of people and places and places around him, as seen through his highly personal, jaundiced-coloured spectacles and it is this that makes him so hard to classify or place in the history of English, let alone European, painting. Michael Ayrton has an interesting point of view:

AYRTON: I should have thought the English Utrillo is probably the place I should describe Lowry as fitting. I think the point about Utrillo is that his quality, which at the moment is rather out of fashion, is a sense of the ambience of Paris, the quality of the plaster walls, of the quality of the rooftops, of the quality of the city itself. The figures in Utrillo's paintings which were not as well drawn as those in Lowry's, always seem too haphazard, and not in fact to be the centre of the situation. Nevertheless, they inhabit the place, and Lowry, like Utrillo, paints inhabited places. He is to me a city painter; he's an English city painter, whereas Utrillo is essentially the city of Paris painter, of the early twenties – the early part of the twentieth century. I've always thought of them together, though when I first encountered Lowry's work, Utrillo was a kind of highly-prized myth who drank himself to death and was drinking himself to death, and all sorts of glamorous things like that, while Lowry seemed infinitely more English, infinitely more down-to-earth, and infinitely less likely to indulge in any of the bohemian chi-chi which attaches to the legend of Utrillo. Nevertheless, there is, I think, a common chord there. A sense of place, and of urban place, in a specific kind of way, and both have the quality of the self-taught. It's not the same as primitiveness, but it is self-taught.

ROSENTHAL: Self-taught but not primitive. I asked Professor Gombrich whether there were any links between Lowry and Europeans like Douanier Rousseau, at least in terms of imagery:

GOMBRICH: Yes, there may be some links in the way in which he isolates individual figures, in which he keeps his painting very legible, in that sense, perhaps like a children's drawing, but this is only the scaffolding as it were, for a very subtle distribution of shapes and forms.

ROSENTHAL: And this is how Herbert Read sees Lowry against the background of twentieth-century English painting:

READ: I think he's a lone wolf in the sense that he is not particularly interested in the main trends or movements of contemporary art, and doesn't fit very naturally into them.

But there are always in any period lone wolves who stand out from the mainstream, who stand apart from the crowd. They have their place in the contemporary scene. They are, let us say, influenced by the same factors perhaps that influence and create the typical movements of a period. But for some reason, some sense of independence, or sense of isolation, they decide to go their own way and to paint in their own way. And they can be some of the most typical artists of their period. One only thinks back to examples like William Blake at the beginning of the nineteenth century. He occupied a similar kind of isolated position in English painting, and yet when we look back over 150 years or so, we see that he did belong to the period, was part of the romantic movement, and I think 150 years hence Lowry will be seen to be part of the general trend of modern art. But that is not the same thing as belonging to a specific movement.

ROSENTHAL: That Lowry is a lone wolf is undeniable, but I wonder if Lowry has ever been influenced by any other painter or whether in turn he has himself exerted an influence? Michael Ayrton does trace some influences, but of an indirect kind:

AYRTON: I would be very hard put to it to know who has influenced Lowry. Oddly enough, I detect a faint influence of a long-forgotten artist, Ethel Walker. Particularly in his painting of the sea, but this may be pure fantasy on my part. I think Lowry belongs to an English tradition which is essentially a provincial tradition containing such artists as Joseph Wright of Derby, for instance, but I very much doubt if there's any direct connection. I strongly suspect, that like many self-taught painters, though there is influence, it is unconscious, and though there is derivation, it is taken in as influence often is by self-taught painters in a complete unconscious and unaware fashion. I don't see any direct derivation from Lowry.* In terms of his influence, I would have thought that he had influenced painters like George Chapman, I would have thought even, perhaps, Josef Herman owed something to Lowry. It's very much a specific English topographical tradition he belongs to. And this is by no means a very fashionable form of expression now. But I have a strong suspicion that it's quite a permanent one.

ROSENTHAL: Lowry is certainly unfashionable, yet as for other unfashionable figures before him, the tide has turned, and few English artists are more popular today. Perhaps in this he is wholly English traditional, out on a limb and at the same time accepted in the end as part of the common body. Does he perhaps after all belong to the loosely knit English tradition? That's not quite the way Edwin Mullins sees it:

MULLINS: I think he clearly doesn't. He doesn't belong to anybody, you can't place him alongside any other English painter, and say he owes this, that and the other to him. In the early paintings you can see something of the influence of Whistler, something of the influence of English impressionism, but this is a very fleeting influence. The moment he acquires his own style of presenting figures all influences really vanish. But I do think at the same time that he belongs to a different kind of tradition, which is that of the English isolated eccentric who's gone his own way, and one would mention artists like Richard Dadd, Blake is an obvious example, Stanley Spencer a more recent example, who may have nothing in common between them, except that they are all isolated freaks, one hates to call Lowry a freak because no one as a human being is less of a freak, but what they contribute to art is nonetheless freakish by its being so totally isolated from its surroundings. This seems to be a particularly English contribution to art. I can't define it, I can't even pretend to explain why it should happen. There must be something about English life which is particularly conducive to this sort of art, and I think it's a very valuable part of the English artistic tradition.

ROSENTHAL: And what does Lowry himself think about his work? I asked him if he thought it was naïve:

* It was assumed well into the 1960s and before the first appearance of Shelley Rohde's biography in 1979 that Lowry had had no formal art education. It is perhaps interesting to note that Michael Ayrton himself was a virtually self-taught painter and sculptor.

LOWRY: Well, I don't think they are. I drew the life, but I – well, put it this way, when I started to try to create the industrial scene, I did a lot of little figures and little drawings, sketches, and they looked like they do look, you know what I mean. And I thought, well, it's got to be, so there we are. That's all. If I'd painted a portrait from life, well, I don't know ... as I don't do any paintings from life, I just don't know what's happened. I don't know. But if they all thought of things about me ... well, and sometimes I laugh, and say just fancy that! I can't think whether they're naïve or not. I don't intend them – I do them as well as I can, to express what I want.

ROSENTHAL: How much formal training did you have, and how much did it stick with you?

LOWRY: Well, the training lasted me all my life, really. I did the anatomy, and I did a very useful – I draw the figures as well as I need to draw them. As well as I can draw them in a way to suit my purpose. But an ordinary live figure ... that would bore me to death. You see, I don't want to do it. You can't photograph these mill scenes. Can't do that. They're too – you've got to be personal about it. Of course, I thought everybody else would really see it redundant, I did one when I started doing them, now I said to myself, I don't think anybody's ever done this mill scene business – as far as I can see Stanley Houghton wrote about it a little, as writing it, the *Hindle Wakes* man, you know *Hindle Wakes* – he was very good, I was very interested in him.[2] And I started idly to do them, and then I said to myself if I can just get these things established, probably I'd clear out. Because I didn't intend to paint all my life, you know. I only expected to get out about 1948, but by then I'd mixed up in it and couldn't stop. But the last five years I'd been very fed up with it. I'd wanted to stop.

ROSENTHAL: Do you find beauty in paint itself?

LOWRY: Well, if I could press a button, and have it done, I'd like to do that, you know. No – it's all the job, an income sort of job – painting, but it's got to be done, and you do it as well as you can, always as well as you can. If I could press a button and have it done of course, I'd like to do that. I'm not one for painting for painting's sake. But, as I say, if I could press a button I'd like to do it you know. I'd save myself the trouble.

ROSENTHAL: Lowry likes phrases like that. He told us over lunch that he was tired, and, after a suitable pause, that he'd been tired now for forty years. In fact, it's all too easy to see Lowry as an eccentric from both a human and an artistic point of view, easy since that basically is what he is. But it is in many ways a calculated eccentricity, which only partially hides the man underneath and hardly hides at all the very considerable painter that he is. Lowry stands apart in more than the lone wolf sense. He is, as Professor Gombrich says, wholly individual:

GOMBRICH: I feel very much that what distinguishes Lowry and makes his contribution particularly precious at this time is that he never tries to follow a fashion; he did not try to be original, he just was original. And he never tried, as far as I am aware, to be ahead of his time, or to follow a new trend, to jump on any bandwagon; he just was himself. And in this way he became an individual and great artist.

* At the time of publication of this book that fifty years will almost have elapsed. It is up to the reader to decide whether that prognostication by a then relatively youthful writer on art has proved valid.

ROSENTHAL: A great artist. In his way Lowry is that. He has made the harsh landscape of the industrial north take on the beauty which was its ravaged birthright. He has taken the scurrying crowds of the mill towns and turned them into individual streams of the life force and, when his sardonic eye has settled on some wretched derelict or down and out, he has extracted from him not only the obvious pathos, but also a kind of triumphant humour entirely lacking in self pity. Modern art and its presentation always raises a great deal of dust, but Lowry's has for a number of reasons mostly connected with his relatively late discovery and the unfashionableness of his work, raised no dust at all, so that one can already see him with a fair amount of clarity and detachment.* I think that in fifty years time, when all the dust around him has settled, the work of L. S. Lowry will be seen as some of the most original and some of the finest English art of this century. But if that's too solemn a thought, perhaps we should let Lowry have the last word – provided that we remember that neither the work nor the man is nearly as simple as he'd have us believe.

LOWRY: People call me a Sunday painter, well I suppose I'm a Sunday painter who paints every day in the week.

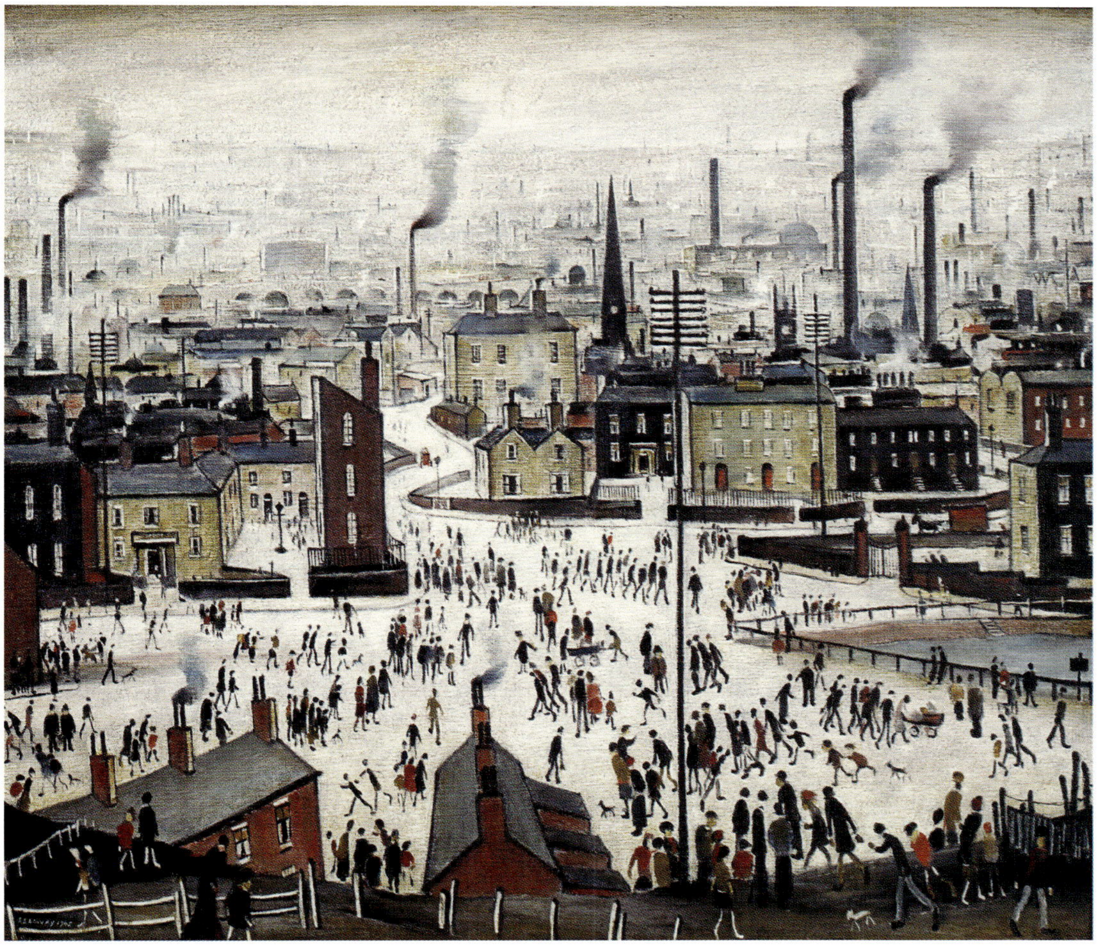

A Lancashire Town, 1945, oil on canvas, 54.6 × 64.8 cm.

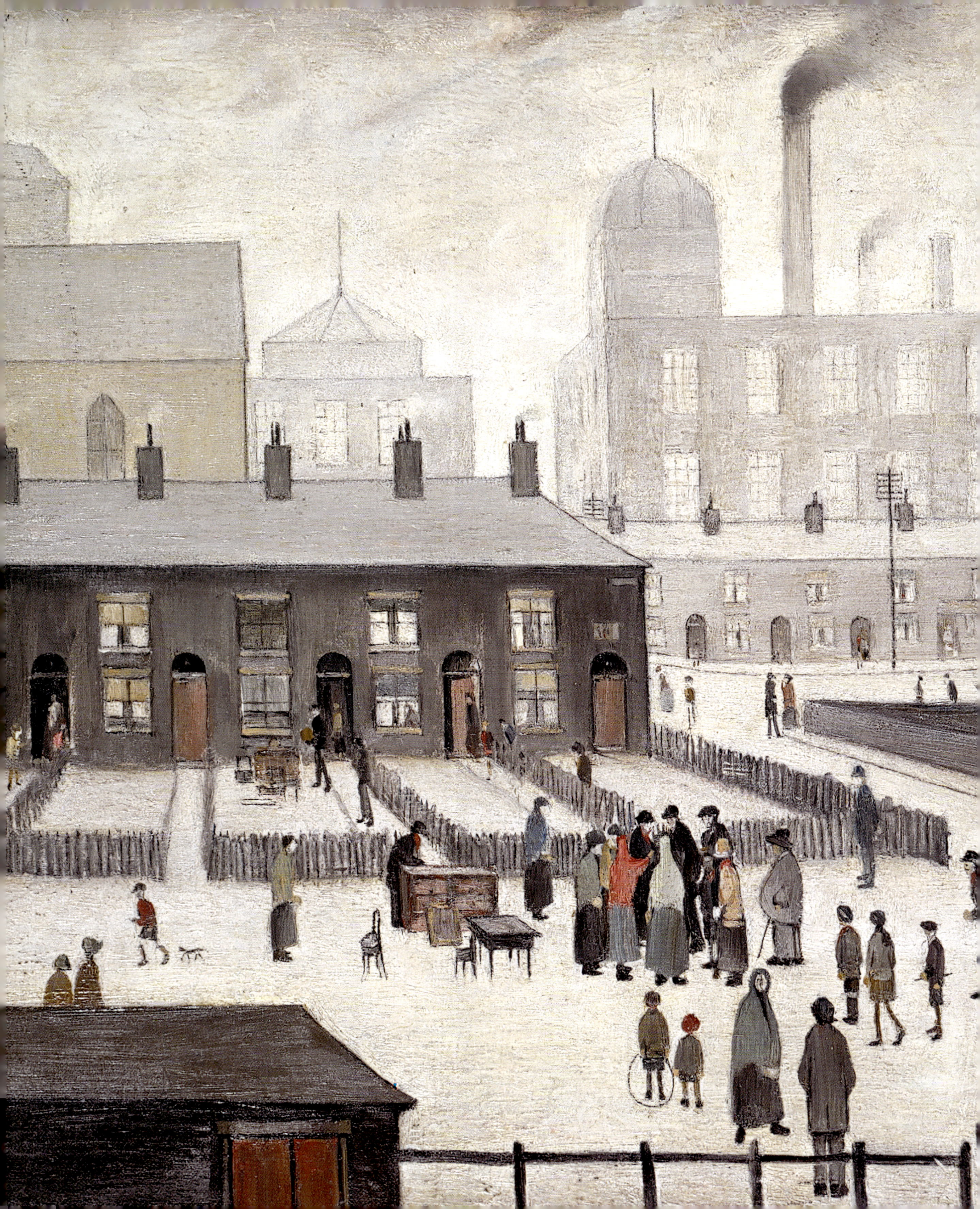

CHAPTER 2

LOWRY IN PERSPECTIVE

His distillation of beauty from the shabbiest and meanest subject that the world has to offer is in harmony with the spirit of his age, but his choice of the locality in which he performs this remarkable operation is an anachronism.

John Rothenstein[1]

L. S. Lowry was, and remains one of the most enigmatic figures in the history of British art. On the whole, those who knew him as a painter were unaware that, from late boyhood to a normal retiring age, (then 65) he was a rent collector and man-of-all-work clerk for the Pall Mall Property Company in Manchester. Unlike Henri Rousseau (nicknamed by Alfred Jarry as *Le Douanier*, i.e. The Customs Officer, because his day job involved working at one of Paris's numerous toll booths), he was never taken up by his leading contemporaries, nor was he nicknamed 'The Rent Collector'. Although Lowry was frequently labeled as either Naïve or Primitive, he was not self-taught, nor was he a creator of fantasy.

He was in fact, while taking many liberties with topography and the depiction of human beings, a painstaking realist, so that, as well as an enigma he was also a master of paradox. Born on 1 November, 1887 and dying on 23 February, 1976 he was in his later years both critically and commercially successful and, had he wished to accept the public honours offered to him, could have been what is now so horribly called a celebrity. Harold Wilson (who owned one of his paintings) offered him a knighthood but he declined, as he did Edward Heath's offer of a CH.

Now, 35 years after his death, his reputation as enigma and paradox has become greatly reinforced. At auction, the prices of his paintings are spectacularly high with certain classic pictures fetching between two and three million pounds each. But in those years that have seen his prices soar and his popular esteem grow with an entire arts centre, with two theatres and an art gallery, built bearing his name in Salford, and a huge variety of merchandise being briskly sold with his most celebrated images superimposed on mugs, pens, notepads etc., his critical reputation has more or less not so much crashed as disintegrated.

I have been writing or broadcasting with and about Lowry for half a century but for the last decade or so I have followed a painful little ritual. Whenever I have written an article about Lowry for journals ranging from *The Spectator* to *The Reader's Digest* and *The Daily Mail* I have always phoned the Information Desk at Tate Britain to ask "Which of your L. S. Lowry paintings are on the walls at the moment?" The answer has, after the clicking sound of computer keyboards being fingered, always been the same: "None on display at the moment". On one occasion the person on the phone tried to be helpful and said that *The Pond* (page 108) was currently on display at Tate Liverpool. Oddly this made

Detail from *The Removal*, 1928, (p.44).

me even more depressed, since this looked as if Lowry had been moved from the "past it" section of this great museum, which has a superb collection of Lowrys in its store-rooms, to the "regional artists" section, Liverpool being, as it were, just down the road from Manchester and Salford. The only conceivable explanation for this neglect of one of the few 20th-century British masters has to be either the curator's lack of interest or, possibly, even an actual dislike of Lowry's work at the top of the Tate structure in the shape of Sir Nicholas Serota. He and my unrelated namesake, Sir Norman Rosenthal, who ruled at the Royal Academy as Exhibitions maestro from 1977 to 2008 and who I know actually dislikes Lowry's work, had in effect been the two main impresarios of 20th century art exhibitions in this country outside the National Gallery with its understandable bias towards the old masters. When I first began writing about Lowry there were lots of other art critics who admired him but old art critics don't just fade away. They either die, as was the case with one of Lowry's staunchest supporters Eric Newton or, as happened with another Lowry enthusiast, Edwin Mullins, who became a notably successful maker of documentary films on art for the BBC and Channel Four and then a novelist and historian. I think it is reasonable to claim that the only regular print art critic who admires Lowry today is Andrew Lambirth of *The Spectator*. The rest maintain at best critical silence and at worst actual contempt.

There has, of course, always been a conflict between the narrow appeal to the cultivated few and the adulation of the mass of the population. One cannot say that Lowry is a great artist because there are coffee mugs with his work printed on them or that a man whose prices exceed three million pounds has to be a genius. This way madness lies and Tretchikov's *Chinese Girl* that adorns a million bedsits, becomes another Michelangelo or Jack Vettriano is the Rembrandt *de nos jours*.

Lowry, like all true originals, is *sui generis*. Like William Blake or Samuel Palmer or Stanley Spencer his work is instantly recognizable and has neither obvious ancestors nor heirs. While Blake was inspired by an entire mythology of unforgettable humans and beasts the other three were irrevocably formed and inspired by their location, their neighbourhood whether in childhood or in early adult life. Palmer's Shoreham affected him relatively late (he was nineteen when he got to Shoreham) and to some extent early Graham Sutherland was indebted to Palmer. But Spencer's Cookham was an early and permanent obsession while for Lowry it was Salford and Manchester which gave him all the material, whether topographical or human, that he needed to form himself as an artist.

Salford, then as now, was an independent city although it has been lumped by the ignorant as an extension of Manchester and is still regarded by many as part of what is known as Greater Manchester. That it is part of the North Western metropolis of Manchester is undeniable, for there is no discernible border between it and Manchester; as there is none between Manchester and Stockport. So, for the purposes of the book, Salford denotes not only Salford but also Manchester and Stockport which also provided Lowry with many of his most iconic images, as did individual suburbs and small towns like Eccles and several other towns and villages which were either a long tramp on foot – Lowry was a great walker – or a short bus or train ride away from his Salford heartland.

That, in aesthetic terms, this unpromising region should have so attracted Lowry and should have been recreated in paint with such beauty has always been a puzzle. In 1945 the anonymous art critic of *The Times* suggested that in an earlier period Lowry could have been a "Wiganish kind of Corot"[2]

John Rothenstein was one of the first important art world figures (he was Director of the Tate Gallery from 1938 to 1964) to recognize Lowry's gifts and was responsible for the Tate's numerous and exceptionally well-chosen collection of Lowry paintings. Rothenstein wrote perceptively about Lowry:

> But as the vision he had at Pendlebury eventually permeated every part of his being, the search for foliage and blades of grass seemed to him a little absurd. If he wanted to paint foliage and grass, he reflected, he could take a tram out to where they grew unstunted; if he wanted to paint Manchester and Salford why should he take for subject what, of all things, was least characteristic of them? So he looked these two appalling places full in the face, and concerned himself more and more exclusively with their most characteristic features: the massive mills and the contrastingly flimsy dwellings of those who worked in the mills; the grim twilight areas of disorderly dereliction; the chapels, the pubs, the sweetshops, where they try to forget their work. It is significant that he rarely painted the most modern mills, and never, I think, the new housing estates, for his real subjects are the bleak pervasive vestiges of the Industrial Revolution. Lowry never represents what he has not seen, yet what he shows us is not a portrait of our own age of equality and planning, when the impact of relievable misfortune is pillowed by social security, when a drab uniformity is replacing squalid disorder. Squalid disorder is what he constantly depicts, and the poverty that accompanied the production of wealth on a scale imcomparably greater than any previous age had known – a poverty measured not only in terms of wages but in terms of life itself. There were not splendid church services or civic spectacles – no symbolic marriage of the Mayor of Manchester to the Ship Canal; no civic games, no complex of beautiful buildings such as ameliorated the harshness of life in earlier civilizations.[3]

Salford today bears little resemblance to what Rothenstein wrote about it in 1956. The factories with their great chimneys no longer exist, the filthy waterways are now clean and prettied up and, on a good day, play host to rowing eights. The slum appartments and dingy shopping streets have all been pulled down and replaced by multi-storeyed towers of 'luxury apartments' and row upon row of identical little red-brick houses all with a garage and a pocket-handkerchief garden. Whoever was in charge of the re-building of the city must have had a built-in dislike of human beings en masse and a need to deprive them of the usual little gracenotes of urban living. Most of Salford is within walking distance of Old Trafford cricket ground and Manchester United's stadium and there are now also several large post-modern office blocks. When I became a regular visitor to study the Old Trafford Test Match or the progress of the Lowry building, or preferably, both on the same visit, staying in a fairly cheap chain hotel, it was to say the least daunting that there were no food shops in the area, no newsagents, no pubs. Apart from the hotel restaurant and bar and before the Lowry went up in 2000, with its attendant branches of Pizza Express, Starbucks etc., you had to walk between half and three quarters of a mile to get fed and watered. No wonder the biggest part of the hotel was the car park. What the present day Salford utterly lacks is character. It is relentlessly dull and, except in the area of the Lowry complex, barren and inhuman; there is no way in which it could possibly nurture an artist of any kind, let alone one of Lowry's genius.

To begin to understand Lowry you have to know about the Salford which was his stamping ground, where he spent countless hours and many days in his grubby mackintosh, rent book in one pocket and sketching materials in the other, ranging from formal little sketching pads to the backs of envelopes and unanswered letters.

One can see what Salford and its inhabitants looked like and how they lived their lives by careful study of his paintings but one can also learn a lot by reading the work of two immensely gifted writers. If every picture is worth a thousand words then, surely, there are many passages of less then a thousand words which can leap off the page and make you understand not just the writer's words but also make you start and say, 'ah, that's pure Lowry'.

If one only reads the opening paragraph of Walter Greenwood's 1933 novel *Love on the Dole* one cannot help but see Lowry plain.

> They call this part 'Hanky Park'. It is that district opposite the parish church of Pendleton, one of the many industrial townships comprising the Two Cities. In the early nineteenth century Hanky Park was part of the grounds of a wealthy lady's mansion; at least, so say the old maps in the Salford Town Hall. The district takes its name from a sloping street, Hankinson Street, whose pavements, much worn and very narrow, have been polished by the traffic of boots and clogs of many generations. On either side of this are other streets, mazes, jungles of tiny houses cramped and huddled together, two rooms above and two below, in some cases on one room down and aloft; public houses by the score where forgetfulness lurks in a mug; pawnshops by the dozen where you can raise the wind to buy forgetfulness; churches, chapels and unpretentious mission halls where God is praised; nude, black patches of land, 'crofts', as they are called, waterlogged, sterile, bleak and chill.[4]

That last sentence immediately conjours up the bleak two-dimensional image of Lowry's painting *An Island* (page39) which the contemporary novelist Howard Jacobson (himself a Mancunian), described as Golgotha.[5]

The ruined, rather grand house is the sort of dwelling that a slave-driving factory owner of Greenwood's time might have lived in. Greenwood's 1933 description of lesser dwellings, of which Lowry painted hundreds, could have been written by Lowry himself, had he been a novelist rather than a painter.

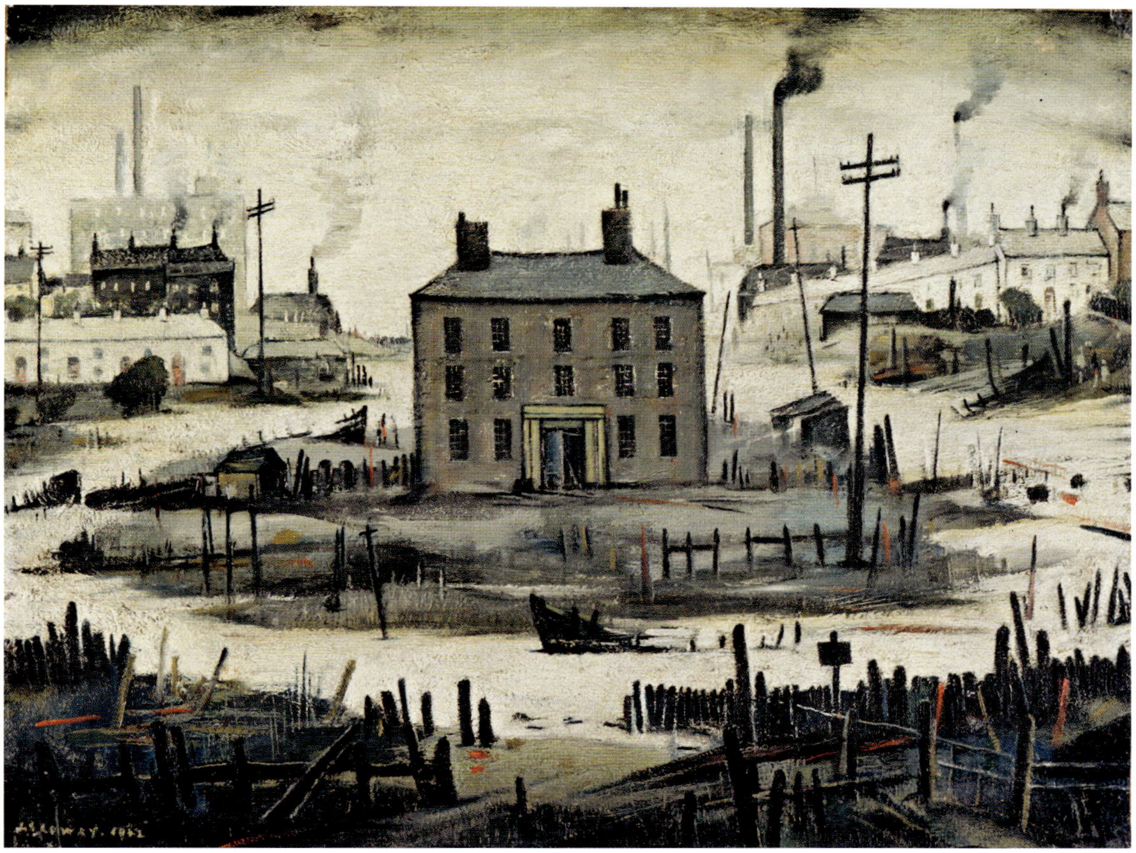

An Island, 1942, oil on canvas, 45.6 × 60.9 cm.

The identical houses of yesterday remain, still valuable in the estate market even though the cost of their building has been paid for over and over again by successive tenants. The houses remain: streets of them where the blue-grey smoke swirls down like companies of ghosts from a million squat chimneys: jungles of tiny houses cramped and huddled together, the cradles of generations of the future. Places where men and women are born, live, love and die and pay preposterous rents for the privilege of calling the grimy houses 'home'.[6]

And these words might have been written by a Greenwood who was studying a painting of Lowry's in the same period. Harry, an office worker, a humble clerk, still only a boy, wants to work in a factory, to become a man:

> He stared at it, unblinkingly. He had seen it before, often enough, but not in the light of the present as something in which he wished to be absorbed. Awe glowed in his intent eyes.
>
> Three huge chimneys challenged the lowering sky; three banners of thick black smoke gushed forth from their parapets, swirling, billowing, expanding as they drifted, with 'unperturbed pace' to merge, imperceptibly into the dirty sky. A double row of six smaller chimneys thrust up their steel muzzles like a cannon trained on air raiders. Tongues of flame shot up, fiery sprites, kicking their flaming skirts about for a second

> then diving again as instantly as they had appeared. An orange glare reflected dully on the wet slates of the foundry.
>
> The colossal building itself sprawled sooty and grimy over a tremendous acreage enclosed within a high brick wall. Within was laid out in streets numbered in the American manner, 'First Street', and so on to 'Forty-First Street'.[7]

There are at least a dozen Lowry paintings reproduced in this book that might have been designed by Greenwood.

Sadly there is no record of these two men, who had so much in common, ever meeting, although Lowry's indefatigable biographer Shelley Rohde reported that Greenwood once called on the Lowry household and, knowing that Lowry worked in the attic, knocked repeatedly until Mrs Lowry opened her bedroom window and told him to go away. He retorted that he had come "to see your Laurie" whereupon Lowry's mother replied: "He's out. Go away. Leave us alone" as she slammed the window shut and the lace curtain twitched back into place.

This was not the only injury inflicted on Lowry by his mother but, in terms of the intellectual posterity of the industrial North West, it was surely among the most regrettable.

Whenever one looks at Lowry's painting of the massed entrance of workers into a factory or a mill or his versions of their exodus from those terrible buildings one thinks of the economy of Greenwood's prose as he paints that kind of scene in words as telling as some of Lowry's pigments.

> Suddenly, from the side of one of the tall chimneys appeared a plume of steam vapour instantly followed by the deep, loud, hoarse note of a siren. The warning signal telling the men that only five minutes separated them from the time to commence work. The great gates slid back. In concert the vast assembly seethed about the opening and spilled into the enormous rail-lined patterned streets and yards, spreading in all directions like an army of ants in panic.[8]

This is pure Lowry for the start of the working day and Greenwood's description of the end of the day's toil, with its early noon release on a Saturday, is masterly and highly visual.

> Noon.
>
> The Great exodus from Marlow's began. Twelve thousand boys and men surging through the gates, a black, agitated river of humanity breaking into a hundred tiny streamlets and scurrying off in all directions. Lines of empty stationary tramcars and fleets of charabancs; corporation buses, push and motor bikes: mad rushes, pushings, shovings, cursing, jangling of tram bell, honkings of motor horns; 'Gerrout of it, y'dreamy-eyed sod, y'...' changings of gears, rattlings of tramcar wheels, clouds of pungent exhaust; 'What a bloody stink ...'
>
> Ragged boys calling the midday sporting newspaper: 'One o'clock ... One o'clock edition,' football and racing talk. Everybody all smiles on account of wages in pockets and because they wouldn't see any more machinery until Monday morning.[9]

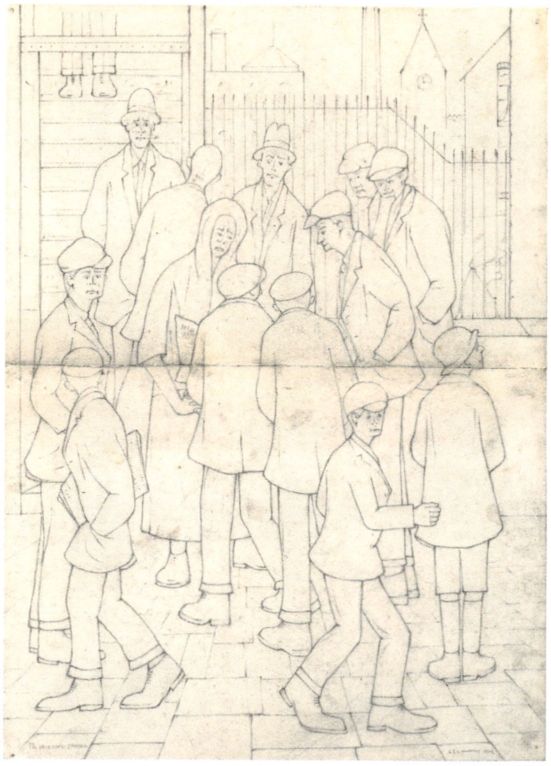

Drawing for *The Midday Special*, 1926.

There are several Lowry pictures which capture this atmosphere and his feeling for, and handling of, industrial crowds constitutes a unique talent for depicting the bustle and energy of a North Western industrial city between the wars. But Lowry was far more than a recorder of moods. He could also capture with uncanny skill the working of small groups of people as in his picture, which might have been made for Greenwood, called *The Midday Special* (above) with its intimate depiction of impatient curiosity by a handful of people taken out of one of Lowry's or Greenwood's exodus crowds.

Love on the Dole is of course not just a novel about factory life. Its parallels with much of Lowry's work are due simply to two artists in different disciplines tackling the world around them. Lowry was not a notably political man. He was probably midway between being a Conservative and being conservative. He was adamant about the iniquities of all British governments of either party because he hated being taxed at all about as much as he hated paying what he saw as an entirely disproportionate amount of his hard-earned money to the state, particularly once he was famous and earning a considerable income. It is doubtful whether he possessed any political fire in his belly and he was certainly not a man of the left. He was fascinated by the human products of brutal, non-welfare state capitalism in that they gave him an inexhaustible subject matter. He would never have thought, let alone spoken, as Greenwood's political hero in the novel did when he was preaching his socialist, even Marxist, views to the oppressed of Salford.

> ... And to find the cost of this present system you have only to look at our own lives and the lives of our parents and their parents. Labour never ending, constant struggles to pay the rent and to buy sufficient food and clothing; no time for anything that is bright and beautiful. We never see such things. All we see are these grey depressing streets; mile

after mile of them; never ending ... And the houses in which we are compelled to live are as though they have been designed by fiends in hell for our especial punishment. When work is regular we are just about to live from week to week; there is no surplus. Bur for ever, there hangs over us that dread threat of unemployment. Unemployment that can and does reduce most honest working folk to pauperdom that saddles them with a debt that takes years to repay ... *that* is the price we will continue to pay until you *people* awaken to the fact that Society has the means, the skill, and the knowledge to afford us the opportunity to become Men and Women in the fullest sense of those terms.[10]

He viewed politics and politicians of all parties with a sharply ironic, even jaded, highly satirical eye. Although in terms of artistic technique he owed nothing to the great political cartoonists such as Cruickshank or Gillray and more or less entirely lacked their frequently *ad hominem* savagery over great issues and fraudulent and hypocritical personal conduct, he understood the universal mendacity of nearly all political meetings. If one looks at *The Election*, also known as *The Orator*, of 1950 (page 43) his views are plain enough. They cut through the platitudes of most public meetings with the sure directness and sardonic dry humour of the wonderful postwar radio comedian and professional Northerner, Al Read. This painting has an unusual structure. Many of Lowry's paintings have the subject of the title tucked away in a corner – sometimes even a dark corner – so that the canvas or board is dominated by all the extras who form the onlooking crowd and the key subject, such as *The Fever Van* (page 177), or *The Removal* also known as *The Eviction* (page 44) or *After the Wedding* (page 45) has to be carefully sought out by the viewer much as in Bruegel's *The Fall of Icarus,* where the majority of the picture is of a tranquil rural scene and you have to look hard to find the diminutive Icarus plunging to his doom in the sea with a relatively small splash. So it is with this, in all senses, engaging picture. Several of the crowd are clearly bored and have already turned away from the speaker. The orator has stepped off his rather low soapbox and is tall enough to be able to reach his audience while standing on the ground. Almost dead centre is a strange little man in a knickerbocker suit, flat cap and stockinged legs, who has the look of a jockey, or at least a racing aficionado, but who also looks as if he could be the politician's electoral agent.

Rather disconcertingly the speaker's hairstyle and moustache remind one not of any English politician one can remember but rather the shade of Adolf Hitler, and the moustache sported by the little man in knickerbockers or breeches is definitely Hitlerian rather than Chaplinesque. Not all of Lowry's paintings are so specific about a single human activity as this one, but it does at times work as a paradigm of his views of city life. Drab, uniform buildings, factory chimneys and a tall thin church spire in the background and, at a rough count, nearly sixty human beings, all of them firmly individual, none of them a mere crowd-filler, each of them recognizable from the everyday street life of Salford. This is an immensely theatrical painting and bears out Sir Ian McKellen's view that Lowry, a confirmed theatre lover, was brought up in his youth in a conurbation that boasted some 64 individual

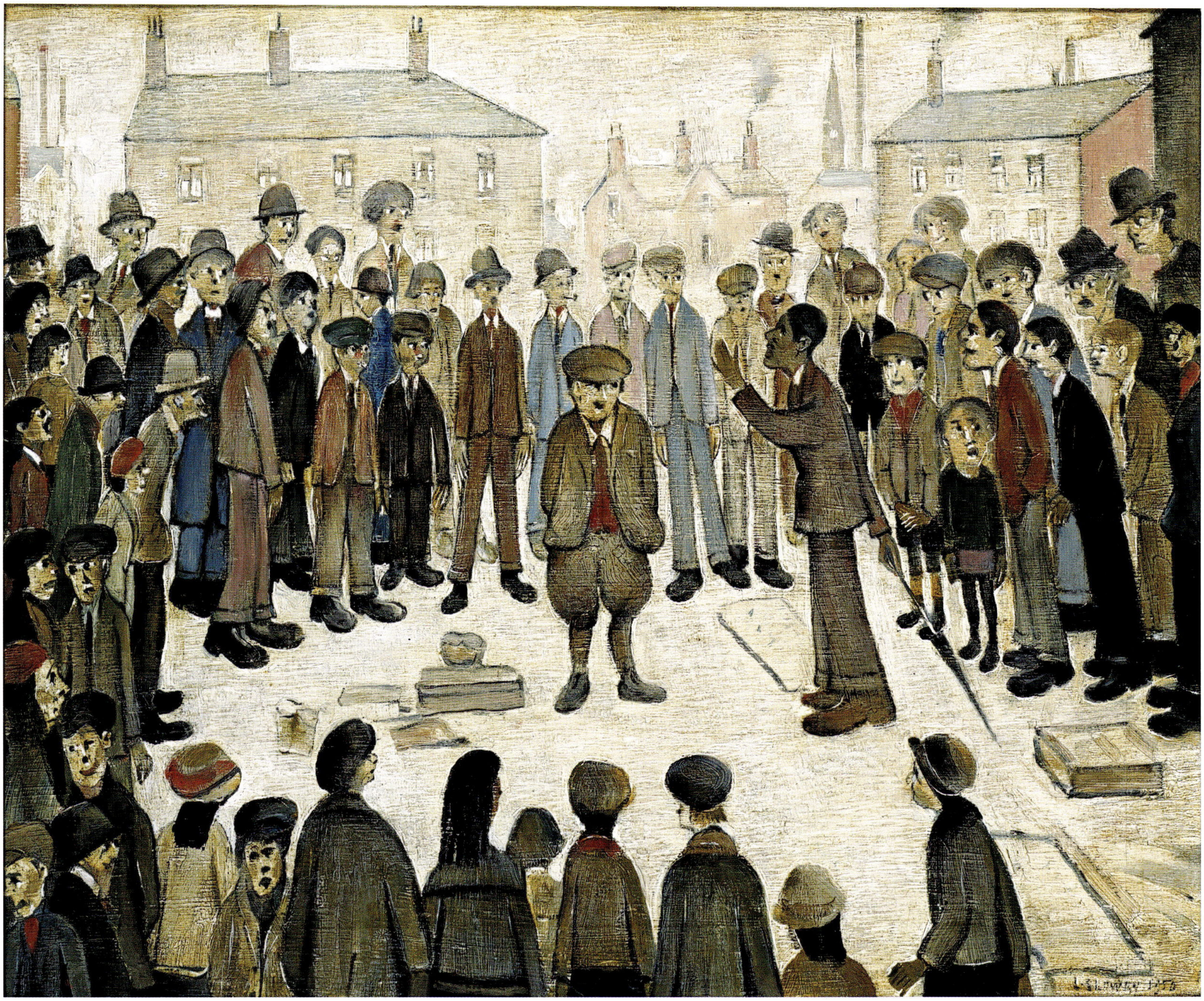

The Election, 1950, oil on canvas, 51.1 × 61 cm.

theatres ranging from vast music halls to small auditoria for chamber plays. McKellen, before he went to Cambridge, where we were contemporaries, was at school in Wigan and Bolton. He attended, as I did, a public debate on 1 February 2009 at the South Bank's Queen Elizabeth Hall. The principal bout was between Howard Jacobson defending Lowry and Brian Sewell attacking him. After Jacobson and Sewell had had their say the chair invited comments

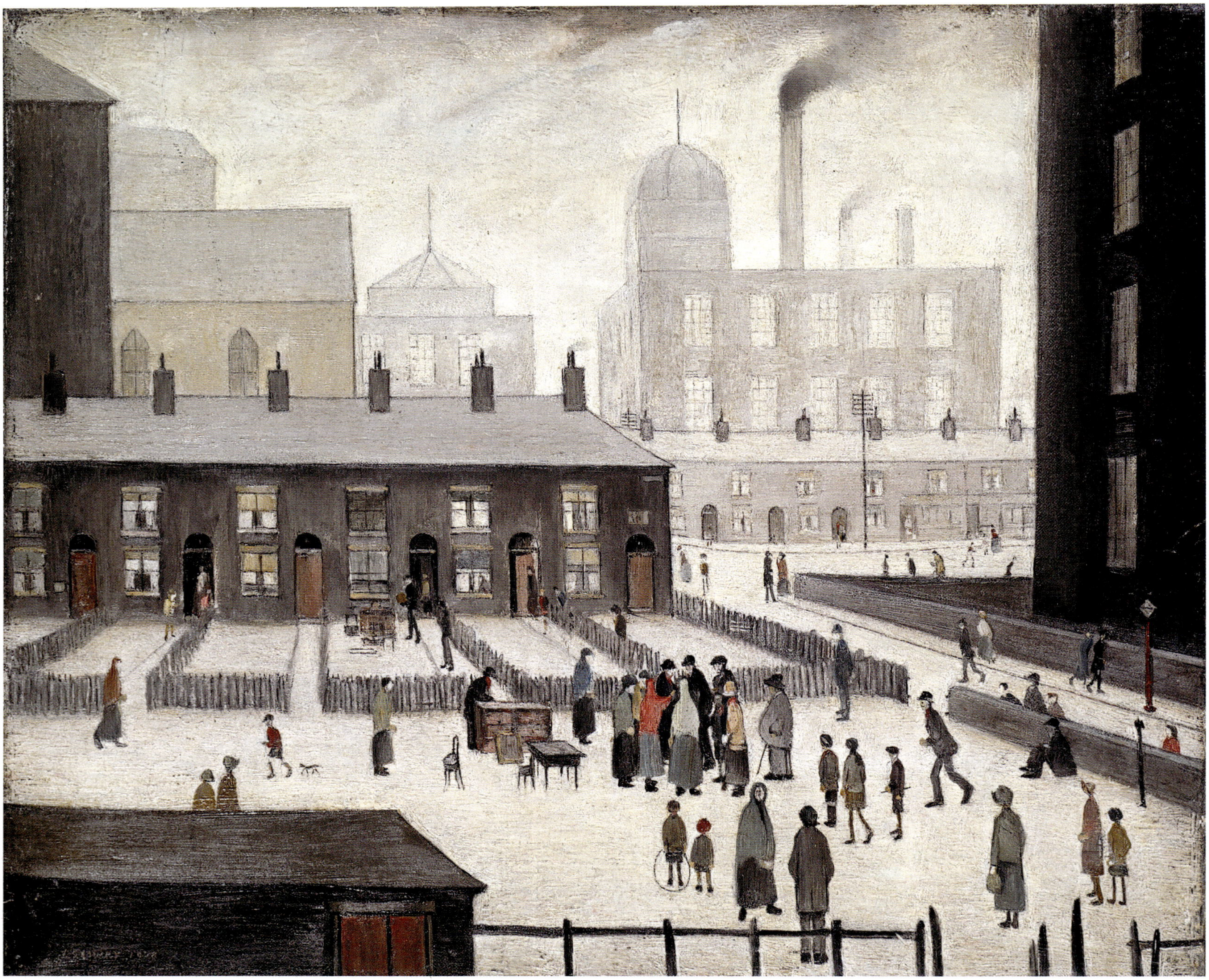

The Removal, 1928, oil on canvas, 43.1 × 53.3 cm.

from the floor, suggesting that speakers could identify themselves – just first names would do. McKellen made his contribution, starting with the words "My name is Ian and I'm from the North". I was on the other side of the hall and could not see the speaker but the voice was familiar enough and I listened with great care as he made the point about the theatre and that one of the keys to understanding Lowry was to look at many of his pictures of the

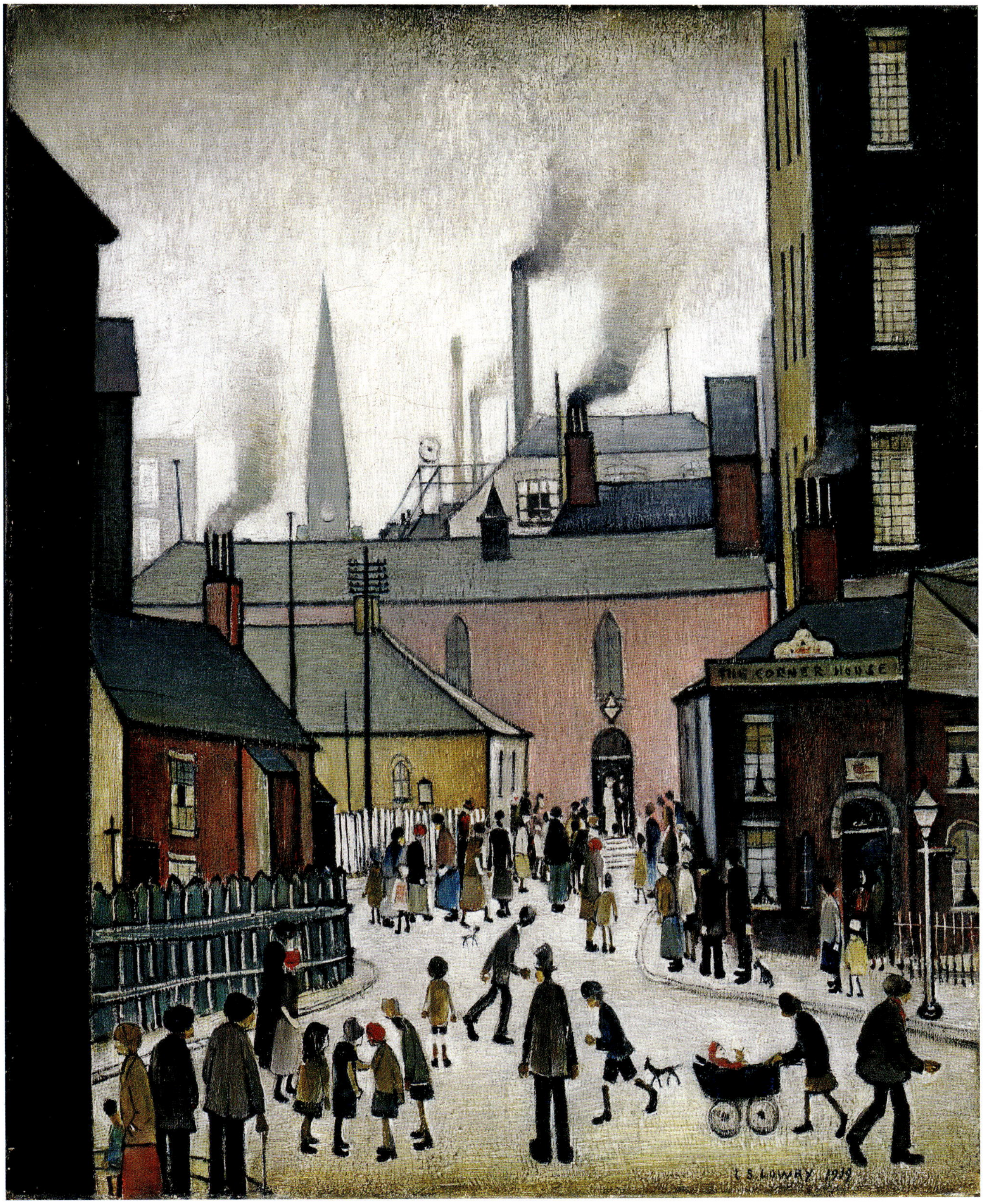

After the Wedding,
1939, oil on canvas,
53.3 × 43.4 cm.

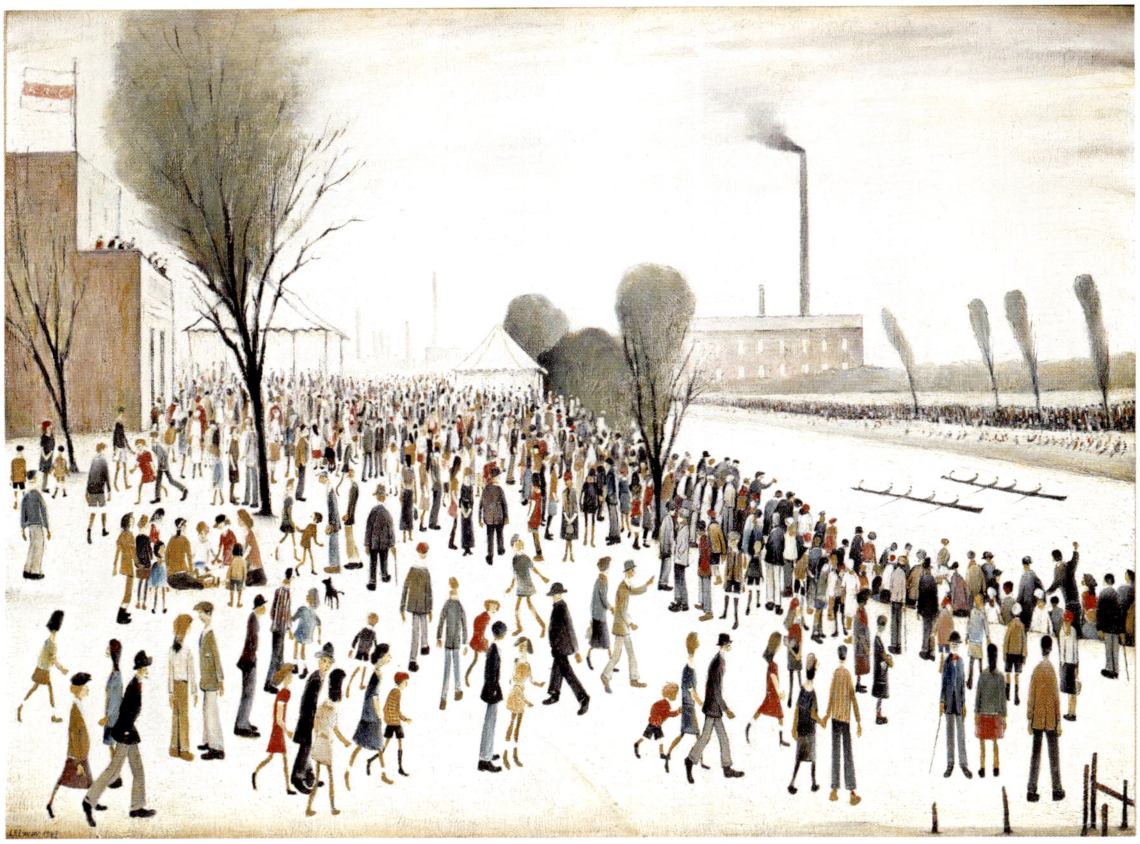

The Regatta, 1949, oil on canvas, 77 × 102.5 cm.

industrial north as if they were behind a proscenium, as if they were in fact staged scenes and events and that often his pictures had a straight line of some sort in the foreground and that line was in effect the front edge of the stage beyond which the action took place in Lowry's mind and in the eyes of the beholder. This is all of a piece with the concept of Lowry developing his art in the period and the area that produced the Manchester School of Dramatists like Stanley Houghton, author of *Hindle Wakes* and Harold Brighouse, author of *Hobson's Choice*.

There is another writer whose experiences of Salford are germane to any appreciation of the city and of its most notable 20th-century resident. If Greenwood's novel is the bible for the first half of the last century then parts of Terry Eagleton's memoir *The Gatekeeper*, his account of growing up in Salford as an impoverished Irish Catholic in the years after World War II (he was born in 1943) and his progression to a Marxist mode of thought while holding distinguished academic posts in Cambridge, Oxford and Manchester, with an honorary degree from the University of Salford, contains some remarkable sketches of the city of Salford and the sheer practicalities of its – and his – poverty before it was razed and re-built into its present anodyne anonymity. His was very much the period of Lowry's prime while Greenwood was at work in effect at the time of Lowry's first important development.

At the age of ten Eagleton, as a pre-pubertal male, was considered by the local Carmelite convent to be safe enough to usher the new brides of Christ through the door out of the waiting room and into the business end of the convent where their hair would be shorn and such terrible frivolities as Marks and Spencer's knickers would be forbidden for ever. The gatekeeper's other principal duty was to admit the parents of the hapless postulant nun for their last visit and sight of their beloved daughter.[11]

Life at Engleton's primary school was less exotic and a good deal less comfortable than his convent duties:

> There was not much of this metaphysical conundrum in 1950s Salford. The boys at my primary school were sometimes so famished that they shoveled great mounds of beetroot into themselves at lunch, then spewed it up again in steaming maroon heaps on their school desks. A lot of them would have known alcoholism and grotesque physical violence at home, and were dripping with all sorts of dark, horrifying sexual knowledge. I was a puny, livid-faced Oliver Twist among these scabby-kneed roughs, dispensed from being regularly bullied because I was chronically ill ...
>
> Some of them seemed as immune to physical pain as a stove-pipe. They could endure any amount of punching and caning, not least at the hands of a teacher known as Miss Arseole, whose real name I can now retrospectively reconstruct as Miss Horsehall. You could have crushed their testicles in a vice and they would not have whimpered, but they howled inconsolably if they ripped their shirts in a fight, since this meant confronting the wrath of parents who had no money to replace their clothes. I was the only child who wore a coat to school, on account of my delicate health, which marked me out as sinisterly as if I had arrived at school in a Bentley with a caviar lunch tucked under my elbow. The coat made me a target for violence as surely as flaunting some obscenely taunting slogan on my chest, though it also signaled that I was a kind of moral cripple, and so inhibited the aggression it provoked.[12]

Eagleton recalls that one day his mother came across L. S. Lowry sketching in the street but culture in Eagleton's Salford childhood was a rare, as well as occasionally misunderstood, commodity. At one stage the Salford Council wanted to brighten the place up:

> Eventually, one councilor proposed erecting a few pagodas in the local park. The suggestion met with general approval, until the mayor rose heavily from his seat. "It's all very well having these 'ere pagodas in t'park", he growled, "but what I want to know is this. *Who's going to feed the buggers?"* It was the same mayor who, while conducting a visiting dignitary around the city art gallery, proudly assured him that all the works on exhibition were 'hand-painted'.[13]

Like many another bright Salford Catholic lad the young Terry was mildly duped into trying out life in a seminary. He records this episode and the Church's failure to ensnare him hilariously. As he puts it: "Not long afterwards I returned home to my crestfallen parents, a spoiled priest". Yet, as the book makes clear, for all its gentle, and occasionally not so gentle, mockery of his Salford childhood Eagleton is somehow proud of the place, scrupulously listing, apart from Lowry, some of its most distinguished products: including Albert Finney, Shelagh Delaney, Peter Maxwell Davies and Mike Leigh.[14]

For much of Lowry's life, Greenwood and Eagleton depicted a Salford of grinding, soul-destroying, even life-threatening poverty in powerful prose which never descended to pity but which was essentially fairly incendiary, left-wing writing, writing intended to cause both pity and anger in the mind of the reader. Lowry was born and brought up in that segment of society which George Orwell, with his division of England into three classes above the manual worker, namely lower-middle, middle-middle and upper-middle would have challenged even Orwell's skills in categorization. Lowry was never poor, never unemployed. Life with his parents as an only child was an odd mixture of hard-driving towards success and a total absence of encouragement. His father was a failing businessman, his mother a pianist who, lacking the necessary talent for the concert platform, gave piano lessons to bring in some money. She it was who put little Laurie into a private school with a proper uniform and insisted that they moved to houses in better neighbourhoods to improve their local standing at increased rents that they could not afford. Mr and Mrs Lowry's aspirations were to belong to what Orwell would eventually call the middle-middle class, aspirations which the young Lowry neither admired nor shared.

While he never shared the lives of the poor, whether children or adolescents or adults, he certainly knew how they lived. As a rent collector how could it be otherwise? Yet his depiction of Salford's (and Manchester and Stockport's) poverty and dereliction completely lacks the sociological, analytic disapproval of a Greenwood or an Eagleton. There is, as they used to say in Hollywood, no 'message'. He never set out to manipulate the spectator's political views or his emotions. He simply recorded what he had seen all his life and what interested him, whether mills, factories, tenement slums, winding streets of tiny back-to-back houses and the people who worked and lived in them. These are the typical subjects which spring to mind when Lowry is mentioned; what conjures up that sloppy, lazy phrase used by those who cannot really see what he is doing, the 'matchstick men'. The proliferation of the 'industrial' paintings, with their dense crowds of miniature people, causes people to be unaware of, or at least less interested in, the many seascapes and studies of all kinds of boats, the frequently, uninhabited landscapes, the literally thousands of drawings of towns and villages all over Britain, many of them sketches for fully-fledged paintings.

Most of the dwellings, workplaces and people lacked beauty. Hard physical labour and abject poverty do not show people at their best and the combination of the generally vile climate of the region and what we now call carbon emissions makes the majority of industrial buildings and slum dwellings look drab almost beyond endurance. Lowry's self-imposed highly restricted palette of only five colours is not in itself an aid to prettiness. Yet there is no gainsaying that out of this unlikely mixture of the drab, the poor and the ugly, Lowry made art of great beauty. This might well be what John Rothenstein called an anachronism yet it is also a form of truth, the truth of Lowry's uncanny, wholly accurate visions; accurate that is from an artistic point of view but, frequently, inaccurate from a purely topographical

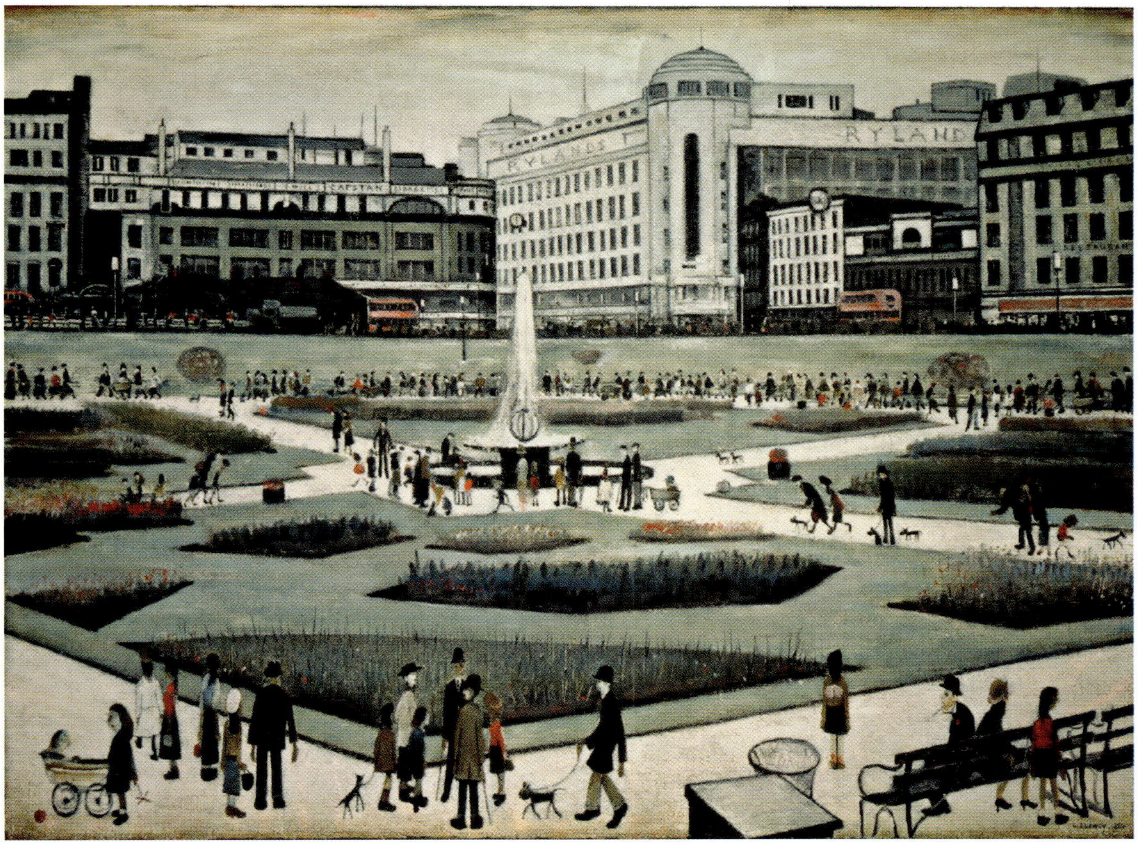

Piccadilly Gardens, 1954, oil on canvas, 76.2 × 101.6 cm.

viewpoint. Many of Lowry's finest city-scapes and crowd scenes are not wholly real; they are analogues of urban nature but they are rarely, unless commissioned for a particular patron, as in his essentially rather unsatisfactory version of Manchester's *Piccadilly Gardens* (above), faithful depictions of a town or city reality. His most interesting views are of towns, cities, even urban landscapes such as *The Pond* (page 108) in which he imaginatively selects fragments and sketches of places and buildings he has observed and even drawn on his various walks and train and bus journeys to meld them into a pleasing whole which is in every way faithful to the spirit of place but which really exists only at first in his head and then later on canvas or board.

As the distinguished left-wing art critic John Berger has pointed out, Lowry's purpose in painting dirt, squalor, poverty and the atmospherically destructive factories and mills was not done as a protest against the ravages of the Industrial Revolution. Although his work had its manifest parallels with the writings of Greenwood and Eagleton and, possibly, Berger himself, Lowry had absolutely no sense of political mission; there was no 'message' in his painting, only a way of seeing what others had dismissed as ugly and unworthy of either study or affection and which he saw as not only a valid and vibrant form of life but a landscape of real beauty.

To return to McKellen's aperçu about the theatrical life of Greater Manchester when Lowry was growing up, the theatre was of greatimportance to him and it is interesting to note that his particular theatrical tastes were not for tragedy or Shaw's wordy plays of ideas but for the Manchester School with which he grew up. In so far as the Manchester School had any sense of unity among its creators as opposed to the journalistic convenience of a neat and tidy label – and hence idiot's guide to classification – about as helpful as the "Kitchen Sink" school or the "Scottish Colourists", then the sense of unity was one perfectly matched to Lowry's mind. The best of the plays were sardonic, ironic, satirical and, above all, if well performed, extremely funny.

It is difficult to understand and appreciate fully the scenes of working-class life and Lowry's recording of public incidents which please the crowds of onlookers while acutely discomfiting the handful of participants. In the recordings of Lowry that I made (see Chapter 1) one could shut one's eyes and imagine that one was talking not to a great painter but to a great comic like Al Read. Time and again in his best pictures he visually captures the tone of Brighouse or Houghton. In *Hindle Wakes*, Stanley Houghton takes that old Victorian cliché of the impoverished mill girl whom the young cad charms, seduces and does her wrong. But, at the end, after the rich cad's family have leaned on him to do his duty and marry the girl, Fanny, humiliates all the toffs by saying that she'd enjoyed her weekend of fun and had not the slightest intention of or desire to marry her seducer, who is clearly unworthy of her. As social comment – and as a clarion call for feminism (the play was first performed in 1912) it is powerful stuff, having much in common with Ibsen's *The Doll's House* written in 1879 except that it is far more overtly satirical and is supremely funny.

Equally well crafted and equally slyly funny is Harold Brighouse's 1915 play *Hobson's Choice*. It is known that Lowry was immensely impressed by *Hindle Wakes* talking about it enthusiastically in his later years. His connection with *Hobson's Choice* is less clear but, as it was first performed during World War I, a conflict Lowry managed to avoid, it is more or less impossible to imagine that he did not know it. *Hobson's Choice*, like *Hindle Wakes*, also had a serious message about youth versus age and about the ties and betrayals of family life. Indeed one theatrical reference book states firmly that the play is 'a kind of plebeian *King Lear*'. Be that as it may, Lowry's satirical comedic style would have been a credit to Brighouse and Houghton. Like them he could take dramatic and uncomfortable incidents and make you laugh just as you, like the inevitable group, or even crowd, of spectators gathered to watch something deadly serious (and simultaneously richly comic), were clearly seeing the funny side of someone else's tragedy. Look at the 1927 painting *The Arrest* (page 51). It shows some plain clothes policemen outside a private house, labeled no. 29, apprehending a wanted man. Lowry has given the street the improbable name of *Police Street* and there are happy gawpers in the windows of number 29 and on the pavement and the roadway. You feel that at any moment the Keystone Cops will show up and that Lowry was chuckling with pleasure when he had finished the picture.

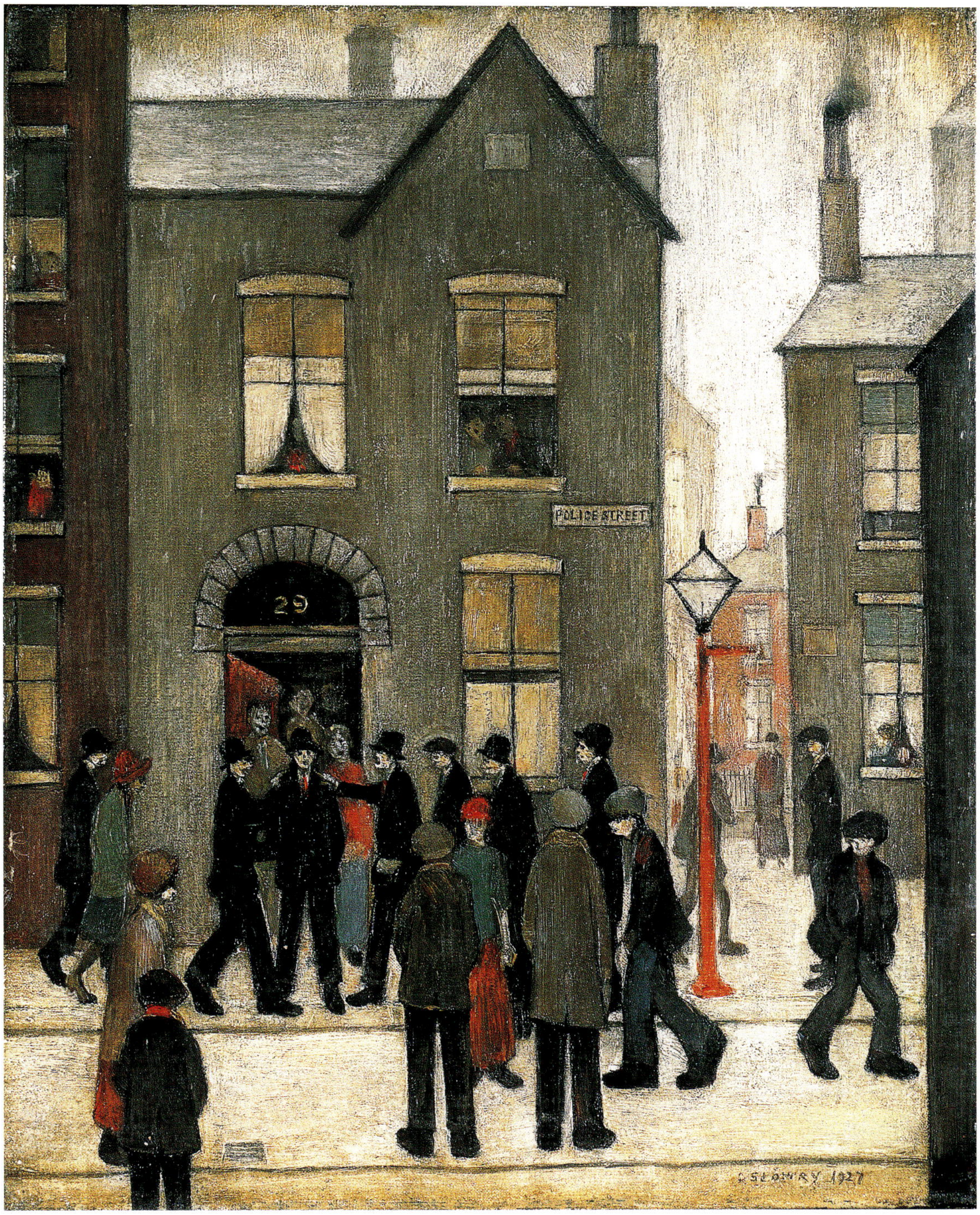

The Arrest, 1927, oil on canvas, 53.3 × 43.2 cm.

In a later painting of about 1935 he depicts *A Fight* (page 52) outside a lodging house displaying in a window its nightly rates for beds at '4d and 6d per night (the equivalent of today's 2½p). One of the onlookers, a man in a blue suit, bears an uncanny resemblance to Harold Macmillan and the only woman among them is smartly dressed and watching covertly over her shoulder having just walked past the participants. It does not look as if

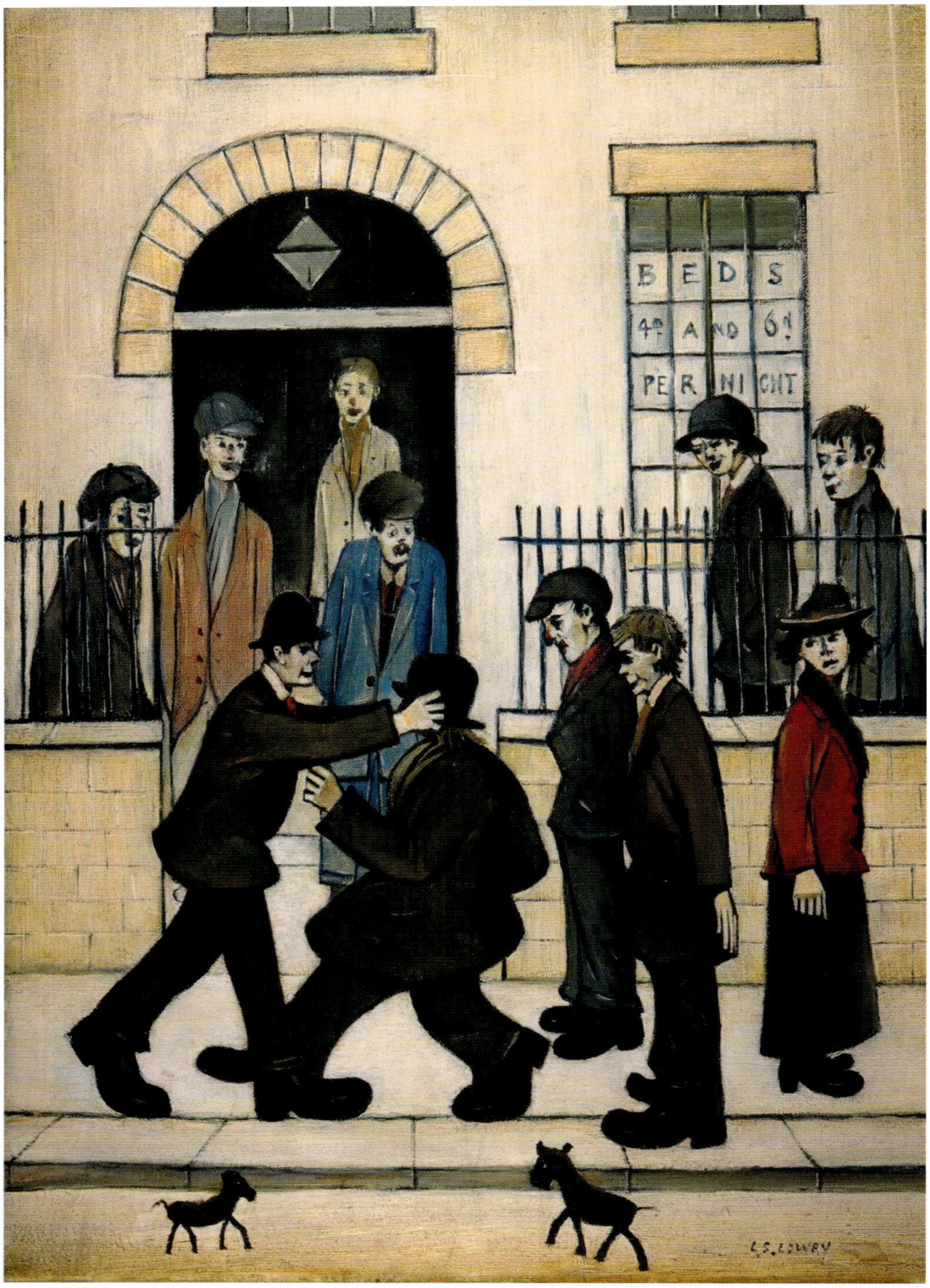

A Fight, *c.* 1935, oil on canvas, 53.2 × 39.5 cm.

the fight will last long as the taller and fitter looking of the two men has already pulled the shorter and fatter one's bowler hat over his ears and has a longer reach. In the gutter there are two classic, exiguous Lowry dogs who, in their postures, are like a mirror image of the two assailants squaring off to each other. *A Fight* is a violent street scene and could just as easily be a scene from a play. Like so much of Lowry's work involving people it is intensely theatrical and imbued with his sardonic sense of humour.

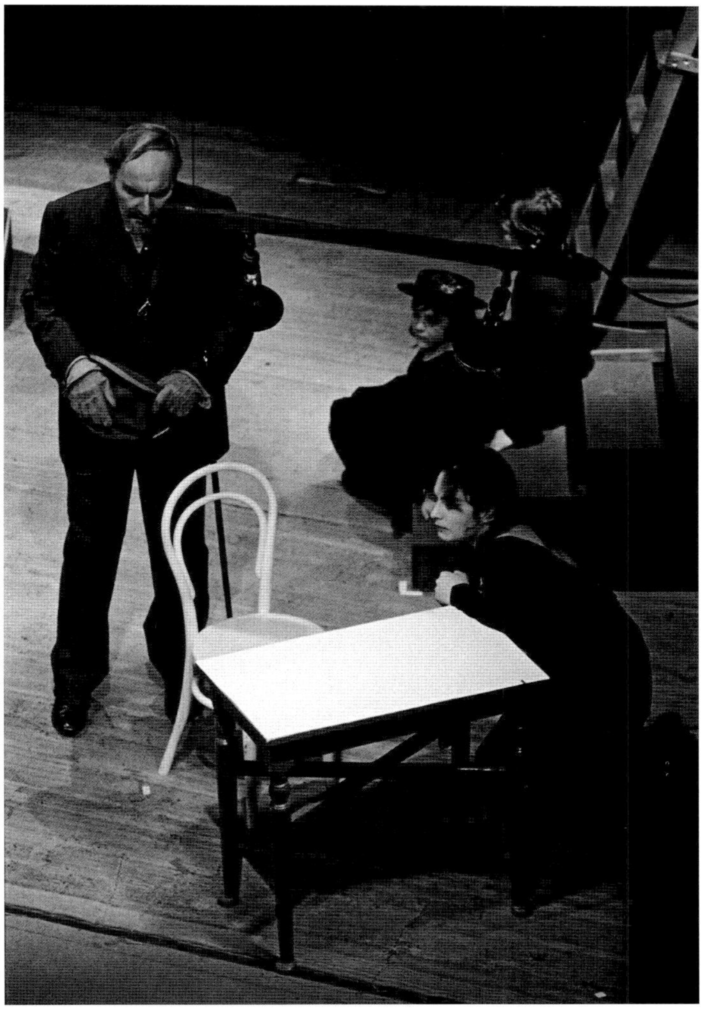

Pirandello's *Six Characters in Search of an Author*, with Ralph Richardson, 1963 revival production Mayfair Theatre. Photograph by Anthony Crickmay.

One of the more surprising aspects of Lowry's relationship with theatre is, at first glance at least, his passion for Pirandello's *Six Characters in Search of an Author* (above). Yet, on analyzing the link, it becomes perfectly natural. Lowry was introduced to the play by Sheila Fell whom he often took to the theatre on his visits to London (see Chapter 13, LOWRY AND WOMEN). She suggested that they went to a production of Pirandello's masterpiece starring Ralph Richardson and using a new translation by Frederick May, which opened at the Arts Theatre Club on 23 June, 1954 and transferred to the St James's Theatre for a long and successful run on 20 July, 1954. According to Rohde, Lowry told his friend Frank Mullineux that this was:

> The only time in my life I have been strongly influenced by a play. I went to see it nine times. By the third time I had become interested in the child with long hair. By the fourth I thought 'I'm gone, I'm gone – I'm, bats about this child'. Then I became interested in the six figures. I had got it bad. The visual aspect of the characters

> fascinated me. Then the child had to have a rest after such a long run and the second child didn't impress me like the first. Years before I had seen *Hindle Wakes* and that was an influence, an artistic influence; but this play was different, it affected me, it mesmerized me.[15]

Sheila Fell had observed Lowry's obsession with the play at the closest possible quarters, simply by sitting next to him at more than one performance.

> When the six characters moved en bloc, very slowly, in their black Victorian clothes, from back to front of stage, he was enraptured.[16]

Fell also remembered him for humanity as well as his painterly genius:

> I miss his wit; I miss his humour; I miss him. He was a great humanist and no one ever seems to mention that. To be a humanist one has first to love human beings and to be a great humanist one has to be slightly detached from human beings after having had great love for them; which is exactly what he was.[17]

If one follows the thought of Fell's eulogy of Lowry and links it with his falling under Pirandello's spell in *Six Characters in Search of an Author* one can see why that spell was so powerful. There is not space enough here to analyze *Six Characters*. It would take a team of theatre critics and a further team of philosophers many days to unravel all its different layers of meaning starting with the fact that Pirandello's play, written in 1924, begins, ostensibly, with a group of theatrical professionals from director to stage manager, about to rehearse a play called *The Rules of the Game*, a drama written by one Luigi Pirandello in 1913.

If the 1950s and 1960s were key decades in Lowry's *oeuvre* they were also the key decades of an *avant garde* theatrical movement known, thanks to Martin Esslin's seminal book, as *The Theatre of the Absurd*, first published in 1961 and revised in 1968. It was the first, and remains the best, account and analysis of the plays of Samuel Beckett, Harold Pinter, Arthur Adamov, Jean Genet, Edward Albee, Eugène Ionesco and others, all of whom were highly individual and were in no way part of a formal group. But they had in common a sense of menace, a radical sense of structure which played havoc with the Harley Granville Barker, George Bernard Shaw concept of the 'well made play'. All they really had in common was the ability to evoke laughter, some of it partly tearful and some of it deeply nervous. And of course the most highly developed sense of the absurd, itself more or less indefinable, but one of those concepts or qualities you immediately recognize when you are face to face with it.

Re-reading Esslin's book in a reprint of 2001 it was, after a diligent search of the index, distinctly odd to find hardly any references to Pirandello who, surely, was the 'onlie begetter,' a whole generation earlier, of the Theatre of the Absurd. By one of life's odd coincidences as I write this in my office, round the corner from the Haymarket Theatre, Ian McKellen is currently starring there in a revival of *Waiting for Godot*. Esslin quotes some reactions to the Paris première of the French version when Anouilh, no absurdist he, saw *Godot* as 'equal in importance with the first performance of a Pirandello play in Paris 1923'. Ionesco, according

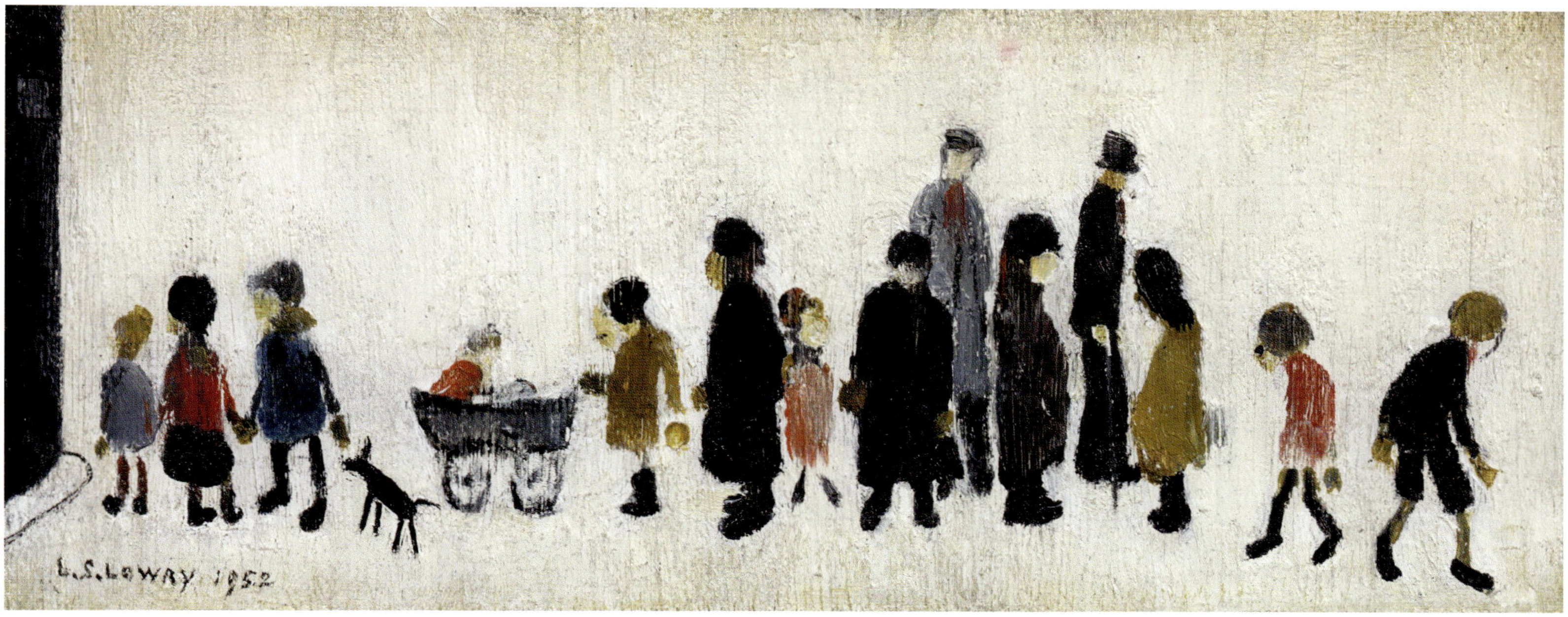

Street Scene, 1952, oil on board, 12.7 × 33 cm.

to Esslin, laid about his ancestors with vigour, dismissing Pirandello as 'outmoded' while still seeing himself as part of a tradition which included Pirandello, Shakespeare, Kleist and Büchner, 'precisely because these authors are concerned with the human condition in all its *brutal absurdity* [my italics].[18]

Lowry was a well-read man as well as a keen theatregoer. I don't believe that he went so repeatedly to see *Six Characters* because he found it difficult to understand. Doubtless the Victorian stage picture and the girl mentioned by Sheila Fell were part of the attraction, but it was surely the profound absurdity of the plot and the characters which made him laugh, made him wonder about himself as well as the people on the stage.

> DIRECTOR: Let's drop it, let's just drop it! You understand, dear sir, that without an author ... I could put you in contact with someone, an author who ...
> FATHER: No, no. Look here: you're the one!
> DIRECTOR: Me? You don't know what you're saying!
> FATHER: Yes, you! Why not?
> DIRECTOR: Because I have never been an author before!
> FATHER: I beg your pardon, but I don't see why you can't do it now! It doesn't take much. A lot of people do it. And your job would be facilitated by the fact that all of us are already here, alive right in front of you.
> DIRECTOR: But that's not enough.
> FATHER: What do you mean it's not enough? When you can actually see us living out our drama ...
> DIRECTOR: That's fine! But you still need someone who will write it.[19]

You need only substitute 'painter' for 'author' to see the complexity of Lowry's own feelings about his craft and his relationship to it. This little scene is manifestly absurd as well as

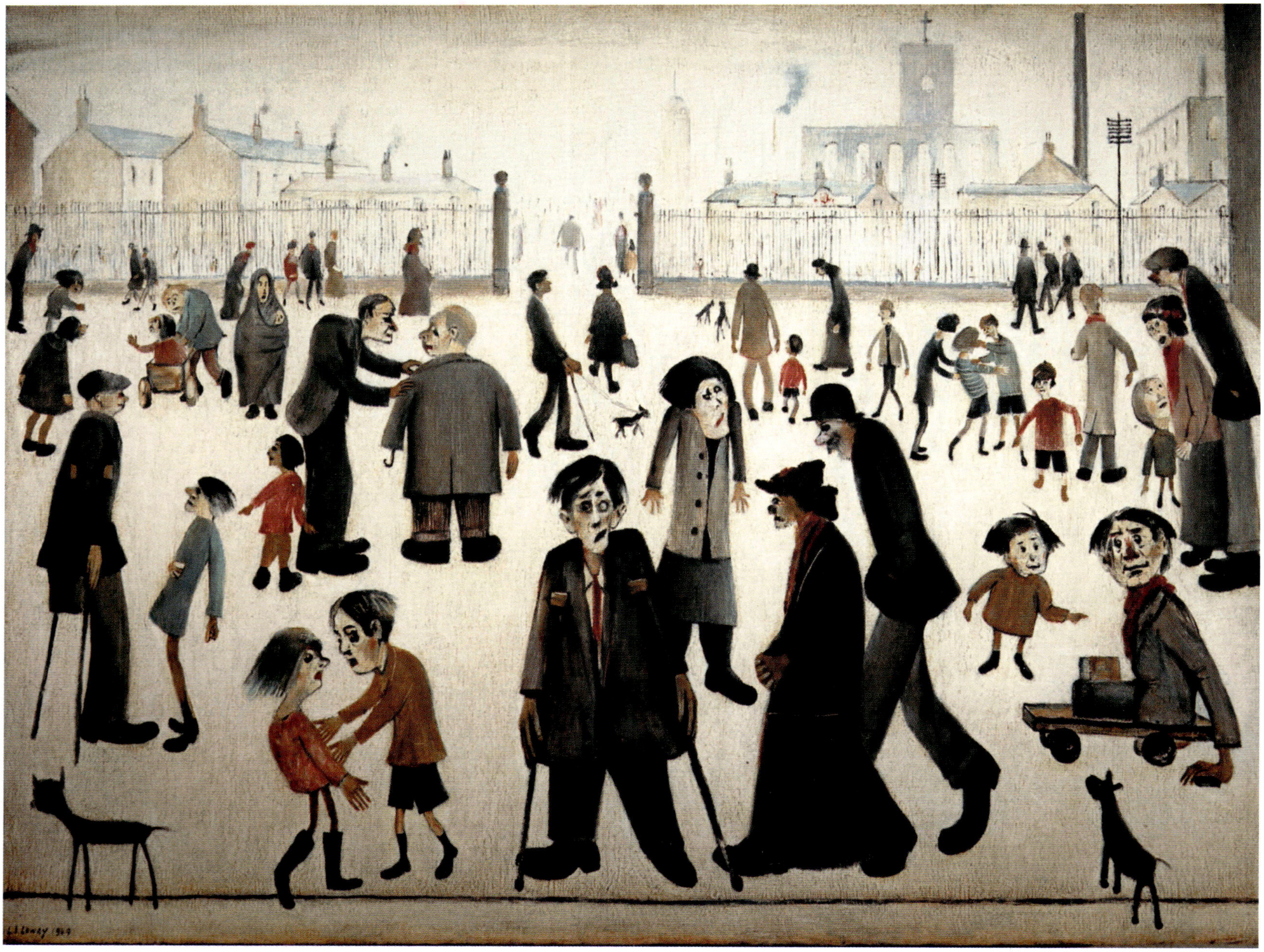

The Cripples, 1949, oil on canvas, 76.3 × 101.8 cm.

comical and right at the heart of the conflict which affected Lowry for so much of his life as an artist. Was he just a rent collector who painted in all the hours he spent away from his day job? Was he 'a real artist', as he himself believed, or was he a naïve painter whose work was that of a hobbyist?

The editor of the Penguin edition of *Six Characters* writes: "... the comedy is built around 'situations', lacking logical development, which are continually interrupted and contradicted."[20]

Again, this conjures up so many of Lowry's paintings: they are, like a good stage set, realistic but they are not real. If one looks at *The Cripples* (page 56) one can immediately see how, for all its human warmth and sympathy, the dominant feeling is for the absurdity of the situation. While one can imagine a scene from one of the more malign films of Luis Buñuel which would gather together this veritable army of the disabled and the mutilated it would be in the furtherance of the plot and might even be logical. But Lowry's concatenation of cripples, like a convention for the halt and the lame, is actually absurd which is what makes it funny and enables one to smile without guilt and simply admire the absurdity, as well as the painterly skill of the artist. Lowry was famously challenged about this picture by his friend and fellow artist David Carr who said that there simply weren't that number of cripples around. So Lowry and Carr set off to find and count them, Carr giving in when the total had reached three figures. In fact Carr had asked the wrong questions. If he was challenging Lowry's veracity he should have asked how can you have seen so many cripples *all so concentrated in one spot*?

The sense of the absurd in Lowry is probably, apart from his devotion to the inherent beauties of the industrial landscape, one of the strongest aspects of his emotional commitment to painting and indeed his overall view of life with its practical jokes and its pricking of bubbles of pretension.

Lowry did not, of course, *need* Pirandello to teach him about the absurd. He could find the absurd for himself, and mercilessly expose it, from early on in his career as in the completely ineffectual struggle between the two contestants in *A Fight* (page 52) dating from about 1935, more or less two decades before he saw *Six Characters*. On the other hand one of his best-loved images, *Man Lying on a Wall* of 1957, is, as it were, post-Pirandello (page 58). Lowry claimed to have seen the subject of this painting from the top of a bus, which is perfectly plausible, but, by deliberate design, he emphasizes its absurdity by turning an anonymous man enjoying a quiet fag and a very uncomfortable 'lie-down' and escape from work into an oblique self-portrait. The painting is signed in the usual way, L. S. Lowry, but the briefcase is decorated with Lowry's initials. Lowry, as a non-smoker as well as a teetotaler, has given the man a cigarette which he is smoking, given his lying flat on top of a narrow wall, in a thoroughly dangerous position. As with other absurdist works of art, whether visual or dramatic, no good will come of this except for the sheer comic joy of viewing the picture which is, understandably, one of Lowry's most popular subjects.

Lowry is a difficult artist to analyze and pin down. He does not fall into any known classification of what constitutes 'art'. Once he has gone through his extremely lengthy juvenilia stage and found his *modus operandi* and his unique style, he does not either develop in a conventional way. Nor does he change either his style or his subject matter in the way in which other 20th-century artists change theirs almost as frequently as they change their clothes. A painter like Sidney Nolan divided his work thematically in effect by discovering a new subject to paint exhaustively, such as the outlaw Ned Kelly or the classical myth of Leda and the Swan, but he rarely dropped any subject completely, no matter how

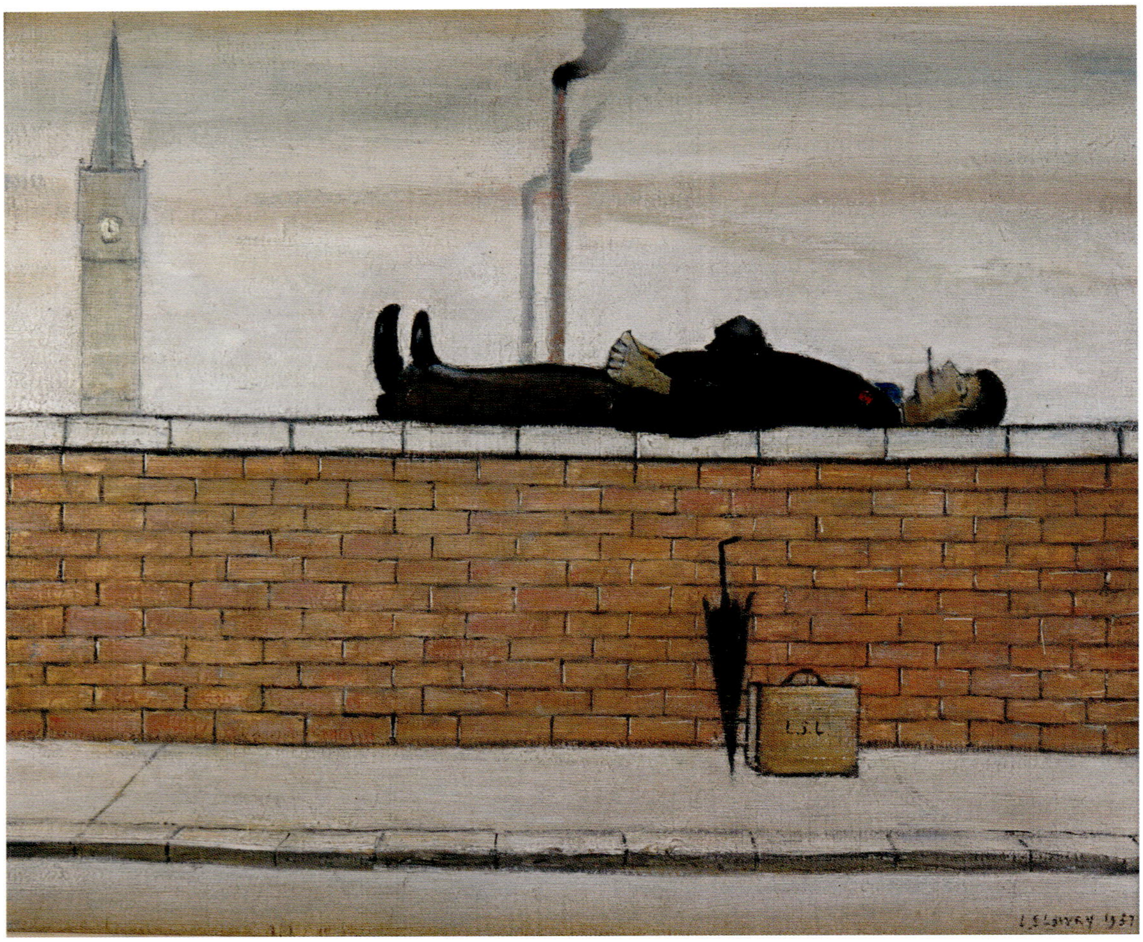

Man Lying on a Wall, 1957,
oil on canvas, 40.7 × 50.9 cm.

comprehensively he had tackled it. He painted Ned Kelly more or less on his deathbed. Mondrian is an example of a man who changed style and subject matter throughout his life but did so in a manner that is simultaneously both gradual and inexorable. Thus if one is lucky enough to see a large Mondrian retrospective hung in a purely chronological sequence one can watch the early, dark, Dutch landscapes with their heavy windmills slowly morph into abstraction and the highly sophisticated, mathematically challenging rectangular compositions which are his iconic works and which, in turn, morph into the frantic, almost frenzied, patterns of the final pictures like *Broadway Boogie-woogie*. Picasso on the other hand quite selfconsciously changed style and subject-matter every few years, thus making life impossible for critics who had to work out the puzzles of his painted neologisms and cope with the most radical changes in his work as he grew disenchanted with a wife or a mistress muse and switched to a new one.

Lowry's *œuvre* offers no such convenient parallels. Once he had learned his craft, had become a serious and professional artist, having made his personal discovery of the unexpected beauty of his surroundings, he stuck to the industrial landscape and the crowds that populated it and added the human theme to the topographical and the architectural strands of his imagery. When, much later, he felt that he had said as much as he could about the densely-populated industrial scene, he made the one radical change of his life, to paint individual human figures and people in small groups so that, while preserving his curiosity, he could concentrate more on character and discernible relationships between smaller numbers of people. While this was indeed a radical change of subject matter there was no equivalent change of style. A group of three children and a couple of dogs was just as unmistakably and immediately recognizable as 'a Lowry' as any mill or factory scene or study of a viaduct or a flight of steps.

He also painted rural landscapes, beaches with bathers and yachts, some pure, uninhabited seascapes and had a vivid interest in what goes with the sea: big ships, docks, piers and ferry boats. He treated the sea as a living thing, something to record in all its different moods and indeed something to fear almost as much as he was fascinated by it. And that, apart from the occasional portrait study or rather gloomy, Munch-like interiors and studies of sickness and death, was the sum total of his *œuvre*. But what a large and powerful and instantly recognizable output it was. His oil paintings alone are to be counted in four figures. His drawings, ranging from little pocket sketch books to large, immaculate records of bridges, staircases, town squares, railway stations, country roads and farmhouses also exist in the thousands. As a paragon of industry he rivals Sickert but you only have to recall Sickert's hyperactivity with wives, mistresses and models – appendages which Lowry avoided – to comprehend his workaholic tendencies.

Yet all his life he painted and drew as he wished and what he wished. He rarely undertook commissioned work, whether formal portraits or records of particular places and nearly always, when fulfilling his commissions, produced work inferior to what he had thought up for himself.

L. S. Lowry had no real artistic ancestors. There was a brief but significant inheritance from his sometime teacher, the French artist Adolphe Valette (1896–1942) but Lowry rapidly absorbed and then shook off Valette's influence. There are those who see Lowry as a somewhat eccentric follower of Sickert and as someone who had much in common with Charles Ginner and Robert Bevan. There is certainly a similarity between Lowry's 1925 *Self Portrait* (page 7) and Robert Bevan's stablelads but that again, like the ghost of Valette, is only a brief shadow which did not last long. Although it is interesting to note that Bevan (1865–1925) was also, although not on quite so generous a scale as Lowry, a compulsive user of white in a multiplicity of shades and textures. Nor did Lowry have any artistic progeny. The big auction houses and those dealers who specialize in Lowry all report that they are offered on average at least once a week a fake Lowry which is no more than a tribute to his popularity. But, while he had many disciples whom he mentored and encouraged in other ways, he had no pupils and no followers. He was, quite simply, a unique, eccentric English artist.

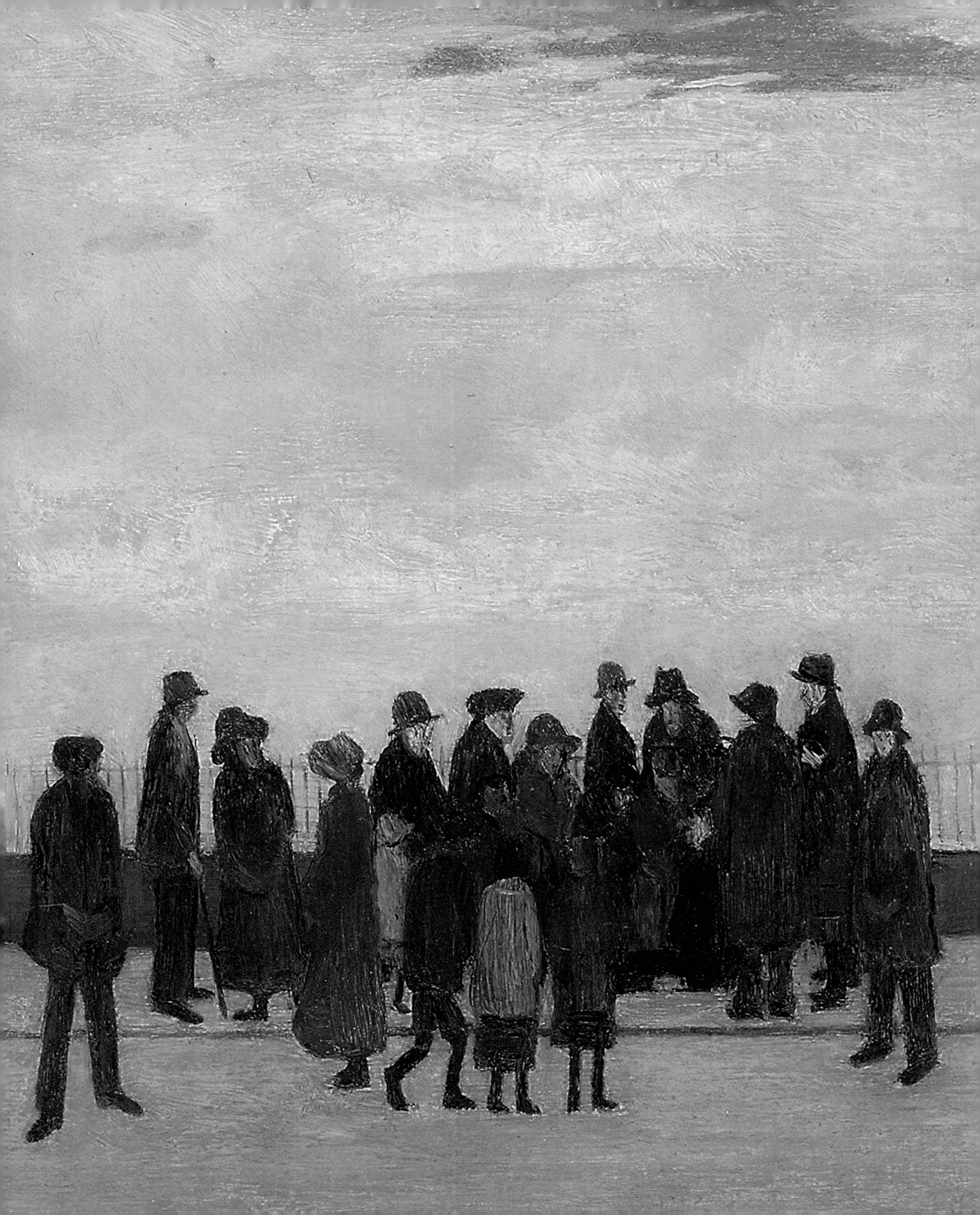

CHAPTER 3

BEGINNINGS

It is consonant with this that one of Lowry's first art teachers was from somewhere else – Adolphe Valette, a Frenchman steeped in the Impressionists and with a devotion to the picturesqueness of Manchester that might well have had a lasting influence on Lowry. There are some rather wonderful Valettes in the Manchester Art Gallery, showing that Manchester could be made to look as dreamy in the mist, as exquisitely deliquescent as any French city beloved of the Impressionists. Lowry didn't go in that direction himself, but to learn what's not for you can be as important as learning what is.

Howard Jacobson[1]

Painters are as varied and as different from each other as any other profession or group of people of similar interests. As with sculptors, writers or musicians there are dedicated professionals who progress sometimes by giant steps, sometimes almost surreptitiously. From the burgeoning talent laid bare by formal teaching, to middle age and some kind of pinnacle of artistic achievement, achieve success and progress to old age and death with their gifts, if they are lucky, undiminished.

There are also artists in all media who spring fully-armed from some indefinable or unfathomable source of intellect, even of genius. The obvious exemplar of this in the twentieth century was Picasso who, even in his teens, overtook his painter father in both technical skill and originality. His father had, symbolically at least, handed over his brushes to his son when Picasso was thirteen. In the nineteenth century, both closer to home and not in any way a genius, but certainly a highly-gifted artist, there was Sir John Everett Millais (1829–1896) who was a true prodigy even if shaped by, and wholly part of, the world of the Royal Academy Schools in 1840, where he was accepted as a pupil when he was only eleven years old. In 1848, i.e. not yet in his twenties, he was, with Holman Hunt and D. G. Rossetti (who was a century later to have such a powerful appeal for Lowry) a co-founder of the Pre-Raphaelite Brotherhood and was elected President of the Royal Academy when that institution was still an effective and distinguished voice for the cream of British artists.

For Lowry there was no sudden efflorescence, no brilliant explosion of talent. There are no extant childhood paintings or drawings to show at least some artistic promise. None of the schools he attended, whether state or private, would have paid much attention to art in their curricula, not even the faintly absurd private school which Mrs Lowry's social pretensions inflicted on little Laurie who hated the compulsory school uniform and was relieved when the family's dwindling finances necessitated a retreat from the pretensions of Victoria Park (still very pretentious when I walked through it as a child during the war) to the unsnobbish dependability of boring Pendlebury and an ordinary non-uniform-wearing state school.

Detail from *Sudden Illness*, 1920, (p.73).

Above all there was no encouragement for Lowry at home as far as art was concerned. No wonder he found it difficult to enter a decent art school. Where and when and how could he have put together a portfolio to smooth his path through the entrance procedures? There are no easy explanations for the presence within Lowry of the need to draw and paint. No trace of a hereditary gift, no parental guidance, let alone enthusiasm. Only a wish for Laurie to get himself onto a safe bottom rung in a job which required no qualifications but which would help to put bread on the table. One can only supply one's own conjectures as to why he had little sketch books in his raincoat pockets, why the envelopes of unanswered letters ended up in the pockets of his jackets and why, when his ever-observant eye lit upon something in the streets of Manchester or Stockport or Salford which he tramped along in his work as a rent collector, a sketchbook or an envelope and a pencil, or later on a pen, would emerge and he would record what he had seen, what had aroused his interest. Rarely can any artistic career have triumphed over such flimsy equipment and with so little outside help. At least, once he had found his niche at the Pall Mall Property Company, he had some sort of security, was promoted and stayed there until he reached retirement age and took his pension when he was 65.

Lowry, in his later years, when I knew him, was a robust man, physically very alert and, when it came to the business of applying oil paint to board or canvas, possessing the enviable hand/eye coordination of a great sportsman. It's hard therefore to imagine that he was a sickly baby and that, in 1916, he was told at his call-up medical that he was flat-footed (given his daily mileage as a rent collector) and that when he was called up for actual military service he would not be sent overseas but put on 'garrison duty only'. His summons to Bury Barracks said he was due there on 22 August, 1916, which was the following Monday and which Lowry and his parents felt was a bit soon, Lowry maintaining that he had been promised two months' notice so that he could sort out the inevitable disruption to his life. Lowry then enlisted the support of a friend of his father, a Justice of the Peace, who wrote a supporting letter to the military authorities who obliged him by shelving his summons and failed to send him a new one so that Lowry avoided any service in World War I. To be fair, in World War II he acted as a fire-watcher during the blitz which disrupted many lives (including that of my own family) and, as Lowry's wartime paintings so brilliantly show, destroyed huge areas of factory and other industrial buildings as well as countless homes.[2]

It was during his apparently endless pupilage that he befriended a fellow student some thirteen years younger than himself who eventually became James Fitton R.A. He also had a friendly relationship with a couple called Frank and Mary Fletcher and in 1919 presented Frank with a portrait as a surprise for his birthday. Unfortunately Fletcher hated the portrait, his wife felt much the same and it ended up behind the wardrobe. The friendship suffered accordingly.[3]

But probably the key event of Lowry's early years in his pursuit of his art was his encounter and subsequent long professional relationship with Adolphe Valette.

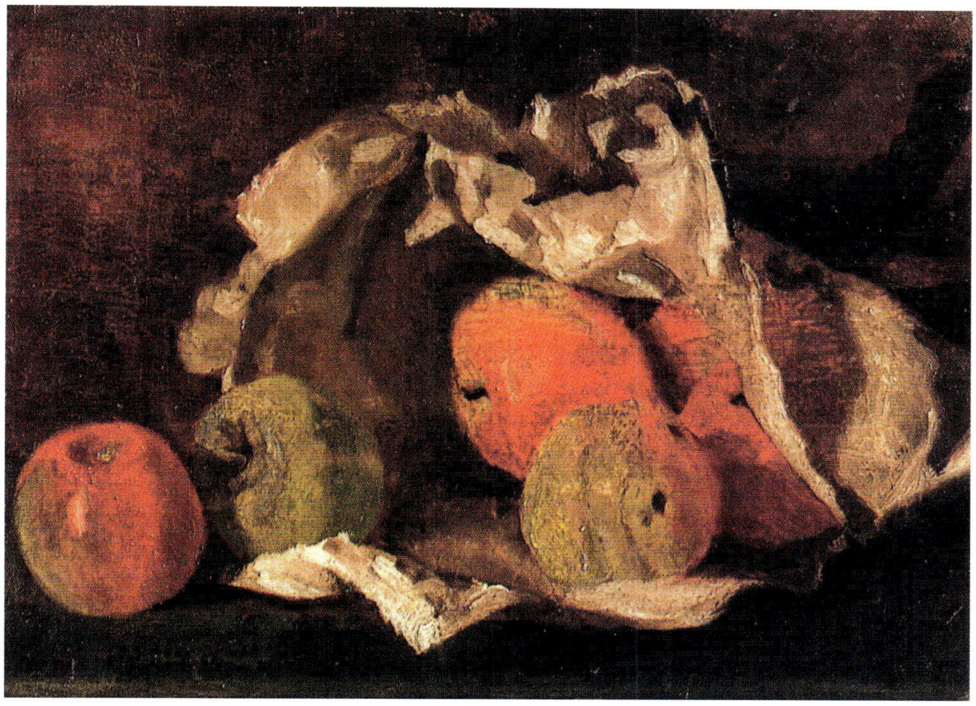

Still Life, *c.*1906, oil on canvas, 23.5 × 33.5 cm.

It is instructive, although not particularly enlightening, to look at Lowry's juvenilia, at the fruits of his relatively late and certainly lengthy pupillage at the various art teaching institutions in Manchester. It is also ironic to recall the long-term disapproval, or at the very least, lack of enthusiasm, (with the notable and even noble exception of his friend James Fitton), from the stuffier representatives of the Royal Academy.

There is something distinctly amusing in their pomposity which was, at least in part, based on a genuinely held belief that Lowry was merely an untaught amateur and not, like them a professionally taught and thoroughly professional and true artist. Yet when one compares Lowry's prentice work, those endless boring studies of odds and ends of classical sculpture and the rather stiff drawings of the life models one is inexorably reminded of the drawings of the pupils of the Royal Academy Schools in the same period.

Lowry was, for all sorts of reasons, a late developer. He had been 'a working man' for several years before he was even accepted at a reputable art school. His first job was as a clerk in a Chartered Accountant's practice in Mosley Street, Manchester where he worked for four years from 1903–1907. In 1907 he got a more interesting job as a claims clerk with the General Accident Fire and Life Assurance Corporation which produced an income of about a pound a week. During his early years with the accountants, he was rejected as a full-time student at the Manchester School of Art. But in 1905 a connection of his father's, Reginald Barber, Vice-President of the Manchester Academy of Fine Art, helped Lowry to get accepted as a part-time, i.e. evening class only, student in 'preparatory antique and freehand drawing'.

This enabled him to obtain further tuition from 1905–15 at the hands of a minor American artist called William Fitz and, more significantly, was accepted, also in 1905 as a pupil in the Life Class of Adolphe Valette, a genuinely gifted French artist who divided his life between Manchester and France. Valette was born in Saint Etienne in 1876, i.e. some eleven years before Lowry, and died in Lyon in 1942. 1905 was the year in which he was appointed 'Master of Painting and Drawing' at Manchester's Municipal School of Art and it is not unreasonable to suppose that the largely fortuitous contact between these two widely different men was the most important moment in Lowry's life so far. Little was known until recently about Valette – there is no entry for him in Grove Art – but, happily, Cécilia Lyon published an excellent monograph on him which throws much useful light on Lowry.[4]

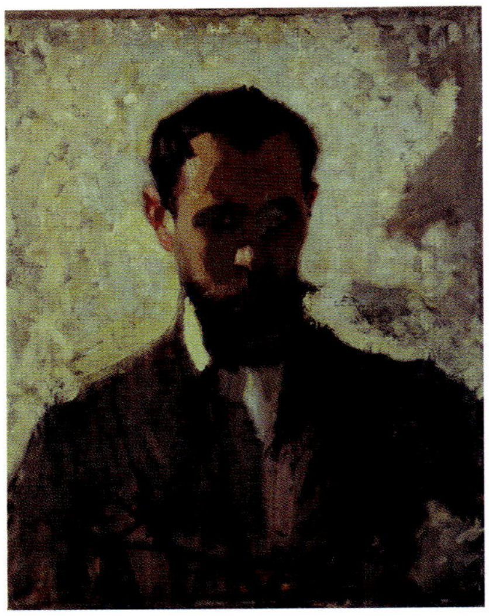

Self Portrait, by Adolphe Valette, 1912, oil on canvas, 60.8 × 48 cm.

One of the most interesting aspects of Valette is the enormous difference between his work in France and what he did in Manchester. Valette was, as far as his attractive, Post-Impressionist paintings were concerned, really much closer to late Impressionism, i.e. not at all academic but sufficiently loose and brightly coloured to be seen as simply a late flowering of the original Impressionist movement. He was in essence a perfect illustration of the French phrase, a 'petit Maître'. But, while he continued in his quiet Impressionist style when he lived and worked in Manchester, it is his completely different paintings of the dark city and its industrial scenes which profoundly affected and influenced Lowry and which show him to be an original and highly talented painter in a way that makes him a true original who has properly earned the prominent display of his works which, happily, constitutes part of the core collection of the Manchester City Art Gallery a century or so after their creation.

Howard Jacobson's phrase in the epigraph to this chapter that Valette 'could make Manchester as dreamy in the mist, as deliquescent as any French city beloved of the Impressionists' is wonderfully apposite. Lyon draws an interesting parallel between Valette in Manchester and Monet in London when Monet, who loved London's smog, hated Sundays because the relative lack of smog made the air too clear.[5]

Given the notoriety of Manchester's climate even today and the smog and the pollution created, at the time of Valette's stay in the city, by the then vibrant if filthy industrial sites so near the city centre, even Valette must have been satisfied with the gloom, the darkness and the softening of outlines in his best paintings, such as *Bailey Bridge, Manchester* of 1912 (page 65). One could be forgiven, on first discovering it in Manchester City Art Gallery, for assuming that Whistler had travelled far north of his beloved Chelsea. Valette's handling of the reflection of light, or the dirty water under the bridge and the hopeless struggle of the sunlight to pierce the gloom of clouds and buildings partially obscured by the smoke of the nearby factory chimney, is in no way inferior to some of Whistler's depictions of the Thames and its many bridges.

Valette's painting of *India House, Manchester* (page 65), also done in 1912, surely foreshadows Lowry's *View of Peel Park* and, again, makes one think of Whistler. But Valette did not have to have rivers or canals in his pictures. He was just as effective on, as it were, dry land

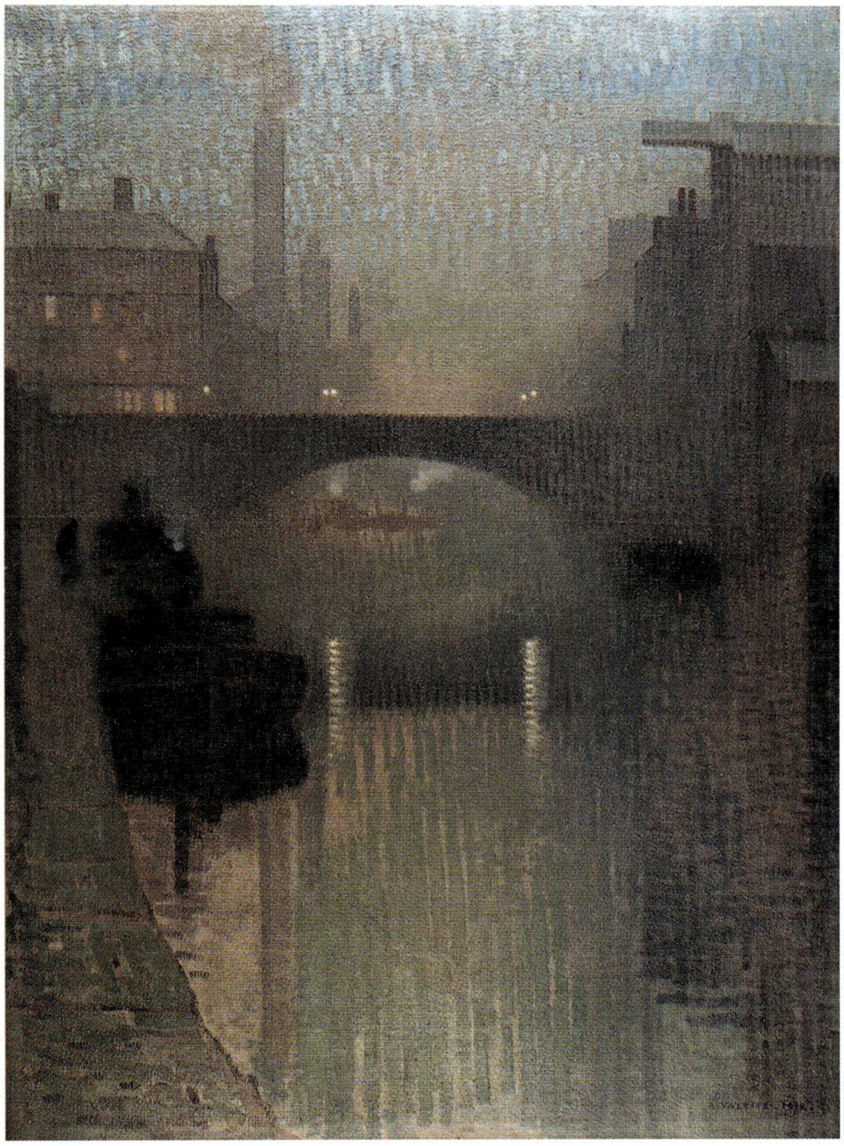

Bailey Bridge, Manchester, by Adolphe Valette, 1912, oil on jute, 179.2 × 138.9 cm.

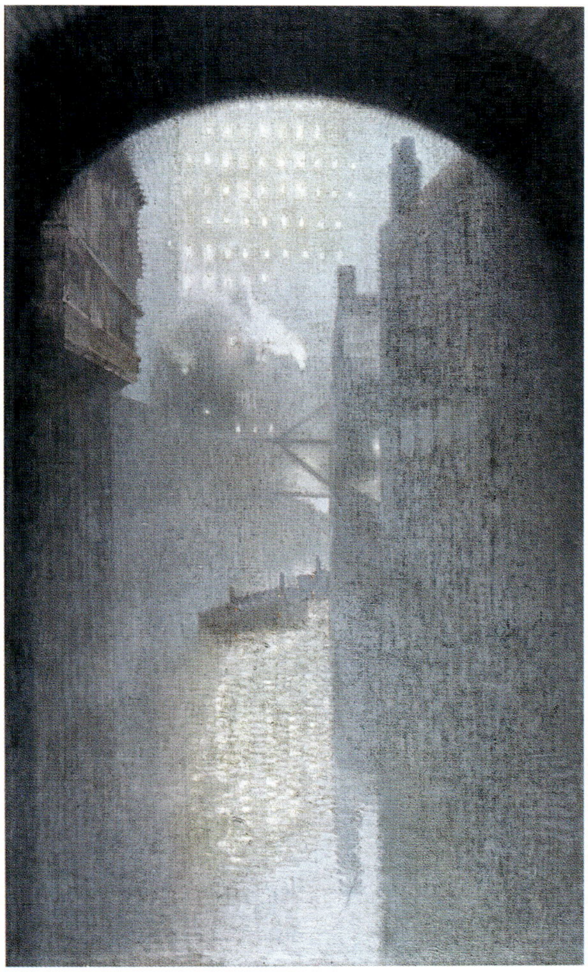

India House, Manchester, by Adolphe Valette, 1912, oil on linen and jute, 142.4 × 86.1 cm.

and his two huge paintings (each is 115.5 × 155.3 cm.) of the cab rank at Manchester's All Saints (1910 and 1911) have, according to Lyon, a movement towards Pointillism.[6] While not nodding quite as assiduously towards Whistler, *Old Cab at All Saints* (page 66) is, with all the known fruits of hindsight, a Lowry painting done in the Edwardian era and a whole generation ahead of Lowry's official style becoming firm. The jaunty pipe-smoking cabbie on his driving seat looks forward to Lowry's *Man Lying on a Wall* (page 58). The horse, concentrating on the contents of its nosebag is done with some of the humour of Lowry's many dogs. The tightly knotted groups of people surrounding the cab, which is simply waiting at its rank for a passenger, are also like forerunners of the human need for the proximity to one's fellows described in Chapter 8, LOWRY AND CROWDS.

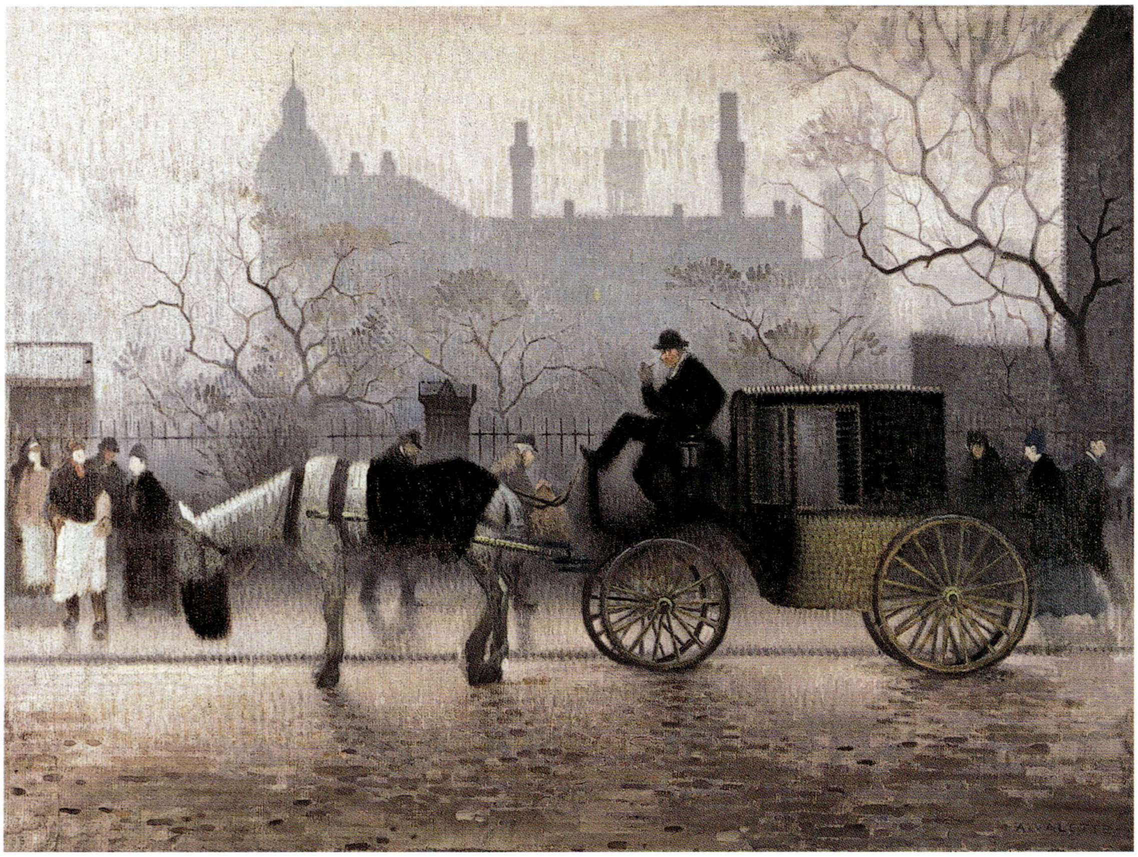

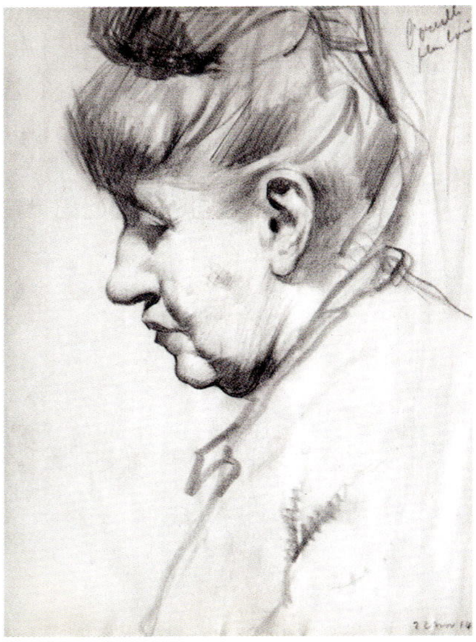

Portrait of the Artist's Mother, by Adolphe Valette, 1914, drawing on paper, 24.8 × 19.2 cm.

Old Cab at All Saints, by Adolphe Valette, 1911, oil on linen and jute, 115.5 × 155.3 cm.

While Valette eschewed *grisaille* as a technique, his Manchester paintings were done with a relatively restricted palette; not with the rigidity of Lowry's self-imposed discipline of only five colours, but, with Valette's fascination with Manchester's semi-perpetual darkness. In his best pictures there was too little sunlight to brighten the skyline and to adhere to the greyness of the city's monumental architecture.

It is difficult not to see Valette's spirit in the predominantly grey buildings and sky in Lowry's 1921 painting at Salford of *The Lodging House* done in chalk on paper but definitely a painting and not a drawing in its artistic effect. *The Lodging House* is also an early example of Lowry's obsession and skill with crowds (page 67).

One can see why Lowry attended Valette's classes for over ten years, a huge length of time for an art student, even one of mature years.[7] Lowry may well have picked up his interest in painting manual workers, not only from his natural environment and perambulations as a rent collector, but from a Valette painting of Albert Square done in 1910 (page 68) in which, apart from another cabbie, plus cab and horse, in the middle ground, the foreground is dominated by a stooped, elderly man trundling a handcart full of bottles of wine. His is a posture one can later find in at least a dozen Lowry paintings from the 1930s onwards; Lowry was certainly aware of his debt to Valette:

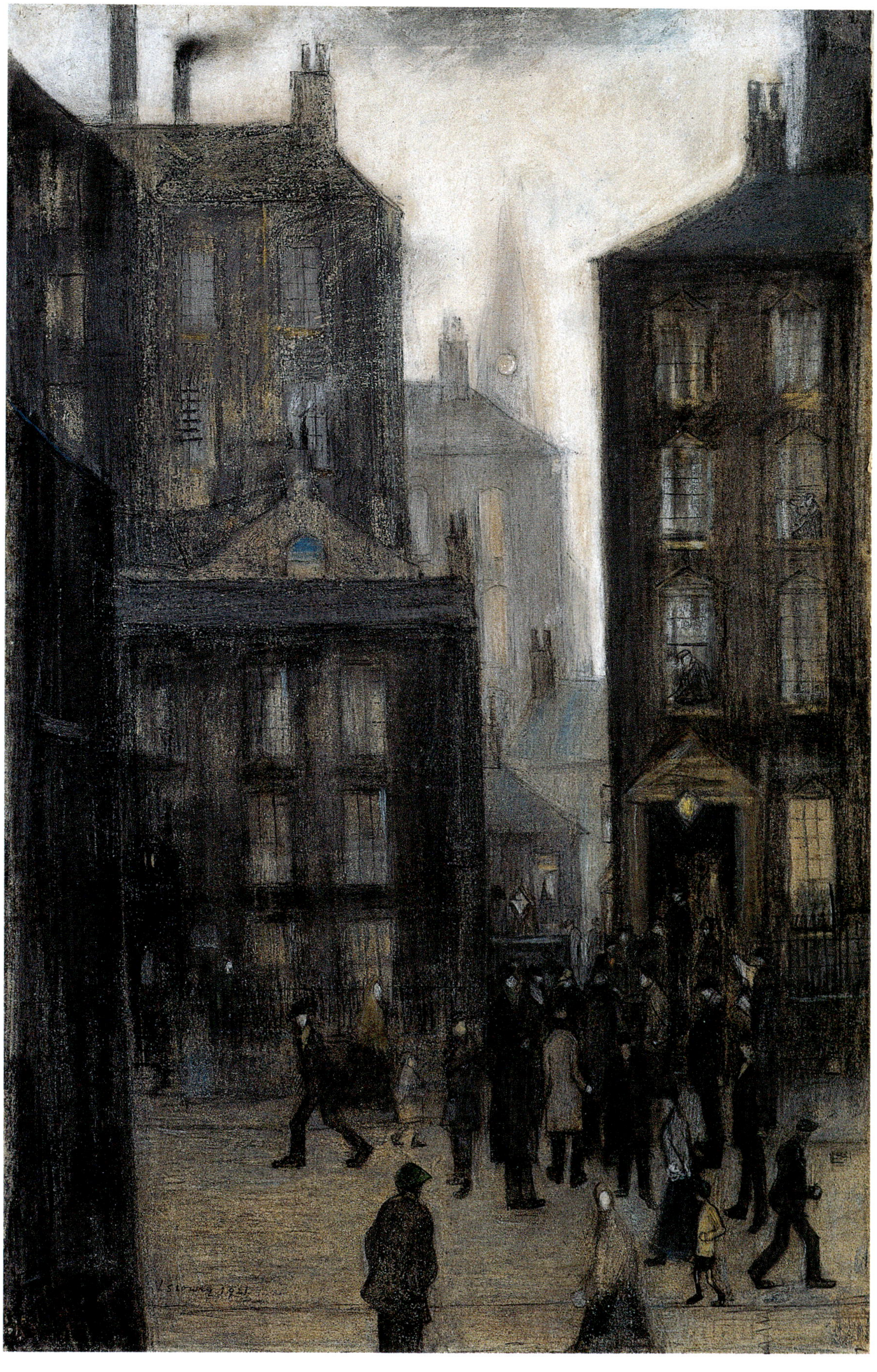

The Lodging House, 1921,
pastel on paper, 50.1 × 32.6 cm.

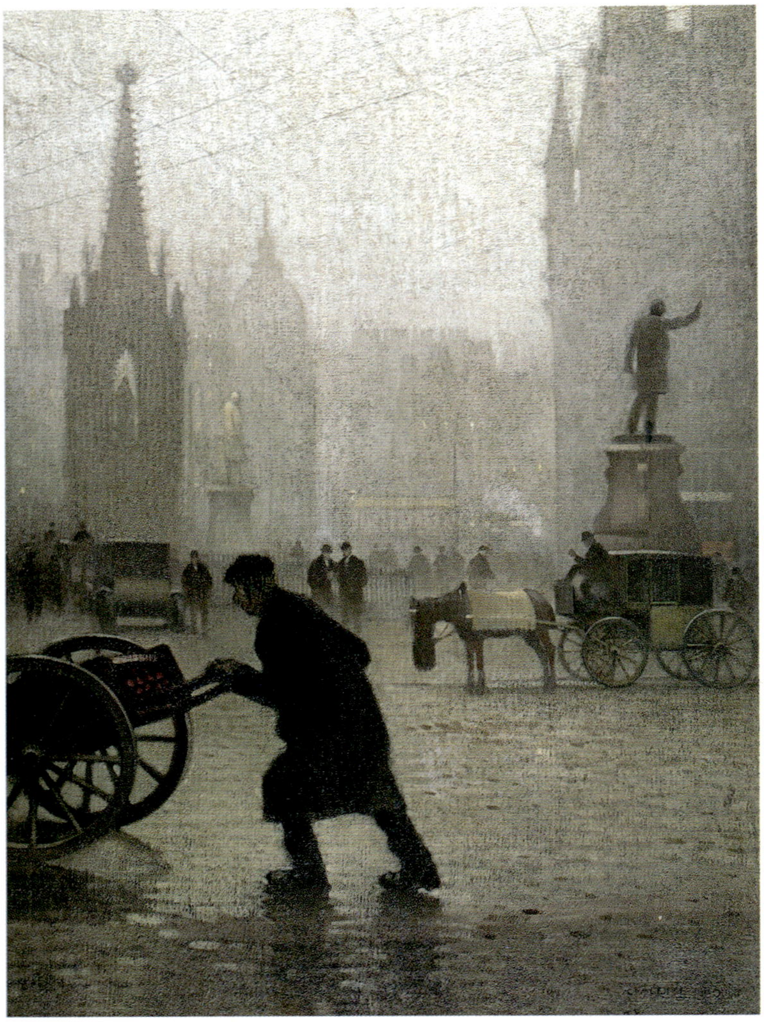

Albert Square, Manchester, by Adolphe Valette, 1910, oil on jute, 152 × 114 cm.

> I cannot over-estimate the effect on me at that time of the coming into this drab city of Adolphe Valette, full of the French Impressionists, aware of everything that was going on in Paris. He had freshness and a breadth of experience that was a very wonderful thing, as I saw it done by himself and his friends. I had not seen drawings like these before – for artistry. They were French life-class drawings, and he painted and drew in the same way. I was fascinated by it, and whilst I never drew in that way – I couldn't have done, it wasn't my way of drawing – I greatly admired him and they helped me very much. They were great stimulants.[8]

Lowry also sensed that Valette respected his burgeoning gifts, although remaining unaware that Valette had once visited Lowry's father to assure Mr Lowry that his son had talent and that he should allow him to continue his art studies.

Valette prospered in Manchester. He was promoted in his teaching role and taught at Bolton as well as Manchester. He had a number of exhibitions which began to sell out and, in 1928, sold nine of his best canvases to the Manchester City Art Gallery before deciding, in the same year, to move back to France where he stayed until the end of his life in 1942. While he himself did not return to Manchester after 1928 he continued to sell his works there until he died.

Although by 1928 Lowry, who was then 42, was beginning, artistically at least, to be his own man despite a career which was professionally tedious and unchallenging and a domestic life for which the kindest adjective would be stultifying.

The family, unable to satisfy Mrs Lowry's overwhelming bourgeois ambitions, had to leave the 'exclusiveness' of the unaffordable Victoria Park for a far more modest existence in Pendlebury. By 1932 Robert Lowry, a failure in business, was dead of pneumonia aged 74. Thus, with the occasional help of a series of maidservants, few of whom, even in those financially straitened times, could put up for long with the bossy demands of the professional invalid who was Elizabeth Lowry, her son had to combine the triple tasks of carer, wage-earner and perpetual art student. Mrs Lowry became 'bedfast' on her husband's death and, until her own death, the only love-object in her life was her bed. Her invalid life continued for another seven-and-a-half years and it is an extraordinary tribute to the endurance of the human spirit that Lowry's personality survived intact living with this unloving hypochondriac in conditions which his biographer described as 'a burden willingly undertaken and miraculously performed, but it was to drive him to the brink of derangement'. In addition to the problems of dealing with his mother, Lowry also had to disentangle his dead father's affairs. "Laurie," writes Rohde, "realized for the first time how tenuous a path Robert had trodden between solvency and bankruptcy." Happily, this middle-aged, unfulfilled man was remarkably robust and, almost miraculously, financially shrewd and, despite his modest income had, without the gamble of the stock market, made sufficient investments and savings to shield his mother from knowledge of her husband's financial fecklessness and keep the by now modest household safe from the bailiffs. Elizabeth Lowry continued to tyrannize from her bed until 12 October, 1939; her devoted son was already 52. In a life full of irony Lowry had just achieved his first success with an exhibition at Reid and Lefevre. He was on his way, but as Shelley Rohde writes in what I suspect is a shrewd psychological assessment:

> At home the show had changed nothing; and his mother's assessment of him was his assessment. Having been raised in the belief that she had an instinctive eye for beauty, he acknowledged her [negative] judgment [of his work] to be true and valid; If she saw only ugliness in what he did, then ugliness there must be, despite what others said; only her conversion to his vision would bring him fulfilment;[9]

Instead she died on him and, as by then Britain was at war, Alex Reid told Lowry that he felt obliged to close his gallery indefinitely and that he was therefore forced to cancel Lowry's show planned for the Spring of 1940.[10]

It is not surprising, in this accretion of disastrous events, that Lowry at the very least fell into a deep depression and, at worst he had a nervous breakdown. From this he was scrupulously and lovingly rescued by his devoted friends Harold and Edith Temperley, who took him to their house in Cheadle Hulme.

If I have concentrated in this chapter on Lowry and Valette it is because Valette was the only senior painter/teacher who took Lowry seriously and, literally alas, the only person who provided the encouragement and the occasional approval, sometimes shading over into praise without which any tyro painter cannot survive psychologically.

If one looks at the work of Lowry's much extended study years one sees relatively little of the major artist who took so long to emerge. There is a rare, possibly unique, figure study of a naked woman done in 1912 and there are several family portraits in pencil or oil done presumably because they were both available as sitters and did not charge modelling fees. The pencil sketch of his mother done about 1920 (below) is not nearly as scary as some of the representations of her, doubtless because her usual air of wincing disapproval could not survive the fact that her eyes are shut and she might well be asleep, looking like a feminine version of W. B. Yeats.

In *Country Lane* of 1914 (page 247) one can see that Lowry was aware of Impressionism and Post-Impressionism, although if this loose, vividly-coloured piece of heavy impasto resembles any other artist in technique then it is either late Jack Yeats of the 1940s–50s or

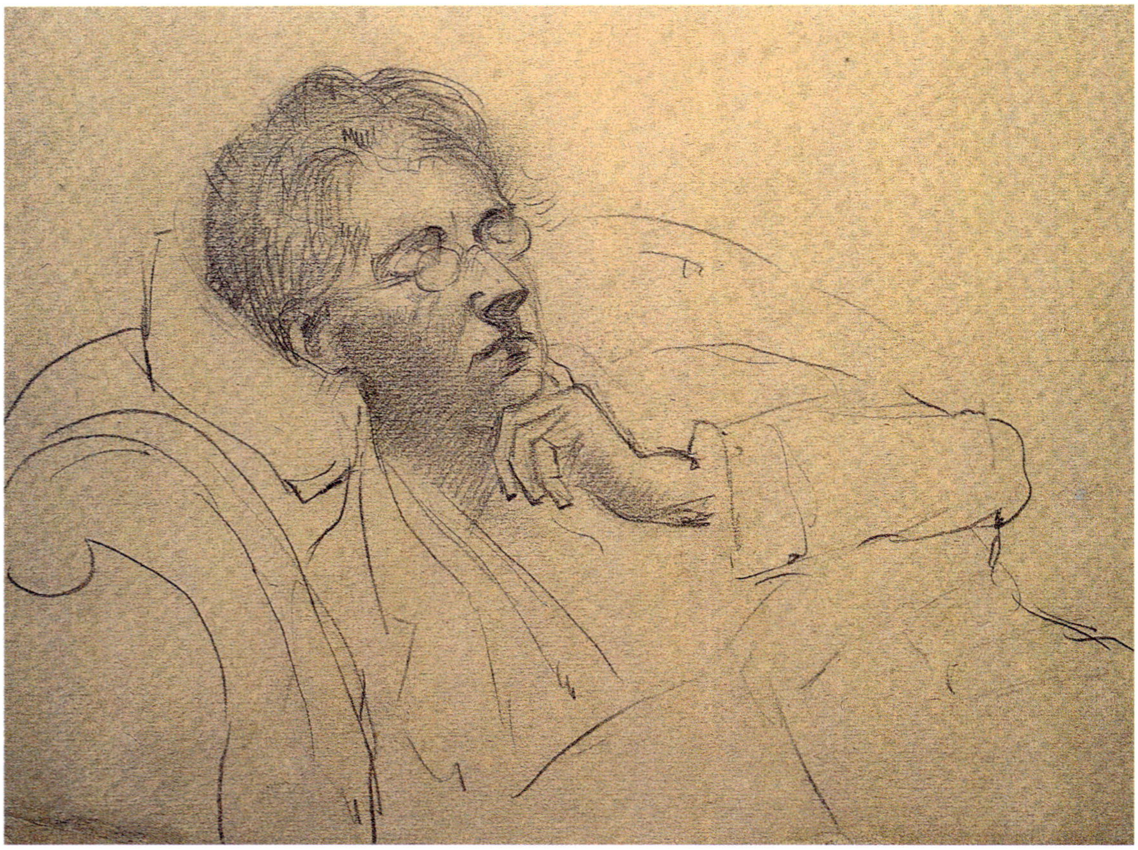

The Artist's Mother, *c.*1920, pencil on paper, 24.5 × 37 cm.

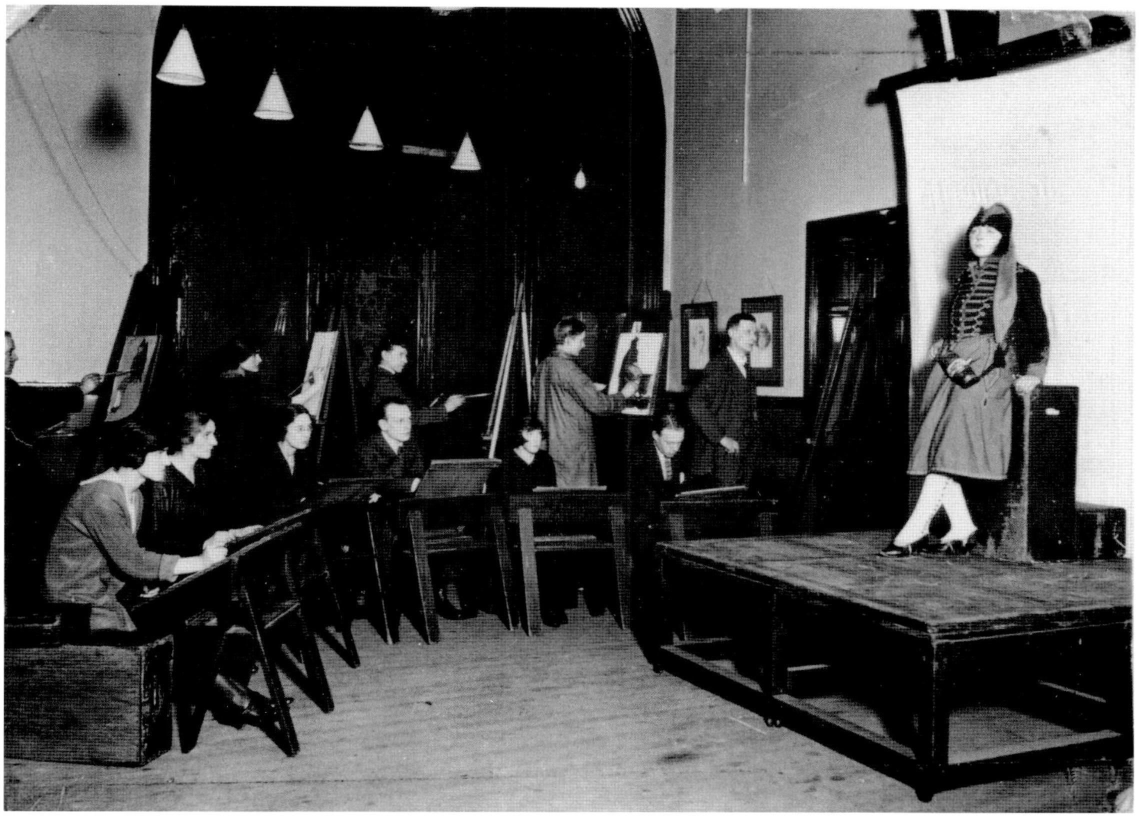

Photograph of Lowry standing (to the left of the model) as a student in the life costume class at Salford School of Arts, *c.*1925.

the vivid, almost brutal Expressionism of Chaim Soutine so that we have the oddity of the student Lowry making pictures that *anticipated* rather than derived from two infinitely more respected near contemporaries. There is no possibility of Lowry imitating two artists one of whom (Yeats) was not yet a fully-fledged painter, who had not yet developed his final style and the other who, at that time, was unknown in England outside the sophisticated Metropolitan art circles of London.

There is some merit in the oil portraits of his parents, his father in 1910 and his mother in 1912, two paintings which he kept by him until his death although they are essentially student works; there is no evidence yet of a real personal style but only a decent, well-taught academic approach to these vital subjects. It was not until the 1920s that we can see the breakthrough in his art, the creation of a style which made his work instantly recognizable.

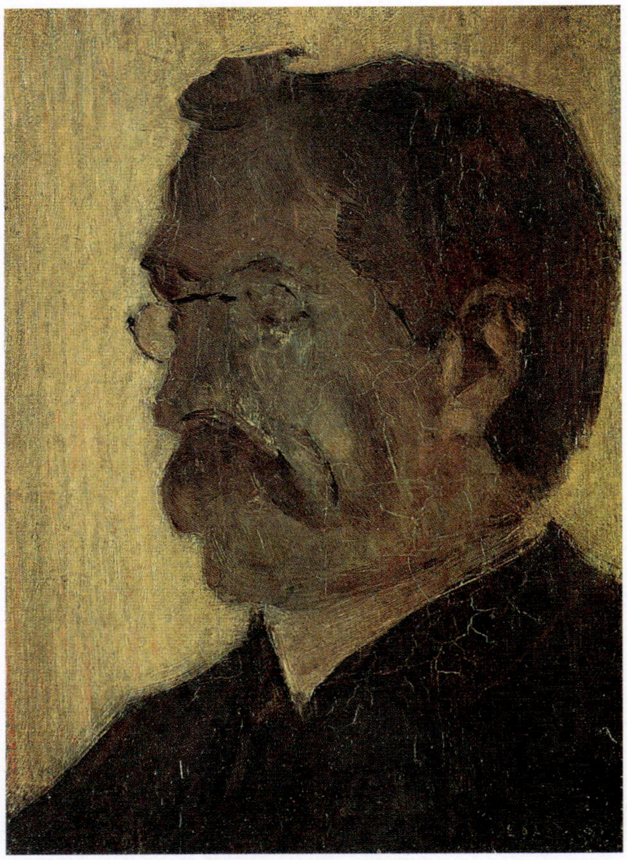

Portrait of the Artist's Father, 1910, oil on canvas, 41 × 31 cm.

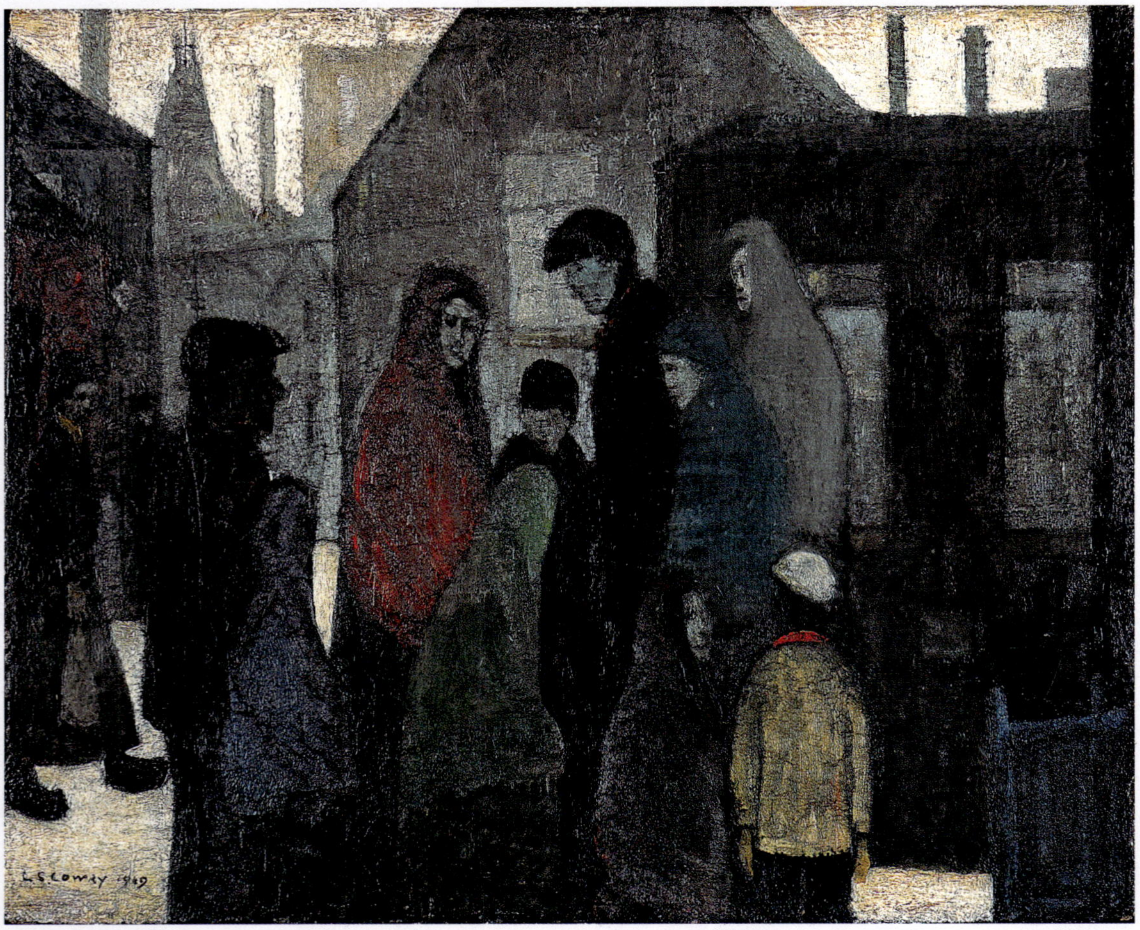

Pit Tragedy, 1919, oil on canvas, 39.4 × 49 cm.

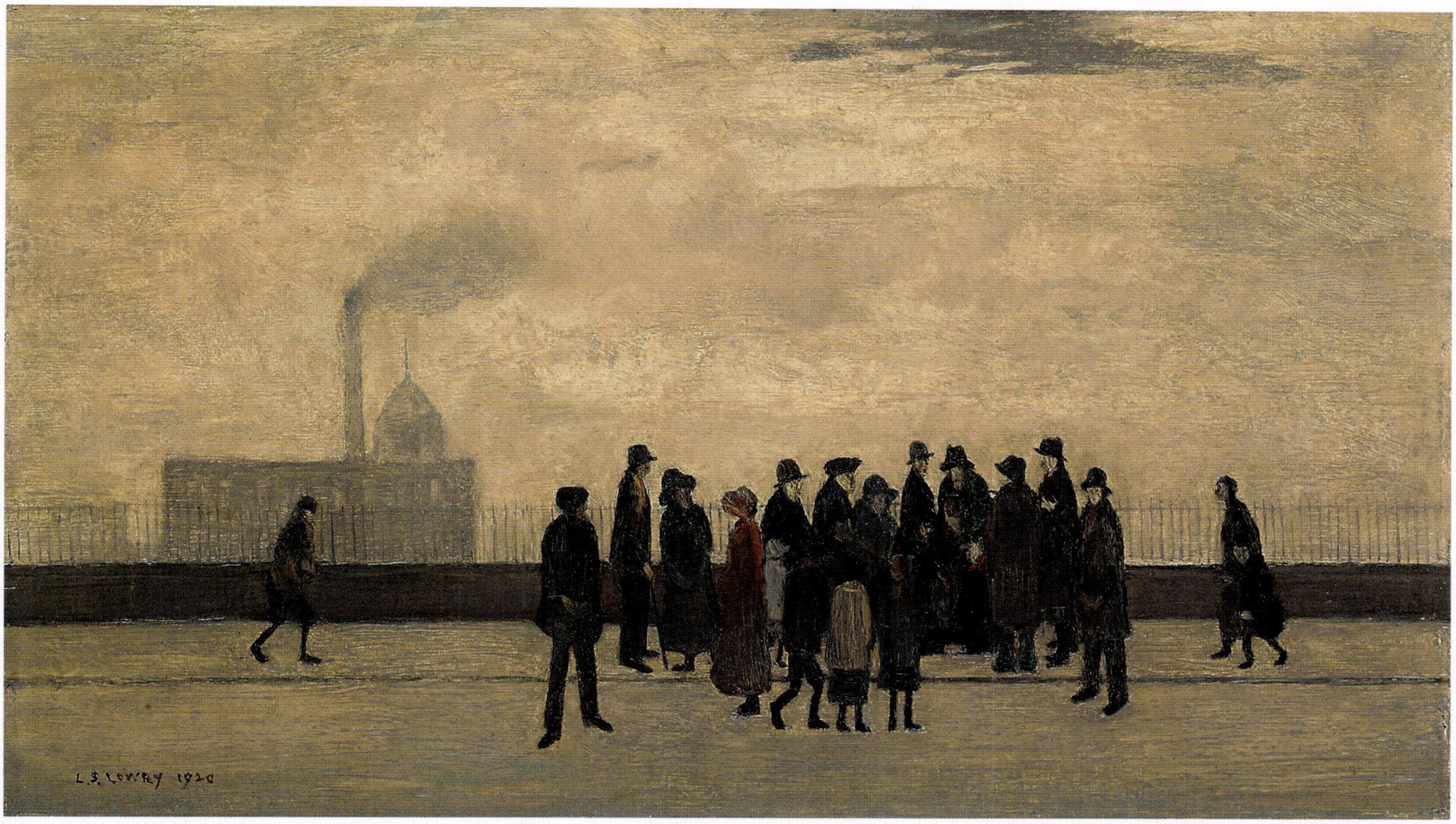

Sudden Illness, 1920, oil on panel, 25.5 × 45.6 cm.

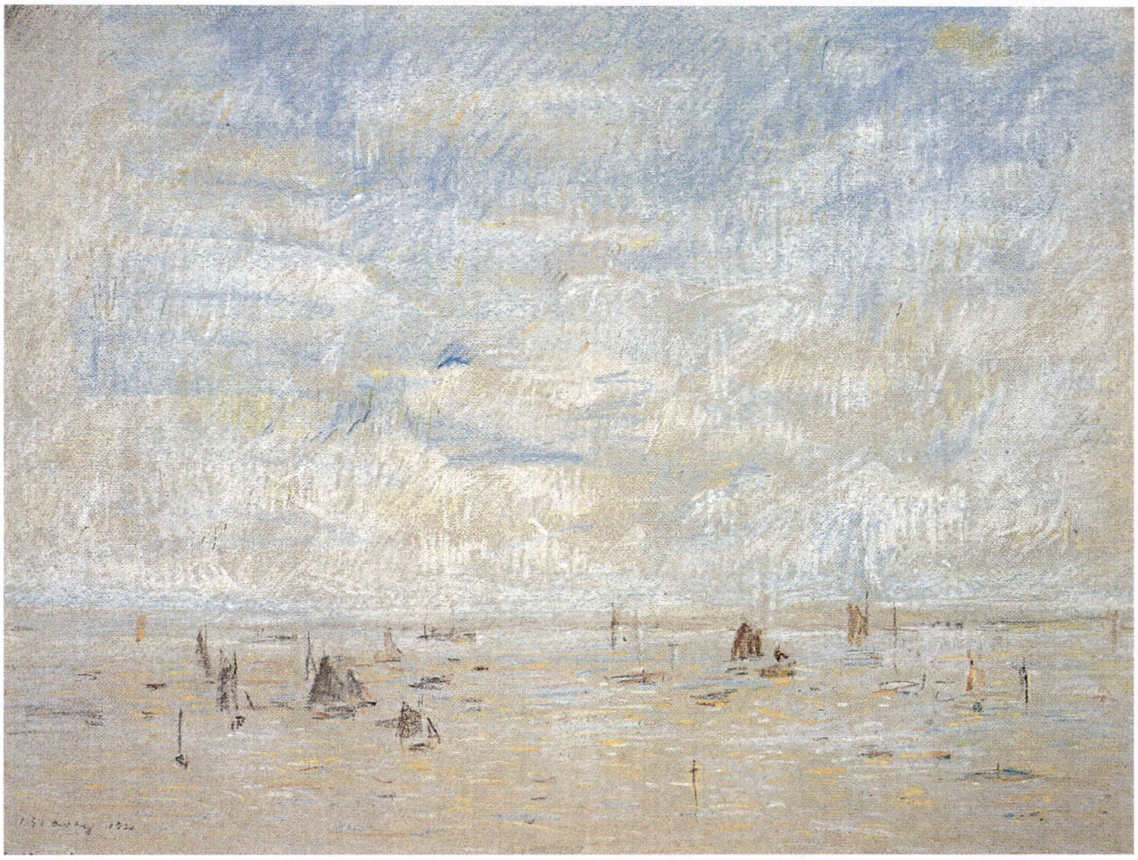

Yachts, 1920, pastel on paper, 28.4 × 38.2 cm.

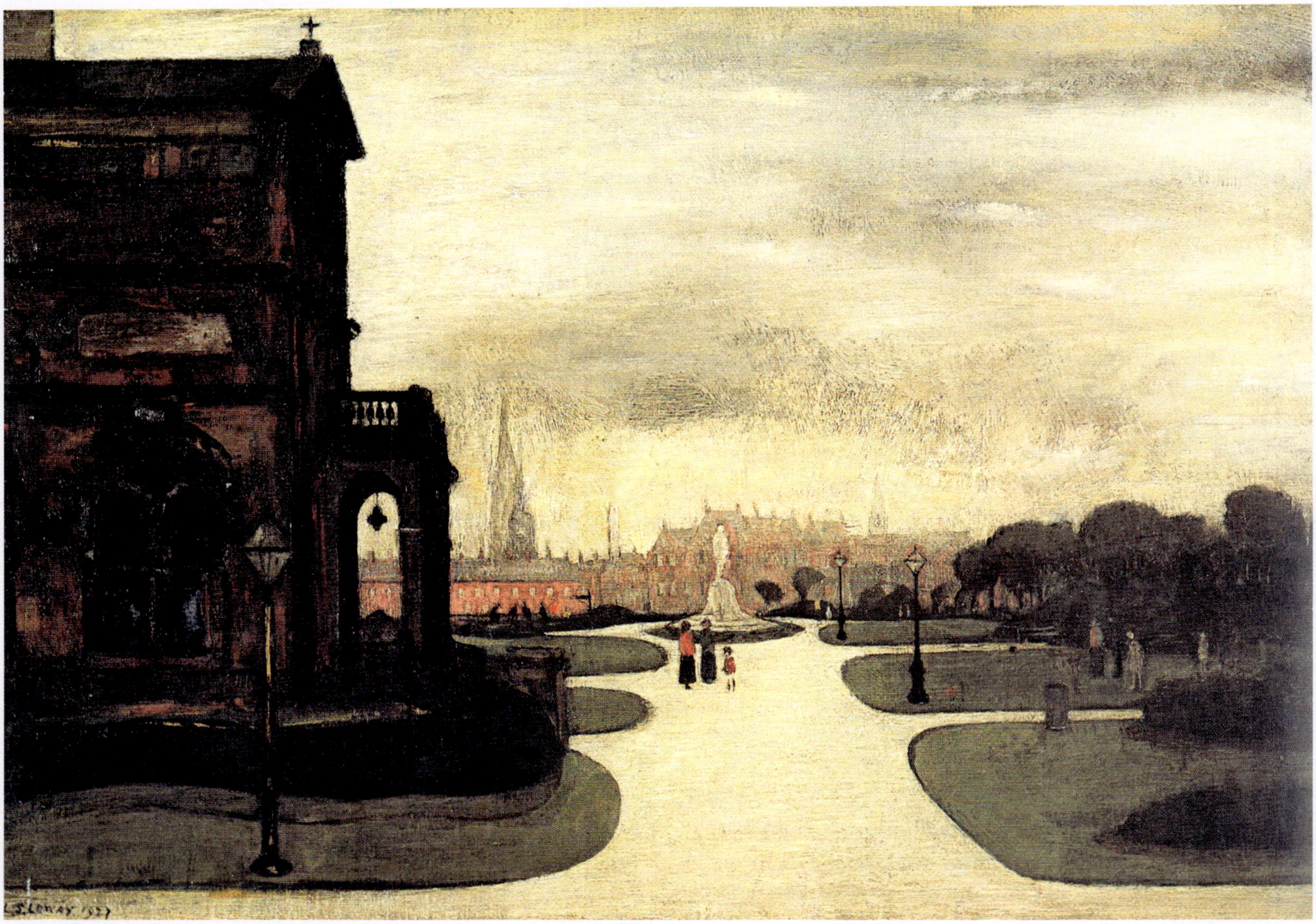

Peel Park, 1927, oil on board/panel,
35.5 × 50.5 cm.

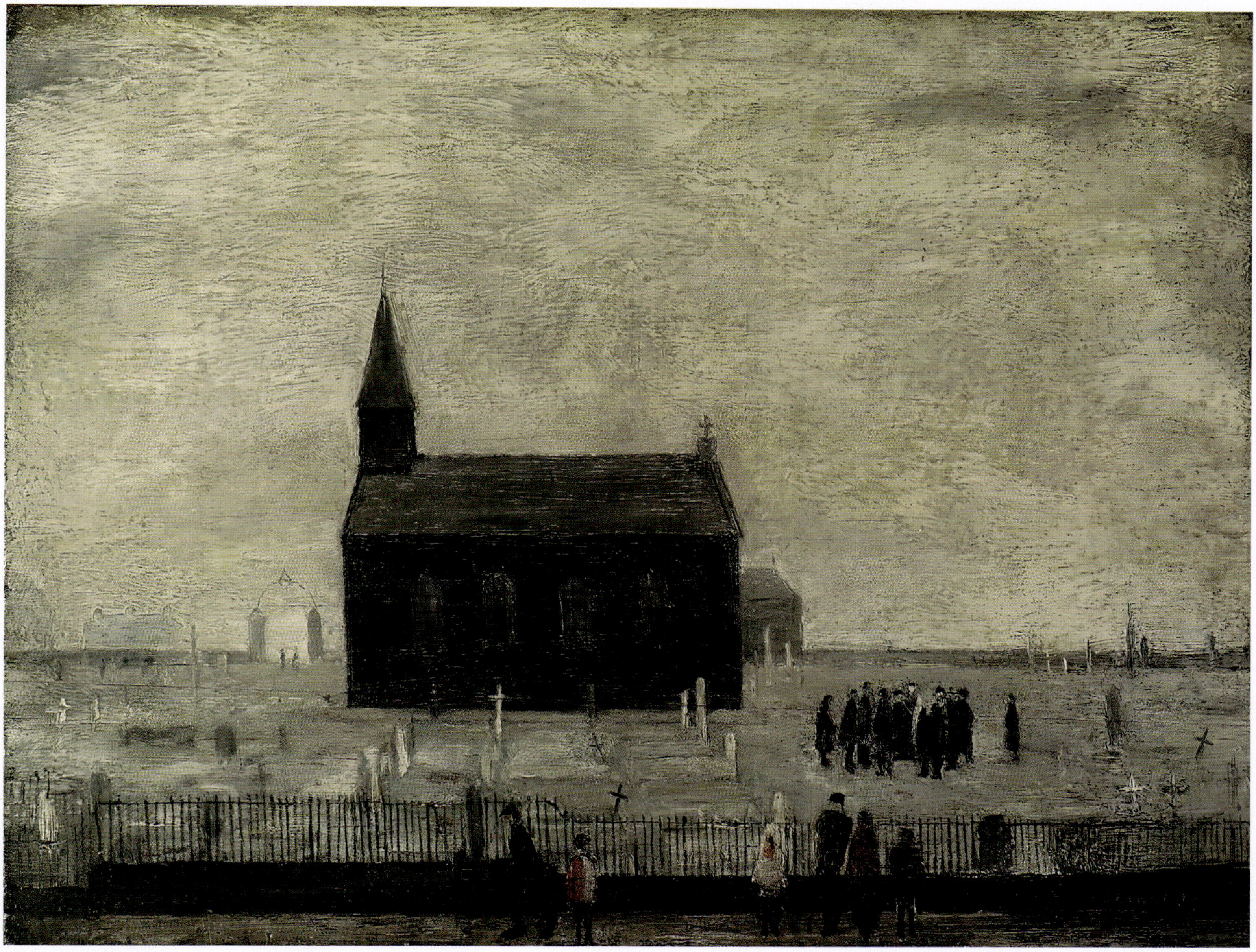

The Funeral, 1928, oil on panel,
36.3 × 47.7 cm.

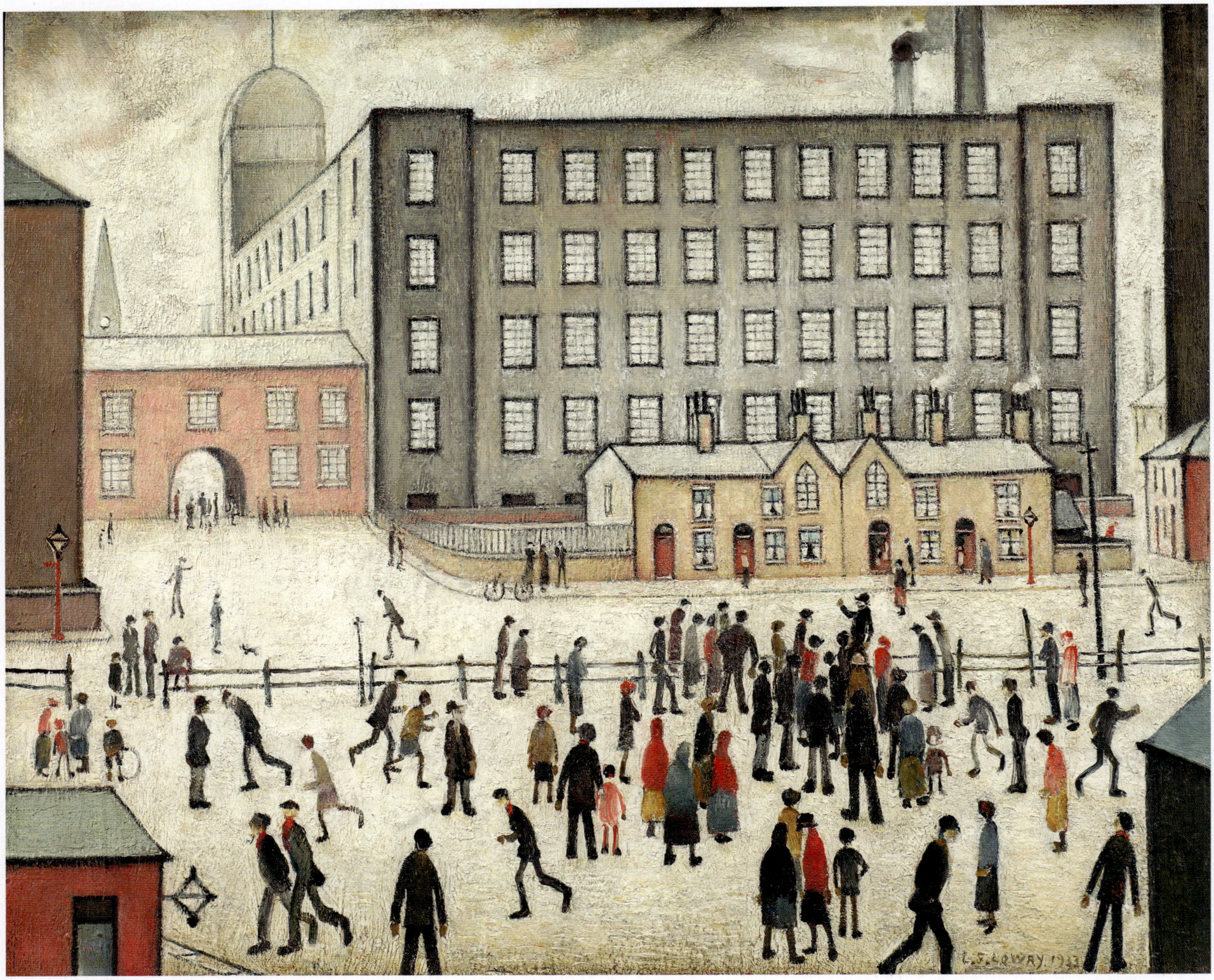

The Interval, 1933, oil on board,
43.8 × 53.3 cm.

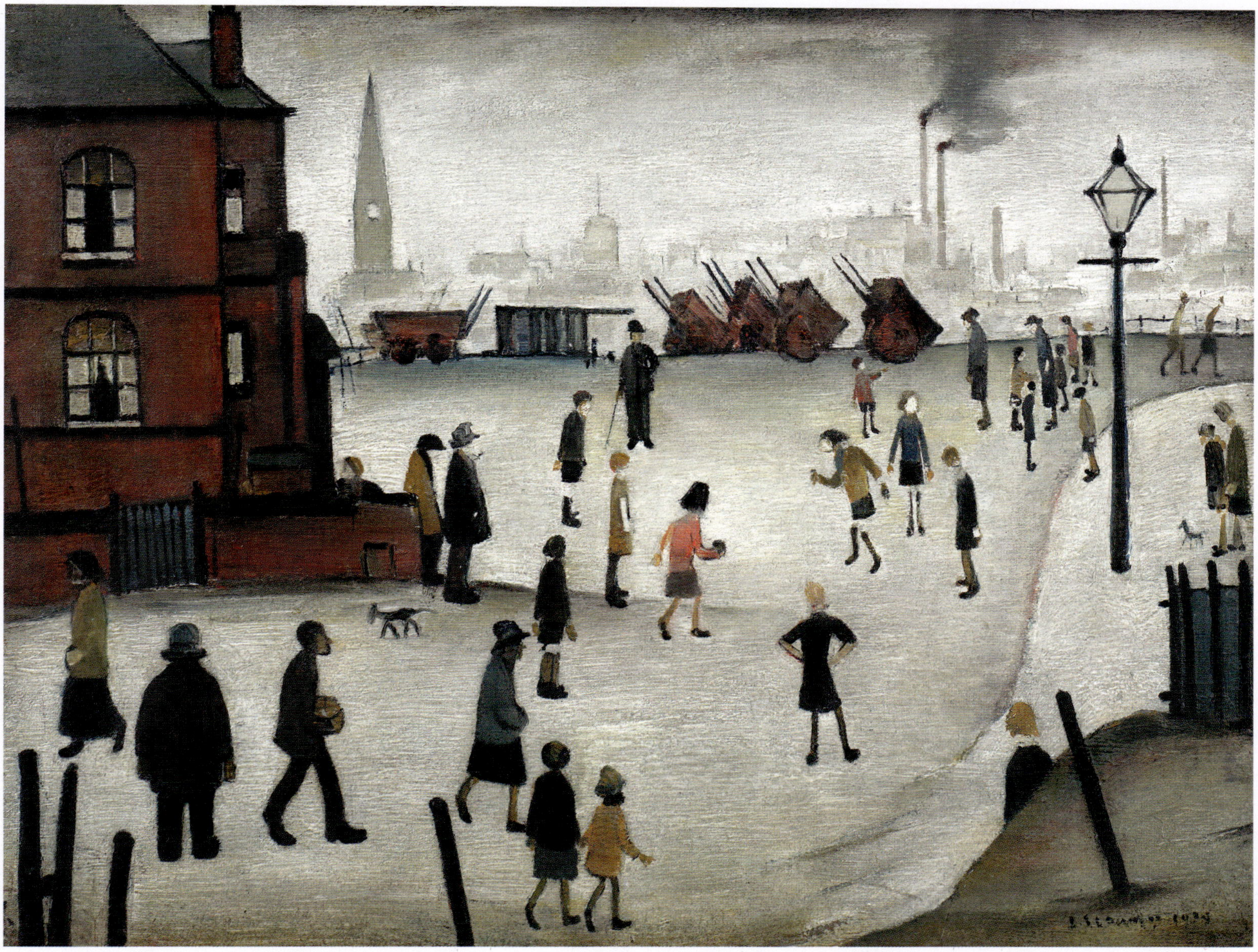

Rounders, 1934, oil on board,
38.1 × 50.8 cm.

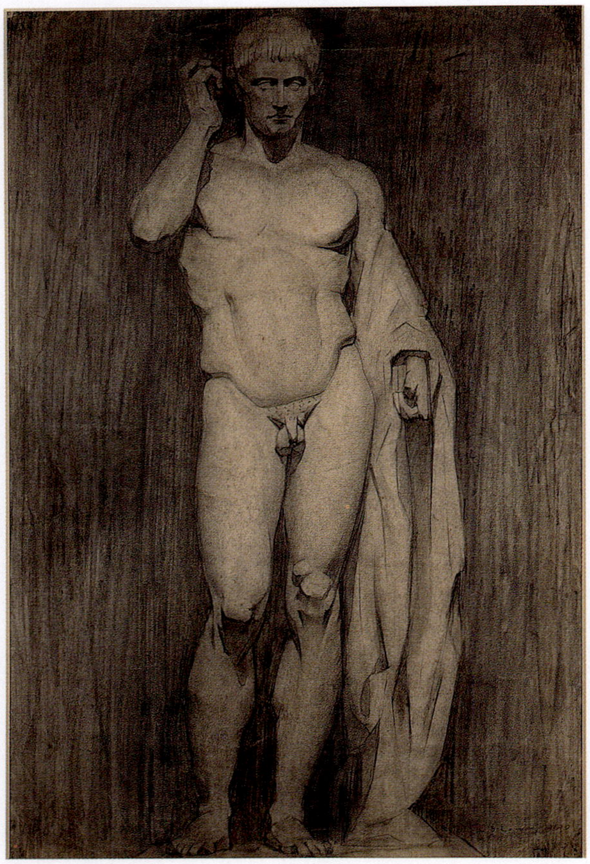

Nude from the Antique, c.1911, pencil on paper, 54.2 × 35 cm.

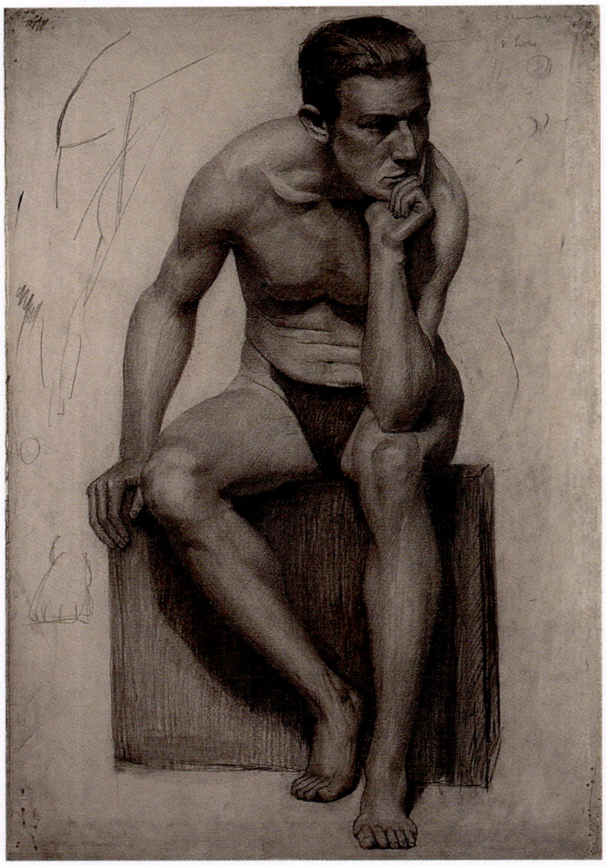

Seated Male Nude, *c.*1914, pencil on paper, 54.8 × 34.9 cm.

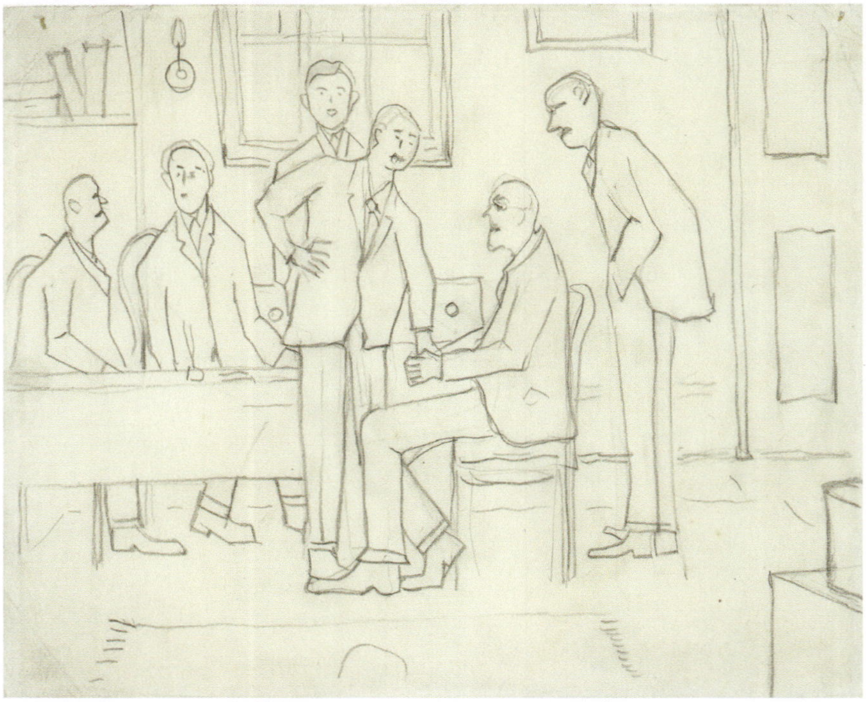

Board Room Scene, *c.*1920, pencil on paper, 20.2 × 25 cm.

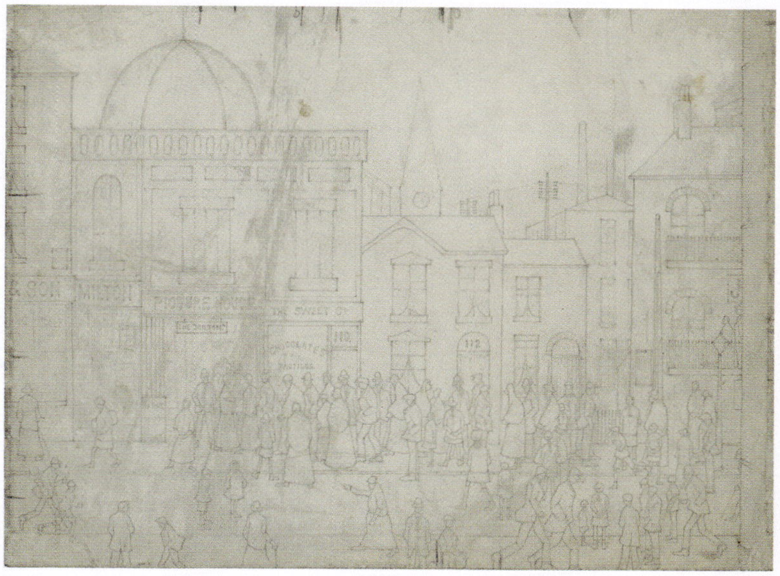

The Milton Picture House, *c.*1920, pencil on paper, 27.2 × 36.7 cm.

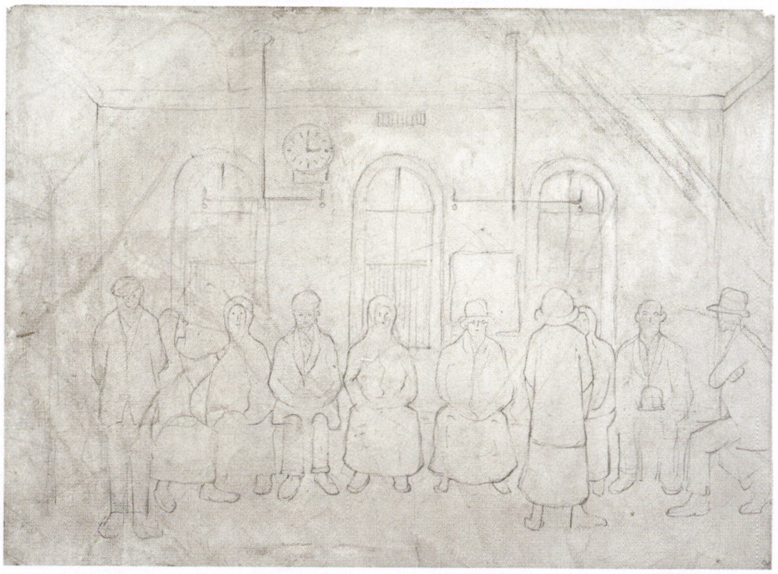

Drawing for *The Waiting Room*, *c.*1920, pencil on paper, 26 × 35.2 cm.

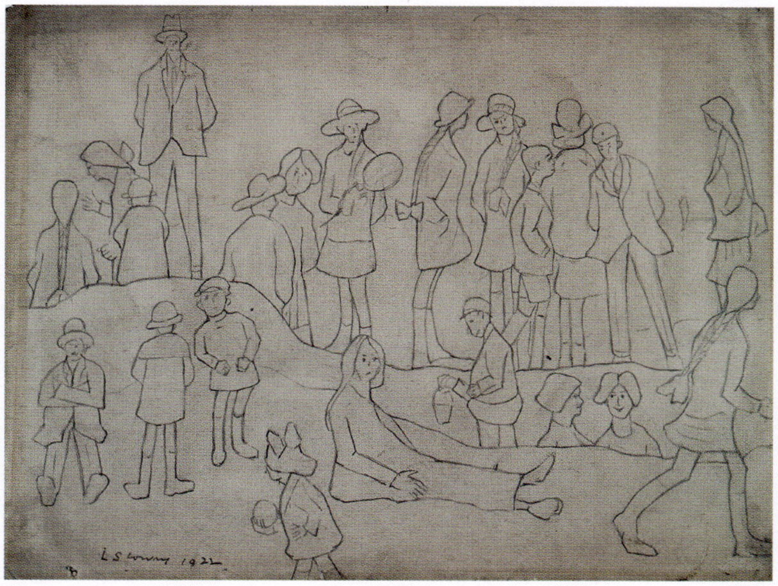

At the Beach, 1922, 26.5 × 35 cm.

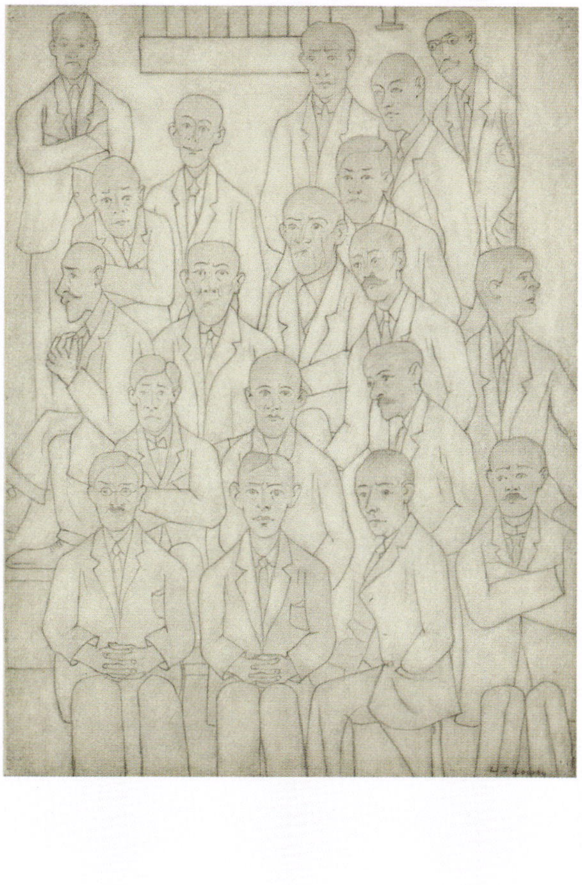

Untitled – Group of Men in Suits, (undated), pencil on paper, 35.5 × 26 cm.

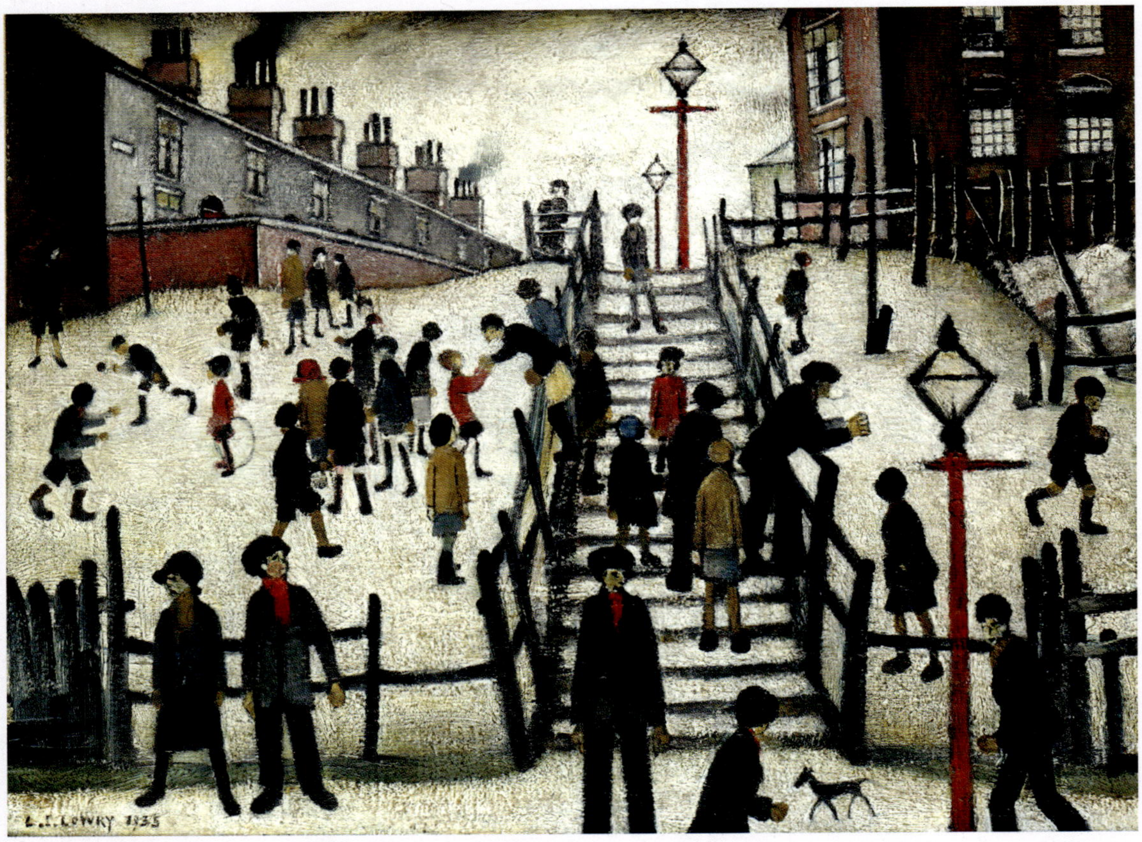

The Playground, 1935, oil on panel, 39.4 × 52.6 cm.

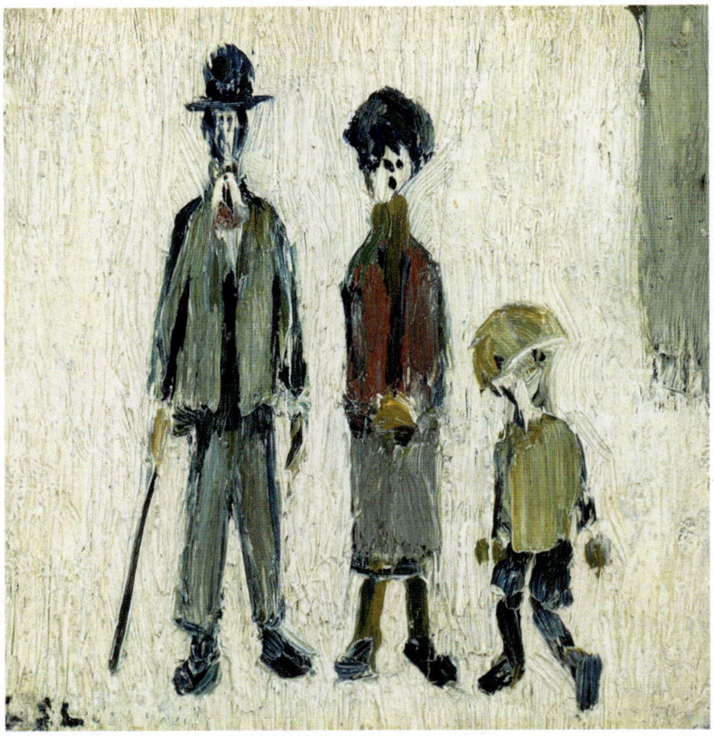

A Family Group, (undated), oil on board, 7.6 × 7.6 cm.

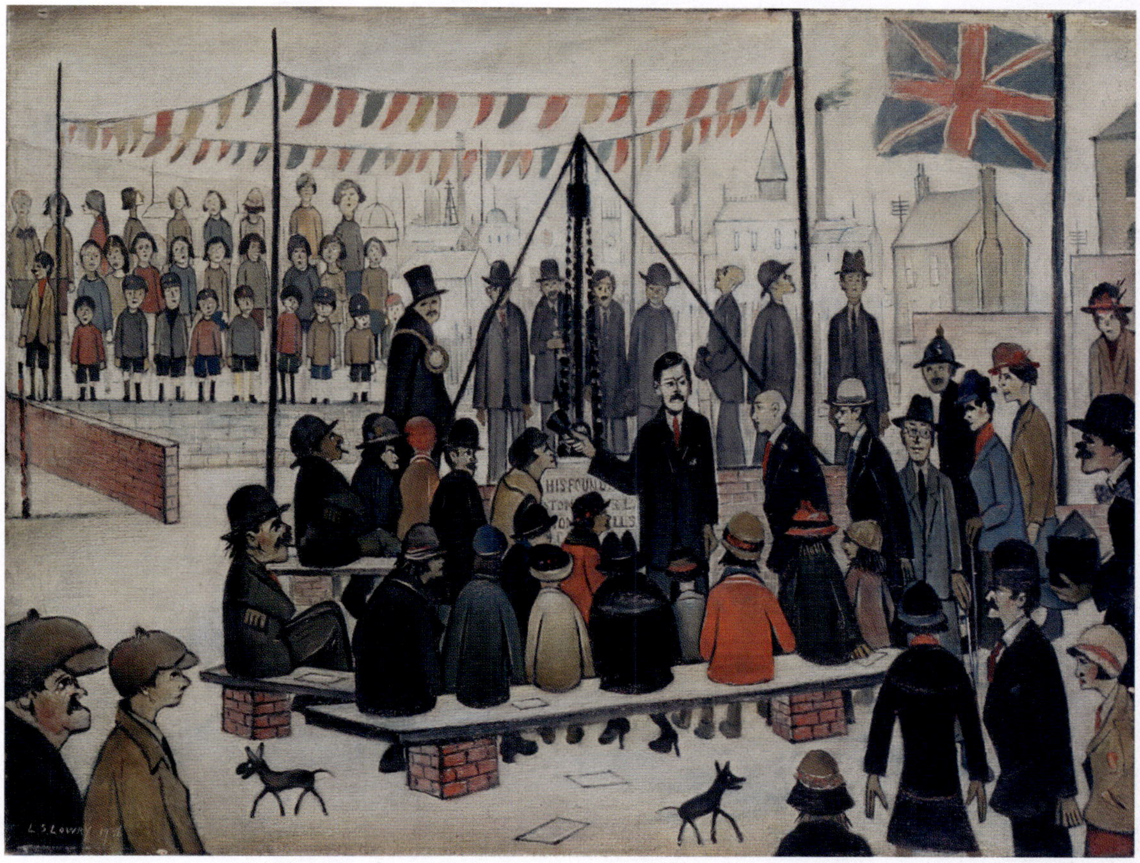

Laying a Foundation Stone, 1936, oil on canvas, 45.7 × 61 cm.

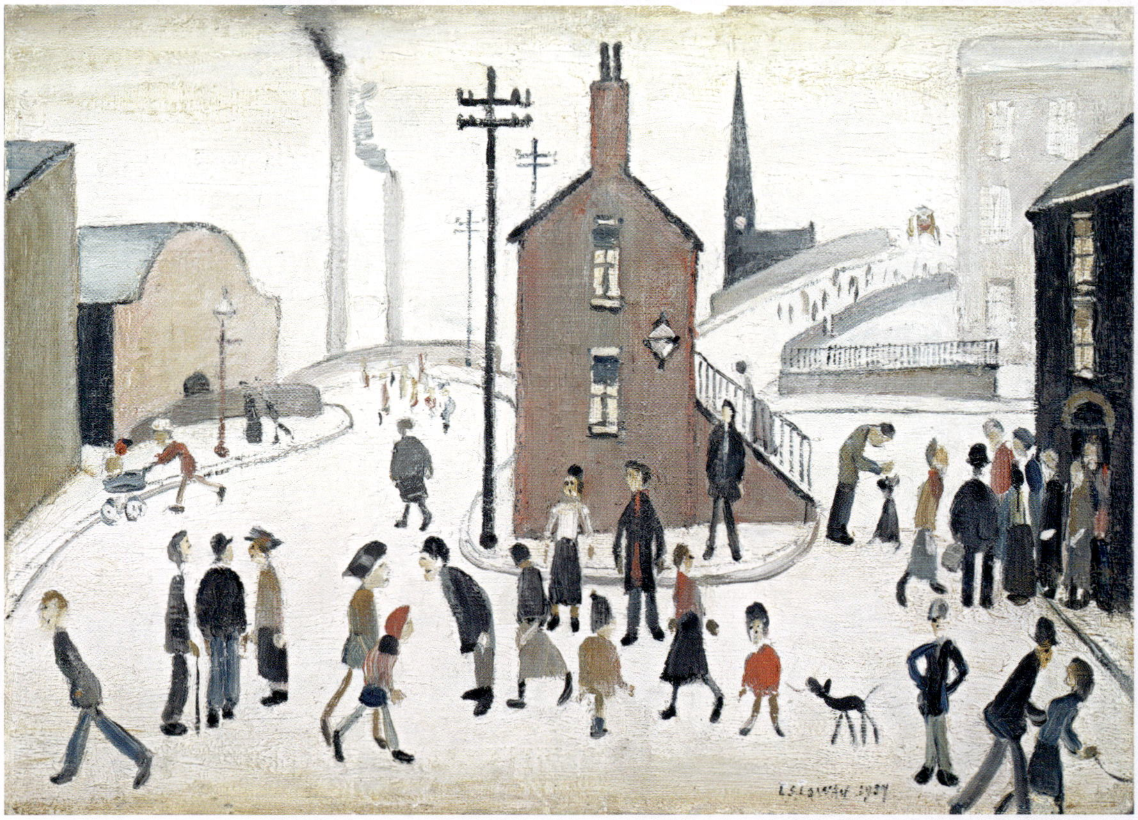

Street Scene, 1937, oil on canvas, 40.3 × 50 cm.

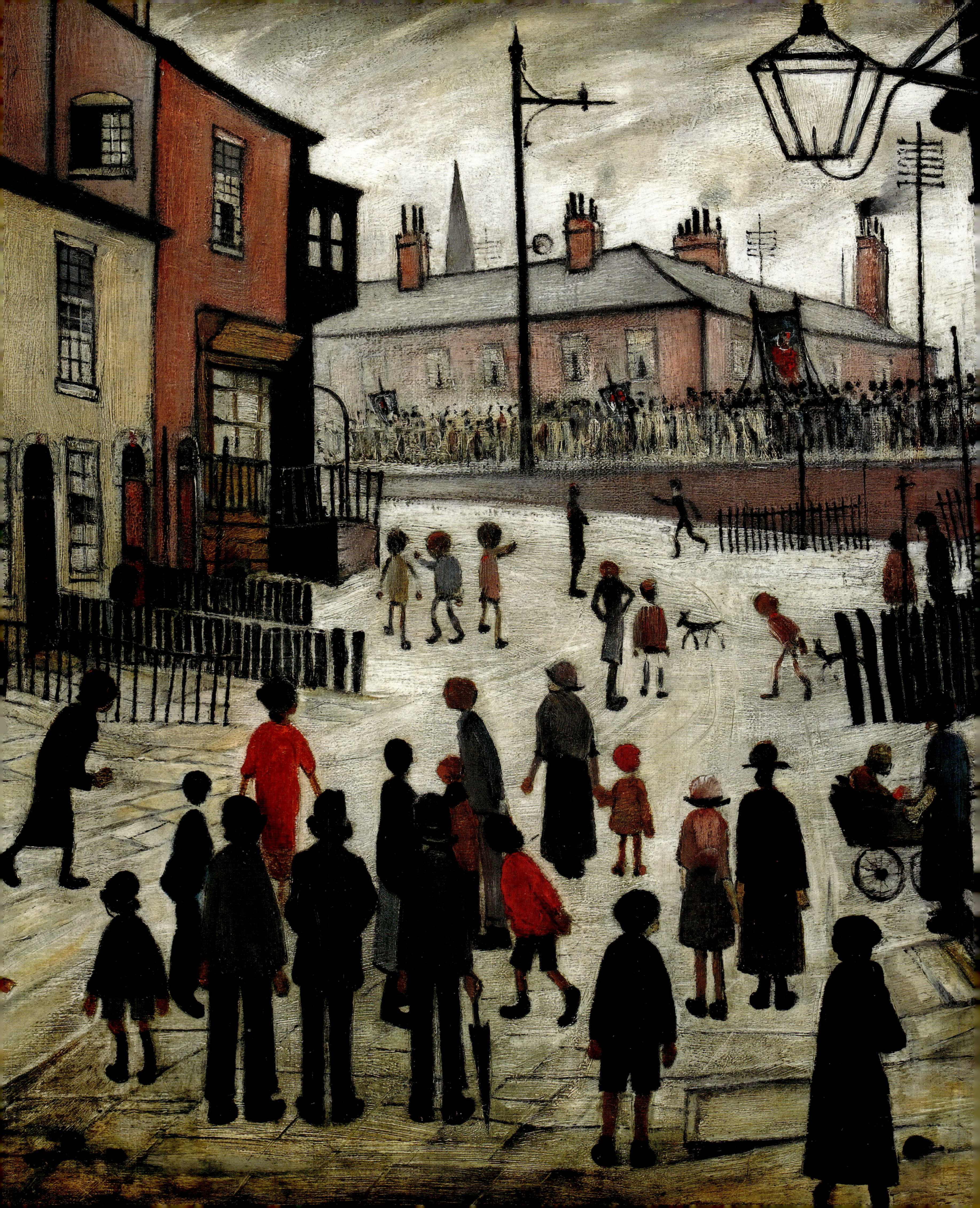

CHAPTER 4

THE ROAD TO SUCCESS

> *I was with a man and he said, look, and there I saw it. It changed my life. From then on I devoted myself to it. I have never tired of looking. It is always fresh.*
>
> L. S. Lowry[1]

Lowry was a great talker and firmly believed in telling people who might be of help to him and his career what he thought they would like to hear. Even in the quotations from him in this book there are, to say the least, inconsistencies, but how dull would a plethora of his utterances be if, for every one of his interlocutors, he religiously set out exactly the same tale in precisely the same words.

The words from the epigraph above are part of a longer episode in Maurice Collis's pioneering book on Lowry published by his dealers in 1951 as an aid to sales and, in reality, simply a longish critical essay-cum-interview accompanied by a few reproductions. But it is worth setting out at some length:

> Suddenly, I began to understand and I said to Lowry: 'Everyone who has written about you has always said that in your paintings you created beauty out of the ugliness of mean streets. But these streets are not mean; they have a strange hardihood, a subtle beauty.'
>
> He seemed very pleased and with great earnestness replied: 'That is it. I was inspired by their beauty. That is why I come here so often to revive myself. At first, when I was young, I did not see the beauty. I used to go into the country painting landscapes and the like. Then one day thirty-six years ago, I suddenly saw it. It was not in this place, but in Salford, in Pendlebury, for there, too, are a few corners like this. I was with a man and he said, look, and there I saw it. It changed my life. From then on I devoted myself to it. I have never tired of looking. It is always fresh.'[2]
>
> One day he missed a train from Pendlebury, and as he left the station he saw the Acme Spinning Company's mill. The huge black framework of rows of yellow-lit windows stood up against the sad damp-charged afternoon sky. The mill was turning out and hundreds of little pinched, black figures, heads bent down (as though to offer the smallest surface to the whirling particles of sodden grit) were hurrying across the asphalt square, along the mean streets with the inexplicable derelict gaps in the rows of houses, past the telegraph poles, homeward to high tea or pubwards, away from the mill without a backward glance. Lowry watched this scene (which he had looked at many times without seeing) with rapture: he experienced an earthly equivalent of some transcendental revelation. Recalling the experience more than thirty years later he exclaimed to me with wonder, 'And to think that it had never occurred to me to do Manchester subjects.'[3]

Detail from *The Procession*, 1938, (p.99).

In fact the moment of 'revelation' became a classic Lowry anecdote passed from writing hand to writing hand. The liveliest version is quoted by Rohde as being from an article by Harry Hopkins in the magazine *John Bull* dated 16 November, 1951, i.e. six years after Collis and nearly two decades before Rothenstein. It reads:

> Lowry had just missed by a second a Manchester-bound train. "I remember that the guard leaned out of the window and winked at me as the last coach disappeared from the platform. I was very cross about that. I went back up the steps. It would be about four o'clock and perhaps there was some peculiar condition of the atmosphere or something. But as I got to the top of the steps I saw the Acme Mill, a great square red block with the little cottages in rows right up to it – and suddenly, I knew what I had to paint."[4]

I suspect Lowry himself honed the story over the years. After all the vision took place In 1915 or 1916 and *si non e vero e ben trovato*. Had Lowry not had the vision, this seminal act of perception, he would surely, as his juvenilia so clearly demonstrate, have become another competent painter of academic land and seascapes. One need only look at the early seascapes, particularly those that are solely of the sea and the horizon or, inhabited by trim little yachts, as opposed to the docks and harbour scenes with large ships and crowds of people, to see that they are distinctly pretty and at times reminiscent of Boudin on a good day and are really not at all Lowry-like. No wonder that the only one of her Laurie's paintings Elizabeth Lowry approved of was one of his Lytham seascapes full of toy-like little yachts.

It is worth quoting at length from Collis and Rothenstein, partly because both were perceptive students of 20th-century British art and shrewd critics, and because they saw – and sympathized with – what Lowry was trying to do in a world which was, with a few notable exceptions, if not actually hostile, then certainly indifferent to his art. In 1927 The Tate Duveen Fund bought Lowry's *Coming out of School* (page 85) but, as if it was to be a precursor of the Tate's subsequent ambiguity about Lowry, the painting was not hung there until 1949 even though Rothenstein had become Director of the Tate in 1938.

Collis gives an interesting account of sitting and talking with Lowry watching a typical Salford park scene with children playing their games on the municipal slides and roundabouts.

> The children continued in front of us with their games. 'I have often painted this scene', he said. Though the scene itself or elements in it looked like a Lowry painting, the children and those old people who were about did not look like Lowry figures. As if divining my thought he said: 'Though I have painted this scene of the children with the slide and the roundabout, I imposed my mood on it., My mood was thrown over the children, is over the people in all my scenes. I could not, I did not want to, paint them as they appear. The truth is that I was not painting them. I have been called a painter of the Manchester workpeople. But my figures are not exactly that. They are ghostly figures which tenant these courts and laneways which seem to me so beautiful, they are symbols of my mood, they are myself.'

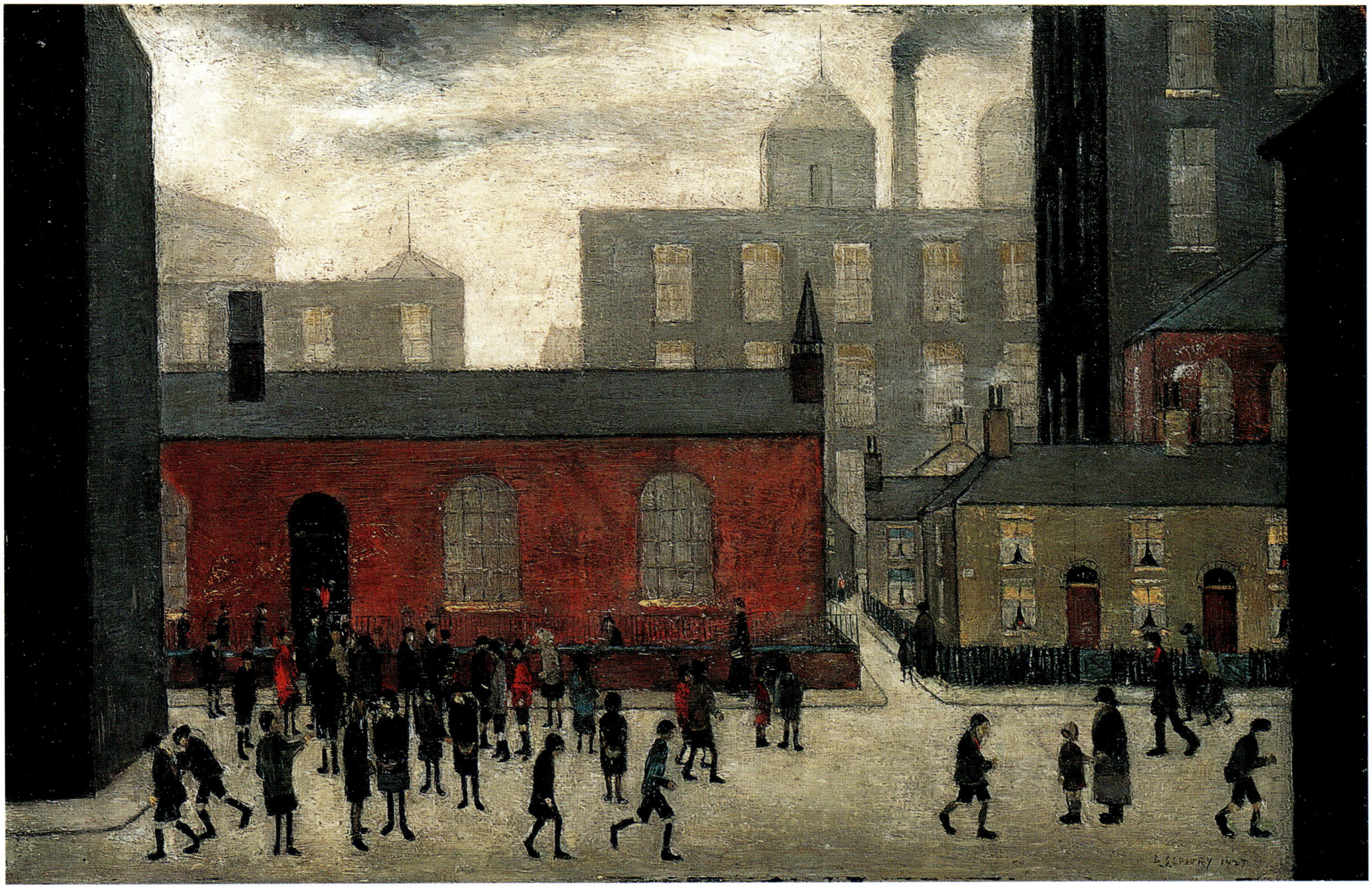

Coming out of School, 1927,
oil on plywood, 34.5 × 54 cm.

And he went on: 'From the beginning I looked at the life around me in this mood, for I was always a solitary, even among the intimates of my youth. Before 1915 I did not know how to express my mood. My figures then were naturally drawn. Tomorrow, when we go to my studio, I will show you examples. I had to abandon that way of drawing when I discovered my subject in 1915. I wanted to paint myself into what absorbed me. Natural figures would have broken the spell of it, so I made them half unreal. Some critics have said that I turned my figures into puppets, as if my aim were to hint at the hard economic necessity that drove them. To say the truth, I was not thinking very much about the people. I did not care for them the way a reformer does. They were part of a private beauty that haunted me. I loved them and the houses in the some way, as part of a vision. It would have been anybody's view of Manchester. But my whole happiness and unhappiness were that my view was like nobody else's. Had it been like, I should not have seen what I did. What I saw became my companion. But a man cannot

> always live with his imagination. Though much comforted by my art, it could not make my solitude less. Indeed, as time went on, I was more and more alone.'[5]

There is in this passage an acute self-knowledge of both his art and, in the second paragraph about being a solitary, his psychological make-up. Artists who subsume their life into their work are ten a penny; most analysis of such people is merely simplistic psycho-babble. But here Lowry is admitting to the imaginative element, the deliberate lack of realism, in his work. This in turn is borne out by the contrasting lack of beauty in the *non-imaginative* works, e.g. the commissioned paintings where the unspoken agreement within the patron/painter contract is that what the artist has to do, as in his painting of, say, *Piccadilly Gardens* (Manchester) (page 49) or *Piccadilly Circus* in London (page 87), is set down what the viewer of the cityscape can clearly see and *not* to indulge himself with his imaginative skills.

Collis has also tactfully recorded his view of Lowry's long mutual dependency on and with his mother, as revealed in a talk with Lowry in a more or less derelict open space in Salford called Stump Park.

> After I had looked for some little time at Stump Park, which I could perceive had the same subtle beauty as the courts off the Oldham Road, we walked on to his parents' house in Station Road, a semi-detached villa with a garden at the back, like thousands of others in the suburbs. 'I lived there with my mother from 1909 until her death in 1939', Lowry said. 'After that I stayed on alone, until in 1948 I bought my present house at Mottram-in-Longdendale, where I shall be taking you this afternoon. My mother never cared much for Pendlebury and made no friends and few acquaintances. For the last years of her life she was an invalid and never went out of the house. I used to look after her with the help of one servant' He spoke with a gentleness that was very moving. And I remembered Mr. Reid had told me how Lowry, on his flying visits to London at the time of his first exhibition, used to catch the afternoon train to Manchester so as to be in time to cook his mother's supper. As we stood gazing at the house (for we did not go in) he said: 'Will you say when you write how much I owe to my mother, for I would like that to be in the book?'[6]

While it is easy, even quite comfortable, to perceive Lowry's sudden vision of the Acme mill as the main event in his artistic life and progress, it was, in cold reality, merely a nudge into a particular journey. It did not of itself create the road to success. Lowry lived a non-metropolitan life and had no dealer committed to making him critically acclaimed, talked about and bought at ever more staggering prices. While Lowry worked by day at Pall Mall Properties and by night in his primitive domestic studio there was no Jay Jopling to add compulsively ever longer rows of noughts to his prices, no Charles Saatchi to see him as the hot number of the future and therefore worth buying up half his output before selling him at his financial peak. No one could, even if he would, turn the ugly duckling L. S. Lowry into the almost supernaturally rich swan Damian Hirst or the cynosure of all PR men's eyes known as Tracy Emin. Life simply wasn't like that. Ask the shades of William Nicholson,

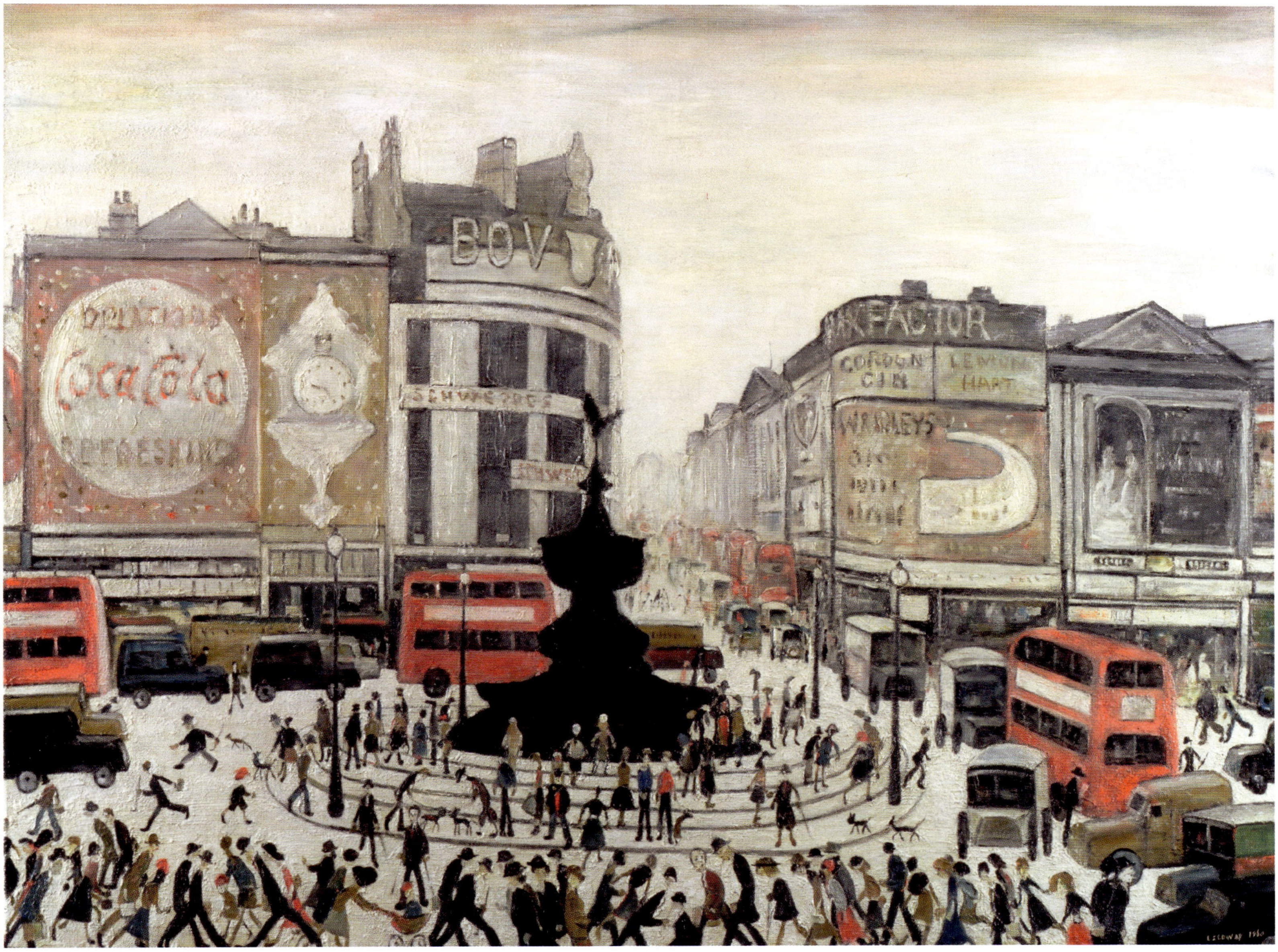

Piccadilly Circus, 1959, oil on canvas.

Jacob Epstein, Matthew Smith, Wyndham Lewis *et al* how long and hard you had to work to earn even a comfortable existence in the inter-war years, let alone during and after the second World War. Even a giant like Lewis was, towards the end of his life, more or less a pauper and it was only the generosity of T. S. Eliot that provided the occasional bottle of champagne or pot of *pâté*.

Lowry's path to success was not only very slow but was also a series of isolated little byways rather than a straightforward path. There is something almost unbearably poignant in learning that in 1952, aged 65, he retired from Pall Mall with a pension of £200 a year, both a common and a commonplace ending to the life of multitudes of ordinary working men at that time.

In February 1919 Lowry had submitted two paintings and a drawing to the Annual Exhibition of Manchester City Art Gallery. All were accepted; *Portrait of an Old Woman* (15 guineas), *Landscape* (6 guineas) and *Pencil Drawing* (4 guineas). None sold. But Lowry received his first press notice from Bernard D. Taylor in the *Manchester Guardian*. Connoisseurs of press brevity will appreciate that the relevant passage from the *Guardian* read in full: "There are good portraits by Messrs Barber, Lowry and Roberts", and one can judge Taylor's objectivity by the fact that the three artists are listed alphabetically. Lowry did not thereafter submit work until 1932 when the Art Gallery invited him to enter his work because of various minute edgings up the greasy pole of artistic recognition. One of the signs of recognition consisted of a sentence attributed to an itinerant painter in a successful novel by Howard Spring (who had become a patron and friend of Lowry), *Shabby Tiger*: "There are only two painters in Manchester with any guts at all – L. S. Lowry and Myself."

Lowry's first purchaser was a 17-year-old girl who bought a drawing for 7s 6d and another at the same price and Lowry did a small painting of ships at sea for her and charged her £1.10s, observing later: "It wasn't a bad price then you know."[7]

But Lowry's mother managed to disparage even this small success and Lowry was determined to make a bonfire of all his drawings to date. He was prevented from doing so by a new friend, a bank manager, who subsequently took Holy Orders and became the Reverend Geoffrey Bennett and Lowry's first proper patron, who accepted the gift of all the drawings, thus not only saving them from destruction but turning them into the nucleus of a major Lowry collection.

In June 1933 Lowry had two paintings accepted for the Royal Academy Summer Exhibition: *A Street in Stockport* and *The Procession* (page 98). Unhappily for Lowry, the *Manchester Evening News* that revealed this honour also outed Lowry as an employee of a property company and ended their report with the words 'Art to Mr Lowry is the antidote to a day of strain at a city desk'. Lowry, normally a quiet, controlled person, seized his coat and stick and marched, furious, to the newspaper and managed to extract an undertaking not to mention his day job ever again, fearing that it would attract – and only to his detriment – the label of Sunday painter he so abhorred. Rohde reports that this attack worked and, almost miraculously, no other newspaper picked up on the story in Lowry's lifetime. Only in 1976, half a year after Lowry's death, did the *Manchester Evening News* return to the matter of Lowry's work for Pall Mall, ironically just in time for notes to this effect to be hurriedly inserted into the Catalogue of the Royal Academy's tribute retrospective exhibition. As Lowry's fellow Academician and friend James Fitton reported, the stuffed shirts at the Royal Academy immediately leaped upon the disclosure and tried to write off Lowry as an amateur who never painted shadows because he painted under electric light thus proving that Lowry's paranoia about how he had made a living was all too well-founded.

After World War I Lowry enrolled and studied intermittently at Salford School of Art where he attended the Life Class taught by the *Guardian's* Bernard T. Taylor. Remembering Taylor's one kind word in his review Lowry ventured to show him some of his early industrial crowd scenes which Taylor did not like and said so. He chided Lowry for making his pictures impenetrable and unattractive with their permanently dark backgrounds. 'Can't you paint the figures on a light ground?' asked Taylor. Lowry responded: 'How do I do that?' 'That's for you to find out'.[8] Lowry was unhappy but Taylor had done exactly what all good teachers do, namely to force the pupil to work the problem out for himself. This in turn lead to Lowry's celebrated 7-year experiment with white on board, which he began in 1924 and which gave him the result in 1931 which marked his work for the rest of his life. This is fully described in Chapter 10, LOWRY'S TECHNIQUE.

Lowry's life and work are full of irony and serendipity. While his local shows in Manchester and Salford produced no sales, he was considered good enough to show, at the Paris Salon, *Election Time* in 1930, nine full years before he had his first London exhibition. It is quite difficult to imagine the effect of *Election Time* (page 90) on the French who certainly failed to buy it. But with all the joys of hindsight it is impossible to see it today as anything other than an archetypal Lowry painting. The inevitable white background is stuffed with action. The political orator, whom, in Lowry's eyes, one knows to be insufferably pompous, is the heart of a classic Lowry crowd scene, dense in the upper left where it can hear clearly what the windbag is spouting and the thinning out in the middle as the crowd either passes by or moves into the painting's foreground to talk among themselves, whether about electoral politics or other interests. As always with Lowry's crowds no two figures are alike; each is a robustly delineated individual. The painting also has an easy mix of formality, the speaker on his podium, two or three people seated on chairs, presumably stewards in case things turn nasty, and then the casual, faintly mocking postures of the dispersed audience. This is so like so many outdoor election meetings that you know Lowry has been accurate in his observation while having reserved for himself the absolute right to invent and put in people whom he has seen elsewhere or whom he has simply pulled out of his imagination.

In October 1921 an architect called Rowland Thomasson put on, at his offices in Manchester's Mosely Street, a show of his own and his friend Tom Brown's watercolours and simultaneously gave Lowry his first proper exhibition, consisting of twenty-five oil paintings and two pastels. Priced, according to size, at between five guineas and £25, none sold. Inevitably some of the best pictures on view are now in private and major public collections such as Salford's The Lowry, and many are now worth a few hundred thousand pounds. For Lowry the most momentous aspect of the show was the *Manchester Guardian* review by Bernard Taylor which, by virtue of its apposite shrewdness and sympathy, is well worth quoting here in full. His take on whether Lowry is a primitive or a realist, some ninety years after he wrote it, still highly valid;

> The third contributor, Mr Laurence S. Lowry, has a very interesting and individual outlook. His subjects are Manchester and Lancashire street scenes, interpreted with technical means as yet imperfect, but with real imagination. His portrait of Lancashire is more grimly like than a caricature, because it is done with the intimacy of affection. He emphasizes violently everything that industrialism has done to make the aspect of

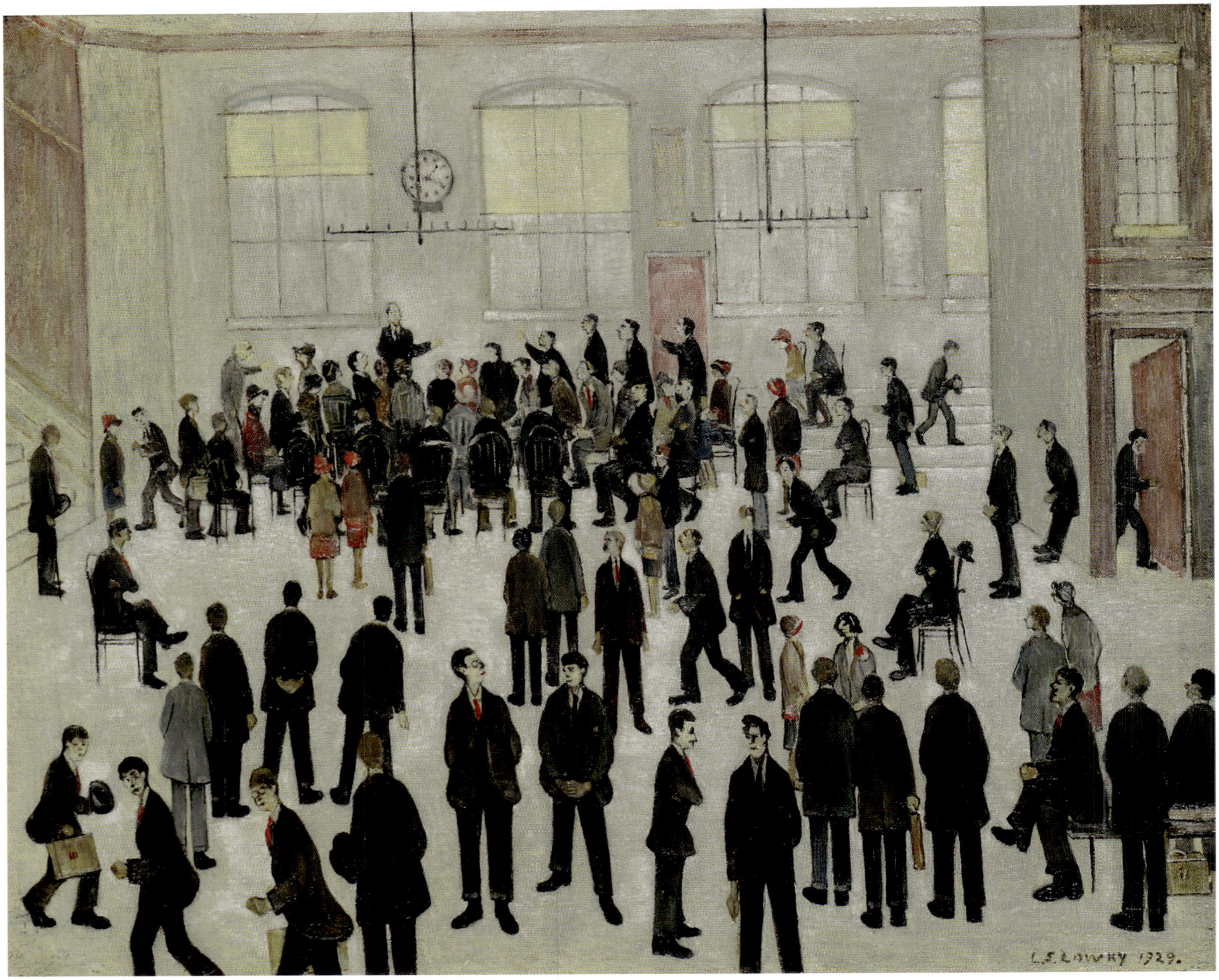

Election Time, 1929, oil on canvas, 41.9 × 50.8 cm.

Lancashire more forbidding than of most other places. Many of us may comfort ourselves a little with contemplating suburban roads, parks, or gardens in public squares, or with the lights and colours of morning or sunset. Mr Lowry has refused all comfortable delusions. He has kept his vision as fresh as if he had come suddenly into the most forbidding part of Hulme or Ancoats under the gloomiest skies after a holiday in France or Italy. His Lancashire is grey, with vast rectangular mills towering over diminutive houses. If there is an open space it is of trodden earth, as grey as the rest of the landscape. The crowds which have this landscape for their background are entirely in keeping

> with their setting; the incidents in the drama of which they are the characters are also appropriate. "A Labour Exchange", "The Entrance for Out-patients", "A Quarrel in a Side Street", "Ejecting a Tenant" are titles which will give a clue to the subjects of the pictures;
>
> We hear a great deal nowadays about recovering the simplicity of vision of the primitives in art. These pictures are authentically primitive, the real thing, not an artificially cultivated likeness to it. The problems of representation are solved not by reference to established conventions but by sheer determination to express what the artist has felt, whether the result is according to rule or not. The artist's technique is not yet equal to his ideas. If he can learn to express himself with ease and style and at the same time preserve his singleness of outlook he may make a real contribution to art.[9]

Although nothing was sold at the time of the shows, Taylor's generous and, above all, perceptive review had a catalytic effect. Taylor got James Bone, then the *Manchester Guardian's* London Editor to come and see the Manchester exhibition. He was sufficiently impressed to spread the word across the paper so that, from then on, Lowry was consistently supported by various sections of the newspaper including reproducing three of his paintings in a supplement to celebrate Manchester's Civic Week. The *Guardian's* Literary Editor, was equally impressed, went on to buy one of the three and Lowry was so grateful that he insisted on giving Arthur Wallace another picture as a gift.

The Director of the Oldham Art Gallery, W. H. Berry, also much taken by Lowry's work, invited him home for Sunday lunch. This turned out to be a serendipitous event of momentous importance. Berry's wife, Daisy Jewell, was heavily involved in the London art world as head of the framing department of James Bourlet & Sons, then as now a dominant supplier of such vital services to artists as storage, packing and safe transport, both at home and abroad, as well as framing. Daisy Jewell became a Lowry fan and set about masterminding a career for him in London where she worked during the week. She introduced Lowry to a director of Bourlet, Armand Blackley, who also became a fan of Lowry's. He and Jewell, from 1923 on, worked heroically sending his pictures to France (five showings at the Salon) and all round Britain even though they all ended up unsold and returned to Bourlet's warehouse. It was through Daisy Jewell and her sister, who also worked in the art trade, that Lowry could add to his burgeoning CV exhibiting at the Paris Salon d'Automne, the New English Art Club, the Irish Salon, the Goupil Gallery, etc. Thus his work became better known but not, alas, better liked.

There were just enough occasional minor sales to cover his costs, but, without his Pall Mall salary and the fact that he still lived at home, he would have been more or less destitute. The sale of *Coming Out of School* to the Duveen Fund in 1927 was a happy omen, but really only a straw in the wind. Unfortunately, the Tate did not show it until 1949, by which date, and under Rothenstein's Directorship, the Tate had already made the other, and its own, purchases. (The Duveen Fund had been established not to fund British works of art directly onto the Tate's walls but to enable contemporary British works of art to be displayed and bought for presentation to local museums and for touring purposes.)

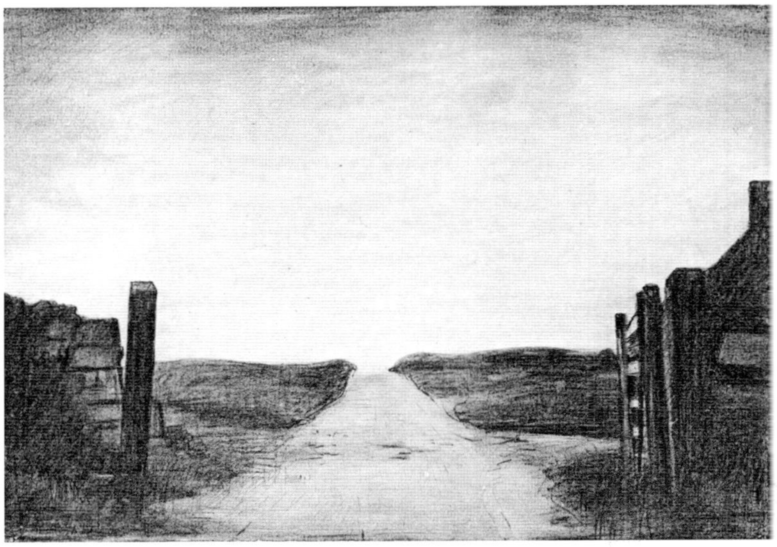

Near Belas Knap

One significant purchase, albeit in the form of a commission, did come his way. His friend, the writer Harold Timperley had been commissioned by Jonathan Cape to write about the Cotswolds. This was published in 1931 under the title *A Cotswold Book* and Timperley insisted that it be illustrated with drawings done by Lowry.

Lowry who, all his life until he got too frail, was an assiduous traveller round Britain, certainly did his homework for this task. There are some 12 drawings, very well printed in what appears to be black and white photogravure well reproduced. Four of the best are shown here: *House at Naunton, Near Bellas Knap, Brockhampton* and *A Cotswold Bridge.* All are easily identifiable as being by Lowry if one has in mind the many hundreds of his topographical sketches and full-scale drawings

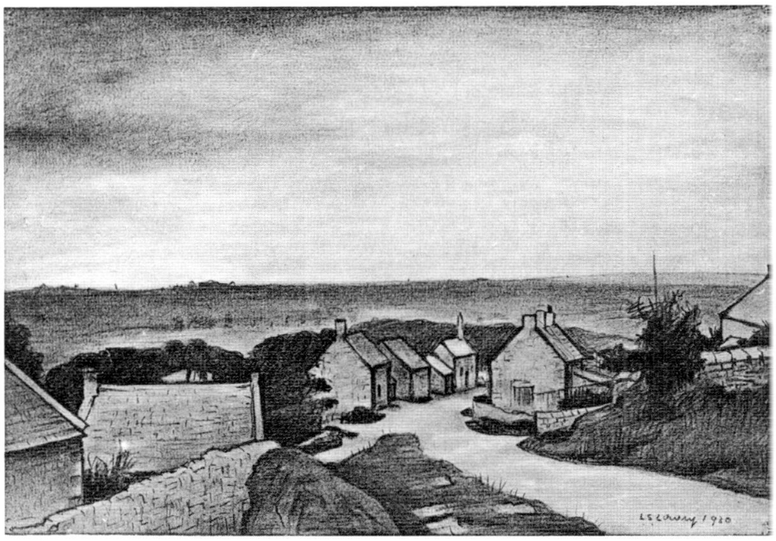

Brockhampton

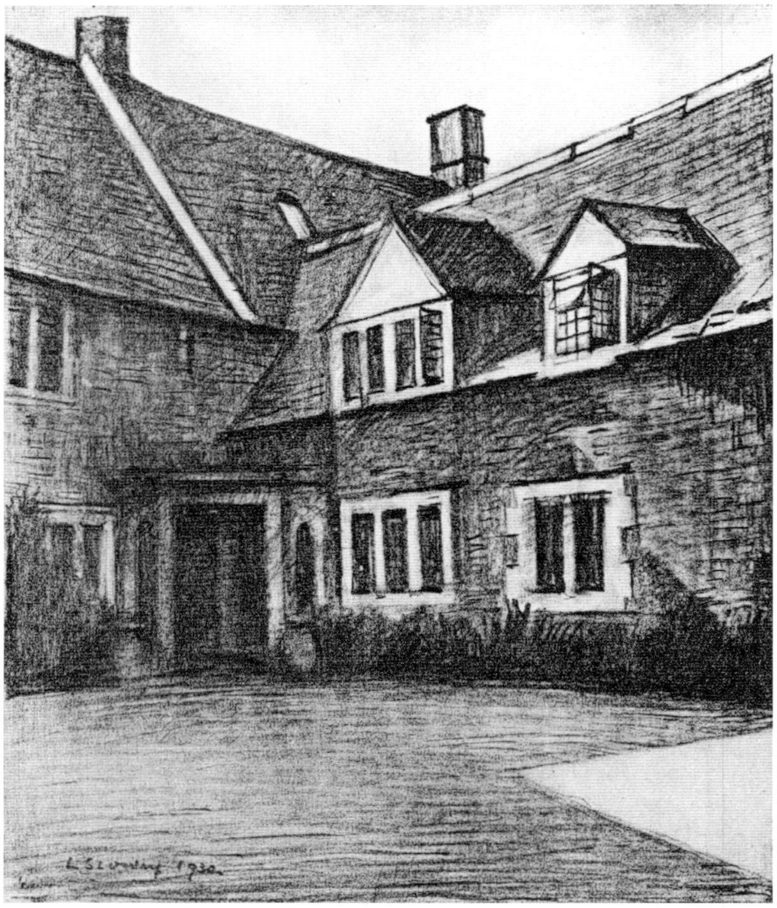

House at Naunton

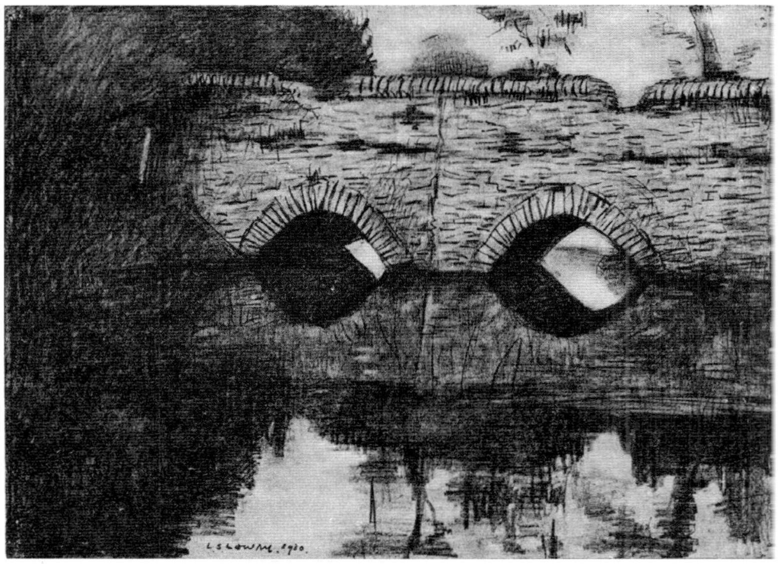

A Cotswold Bridge

of the Manchester and Salford streets and suburbs he knew and studied so well. All are perfectly competent academic studies of typical Cotswold scenery but lack that instant spark of recognition you get in similar works by other and more prolific book illustrators such as Edward Bawden, Eric Ravilous and Edward Ardizzone. But they all delighted in illustration and book illustration most of all. For Lowry it was a one-off and since the work was at best poorly paid one can see why Lowry did not encourage further book publishing ventures although he responded eagerly enough when offered sizable sums for so-called "Original Artist's Prints". Nonetheless when one looks at, say *Near Belas Knap* it is good to see him tackling rural byways with the same concentrated interest as a street in Stockport or a square in Eccles.

Timperley paid Lowry a fee of £30 out of his own Cape earnings, (about £1,200 in today's money) which for twelve pencil drawings by a commercially unsuccessful artist was a very reasonable fee. In fact Timperley did not do much better for his text and when Cape commissioned a further volume, *A Shropshire Book*, they insisted on using photographs so that Lowry's anticipated business partnership with Timperley was rather short lived.[10]

In the spring of 1930 Lowry had his first, separate, one-man show in Manchester at the Round House in Every Street "at the Special Request of the Manchester University Settlement". It consisted of some 25 pencil drawings of Ancoats a district of Manchester which he often visited and drew copiously. All carried the same price, 3½ guineas unframed or 4 guineas framed. Bernard Taylor having died in 1928 the *Guardian's* highly favourable review was written by someone else and was unsigned. By the second day (26 March) every drawing had been sold, many to Manchester's great and good, including Professor J. L. Stocks and his wife Mary (later Baroness Stocks). Another was bought by the wife of C. P. Scott the Editor of the *Manchester Guardian* and one of the drawings was wanted by both Margaret Pilkington (Director of the Whitworth Art Gallery) and Lawrence Haward (Curator at the Manchester City Art Gallery). This represented, once the two claims were settled, Lowry's first sale to a Manchester institution and the following September Haward bought Lowry's great 1926 painting *An Accident* (page 94) after having haggled the asking price (as most English public galleries inevitably do) down from 30 guineas to £26. This is a superb painting bearing out Lowry's view that for a good crowd you need either a quarrel or a body. Against a good, light, white background we are given all the classic ingredients of a top-drawer Lowry. The sky is complex and turbulent, to show off the inevitable mixture of dark clouds and even darker plumes of smoke from the soaring chimneys in both back and middle grounds. With the factories looming behind them there's a strange, truncated terrace of four houses, all neatly curtained with their façades rendered in a deep, brownish ochre. They in turn look out upon a vast open space filled with about seventy people either quite close to the dense crowd at the right staring, presumably, at the body, or distant from it but about to converge on those with the best view who must surely take the totality of the crowd to over a hundred people.

They have all been drawn to the idea of a dead body, although, as if governed by the formal rules of Greek tragedy, no corpse is visible. We would have to rely for a description on

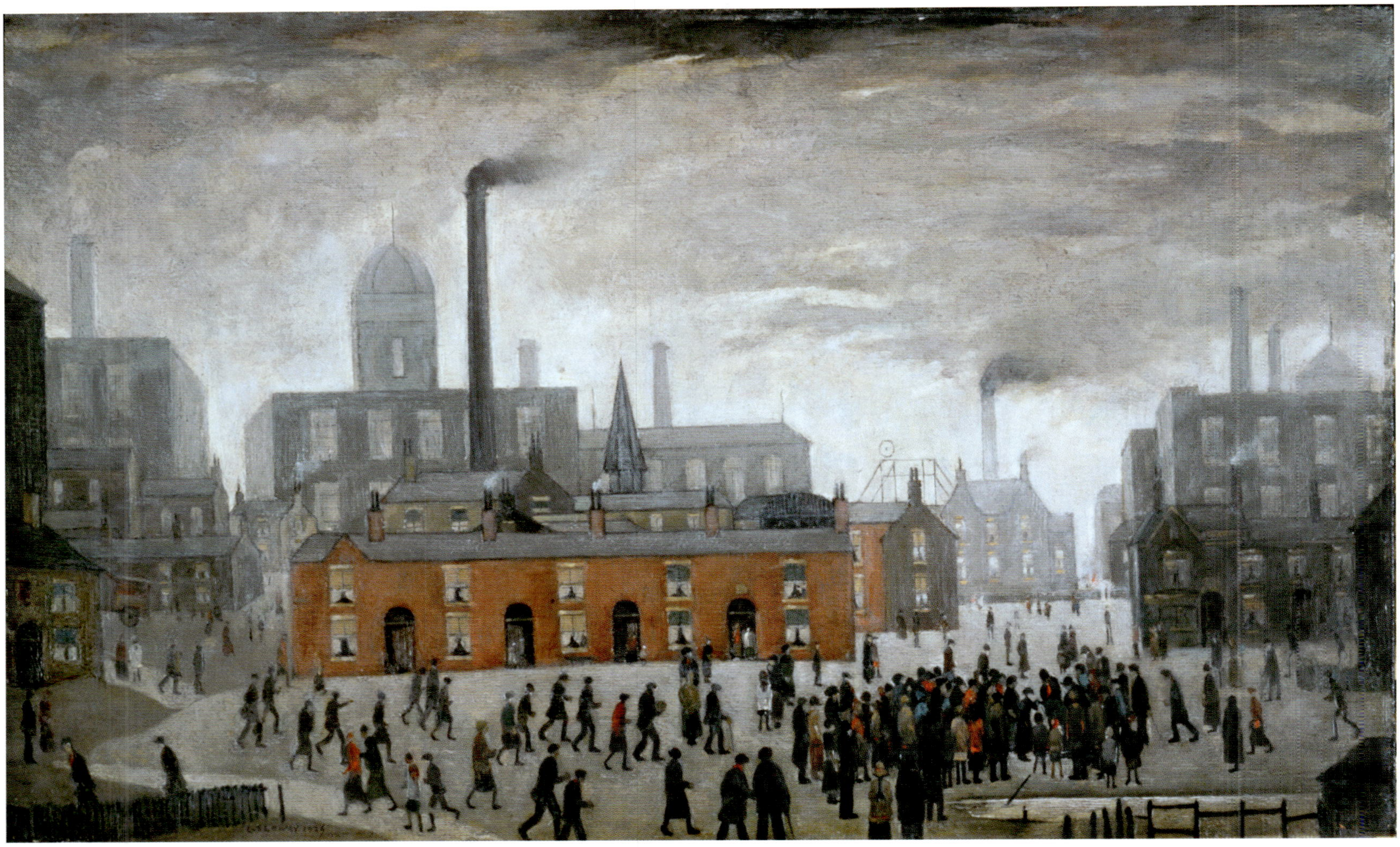

An Accident, 1926, oil on panel, 36.3 × 61 cm.

the account by someone who actually saw "it" happen whatever "it" actually was. Certainly the tightly-knit group "concealing" the body are united by their universal curiosity and their equally universal morbidity. Yet there is no body visible. Just as in Lowry's paintings of his mother's bedroom, while Edward Munch would surely have a ghastly, pallid, haunting corpse lying in or on the bed so Lowry, doubtless still mourning Mrs Lowry's demise, cannot bring himself to have the bed inhabited in any way. Even in another great work, *The Fever Van* of 1935 (page 177) we don't see the patient. We see the doors of the fever van wide open, we see the morbid, gawping crowd but we don't see a bedraggled child with scarlet fever or an adult with terminal tuberculosis. For Lowry himself it is enough to analyze the crowd so that we – and he – can imagine the victim who is the cause of the crowd. Lowry, writing in 1950 to the Manchester City Art Gallery, *inter alia*, about his painting technique for *An Accident* said: "As to the subject, it was a case of a woman found drowned (suicide) some years ago in Pendlebury".

Be that as it may Lowry ensures that there is no visible corpse. The woman is completely hidden by the closed crowd and the only hint of a watery grave is what looks like a large puddle at the front edge of the painting. In other words the real horror of the story is concealed from us.

Haward went about as far as a provincial curator could in "commissioning" work from a local and living artist suggesting to Lowry that he should draw some studies of the topography and inhabitants of Manchester's Piccadilly. Lowry asked whether Haward had any particular visual aspects in mind and when Haward told him what they were, Lowry set off to work precisely to order. But Haward, in effect, rejected them by suggesting that Lowry should do something different. This understandably offended Lowry who, reasonably enough, stood on his dignity – he was by then 43 – and responded: "I am afraid that I cannot spend any more time on this subject."[11]

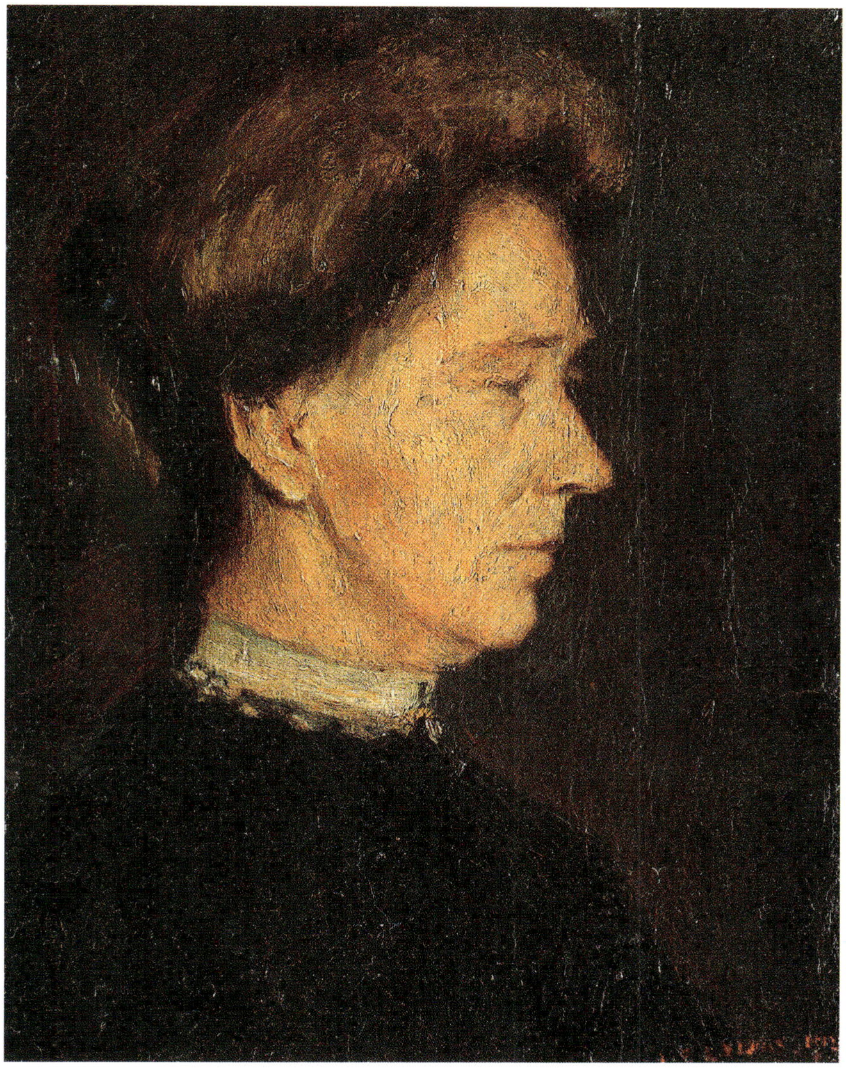

Portrait of the Artist's Mother, 1912, oil on canvas, 46.1 × 35.9 cm.

While teenage, would-be artists often have parents who discourage their ambitions in order to steer them into more lucrative and, above all, safer occupations, Lowry, a middle-aged man with a modest but safe career with a reputable property company, did not need that discouragement from his parents. To be fair, his father was, on occasion, moderately encouraging and correspondence unearthed by Rhode even shows that he was actually aware of, and indeed proud of, his son's artistic talent. But, inevitably it was to his mother that Lowry turned for domestic encouragement. Yet when Lowry disparaged himself in order to provoke some comforting praise from Mrs Lowry the most she would say was 'Well, you never can tell'.[12]

Once, desperate for a few words of praise, after she had withheld comment on his latest work, he asked her "Well, what would you like me to paint?" To which his mother replied "Little boats at Lytham". Ever the dutiful son he made such a painting and gave it to her. By some miracle, or perhaps from genuine pleasure, (how can one tell with such a cold, controlling woman?) she admitted to liking it. Thus, quite truthfully (since in the land of the blind the one-eyed man is king) Lowry could describe this painting, *Sailing Boats*, 1930, as his mother's favourite picture and he put it on his sitting-room wall, next to his portrait of her, where it stayed for the rest of his life. It is in fact an attractive work, full of light and like some of his other paintings based on his visits to this classic Lancashire coastal holiday resort, there is a Boudin-like touch to both subject matter and technique.

In my view there was only one moment when Mrs Lowry's negativity towards the conjunction of her only child and the world of art was justified. That was when in 1939 (the year of her death) Gordon Phillips of the *Manchester Guardian* invited Lowry to write art criticism for the newspaper. Naturally enough, Lowry showed Phillips's letter to his mother who, said Lowry, "Laughed and laughed and laughed" and, having recovered her habitual, severe composure, said "You could never do it, Laurie. The show would be over before you could get it properly phrased". Wisely therefore, Lowry declined the *Guardian's* offer. Wisely because, while Lowry was certainly a shrewd judge of art, both ancient and modern as his acquisition of pre-Raphaelite paintings and drawings and first–rate works by Lucian Freud and Sheila Fell indicates, his written use of language as even his best letters to David Carr demonstrate (see Chapter 7) was really rather stiff and lacked the fluent ease necessary for any *Guardian* writer on art and culture in general. To be fair Lowry was a superb *talker* about art, shrewd and to the point, and his account of the *Guardian's* approach and his mother's reaction to it was one of his favourite self-deprecating anecdotes.

To those who knew him Lowry was a very robust man with tremendous inner strength. In 1932 he had to cope with his father's death which in turn led to his mother taking instantly to her bed where she remained, entirely dependent on her son until she died in 1939. As if trying to succeed as an artist, holding down a full-time day job and looking after a self-willed, chronic invalid were not enough cumulatively to break any man's spirit, the death of Robert Lowry revealed, within days, that he had been a feckless spendthrift who died with huge debts ranging from unpaid rent to substantial unsecured loans, all of which Lowry had to, either by law or by what he saw as his moral duty, pay off as and when he could.

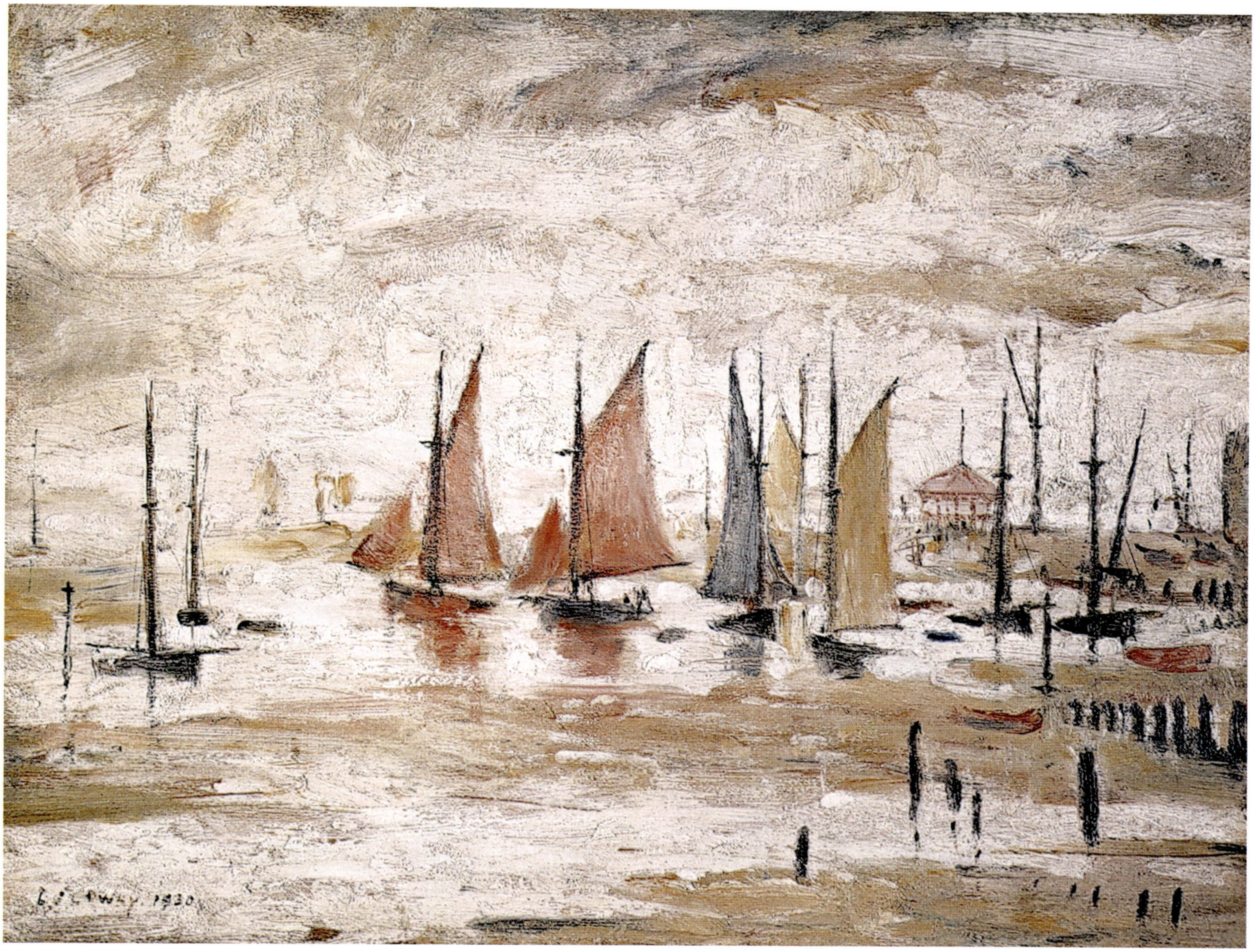

Sailing Boats, 1930, oil on canvas, 35.5 × 45.5 cm.

But it was not all bad news since two months after his father's death he had two paintings accepted by the Royal Academy which, in those inter-war years was still the pinnacle of achievement in Britain as far as both exhibiting and membership were concerned. Two years later, in 1934, Lowry was elected a member of the Manchester Academy. Also in that year he was made a member of the Royal Society of British Artists so that he was able to put RBA after his name. One by-product of that membership was the purchase from the Arlington Galleries (where the RBA members exhibited) of *The Procession* (page 98) by Oldham Gallery where his early mentor W. H. Berry, (the husband of the indefatigable Daisy Jewell) was Director.

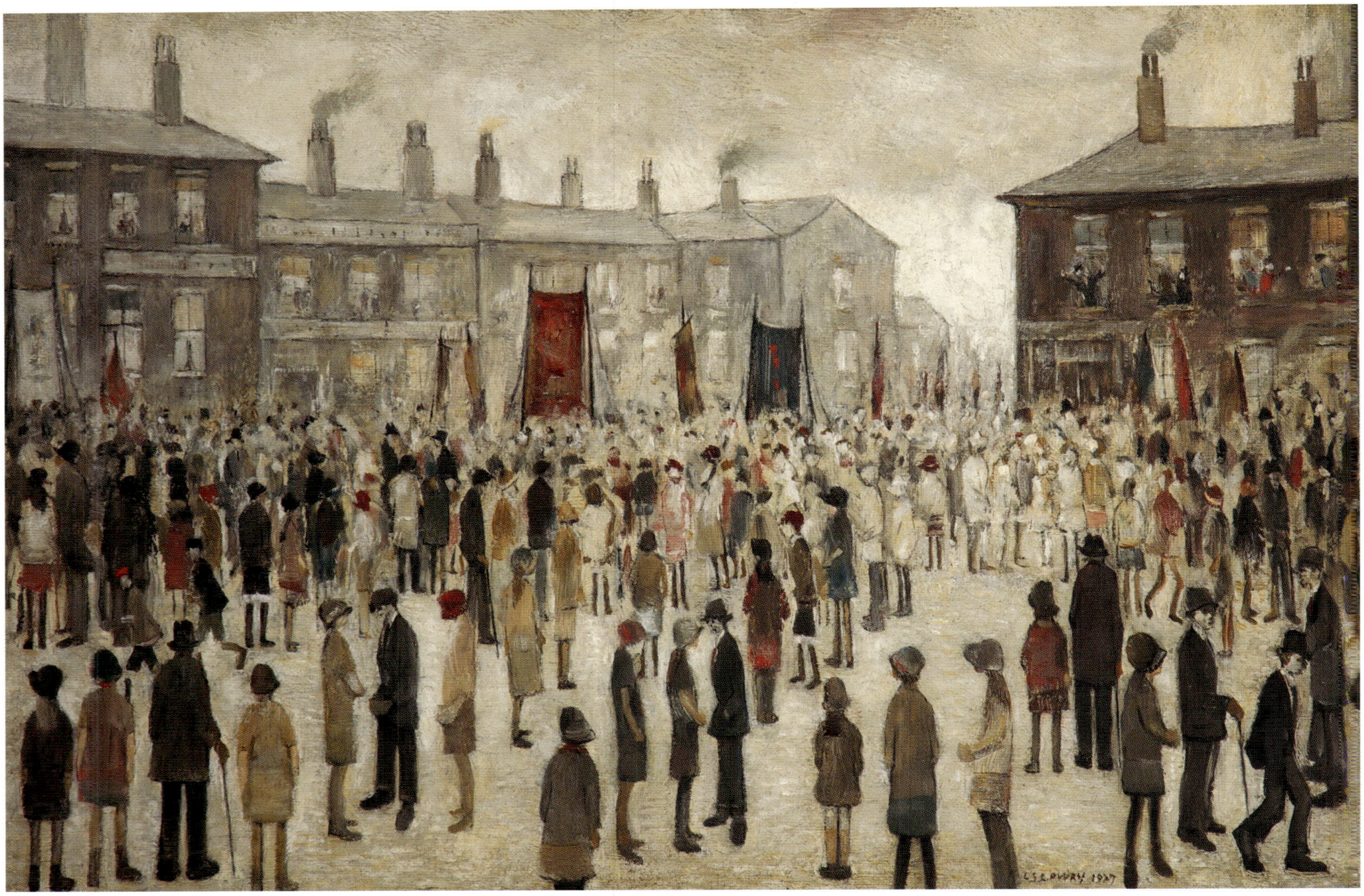

The Procession, 1927, oil on plywood, 35.5 × 54.5 cm.

The Royal Scottish Academy also bought a painting in 1934 and, in 1936, Salford bought its second Lowry, *St Simon's Church* (page 100). In January 1935 he got a favourable review from the powerful art critic T. W. Earp in the *Daily Telegraph*.

In this period after the death of his father there were some particularly grim paintings executed, including the self-portraits and portraits of other middle-aged or elderly men with strained faces, burning, often red-rimmed eyes, all at least a little tinged with at best deep depression and at worst madness. Given the background of his life at this time it is tempting to see all of these as, if not actual self-portraits, then at least representations of the turmoil of his mind and the turbulence of his spirit much as, earlier, Van Gogh had portrayed his own distress in the paintings he made of his own features.

There is also a noticeable darkness of the spirit in his invented landscapes such as *The Lake* (page 101) of 1937. It is, of course, mere coincidence that there exists such an accurate prose evocation of this quintessential Lowry painting, a work of quite haunting power from

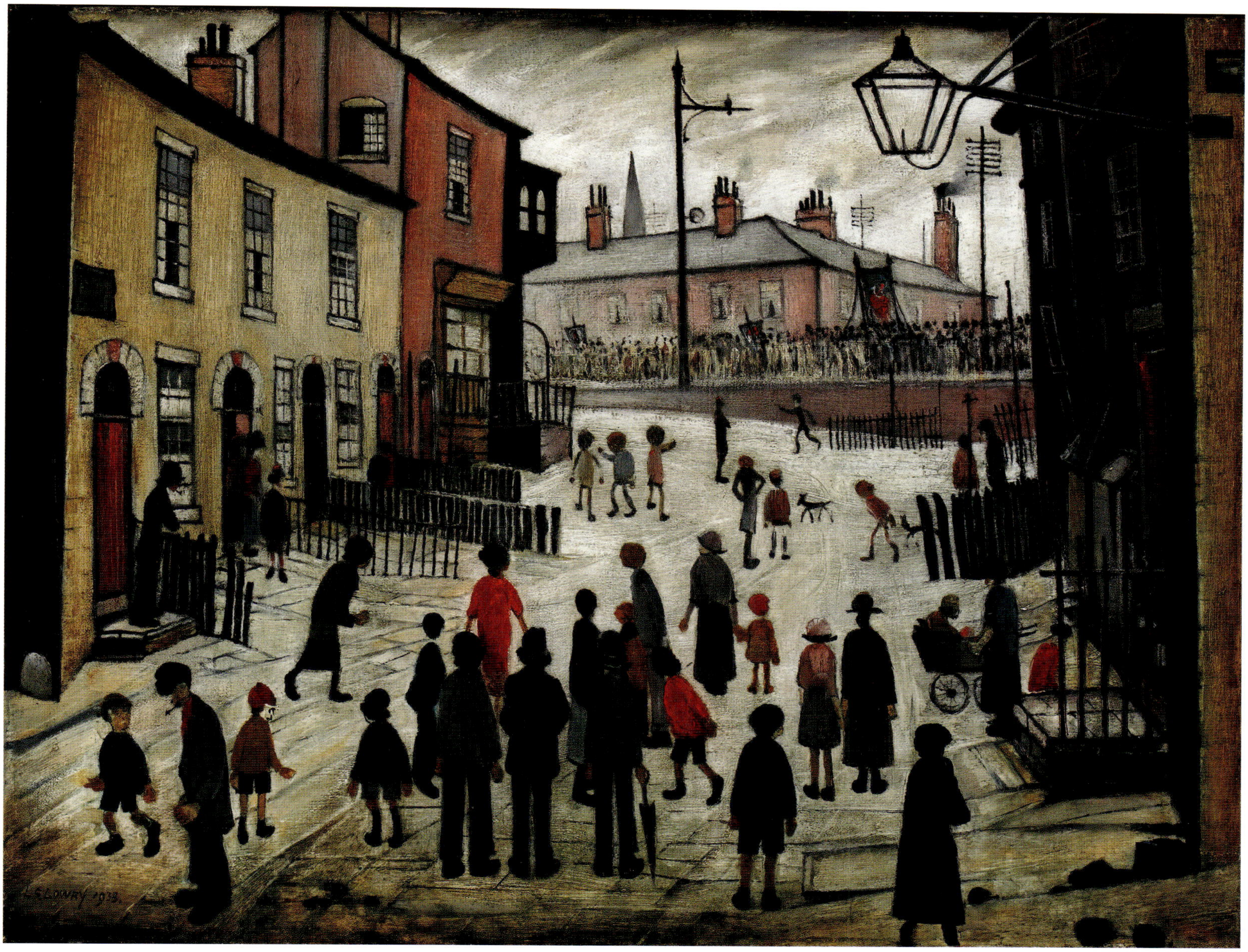

The Procession, 1938, oil on canvas, 46 × 61 cm.

which any element that might seem pretty or containing any kind of human warmth or any scintilla of pity have all been banished.

There is no evidence that I can find that there was any form of contact between Lowry and George Orwell. Lowry does not figure in the cumulative index of Peter Davison's monumental 20-volume edition of *The Complete Works of George Orwell* and we know that Lowry was no socialist, even if we can only assume that he may well have voted Conservative and was certainly, with a small 'c', a conservative human being. It is therefore unlikely that Orwell was aware of Lowry and virtually impossible that Lowry could have read Orwell's *The Road to Wigan Pier*, published in its Left Book Club edition only in 1937, the year in which *The Lake* was completed. But there is a passage in the Orwell book which, rather like some of the prose by Walter Greenwood quoted in the introductory chapter, seems to do in words almost exactly what Lowry does with paint. John Berger has quoted this paragraph in his essay on *Lowry and the Industrial North*[13] and I can see no way of omitting the crystalline clarity of Orwell myself.

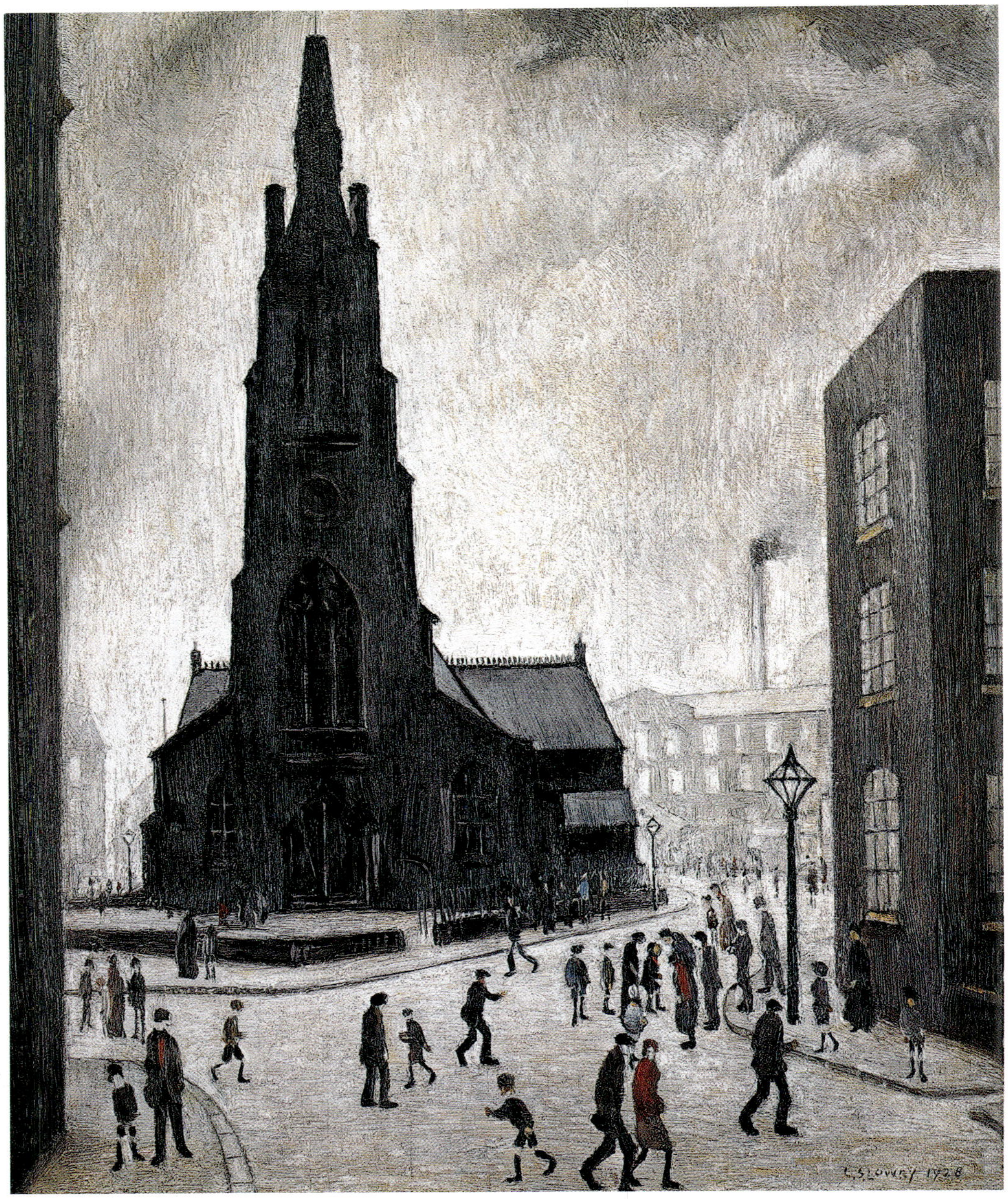

St Simon's Church or *A Street Scene*, 1928, oil on board, 43.8 × 38 cm.

> I remember a winter afternoon in the dreadful environs of Wigan. All round was the lunar landscape of slag heaps, and to the north, through the passes, as it were, between the mountains of slag, you could see factory chimneys sending out their plumes of smoke. The canal path was a mixture of cinders and frozen mud, criss-crossed by the imprints of innumerable clogs, and all round, as far as the slag heaps in the distance, stretched the 'flashes' – pools of stagnant water that had seeped into the hollows caused by the subsidence of ancient pits. It was horribly cold. The 'flashes' were covered with ice the colour of raw umber, the bargemen were muffled to the eyes in sacks, the lock gates wore tears of ice. It seemed a world from which vegetation had been banished; nothing existed except smoke, shale, ice, mud, ashes, and foul water.[14]

According to Rohde, Lowry, referring to this period of his life, said of his paintings at that time, surely including the brutal if imagined reality of *The Lake* "I did them to let off steam. I was out of my head in those days, out of my head, you know."

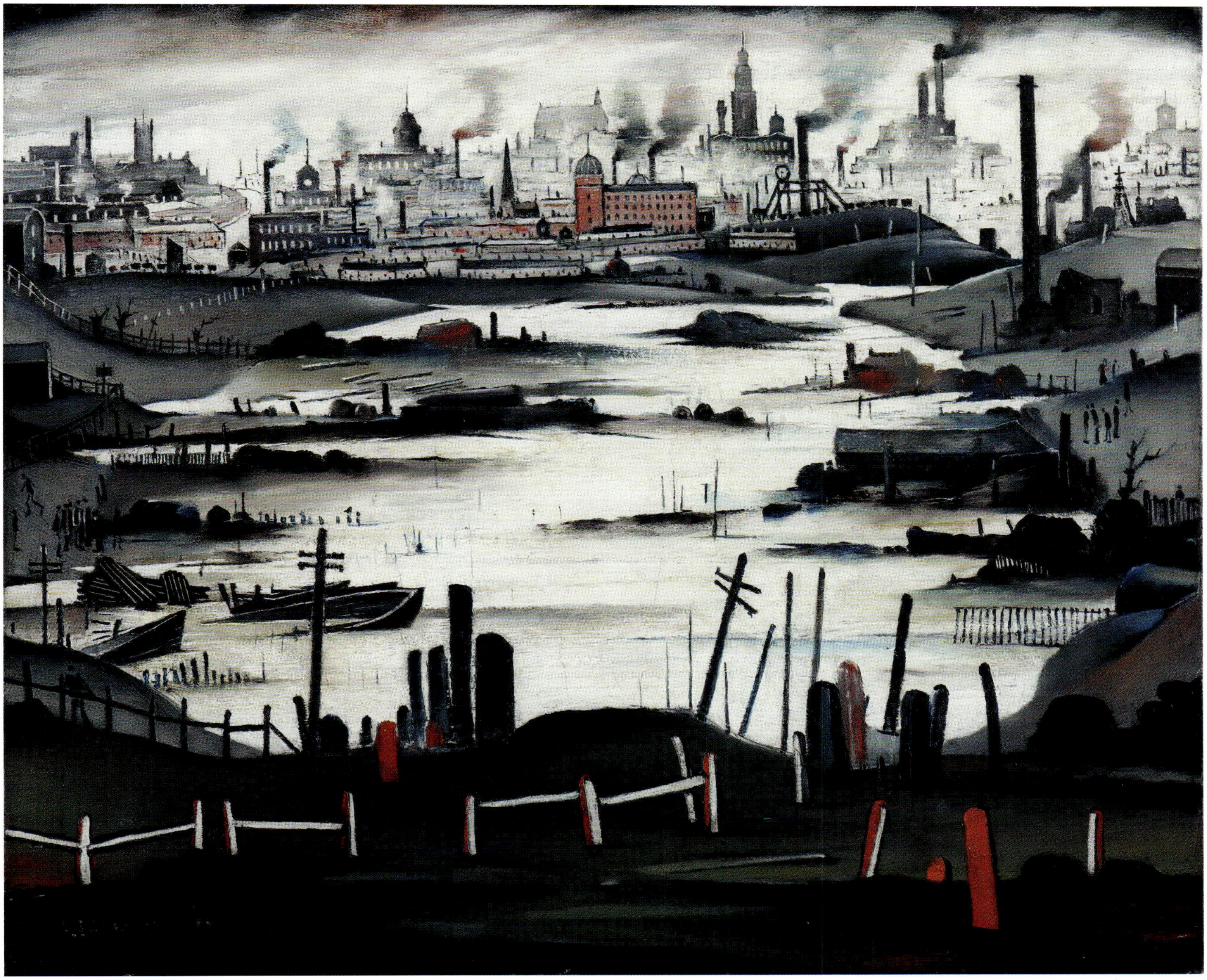

The Lake, 1937, oil on canvas, 43.4 × 53.5 cm.

However, as the significant memberships and purchases listed above make clear his life was not wholly negative. Success was slowly accruing. And in 1938 Daisy Jewell discovered that A. J. McNeill Reid, a Director and Partner in the powerful gallery Reid and Lefevre was going to visit Bourlet's. She cunningly left a few Lowrys lying around which caught McNeill Reid's eye and also captured his interest. He told Daisy Jewell to send half a dozen round to his gallery and, provided his partner MacDonald also liked them, they would give Lowry a show.

It was not to be instant riches for Lowry but it was the beginning of success and reasonable prosperity.

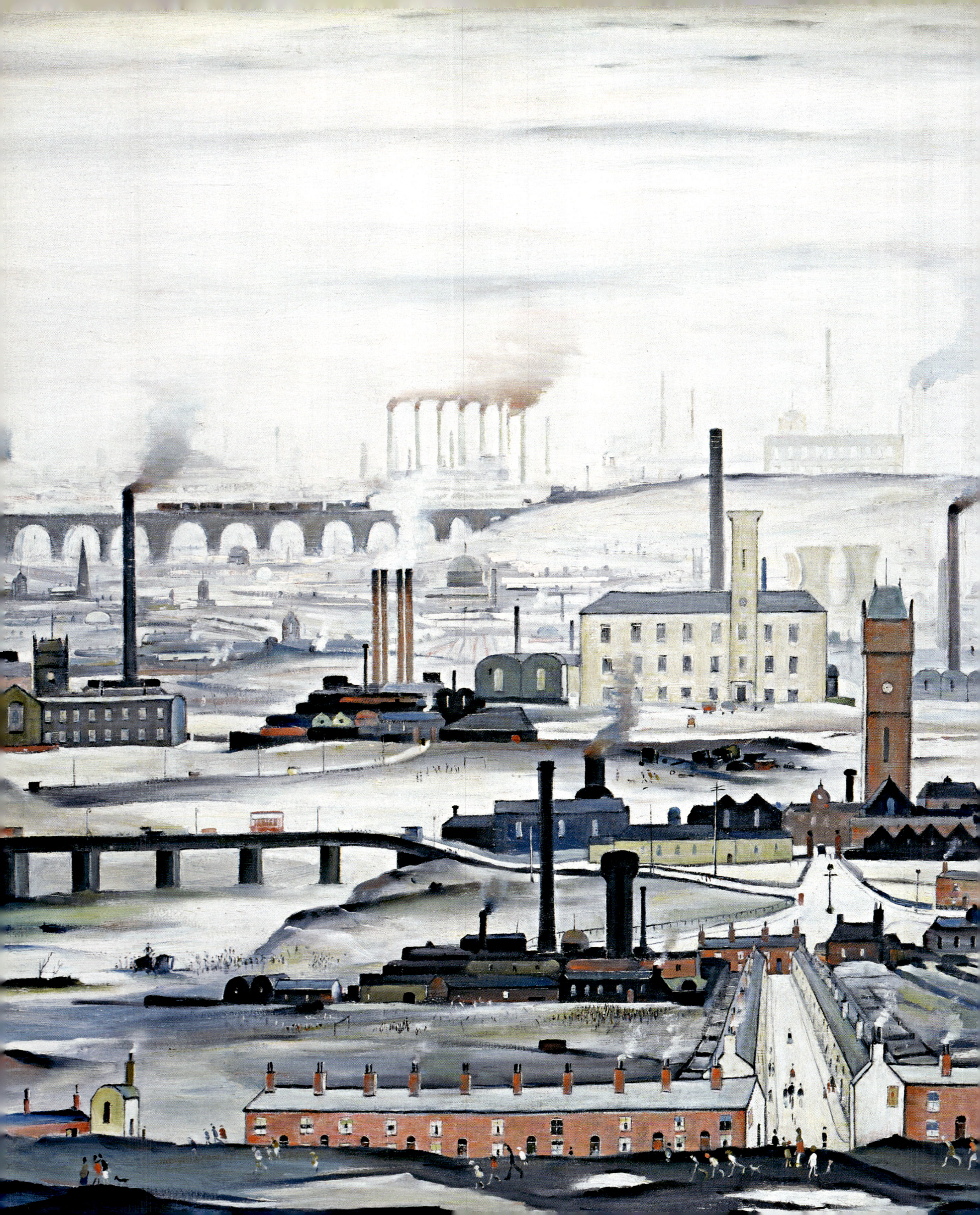

CHAPTER 5

LOWRY ESTABLISHED

The unreliability of his story-telling should be set against the honesty of his paintings … Lowry's deep truthfulness to his subject is one of the attributes which lifts his work from the provincial to the universal.

Andrew Lambirth[1]

Lowry's acceptance by Reid and Lefevre was a watershed of his life and art. Reid's partner liked Lowry's work as much as Reid and Reid wrote to Lowry in May 1938 saying he would be happy to give him a one-man show in the following January, making it clear that he wanted about 25 pictures, all of them new. Lowry had to explain that (a) in that time he could not possibly produce that many *new* and completely finished pictures. The most he could do would be ten new and the rest from the stocks held at Bourlet and (b) most of his best pictures were kept and worked on by him for several years. To Reid's credit he accepted this situation. But then this was, in terms of modern or contemporary art, the closest London had to the legendary dealers of Paris such as Kahnweiler or Wildenstein although on a much more modest scale. Reid and his father Alex had been instrumental in helping to build a collection for the Glasgow tycoon, Sir William Burrell, whose Burrell Collection is now one of Glasgow's most significant cultural ornaments. Alex Reid had spent much time in France, at one stage sharing student lodgings with Van Gogh. He had also formed a close friendship with Whistler who became Reid junior's godfather, hence his middle name McNeill.[2]

When the Lowry exhibition was ready, and after Daisy Jewell had held Lowry's hand and exercised a calming influence over this nervous middle-aged man who was at last having an opportunity to shine in the metropolis, she saw to it that all the leading art critics of the day were sent fulsome invitations to their private addresses rather than merely to their newspapers and journals.

Unsurprisingly the critical reception of the exhibition was mixed. One of those who disliked the show was the then teenage prodigy, the painter, sculptor and writer Michael Ayrton who was, when only eighteen at the time of the show, writing for *The Spectator* he wrote that "I resent the Lowry automaton so fiercely that I must concede part of his actuality by the very degree of my revulsion, but I am inclined to think that some part of Lowry's convention rises out of his inability to draw the human figure". There is, in this caustic comment, considerable irony. Had Ayrton had the opportunity to see some of Lowry's painstaking academic drawings, done at his several art schools, Ayrton, himself a formidable draftsman who had studied in Paris under Pavel Tchelitchev, *before* his stint at *The Spectator* would surely, while conceding their competence, have excoriated their sheer, basic orthodoxy,

Detail from *Industrial Landscape*, 1955, (p.109).

their dullness, and would have re-doubled his scorn for Lowry the draftsman, while still disliking the paintings. According to Rohde, Lowry would complain to his later patron, Monty Bloom, about Ayrton's cutting remarks and then have a little gloat at the fact that at that stage of his career Lowry's prices were about ten times as high as Ayrton's.[3] But the deepest irony, at least for the author of this book, is that Michael Ayrton was, in middle age, some fourteen years older than me and was a most significant and important mentor to me in terms of both art and art history. He had by then completely changed his view of Lowry and was a most willing and subtle enthusiast for his work as his contributions to the Third Programme radio symposium that I put together for the BBC (and which is, in a slightly edited version, reprinted in Chapter 1) clearly shows.

At the other end of the opening critical spectrum in January 1939 was Eric Newton, the most learned and humane newspaper art critic, then writing for *The Sunday Times*. Newton's words still resonate and apply to Lowry's *œuvre*: "Mr Lowry has formulated his own creed and consequently he will fit into no pigeonhole. His vision is personal to himself … and owes nothing to any other artist. Like Cézanne he has gone straight to life … and his only concern as an artist is to translate this attitude to it into paint. He belongs to no school, but he may ultimately be the founder of one."[4] Some seventy years after Newton wrote those words only the prophecy of a school now seems out of place.

If the critical reception was mixed, the commercial aspect was much more uniform. Sixteen of the paintings sold, mostly to private collectors, at about £30 each. Allowing for seventy years of inflation that is about £1,200 each but even inflation statistics are fallible or, in this case, quite unrealistic since today no distinguished West End art dealer with current overheads could afford to sell well-received oil paintings at £1,200 each and hope to thrive. But, for the time, £30 was good going. The mighty Shell commissioned a painting and the Tate, to which Rothenstein had only recently been appointed Director, was interested and the wise and wily Daisy Jewell suggested that their interest be stimulated by a £15, i.e. half-price, offer. At that price Rothenstein was able to persuade the Tate's Trustees and the Tate acquired one of Lowry's finest works from the 1920s, *Dwellings, Ordsall Lane, Salford*, dated 1927 (page 105). This was recognition of a high order, even if later than its recipient desired. The Tate purchase gave him much confidence and he was sufficiently grateful that in 1957 he gave the Tate his preliminary drawing for this archetypal early cityscape. In some ways the pencil study is almost as *finished* a work as the oil painting. This is no hurried sketch but a very carefully composed and calculated picture whose studious detail must have made the execution of the oil painting a relatively simple task compared to those city scenes which were partly real and partly imaginary.

For obvious reasons the pencil sketch is pure black and white but the finished painting is an almost Whistlerian symphony in near monochrome. There is a tinge of sulphurous yellow in the sky and three or four patches of red in the clothes of the people. They, unusually for a major Lowry painting, are not a crowd. There is no dense gathering of humanity, partly perhaps because there is no extraneous event such as a drowning or a fight to stimulate a

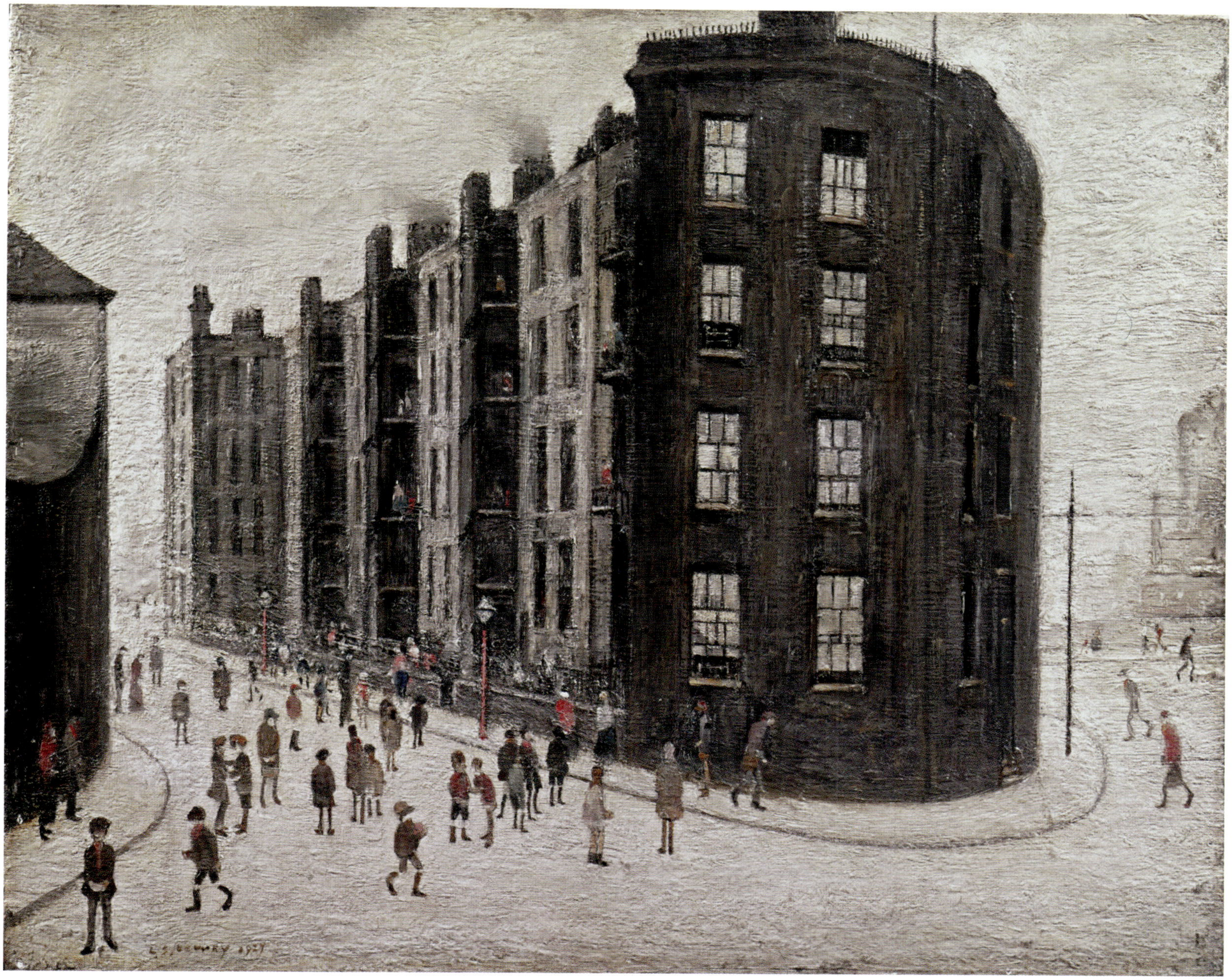

Dwellings, Ordsall Lane, Salford, 1927, oil on wood, 43.2 × 53.3 cm.

crowd in the first place. There are simply a few children playing in the street and a lot of adults walking either to get from A to B or simply strolling along aimlessly.

What counts here is the Whistlerian symphony of black and grey and Lowry's beloved white. Although the painting measures only 45 × 53.5 cm., it is in form, if not in size, a monumental work. In reality only four storeys high, the building has the impact on the street of a skyscraper. Despite having been built as flats for human beings the building has neither humanity nor indeed any human scale. If Le Corbusier had been around then as a fully-fledged architect, the *Dwellings* would have borne out his notorious dictum that a house is a machine for living in. The building exemplifies soullessness although the picture does not. The soot-blackened façade, the grey panels caught in a beneficent light, the short, stumpy plumes of smoke emanating from the chimneys that serve fireplaces that would not yet have heard of smokeless fuel, but would burn the cheapest available, dusty and fragmentary, coal or coke; all this turns a block of flats into a truncated factory without any towering chimneys to propel the inevitable smoke skywards. Add to this the vast acreage of sky and the huge space that surrounds the Dwellings, so that Lowry can exploit his extraordinary use of white as his major colour, and you have a painting of weird and enigmatic beauty.

The Dwellings were actually misnamed by Lowry as they were on Oldfield Road and consisted of two brick buildings containing respectively 12 "houses" and 48 "houses", erected for artisans in 1893 by the Yorkshire and Lancashire Railway Company. They were demolished round about 1970. Lowry was much taken by the Dwellings: "I'd stand for hours on just this spot … and scores of little kids who hadn't had a wash for weeks would come and stand round me. And there was a niff too."[5]

That old workhorse of a phrase "size doesn't matter" inevitably springs to mind when one contemplates certain of Lowry's bigger pictures. The phrase, with its frequently implied connotation of sexual equipment is now prone to give rise to sniggers or be so reduced in impact and considered to be such a cliché that, whether used in writing or in speech it needs to be protected by loud or large quotation marks. This is a pity since it still evokes all sorts of conundra and philosophical queries when used in connexion with art. Is an exquisite miniature portrait on parchment, barely an inch high, less of a work of art than a twelve-foot high equestrian royal portrait by Van Dyck or Velasquez? Joseph Albers probably, in mere statistical terms devoted about 90 per cent of his painterly energy to his *Homage to the Square* series of paintings and prints. After he had been in America for some years an earnest graduate student asked Albers whether his recent increase in the regular dimensions of all his square on square paintings was due to Albers having finally come to terms with the sheer vastness of the United States as opposed to the moderate size of his native Germany. In one of the more memorable put-downs of twentieth-century art history Albers replied that the student's idea was palpable nonsense and that the increase in acreage of the squares, (which applied only to *some* of the recent paintings and not to *all*) was that Albers had acquired a new station-wagon which was big enough to transport the larger size of these pictures, thus giving Albers the freedom to increase their size when he felt like it.

With Lowry the issue of size is rather more complex. The bulk of Lowry's oil paintings are quite small in area. Many, particularly the studies of individual humans, or small gatherings of two or three people, are often less than a foot wide, sometimes as small in height as well. There are dozens of cityscapes on canvases or boards of approximately 50 cm. high × 36 cm. This is in fact a size that suits Lowry and one never feels that it is cramping his style or that he is constantly yearning, if one can put it this way, to work on a wider canvas.

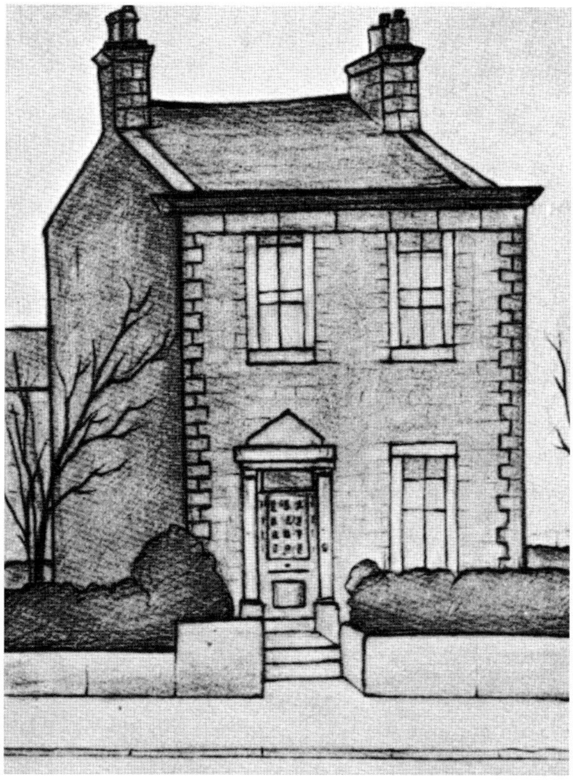

The Elms at Mottram-in-Longdendale where Lowry moved 'temporarily' in the late 1940s and stayed until he died. He drew the picture especially for a *House and Garden* series in 1958.

There can of course be several wholly pragmatic reasons for Lowry's choice of his favoured sizes. He never had a spacious, high-ceilinged studio with large doorways. He painted in a modest room, whether an attic or a parlour in a series of small houses. Even when he was earning enough to live comfortably and felt able to leave the family house, by which time of course he had no family, it was to the grim little stone house in Mottram-in-Longdendale which even the most linguistically-gifted and imaginative estate agent could not describe as a desirable residence.

Lowry himself had no illusions about The Elms as this ugly dwelling was called:

> Heaven alone knows why I came to this place. I absolutely loathe it! I hate the house I live in now ... A friend of mine said "If you tried hard and sought diligently for years on end you couldn't have found a more unsuitable house", but here I am and here I suppose I'll end my days.[6]

Furthermore, until he found success, he would have found the increased outlay on artists' materials too burdensome to support larger pictures and it is a foolish painter who embarks on a mass of large canvases if he is not even selling his small and medium size works. Thus it takes all sorts of confidence to tackle the monumental and, while his 1939 Reid show was a success, it only produced a few hundred pounds and Hitler and World War II were only a few months away and created for both lesser and greater artists than Lowry an unfortunate commercial vacuum since, while it was an undoubted honour to be an official war artist it was not exactly a lucrative activity.

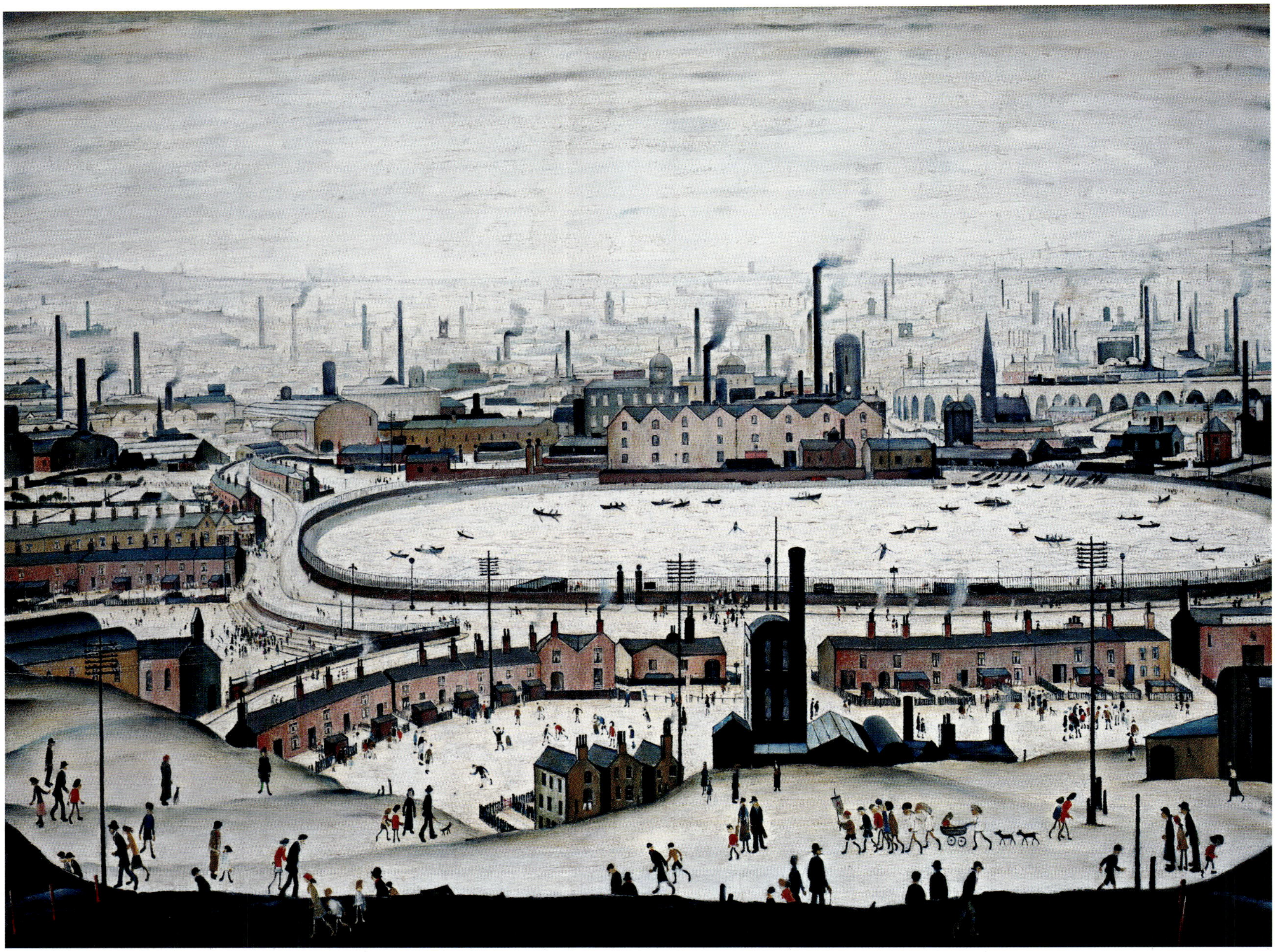

The Pond, 1950, oil on canvas, 114.3 × 152.4 cm.

Yet it was, if one discards the war years, only five years before Lowry produced one of his undisputed masterpieces and it was, by his own standards, huge: 114 × 152.4 cm. or 46½ × 62 ins. Painted in 1950 it was a Chantrey Bequest purchase by the Tate only a few years later. As we have seen with Albers' *Squares* there are some painters who, when their canvases get bigger, simply paint their usual subject but, as if using a pantograph – in those days, a computer today – simply enlarging each of the usual elements; Lowry was not like that. *The Pond* (above) and a painting five years later, *Industrial Landscape* (page 109) with, to a millimetre, the same dimensions as *The Pond*, was also a Chantrey Bequest purchase by the Tate in 1956. Both are not bigger than the usual bustling Lowrys, in terms of the number of

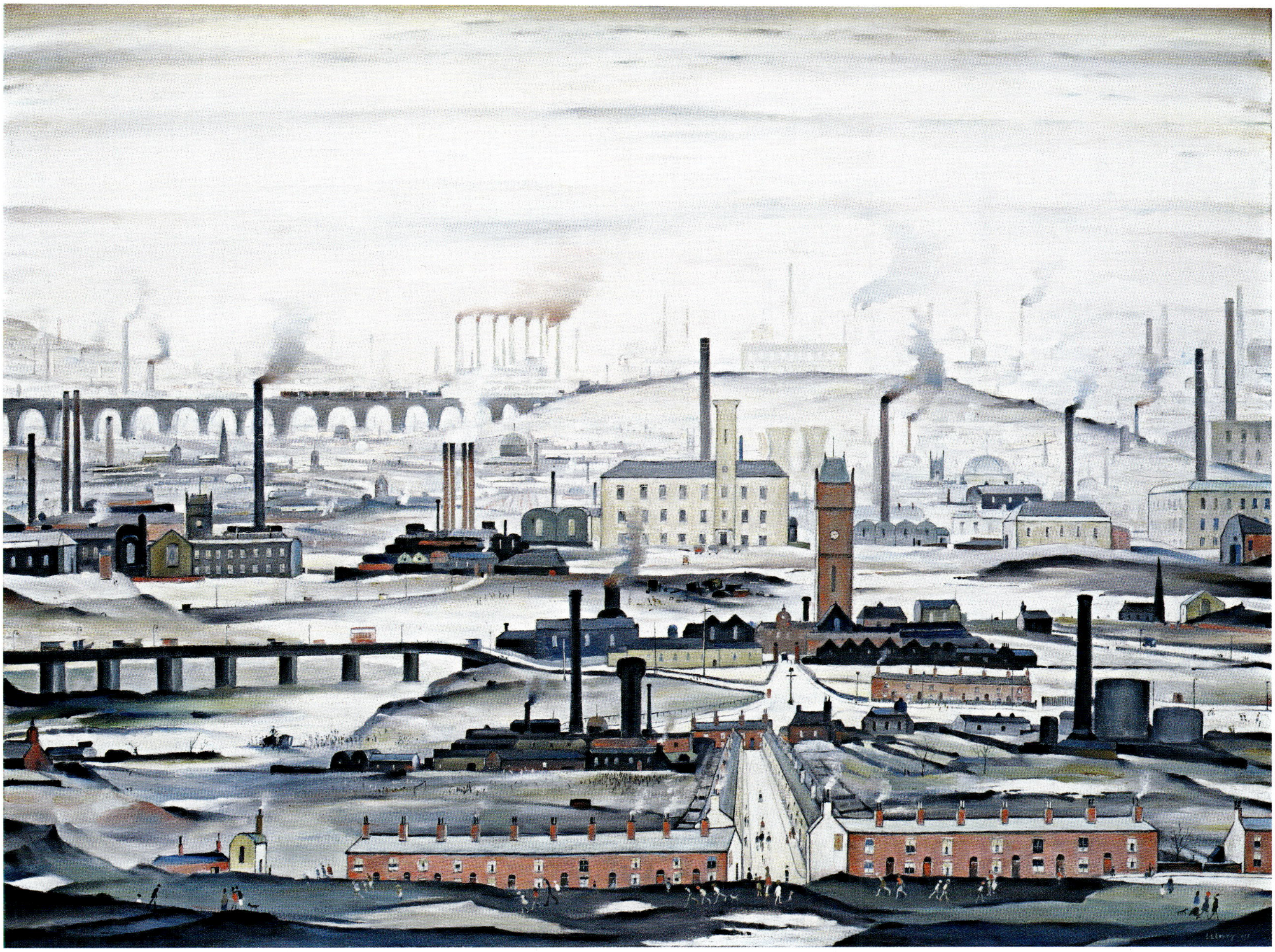

Industrial Landscape, 1955,
oil on canvas, 114.3 × 152.4 cm.

the elements included. But they are much bigger in scope. The extra size of the canvas has enabled Lowry to expand the entire view. There's more of everything and here everything is sky, water, factories, chimneys, rows of houses, little boats on the water of the pond. The only thing where the output is not increased is, oddly, the people. There are in *Industrial Landscape* hardly any people, as if Lowry is making a different point; that here it is the landscape that counts, that, in his hands, establishes a cumulative beauty for which he does not need masses of people and even in *The Pond* the human population is relatively sparse, sparse that is for such a scene of such a size, at a rough count perhaps only a hundred clearly visible in the foreground. Both large paintings do inevitably have vast spaces of Lowry's

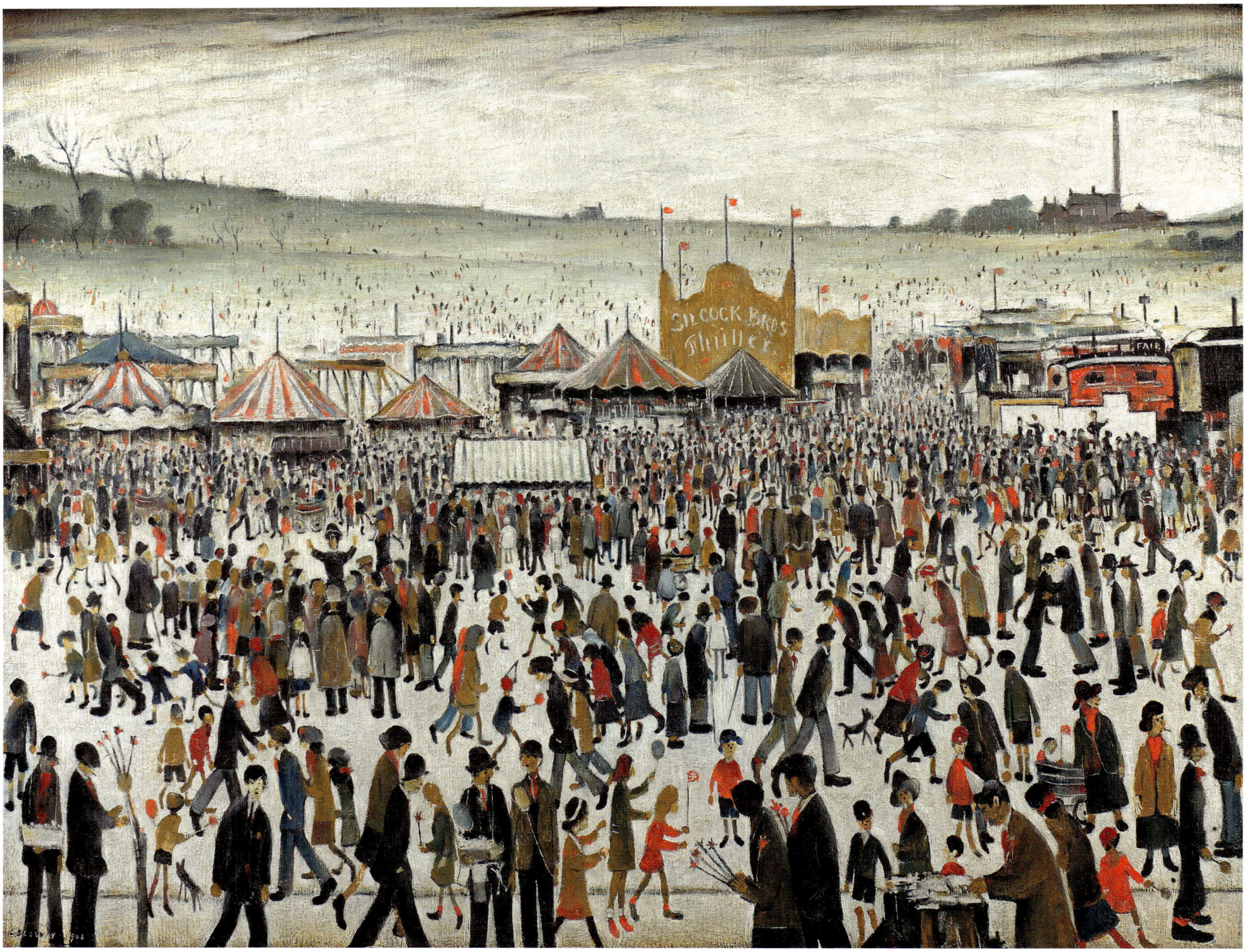

Good Friday, Daisy Nook, 1946, oil on canvas, 76.2 × 101.6 cm.

multi-hued, ever-subtle background colour and both recall Julian Spalding's brilliant *aperçu*: "The white in Lowry's pictures, like gold in an icon, represents light and space: it is the ether of his imaginary world.[7]

Whereas in *Good Friday, Daisy Nook* (above), painted in 1946 and measuring 76.2 × 101.6 cm. the number of people in that crowded and hyper-animated fairground in what is, to date at least, the most expensive Lowry ever sold, at £3.77 million (in 2007), is by this author's eyes at least, literally uncountable with any hope of accuracy. The surface of *Good Friday, Daisy Nook* is less than half that of *The Pond* which has nothing whatsoever to do with the relative merits of the two paintings but merely makes the point that size for Lowry was an arbitrary matter of little importance to him, other than an indication of the space he had available to him to fill as he wanted in terms of his admixture of reality and imagination.

Reid thought well enough of Lowry's debutant success to promise him immediately another show 'next year'. Alas, the show apart, 1939 was an *annus horribilis* for Lowry. The outbreak of war in September led Reid, in common with other art trade professionals, to get out of the trade altogether or at least severely to scale down their activities. Reid wrote to Lowry that the gallery would close "for an indefinite period ... I feel I would be much better employed making munitions than standing about in a picture gallery ... We will therefore, I am sorry to say, have to cancel your show which was fixed for next spring."[8]

For any artist in mid career this was a disaster. For one who had entered his fifties, at last had a success in London and who was, to put it bluntly, a depressive, still living at home with a mother for whom burdensome would be the mildest possible epithet, the imminence of World War II was catastrophe. To many another man such a domestic life would have been perpetual torment, not least because Mrs Lowry could not, or one suspects, would not recognize her son's talent and distinction. The success of his first London show apparently meant nothing to her and there is no record of any kind word or praise from mother to son who looked after her with such devotion. When she died on 12 October, 1939 Lowry was devastated by the loss of the only woman he had loved. He had what we can see today as a more or less complete nervous breakdown and his return to sanity was largely due to the chance discovery of him looking at his beloved pre-Raphaelites in the Manchester City Art Gallery by his friend Harold Timperley who got him back to his house in Cheadle Hulme where he and his wife took him in, made sure he ate, dragged him out on long walks, played music to him and gradually restored him to some form of mental health if not to total sanity. Only Lowry himself could do that, long before the practice of psychoanalysis and the talking cure were available to the professional classes although not within the grasp of a rent collector whose art was at last being recognized, but whose profitability still eluded him, all the more so for the six years of war and austerity that followed his London debut to dash the cup from his lips.

So he went on with his day job and, being too old for military service, became a night-time fire watcher. And eventually he resumed painting every hour that he could. Moving house did not appear to be a valid option for him which could not have done much for his disposition. It was not until 1948 that he moved to the fairly hideous house in Mottram which he was honest enough to recognize as the little horror it really was. But at least it was not the hardly more attractive dwelling in which he had been cooped up with his mother. Their life together may remind any conventional family man possessed of the smallest grain of black humour of Alfred Hitchcock's *Psycho*.

When, at least partly healed by the saintly Timperleys, Lowry returned to Pendlebury's Station Road, he was the richer for his mother's bequest of just over one thousand pounds. He followed the sound advice of Mrs Lowry's doctor who recognized, before her death,

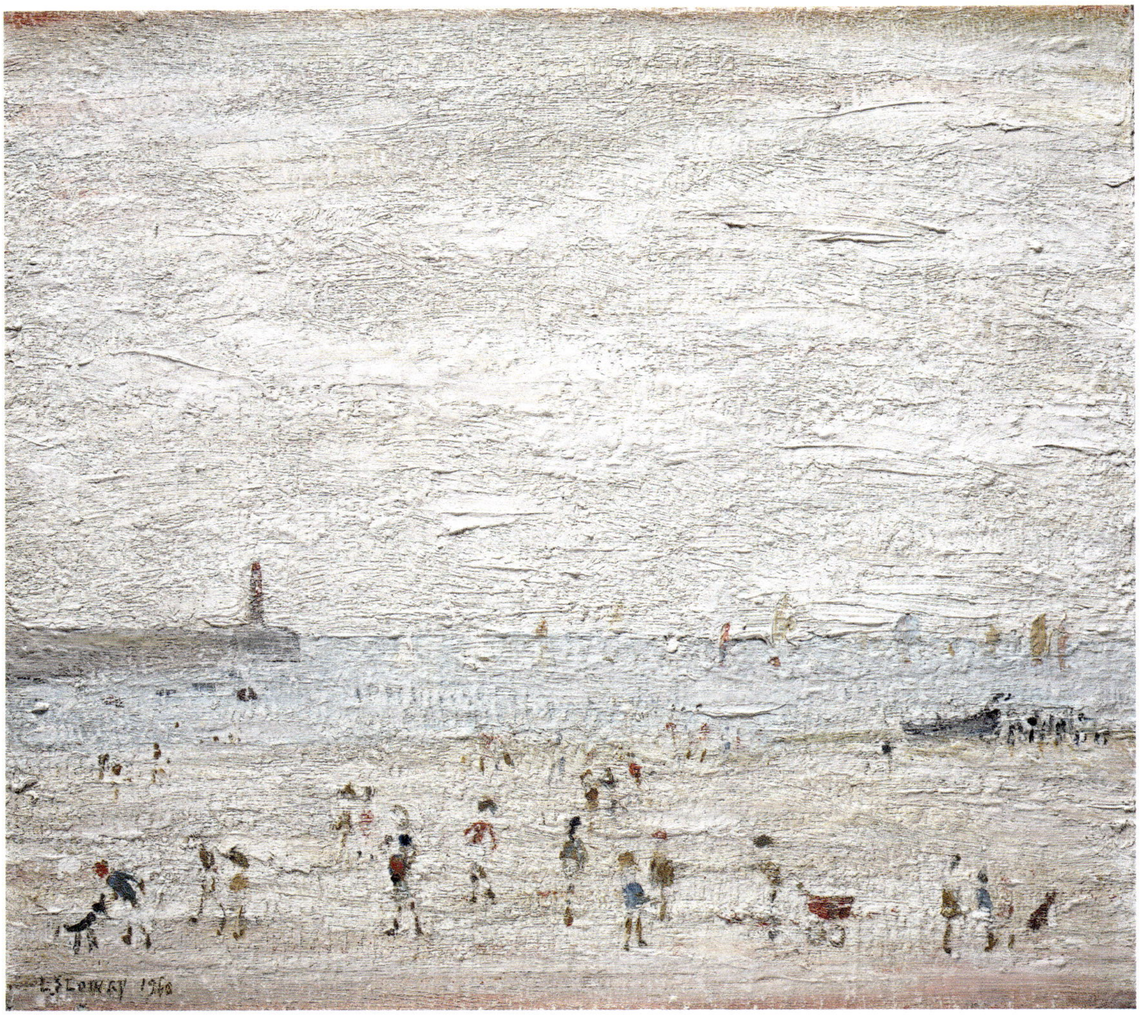

Spittal Sands, Berwick, 1960,
oil on board/panel, 47 × 51.25 cm.

that it was Lowry himself who was in great danger and warned him "Take a break or have a breakdown" and doubtless this helped him to endure her death without giving up his own life. He travelled to places like Thurso, Peterhead and Berwick-on-Tweed, the latter town much loved and painted by him and which, on a much lesser scale than Salford, but still effectively, has provided a fine artistic shrine to him and there are some fine paintings of this border town, for example, *Spittal Sands, Berwick* (above).

Back in Pendlebury, and after the funeral, he moved his studio from the attic to the dining room and decorated the parlour with the oil portraits of his parents and the self-portrait of a young man in a flat cap.[9]

Not for a moment can one compare the quality of Lowry's painting with that of Edvard Munch, who occupies a pinnacle in the history of European painting even higher than that occupied by Lowry in the history of British art. But it is instructive to compare their jointly held fascination with death, even a certain morbidity in their work. Significantly neither

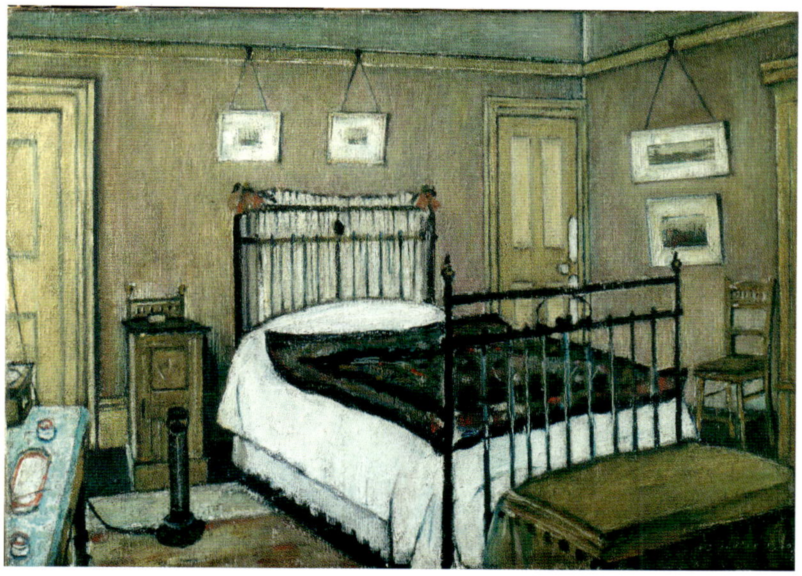

The Bedroom, Pendlebury, 1940, oil on canvas, 35.8 × 51.2 cm.

married nor ever had a long permanent relationship with a woman although there is no reasonable sexual comparison between the virgin Lowry and the compulsively womanising Munch. But both commemorated death in some of their finest works, Munch doubtless because he came from a large family who lived in an era when medicine was primitive and tuberculosis was rife. Lowry, an only child from a small family, saw how frequent and widespread were deaths from tuberculosis (think of *The Fever Van*) and from sheer poverty he could not possibly escape during his day job as a rent collector. Also one cannot doubt the depths of despair in Munch's many paintings of invalids in sick-rooms and the horrors of losing his beloved sisters before their time. For Munch there were many deaths and incipient deaths which he painted with a frequency which surely at least shades into morbidity.

For Lowry, as we've seen, there was, despite *The Fever Van* (page 177) and *An Accident* (page 94) which featured disease, or even suicide, only one death mattered and that was of the only woman he really loved, no matter how unproductive that love was nor how one-sided. According to Rohde and Andras Kalman, Lowry locked the door to his mother's bedroom and then made a painting of the room from memory a year later. Unlike a Munch touched by illness or death it is of a bare room, completely and neatly furnished, the bed immaculately made up (above). The bareness of the room consists in its not being inhabited. Yet for seven years it was lived in every day and all day by a professional invalid, a room constantly visited by Lowry from the day she became 'bedfast' till the day she died, like so many of her kind aged 83, a considerable achievement even for a healthy woman in 1939. Mrs Lowry, perfectly understandably, has had a bad press and Lowry's suffering at her hands was grievous. But one wonders how near the unspoken, possibly unspeakable truth, Andras Kalman got in his note on the painting when he wrote "Certainly he suffered black despair after her death, but did it not also come as something of a release?"[10]

Was Lowry's obliteration of Mrs Lowry from her eminent domain, the place from which she ruled over her bit of Station Road, where she maltreated her long-suffering servants and tortured her dutiful, loving son by withholding all praise and love, just possibly the worm turning at least a little? If he could not get her out of his system, could he not by producing this meticulously chilly rendering of a room he suffered in so acutely exorcising, by abolishing her physical presence, her utterly un-maternal treatment of him?

But, after the relatively brief period of breakdown after his mother's hardly unexpected death, Lowry was, with all the restrictions of first the phony war, and then the real thing, back to painting. The wartime restrictions probably, with their stringent black-out and curfew rules, were not as irksome for Lowry as for other workers since the houses available for rent collection were surely diminished, leaving him more time for painting in his new 'studio'. Conversely his two or three nights a week of fire-watching on the rooftops of Manchester department stores such as Debenhams or Lewis's would have tired him out and curtailed his nocturnal painting hours. Nonetheless Lowry produced some remarkable work, both during and after the war, seeing in the destruction of blitz and bombing raids a new set of images of city and townscapes. In these his previous habitual inventiveness, in which he made up towns and cities that existed partly in his endless perambulation of familiar streets and partly in his remarkable, even fantastical topographical imagination, was elaborately stimulated by the results of the bombing.

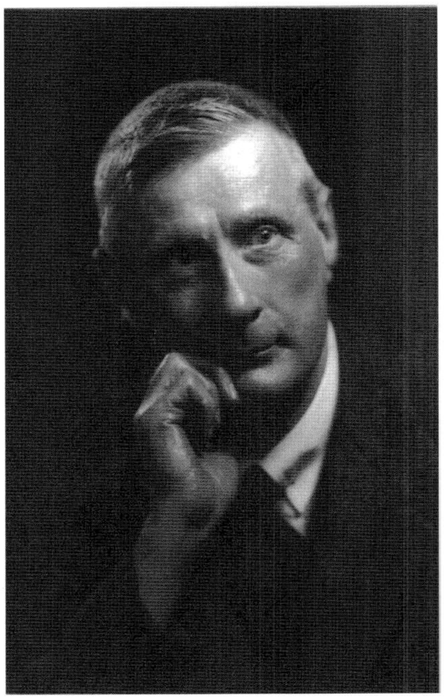

Photograph of Lowry, (undated), by F. W. Schmidt.

Lowry's war paintings were the antithesis of his two principal contemporaries in this field, although it is doubtful that Lowry was much aware of either Graham Sutherland or John Piper, let alone aware of any competitive spirit in their rendering of Britain's destruction by the Luftwaffe.

Both Sutherland and Piper, by co-incidence born in the same year, 1903, and both educated at the minor public school Epsom College, produced some of their best pictures during and after the war. (1903 was clearly a vintage year for the birth of British artists, since it also saw the arrival of Edward Bawden, Ceri Richards and Eric Ravilious.) In the age of austerity that followed victory in 1945, war damage, particularly in cities, survived unrestored well into the 1950s. Since both Sutherland and Piper were highly talented and as highly individual in painterly style, each possessed his unique thumbprint which was unmistakable and as instantly identifiable as Lowry's. Yet, in an odd way, their thumbprints did somewhat invalidate some of what they did during the war. With Piper it was a wholly irrepressible urge towards, at worst, a prettification of even the most shattered buildings and street which gave even his best war pictures an overwhelming sense of decoration which went a long way towards minimising the horrors depicted. In the case of Sutherland there was in almost everything he did, apart from his formal, commissioned portraits, a distinct touch of anthropomorphism carried over from his exhaustive landscape studies and obsession with vegetation which frequently took on board ambiguously human or animalistic twists.

For Lowry the war damage wrought on his territory presented him with, perhaps for the first time, a range of subject matter that he could paint and in which he could express only exactly what he saw and what he felt. There was no need to start with a blank, if prepared canvas or board, and then work out, area by area, building by building, open space by open space, whether the product of a pencil sketch or whether a product of his imagination. Simply to set down what he saw was sufficient not only to make up an interesting painting but all that he needed to express his emotional reaction freely and frankly.

Having, as a child, lived through the Manchester blitz which Lowry had watched from the rooftops while my family and I cowered in a steel shelter erected in our cellar in Withington, I can vouch today not only for the artistic merits of Lowry's blitz paintings but also for their topographical accuracy. Our landlord's property survived structurally although all our windows were blasted out a couple of times and it was a commonplace to pass on the way to school the next day scenes like that shown in Lowry's 1942 *Blitzed Site* (below). Barely standing shattered walls looked ready to collapse totally, red-tinged. Not yet wholly extinguished fires flickered ominously, even if harmlessly, just as Lowry has depicted them. Owners and tenants stood looking fearfully at the wreckage of their homes while others looked for anything that might be saved or even scavenged since who would know if the owners were alive or not. There are no jolly propaganda pictures here; no *faux* cheerful Cockney sparrows posing for photographers. Just once-solid Mancunian houses transformed

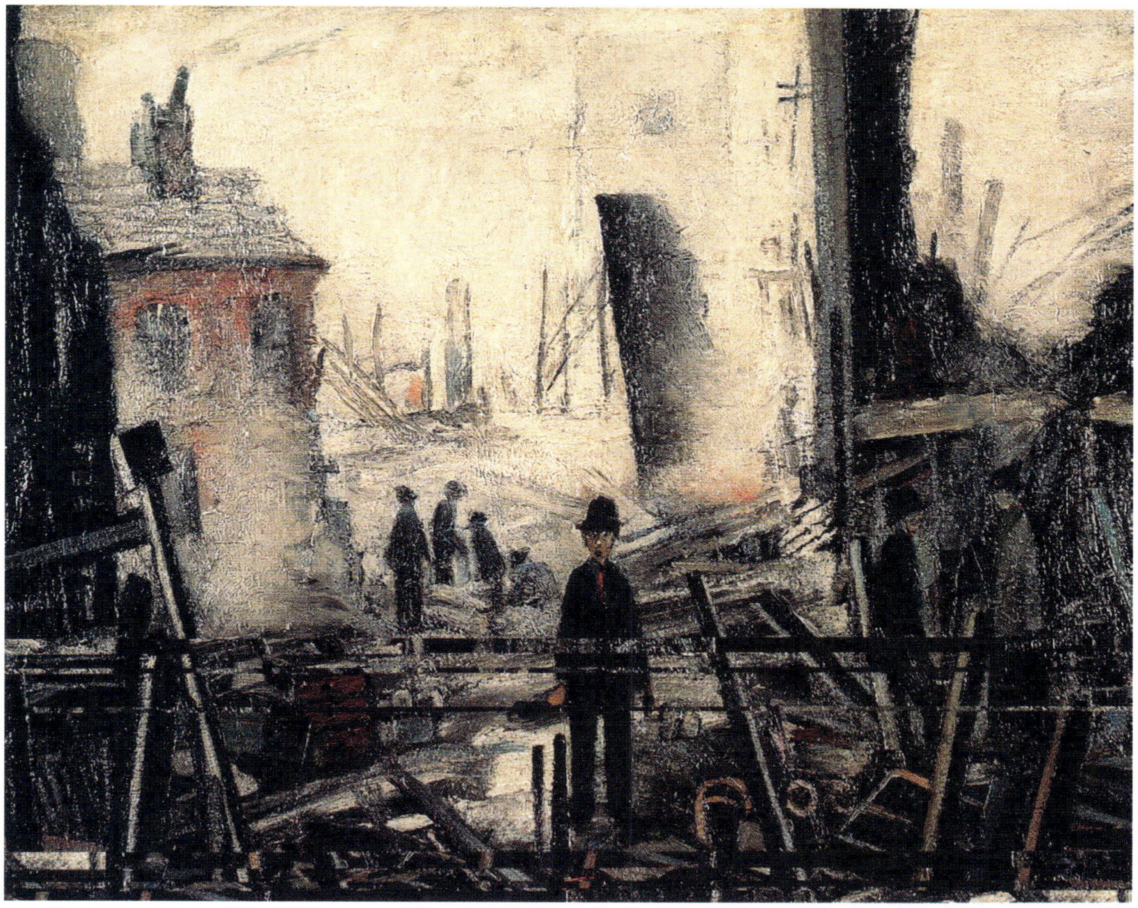

Blitzed Site, 1942, oil on canvas, 23.5 × 33.4 cm.

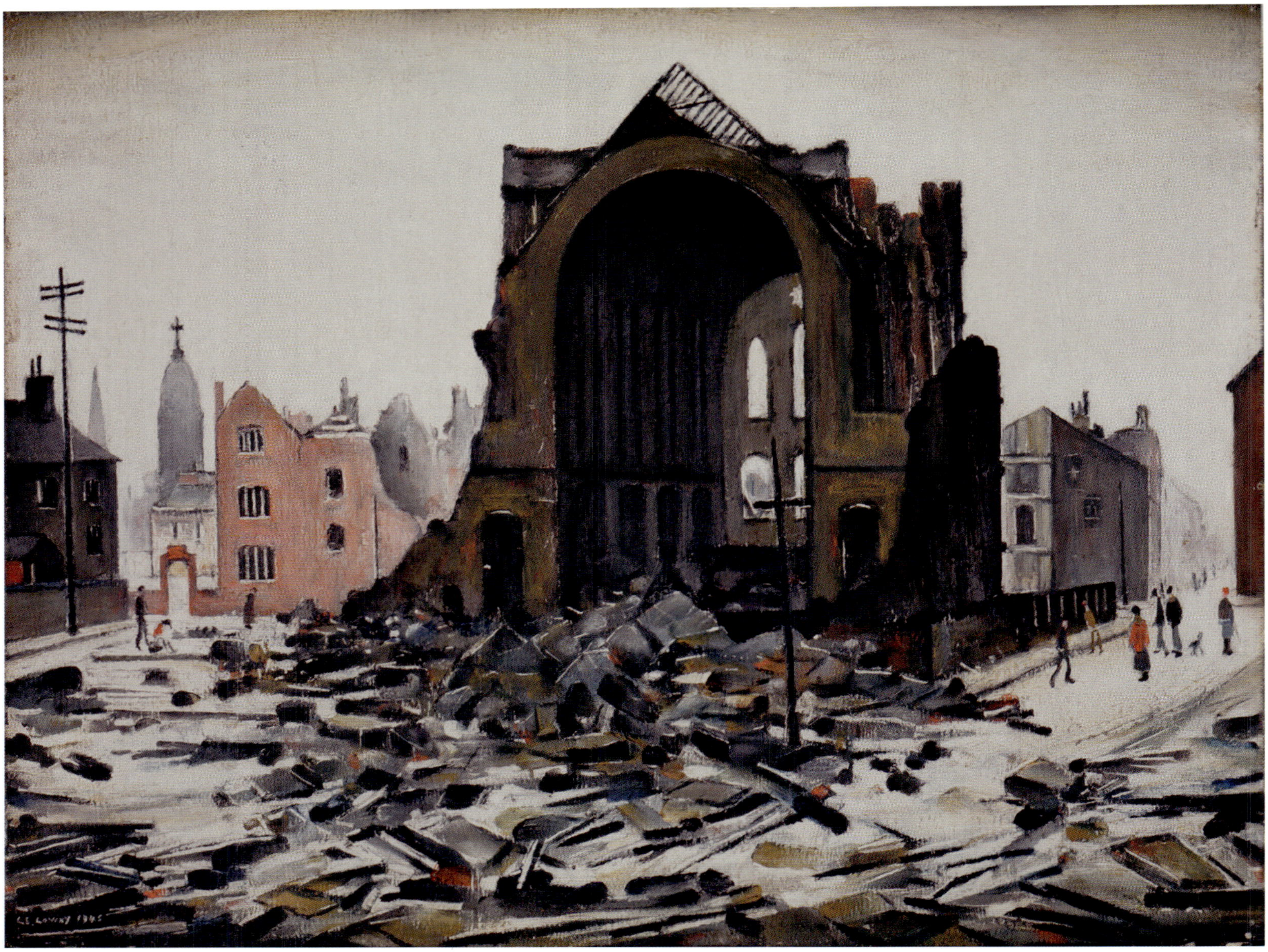

St Augustine's Church, Manchester, 1945, oil on canvas, 46 × 61.3 cm.

into rubble and once solid Mancunian citizens suddenly made homeless and even destitute; knowing what had hit them but not knowing what to do.

Those who do not understand Lowry, or the beauty of his subject matter, are perfectly capable of describing one of his typical and best city-scapes or street scenes as 'gloomy' or 'bleak'. Those who do appreciate him see these pictures as beautiful renderings of a beautiful world. But *Blitzed Site,* while aesthetically superbly painted, is full of doom and gloom, a work of true bleakness and bleak truth.

While *Blitzed Site* is pervaded by a frightening immediacy, as if Lowry had painted what is effectively the morning after, another war-time painting, *St Augustine's Church, Man-chester* (above) of 1945 tells another story altogether, a different emotion recollected in tranquillity if the word tranquillity can be applied in such a context. The majestic church, like Manchester Cathedral and all the other older churches of the city had a blackened exterior, from the city's industrial pollution. It was bombed in 1940 and was painted by Lowry some five years later when the only remedial work would have been the making safe of the main structure so that the shell of the church would not collapse upon the unwary. The detritus of a massive bombing explosion is still there because, with a war to be won, there was neither labour nor money to spare for something as non-essential as yet another church of any denomination. The shattered nave has somehow remained standing with its corona of skeletal ceiling timbers above it. The once magnificent stained glass windows are now only window-shaped gaping holes, the foreground an unstructured pile of the wreckage of pews, scorched cushions and kneelers, a poignant, solitary wooden cross stuck into the ground, in an ironic parallel position to the untouched church tower, surmounted by its own healthy cross in the left background of the painting.

There is a pronounced contrast here between the apparently spontaneous *Blitzed Site* and the carefully observed *St Augustine's* done after years of observation and, since it gives Lowry an opportunity to *organize* the composition and add any flourishes he fancies to the main event, making one wonder whether the whole, spired background church and its close, pointed-spired neighbour are really there and really precisely in those positions or whether Lowry is inventing again. At least the people are in more cheerful mode and their clothes more full of colour then usual. It is also interesting to compare this powerful version of a destroyed church with the much earlier painting, *A Street Scene, St Simon's Church* (page 100) of 1928, already a most artful composition and one apparently lacking any embellishments from imagined add-ons.

Possibly the most striking picture from the wartime years and their aftermath is the fabled *Good Friday, Daisy Nook* of 1946 (page 110). This remarkable example of Lowry's capacity for taking infinite pains and for creating a seething mass of wholly differentiated people is celebrated, in our materialistic age, because it is, at least at time of writing, the most expensive Lowry ever at £3.7 million. Lowry's devoted sometime dealer, the late Andras Kalman, wrote that: "Lowry could only have painted this picture after his mother died – he wouldn't have had the time or inclination before that when she was ill."[11] This is a shrewd assessment but it does not entirely exclude my own view that with Lowry, however traumatic the loss of his mother was, by 1946 she was seven years dead, as long as his buried piece of wood painted in white. To know Lowry at all was to know that, despite the carapace of his 'grumpy old man' pose, cheerfulness had a habit of breaking out. Might one not therefore at least speculate that the eruption of bustle and humour which is *Daisy Nook* is Lowry at last shrugging of the unrelieved pain and sorrow of Mrs Lowry's death and, at the distinctly ripe artistic age of almost sixty he had learned how to enjoy himself as an artist and to replace some of the gloom with gaiety and *joie de vivre*?

In fact Lowry survived the war rather better than the buildings he painted. Reid's Cassandra-like prophesies turned out to be exaggerated and Lefevre gave him a show in 1943 which he shared with Josef Herman. Lowry sold six pictures, including one to his most stalwart critical proponent, Eric Newton and showed one of his most endearing human characteristics when, Herman having sold none, Lowry bought one of his best paintings and, in 1955, when he again shared an exhibition with Herman, bought another which he presented to Salford Art Gallery. Only successful artists can do that sort of thing and Lowry's real success dates from 1945 after the war had ended. His 1945 one-man show at Lefevre was a more or less complete sell-out and, even after dealer's commission, showed a tiny profit for the first time in Lowry's life and this was the first year that his earnings as a painter had exceeded his income from Pall Mall. More importantly from a career point of view one of his early paintings, *A Fylde Farm,* was bought by Queen Elizabeth (subsequently the Queen Mother), probably the only member of the House of Windsor in the last century with anything approaching a sophisticated taste in painting. If 1939 was his *annus horribilis*, then 1945 was his *annus mirabilis* as, in addition to royal patronage, this man, whose formal education was almost non-existant, was given an Honorary M.A. by Manchester University. Unusually for such occasions, when the presenter tends to restrict himself to well-meaning but hollow platitudes, the oration in favour of Lowry's degree was robust, even outspoken and very much to the point:

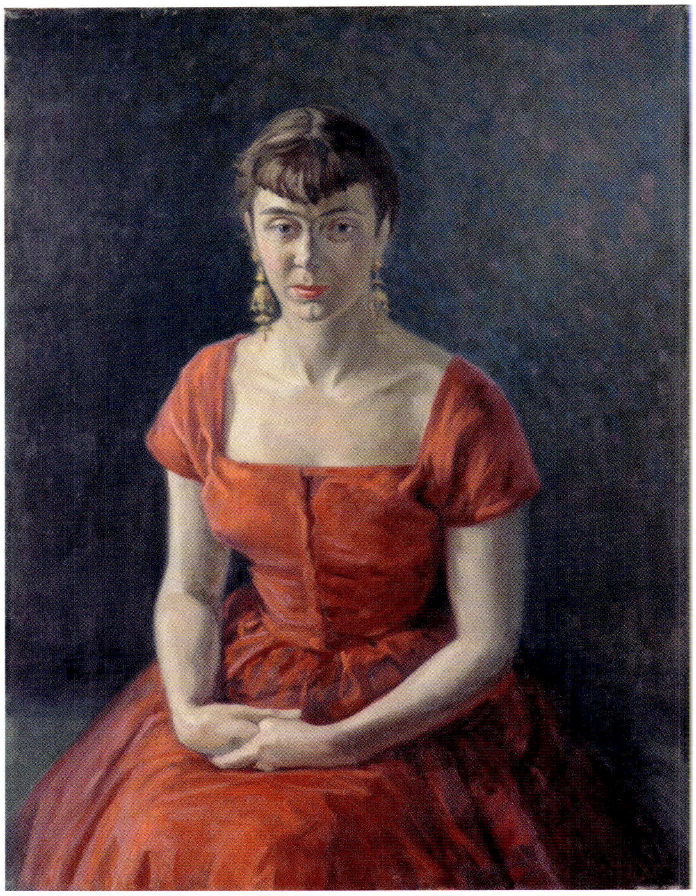

Portrait of Margo Ingham, by Ian Macdonald Grant, 1951, oil on canvas, 91.6 × 70.7 cm.

> His work is marked by a ruthless sincerity which prevents it from falling into mere prettiness or sentimentality; while the artist's obvious and deep affection for his subjects ensures that the picture, however grim, shall never be sordid. He confers beauty on the seemingly unattractive by the affectionate understanding which he brings to its portrayal. The quality of his work is increasingly recognized all over England: Only here in his own county and among his own people is he a prophet not yet sufficiently honoured. That defect we now in a measure make good.[12]

Lowry was also taken up by a flamboyant local businesswoman and cultural entrepreneur called Margo Ingham (above), who, with her husband Ned Owen had started the Manchester Ballet Club which also doubled, during the day, as the Mid-Day Studio before moving to a cellar in Mosely Street where the two resident mice were known as Modigliani and Hobbema. She wanted to give Lowry a proper Manchester exhibition but lacked the necessary financial resources, so, in 1948, she got Lefevre to back the show and persuaded Eric Newton to open it and to give a radio talk on Lowry's work for the BBC Home Service (today's Radio 4).

Newton, always an out-spoken man for whom out-spokenness was a form of integrity when, for lesser men, it was so often a mask for rudeness, spoke passionately in Lowry's cause:

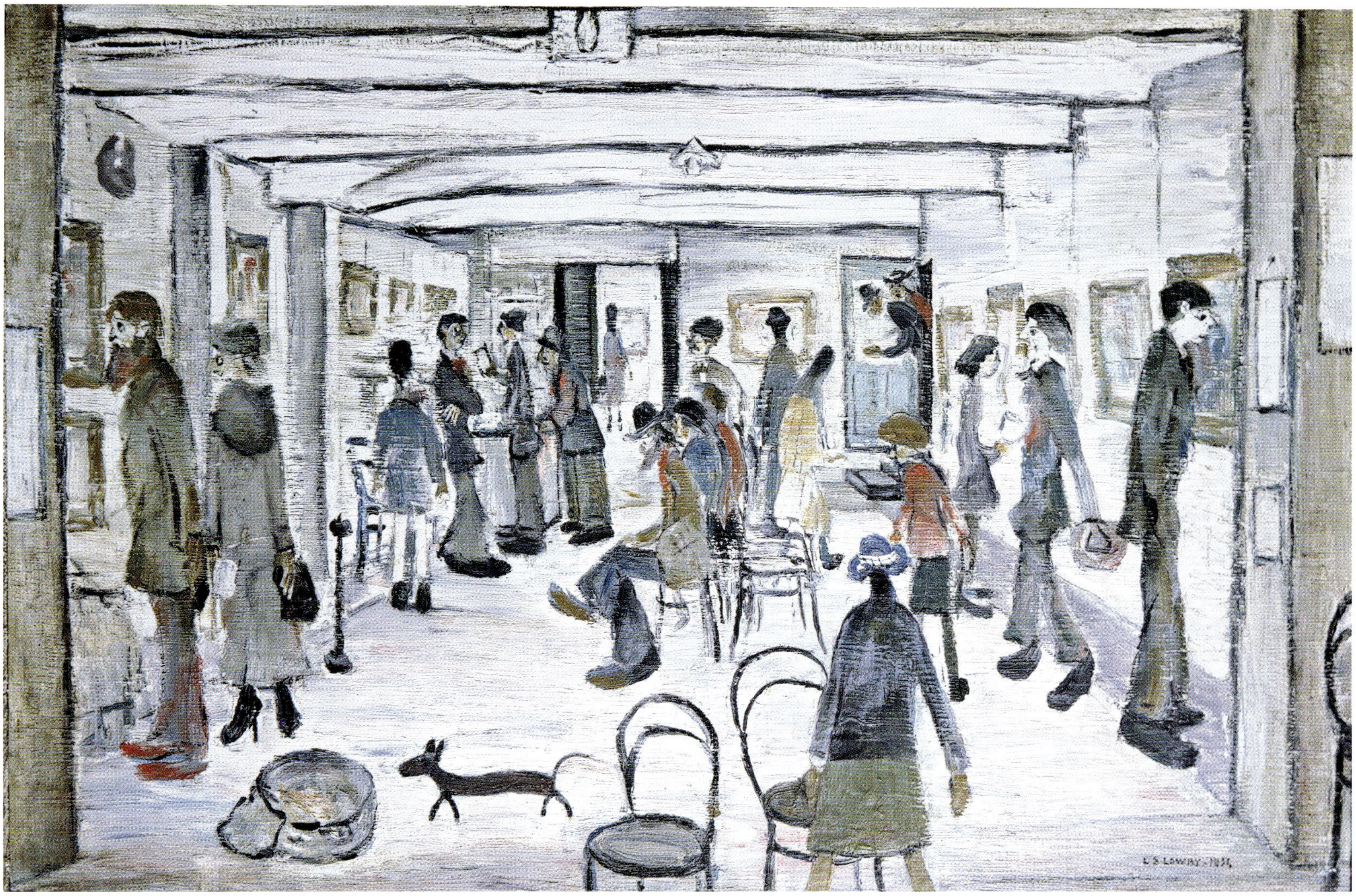

The Mid-Day Studio, 1952,
oil on board, 14 × 25.3 cm.

> It is strange that an artist who was in his early thirties when he began to know exactly what he wanted to paint should have to wait till he was sixty before holding his first one-man show in his native city. It is stranger still when one remembers that almost the whole of his art during those thirty years has been dedicated to that city … If paint is to express a lifetime of devotion it must be handled as though it were precious, put on with enormous respect. Lowry does that and the visionary in him is revealed in the movement of his hands as well as in the quality of his mind.[13]

Newton gave a stern instruction to all of Manchester to visit the exhibition, his exhortation worked and local citizens and bigwigs went and looked and bought. And so, at last, the prophet had a comforting mixture of honour and profit in his own land.

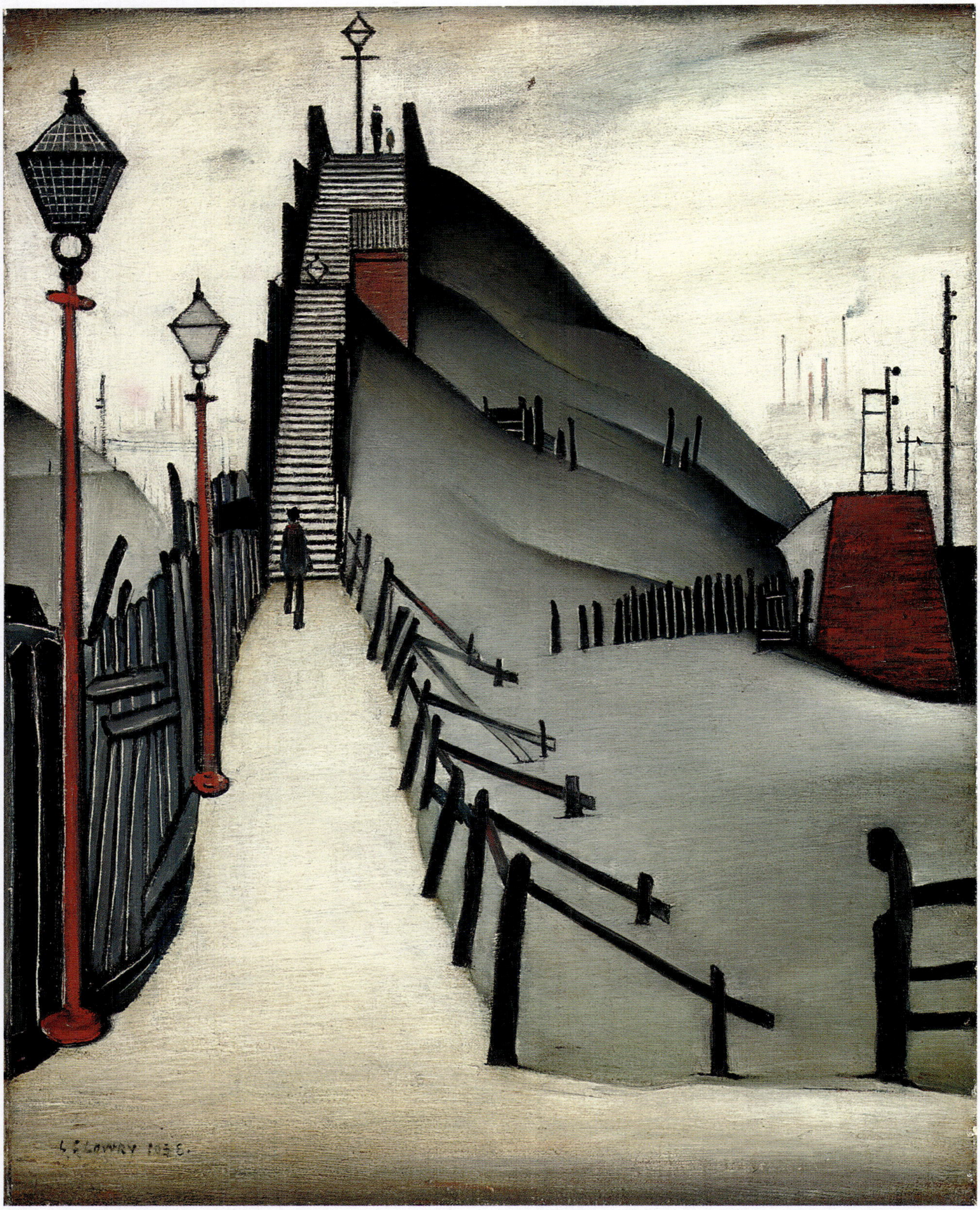

A Footbridge, 1938,
oil on canvas,
53.3 × 43.2 cm.

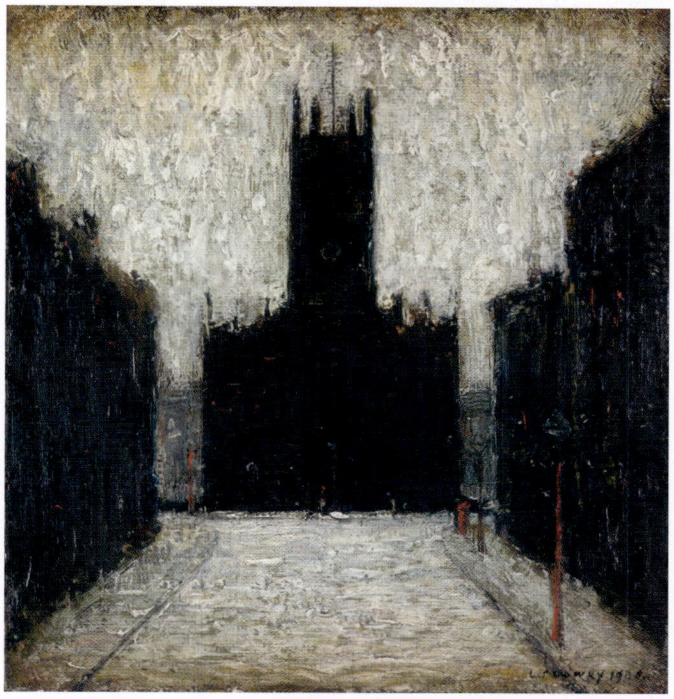

St John's Church, Manchester, 1938,
oil on board, 31 × 30.3 cm.

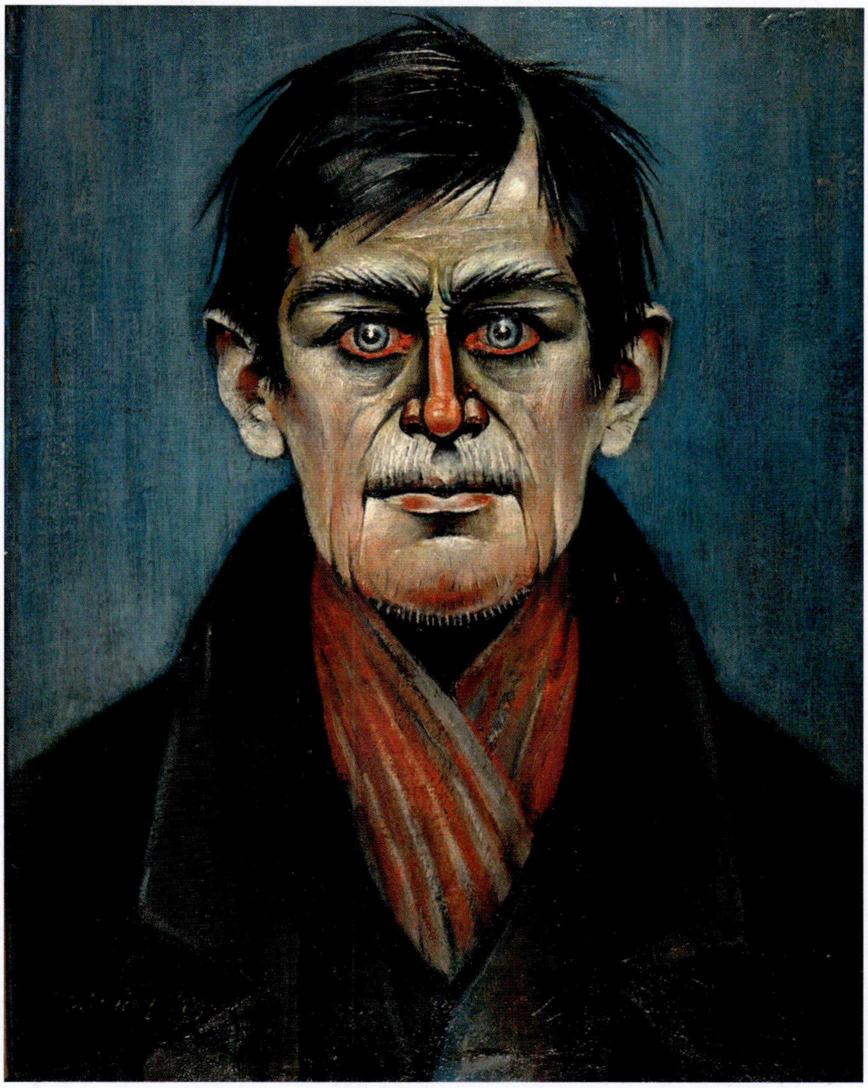

The Head of a Man, 1938,
oil on canvas, 50.7 × 41 cm.

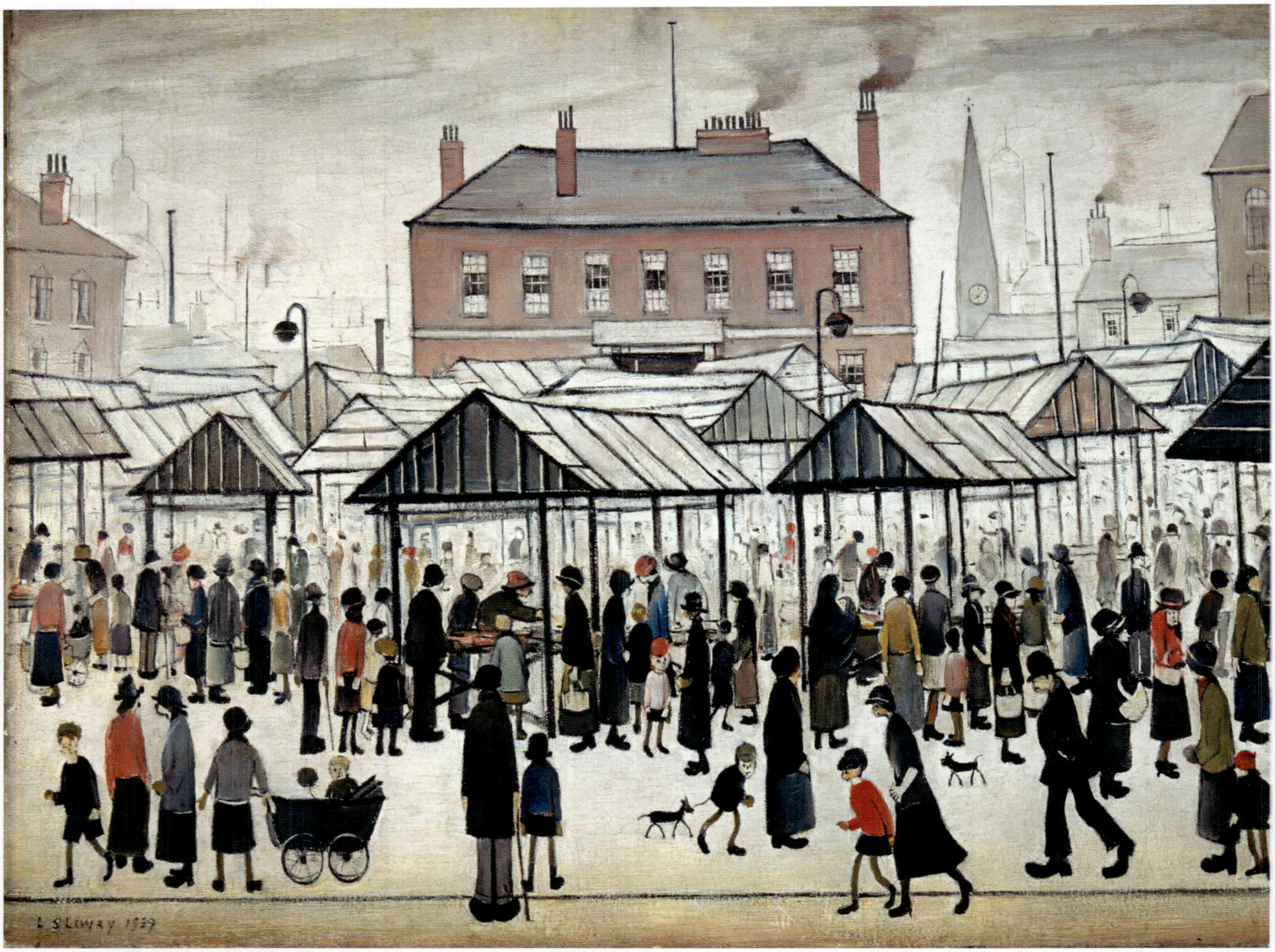

Market Scene, Northern Town, 1939,
oil on canvas, 45.7 × 61.1 cm.

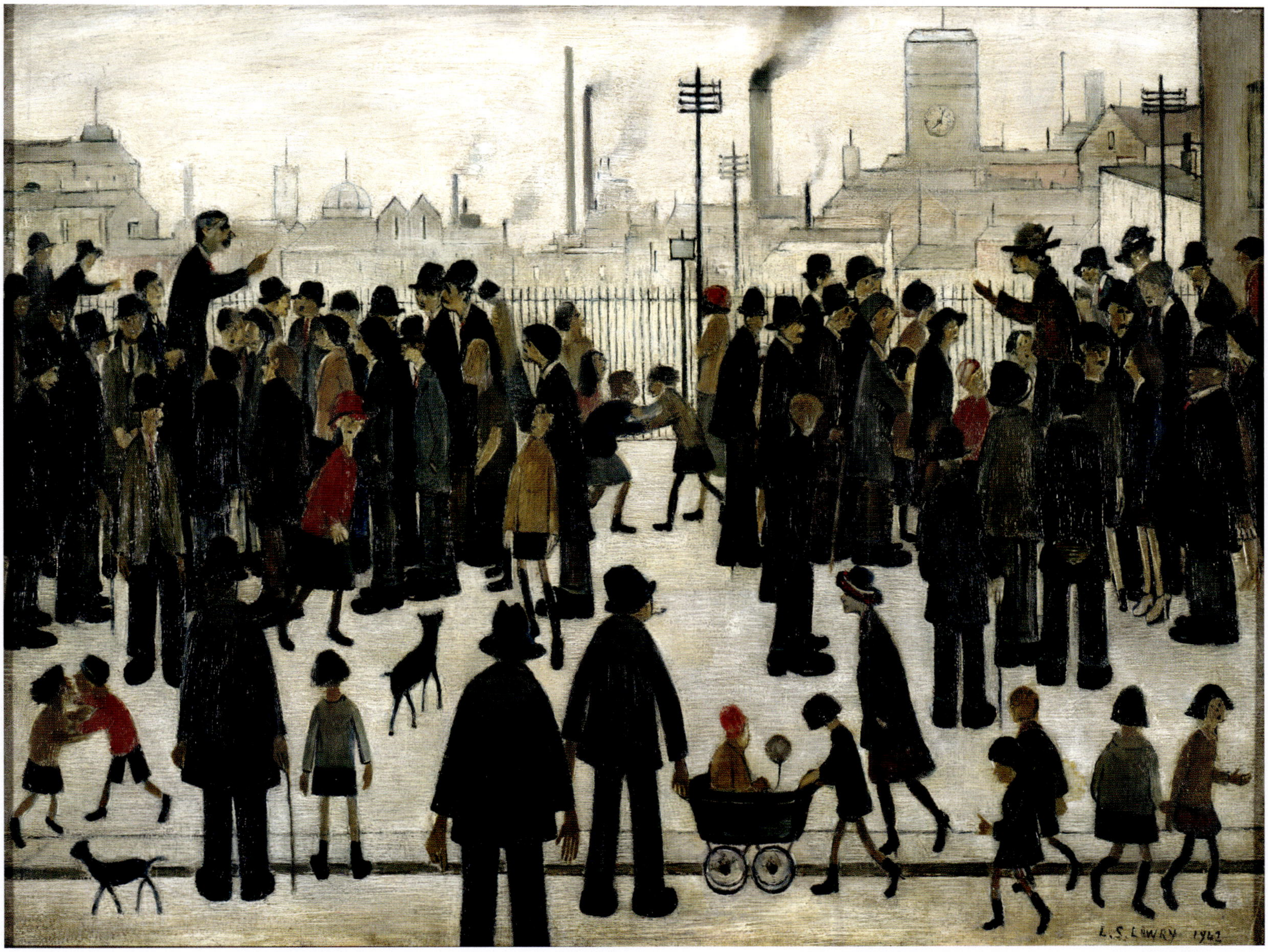

The Rival Candidates, 1942,
oil on canvas, 45.8 × 61 cm.

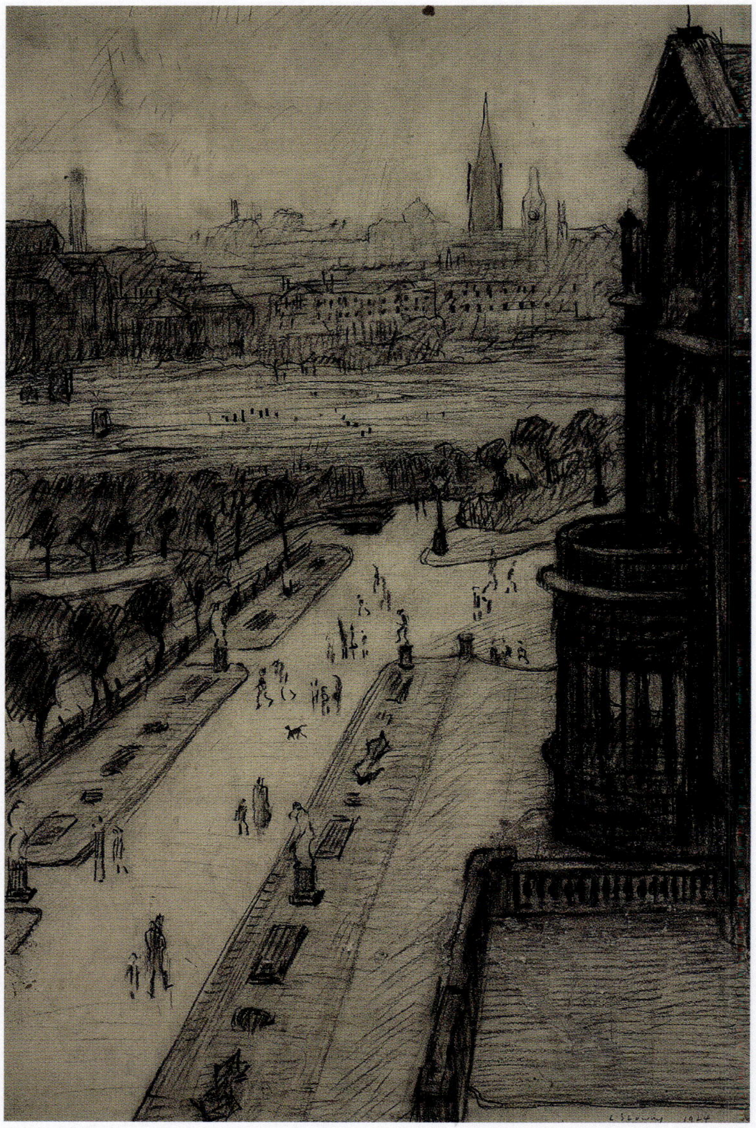

View from the Window of the Royal Technical College, Salford, Looking Towards Manchester, 1924, pencil on paper, 54.4 × 37.5 cm.

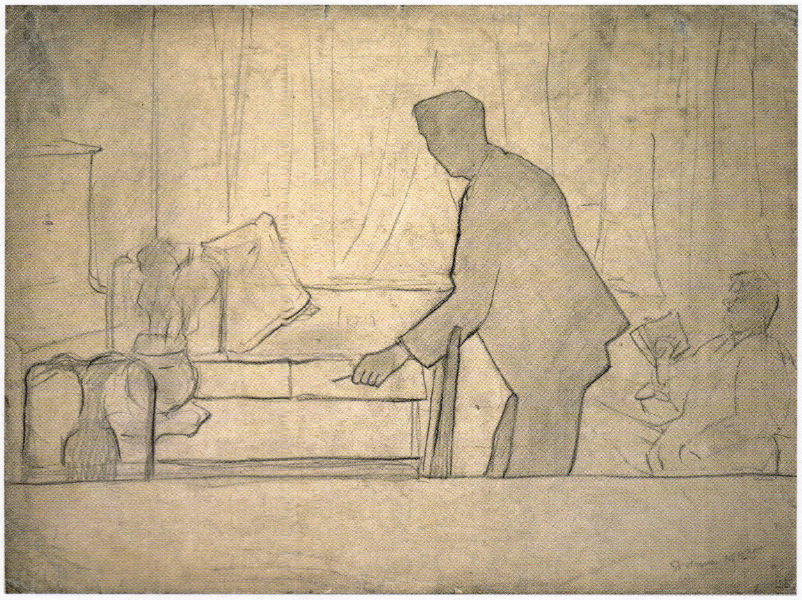

Self Portrait in a Mirror, Lytham St Anne's, 1925, pencil on paper, 27.5 × 36.5 cm.

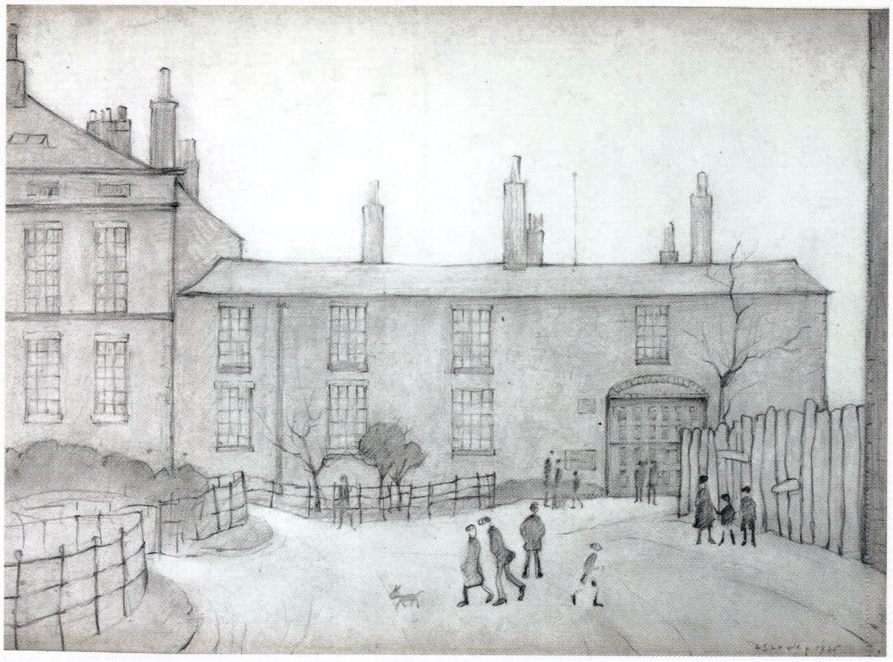

Leaf Square, 1925, pencil on paper, 34.8 × 24.5 cm.

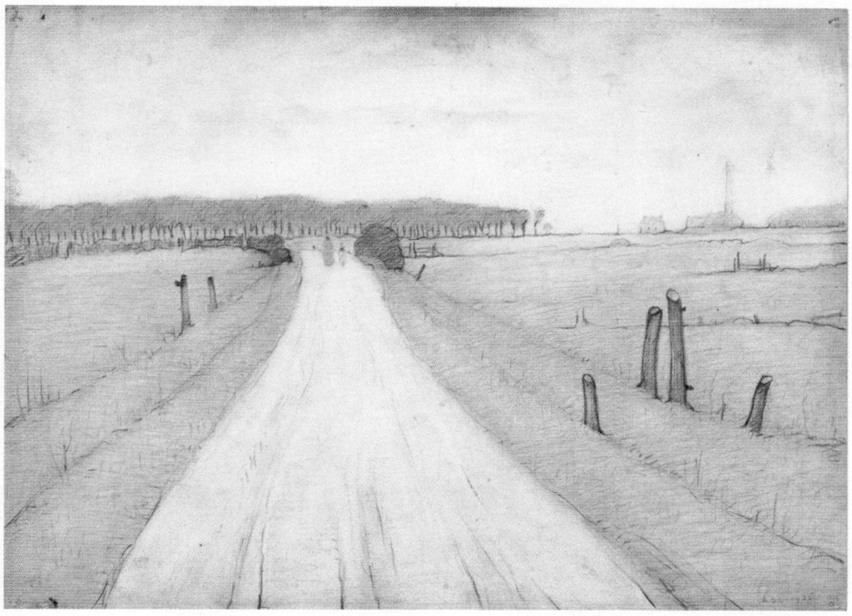

Country Road, 1925, pencil on paper, 24.5 × 34.7 cm.

By the County Court, Salford, 1926, pencil on paper, 24.6 × 34 cm.

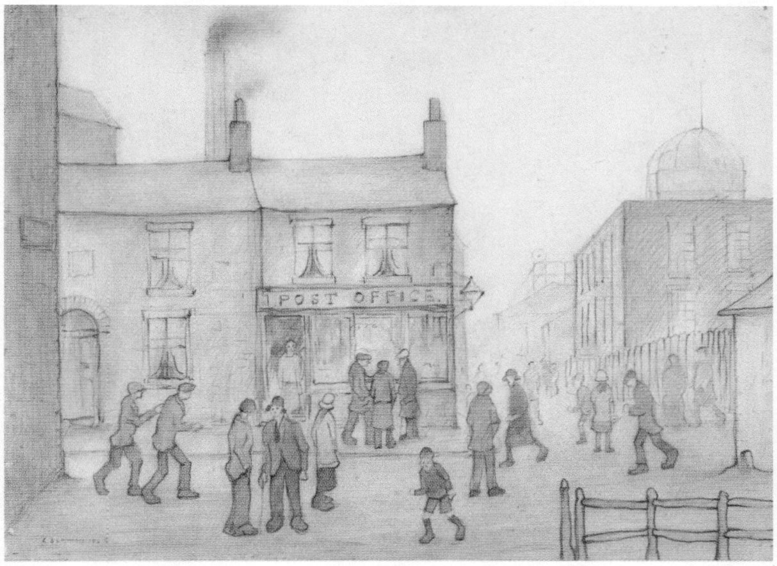

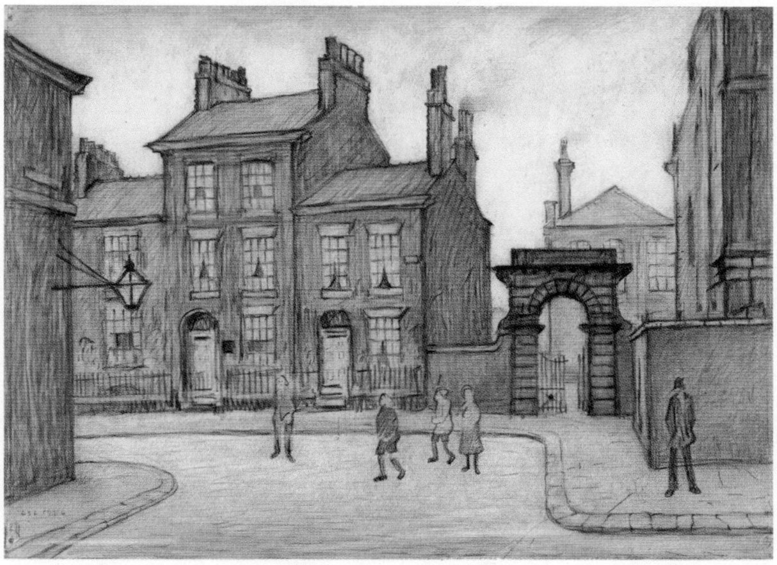

The Post Office, 1926, pencil on paper, 27 × 37.3 cm.

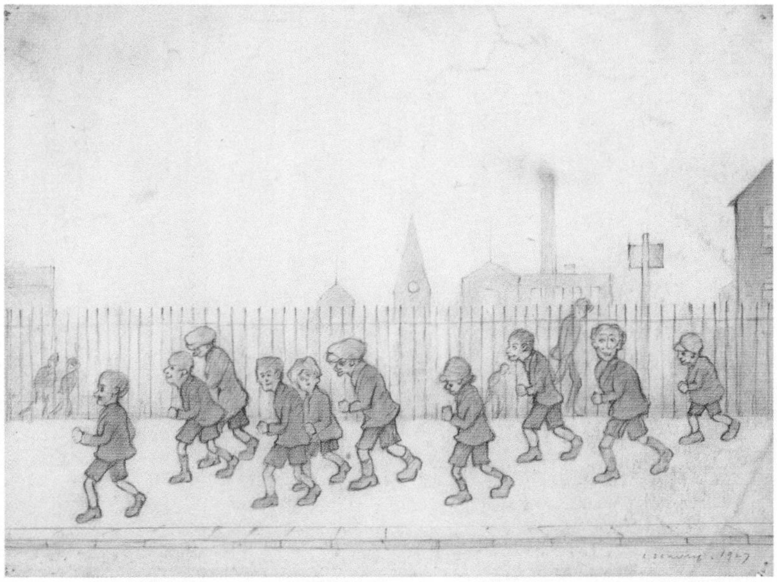

Children Running in Front of Fence, 1927, pencil on paper, 26.3 × 36 cm.

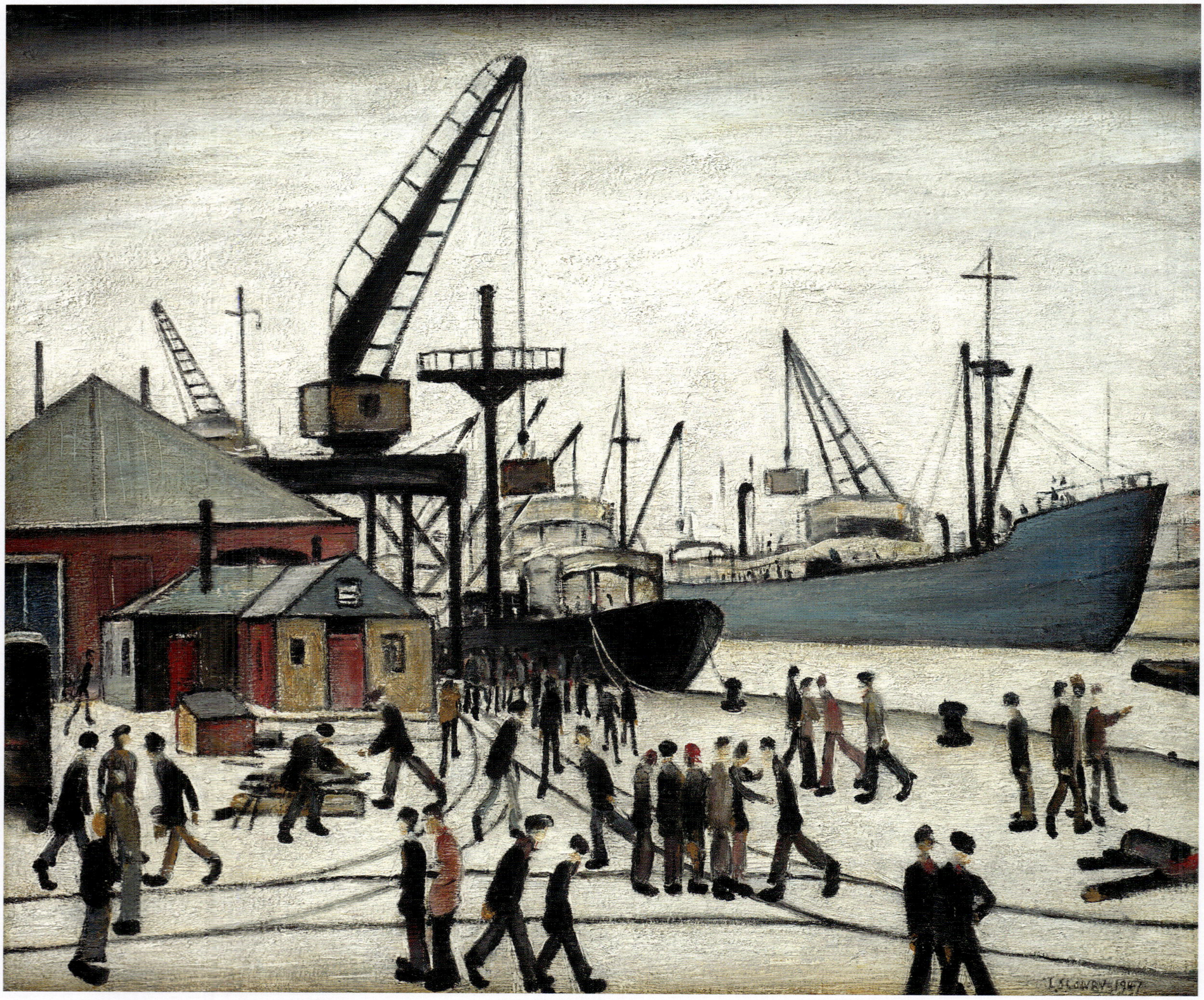

Glasgow Docks, 1942, oil on canvas,
68.9 × 79.4 cm.

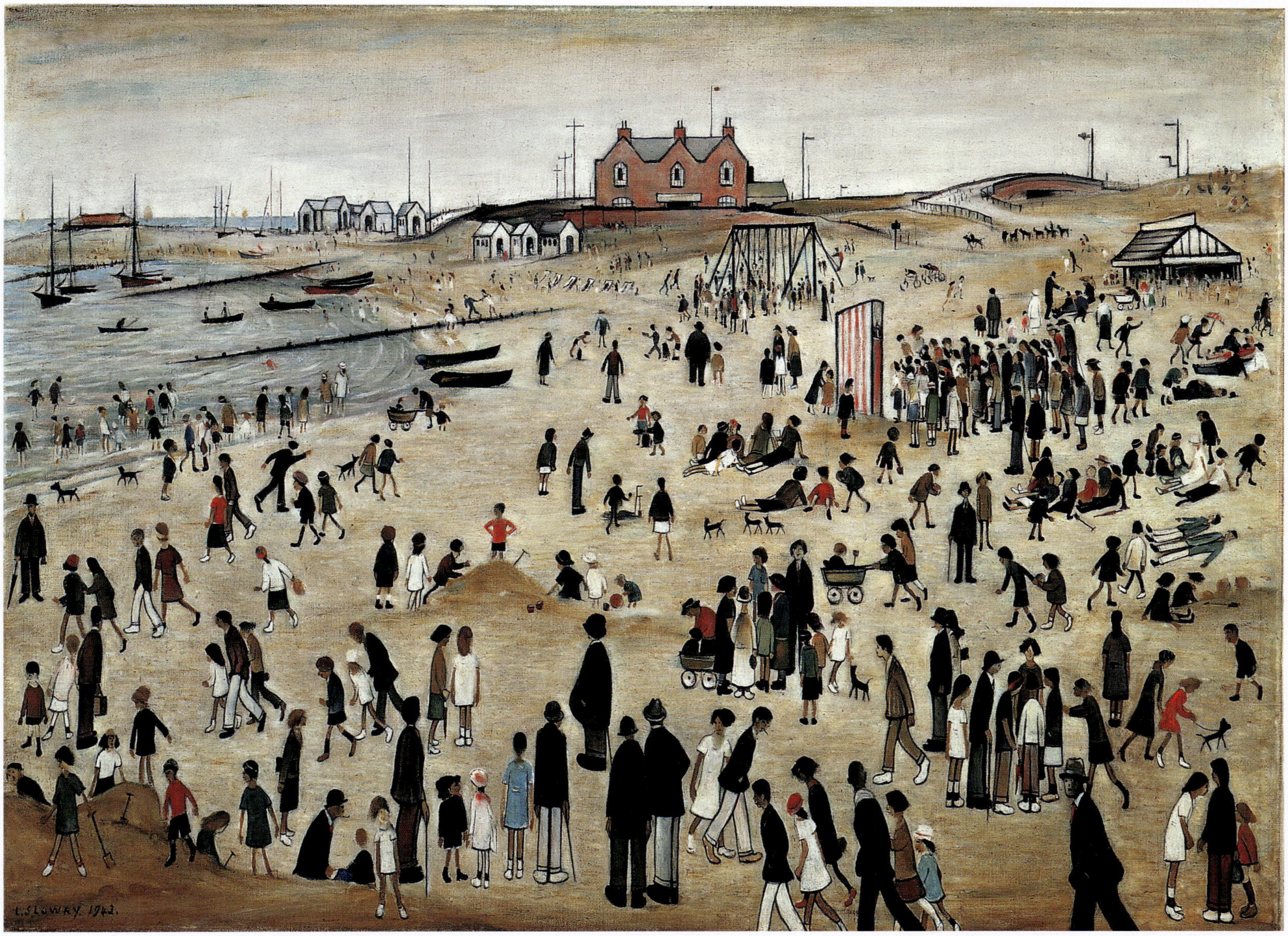

July, The Seaside, 1943, oil on canvas,
66.7 × 92.7 cm.

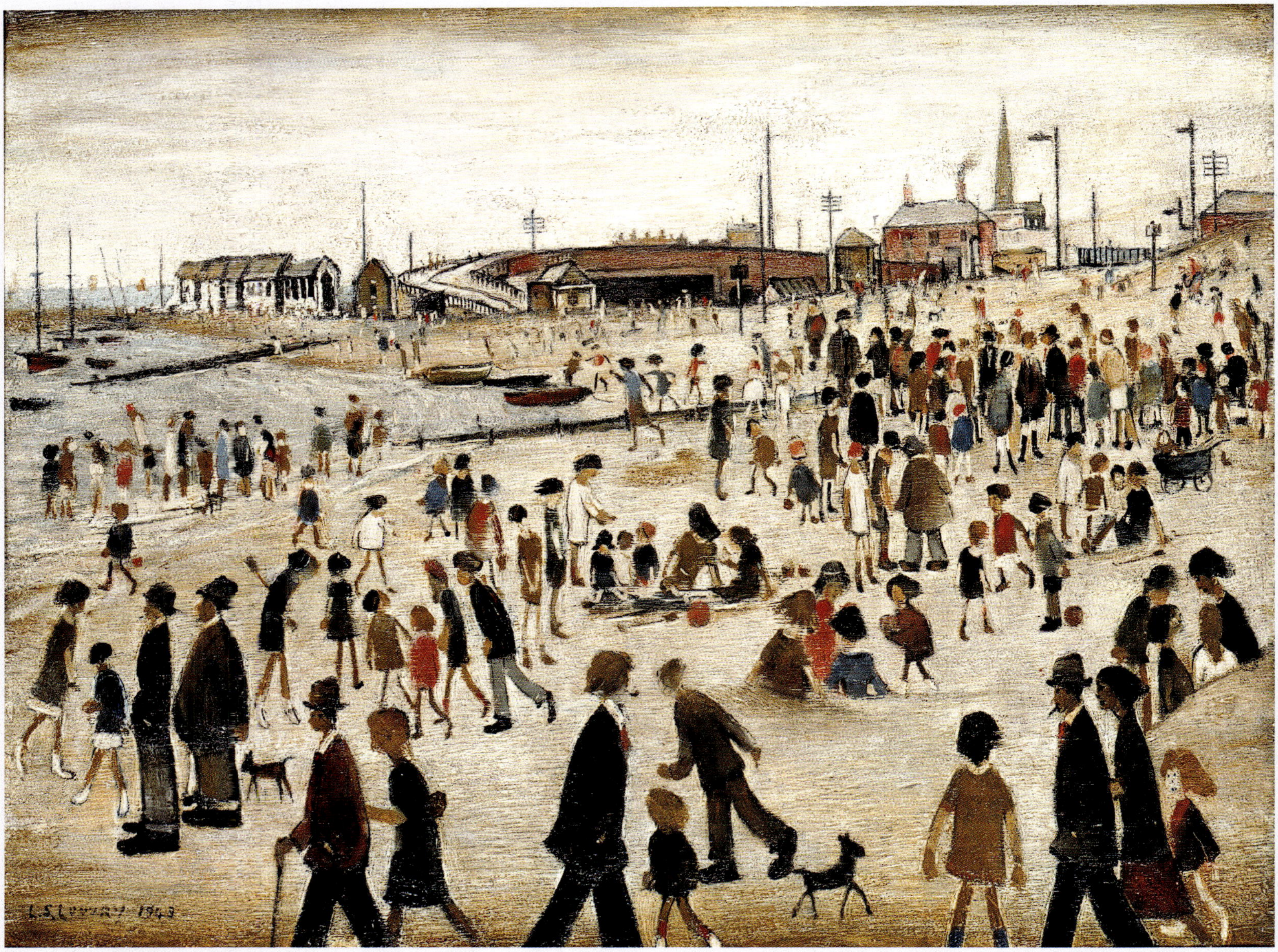

Beach Scene, 1943, oil on canvas, 46 × 61 cm.

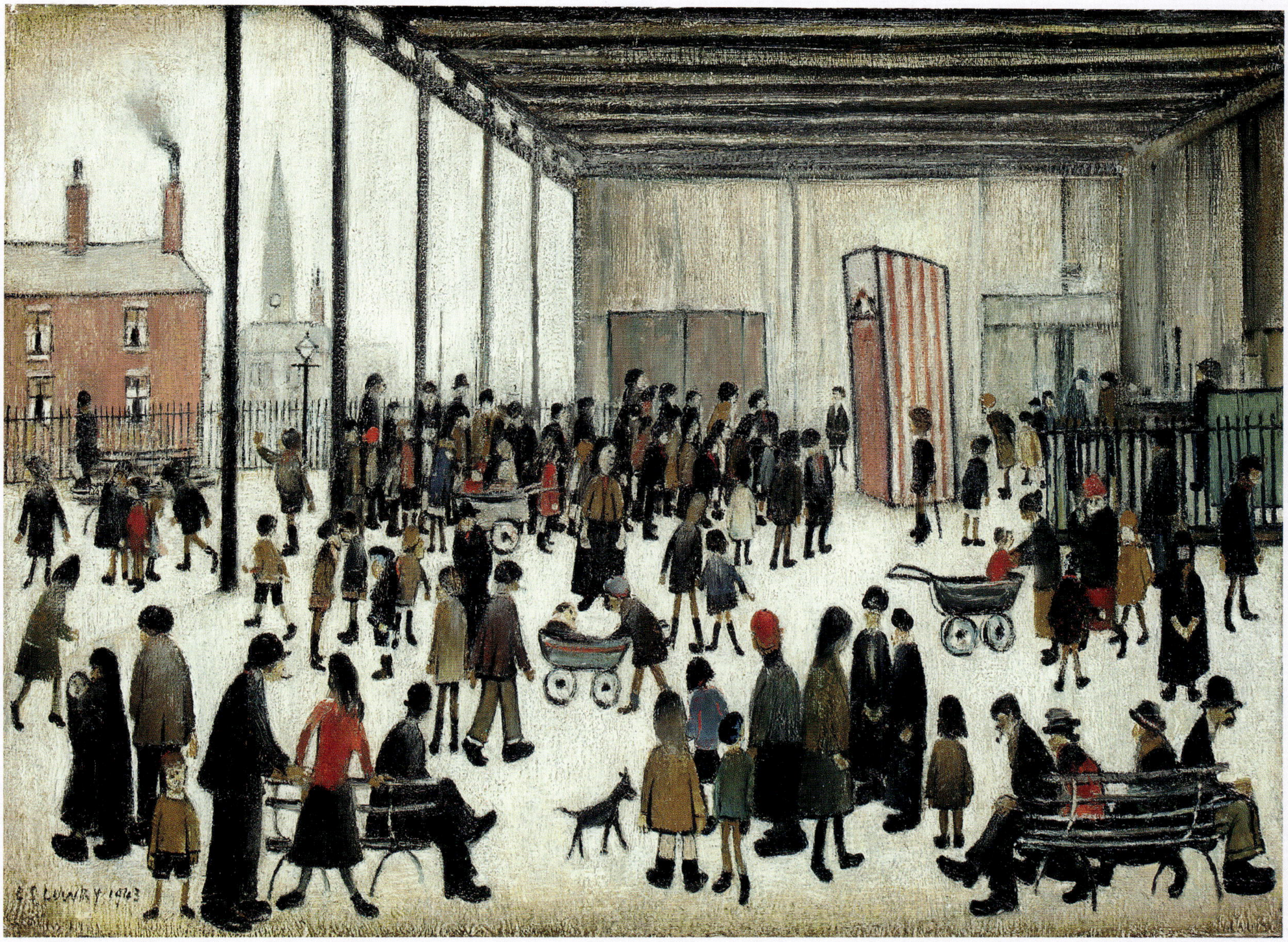

Punch and Judy, 1943, oil on canvas,
40.6 × 55.9 cm.

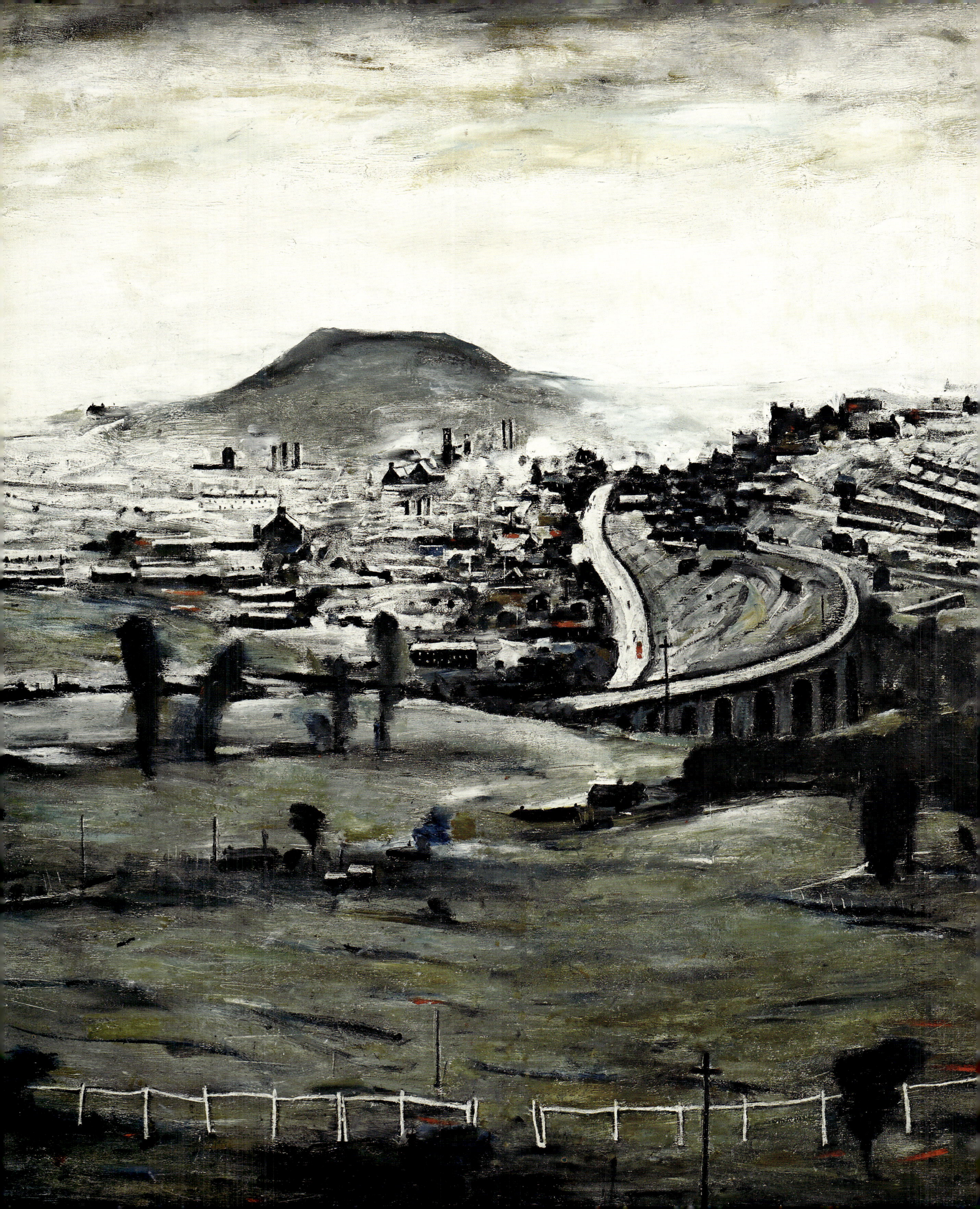

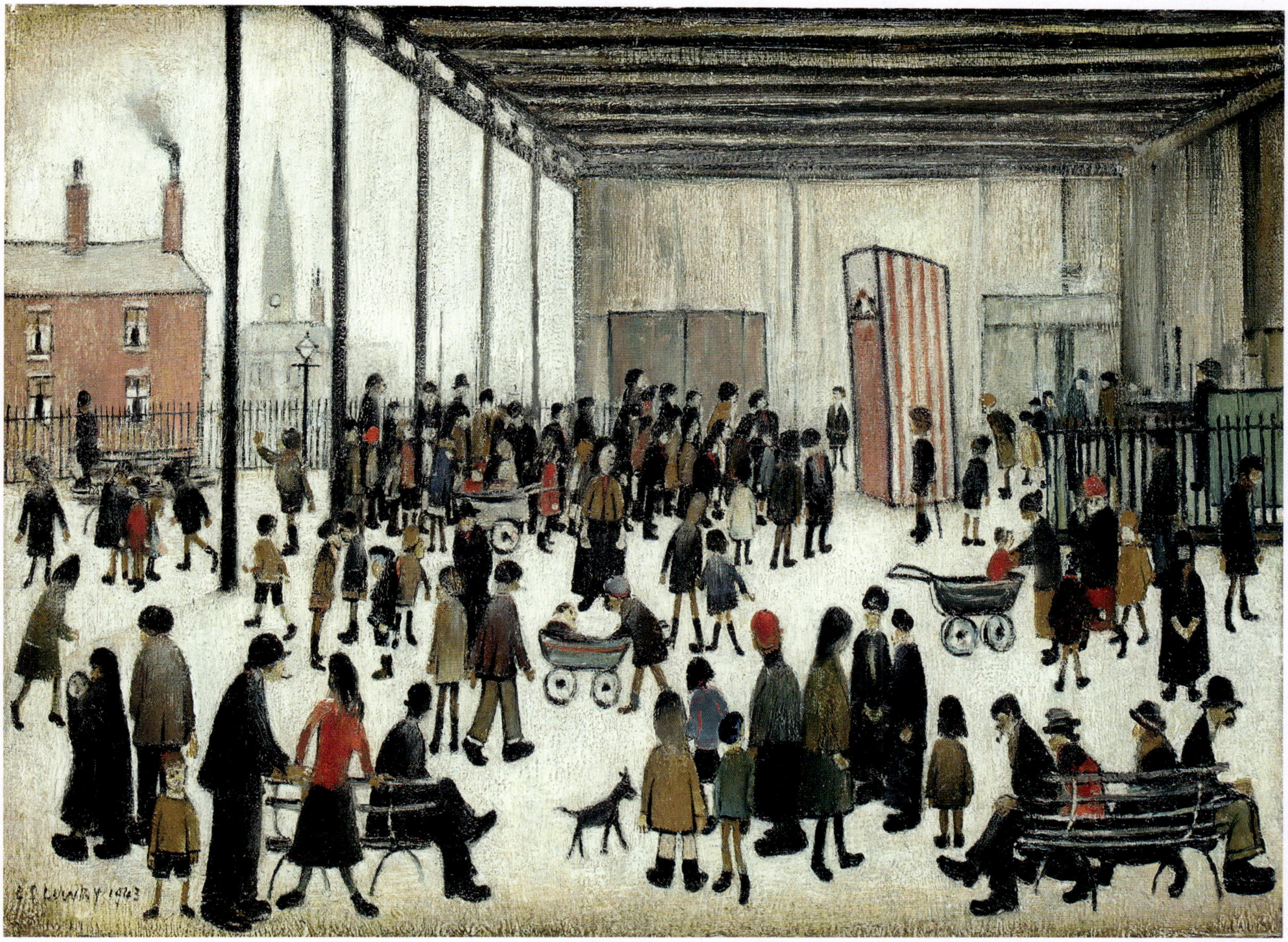

Punch and Judy, 1943, oil on canvas,
40.6 × 55.9 cm.

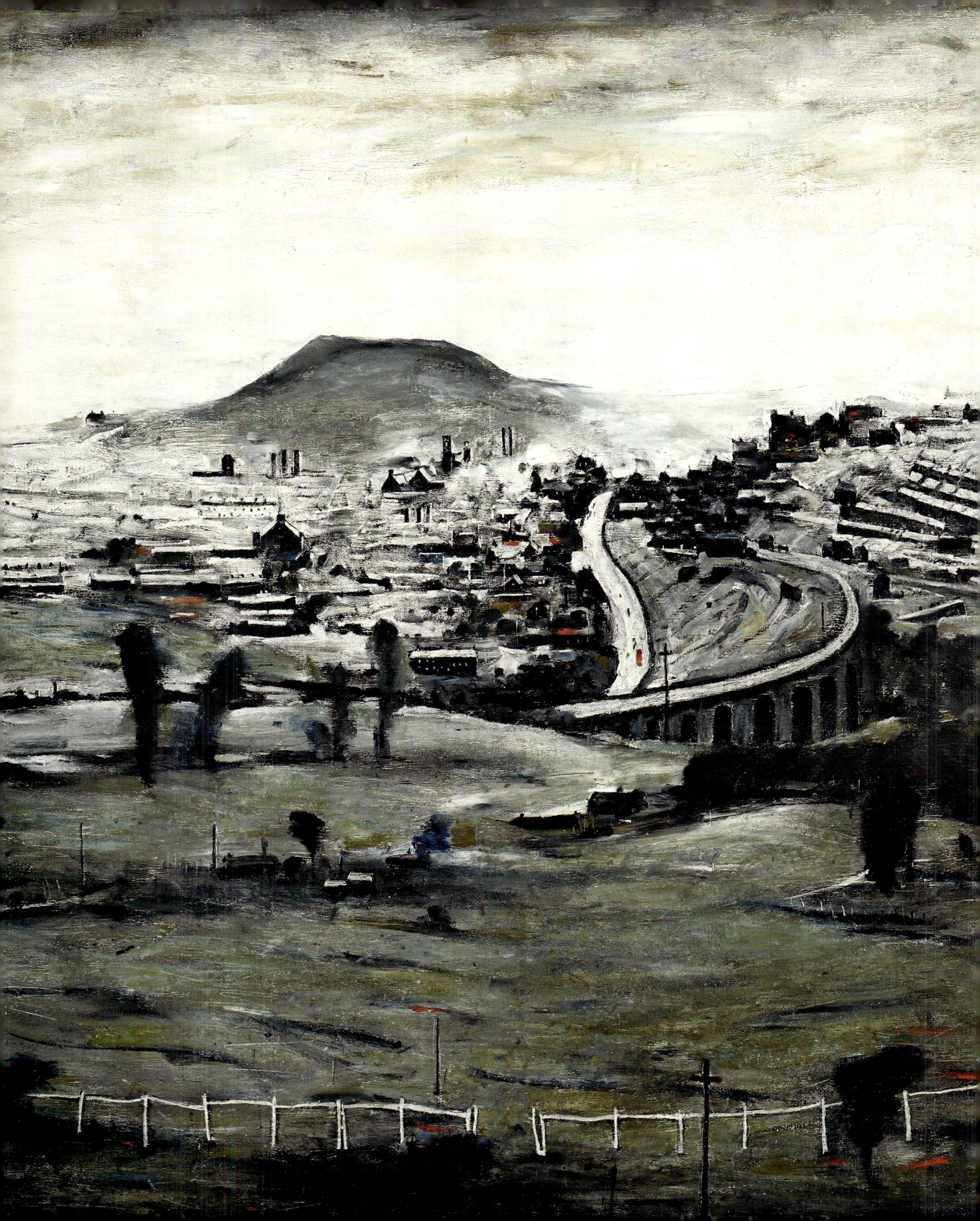

CHAPTER 6

ENTER MONTY BLOOM

Lowry liked anything that showed enough spirit to fight back, including cripples offended by his perpetual staring. The figures in his pictures are isolated not because they are pathetic and lonely, but because they are alive and independent. It is Lowry's unquenchable spirit of fun that gives his paintings their bright, audacious presence.[1]

Julian Spalding

Tolstoy's great aphorism about all happy families being happy in the same way while all unhappy families are miserable in totally different ways might well be transferred and adapted to the lives of artists. Success for most artists is much of a muchness while failure, or at least the ostensible lack of success, is always a uniquely designed package of misery peculiar only to the victim under the microscope. From the fictitious madness of the fictional Frenhofer in Balzac's small masterpiece *Le Chef d'Œuvre Inconnu,* probably the greatest work of fiction about an artist's life ever written, to the real agony and ecstasy of Van Gogh, the world of art is littered with every kind of human vicissitude from the global triumphs and Midas touch of Picasso to the many unknowns who starved and died in their wretched, if clichéd, garrets.

As we have seen, Lowry had more than his fair, or unfair, share of garret life, albeit in a garret in his parents' house. Had it not been for the frequently bizarre labour on behalf of the Pall Mall Property Company, Lowry, in the poverty-stricken 1920s and 1930s, would probably have starved. It was a world that lacked Arts Council bursaries simply because there was no Arts Council. There was in Lowry's circle no Mæcenas like Charles Saatchi to see that he was decently fed, watered and housed in exchange for his best output.

Yet Lowry survived to experience modest success in 1945 and thereafter a gradual transposition into mild prosperity or at least a prosperity that forced him to pay a lot in income tax at the extortionate rates of the period, something that put a lot of iron in his soul and evoked constant grumbling about the Government's (any Government's) fiscal greed. (For those under fifty who might read this book, the top rate of income tax for someone earning as much as Lowry did in his belated prime, was 19 shillings and sixpence in the pound, a wallet-wrenching 97½ % of his top earnings unless he had an unusually creative accountant.)

While Lowry's success grew so did all the obvious glittering prizes: honorary doctorates – no more M.A.s; an exhibition at Lefevre where in 1961 every picture was sold even before the show had opened; election as an Associate Member of the Royal Academy in 1955 when he was 67, i.e. already an old-age pensioner. (Full membership as an RA came to him just in time, in 1961, when he was already 74. As eligibility for election to full membership ended

Detail from *Bargoed*, 1964, (p.147).

when a candidate reached 75, this was a damned close run thing. Lowry stuck to his habitual cussedness and rarely made use of the Academy and its occasional Lucullan feasts.

Lowry was made a Freeman of Mottram-in-Longdendale in 1955 and, rather more memorably, of Salford in1965. In Coronation Year, 1953, apart from his Moscow Embassy-bound painting of the Coronation procession in the Mall, Lowry entered a painting competition sponsored by the Football Association. There is still some mystery as to how and why Lowry's painting was entered. It could well have been entered by Lefèvre where it was simply in stock, rather than on display. (This was many years before a passionate interest in the great working class game had become obligatory among politicians and the so-called "chattering classes", whose interest in sport had been for decades restricted to cricket, golf and tennis). Be that as it may, Lowry wrote to David Carr on 28 October, 1953: "It has won a prize ... I was never more surprised in my life when I heard the news ... So now I have lost my record of not having ever won anything".[2]

The painting is called *Going to the Match* (page 133) and, interest in money being what it is, it became a subject of sensation, not in Coronation year when it was painted and when it won the prize, but around the time of the Millennium when it was sold at auction for not much less than £2 million to the Professional Footballers' Association in Manchester. They, quite rightly, have ensured a wider audience for it by lending it to the Lowry in Salford. Andras Kalman had it through his hands a few times and was very pleased when one of his sales reached £1,000. In his delightfully reminiscent book with Andrew Lambirth he has written:

> When as a young man I had a night job in a tannery, every day I used to pass this scene – Burnden Park, the ground of Bolton Wanderers Football Club, one of the oldest teams in England. This is where football really started – Preston North End, Blackburn Rovers, Manchester United. I have been to the ground. The crowd would have got off the buses and made their way to the turnstyles. Lowry was conservative in his appearance and views. He didn't like louts or the changes in football or cricket matches, the rowdiness and vulgarity, the commercialism. I went a few times to football matches with him when there was no worry about violence, when the scene was really like this.[3]

Going to the Match is an exceptional painting and its then record price reflects its quality not merely its appropriateness to the eventual buyer. In fact, its appositeness, if superficially judged, is not only unusual, rather like a piece of programme music such as Handel's *Music for the Royal Fireworks*, but a rare example of the *pièce d'occasion* whose integrity and grandeur eclipses the occasion itself. To a Mancunian like myself, while the architecture is very different, the painting evokes, in its barely suppressed excitement, in its sense of a huge crowd in directed and purposive motion – quite unlike Canetti's unthinking and fundamentally purposeless crowds – the parallel scene outside Manchester United's ground, or even, in crowd terms, the holy of holies of the first day of the Roses match at Old Trafford. To any Lancashire man in those days the battle for cricket supremacy at Old Trafford was not a Test

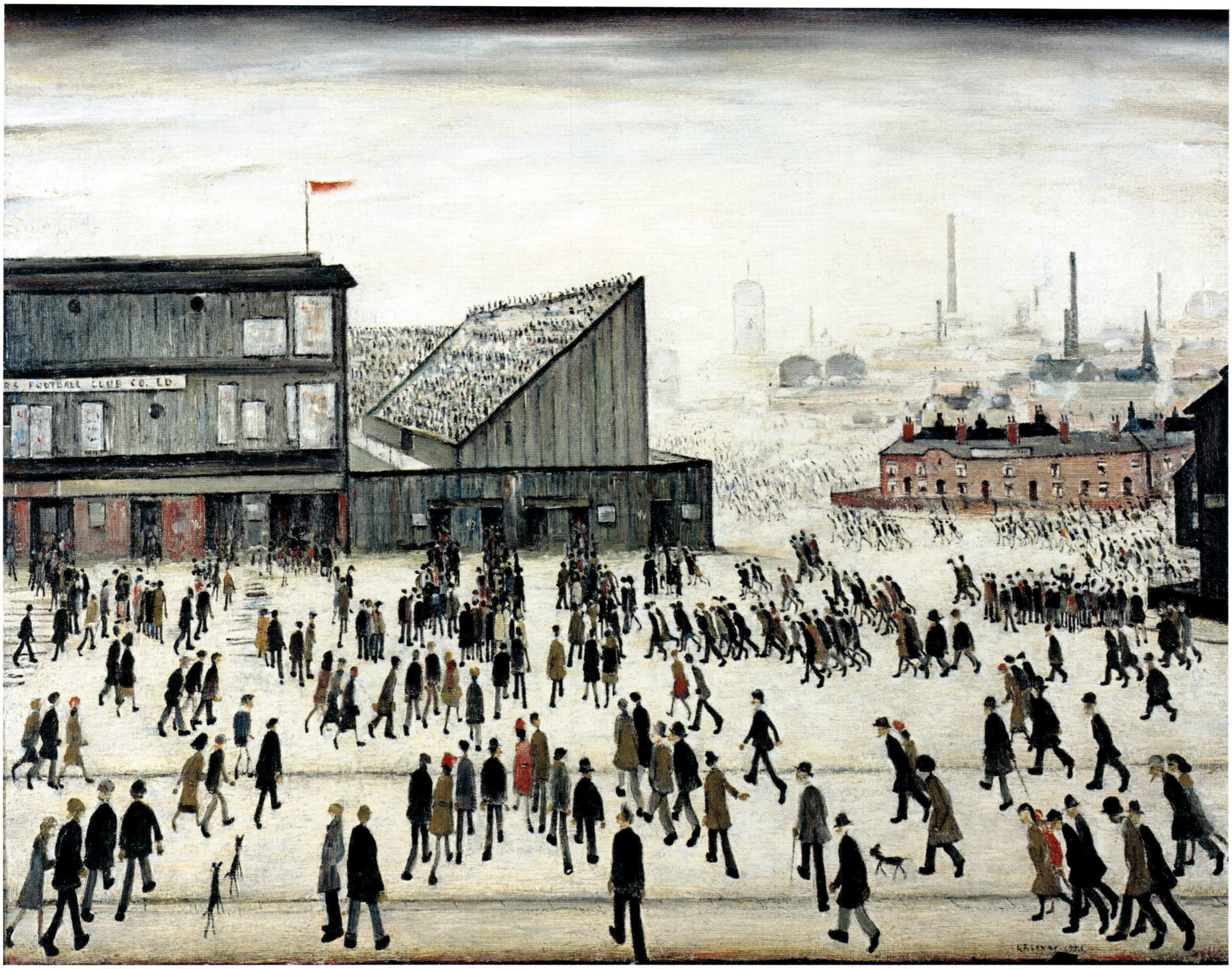

Going to the Match, 1953,
oil on canvas, 71 × 91.5 cm.

Match but a County Championship match, spanning a Bank Holiday weekend, between the red rose of Lancashire and the enemy across the Pennines sporting the white rose of Yorkshire.

Of course Lowry was recording a football crowd, not a cricket match, although he did paint one or two cricket matches in progress, and this is definitely Bolton not Manchester but there is a strong generic, as well as specific, local atmosphere in this painting, albeit one shaped very precisely by the year in which it was painted. One cannot second guess Lowry's mood or his political purpose, if he had one, but there is a world of difference between the

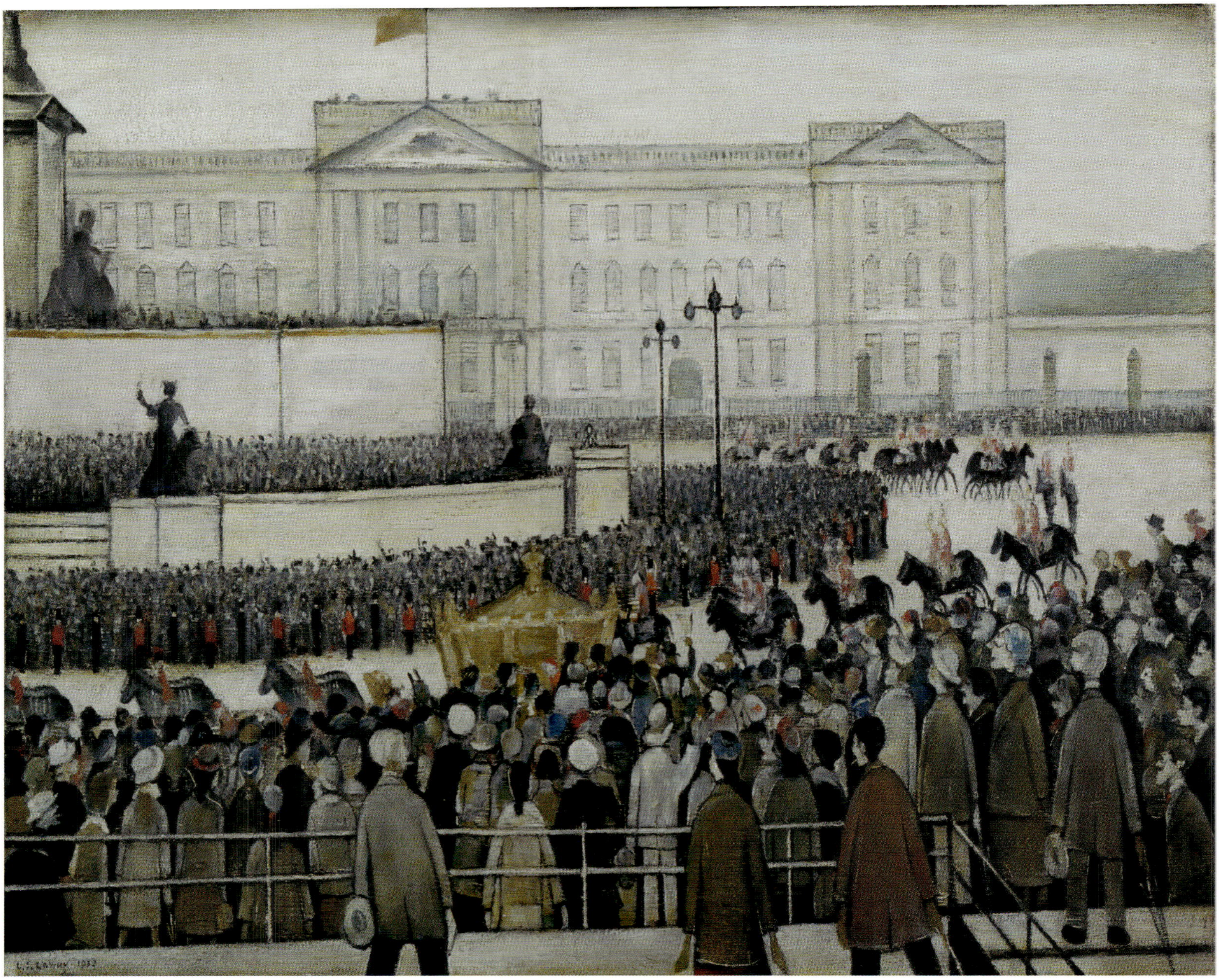

Coronation Procession in the Mall, 1953, oil on canvas, 50 × 63 cm.

faintly drab realism of the football stadium and its environs and the flash and filigree of his commissioned *Coronation Procession in the Mall* done in the same year. Lowry was not much interested in either the Queen or her over-elaborate Coronation procession. But he was very interested in the Bolton stadium and the people who queued at its turnstiles. This was an ugly but utilitarian building that was a source of entertainment at then a modest price and replete with the highest excitement for the common men and women he painted so often and in such detail. How Lowry (and indeed Andras Kalman) would have hated the current lavish and ruinously expensive football stadium owned by Manchester United, let alone the glitzy monstrosity of Arsenal's Emirates Stadium, and how scornful he would have been to learn that Test Matches at Lord's and the Oval had ticket prices touching the £100 mark.

Although Lowry did not set out in *Going to the Match* to paint a historical scene I suspect that he was, at least, in juxtaposition with his Coronation picture, making a generalised point about the place of the common man and how his mid-20th century brand of bread and circuses meant so much to him and why and how it brought some colour and joy into an essentially drab existence. Perhaps the Professional Footballers' Association were struck by the same perception of this painting. Critics are often asked, about a particular artist, which is your favourite picture? Having spent more than half a century studying and enjoying L. S. Lowry, I can at least relish the irony that, as a devout cricket-lover and as someone who positively hates Association Football as a corrupt and deeply corrupting industry almost destroyed by greed, if I could own just one of the paintings in this book it would, without a short list or any hesitation, be *Going to the Match*. It is a painting in which most of Lowry's tics and mannerisms are either only lightly sketched – the chimneys and church spire in the right hand background – or simply dispensed with – no narrow streets, no shops or pubs.

What he concentrates on is the ugly but wholly utilitarian stadium, the multiple turnstiles each with its own queues, the vast but scrupulously regimented crowd, each group bent upon its own turnstile if close to the stadium or, if further away, united by the common purpose of getting in on time. And, typical of the mordantly observant Lowry, a group on the right, perversely not marching towards the stadium but grouped around, and concentrating on, an orator on a soapbox peddling either religion or revolution and surely enjoying the attention which might, just might, divert them from the sinful enjoyment of a big match.

As so often a huge proportion of the painting's surface is full of Lowry's, multi-purpose white, so subtly and carefully applied and differentiated as to seem like an entire palette. Most interesting of all is the posture, bending forward, of the crowd advancing on the football ground. The only indicator other than their postures is the flag, or windsock, flying from the stadium roof to indicate both the direction and the force of the wind. But apart from that, Lowry indicates that this is a gusty day. The majority of the people on the left and in the centre are more or less wholly upright. On the other side, more or less from the centre of the canvas to the right hand edge the crowds are all bending forward, from right to left as they fight the wind which is blowing hard at them so that they need to bend into it in order to remain upright and traverse the flat land to reach their target. It is a perfect example of a painter manipulating his vast stage army like puppets, giving them a common struggle, a common purpose, without showing us the multiple invisible strings he controls with such virtuosity.

While Kalman and Lowry's sentiments about going to football matches ring absolutely true, there is not much point in mourning a past which has gone and will never return; but Lowry's painting is still, nevertheless, a reminder of a more innocent age yet also one in which the players were paid just about a living wage and that only for the season, from September to April, and were then laid off, wageless until the next season came round. If they were particularly talented (and lucky) they might also in the summer months play cricket for their county, or as professionals in the Lancashire Leagues and, if even luckier, could, on retirement take over a pub and survive to a decent old age. But just as many could end up destitute and living on such charity as a pre-Welfare State might provide. No footballer of the period would own a mansion in Alderley Edge, let alone drive a Bentley with a BMW or a Jaguar for the WAG. Lowry would indeed have hated all that.

As it happens, on the day that I wrote this section of the book, *The Times* reported, with a long obituary and two additional feature articles, the death of a footballer and football manager Sir Bobby Robson, at a considerably greater length than that devoted to the much earlier demise of L. S. Lowry. On top of that, *The Times* also included in its issue of Saturday, 1 August, 2009 a twelve-page supplement dealing in relentless detail in its entirety with Robson's life. One can all too easily imagine what Lowry would have made of it all, not least because Lowry was a man who liked the North East of England possibly even more passionately than his beloved, native North West.

This is where Lowry's character is so interesting. The Elms was the house of a man who had no money (which was still the case when he moved there in 1948) and who, when he had, for the time, quite serious money, never spent it on either frivolity or on himself. He didn't trade up to a large house; he did not acquire a trophy wife; he continued as a teetotaller and a non-driver and never owned a car. As we see in the chapter on women, he was a materially generous mentor to several young women, much to their advantage but never, as they say, took advantage of them. His luxuries were to travel in Britain whenever and wherever the spirit moved him and he did spend considerable sums on works of art, notably on the pre-Raphaelites. But he also bought pictures by his protégées such as Sheila Fell and his needy friends such as Josef Herman and then, in order to further *their* careers, rather than merely decorating his own walls, presenting his purchases to reputable museums.

There were also other trappings of success offered to him, but mostly either refused or accepted without any pleasure, such as having a postage stamp showing one of his paintings. The GPO (now The Royal Mail) used *Coming out of School* (page 85) on the 1s 6d stamp but one cannot be sure what gave him more pleasure, the exposure thus granted to one of his paintings or the ill-feeling among some of his fellow RAs that this (rather than one of their paintings) should put this wretched near amateur artist in the same bracket as Stubbs or Gainsborough. Lowry's carapace of disapproval could, when properly exercised, reveal the odd curmudgeonly phrase.

As for the various attempts to make Lowry respectable by including him in this country's six-monthly Honours List, various governments, rightly seeing that a gong for Lowy would look good for those who bestowed it, tried and tried again but all misjudged their man. Harold Macmillan offered an OBE in 1955, Harold Wilson upped the ante in 1960 with a CBE and, in 1967 tried again with an offer of a Knighthood. All were rejected and there

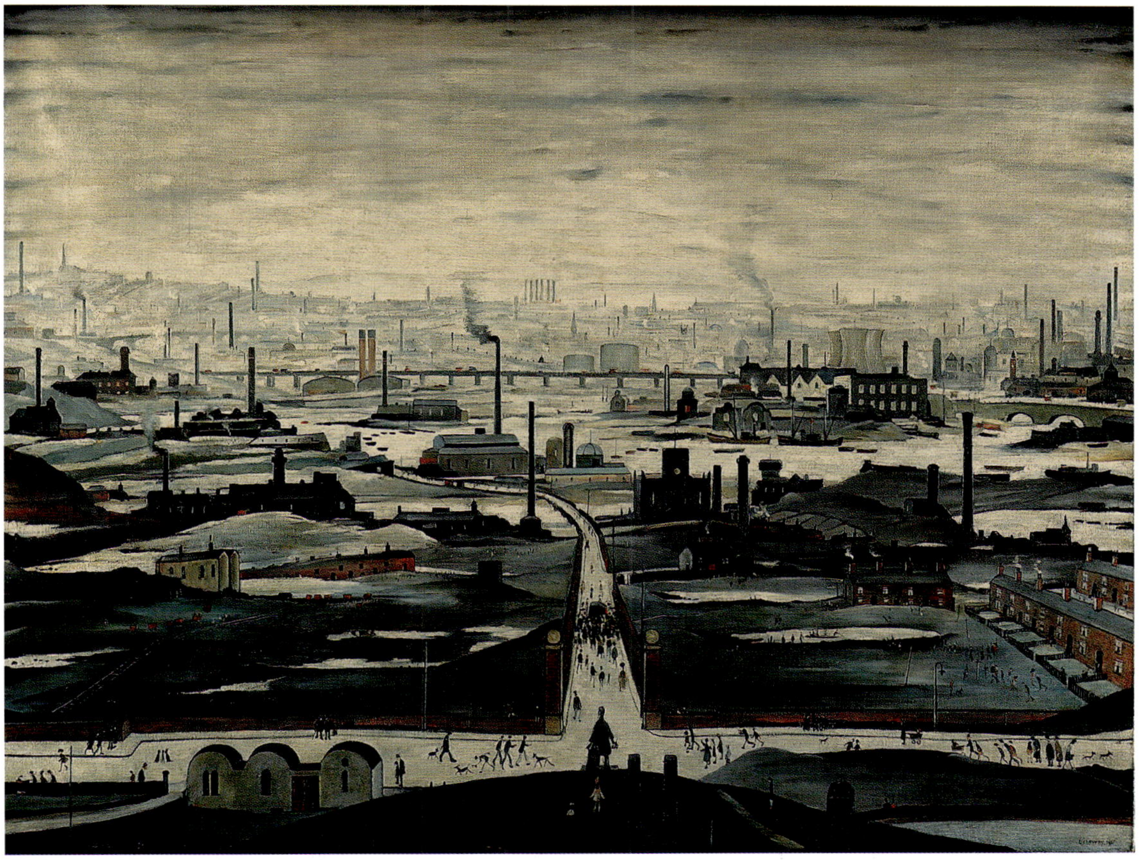

Industrial Landscape, 1953, oil on canvas, 45 × 60 cm.

is no record of his being offered the grandest decoration of all, the Order of Merit, which restricted as it was to only 24 living members, had included, among contemporary artists, Henry Moore, Ben Nicholson, Sidney Nolan, Augustus John and Graham Sutherland. The closest Lowry came to that was the *proxime accessit* for those who could not make it to the OM, the Companion of Honour. That decoration was offered by Edward Heath in 1971. Someone on Heath's staff, aware of the past, had drafted a particularly tactful letter which clearly left the door gently open for yet another refusal, which was precisely what Lowry sent back to Downing Street including the words: "I have at all times tried to paint to the best of my ability and I would only hope that any remembrance people may have of me when I am gone may be based on my work rather than on any decoration I may have collected on the journey".

Lowry's response, firm as it was, was also quite tactful. He was more outspoken when explaining this, to Maitland at least, incomprehensible conduct. Professor Hugh Maitland, a relatively young, Canadian academic had asked Lowry whether he had deemed the first offer – of an OBE – as too trivial to accept. Lowry's response was: "Not at all. They offered me a knighthood and I wouldn't touch it. I think it would be very degrading … I think it's laughable. I've very strong opinions about honours. They are ten a penny. They are fifty a penny. I didn't want it at all. I was shocked. I'm not a socialist, I'm a good Conservative. But I didn't want a title."[4]

Conservative, even with a capital C, he might well have been and if one had to guess at how he voted it would not be at all difficult to see him voting for Macmillan or Heath but when one looks at paintings of political events, soapbox orators, even directors' meetings, Lowry's deep contempt for all things political, regardless of party allegiance is manifest and, when he paints people en masse he is always on the side of the people and against authority.

If one looks back to an early painting, *The Removal*, of 1928 (page 44) one can see at a glance that it is not a removal that he has recorded but an eviction and there is no doubt where his sympathies lie. As Andras Kalman has shrewdly pointed out : "In Lowry's paintings there are never any references to the big houses that were actually quite often close by – the owners' houses. He only painted the houses for the workers."[5] Actually Kalman's generalization is not entirely true since Lowry did sometimes paint large detached houses but his feelings about them were made plain by painting them, if not in ruins, then at least in poor condition, requiring the attentions of builders and decorators.

Lowry, being Lowry, usually got away unscathed if his political "message" was too obviously sympathetic to the lame and disabled because of the saving grace, as in *The Cripples* (page 56), of his humour, sardonic and almost brutal as it could occasionally be. Sometimes he would go too far in mocking a patron as when he painted the laying of a foundation stone in the presence of some Manchester or Salford bigwigs where the satire of their municipal pomposities became evident even to the most bovine and self-satisfied worthies who felt, with some truth, that Lowry had mocked them for posterity. Which indeed he had.

On 11 October, 1961, when Lowry was 73, there took place a kind of apotheosis as well as a day of judgment. This was the day of the Lefevre sellout, before the official opening, of all the paintings that comprised his seventh one-man show. Cheque books were being waved in vain. Gallery staff had to limit even well–established old clients to one painting each and, according to Shelley Rohde the exhibition made it to the front page of *The Daily Herald* describing the sort of thing that "usually happens to artists only after they are dead." Some forty years after his first, entirely sale-free, one-man show in Mosely Street, Manchester, the sell-out in Bruton Street must have been for Lowry a massive justification for his artistic life. On that morning, within an hour, more than twelve pictures went at prices up to £1,000. (To put that figure into current perspective my salary as a middle-ranking executive in an art-book publishing house in the same year had just been raised to £1,000 a year.)

For many of the biographical facts in this book I have relied on the indefatigable Shelley Rohde so that it seems appropriate to quote her verbatim on this momentous event:

> It would seem that one of the major causes of the almost hysterical demand for the long-neglected industrial scenes lay in what was assumed to be the artist's perversity, but which it would be more accurate to call his integrity. Now that final acceptance had at last been achieved, he had, to all intents and purposes, abandoned his subject. The vision had faded and died.[5]

In other words, almost exactly forty years after his first public failure in Mosley Street, he had had a huge triumph in Bruton Street where much the same sort of picture that had been rejected, even dismissed, in Manchester was being almost fought for by wealthy *cognoscenti*.

It was, for the 73-year-old, with his dry, sardonic sense of humour and his always highly dignified sense of his own self and his iron-clad integrity, the perfect last laugh view of his life and work. He had finally made it with the industrial scenes which at first no-one but he himself appreciated. So be it. He made it clear that he wished to make no more such pictures. It had taken four decades to persuade the world that what *he* considered to be beautiful really was beautiful and he had had, and done, enough of that.

Being Lowry he could not resist being pawkily anecdotal about it all. A favourite tale was of a young man who hesitated too long in deciding to buy an industrial picture. So he retired Lowry-less but came back later to see if there was still a picture he could admire and buy. "Oh no," said Lowry "You're too late." "Ooh, I loved that."[7]

Lowry remarked that:

> In London all they want now are pictures with lots of little figures on them. Well there are no little figures on them so they'll have to do without. It's very sad. People write you know and say 'I'd like a mill scene' and I write back and say: 'I can't do it, and it wouldn't be any good if I did do it'.[8]

Lowry's biographer makes a case that his decision to abandon the industrial scene was neither abrupt nor an act of revenge for the many slights of the past, but arrived at gradually between 1948 when he left Pendlebury for Mottram-in-Longdendale, thus losing his topographical background and stimulus, and 1952 when he retired from Pall Mall, thus severing his forty years or more connection with the shabby streets of Manchester and Salford. He is on record as telling Professor Maitland that "My interest evaporated spiritually in about 1951 when I realized my work was *everywhere*".[9]

Perhaps more to the point is a remark of Lowry's to Frank Mullineux: "The strange thing is that when the industrial scene passed out in reality, it passed out of my mind. I could not do it now, but I have no desire to do it now, and that would show".

I suspect that there were two key reasons for Lowry's abandonment of what had brought him, at last, renown, a degree of fame and a lot of money for a man with no family commitments. One is the fairly obvious one of boredom allied with the risk of his public reputation becoming that of a one-trick pony with the two intermingling in his always self-aware mind. The other, to use Lowry's own words "the industrial scene passed out in reality". For all the topographical liberties Lowry took with reality he still needed the real thing as a spur to painting it. No matter how many brilliant – or merely workmanlike – sketches he'd made in his notebooks, there was, for his industrial oil paintings, no substitute for the dingy street, the filthy canals, the smoke-belching chimneys, the endless pubs and shops and factories. So many of the mainstays of his canvases had been, literally, blown away by the Luftwaffe until

1945 and, between 1945 and 1955, much of what was left more or less upright was cleared away by municipal and commercial builders. So that, were Lowry to come back resurrected he might just about recognize Manchester's great public squares which, particularly at night, still look remarkably like the paintings of Adolphe Vallette but contemporary Salford would seem as strange and improbable as visiting Mars; a Mars whose only recognizable buildings (from Lowry's point of view) would be a few churches. There would be no domestic dwellings, no factories, no chimneys and he'd be very hard pressed to identify the currently, squeaky clean waterways and canals. Only the Lowry arts complex and the Imperial War Museum of the North would spark off Lowry's interest but would also surely baffle him from both an architectural and a utilitarian point of view.

By 1956 even Lowry's dealers were aware of either Lowry's decision or at least of its imminence. McNeill Reid wrote letters that mingled fishing and, understandably, cupidity. His goose's golden eggs were obviously in short supply: "I do not suppose you have any tiny industrial paintings lying about. There seems to be a considerable demand for that sort of thing". But Lowry was not, (when indeed had he ever been?) a persuadable man. Later he told Tyne-Tees Television: "I could have kept on doing industrial scenes, but I don't do them because I don't think I could do them *sincerely* and it tells, you know, in the work".

All of which goes to show that Lowry was slowly but resolutely taking steps to retire from what he had fought so hard for, to give up, in effect, not just a single, if overwhelming, theme but an entire way of looking, seeing and celebrating in paint a landscape and a way of life that had not just fascinated him for nearly half a century. It had obsessed him, had entered his bloodstream and, finally, he had had enough.

As he put it "I feel more strongly about these people than I ever did about the industrial scene. There but for the grace of God go I".[10] Rohde quoted this statement of belief, in effect a *credo*, as if it was a simple truth attached to her view that Lowry:

> Now he had a new obsession: his single figures, his grotesques. The struggling, surging, misshapen homunculi who had lived for so long in the shadow of the mills emerged at last from their background to stand alone, as he stood alone. If he saw them as odd, it was because he felt himself to be odd; if he saw them as different, it was because he felt himself to be different; if he saw them rejected, it was because, despite all his current acclaim, he still saw himself rejected.[11]

Lowry immersed himself in painting relatively small pictures of single figures, couples, even groups of five or six people at a time, in all of which there is a hint of a wall here, a staircase there, an occasional impression of a road surface but never a whole street or a square or a factory dominated space. Rohde stresses that Lowry now identified himself with these struggling, often tragic individuals having abandoned the industrial community that had created them.

While it is possible to *read* these people in this way, where one must differ from Rohde is in her apparent belief that the industrial scene has been abandoned and that these people

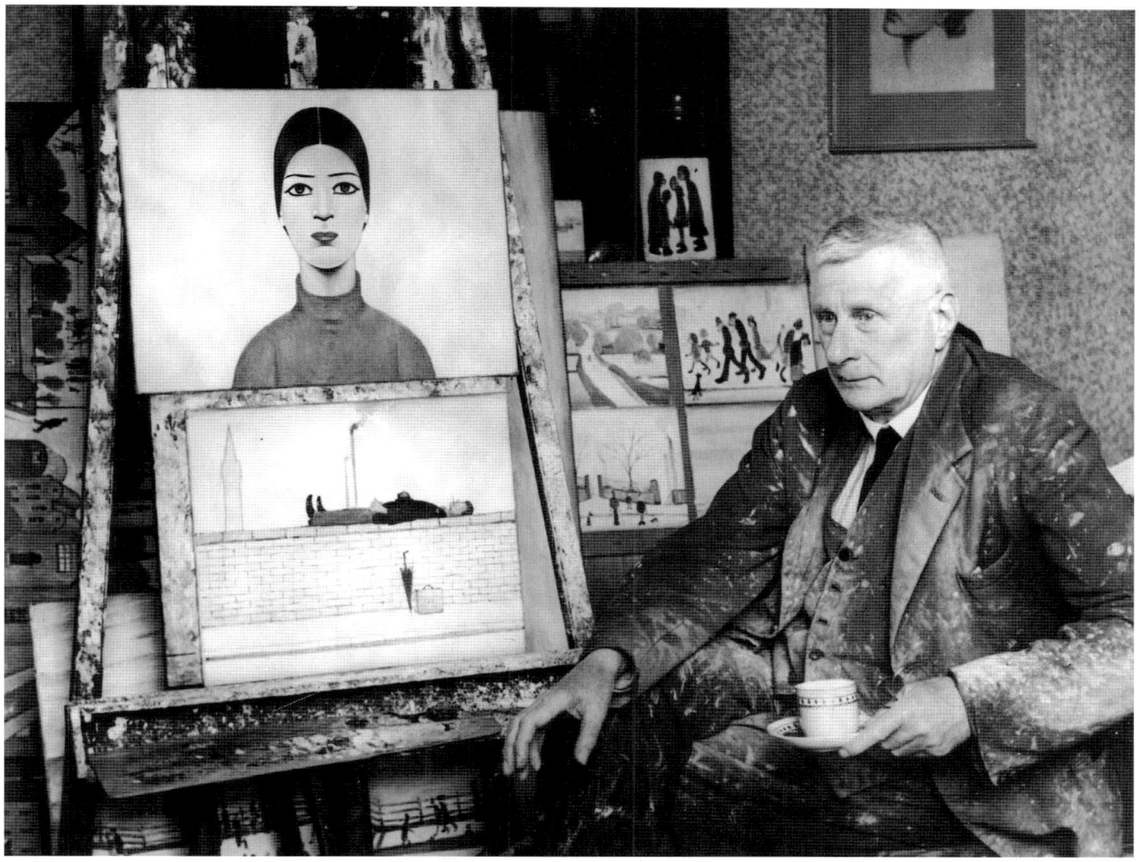

Photograph of Lowry in his work room, with a cup of tea, (undated), by Tom Stuttard.

have replaced it. But this surely is a typical authorial inversion of carts and horses. One would never say that Picasso had abandoned Cubism to adopt his neo-classical phase or that Matisse's late *papiers coupés* were a replacement for his North African women. In Picasso's case, as has been often noted, he changed styles more or less as and *when* he changed the woman in his life and Matisse had recourse to the magnificent paper cutouts only because arthritic hands prevented normal brush on canvas painting. The principal artistic fact about Lowry's work before he abandoned the industrial scenery is that he fought from first to last, as those early almost lyrical accounts he has given of his discovery of the Acme Mill clearly show, to recognize the beauty of the mills and their surroundings. And then to get others, preferably if they bought his pictures and *even if they did not buy*, at least to share his appreciation – as early critics and supporters like Rothenstein and Collis did – of that mysterious dark beauty which so many unthinking people saw only as industrial ugliness.

Also important in this issue is the complete absence in Lowry's work of what is known loosely, and rather contemptuously, as *agitprop*. If ever there was a subject area of British art that could lend itself to agitprop it was surely Lowry's industrial North-West. One could readily accuse Walter Greenwood's novel *Love on the Dole* of being classic agitprop, in that every page is about courageous but helpless workers being physically, politically and emotionally crushed by brutal employers and much of the drama of the Manchester School, which Lowry so enjoyed, is also about courageous but lowly workers proving to be better people than the boss class which exploits them.

Yet in Lowry's paintings there is not a scintilla of left-wing politics, apart from the fact that we know that Lowry was in his way of life very conservative and, were we able to plumb the secrets of the Ballot Box we would almost certainly find a staunch Conservative, constantly moaning about his success turning him into a blood-sucked victim perpetually stolen from by that leech the Inland Revenue.

I believe that Lowry's great shift of subject matter, the biggest and most important of his artistic life, was an odd mixture of boredom with the industrial scene, the knowledge that it was in reality, if not obsolete, then certainly obsolescent, that he had had to fight very hard to convert critics and patrons to his perception of its beauty and that, by the time of the cementing of his success in 1961, he knew that he had won a great victory. And if that sounds negative rather than positive (and this is in no way an attempt to equate Lowry with Picasso), as with Picasso and Cubism or neo-Classicism he had been there and done that. Other than endlessly repeating himself or, worse still, copying himself, Lowry was more than entitled to move on. In his choice of where to move there was also a more positive aspect. As we know, or think we know, if he had any professed political leanings, which judging by the studied contempt he meted out to those public figures or soapbox orators who crept into his work, they were neither to left nor right but to a central core of humanity, the humanity that made him utter the grace of God thought while in no way letting up on the sardonic glee with which he depicted the human oddities who so frequently crossed his path. Lowry himself valued these paintings very highly, more highly than many of his industrial scenes and felt bitter when they turned out to be not only harder to sell but had to be sold more cheaply as well.

The question of prices here has, as nearly always, nothing to do with relative quality. Posthumously at least, Lowry's prices are now very high and you need to be rich to buy a major work. On the whole, when the rich buy a picture by a well-known name they do it, no matter how much they might protest to the contrary, to impress other people. To impress other people it must shout the artist's name across the room so that the least knowledgeable visitors can say immediately. "Oh, you've got a Lowry. Aren't you lucky/clever/filthy rich". (Delete that which is inapplicable.) This is true of any expensive artist. If you splurge on a Van Gogh you have to get sunflowers and not potato eaters, if Renoir a luscious, faintly overweight nude and not a flower piece, if Degas a ballet dancer and not a brilliantly-lit scene in a night-time café. So it is the Lowry industrials which command the highest prices which means that, for want of a better portmanteau word, what we can call the grotesques don't do so well in the auction rooms, which is an irrelevant pity since, as works of art, many of them are at least the equal of the mill scenes.

Perhaps it is relevant here to record that, in the North-West in particular, where you might expect a knee-jerk, almost reflexive enthusiasm for Lowry and his work, there were, and still are, many people who do not admire Lowry. Or, to put it differently, genuinely do not *like* his work. My friend and contemporary the writer and broadcaster Joan Bakewell, whose childhood was in Stockport while mine was in Manchester, wrote about Lowry in her column in *The Independent* on 16 March, 2007, in which she delivered an encomium of his work and even of a burgeoning reputation beyond these islands. She also recounted an anecdote about her father, who had made the epic journey from working class orphan to successful middle-class engineer, an account of her enthusiasm for Lowry and the grim world which furnished his pictures. She writes:

> My parents were born in such places and climbed by their own efforts to enjoy the lusher pastures of golf-club Cheshire. When offered the chance, later in life, of buying a Lowry, they didn't hesitate: 'Oh, no, no thanks. We know what it was like living there; we don't want to be reminded.

For many reasons that seems like the wrong decision, yet one can readily understand it. It is, in its own faintly perverse way, a compliment to the overwhelming impact of a good Lowry painting, where given the wrong circumstances, its powerful verisimilitude is unbearable. (One assumes that the picture in question was a classic industrial scene and not one of the 'grotesques'.)

Lowry rapidly committed his new beliefs to board and canvas and, with total commitment, soon found himself in vigorous debate with his staunch friend Hugh Maitland, who observed to Lowry that, being a medical man himself – he was a professor of Bacteriology – he felt that Lowry was in some way taking advantage of these people when he painted them, regarding them as mere specimens and not as fellow human beings, saying *inter alia* that there was really no sociological reason to paint them.[12]

Lowry was unhappy with that, particularly when Maitland suggested that Lowry "had a certain relish in painting them". Lowry denied this :"Oh no. I thought that somebody ought to do them, And I thought that I would do them because nobody did them. *And all the time I was sorry for them.*[13]

Edwin Mullins, who had organized the Arts Council Lowry retrospective in 1966 got Lowry to admit:

> There's a grotesque streak in me and I can't help it. That's why I don't dare paint the Salvation Army, which I've often been asked to do. I'm not religious, but they do wonderful work, you see. I can't say why I'm fascinated by the odd, but I know I am ... They are real people, sad people. I'm attracted to sadness, and there are some very sad things. I feel *like* them.[14]

There is another aspect of Lowry's switch from industrial to grotesques which one can only treat as conjecture. At its simplest, Lowry stopped doing industrials at about the same time as they brought him fame and riches; in other words at the time when they brought him what he had craved for more than forty years. In the eyes at least of his dealers and his supporters over the many lean years, he switched his attention, his art, his very being, to the

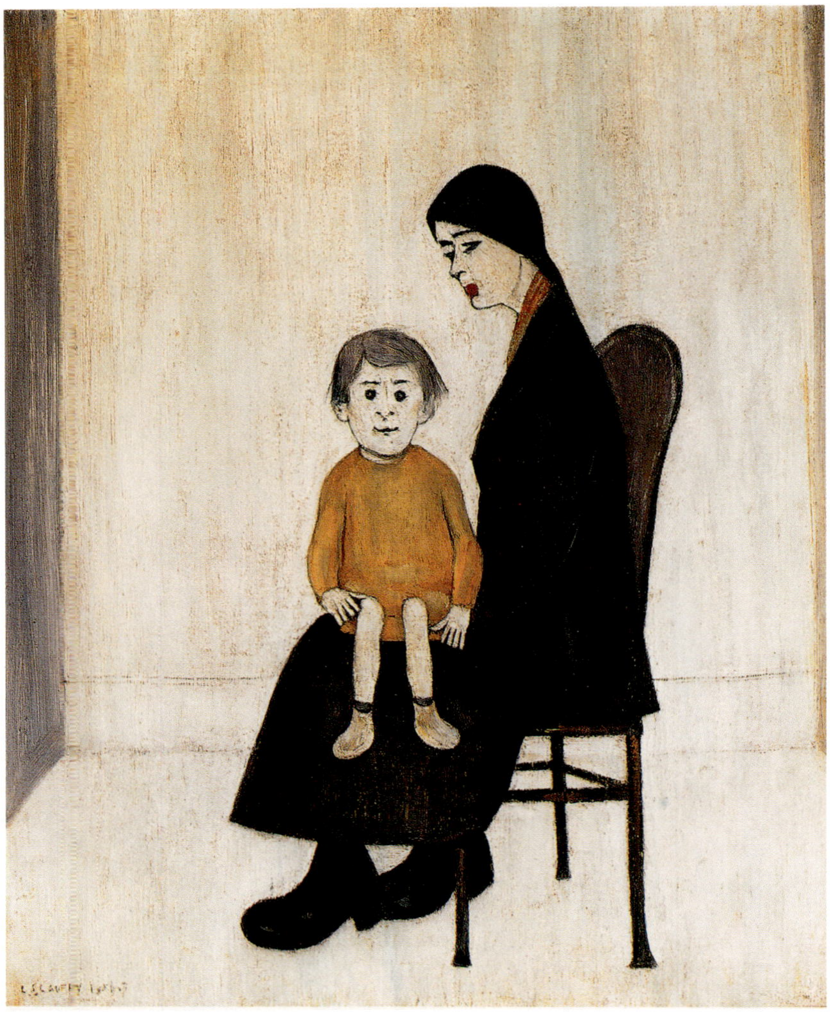

Mother and Child, 1956–7, oil on canvas, 61 × 51 cm.

making of grotesques which no one wanted to buy, let alone liked. Lowry sent one to Reid who sent it back with a query as to whether or not it was finished. It takes a very robust artist to take such treatment from his dealer without flinching. So one cannot really help asking whether there was not something perverse about his decision and its execution. It could bring him neither greater fame nor greater fortune. It could give no pleasure to his followers or to his loyal friends who were, on the whole, baffled by Lowry's conduct. The switch of emphasis, of subject matter and the manner of the painting, distinctly Lowry-ish, but much less carefully structured and composed, because in his concentration on the individual characters, more or less any background would do – and did; all this was not only perverse but it was, in Lowry's hands, wilfully perverse. Lowry was nothing if not self-aware when it came to painting. In effect he was throwing down a massive, paint-encrusted gauntlet and was saying loudly and clearly, either love my work as it is and take me as I am or shove off. Which is what most people did.

At which point enter Mr Bloom. I had wanted, as a committed Joycean, to call this section of the book Bloomsday, but felt that to do so would be, at least in my own atheistic terms, demeaning to Lowry and sacrilegious as far as James Joyce is concerned.

Monty Bloom was a successful Welsh Jewish businessman who observed Lowry at the private view, in Andras Kalman's King Street Gallery in Manchester, of paintings by two chimpanzees named Congo and Betsy who, in best Andy Warhol fashion had their fifteen minutes of fame. The opening was, as they say, in the presence of the artists and Lowry was on his worst behaviour, enthusing to all who would listen:

> Wonderful, marvellous, what fun, what colour – just look at it, isn't it tremendous! Now I really *do* see what action painting is all about. If this is it, well that's fine! And they can't help doing it, can they? That's the great joy; it's so unaffected.[15]

Bloom, an accomplished buyer, seller and re-builder of failing businesses, had been much taken by the Lowry paintings he had seen on television when John Read's film about Lowry was shown and admired the man and his ironic dismissal of the evanescent artistic charms of the chimps. Via Ted Frape of Salford City Art Gallery he had commissioned an industrial landscape from Lowry and therefore felt able to introduce himself. Lowry at once asked him to come and collect his picture, so Bloom drove him to The Elms. There Lowry showed him an industrial which he had in stock, as opposed to the one for which he had accepted a commission. Bloom liked the picture but his attention was distracted by the "grotesques" he saw on the walls. Embarrassed, he started to tell Lowry: "I like the mill scene but I think I prefer those ..." "I prefer them myself" said Lowry and laid down around the easel about twelve of them. Bloom then chose six and asked Lowry if he could buy them. Lowry satisfied himself that Bloom's enthusiasm was genuine and named a price of ninety pounds. Bloom asked if that was for the six, Lowry said yes, Bloom paid and took all six away with him. For Lowry, despite the absurdly low price, this was a special kind of victory. At last someone had appreciated his grotesques and at last he had sold some of what everyone else either scorned or ignored.[16]

If for Lowry the painting of the grotesques became an obsession, so, for Bloom, the obsession was to acquire them. They were the first paintings he had ever bought and, certainly for that period of his life when he was close to Lowry, those were all the pictures he collected. (I have noticed, when looking at Lowrys in private houses, that quite a few enthusiastic collectors buy only Lowrys and where they do not have enough Lowrys to fill all their walls leave the Lowry-less walls bare.)

But the Bloom effect was catalytic in other ways. Bloom was a passionate Welshman and insisted that Lowy visited him in Southport and travelled with him in Wales, with the quite unexpected result that, as far as Wales was concerned it was, at least temporarily removed from the industrial exclusion zone. Not only did Lowry become enamoured, as Bloom was, with the beauties of the Welsh landscape, producing, among other major works, the superb *Hillside in Wales* of 1962 (page 146) now languishing unseen in the Tate's store in Southwark,

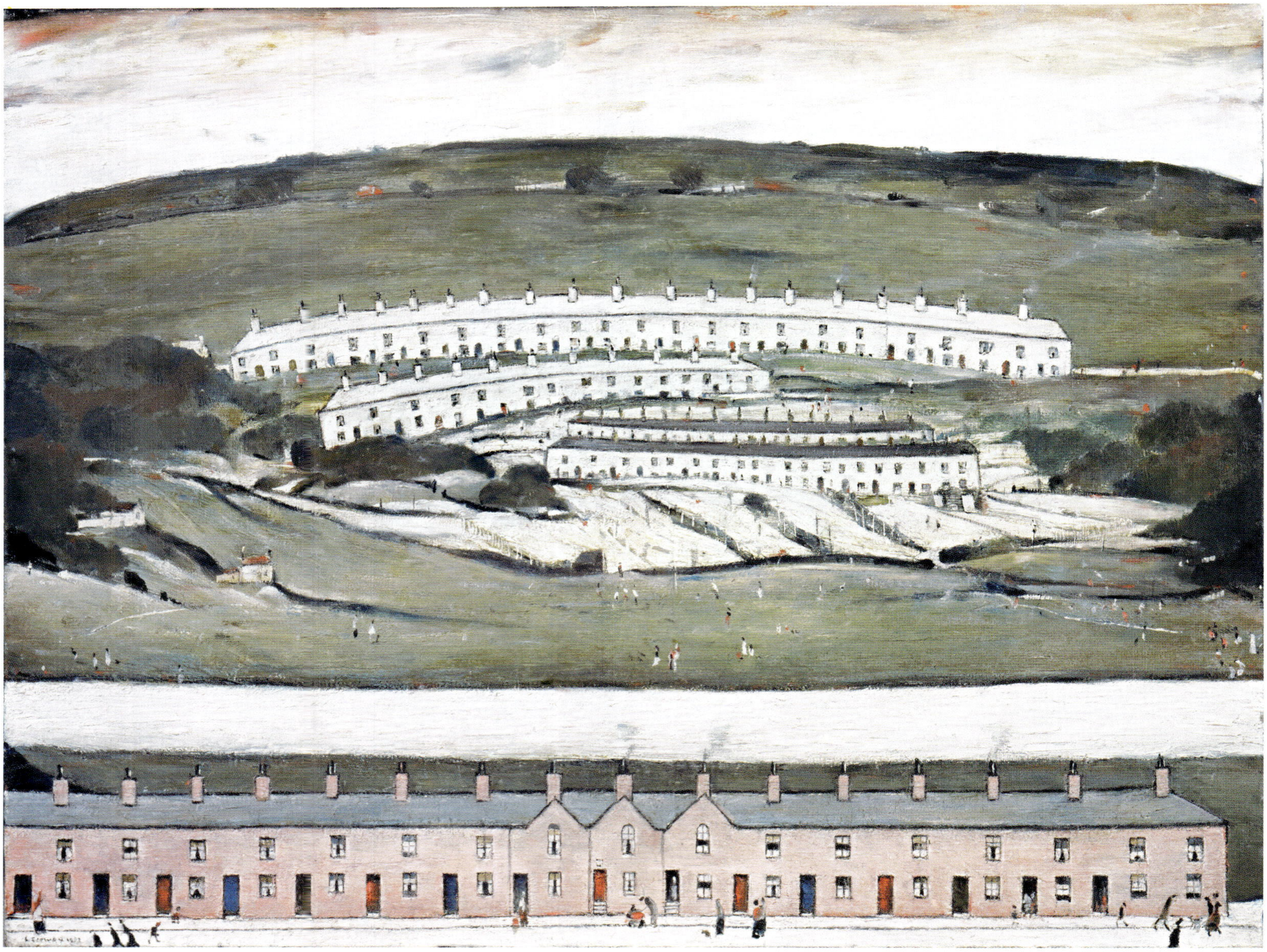

Hillside in Wales, 1962, oil on canvas, 76.2 × 101.6 cm.

but he broke his own embargo on industrials with his 1965 *Bargoed* (page 147) in which the belching chimneys are replaced as the dominant feature by a monstrous mountain-sized, slag heap. The huge foreground is not in Lowry's traditional white, but is painted in a lush, ripe green to point up the essential dysfunction of a vast grassy plain leading up to the cramped little houses, looking like rows of grey Monopoly symbols, leading the eye to the massive slag heap looking like a misplaced Table Mountain.

But the most powerful effect of the Bloom relationship was the sheer volume of his purchases. If what follows reads like the aridity and boredom of statistics then so be it. But to Lowry to have a patron as enthusiastic and assiduous as Monty Bloom would have been,

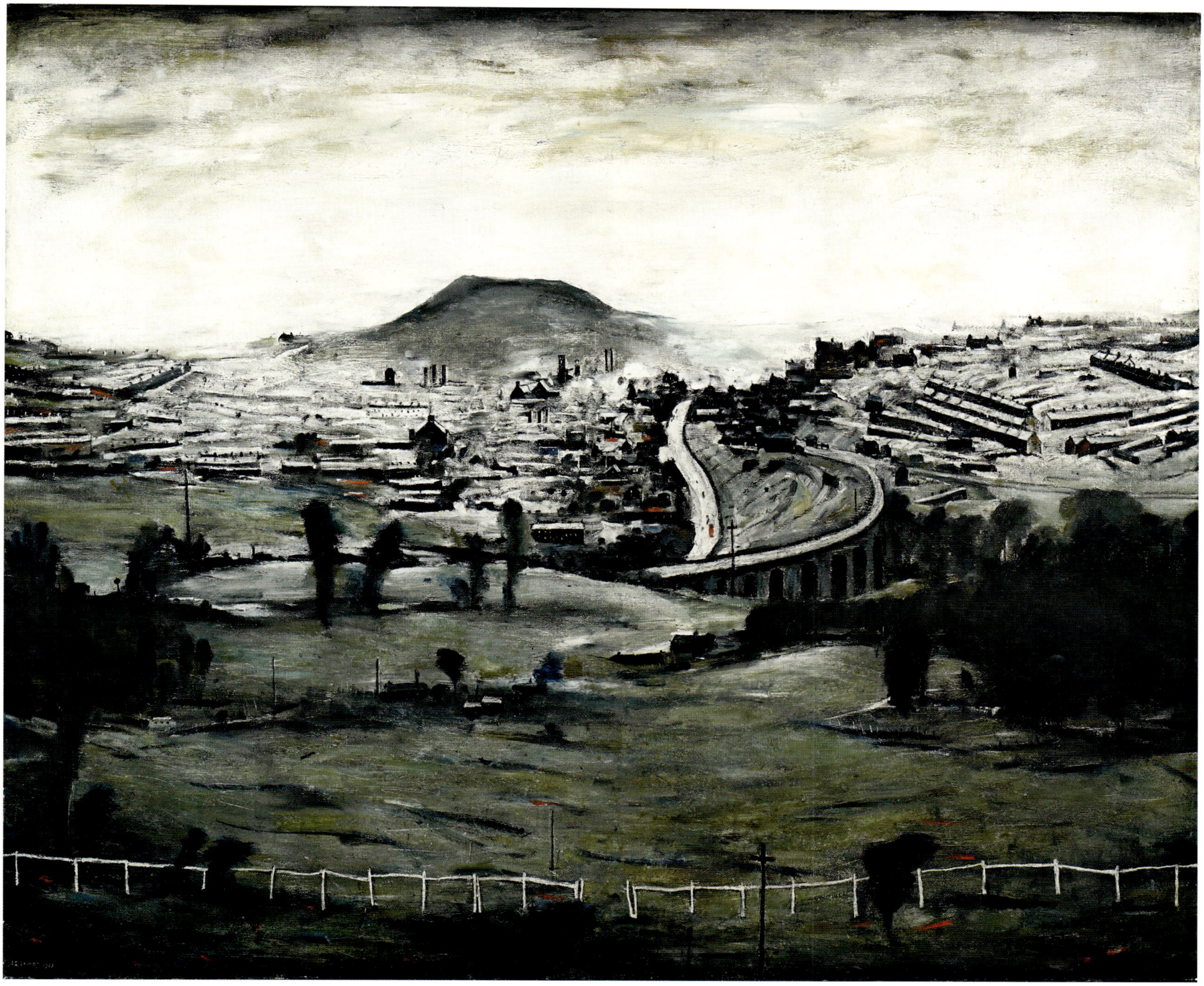

Bargoed, 1964, oil on canvas, 121.5 × 153.5 cm.

if Lowry were that sort of human being, a life-changing experience. But, as we have seen, Lowry was not a man to change his life because of someone else's actions. He carried on exactly as before Bloom's arrival although Bloom's purchases must have been a source of comfort and even pride that what he was doing was not just important but was recognized as such.

Not everything went entirely smoothly. Bloom's wife, at first tolerant, began, as the collection grew and grew, to ask, rather pitifully where they would be able to hang further purchases as the house began to look like the Uffizi. Bloom was reduced to keeping paintings in the boot of his car and at the back of wardrobes and, in one case, lending a particularly fine piece to Salford.

By the mid 1960s Bloom had 60 Lowrys on his walls and another 40 in various storage places. By the 1970s, in sheer numbers his collection exceeded the other major private ones belonging to life-long friends like the Maitlands, the Bennetts, the Leggatts, and even the public collection in Salford, and almost certainly more than Lowry owned himself.[17]

Bloom was not only a compulsive collector; he also had a very good eye, and, as Lowry's reputation went on growing so Bloom, inevitably, was asked to lend from his collection. In 1962 the Graves Art Gallery (the city's municipal gallery) in Sheffield decided to have a Lowry retrospective and, having approached Bloom, visited him in Southport intending to ask to borrow a handful and ended up taking 42 of which they showed 39. In 1964 the Stone Gallery (a private dealing gallery) in Newcastle owned by Micky and Tilly Marshall also went on a pilgrimage to Bloom in Southport, having ingratiated themselves with Lowry by saying that they preferred his individual paintings to his industrials. They had also intended to borrow just a few but on seeing them all on display ended up basing their entire Lowry show on part of the Bloom collection, borrowing 48 pictures in all.

When asked by a London journalist why Mr Bloom had so much of his work Lowry replied: "That's simple. Mr Bloom said 'How much?' and he went on saying 'how much?' And now there are none left".

When Edwin Mullins visited the Newcastle show while Lowry was there, the artist told him "At last I feel I'm getting what I've wanted ... I think I'll die, sir. There's nothing left. I'm old ... Well perhaps not till after the private view".[18]

The power of the impulse to change his basic subject matter was clearly enormous. It was, in all sorts of ways, a momentous decision but, like other momentous decisions, whether in art or in life, there were, with the benefit of hindsight, little signposts for the impending decision quite a long way back. *Family Group* of 1936 (page 149) is definitely not an industrial. It might show an interior with five people in it much as, if one could enter a between-the-wars mill worker's tiny rented house, and be confronted by what Lowry has painted here but, in spirit, it belongs with the grotesques done a quarter of a century later. You can tell by the space occupied by the five figures that this is a tiny, cramped, cottage. There isn't much nourishment on the table; just one mug. The adults and children don't look comfortable. Their clothes which are rather tight and worn as if to conserve meagre heat. The large boy on the right is the spitting image of his father and is tremendously ill at ease, as if some disaster has befallen him at school. The father's face is rigid as he looks sideways at his family, subsumed by fear, a real sense of dread. The wife/mother, painted in profile, is just, but only just, making glancing, tenuous eye-contact so that all the viewer can do is speculate as to the cause of all this despair. A death in the family? A catastrophic accident at the mill? A cut in the already desperately low 1930s equivalent of Unemployment Benefit? The Mill itself going bankrupt? It could be a scene from a play by Harold Brighouse. But, whatever lies behind it, it is surely a fore-runner of the grotesques of the early 1960s and, at that stage in

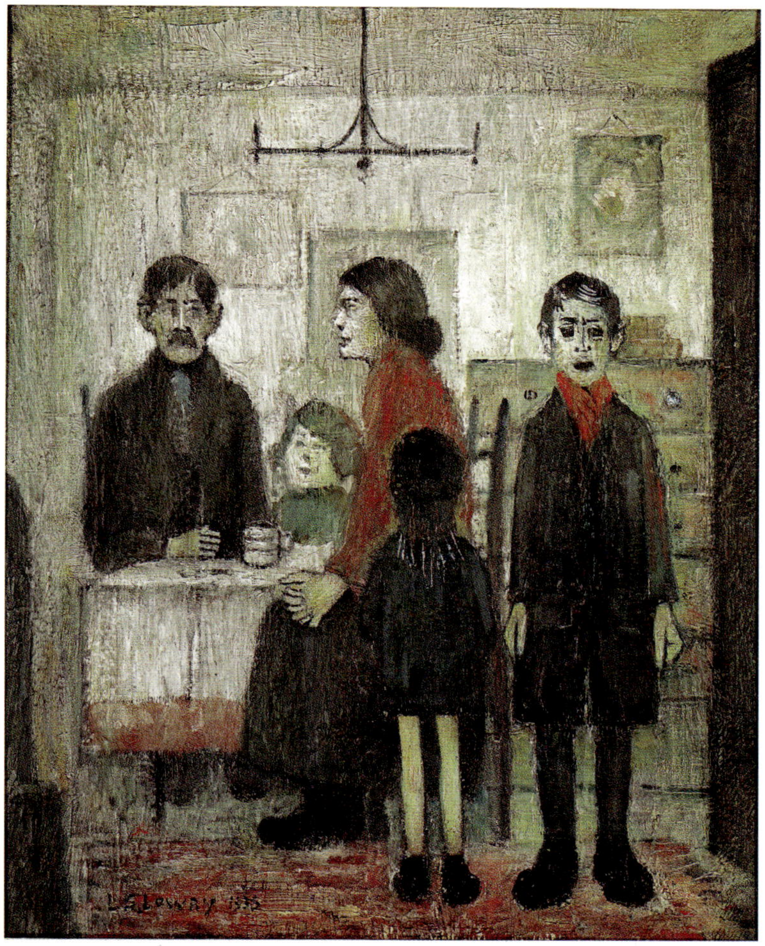

Family Group, 1936, oil on canvas, 45.1 × 34.9 cm.

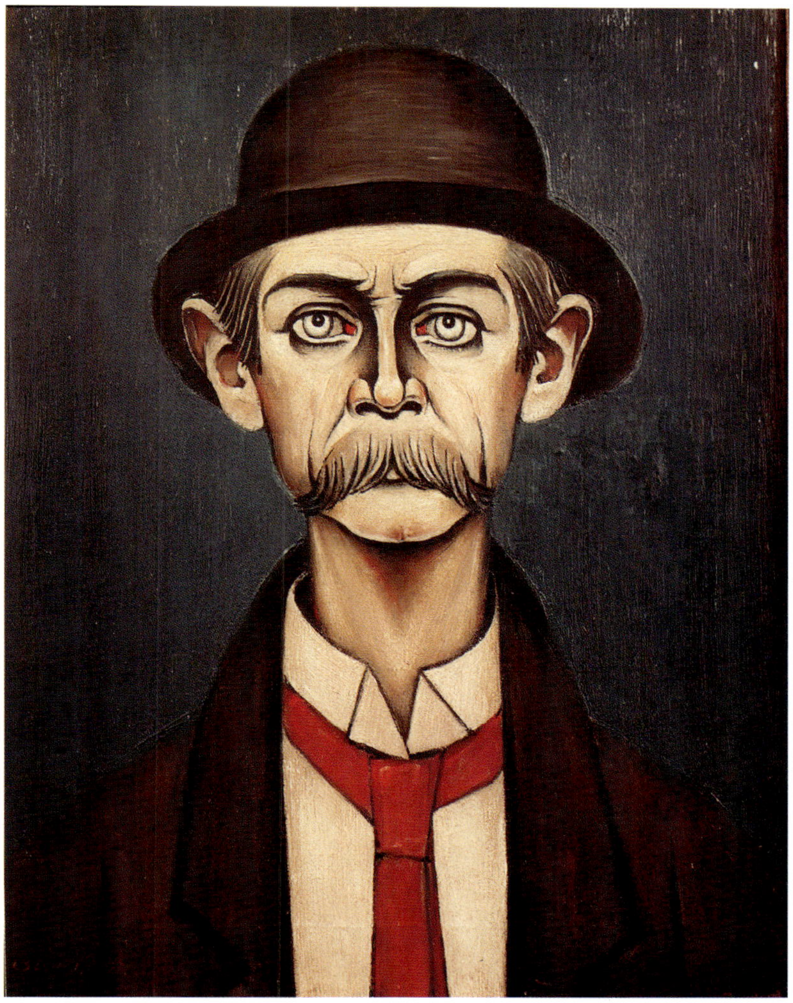

Manchester Man, 1936–7, oil on canvas, 53.3 × 43.2 cm.

Lowry's career – or non-career – it is difficult to think of any other painting by him so replete with raw but yet carefully repressed emotion.

In the same year he also painted the stark, caricatured figure of bowler-hatted red-eyed, inflamed *Manchester Man* (above) who was also a grotesque before his time. 1936 also produced an interesting cross between grotesque and a group portrait of the people waiting to see the Doctor. This usually bears the title *The Doctor's Surgery* (page 150) which makes no sense at all as it is obviously the doctor's waiting room. The dominant figure of the man standing on the left looks very like the paterfamilias of *Family Group* and his finger, covered by an elaborate dressing, is doubtless a souvenir of an accident at the mill. Kalman has pointed out that Lowry loves to paint the back views of children "with their socks up or down"[19] and here there are two, the only characters whose faces you cannot see. The other eleven characters have just as much individuality and personality as you would find in a comparable Daumier and are painted with a similar world-weary humanity. No two faces are alike so that this is no crowd scene. It is barely, even psychologically, a group scene. It is really a series of grotesques gathered together early in Lowry's career so that when he consciously switched away from the industrials he certainly did not have to invent anything new. For all the current observations he made during the 1950s and 1960s of individual oddball human

Always known as *The Doctor's Surgery*, it is clearly actually *The Doctor's Waiting Room*, 1936, oil on canvas, 38.7 × 52.1 cm.

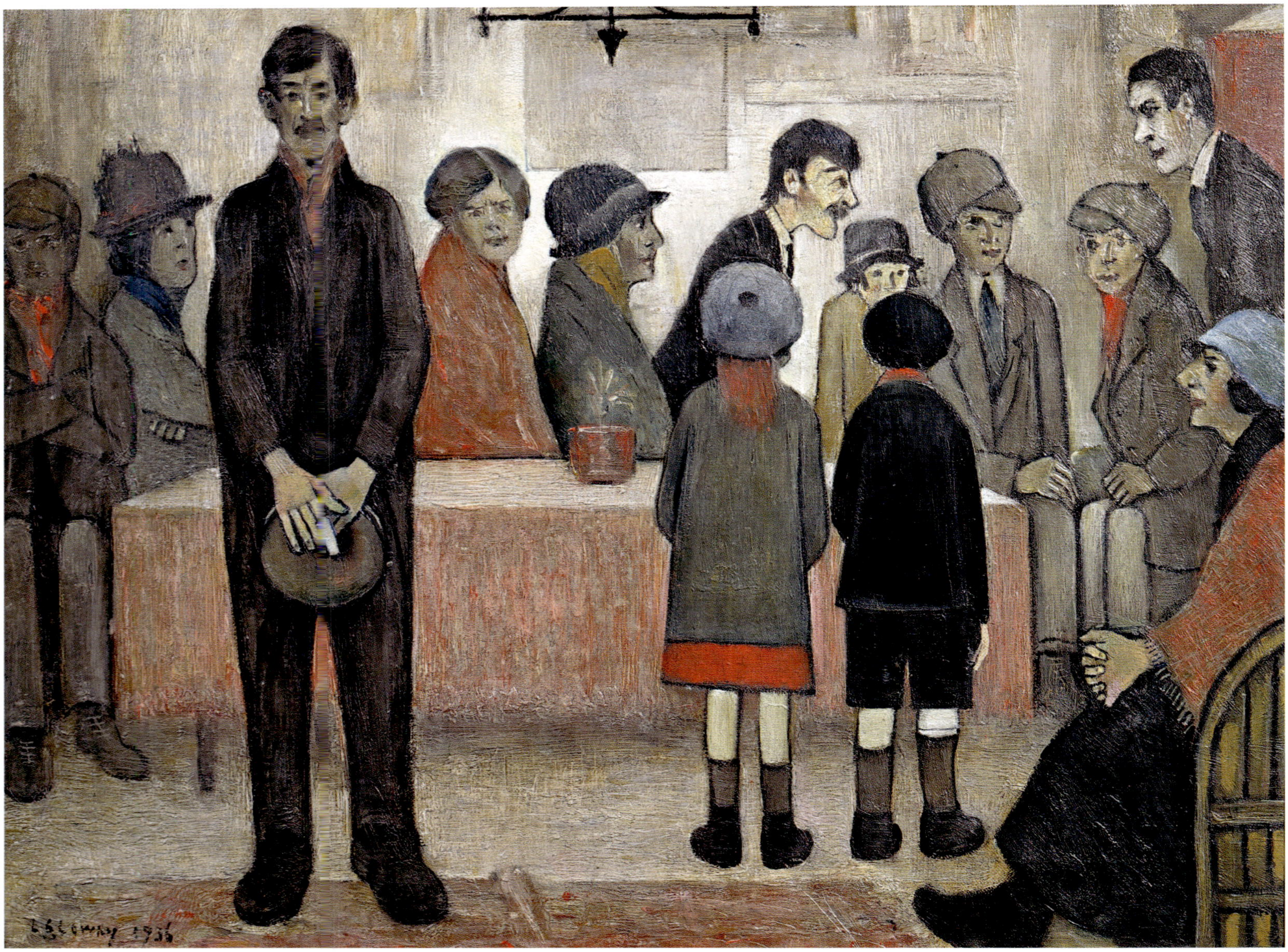

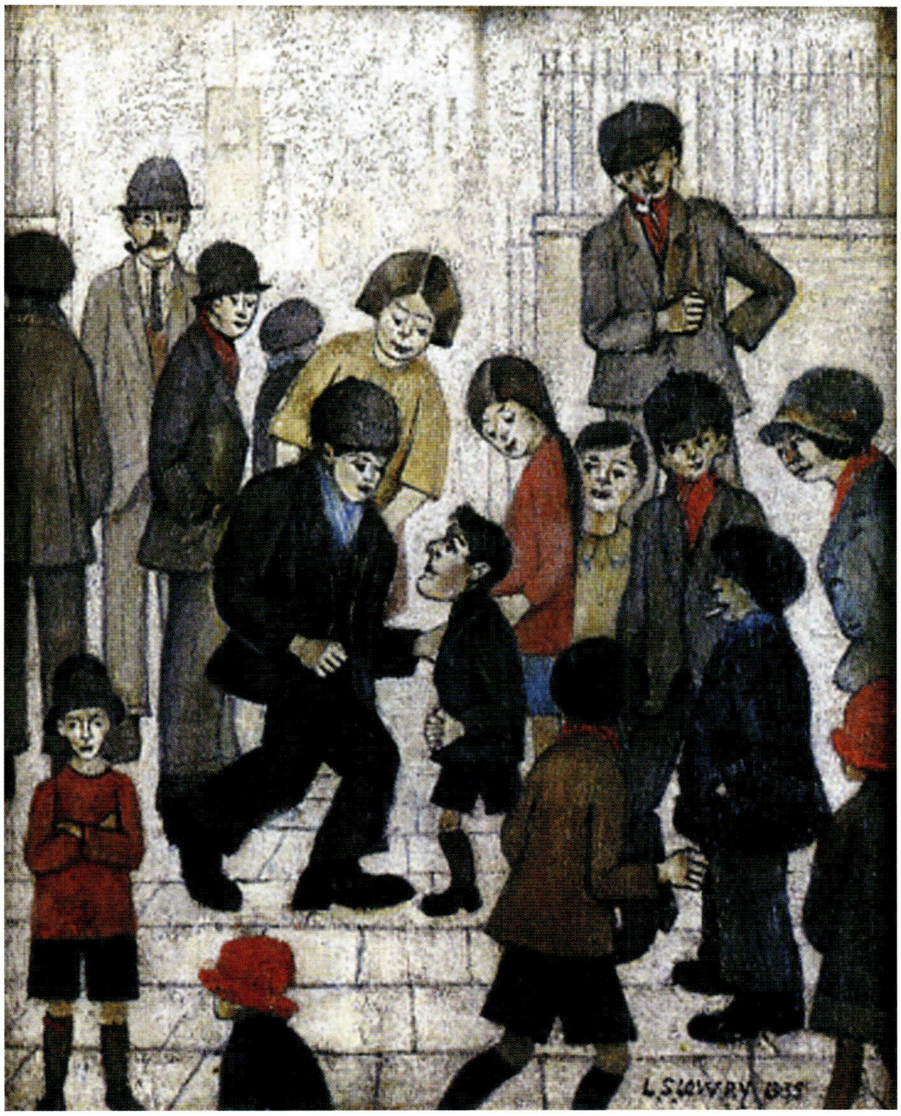

An Argument, 1934, oil on panel, 53.3 × 43.2 cm.

beings, the halt, the lame, the completely crippled, the drunk, even the mad, all had their roots in the reality of Manchester, Stockport and Salford for their immediate physicality. But their deeper roots, not limited to the superficial renderings of their physiognomies, surely go back to these paintings of the 1930s.

In these forerunners of grotesquery he had not yet found his way to caricature. Which is perhaps another way of saying that he had not yet uncovered that vein of cruelty common to so many of those artists who saw the human condition as something one could – and should – laugh at. If this meant, as it did for late Lowry, a strong element of exaggeration then that is as it should be. Exaggeration is the fuel of caricature and Lowry not only practised it but knew he was doing so.

Woman with a Beard of 1957 (page 152) is a perfect case in point. Lowry himself has described how it came about:

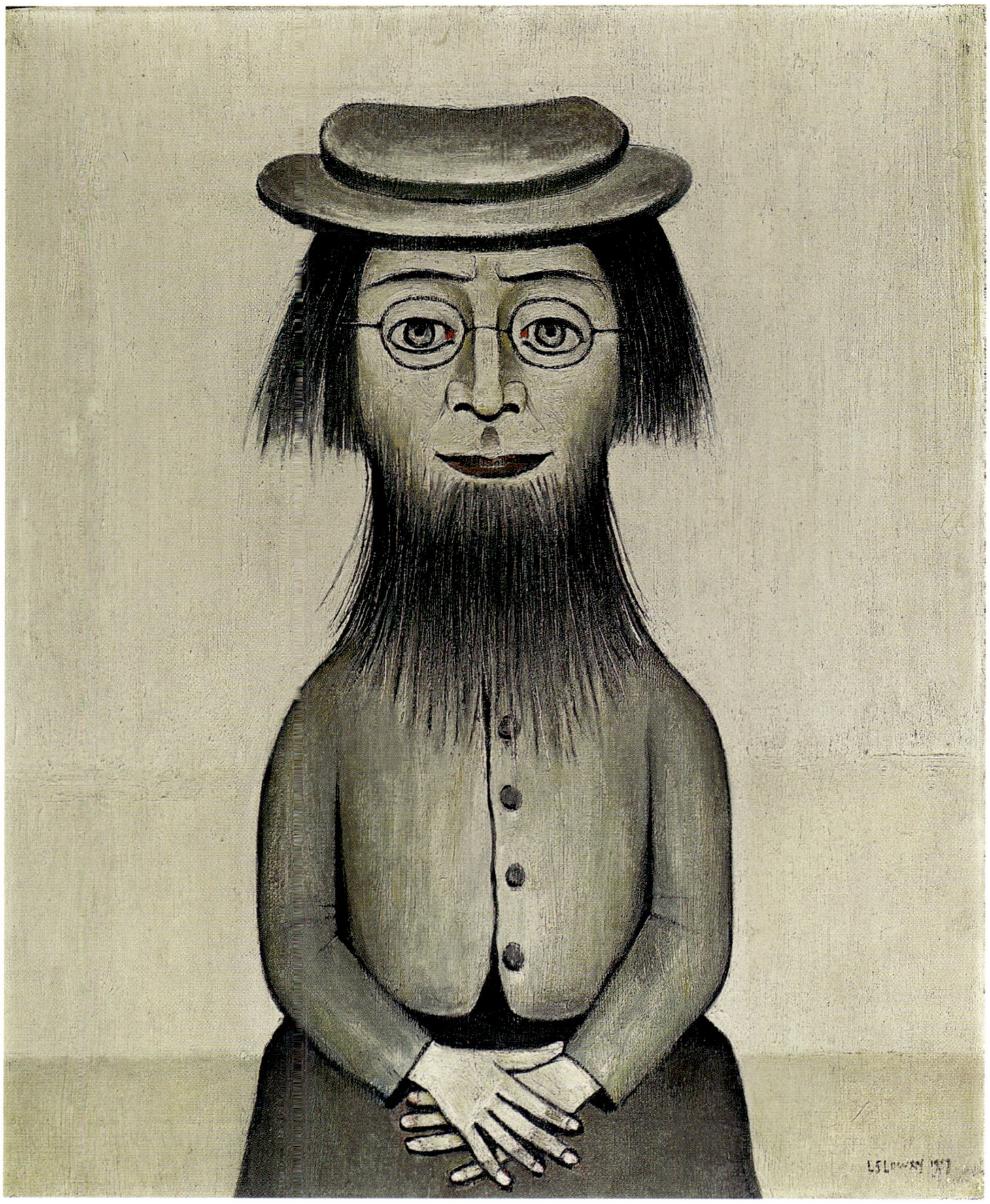

Woman with a Beard, 1957,
oil on canvas, 59 × 49 cm.

> I came on the train, and facing me – facing me – was a lady with a beard, and I couldn't take my eyes off her. I did a quick sketch, but she noticed and said angrily 'What are you doing? What are you drawing?' is how he related the episode to Kalman. To someone else he admitted: "I blushed like a Dublin Bay prawn and showed her my sketch – the one from which I made my painting of her. At first she was greatly troubled but we talked, and by the time we reached Paddington we were the best of friends;[20]

Kalman has expressed the view that "It's probably very exaggerated – she was probably just a whiskery lady".[21]

I'm sure Kalman is right about the exaggeration but then that is the point of the painting. From an ordinary woman with a shaving problem Lowry has made an almost ludicrously

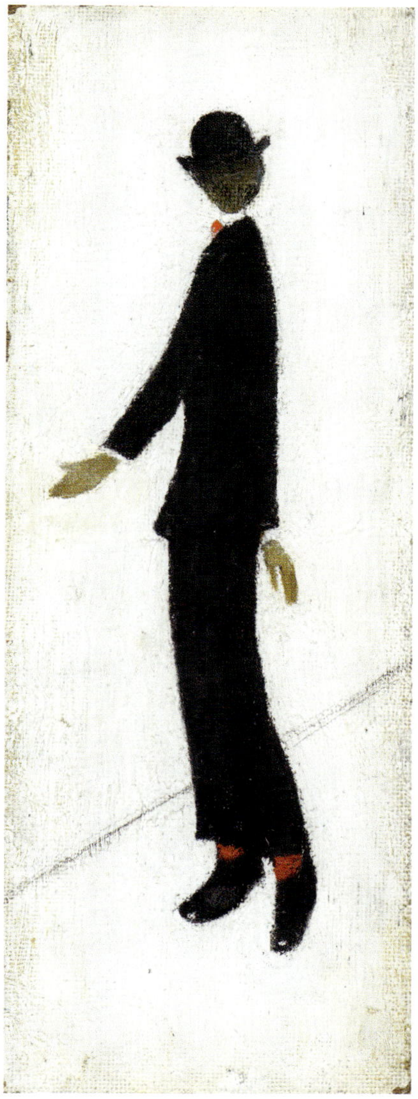

Man with Bowler Hat, (undated), oil on canvas, 52.25 × 31 cm.

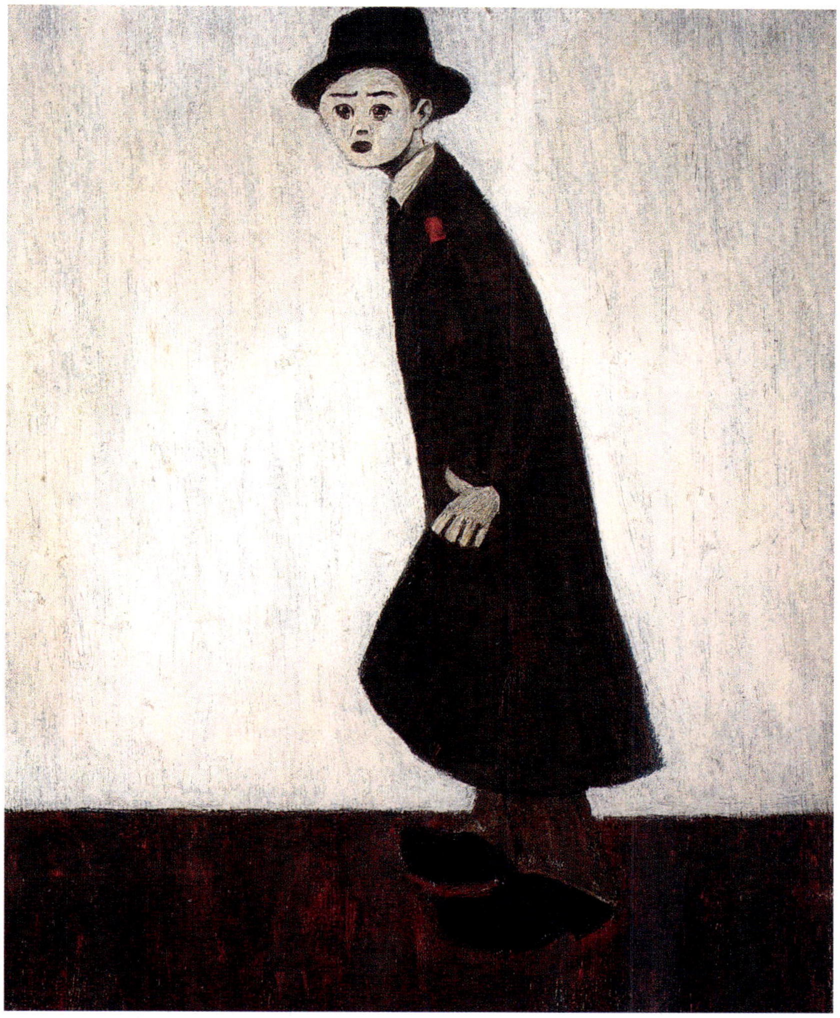

Man in a Trilby, 1960, oil on board, 74.75 × 64.75 cm.

funny picture of almost total improbability. While there are plenty of men who sport beards but shave their upper lip, and thus dispense with a moustache, I've never come across any woman who did that, and, outside the theatrical stage and dodgy 'bearded lady' freak show exhibits at fairs, (which are nearly always fakes), you will never find a woman who would allow herself such a vigorous growth. Although there is a memorable painting by Ribera in the Prado of a luxuriantly bearded woman suckling her child, this is Lowry having a bit of fun and, overall, the face is painted with compassion as well as humour.

In many of the grotesques one can see very clearly the influence of the theatre, in particular the Edwardian theatre of Manchester which Ian McKellen has singled out as a major influence on Lowry's imagery. There are certain paintings of individual human beings which belong far more securely to the theatrical, particularly the music hall stage, rather than the people encountered or observed by Lowry on his rent-collecting perambulations.

If one looks at *Man with Bowler Hat*, undated, (above left) or *Man in a Trilby* of 1960 (above right) and almost certainly painted at about the same time, there is a flamboyant, even faintly exhibitionistic aura, about both figures who would have been quite at home on the boards of the Palace Theatre tap-dancing or singing some sentimental ballad. Both figures are as lean as professional dancers, and although Bowler Hat wears a well-cut suit and

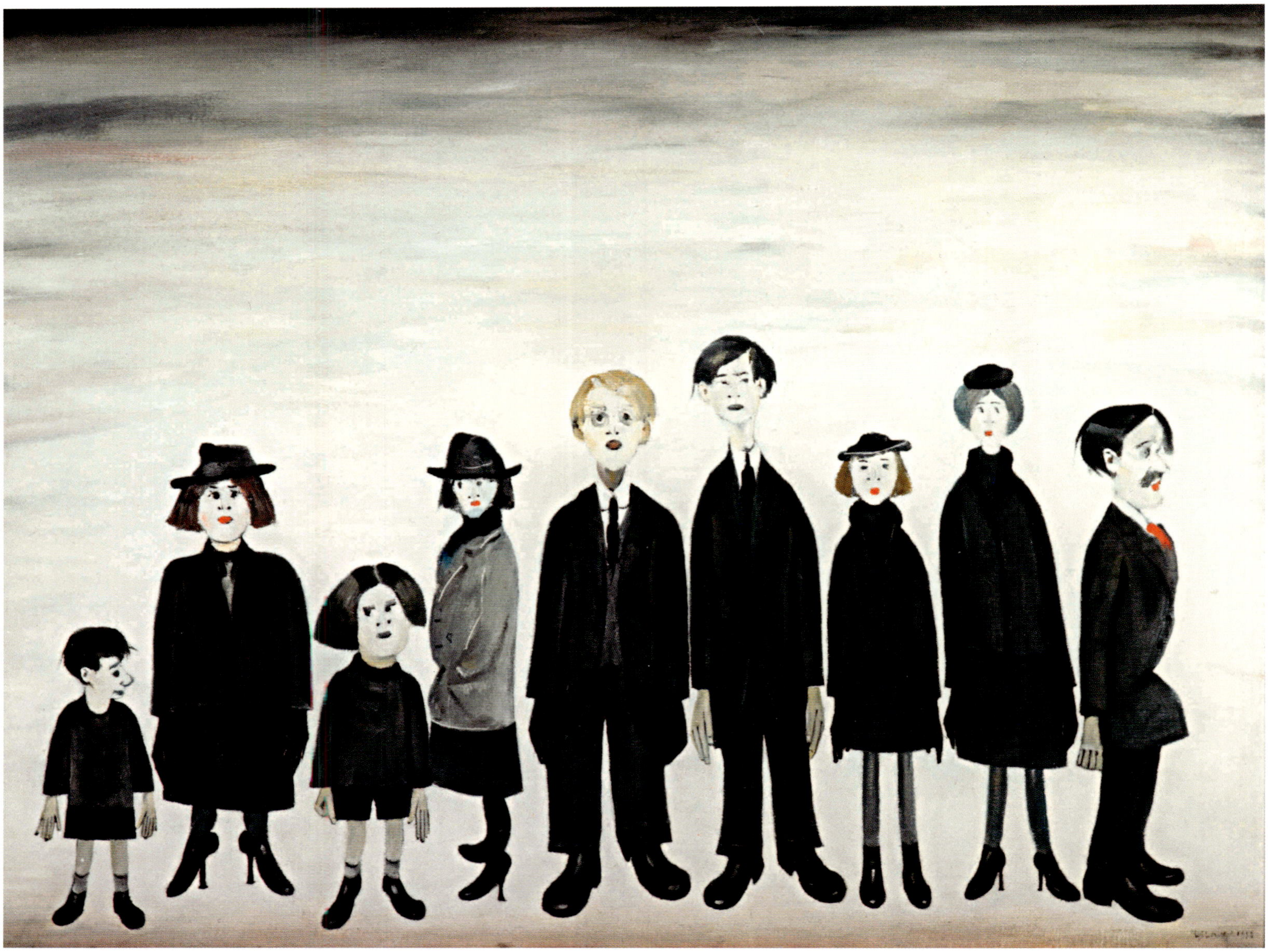

The Funeral Party, 1953,
oil on canvas, 76.1 × 102 cm.

Trilby a well-tailored, very long, overcoat, they could, apart from the sartorial differences be the same person. Bowler Hat's face is hidden while Trilby looks directly at the viewer although there is something mask-like about the face, as if heavily made up with white grease paint, so that he reminds one of the French mime artist Marcel Marceau with his face for once in repose. Interestingly, and indicating that these are almost certainly at least partly imagined figures. There is another picture called *Man with Trilby Hat*, undated, but of the same period which is beyond any reasonable doubt of the same man. He wears a similar overcoat but, instead of the lean, dandified figure in the other picture, Lowry has painted him both shorter and more thick-set. Lowry's viewpoint here gives him a foreshortened vision and the face is painted in a much more rudimentary form, making it even more mask-like than its (assumed) predecessor.

Probably the most powerful of all Lowry's grotesque pictures, as it were, the father of them all is *The Cripples* (page 56). It comes almost as a shock to recall that it is dated 1949 when in fact at that time Lowry was still deeply immersed in his industrials. This simply goes to show that his major decision to switch from industrials to grotesques may have been, when he announced it, both abrupt and apparently arbitrary, but like other decisions and evolutionary changes in an artist's chosen subject matter, the implementation of the decision came from a lot of brooding speculation and careful thought. And if *The Cripples* is the *fons et origo* of the later grotesques, then probably *The Funeral Party* (page 154) of 1953 is a way station on the same journey. After all both *The Cripples* and *The Funeral Party*, while definitely not among Lowry's beloved crowd paintings, are actually quite densely populated and can be seen as signposts to the painting of small groups and eventually of faintly improbable but always diverting individuals. In *Little Girl Seen from the Front* and *Little Girl Seen from the Back* (below), both painted on canvases of the same dimensions, you see the same girl shown as if caught between two facing mirrors. Happily she is not crippled but she might easily be a spare character from *The Funeral Party* for whom Lowry had no room

Little Girl Seen from the Front, (undated), oil on canvas, 78 × 68 cm.

Little Girl Seen from the Back, 1964, oil on canvas, 77.5 × 68 cm.

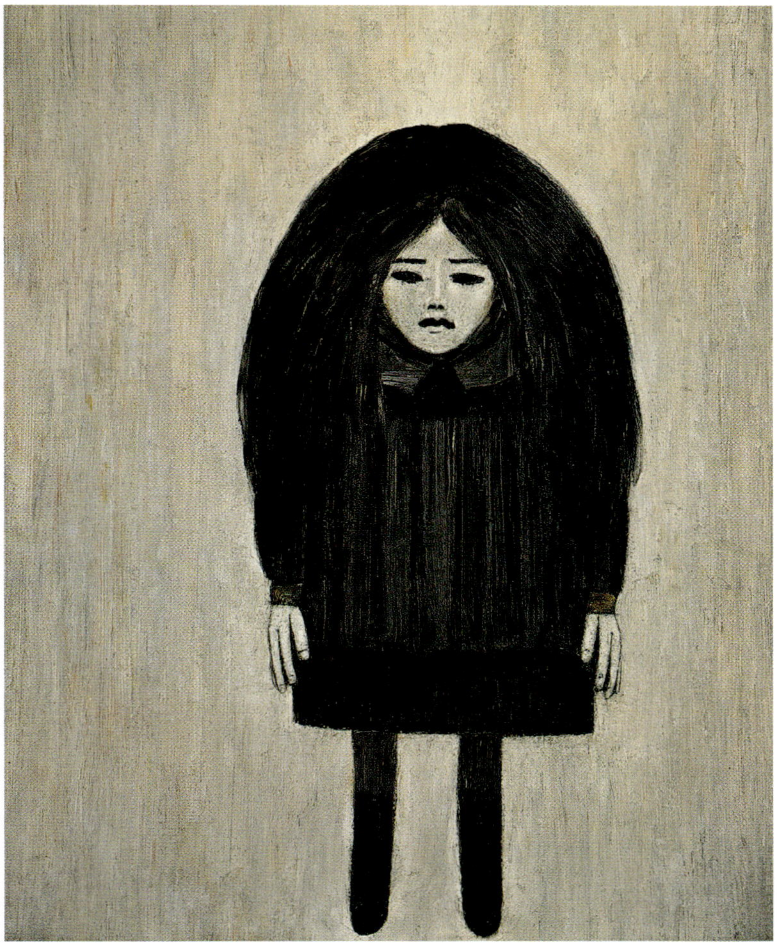

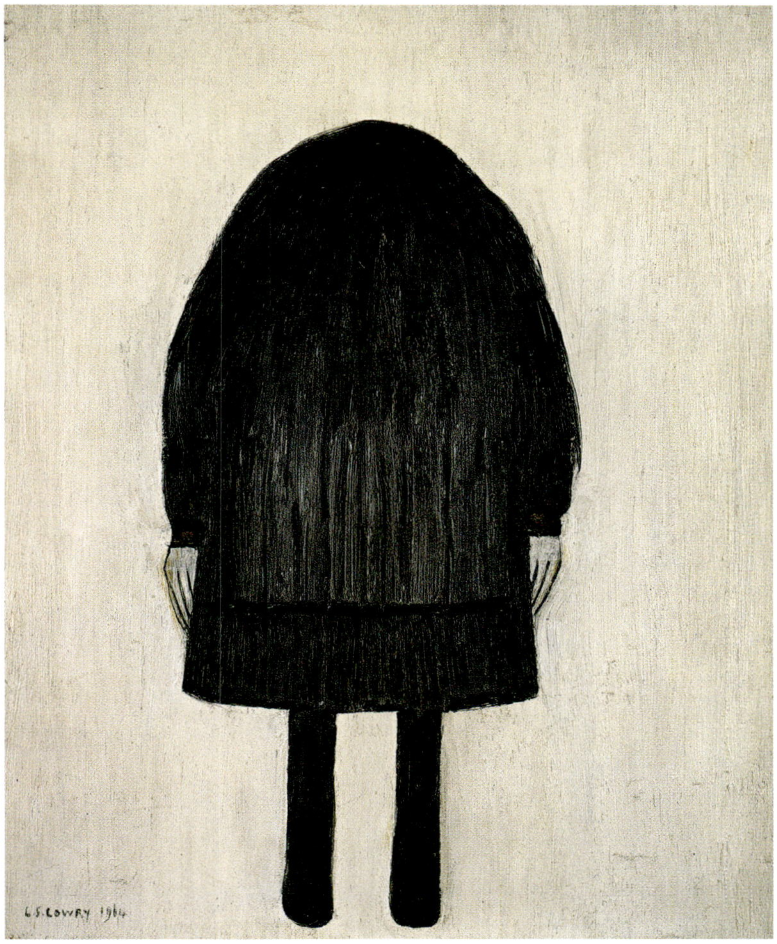

at the time. But she is, for all that, a brilliant invention for a man so dedicated to the use of white paint and the effect of his deep plunge into the density of black is startling. These pictures also testify to Lowry's passion for the work of the pre-Raphaelites in general and Dante Gabriel Rossetti in particular. Rossetti indubitably had a powerful, if multi-coloured and therefore more interesting, hair fetish although it was never quite as improbably luxuriant as the little girl here. But Lowry also had an obsession with masses of female hair and there are plenty of pictures of imaginary women sporting vast amounts of, if not imaginary, then

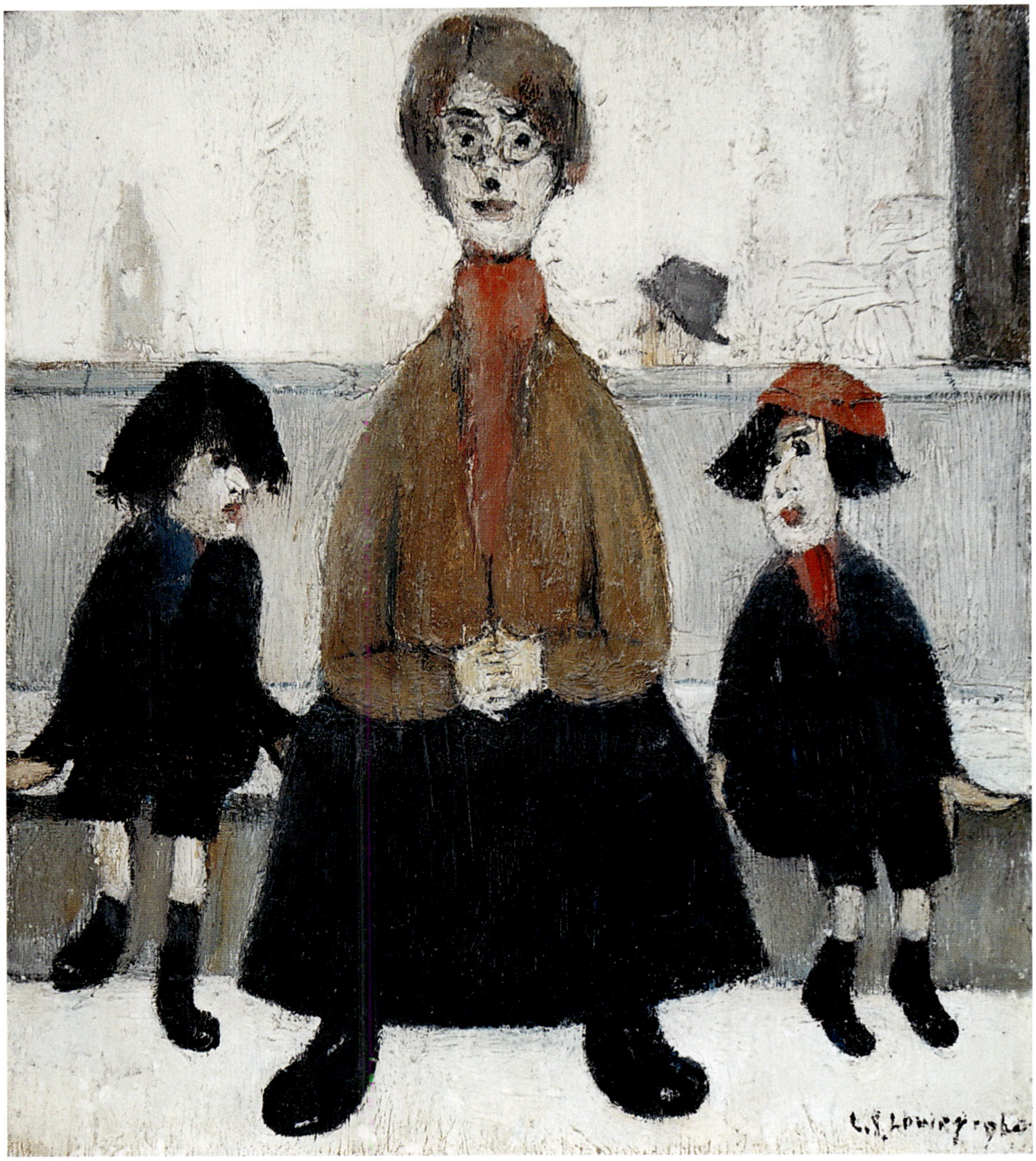

Woman Sitting with Two Children, 1960, oil on board, 27.5 × 24 cm.

surely desirable amounts of hair. This little girl's abundance goes further than any of his other related works which does not mean – oh heaven preserve us from the moronic, sexual excesses of the tabloid press – that Lowry was a pædophile. He just liked women with lots of hair and even he would accept that in these two views of a little girl he has, at least, strayed across the borderline between representation and caricature.

There is one "grotesque" painting, not previously reproduced and held in a private collection which, like so many of these pictures, is untitled, but is dated 1960, the year in which it was bought directly from the artist (page 156).

It is, to state the obvious, a typical Lowry but within its limited space (it is 27.5 × 24 cm.) it crams in many of Lowry's mannerisms and tics. A bespectacled, middle-aged woman sits on a rather uncomfortable ledge jutting out from a wall, (this is definitely not an outdoor bench or seat) flanked by two children of exactly equal height – their heads are positioned very precisely at the same level of the wall against which they are sitting. The one on the right is definitely a boy, wearing a red school cap of more or less the same colour as the woman's scarf. The child on the left, without headgear, is on the whole more female than male, and is almost a mirror image of the boy. Both are in semi-profile, looking towards the centre, their clothes identical except that the one on the right sports a red scarf and the one on the left has a blue one. Blue scarf, although the hair is much the same length and colour as the boy's, does however have a girlish face. On the other hand he or she is wearing the same kind of short trousers as the boy who could he his/her brother. To confuse the issue further, girls at that time and of that age, wore skirts and not short trousers.

If one looks beyond the top of the wall, just over the woman's shoulder there is the head of a man in a battered trilby hat and smoking a cigarette. In the left background one can see the shadowy outlines of some indeterminate, inevitably white sky which, to the right of the picture, adjoining the black pillar on the edge, is painted relatively coarsely, as if applied by his smaller fingers and suggesting some turbulence in the air.

The central figure of the woman is the dominant image but there is absolutely no physical contact, nor any emotional linkage between her and the children. Nor is there any meaningful contact between the children, both of whom seem entirely unblessed by any childhood freedom. I do not believe I am imagining, from the serene, but entirely unengaged countenance of the woman, gazing entirely without emotion through those large spectacles, that this woman looks uncannily like Lowry's portrait of his mother (page 256). This is a very carefully planned and composed painting, as thoroughly ambiguous and thought-provoking as any of the grotesques of this period. One's only surprise is the fact – since it is a very good painting – that it was not snapped up by Monty Bloom as soon as it was finished.

While the market place will doubtless always favour Lowry industrials more than Lowry grotesques, just as it undervalues Lowry's landscapes and seascapes, there is no simple explanation or resolution on grounds of quality for this internal rivalry between the two categories of painting. Neither is 'better than' the other. They are simply different in both subject matter and in emotional involvement.

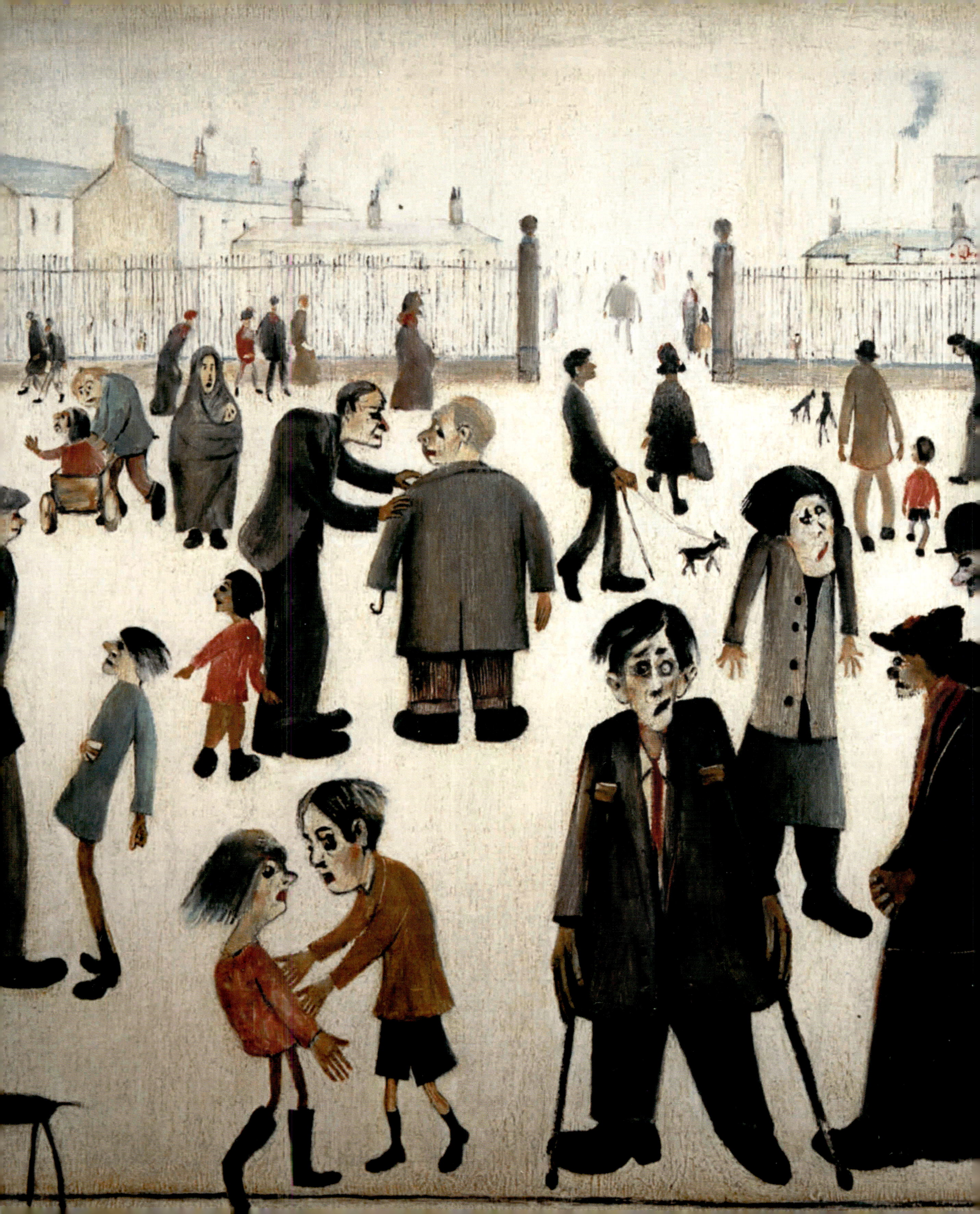

CHAPTER 7

AN INTERLUDE: L. S. LOWRY AND DAVID CARR

... I want to make a name for myself. I have a horror of sinking into oblivion.[1]

David Carr

There is a case to be made that L. S. Lowry is not only a severely underestimated artist but that he is also much misunderstood. I have tried elsewhere in this book to demolish some of the classic misconceptions about Lowry, both artistic and biographical. Some of the misconceptions are simply the fruits of a lack of understanding. That he was a naïve artist, that he was a Sunday painter and so on. All nonsense. Some of the personal, psychological analyses are equally far-fetched. That he did not marry and lived alone meant that he was a recluse, that he was tragically lonely. That he did not marry is dealt with fully in Chapter 13. But he was certainly no recluse and, as I've written elsewhere, he was a solitary which does not mean that he was lonely. He had one peculiarity regarding friendships; he kept his friends in separate compartments of his life; he did not introduce them to each other; he did not keep open house for them or give parties. But, in those days, that was an activity reserved more or less to those higher up the social pecking order and financially better off then Lowry. And, if one has some interesting and close individual friends and if one has been an only child of an inadequate father and a coldhearted but permanently demanding invalid mother, would one not crave the closeness of satisfactory, mutually respecting, individual friendship and might one not decide that those friendships were too valuable to dilute either with other people or too enjoyable as they were without relationships being confused and possibly irreparably damaged by the intrusion of sex?

This is by way of introduction to possibly the most interesting of Lowry's friendships, of paramount interest because it was with a fellow painter of considerable distinction and because it has been, on Lowry's side at least, so well documented. In the library of the Victoria and Albert Museum in London there is a wonderful treasure trove consisting of Lowry's letters to David Carr although, sadly, given Lowry's chaotic housekeeping habits, Carr's replies have not been so carefully preserved, although their relationship began with a long, unsolicited letter from Carr to Lowry enquiring about a possible purchase to follow on one completed acquisition by Carr of *The Mill Chimney* at the Lefevre Gallery in 1943.

Carr was born in November 1915, a son and scion of the Carr biscuit-making dynasty which owned Peek Freans, and lived in palatial Edwardian style in Montrose House at Petersham, near Richmond-on-Thames. Montrose House is a William and Mary mansion built by the Duke of Montrose in the early 17th century. The Carrs were Scottish Quakers and David, like his forbears, was educated at Uppingham and intended automatically for the business. He managed to negotiate time off to read History at Exeter College, Oxford, but left after

Detail from *The Cripples*, 1949, (p.56).

four terms for a tour of Italy, a year in France and an absolute conviction that he would become a painter and not a biscuit-maker.

His father cut him off with a mere £300 a year – about £10,000 in today's money – but his mother supported his ambitions.[2] He studied art briefly at the Byam Shaw School and then at the wonderful East Anglian School of Drawing and Painting at Dedham where his fellow students included the teenage Lucian Freud, Kathleen Hale, the creator of *Orlando the Marmalade Cat*, and Barbara Gilligan whom he married.

Legend has it that Freud and Carr were in the habit of painting and smoking all night and, following an accident, the art school burned down. Local Suffolk myth has it that Sir Alfred Munnings, a former President of the Royal Academy and a notorious hater of "modern art", who lived in Dedham, and had himself driven to watch the fire, called out 'So perishes all modern art. May it all die thus' and other imprecations of similar purport. David Carr made a more constructive memorial to the event in the form of two more-or-less identically-sized oils on canvas in July 1939. Entitled *Dedham Painting School Before the Fire* and *After the Fire*. They were sold recently at Christies South Kensington on 15 July, 2009 almost exactly 60 years after the event Carr participated in and so memorably recorded. (The buyer was Colchester and Ipswich Museums.) The school's joint owners, and instructors, the painters Cedric Morris and Arthur Lett-Haines moved house and school from Dedham to Benton End, near Hadleigh in Suffolk where, inter alia, Kathleen Hale became Lett-Haines's lover and incorporated him as the Katnapper in the *Orlando* books. (Morris had to make do as the Dancing Master.)[3]

At the outbreak of war in 1939 Carr, as a Quaker, was, (like Lowry on health grounds in World War I) excused combat duty and volunteered to serve either in the Merchant Navy or as an ambulance driver in London but was rejected on medical grounds. His first contact with Lowry was the fan letter in 1943 in which he told of already accomplished and possible future purchases. Carr was in fact a very shrewd collector of the work of his contemporaries and this might well have contributed to his neglect by London dealers such as Lefevre who saw him as a valuable connoisseur customer and perhaps therefore ignored his own work which he was, in any case, not overtly ambitious about.

One of his letters to Lowry does survive and is well worth quoting, not least because as a *writer* and stylist he was on a different plane from the barely educated Lowry:

> But unlike you, I try to express my feelings through the buildings alone; the boats, the cranes, the railway trucks are the monsters who live in my world and people it.
>
> Your painting is much more to me than just a decoration on the wall and has given a new vision of town life, and often when not working I wander about trying to see the landscape through your eyes; through the people to their buildings and feel vaguely ashamed of myself for refusing to recognize them in my own work. But it does seem to me that when men build they give their work a character so different from their own souls that I can't begin to fit the two together in a picture. The very problem that you have solved. Please excuse me for talking about my own feelings but I couldn't resist the

> temptation of doing so to someone who understands the soul, the character, or what you will, of those slums and town fringes as you do, in their queer and often ghastly beauty.[4]

In addition to his friendship with Lowry he was close to those pillars of English neo-Romanticism, the two Roberts, Colquhoun and MacBryde and had a long friendship with Prunella Clough who shared his interest, obsession even, in and with industrial buildings and machinery. Ronald Alley perceptively wrote of Carr:

> The theme which now began to pre-occupy him and which runs through all his later figurative works was that of man and machine: not just the beauty and power of machines but their role as the physical extension of our living bodies.[5]

Bryan Robertson, who showed some of Carr's work at the Whitechapel Art Gallery of which he was by far the most important director in the last century wrote:

> He was a maverick, fundamentally an auto-didactic one-man band, and no respecter of authority if it imposed in any way on his own ideas, opinions and activities.[6]

Robertson's description might be applied almost word-for-word to L. S. Lowry. For all Carr's matinée idol good looks, formidable cultural knowledge and sheer charisma of character, he was in many ways made in the same artistic mould as Lowry. Usually friendship is quite awkward if the two parties are too similar. But in the case of Carr and Lowry there is no competition, just a convergence of interests and the shared passions of similar curiosities.

Tragically, Carr learned in 1960 that he had an incurable cancer. He fought it bravely but died on 28 November, 1968. Robertson believed – and so do I – that Lowry had an artistic influence on Carr although in my opinion the reverse was not true. "Lowry in the whites of sea and sky, black horizon lines and cold blue reds and grey green; and Freud, marginally, in the big close-ups of heads and graphic delineation of feature."

Both Lowry and Carr received little recognition and enjoyed little success until late in their careers and lives. Carr in fact died before he had a proper, substantial one-man show in New York in 1969 and his first London exhibition at the Mayor Gallery, in 1987, took place nearly two decades after his death.

The two paintings reproduced here, *Cleaning the Nets, Lowestoft* of 1949 (page 162) and his *Self Portrait and Still Life* of 1947 (page 163) are totally unlike Lowry's but they are in tune with, in sympathy with, what and how Lowry painted and thought.

The bulk of the Lowry letters date from 1944 and 1945 and continue until early 1954. Many of them are simple, functional documents setting out time and place for the next meeting or conveying, in fairly stilted form, seasonal good wishes for birthday and Christmas or New Year to Carr and his family. The letters, sometimes postcards, are all resolutely begun with the words 'Dear Mr. Carr'. Lowry was, even for his time, rather rigorously old-fashioned and any male interlocutor, known or unknown, was invariably addressed in a Johnsonian manner as 'Sir' in conversations. To be fair, Bryan Robertson has noted in his monograph

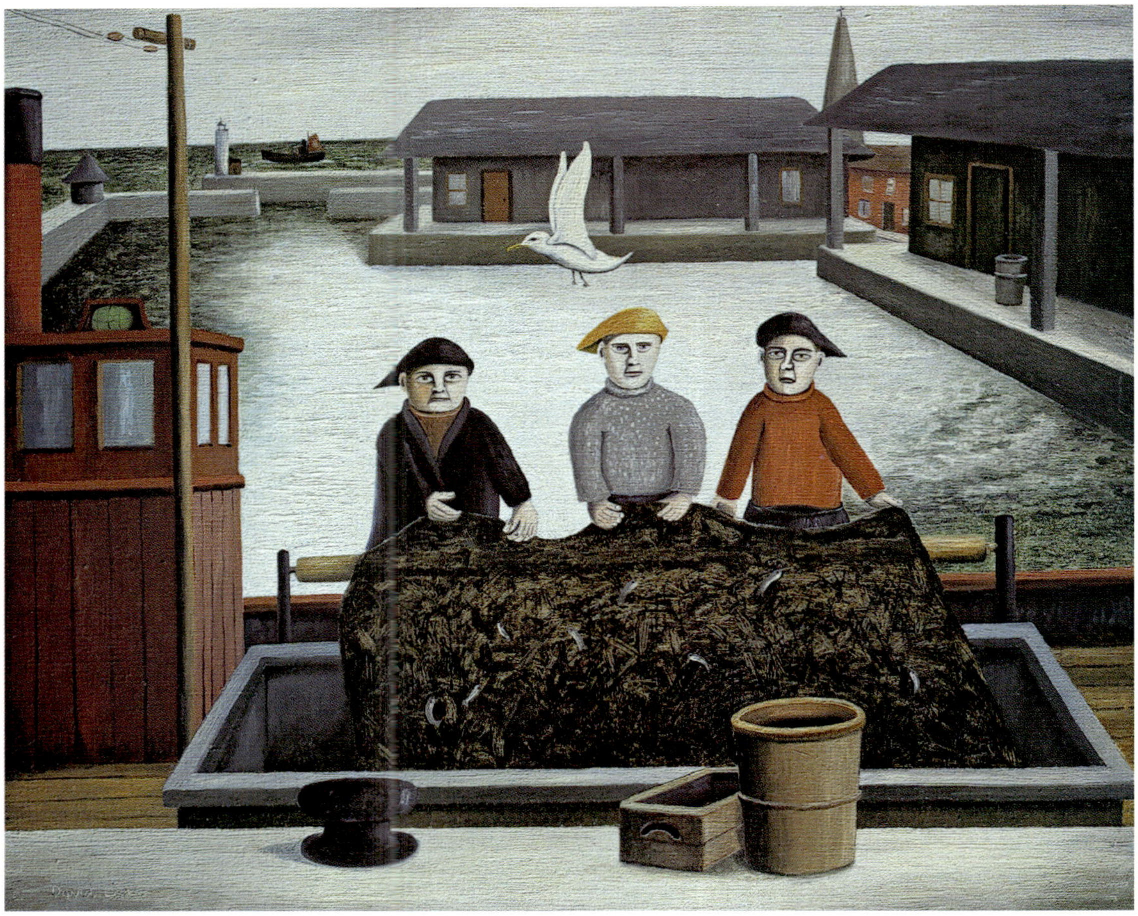

Cleaning the Nets, Lowestoft,
by David Carr, 1949, oil on canvas,
61.6 × 76.2 cm.

on Carr that when Carr and Prunella Clough visited Lowry at Mottram-in-Longendale Carr always addressed Lowry as 'Mr. Lowry'.[7]

L. S. Lowry to David Carr November 24 1944

I am glad that you still like that beach scene. That is what we all want you know: and what you say about my work is very good …

October 8 1945

I thought these drawings might prove interesting to you – how dreadfully crude and ill drawn, weren't they – those very first memory impressions …

22 December 1945

I am full of passion. For some time I have been going down a street in Manchester with a lively level crossing with the oldest of engines crossing the road every time. This engine was blocking up the way. Men with red flags and so on. I think it downed [sic] upon me, as I lay in my little bed one night what a subject it was and I turned to the spot the next day at the same time – no engine – no flags and all clear and that has

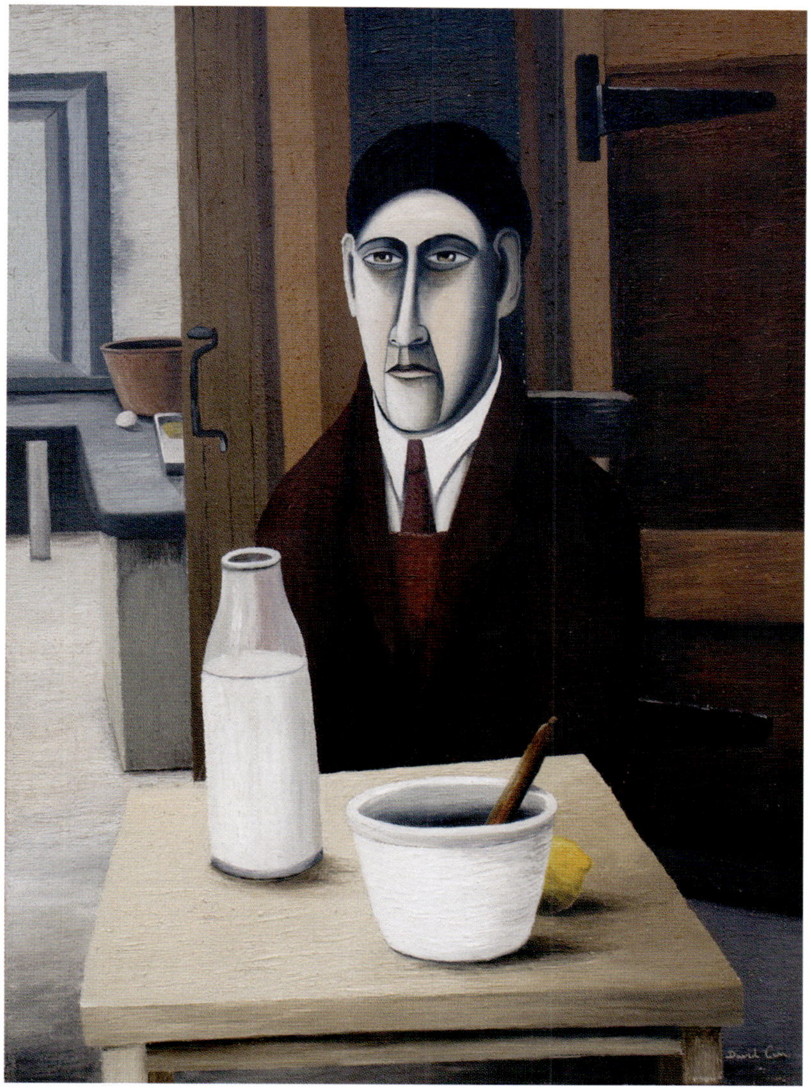

Self Portrait and Still Life, by David Carr, 1947, oil on canvas, 84.5 × 62.7 cm.

happened every time since, it is simply impossible to visualize an engine so dilapidated – a lovely broken down engine – I am a sad man! *[This letter, simultaneously both sad and funny is just like one of the monologues of the North Country comedian Al Read whose speech patterns, on radio at least, were very close to those of Lowry himself.]*

October 20 1946

P.S. I declare I am forgetting to tell you how I got on in the Cotswolds – had a very good weekend – there is plenty of material – I should have to deal with it in my own way – the villages and towns … [appeal] in a certain sort of way to me – I didn't make any sketches then but am going again early next year … The villages are certainly very quaint. The stone (the buildings are mostly of stone) is very warm – I noticed that at once, as quite different from the stone in Lancashire and Yorkshire, which is cold and hard and bleak. *[It is perhaps odd that in the passage quoted above Lowry does not mention his commissioned, and on the whole excellent, drawings he did in 1930 for the book* A Cotswolds Book *with text by H. W. Timperley published in 1931 by Jonathan Cape.]*

7 November 1946

[After a characteristic moan about ageing (he was 59) Lowry writes:]
Thank you for the Glasgow drawings and from what you say, you seem like me to have a passion for grave-yards.

September 13 1948

The 'Cripples' picture is prospering – I have operated on one of the gentlemen in the far distance and given him a wooden leg – I think you would approve. I still laugh heartily at the hook on the arm of the gentleman. That suggestion of yours was a masterstroke.

November 2 1948

Here The Cripples are very good and behaving themselves and none of them are undergoing any operations at present. [*It is difficult not to notice a certain sadistic glee in Lowry's comments on his painterly victims. Furthermore much of the later correspondence is, on Lowry's side at least, full of travel logistics and an ever-increasing valetudinarianism, full of gloom and doom about his body 'breaking up'. One cannot avoid noticing, as one reads further in Lowry's letters, that he is at his happiest and most cheerful when he is grumbling in his health obsessions and misery, is he, one cannot help wondering, acting out his mother's hypochondria with which he lived so long?*]

September 7 1949

I am sorry tho' that you couldn't tell whether those were dogs or horses in the [mixed] show picture – I am afraid I annoyed a member of the show very much when he came to have a look at it … but for the life of me I couldn't bring myself to alter them as they were so much [alive?]

November 6 1952

Yesterday I had a friend and his wife here, who were passing through Manchester who, foolish people, thought they knew everything about my pictures – it completely shook them. They had never seen anything like it. They were holding forth as it were. So I just thought I'd give them something to think about, and their reactions to it were beyond my wildest hopes.

[*Lowry could, when he wished, be quite malicious but alas there is no record of what he shocked this innocent couple with. Lowry was, as we know, a reluctant 'official' painter. So it's not surprising that he wrote to Carr on 28 August, 1953 regarding his* Coronation Picture*:]*
I have nearly finished the picture, just a straightforward view from my seat at the top of the Mall facing the Palace, with part of the Victoria Memorial on the left-hand side. I had to bring in the Coach (or a suggestion of it) with Horseguards following. I wonder what you will think of it. I had to resist the temptation of depicting one or two amusing things I saw that day. It wouldn't have done, no, not quite the thing the authorities had in mind, I am afraid. *[The 'Authorities' acknowledged the picture and sent it to our Moscow Embassy, much to Lowry's delight since he was aware that the Russians liked his industrial paintings therefore believing that Lowry was a Communist.*[8] *According to Rohde*

in her biography published first in 1979 by then the Coronation painting had gravitated to the Embassy's second spare bedroom.]

[Clearly Carr had asked Lowry about his painting techniques because on 25 January, 1954 Lowry responded with an explanation of his huge exploitation of white, a colour much used also by Carr in his oil paintings:]

I nearly always give a canvas a good coat of zinc white and let it dry thoroughly. It may be months – or weeks – before I work on it. And at times, but not often I give it a thick coat of zinc white and work on it while it's wet – but I invariably coat the canvas with this white before I work on it. I never use Foundation White – always zinc. I don't know why really. I simply seem to prefer zinc. I have been speaking of the prepared canvases ... I have never prepared my own – does that tell you what you need to know?

While not a recluse Lowry could be both reserved and shy. When it came to an invitation to stay with Carr and his family – he and Barbara had four children – Lowry resisted, concerned at how he might be received by the Carr's children. But, after appropriate persuasion he yielded, greatly enjoyed himself in the Carr's bohemian, spartan but always lively household and appreciated the children as they appreciated him, even if they tended to see him as a figure of fun who could, with very little persuasion, play games with his false teeth, in those days more or less *de rigueur* among the working class but rarely to be found in the Carr social class. As with so many artists Lowry's carapace of occasional malign glee at the misfortunes of others and his sometimes frosty reserve with new people was simply a protective device to conceal his essentially warm humanity.

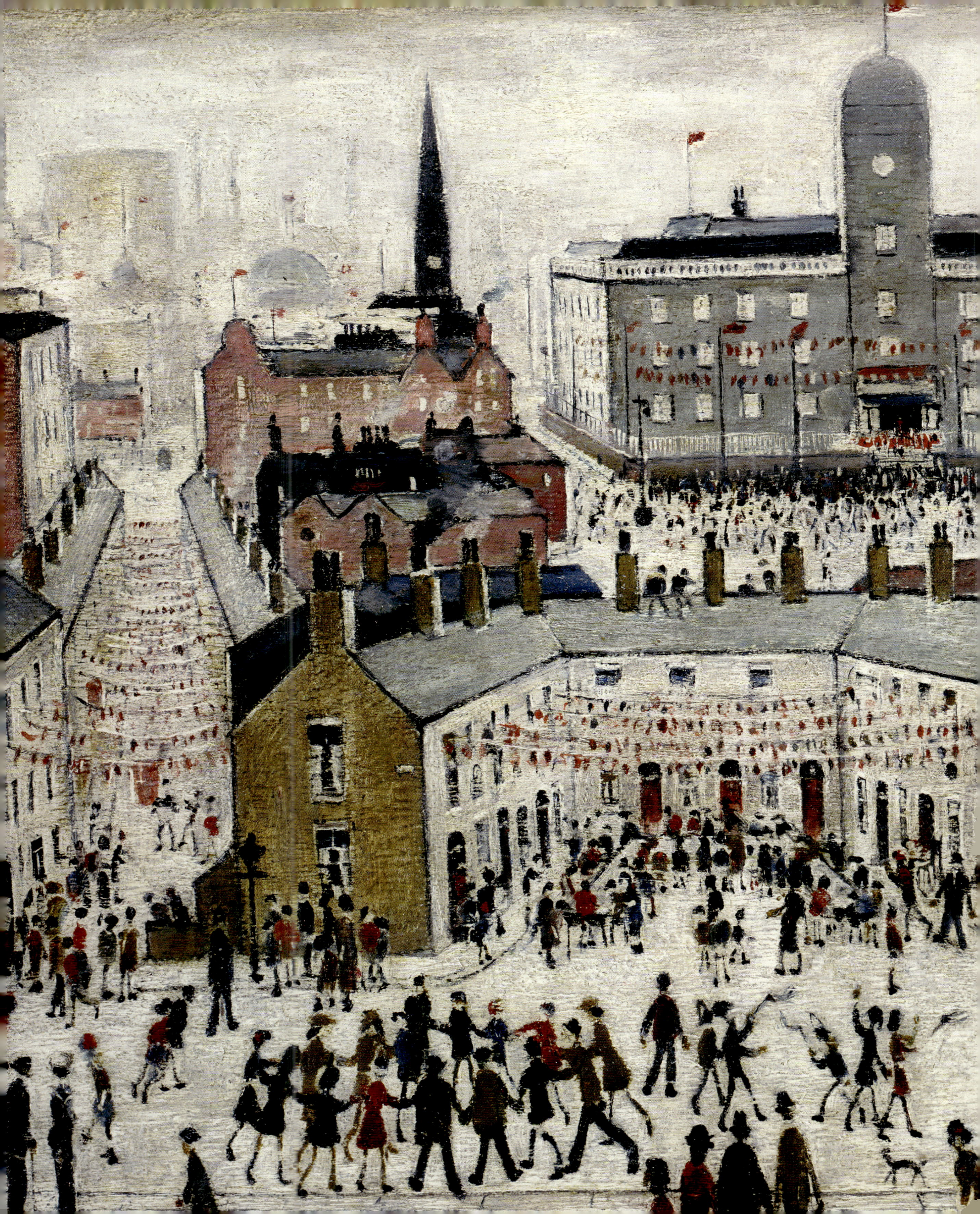

CHAPTER 8

LOWRY AND CROWDS

He observed all these people from under his lashes with urgent repugnance. It always happened like this: he thought he was normal, like everyone else, when he imagined the crowd in abstract, a great, positive army united by the same feelings, the same ideas, the same aims; and it was comforting to be part of this. But as soon as individuals emerged out of that crowd, his illusion of normality shattered against the fact of diversity. He did not recognize himself at all in them and felt both disgust and detachment. What did he have in common with those three sinister, vulgar individuals, that streetwalker, that white-haired old man, that breathless and humble mother. Nothing except this disgust, this pity.[1]

Alberto Moravia

Besides, he liked these contacts with the crowd, unpleasant and uncomfortable as they were, and preferred them to contact with individuals; from a crowd, he thought, as he stood on tiptoes on the platform to breathe more freely, he got the comforting sensation of multiple communion, whether it involved being crushed inside a bus or the patriotic enthusiasm of a political rally. But individuals only caused him to doubt himself and others, like this morning during his visit to the ministry.[2]

Alberto Moravia

The two passages above, used as epigraphs to this chapter, are highly ambiguous if it is a matter of deciding whether the fictitious character who sets these thoughts down is on the side of the crowds or whether he is aloof, and actually dislikes them. The character, Marcello Clerici, whose life is recorded in what is perhaps Moravia's most powerful novel, *The Conformist,* a work far more impressive than the more popular, more celebrated *The Woman of Rome*, is a classic example of a well-off, advantaged intellectual who gets sucked into the Italian Fascist movement. Once sucked in he is compelled to assassinate the distinguished philosopher who had taught him at university and has escaped Fascism to live in exile in Paris.

One might well ask what all this has to do with L. S. Lowry or, indeed, what Lowry has to do with Fascism. Obviously Lowry was not remotely a Fascist but Fascism has always had an appeal for crowds and has thrived, as the history of the 1930s makes clear, by and with and on its establishment and control of crowds. Take the crowds away and Mussolini, Hitler, Franco and Oswald Mosley become joke figures as Charlie Chaplin so brilliantly demonstrated in *The Great Dictator.* Yet, if one were to stop the reasonably well educated

Detail from *VE Day*, 1945, (p.194).

man-in-the-street and asked him what images the name L. S. Lowry conjured up, he would doubtless respond with industrial landscapes full of factories and gigantic chimneys and crowds whether straggling or dense, but definitely crowds. And there's little doubt that Lowry's attitude to those crowds was distinctly ambiguous; certainly as ambiguous as those of Clerici. Moravia's Clerici was in fact, whatever his true feelings, a cold-blooded monster of a man, capable of lust but not love, totally lacking any moral compass, ready to kill for the Party the one man who had helped to shape what little good there was in him, namely his fine intellect. Lowry was not like that at all. He could be reserved and distant until he got to know and trust someone. He was, as has been frequently noted, not as conventionally assumed, a recluse, but definitely a solitary.

This makes his obsession with crowds all the more odd but, as we also know, he *was* an odd, eccentric man. Why else would so solitary, so *independent* a spirit devote so much of his creative energy to the depiction of crowds, possibly one of the most difficult and complex of all forms of painting if one excludes those painstaking artists who specialized in records of battles or other images of soldiers on parade or whole armies on the move.

Perhaps it was Pieter Brueghel the Elder, whom Lowry greatly admired and who has never been equalled in his understanding of the common man and in his almost uncanny ability to fill a canvas with dozens of every type of human oddity who influenced him in that direction; whether merry in mood as in *Peasant Wedding* in Vienna or grotesquely macabre as in the Prado's *Triumph of Death.*

Lowry, like most artists, did not much appreciate having influences attributed to him, particularly if that influence was world famous. But his ever tactful friend and patron, Professor Hugh Maitland, did manage to extract this admission from Lowry as to the power of Brueghel whom he prodigiously admired:

> Oh, it is common sense. [Brueghel] did the industrial scene as he knew it in his day and I did it in my day, so it is natural that critics make comparisons between his work and mine. It jumps to the eyes. When he was alive he saw the industrial scene around him and he did it. Now four hundred years later I saw the industrial scene around me and I did it. And with him, people said 'what are you doing these things for? Nobody wants pictures like this!' and funnily enough they have said the same thing to me.[3]

That is a revealing quotation, partly because Lowry is willingly admitting an influence, even a source for his kind of painting and partly, as the reader of any of the interview transcriptions in Chapter 1 will recognize, Lowry was a man who chose his words carefully and, in this particular case, had no problem in bracketing himself with Brueghel. Note the last words: 'they have said the same thing to me'. An influence is one thing but claiming parity, as he is slyly doing, is absurd. I yield to no one in my personal enthusiasm for Lowry's art but any *comparison* between him and Brueghel is almost too absurd to contemplate and should perhaps not deserve any further discussion. In fairness to Lowry he might, in his linkage to Brueghel, have been in jest.

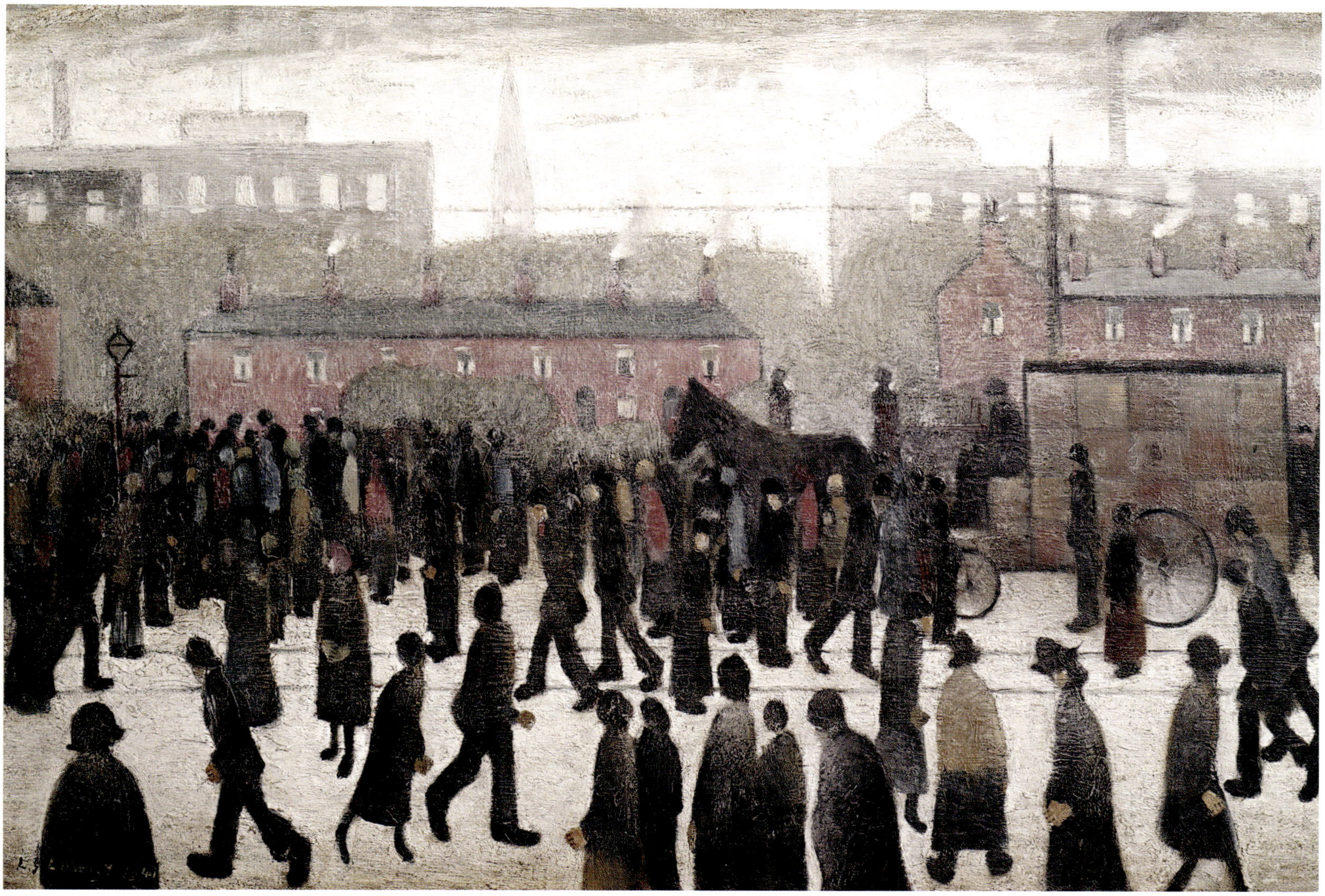

The Old Horse Ambulance, 1941, 43.2 × 61 cm.

Howard Jacobson has written with typical clear-sightedness about Lowry's attitudes to crowds, with such insight that I can even forgive him his use of the phrase 'matchstick figures', normally so anathematic to me:

> But for the most part these matchstick figures hurry off the canvas, the forward slope of their bodies suggesting not just dejection, or the bad weather that is partly instrumental to that dejection, but a sort of propulsion disconnected to their wills, some going left, some going right, the difference in their direction their only distinguishing characteristic, but no reason, really, why those going left shouldn't be going right, and vice versa. Dwarfed by the mills, the chimneys and the chapels, *they are foreground without function*, the very peremptoriness with which they're drawn – for why would one reduce the various and abundant fleshiness of humanity to a matchstick silhouette? – *the proof that their individuality is not what matters to Lowry. They are a crowd, a cluster, a congregation*, viewed by someone who is not of them – not contemptuously or satirically,

> but from somewhere they are not – figures of loneliness themselves, congregating and yet separate, a mystery to the painter. And that's the subject – not their street-corner, ragamuffin heritage vitality, and not their servitude to capitalism – but their mystery.[4]

The ambivalence seen by Jacobson is not unlike that of Clerici in the Moravia passages at the beginning of this chapter.

While Lowry's engagement with crowds is probably the only parallel with Brueghel, if relative quality and painterly skill are brought into consideration, there is one other artist, in this case a near contemporary of Lowry's, whose involvement and re-creation of crowds is, in its sheer ambition and obsessiveness, worth comparing with Lowry. The half-Flemish, half-English James Ensor (1860–1949) was, with Paul Delvaux and René Magritte, one of the remarkable triumvirate of Belgian artists who dominated the first half of the 20th century. in that country. Although Ensor was a compulsive self-portraitist, and painted superb still lifes, his most recognizable works are his savage cartoons, brutally satirizing his *bêtes noires* in medicine and the law. But his greatest works, many dating back to the 1880s and 1890s were of large groups and huge crowds, often watching a seminal event such as an execution, e.g. the oil painting *The Execution* of 1893 or the gathering of *The Cuirassiers at Waterloo*, a coloured drawing of 1891. Occasionally the pictures are quite jolly, as in another large, coloured drawing of *The Baths at Ostend* (1890). His generally acknowledged masterpiece, now confined to the Getty Museum at Malibu (because too fragile and vast to travel), measuring 2.57 metres in height and 4.30 metres wide, shows *Christ's Entry into Brussels*. Painted in 1884, when Ensor was only 29, it is a virtuoso engagement with the art of painting and the nature of humanity *en masse* and one cannot help wondering what Lowry would have made of it and of its creator. But as Ensor's reputation was slow to reach England and the only significant British exhibition of his work was after Lowry died, and as Lowry did not travel abroad, one has to assume that he never encountered Ensor's work. Overall Ensor's attitude to crowds was, unlike Lowry's, unambiguous, although it might be more accurate to suggest that Ensor's primary feeling for crowds was misanthropic which was not the case with Lowry. But where the attitudes of these two great artists differed most strikingly was Ensor's habitual, indeed obsessive, use of masks. Nearly all of Ensor's best paintings of people in groups or crowds show the human figures as faceless, their physiognomy completely concealed by masks. Lowry's people, at least when they are big enough are carefully differentiated and full of individual character and, on the whole, are regarded with friendly curiosity. But they are of course limited to what Lowry sees, or at least thinks he sees. He is, after all, a painter, not a camera. Ensor's masks may conceal the subject's (or the victim's) true facial features, but what he paints in his masks is just as infinitely varied as the faces we are not allowed to see. The emotions of the masks are fully human even if most of them portray the less estimable emotions such as greed, lust, cynicism, envy, simple-mindedness. Ensor is, in his masks, able to create all the follies of man and to expose the darker side of human conduct. He also lacks Lowry's self-imposed restrictions on colour. So that his range and richness of colour allies itself to his vivid senses both of recall and invention to make

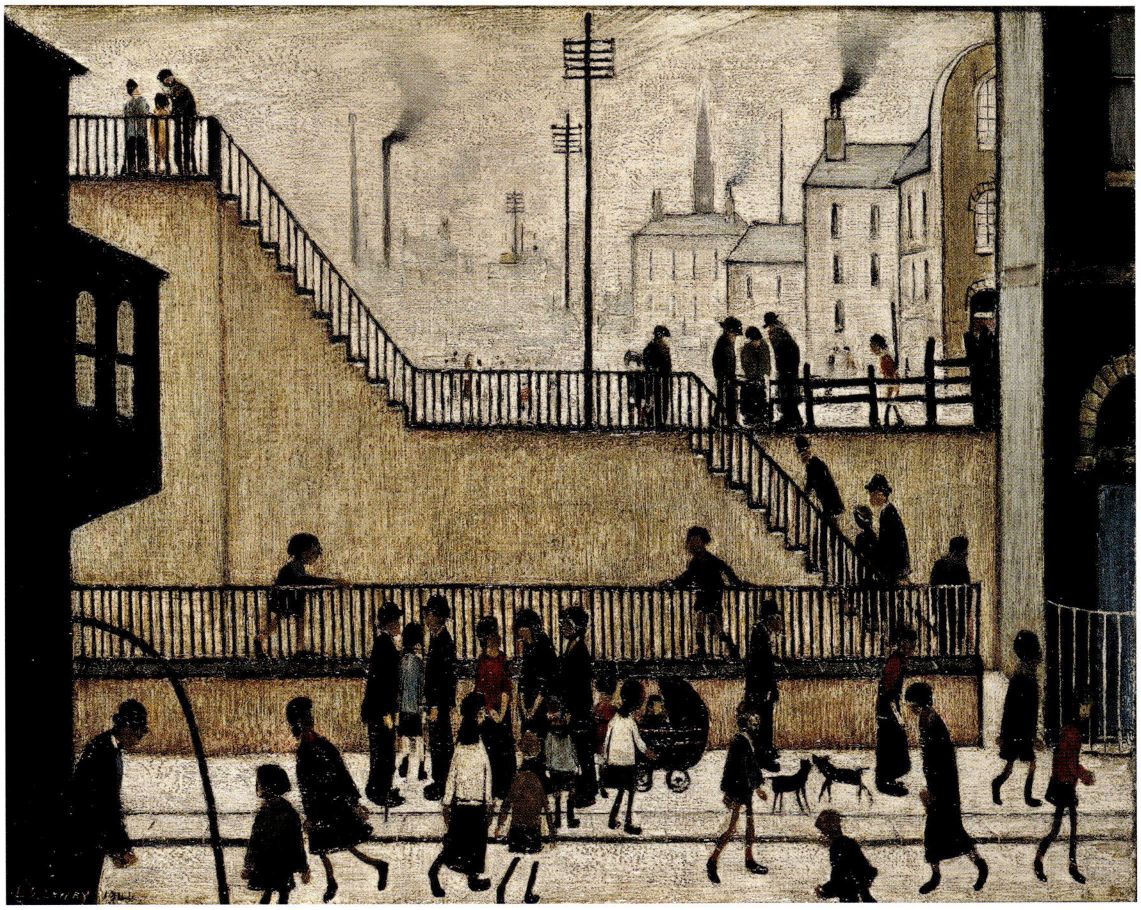

The Steps, 1944, oil on canvas, 41 × 51 cm.

his crowds of masks operate at more numerous and greater emotional depths than Lowry's plain, unadorned industrial faces. But if faced by that old question as to whether one would like, when alone on a dark night, to be suddenly faced by a Lowry crowd or an Ensor crowd I would seek shelter the moment I set eyes on a multi-coloured, sinister Ensor mob.

Kenneth Clark also was quite captivated by Lowry and crowds as in his introduction to the exhibition entitled *A Tribute to L. S. Lowry* held at the Monks Hall Museum in Eccles in 1964:

> All those black people walking to and fro are as anonymous, as individual, as purposeless and as directed as a stream of real people who pass before our eyes in the square of an industrial town.[5]

As we know from the rise and fall of Fascism, power can ebb and flow with crowds. Their capacity for exploitation and abuse of the antithesis of the crowd, i.e. the individual, while themselves being exploited by the charismatic, dangerous leader is terrifying. Lowry's crowds are neither threatened nor threatening. It is chastening to re-read, in the turmoil of the 2008–10 financial catastrophe, the introduction to the second (1969) edition of that sociological classic *The Lonely Crowd* by David Riesman, Nathan Glazer and Reuel Denny. In what is an essentially American study, they thought of English society at the time:

> We can see in the United Kingdom the problems that arise when a society becomes psychologically post-industrial long before the economic infrastructure is sound enough to bear the weight of steadily rising expectations.[6]

These may seem strange words for an art-historical monograph but they do point with almost uncanny accuracy at the Industrial North West that Lowry painted and in which the word *Industrial* is no longer appropriate or even relevant.

Riesman *et al* made huge waves among 'the chattering classes' when their book was first published in 1961, not least for their neologisms and definitions concerning the 'inner-directed' person and the 'other directed man'. (Note that a *person* is inner-directed while a *man* is 'other directed'):

> The inner-directed person is not only chained to the endless demands of the production sphere; he must also spend his entire life in the internal production of his own character. The discomforts of this internal frontier are as inexhaustible as the discomforts of the frontier of work itself. Like the fear of being retired or unemployed in the economic realm, apathy in many sectors of his inner or outer life is felt as underemployment of characterological resources. The inner-directed man has a generalized need to master resource exploitation on all the fronts of which he is conscious. He is job-minded. [*As was probably the case with Lowry.*]
>
> The frontiers of the other-directed man are people; he is people-minded. Hence both work and pleasure are felt as activities involving people. Many of the job titles that exist today existed in the earlier era; many recreations likewise. My effort is to see how change of character is connected with change of meaning in the same pursuits as well as with development of new pursuits.[7]

There is, for all the sociological jargon, an echo here of Freud's definition of a good life, which in much cruder terms says that one should go off to work in the morning looking forward to what the day will bring and then set off jauntily to go home to wife and family in the evening. Lowry, for obvious reasons, was not able to fulfil Freud's dream but he was surely, as defined by Riesman, an 'inner-directed' person. Although *The Lonely Crowd* is in fact very clearly expressed and far more lucid than most jargon-infested sociological writing of the period, I doubt that it would have found a place in Lowry's own library; which is a pity since the actual title concept, the paradox of the lonely crowd is one from which he might have learned something about himself and his fascination with crowds. On the other hand, reading the book might have put him off dealing with crowds altogether. Once Henry Moore was asked by an interviewer whether he had read a recently published study of his art written from a Jungian point of view. Moore, who certainly knew both his Freud and his Jung, shuddered and said that he had not and indeed never would read the book in question. When asked why not he replied that "if it told me what my work was all about and how and why I did it I'm certain that I would not be able to work like that any more".

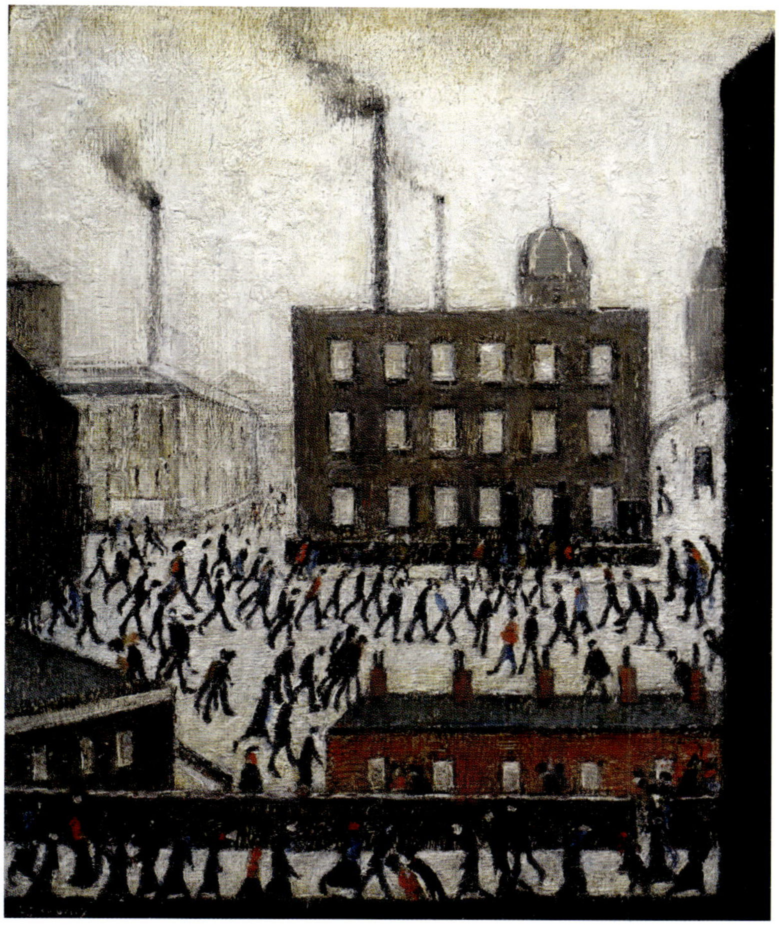

Going to Work, (undated), oil on board, 30.5 × 25.4 cm.

I think that the writer who has most brilliantly tackled the complexity of crowds and their relationship to the individual person is the 1981 Nobel Prize Winner Elias Cannetti (1905–1994). Much of Canetti's *œuvre* consists of short aphoristic or travel books but he wrote two masterpieces, the novel whose English title is *Auto-da-Fé* and his massive and highly original examination of human society through the ages, *Crowds and Power*. This book is quirky, almost, but not quite, implausibly erudite and has universal appeal for anyone interested in mankind's history and development. It is in no way an English book, despite Canetti's long sojourn as a Jewish refugee in this country, and it was written in German. For a book of such intellectual grandeur it is not unexpected that it is no longer in print in England and if you want to acquire a copy you need to get it from America. To the best of my knowledge Canetti and Lowry did not meet and I suspect that each was ignorant of the other's existence.

This makes the resonances of some of Canetti's text with the painting of L. S. Lowry almost uncanny and certainly very stimulating. Take this passage:

> The Englishman sees himself as a captain on board a ship with a small group of people, the sea around and beneath him. He is almost alone as captain; he is in many ways isolated even from his crew.

> The sea is there to be ruled. This conception is decisive. Ships are as much alone on its vast surface as isolated individuals; and each is personified in its captain …
>
> When one comes to consider the character of the sea itself one must remember how numerous and violent are the changes to which it is subject. It is more varied in its transformations than any of the animal crowds with which men have dealings; and how harmless and stable, compared to the sea, are the hunter's forests and the farmer's fields.
>
> The Englishman's disasters have been experienced at sea; his dead he has often had to imagine lying at the bottom of the sea; and thus the sea has offered him transformation and danger.
>
> His life at home is complementary to life at sea; security and monotony are essential characteristics. Everyone has his place which, except to go to sea, he is not supposed to leave for the sake of any transformation; everyone is as sure of his habits as of his possessions.[8]

Lowry was, of course, no sea captain but he was very much the master of his own fate and the nature of his aloneness; his closely guarded isolation, is precisely caught by Canetti in the purest of serendipity. Given Lowry's passion for the sea, a passion largely controlled by his respect for an element he held in awe and which, according to his own words set out in the interview printed in Chapter 1, he actually feared, the penultimate paragraph of the Canetti passage is a palpable hit at a man he did not know and a target he had in no way deliberately sought.

Earlier in the book Canetti writes: "There is nothing that man fears more than the touch of the unknown" and "It is only in a crowd that man can become free of this fear of being touched", and continues:

> That is the only situation in which the fear changes into its opposite. The crowd he needs is the dense crowd, in which body is pressed to body; a crowd, too, whose psychical constitution is also dense, or compact, so that he no longer notices who it is that presses against him. As soon as a man has surrendered himself to the crowd, he ceases to fear its touch. Ideally, all are equal there; no distinctions count, not even that of sex. The man pressed against him is the same as himself. He feels him as he feels himself. Suddenly it is as though everything were happening in one and the same body. This is perhaps one of the reasons why a crowd seeks to close in on itself; it wants to rid each individual as completely as possible of the fear of being touched. The more fiercely people press together, the more certain they feel that they do not fear each other. This reversal of the fear of being touched belongs to the nature of crowds. The feeling of relief is most striking where the density of the crowd is greatest.[9]

This seems very like a plausible explanation for the set-piece crowds Lowry painted in pictures like *Going to the Match* (page 175), a picture of a large crowd with a purpose and yet one in which Canetti's classifications seem not only to be part of Lowry's thoughts but also a clearly visible representation of Canetti's ideas. Such a crowd is different, and its emotional loading is different, from the much looser crowds Lowry represents as merely the people

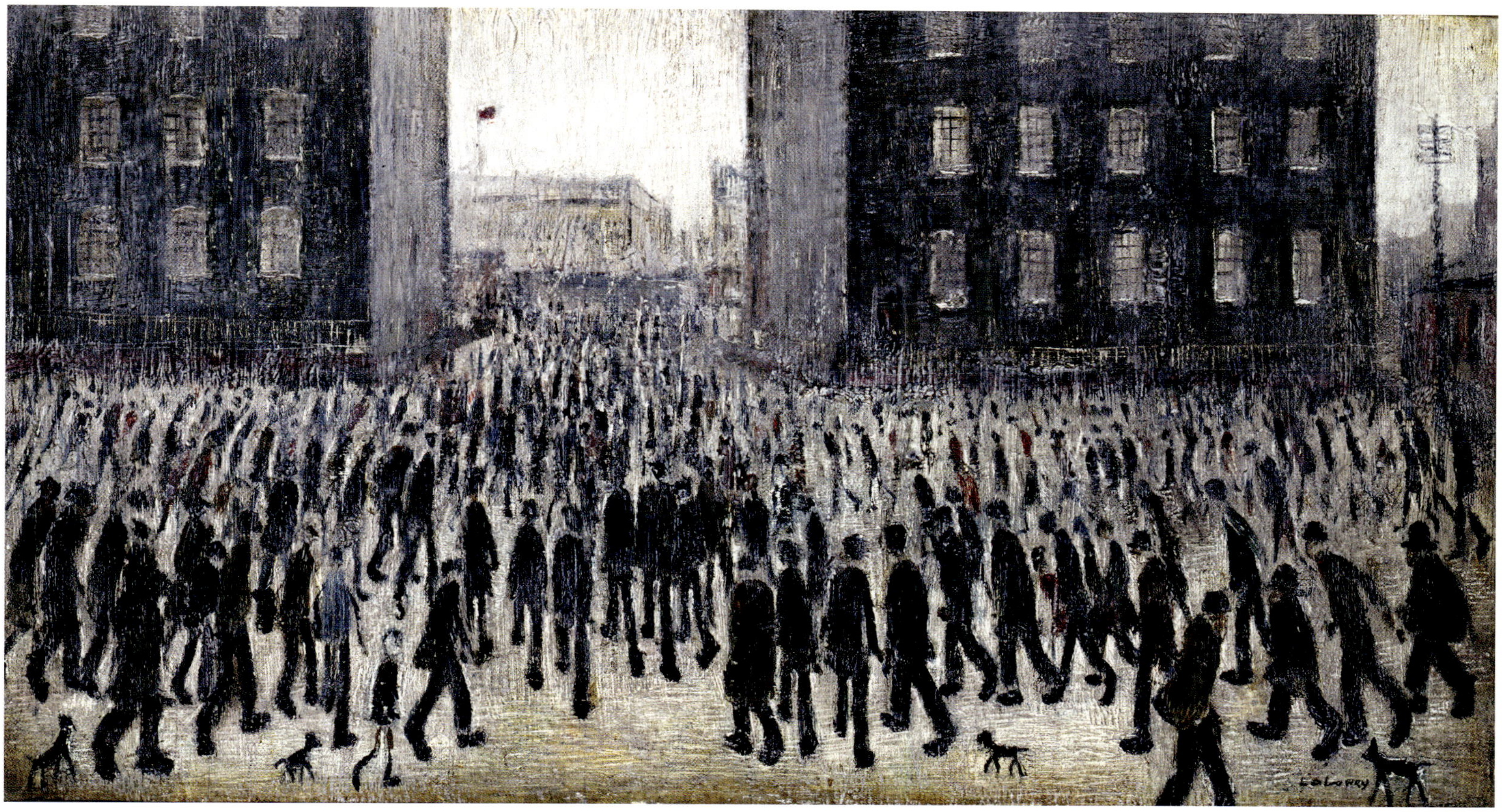

Going to the Match, 1946, oil on panel, 28 × 49.5 cm.

who populate, whether sketchily or densely, the straight industrial landscapes. What Canetti wrote above would almost certainly not apply to the more detailed, less densely populated, less numerous crowds when Lowry is depicting an event being *watched* by a crowd. If the event is the *cause* of the gathering crowd then Lowry's attitude to them is different. Less generalized as in Canetti and much more individualized and specific, as in *The Removal* (or *The Eviction*) (page 44) of 1928 where the crowd is simultaneously *looser* and more *focused*.

But how interesting it would be to speculate that Lowry *had* read and absorbed Canetti, although virtually all his best pictures involving crowds were painted long before *Crowds and Power* was available in English in 1962. One can almost hear one of Lowry's sardonic chuckles as he reads Canetti's early chapter on 'The Open and Closed Crowd':

> The crowd, suddenly there where there was nothing before, is a mysterious and universal phenomenon. A few people may have been standing together – five, ten or twelve, not more; nothing has been announced, nothing is expected. Suddenly everywhere is black with people and more come streaming from all sides as though streets had only one direction. Most of them do not know what has happened and, if questioned, have no answer; but they hurry to be there where most other people are. There is a determination in their movement which is quite different from the expression

> of ordinary curiosity. It seems as though the movement of some of them transmits itself to the others. But that is not all; they have a goal which is there before they can find words for it. This goal is the blackest spot where most people are gathered. … In its innermost core it is not quite as spontaneous as it appears, but, except for these 5, 10 or 12 people with whom actually it originates, it is everywhere spontaneous. As soon as it exists at all, it wants to consist of *more* people: the urge to grow is the first and supreme attribute of the crowd. It wants to seize everyone within reach; anything shaped like a human being can join it. The natural crowd is the *open* crowd; there are no limits whatever to its growth; it does not recognize houses, doors or locks and those who shut themselves in are suspect. "Open" is to be understood here in the fullest sense of the word; it means open everywhere and in any direction. The open crowd exists so long as it grows; it disintegrates as soon as it stops growing.[10]

It must surely be one of the central paradoxes of the life and work of L. S. Lowry that this solitary man obsessively painted people *en masse* and explored them with a humanist approach, possibly without Canetti's formidable philosophical and analytic brain power, yet had the same psychological penetrative understanding. He was also much terser than Canetti, while understanding the same issue. "Where there's a quarrel there's always a crowd. It's a great draw. A quarrel or a body."

It is also interesting that while Canetti was singularly acute about the destructive power of crowds Lowry ignores those aspects. For Canetti:

> The destructiveness of the crowd is often mentioned as its most conspicuous quality, and there is no denying the fact that it can be observed everywhere, in the most diverse countries and civilizations. It is discussed and disapproved of, but never really explained.[11]

Although Lowry lived in a quieter Britain than our own today and we know all too well the capabilities of football crowds turned mindless and nasty even if they are, as Canetti states, 'never really explained', it is plain that Lowry actually liked crowds and neither saw them nor depicted them as dangerous or uncontrollable. Not that his views were wholly rosy. He had no trouble depicting them, particularly when they were focused on some unpleasant activity, as morbidly curious or voyeuristic. This is something one can see in one of his most important paintings, one which bears careful analysis partly because it is central to his work in the 1930s and partly because it could easily have served as an illustration for the English edition of *Crowds and Power* as an example in microcosm of Canetti's broad macrocosmic sweep over humankind's relationships to both power and crowds.

One of Lowry's most typical and most important paintings is *The Fever Van* of 1935 (page 177). Like many of his best works it not only tells a story but is part of our social history and one day perhaps some eager graduate student will do an appraisal of Lowry's work *solely* from the social historical point of view. It would doubtless prove illuminating to historians and sociologists alike.

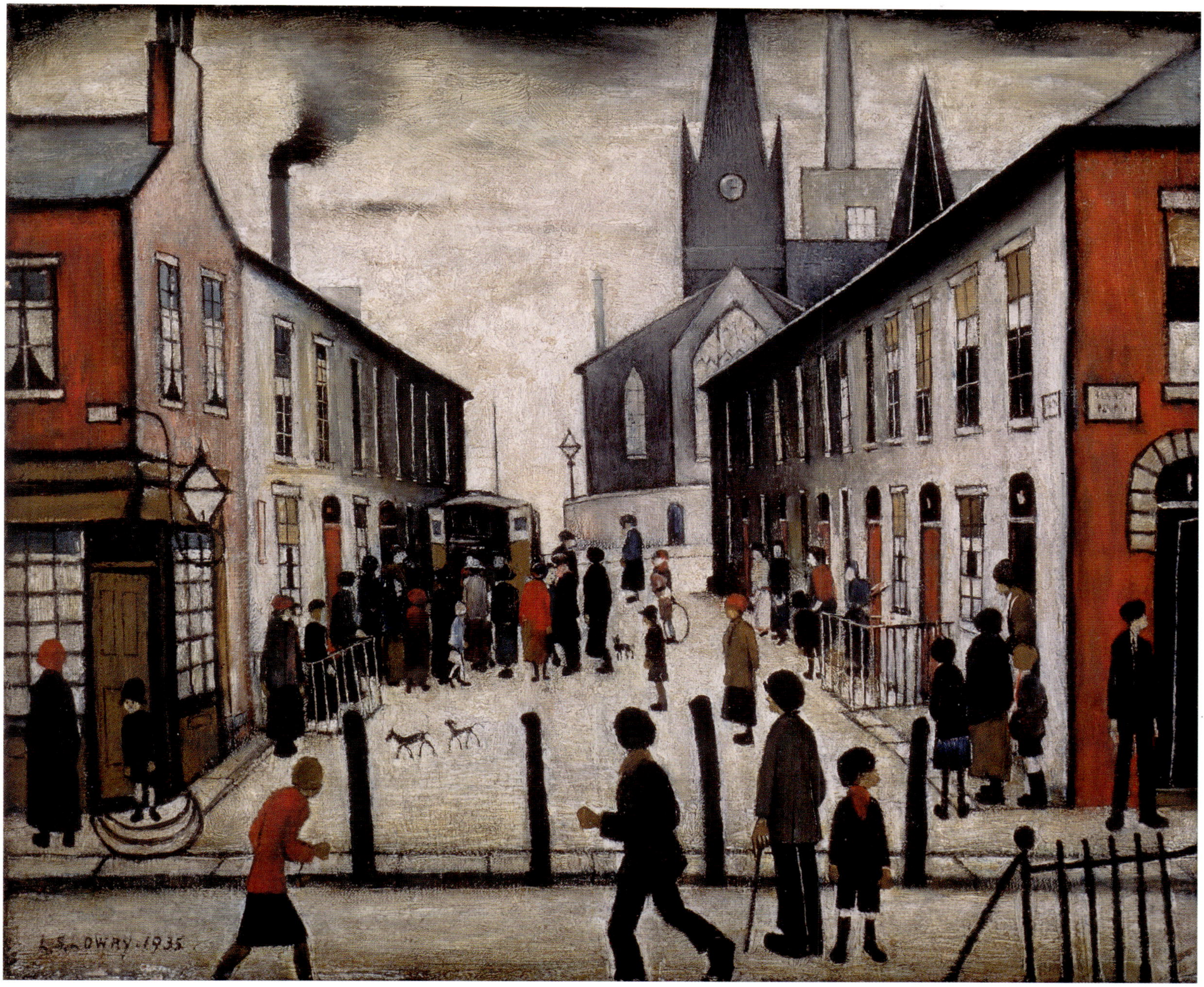

The Fever Van, 1935, oil on canvas, 43.1 × 53.5 cm.

The Fever Van has intrigued me since I first saw it on my first visit to Liverpool, (around the same time as my first meeting with Lowry), but it was only as I began to write these pages that I registered the year in which it was painted, 1935, the year of my birth. I was familiar with the term *Fever Van* and indeed remember them in the poor quarter of Manchester where I spent my childhood. I say poor because that's what it was to anyone who aspired to the middle class or who lives in reasonable comfort today. But the street in which we lived was at least one stage up from the one depicted by Lowry and, while we froze during the wartime winters, we did have indoor plumbing. But the Fever Van certainly called occasionally in our street, one long ago pulled down to make room for an extension to the local hospital's car park. According to some invaluable research of the medical aspects and implication of Fever Vans in general they continued in daily use until the 1950s and Fever Van was simply the North West of England's version of what the rest of the country called an ambulance. The medical information used here comes from an article on the background to Lowry's painting in the Journal of the Royal Society of Medicine by Julia Sarginson and Lucy Guppy.[12]

In those days ambulances would be called out for certain highly infectious diseases such as scarlet fever or diphtheria, not only of fatal potential but capable of spreading like wildfire because of the overcrowding of factory and mill life and the worse overcrowding of tiny houses holding ten or more human beings of varying ages in small, unventilated rooms. When one of these diseases was diagnosed the law and the primitive, pre-National Health Service, medical system was swift and brutal and all too necessary if mass outbreaks or epidemics were to be prevented or at least halted. The Fever Van would arrive and take the patient, regardless of age but more usually a child, to spend as much as six weeks in one of the special isolation hospitals. Once the patient had been carted off, or, if the family was lucky, while the wretched child was being wrapped up and lodged in the Fever Van the crew would fumigate the child's room and possessions, and, often, the whole house.

For Lowry, the peripatetic rent collector, this nightmarish event would have been a fairly common sight, one which told *him* a story, one with which he sympathized and, inevitably, a natural drama to a man who loved the dramatic, whether in theatrical form or simply in real life. The painting is bursting with life while it is recording a very ordinary street with a shop or a pub on the front left corner, the local church at the end of the street and, in shadowy outline, the tall chimneyed factory where most of the male inhabitants would work. It is, of course, a street without vehicles, one in which motor cars did not exist and only a fortunate tenant would own a bicycle.

The crowd of neighbours, like many of Lowry's – and life's – crowds is divided between the densely packed one hovering round the back of the ambulance with its doors ready to receive the patient, and the more spaced-out audience, moved perhaps by pity or reticence who are happy to watch at a distance but are just as determined to miss nothing of the great event (Canetti would have appreciated this crowd). Merely the distribution of the onlookers is masterly. You do not need William Blake to tell you of the fearful symmetry of two sides of the street, in reality two parallel lines but parallel lines which, in this painting are moving towards convergence at the far end.

The Fever Van, itself the centre of the action, is *not* the centre of the picture which is in itself a perfect composition. There is, around the back of the van just enough detail so that you can follow the story but not enough to satisfy the ghoulish interest of the voyeurs you always find attending such events. The handling of the paint is a superb example of Lowry's versatility with his limited five-colour palette so that the painting is as flawless aesthetically as it is daring in its composition as it is masterful in its narrative quality, in its sheer story-telling skill.

The Fever Van is also a perfect illustration of his own words about his fascination with dramatic, even drastic, events:

> Accidents interest me – I have a very queer mind you know. What fascinates me is the people they attract. The patterns those people form, an atmosphere of tension when something's happened … Where there's a quarrel there's always a crowd … It's a great draw. A quarrel or a body.

Doubtless once the Fever Van had been driven off, the crowd, in accordance with Canetti's dictum, would break up and disappear.

One of our greatest art critics, John Berger, in his brilliant essay *Lowry and the Industrial North*[13] published in 1966 saw with great clarity the special character of Lowry's crowds:

> The character of the figures and crowds is also specially English. The industrial revolution has isolated them and uprooted them. Their home-made ideology, except

Railway Platform, (undated), oil on canvas, 47 × 76.2 cm.

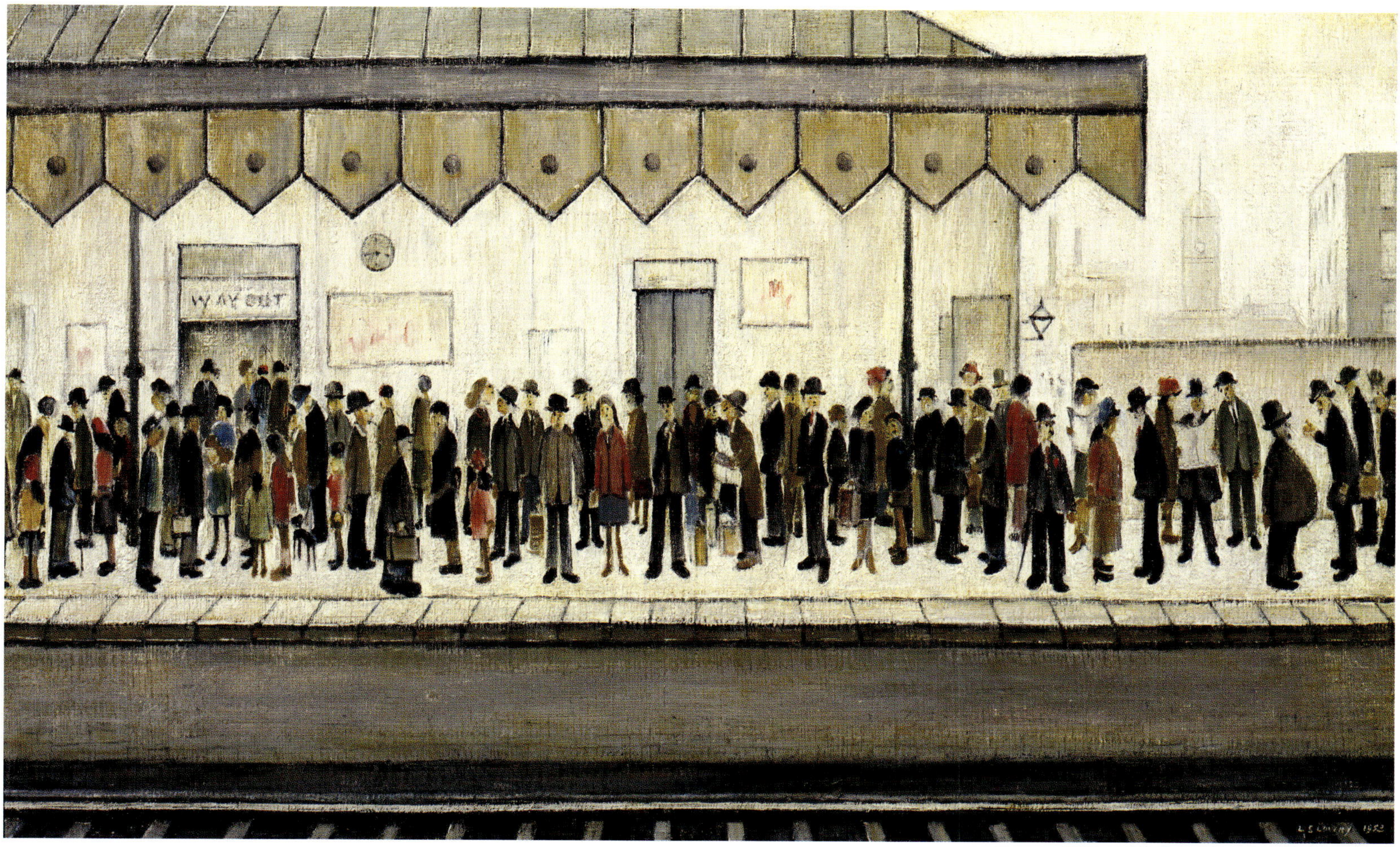

> when they are led and organized by revolutionaries, is a kind of ironic stoicism. Nowhere else do crowds look so simultaneously *civic* and *deprived*. They know each other, recognize each other, exchange help and jokes – they are not, as is sometimes said, like lost souls in limbo; they are fellow-travellers through a life which is impervious to most of their choices.[14]

Berger, also a powerful social commentator, saw from a different angle but with a similar wide perspective the same English decay as that noted by Riesman:

> These paintings are about what has been happening to the British economy since 1918, and their logic implies the collapse still to come. This is what has happened to the "workshop of the world". Here is the recurring so-called production crisis; the obsolete industrial plants; the inadequacy of unchanged transport systems and overstrained power supplies; the failure of education to keep pace with technological advance; the ineffectiveness of national planning; the lack of capital investment at home and the disastrous reliance on colonial and neo-colonial overseas investments; the shift of power from industrial capital to international finance capital; the essential agreements within the two-party system blocking every initiative towards political independence and thus economic viability.[15]

Lowry seemed rarely to paint crowds merely for the sake of bringing off a difficult artistic challenge, as if he wanted to show that Brueghel a thing or two. His crowds in fact varied considerably in accordance with what they were doing. They could be orderly, moving both in unison and positively if they had a strong common purpose such as taking part in a religious procession or enjoying the pleasures of a fairground or simply leaving work, exhausted but with relief, moving in varied directions but definitely getting away from something whose absence they appreciated, as in the 1930 *Coming from the Mill* (page 181). Lowry feels their easing off of tension, yet also shows, in their often bowed postures, the legacy of long hours of sweated hard labour à la Greenwood. Not all of them are thus battered and some are not bowed but merely leaning forward purposefully to propel themselves homewards with greater speed. *Coming from the Mill* shows Lowry at his most thoughtful and, to use a word devalued by its current use, or misuse, *caring*. Yet an image which could so easily be interpreted as, or modified into, agitprop is, as Lowry himself was, many miles away from that ugly and deeply sentimental form of painting which so desecrated Soviet art under Stalin and his gang.

Few other artists have painted such harsh subject matter without a shred of sentimentality. Perhaps only Daumier and Van Gogh in his potato-eater phase could be so perceptive and sympathetic about the poor while painting them so truthfully.

To quote Berger again:

> The extraordinary fact is that *nobody* [my italics], faced with Lowry's pictures whose subject-matter is nearly always social, ever discusses the social or historical meaning of his art. Instead it is treated as though it dealt with the view out of the window of

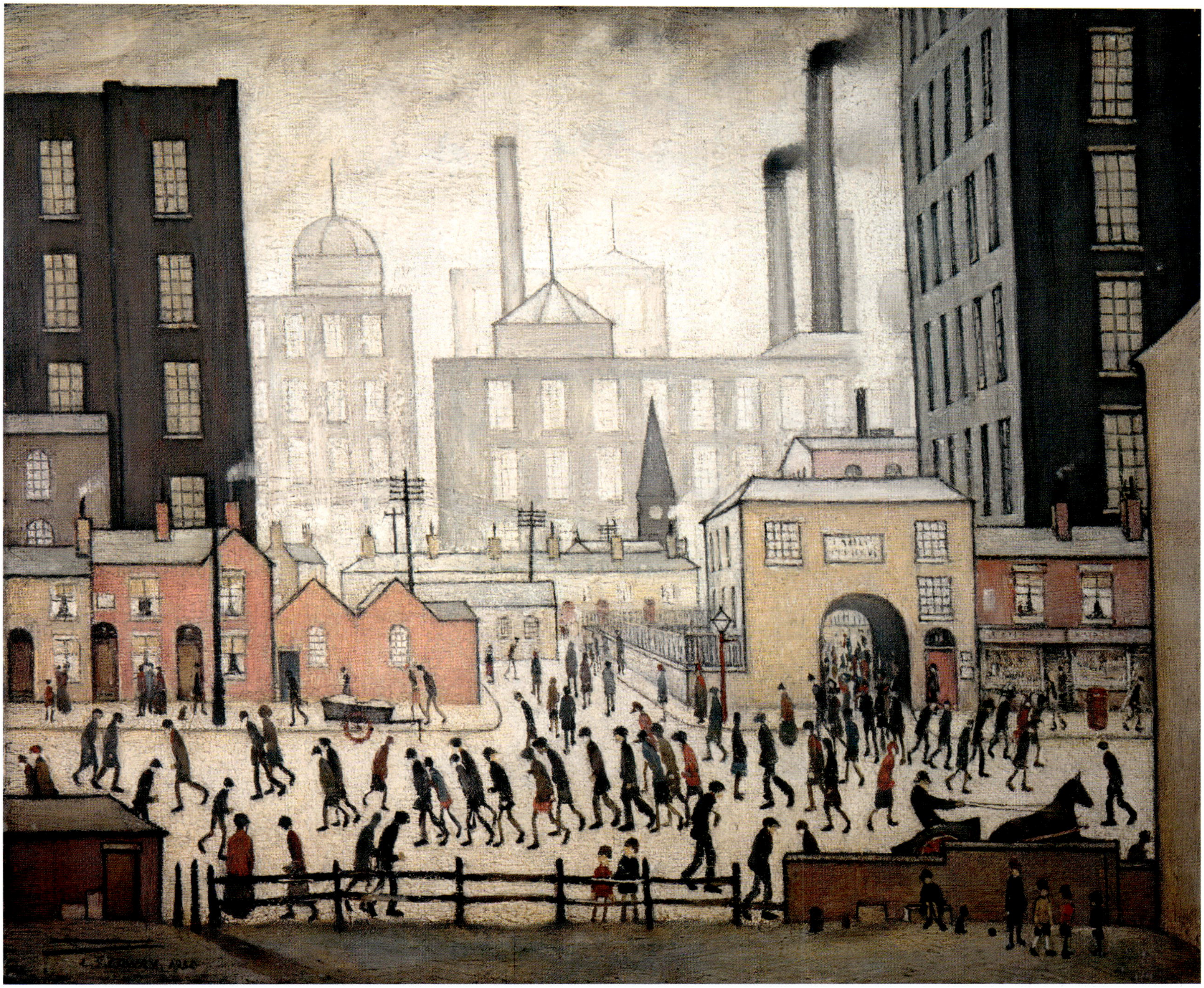

Coming from the Mill, 1930, oil on canvas, 42 × 52 cm.

> a Pullman train on its non-stop journey to London, where everything is believed to be very different. His subjects, if they have to be considered at all in relation to what actually exists, are considered as local exotica.[16]

Lowry was a genius at handling large masses of people in a manner that Canetti would instantly have understood even though he did not paint the violent, mindless, dangerous crowds that Canetti analyzed so remorselessly. But Lowry also had an extraordinary gift for taking small groups of people, too few in number perhaps to constitute a crowd, but enough to establish what they had in common and why the group in the picture was larger and more interesting than the sum of its parts.

A classic example of this is *The Funeral Party* of 1953 (page 154). Michael Howard in his interesting study of *Lowry A Visionary Artist* published in 2000, states firmly that this painting was suggested to Lowry by the 'characters' in Pirandello's *Six Characters in Search of an Author* who come onto the stage dressed in mourning. This seems to me unlikely since Lowry only became so enamoured of the play when he made so many visits to it during its London production of 1954 i.e. a year later than the date of the painting. (This could, of course, be one of the cases where Lowry used a date when he started a picture but, more frequently, when he worked on a particular painting over a period of years, he sometimes signed and dated them in the year of completion.)

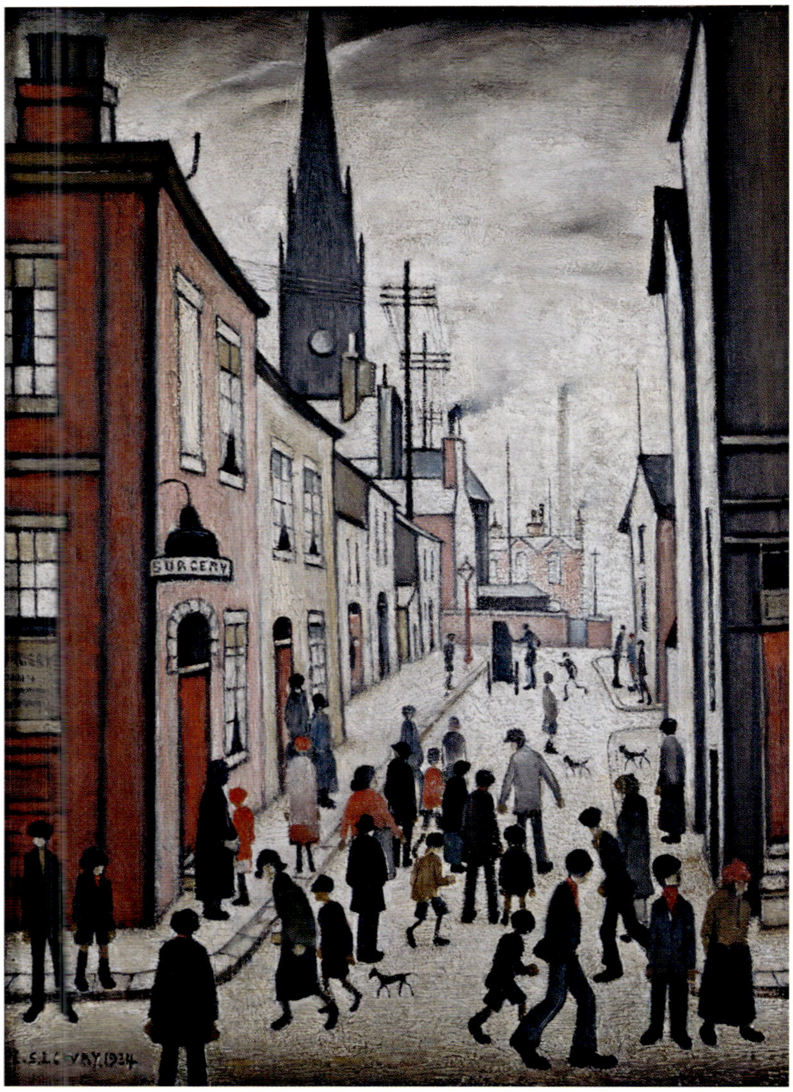

The Organ Grinder, 1934,
oil on canvas, 53.5 × 39.5 cm.

Be that as it may, *A Funeral Party* is certainly a very theatrical painting and the ill-assorted nine adults and children standing stiffly in a straight line could even be a group of actors taking a curtain call, with the little boy at the end on the left and the dark-haired man on the right looking over to a box, while the other seven face the audience in the stalls.

On the other hand most actors practise, at least at curtain calls, a bonhomous togetherness and few paintings of groups, or mini-crowds, like this one have so lacked even a scintilla of bonhomie, let alone togetherness. They surely do not fit in with Canetti but are a classic example of Riesman's *Lonely Crowd.* Lowry does not even set out to unite them, as many funeral parties are, in grief. If one magnifies the image of the young woman fourth from the left you can just about convince yourself – with an effort – that there is a large tear under her left eye but the rest seem resolutely un-tearful, perhaps in shock still, but stoically miserable. The little boy on the left has a faintly comical air while his big sister?, two along, is giving him a sidelong, rather suspicious look as if trying to catch him out in some misconduct.

I suspect that rather than an afterthought on Pirandello this bizarre scene, (incidentally a virtuoso piece of painting in which the black and near black funeral clothes are as vivid as a cinema screen with the intensely varied pallor of the group's faces highlighted by the sea-like tints which he has mixed up with his habitual deep white), has some other origins in Lowry's head. Indeed one could almost believe that the members of the funeral party were posed standing on the seashore by Lowry as the perpetual ringmaster of his characters.

However perceptively Canetti, Clark, Berger and Riesman *et al* wrote about the nature of crowds, power and loneliness, no one has portrayed the intensity of simultaneous mass companionship – and the concomitant role of the solitary – as Lowry in his best crowd paintings. There is perhaps more of domestic incomprehension and separateness in some of Lowry's Munch-like paintings of family life, but, in his major group and crowd pictures no one has so brilliantly depicted people's need to congregate and their even more powerful need to be private, uncommunicative and solitary.

According to my colleague Edwin Mullins, who was sitting one day in the 1960s with Lowry in Manchester's Piccadilly Gardens, he asked Lowry why he was so obsessed with crowds and Lowry replied, after a long pause:

> You see, Sir [he called everyone sir], people think crowds are all the same. But they're not, you know. Everyone's different. Look! [He became very animated, pointing at people walking by]. That man's got a twitch. He's got a limp. He's had too much beer. That woman, she's angry with her child. Those two have had a row; you can see it from their faces ... It's wonderful, isn't it? The battle of life, sir. That's what it is. The battle of life.[17]

Mullins goes on to say:

> Hence crowds were his battlefield, which he survives as a fascinated onlooker – like a war correspondent – even if the battle was often more like that of Tweedledum and Tweedledee.[18]

As so often Lowry knew himself better than an outsider ever could.

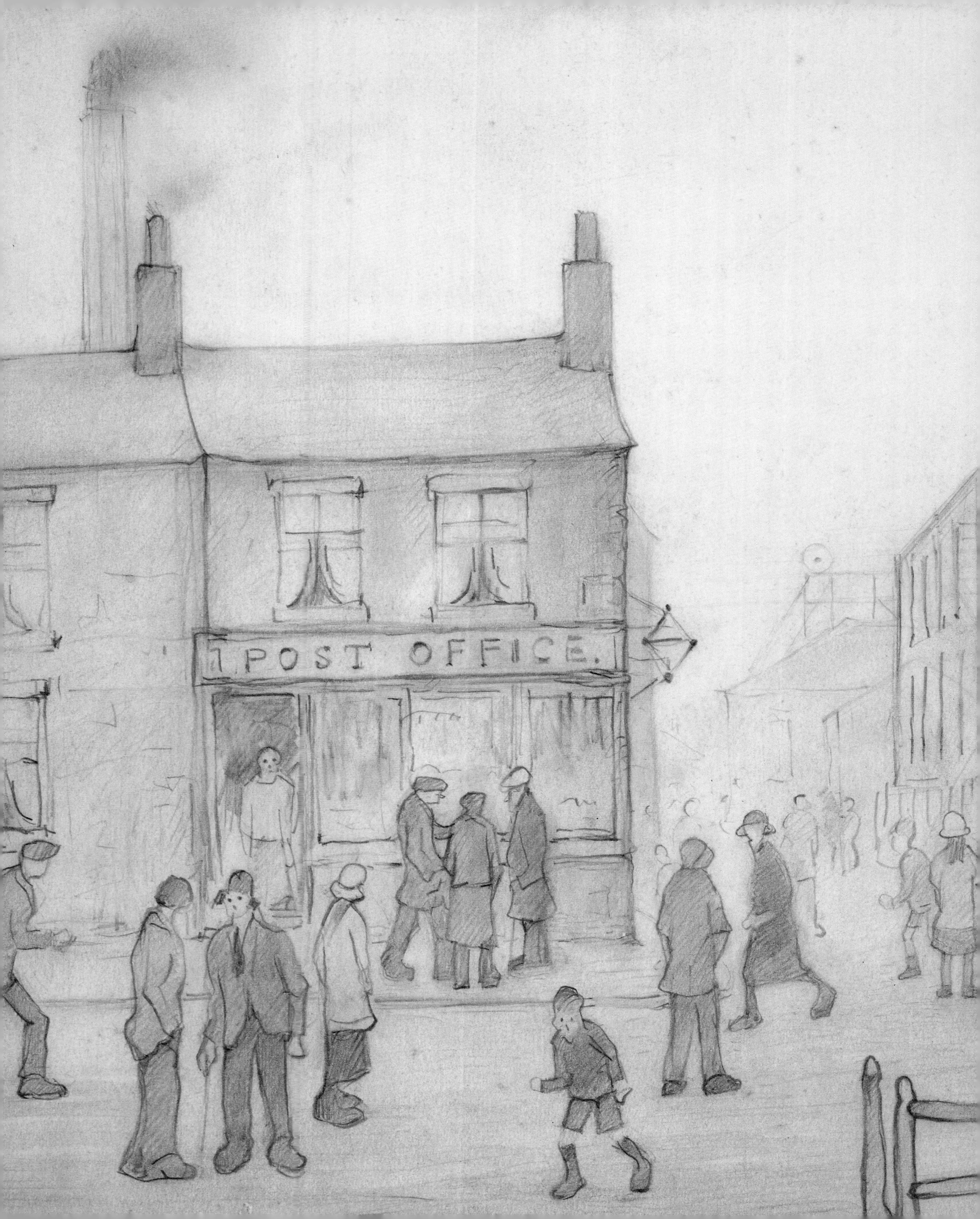
POST OFFICE.

CHAPTER 9

LOWRY AND ABROAD

> *Lowry's provincialism was the proof of his authenticity, a relief from the falsities of the avant-garde. The late and much-missed Peter Fuller, who championed Lowry in the first issue of the now good-as-defunct Modern Painters, saw in his provinciality an example of that 'informed and often intransigent insularity' which constituted the great strength of English painting. In this account, provincialism comes to mean more than specifically or even narrowly local, lacking the sweep and confidence and up-to-datedness of the metropolis – it means finding 'a greater creative stimulus in the* refusal *of those modernities which a capital city is always quick to embrace.'*[1]
>
> Howard Jacobson

Like many Englishmen of his type, class and generation, Lowry did not think much of, or was even interested in, abroad. Unsurprisingly therefore he did not travel there. Given his very precise views and tastes in food it is perhaps just as well as he would surely not have liked abroad other than for its museums and their contents. On the whole abroad did not much take to Lowry either which is no denigration of Lowry or his art. Very few 20th-century English artists have enjoyed much success outside Britain. Francis Bacon and Lucian Freud are the rule proving exceptions, the only two British artists of the period who make foreign auctioneers' pulses race. Henry Moore, Barbara Hepworth, Ben Nicholson and Howard Hodgkin can make a few dealers' tills ring but you'll find hardly any work abroad if you look for Jack B. Yeats, Ivon Hitchens, Victor Pasmore, Graham Sutherland, John Piper, Keith Vaughan, Matthew Smith and many more. Leaving the USA out of this state of affairs it is on the whole a rare excitement to find a significant 20th-century British work of art in a European museum. Other than the odd Francis Bacon or Lucian Freud and some sculptures by Moore and Hepworth there's not much to be found.

I excuse the old Commonwealth from this stricture since British art is well represented there and there are some first rate Lowrys in Australia, New Zealand and Canada. In the USA one will occasionally come across a Ben Nicholson, Moore and Hepworth aplenty and excellent Bacons and Freuds but Lowrys have not yet made any impact, at least in the museum world. There is a recent acquisition by bequest of one superb Lowry from America to the Fitzwilliam Museum in Cambridge but the source is almost certainly a private collector and Cambridge alumnus who took the painting with him on going to live across the Atlantic.

Shelley Rohde states that one of Lowry's paintings was bought by the Museum of Modern Art New York in 1952 but it has not been possible to verify this or even establish that it was indeed bought but had been subsequently de-accessioned. However the Museum of Modern Art did acquire in 1964 a particularly interesting Lowry painting with the aid of

Detail from *The Post Office*, 1926, (p.125).

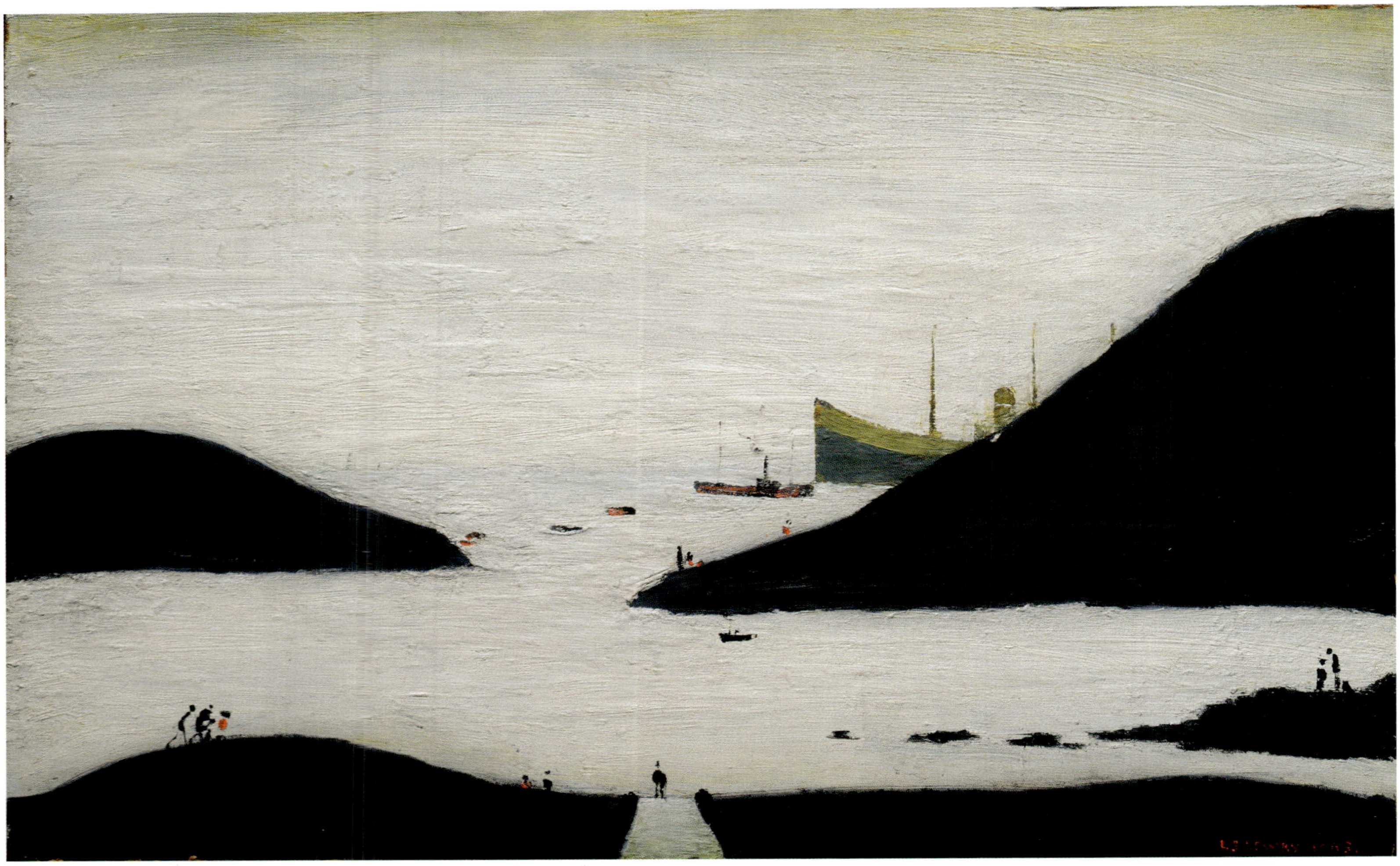

Ships Near Cumberland Coast, 1963, oil on board, 30.1 × 48.7 cm.

the Blanchette Hooker Rockefeller Fund, (above), entitled *Ships Near Cumberland Coast* and painted in oil on board in 1963. It is, for the seeker after the paradigmatic Lowry painting an odd but remarkably appealing hybrid of Lowry's favourite themes. The sea and the ships, realistic and, even in the far distance, sharply outlined, speak for themselves. The land in the foreground and the two promontories facing each other in the middle ground would look equally at home in his occasionally phallocentric Lake District landscapes with their obviously mammary hills so that the transatlantic buyer of the picture is, in effect, getting two Lowrys for the price of one.

The one non-anglophone country where Lowry might have had some success was France. Some shrewd and notably xenophobic French judges of art selected for five successive exhibitions at the Paris Salon and the Salon d'Automne in the late 1920s a number of significant Lowry paintings although, sadly, there were no sales. One of his submissions was *Going to the Match*. At one stage it even looked as if Lowry might have acquired a French dealer. He had been included in the 1931 *Who's Who of European Painters*. Shortly after he had exhibited

A Hawker's Cart and *Going Home from the Mill* at the Salon he received an enthusiastic letter from a publisher/dealer in Paris called Edouard Joseph. He responded immediately, expressed some reservations about costs, but asked Bourlet to send Edouard Joseph *Going to the Match*. Alas, no exhibition materalized, nor did Lowry, himself a punctilious correspondent on business matters, even receive a reply.

Many years later, the wound still raw, he recalled it in a conversation with Edwin Mullins.[2] "I was then forty and no dealer had ever approached me before, but many years later I asked a gentleman who I thought might know about [Edouard Joseph] ... He died. Yes, he'd been going in for an operation when he wrote to me, and had passed away a week later. I've never judged a man for not answering letters since."

As in other matters there is an ambivalence in Lowry. Did he really want international renown? Would he have travelled to Paris or Berlin if shown there or anywhere else outside Britain? One can only ask and then only doubt whether he would. Yet this is the same man who constantly refused the many official honours that were offered him by Downing Street. Would he have declined a knighthood, as he did, if his mother had lived a healthier and longer life? Would he not have thought she might at long last have been impressed by her brilliant but unloved son? If only to drop the name of 'Sir Lawrence' to her neighbours?

There can obviously be no definitive answers to these questions, only speculation. In the end Lowry's reputation rests in Britain only, despite the occasional hopeful forecast of a big breakthrough abroad. In fact most countries with any pretension to culture have museums stuffed and filled high with the work of a local hero. Essentially you can be Akseli Gallen-Kallela whose work I have long admired in Helsinki, but who is, outside a small group of professional art historians, unknown beyond the Finnish border. Or you can be Edvard Munch who left more than 20,000 works to the City of Oslo which devotes literally acres of space to his genius and Munch's international reputation and prices have never been higher. No one knows quite why, other than a public estimation of sheer quality, one artist satisfies only his native country while another transcends national boundaries. I suspect that Lowry, were there an afterlife, would in fact be happy to be a giant in these islands without having a huge reputation abroad.

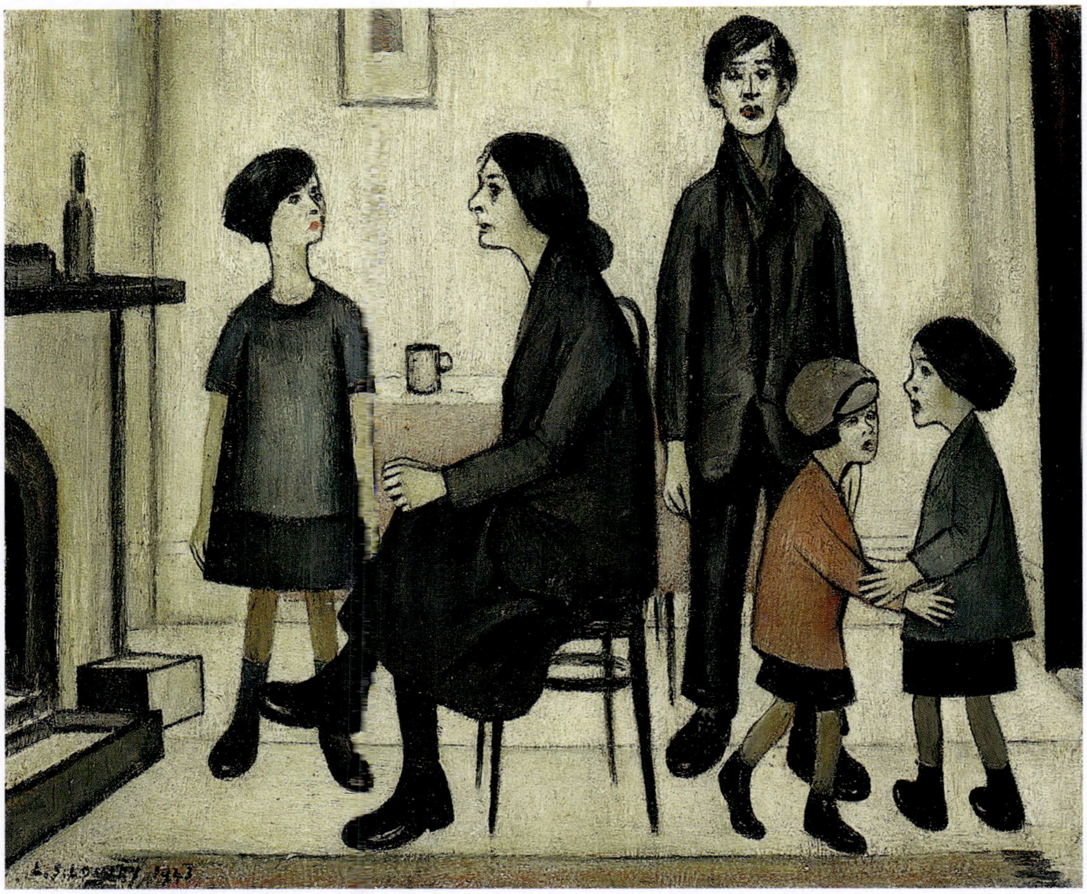

Discord, 1943, oil on board,
42.5 × 52.5 cm.

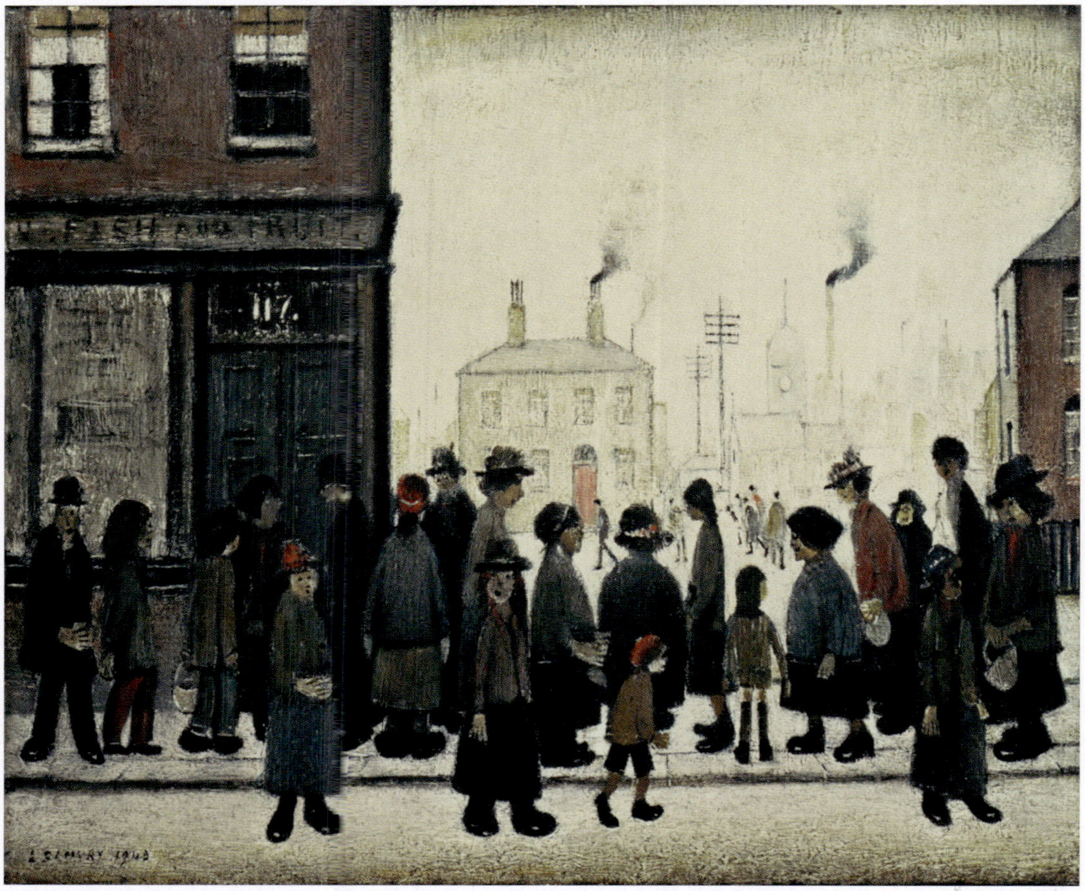

Waiting for the Shop to Open, 1943,
oil on canvas, 43.3 × 53.3 cm.

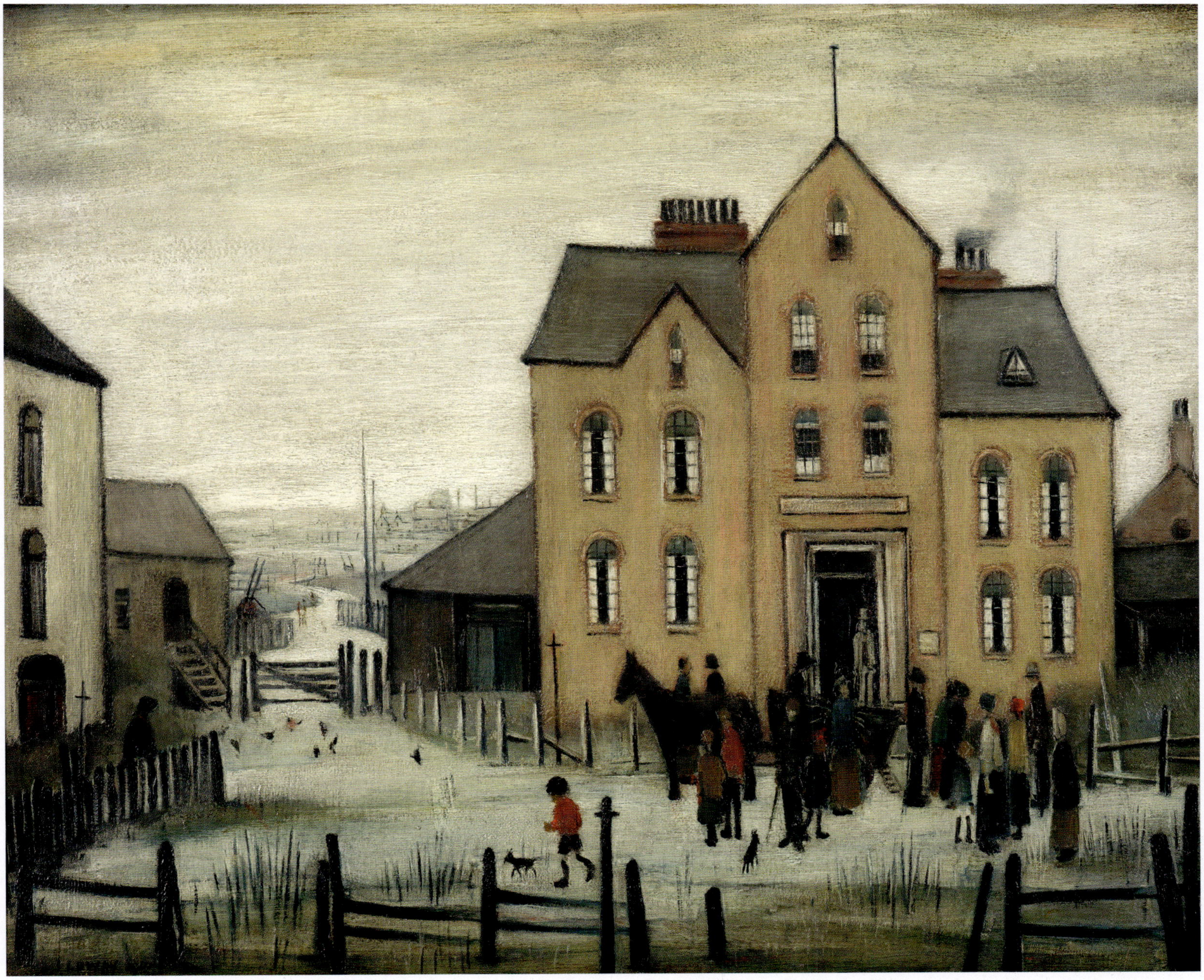

The Mansion, Pendlebury, 1944,
oil on canvas, 42 × 52 cm.

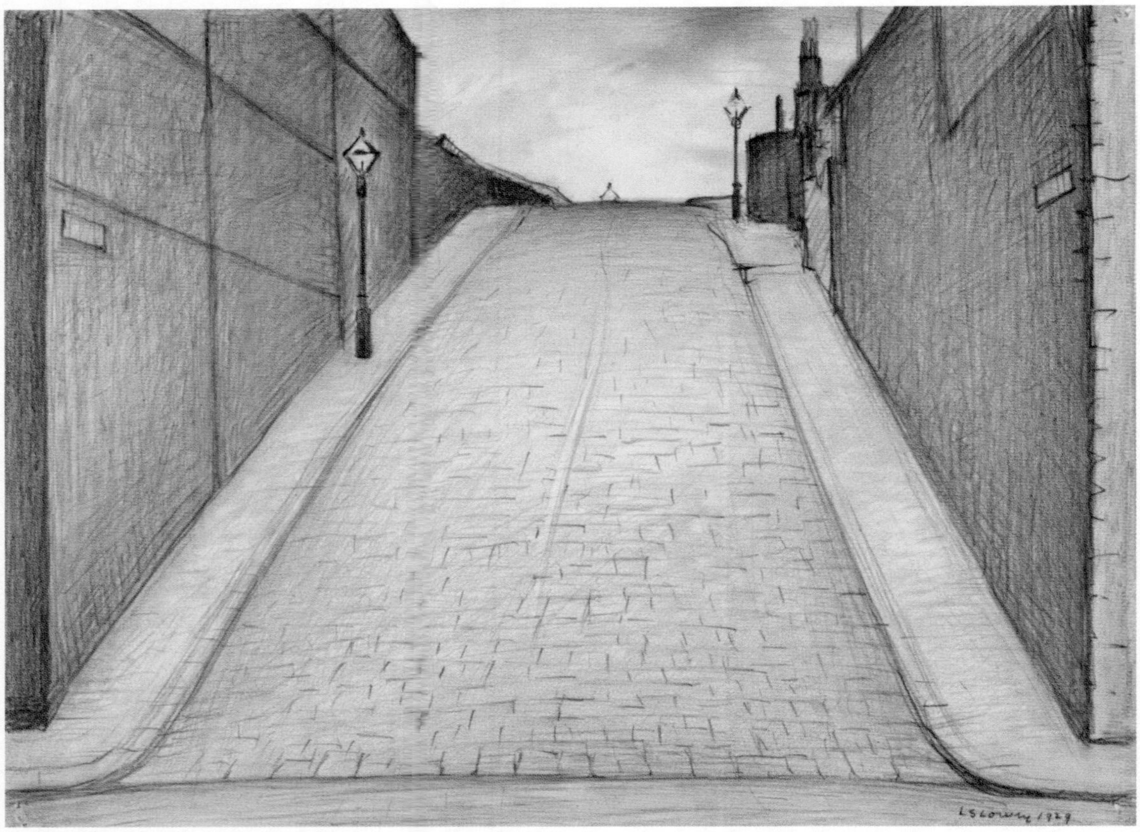

Street Scene, Junction Street and Stony Brow, 1929, pencil on paper, 28 × 38.3 cm.

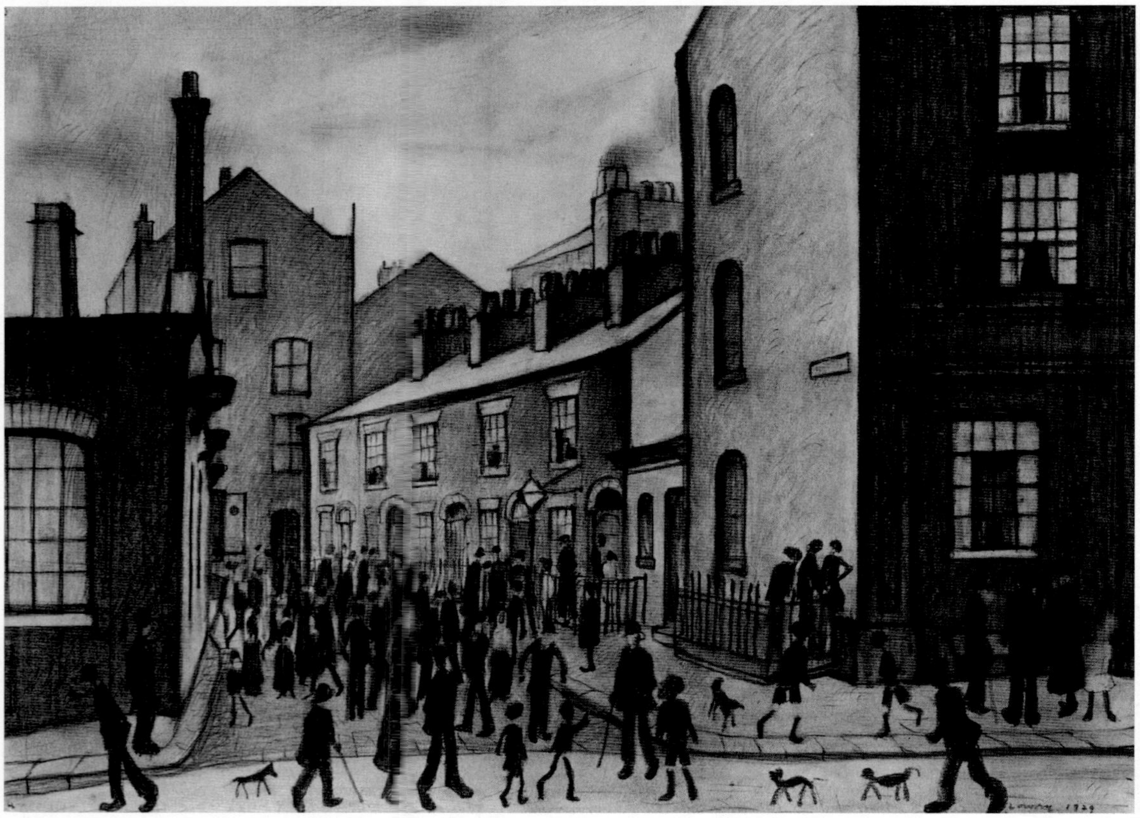

Ancoats, Manchester, 1929, pencil on paper, 27.8 × 38.3 cm.

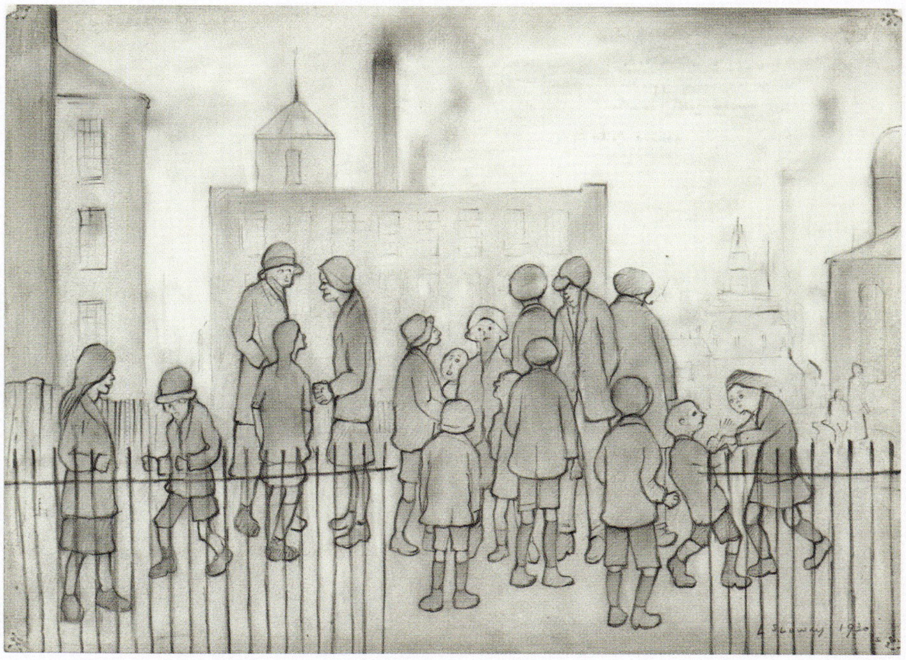

Waiting for the Papers, 1930,
pencil on paper, 24.1 × 24 cm.

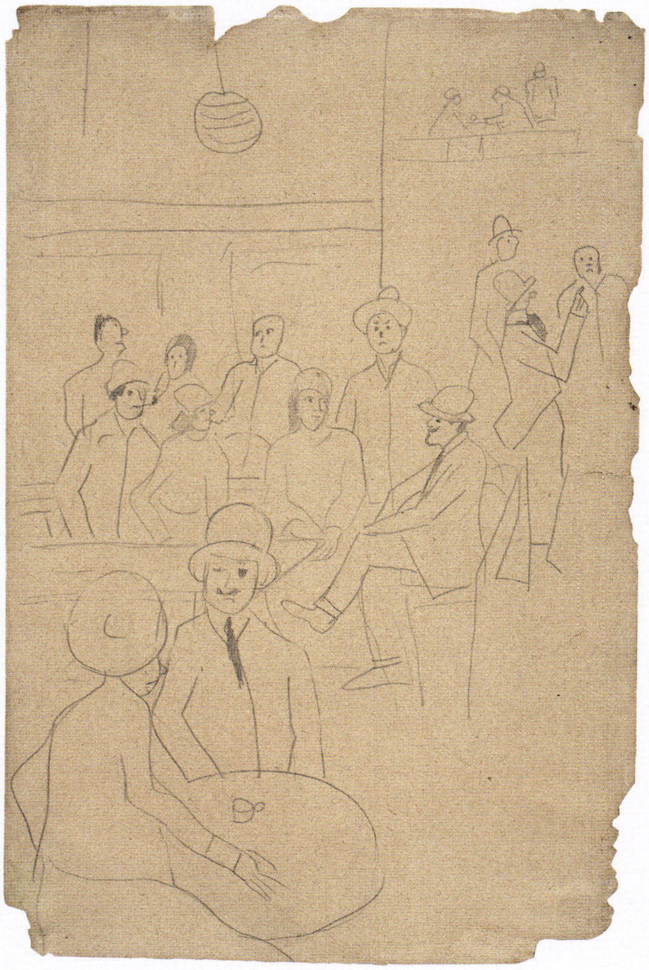

Untitled – Scene in Restaurant, *c.*1920,
pencil on paper, 37.2 × 24.5 cm.

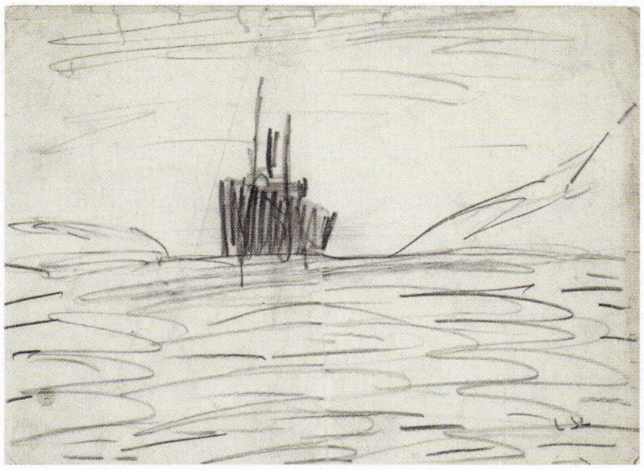

A Ship, 1965, pencil on paper,
17.7 × 24.5 cm.

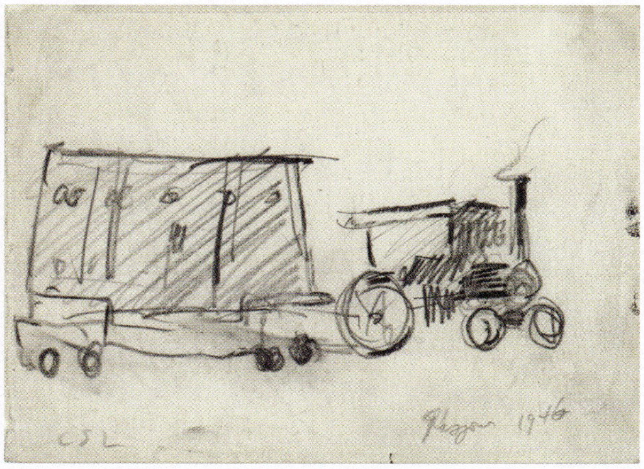

Steam Traction Engine, Glasgow, 1946,
pencil on paper, 12.8 × 17.7 cm.

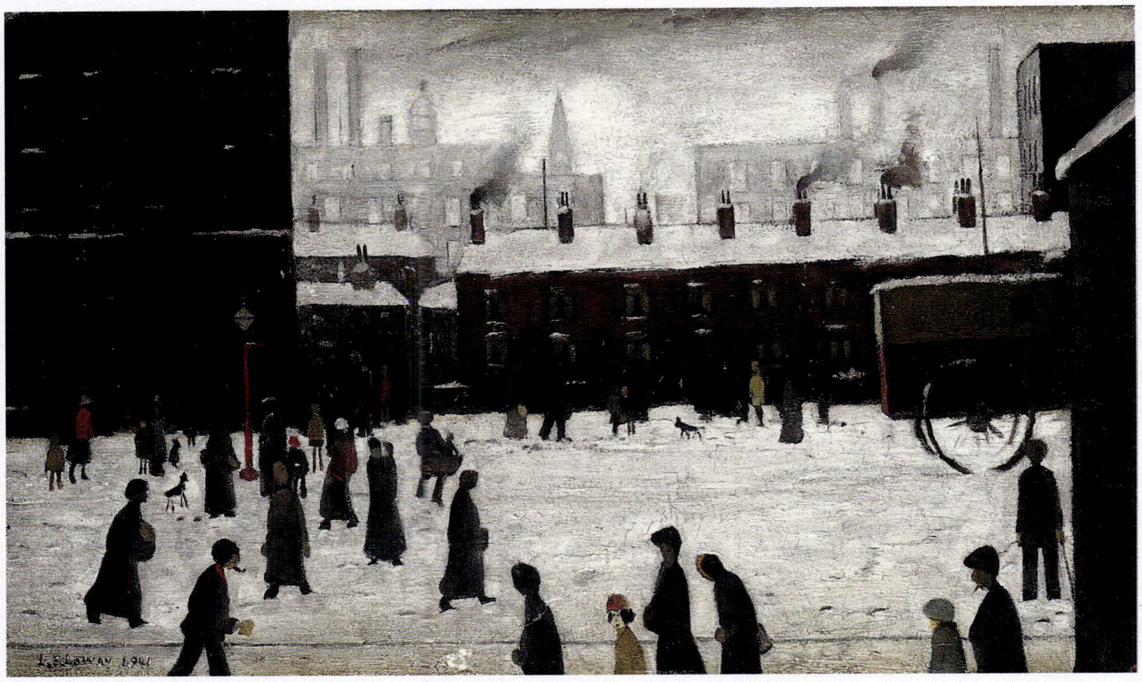

Street Scene in Snow, 1944,
oil on panel, 36.2 × 61.6 cm.

Derelict Barges, 1945, oil on board,
27 × 45.5 cm.

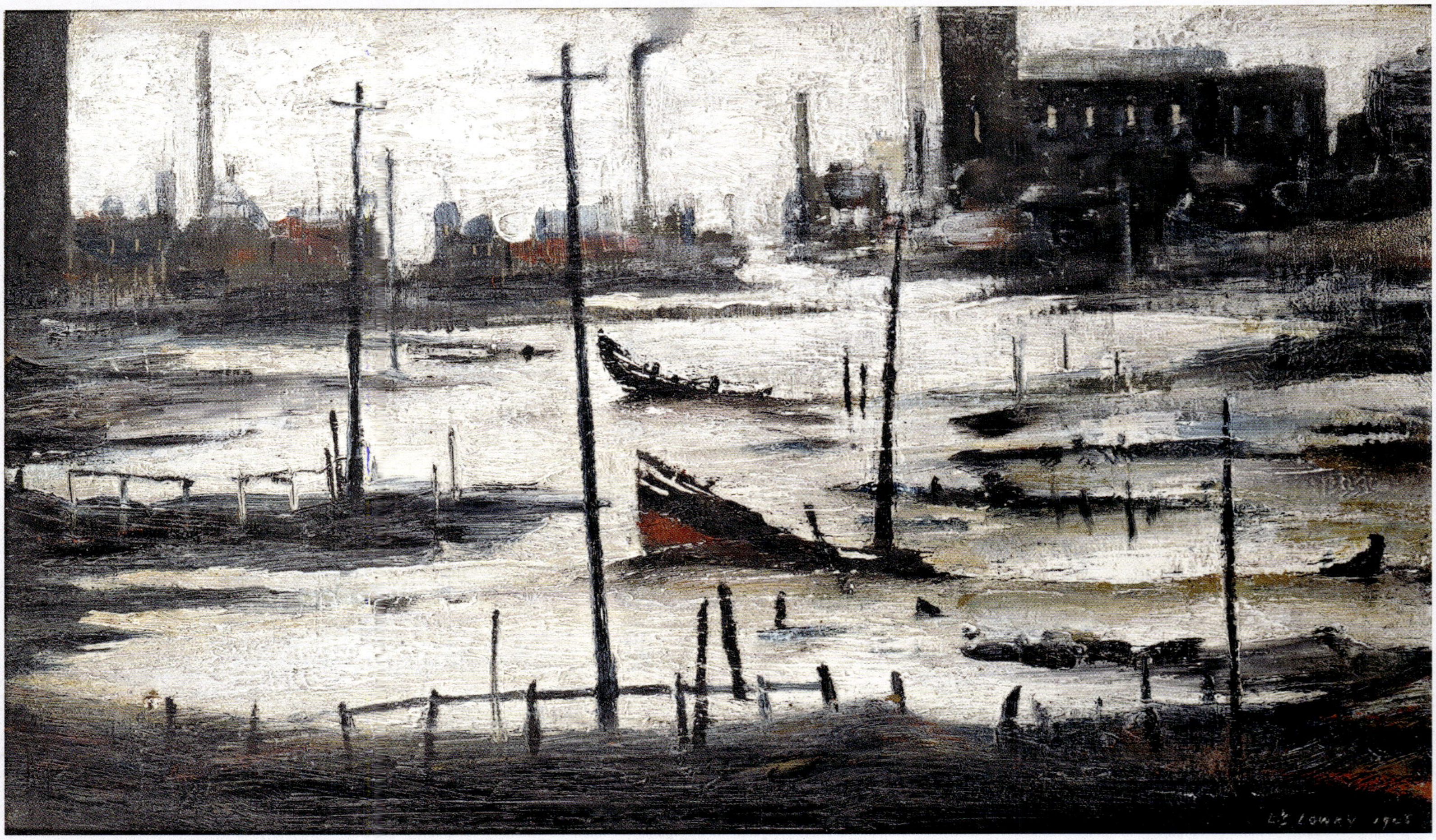

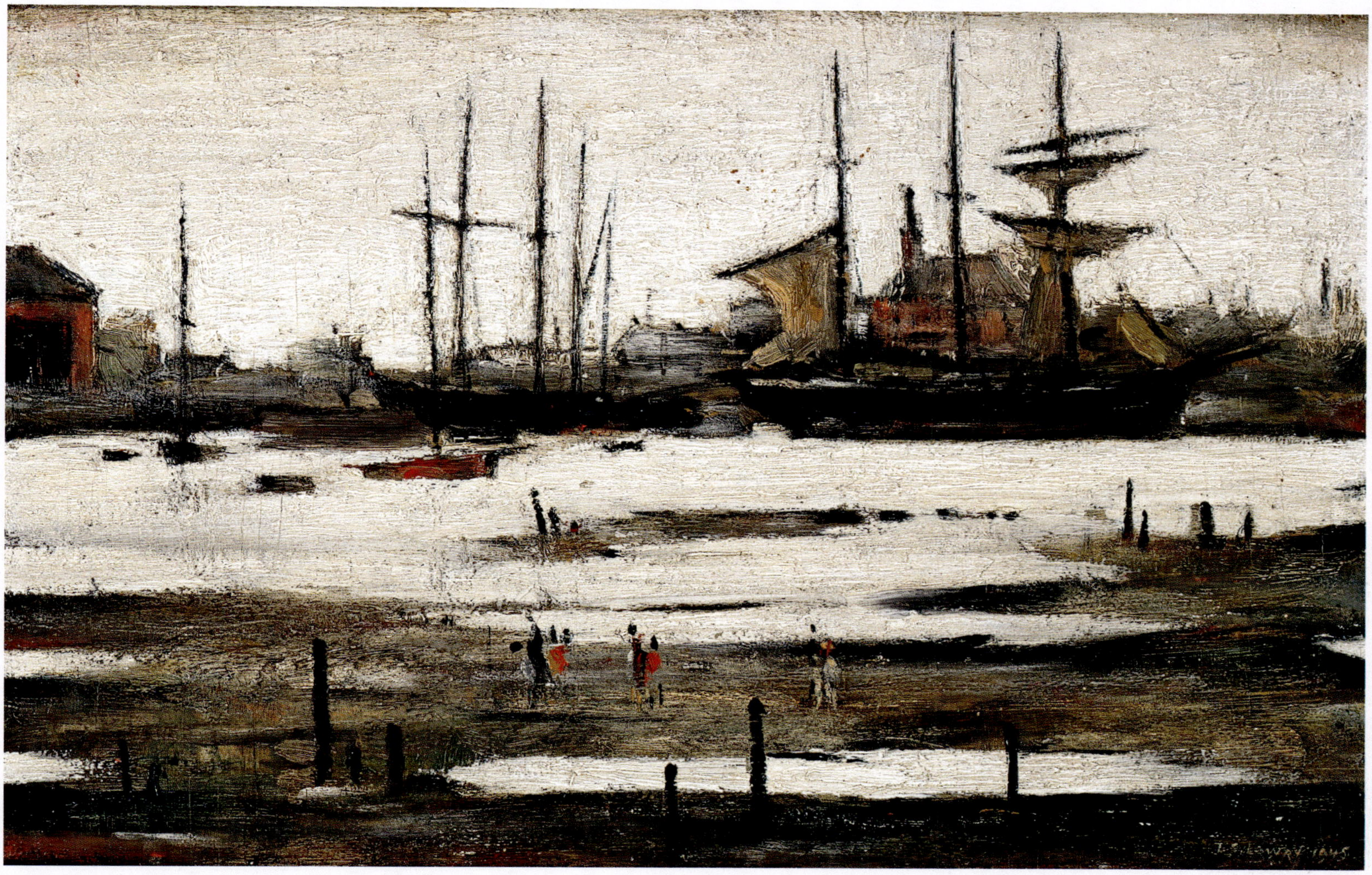

Rhyl Harbour, 1945, oil on board,
26 × 40.5 cm.

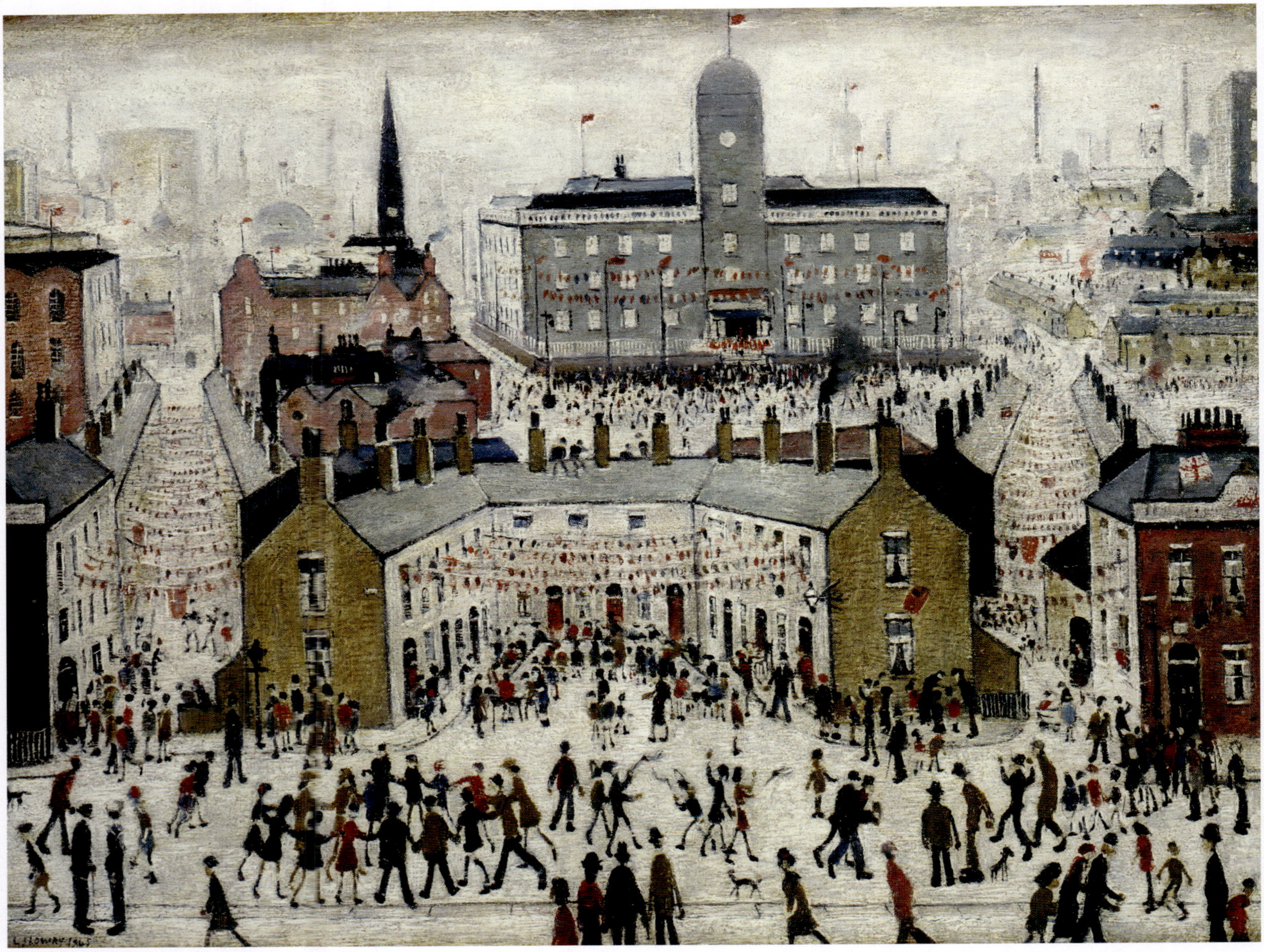

VE Day, 1945, oil on panel,
50.8 × 68.6 cm.

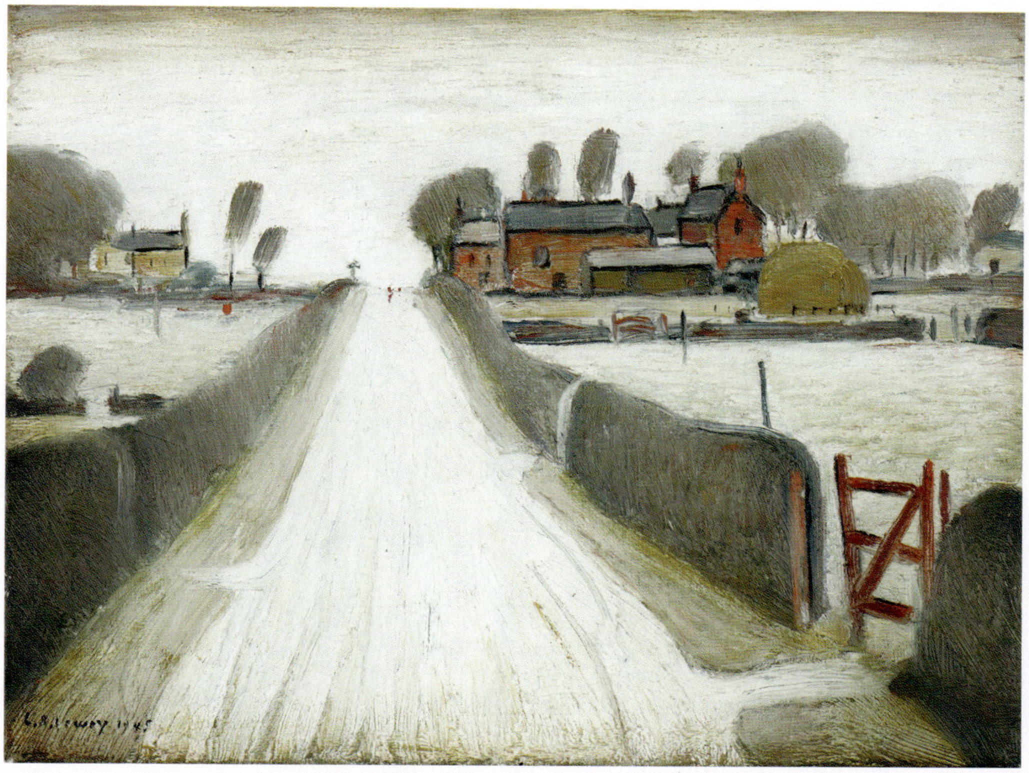

Fylde Farm, 1945, oil on canvas, 38 × 45.25 cm.

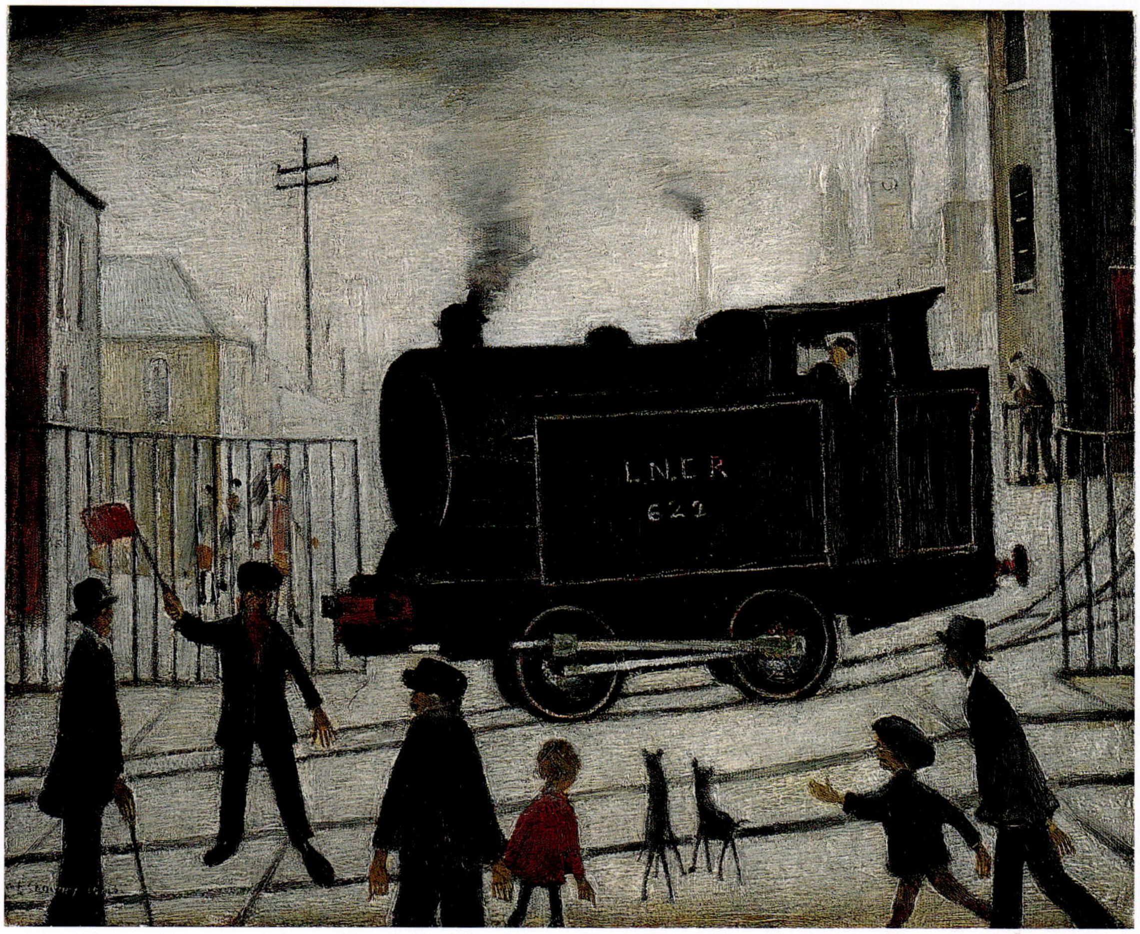

Level Crossing, 1946, oil on canvas, 46.1 × 56.1 cm.

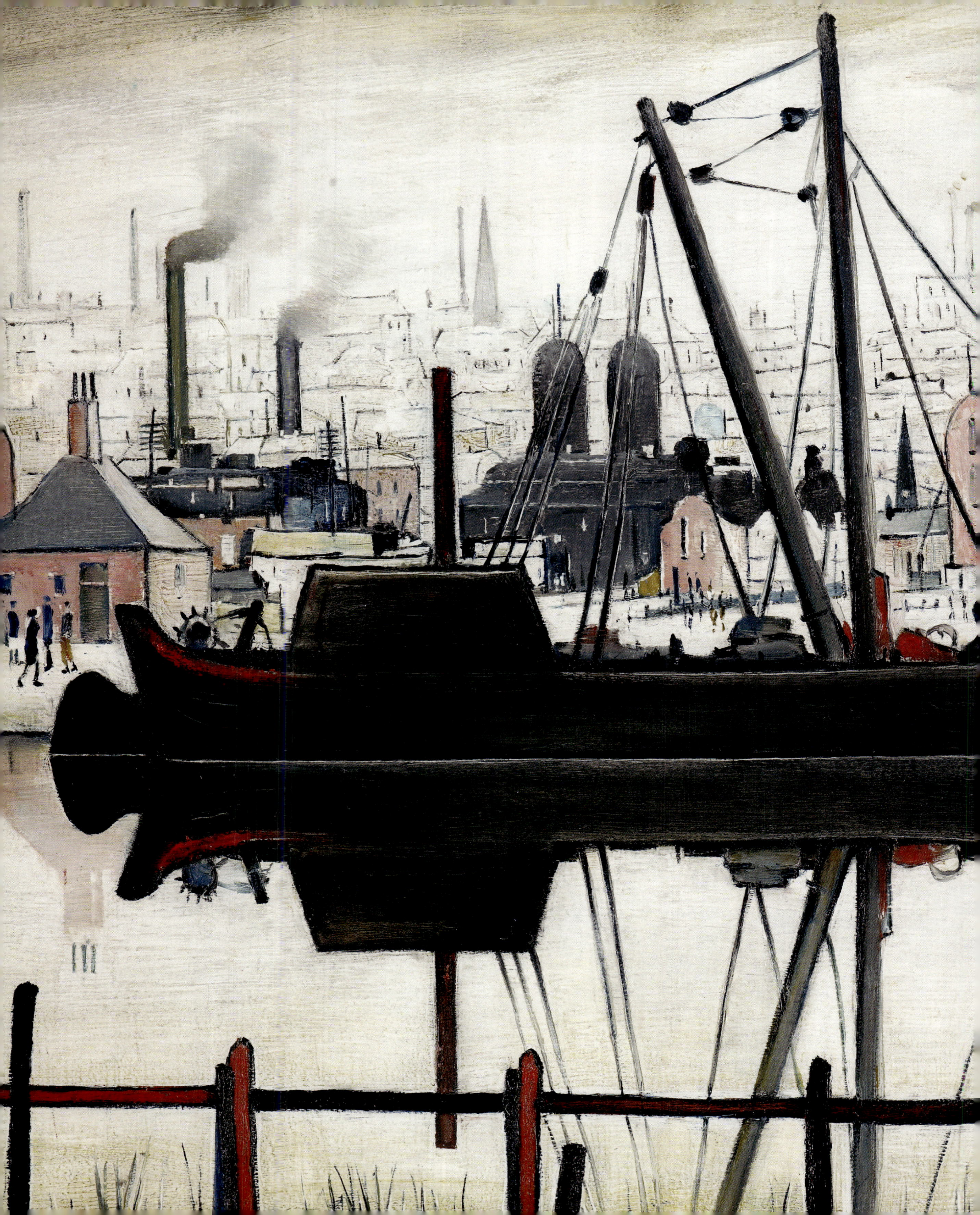

CHAPTER 10

LOWRY'S TECHNIQUE

But now behold,
In the quick forge and working-house of thought.[1]
Shakespeare

Lowry's artistic technique is deceptively simple. Deceptive because it looks easy and limited, which is why he is today one of the most widely forged painters in England. The only other artist I have known who is so frequently forged is the Australian Sidney Nolan who, like Lowry, is expensive and deceptively easy to imitate. Because Nolan's most desired paintings include the square, iron mask of the outlaw Ned Kelly, it is Kelly forgeries that turn up most often at auction houses and at private dealers' galleries. This is because Nolan did many hundreds of pure landscape paintings without a Kelly image which, unless exceptional in quality, are fairly low priced. Consequently unscrupulous people make a tracing of the very simple basic Kelly outline from a genuine Kelly landscape and, with a steady hand and a few brushstrokes paint a Kelly outline on an unadorned landscape and trot off to con a dealer or an auctioneer or, simply, a collector without much judgment and ask for four or five times its original, Kellyless value.

With Lowry it is more complex and the forger, while he may have an endless variety of industrial landscapes to copy, thinks it is fairly easy to do because Lowry used only five colours. Were the would-be forgers more knowledgeable about the sheer difficulty of making a convincing Lowry with that restriction they surely would not try but, ever optimistic in their search for a gullible punter, they turn fake Lowrys out at a great rate. Thus, virtually every known Lowry-dealer, and all the auction houses, get at least one fake offered to them each week and, all too often the fake is offered not by a con-man but by a collector who has been fooled by a con-man, i.e. not actually trying to sell his picture but merely wants an insurance appraisal and is quite shattered when the dealer or auctioneer has to disabuse him. It is not unknown for the victim to offer violence to the bearer of bad news.

In fact Lowry's self-denying ordinance regarding colour is a quite extraordinary limitation to apply to himself. It is true that no one has ever celebrated Lowry as a great colourist, a judgement one could happily apply to Howard Hodgkin, Ivon Hitchens or Craigie Aitchison among others. What Lowry has done is typically paradoxical, given the many difficulties thrown into his path as he struggles to become a significant painter. One can imagine a successful artist having a five colour period in mid-career as an experiment and then, having exhausted the concept, dropping it and moving back, or onwards, with a full palette. I can think of no other major painter who so limited himself. Nor can one see this as a restriction

Detail from *A Coal Barge*, 1938, (p.202).

in pursuit of excellence, or even perfection. In other words, it lacks, for want of a better phrase, the improving benefit of the architects' Golden Section.

The only parallel I can think of is the far more taxing, even brutal, task that Georges Perec inflicted upon himself, to write a full-length novel, *La Disparution*, without once employing the letter E. And if one has, entirely understandably, some difficulty in even coping with the idea, imagine the Herculean labour of Gilbert Adair, who turned Perec's glittering French prose into a sparkling English novel called *A Void*, also without a solitary E. One does wonder whether Lowry was, in his chosen limitation, making life difficult for himself, having to create as it were a language composed only of diphthongs as he mingled his chosen five, or whether he was making life easier for himself in a manner analogous to his dress sense. Lowry restricted his clothing to black suits and black ties so that he never had to worry about which colour he was going to wear when he got up.

Lowry's chosen five colours were; ivory black, vermilion, Prussian blue, yellow ochre and flake white. His obsession with white and what aging can do to it was and remains one of the most widely known of all his charateristics and his celebrated experiment with that colour over a seven-year period is described in Chapter 2. Lowry himself is on record with the words:

> I am a simple man, and I use simple materials: ivory black etc. and no medium. That's all I've ever used for my painting. I like oils. Watercolours I've used only occasionally. They really don't suit me ... dry too quickly. They're not flexible enough. I like a medium you can work into, over a period of time. That's about all there is to say on how I work.[2]

At the risk of being repetitious, Lowry's experiment with flake white was to cover a wooden board with the paint and then place this board in an airtight container for seven years, at the end of which period he took it out of its container. He then painted another board with the same quantity of the same paint so that he could precisely show how seven years of more or less laboratory conditions had affected the texture and the colour of the pigment. Clearly the comparison pleased him and reinforced his enthusiasm for that particular paint. The point is almost too obvious to deserve comment but Lowry left nothing to chance. Every aspect of his art was scrupulously prepared and thought through and, while one should never neglect the association of lies, damned lies and statistics, I am quite certain that among the vast acreage that would be constituted if all of Lowry's paintings were placed end to end, white in some form or other would be the dominant single colour element and, in quite a few paintings, would occupy as much or even more surface area than any other two of his chosen five colours.

Anyone who is anxious to learn just how Lowry painted, without the privilege of having actually watched him at work, must read the booklet, issued by the Lowry Press in 2002 entitled: *Painting a Lowry: Coming from the Mill. A Reconstruction* by Edwin Bowes. In a work of considerable brevity and great sensitivity, Bowes, who was both a painter and a professional conservator, not only produces the best ever analysis of Lowry's technique as an artist, but gives a blow-by-blow account of how he copied a classic Lowry painting in the Salford collection: *Coming from the Mill*, done in 1930 (page 181). It is, in its way, also a forger's charter and, because of the sheer difficulty of the task, also a deterrent to forgery, not least because even to the naked eye it is manifestly not by Lowry and, when exposed to the pitiless process of raking light photography the differences not of colour but of texture and depth of paint leap out at the viewer. This alone should be enough to deter any forger, although given Lowry's prices for his best pictures hope will always spring eternally for the crooked few who still worship at the altar of Van Meegeren, the briefly successful wartime forger of 'undiscovered Vermeers'.

The illustrations on these pages show the original Lowry, the Bowes version, (which is the same size as the original), showing how it has been squared off to facilitate accurate copying, using a grid done over a reproduction, which is then replicated in a larger size over a board so as to ensure that all the ingredients of the original appear in their correct place in the copy.

While a good copyist can work from a reproduction, the result, because based on a two-dimensional object, is never as good as one based on the original painting, which is a three dimensional object, because of the density and depth of the paint on the board. Bowes helpfully tests the materials he has used, including titanium white because, since Lowry's heyday, flake white has become very rarely used now because of its toxicity.

The two other illustrations show the real Lowry photographed with raking light at an angle of 45° to show the depth of the paint and the carefully layered texture which is uniquely Lowry's and immensely difficult to replicate without his hand-eye co-ordination and a total insight into his mind.

Bowes should be read by anyone who wants to know how Lowry thought as a painter and Bowes' completed copy is, as copies go, a brilliant version of singular accuracy. But, as he himself has written, "As Lowry's painting is more than seventy years old [it is now exactly eighty] and covered in a thin layer of surface dirt, the reconstruction has a more crisp appearance than the original".

Lowry's use of white is ubiquitous and copious. The surface of a street can be as white as the sky and if he wants to draw one's attention to the sharp edges of a rectangular building, or the overbearing reaching up to the sky of a factory chimney, he will outline the dark shape with more white to accentuate the sharpness of the *building*.

And, when one looks at one of Lowry's crowds, or a somewhat smaller gathering, they are nearly always displayed against the subtlest of white backgrounds, backgrounds flecked with pink or blue or grey patches. I can think of no other English artist who could create such a subtle and wide range of colours out of a white which is the complete antithesis of any white we know in everyday life, be it a wall, a chair, a sheet of paper, a bedsheet.

Certainly there is no better possible background for the people he painted so obsessively. 'A street ... without people ... is as dead as mutton.' Sometimes Lowry does cheat on his

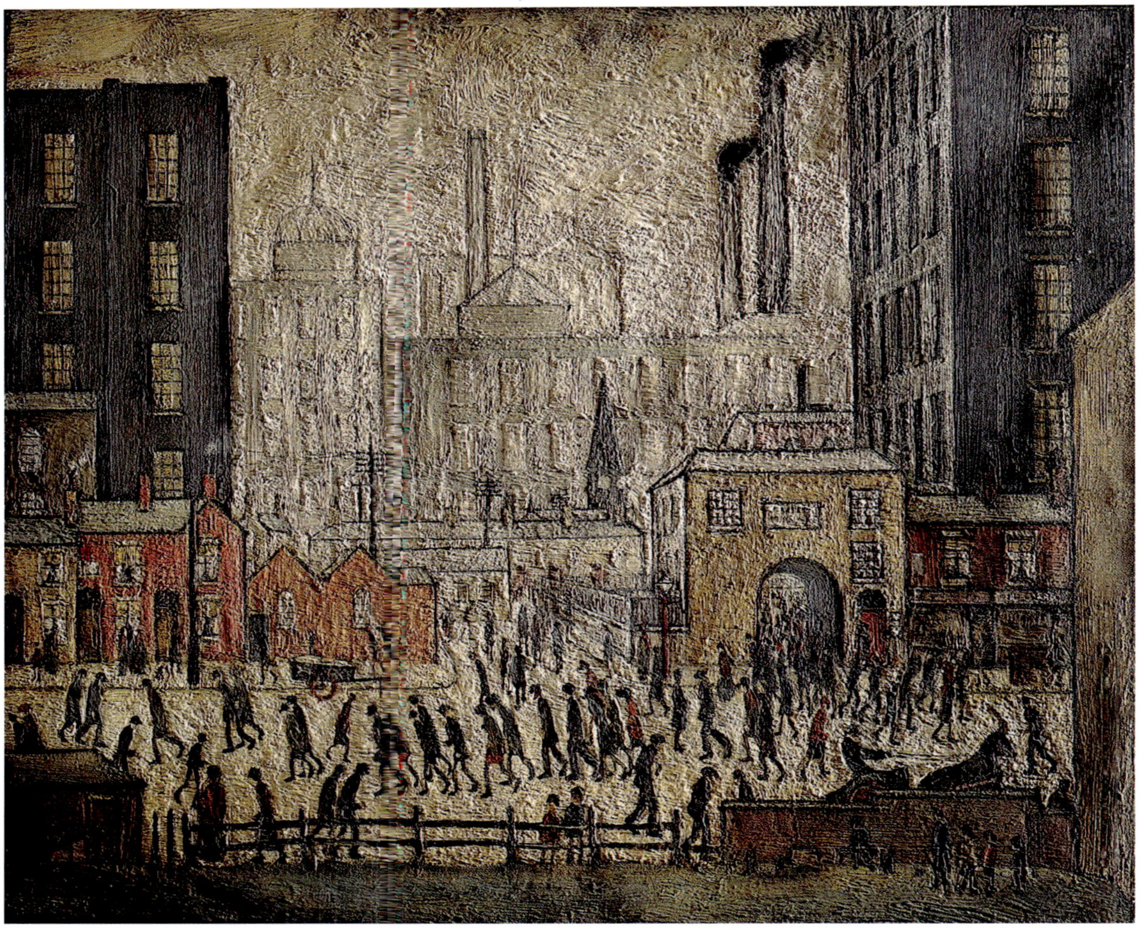

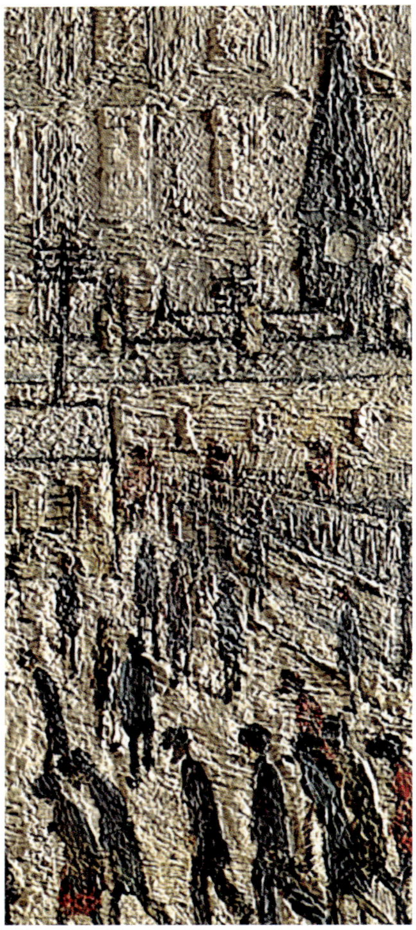

Coming from the Mill, 1930, oil on canvas, 42 × 52 cm., photographed in raking light.

self-imposed narrow colour range. As Bowes has pointed out, in *The Cripples* (page 56), Lowry has used alizarin crimson for the red scarf of the man pushing himself along on a trolley.

As for his love of oil paint he has, as we know, said of his preferred medium:

> I like a medium you can work into, over a period of time. That's about all there is to say on how I work.[3]

Those words of Lowry's provide, in their possibly excessive simplicity, ammunition for Academicians who dismissed him as a naïve or primitive artist but they are certainly both true and self-aware.

Lowry's manifest enjoyment of oil paint as a medium quite often made him move away from the relative flatness and smoothness of his most typical cityscapes and landscapes into the use of a quite heavy impasto. This was often the kind favoured, among his near contemporaries, by such as Jack B. Yeats and Kokoschka and even later artists such as Frank Auerbach although he never went as far as Auerbach whose impasto was, and is, so thick and heavy as to render his subject matter virtually abstract.

When Lowry used impasto it was much cooler in effect than Yeats or Kokoshchka, both of whom used a far wider range of colours. It is reasonable to note that Yeats and Kokoshchka tended to build up their impasto with paint heaped upon paint and pure colour laid on top of pure colour. With Lowry, the impasto was almost a mirror image of what his great contemporaries did in that he built downwards. A very thick layer of oil paint, in his usually subdued range of colours, would be applied and then a third dimension would be added by 'digging' downwards. Lowry would gouge into the paint with a brush handle, or various dimensions of nails to create deep, trough-like lines in the paint which served not as outlines but as lines which actually altered the perspective of the picture and served to emphasize an unusual shape. A classic example of this is a painting of 1953 called *An Old Lady in a Wheelchair* (below). It is quite unmistakably Lowry, redolent of his sly but sympathetic humour and clearly a part of his endless fascination with cripples. Against a white background a rather zany-looking youth is pushing a typically crazy old lady in a wheel chair which, apart from the handle at the back and the two tiny wheels at the front, looks exactly like a dustbin on wheels, surely an effect deliberately sought by Lowry. The thick, heavy impasto of the paint is highlighted by deep striations made by a sharp object such as a stout six-inch nail. For all its old-fashioned association of subject matter it is quite definitely, and very curiously, a strikingly 'modern' picture for 1953.

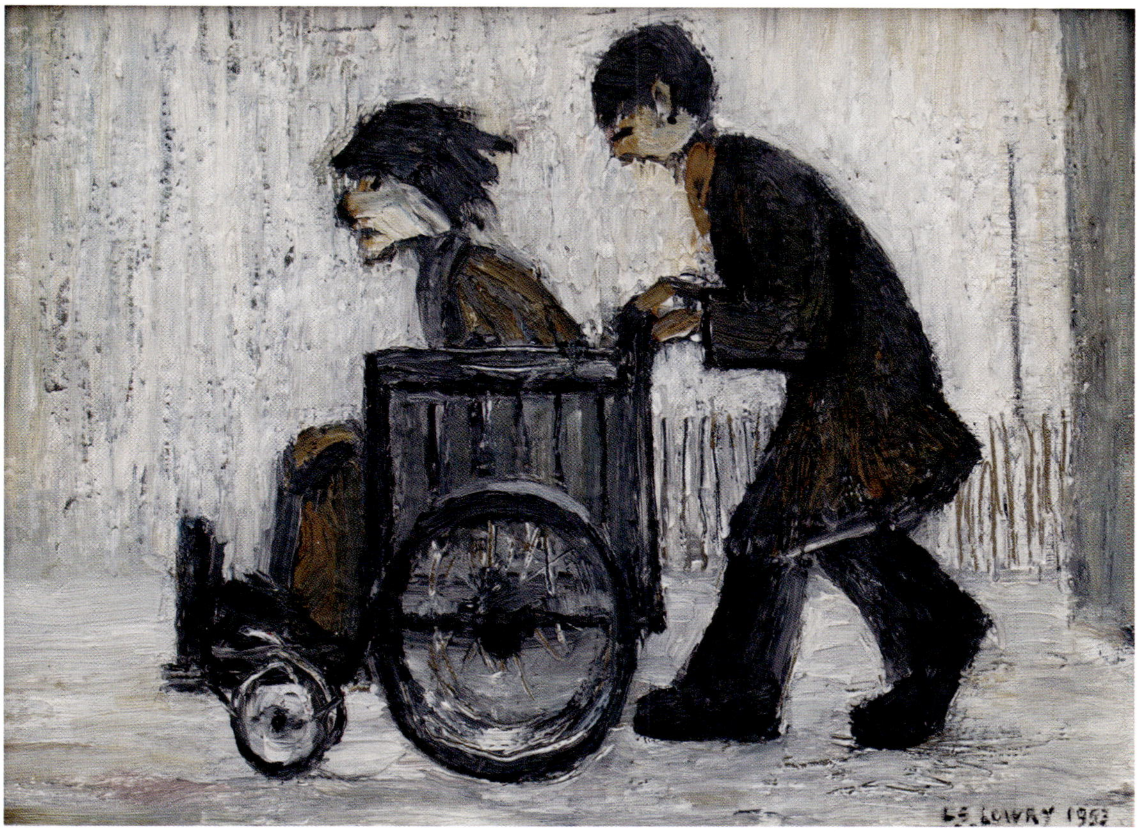

An Old Lady in a Wheelchair, 1953, oil on board, 24 × 33 cm.

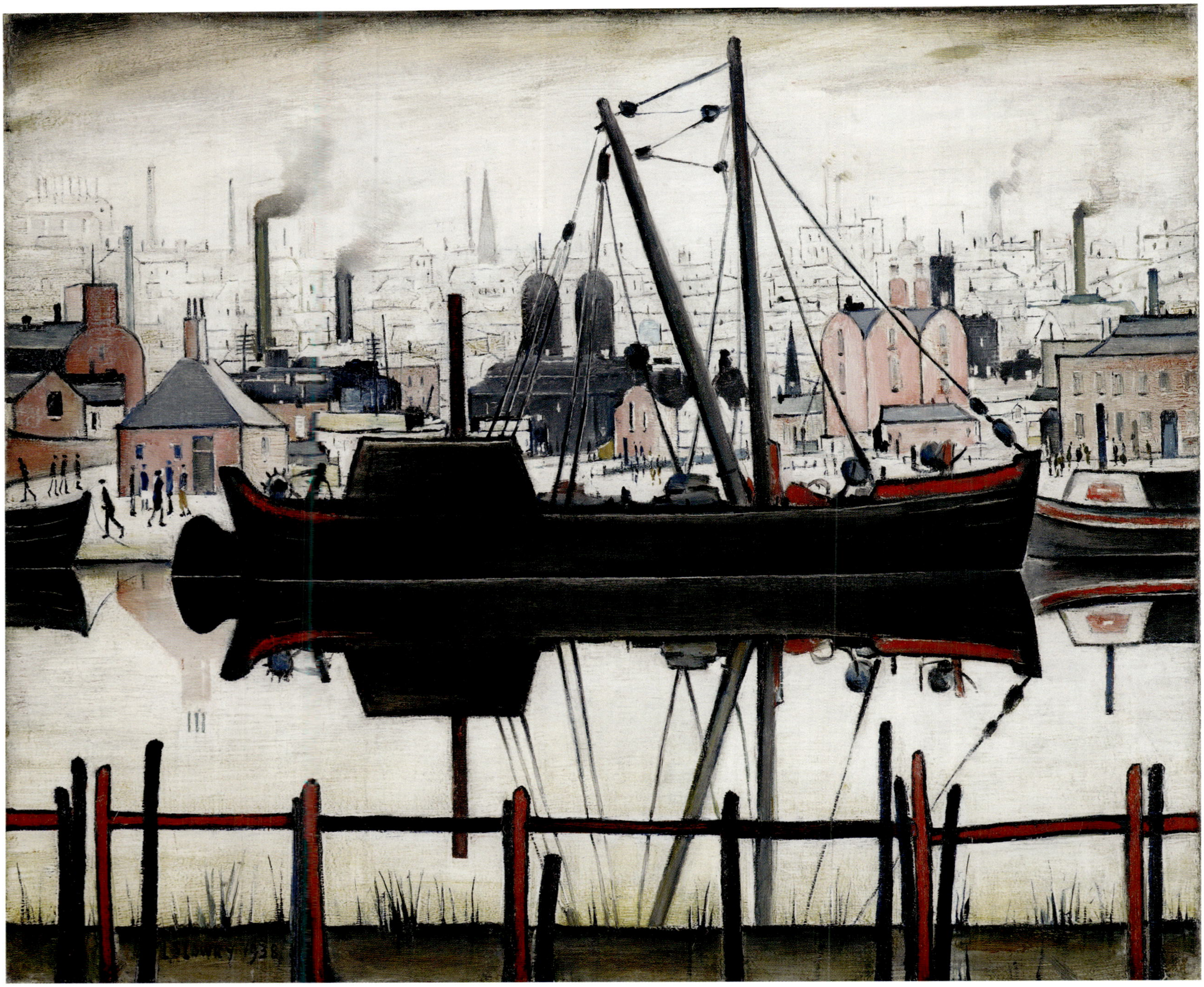

A Coal Barge, 1938, oil on canvas, 43 × 53 cm.

He has also been charged as naïve because he very rarely paints shadows. He does however paint reflexions when the spirit moves him, particularly with ships on water, when he will produce the classic image of a boat on water with its upside-down image reflected directly underneath it (above).

Another criticism, also presented in somewhat admonitory terms, as if telling off an errant schoolboy, is that he painted in artificial light. This is certainly true. He was in no way a *plein-airiste*. He did not possess a proper studio full of windows and skylights, simply because he did not need them and he did not need them because he would not, until he became successful, have been able to exploit them as other painters do. By day Lowry was a rent collector and office worker in a part of Britain where bright sunlight was, even if it could penetrate the ever-present pollution, a rare commodity. In any case, while he sketched in pencil on paper when he was perambulating among the tenants, he painted only at home and only at night with artificial light. This was his right to do if it suited him and if it deprived us of shadows that is a small loss in the face of his talents.

In any case there are other artists who painted by artificial light, such as Caravaggio or Georges de la Tour. Josef Albers, who with all the superior resources of the Bauhaus, followed by the richest universities and art institutes in the world, painted his abstract masterpieces *only* by artificial light in a studio where only electricity could give him the reliable constancy of light he needed for an art which consisted of an endless set of variations on the square, and the quality and power of colour that he sought could only be created with a light which was both permanent and consistent.

That quality was also something Lowry needed and, having seen him at work in the studio at his house in Mottram-in-Longdendale, it was extraordinary what he could do in the relative glare of light from the most primitive of fixtures.

There is a fascinating unpublished manuscript by Lowry's old friend Professor Hugh Maitland and which is now in the Lowry archive at The Lowry Museum in Salford. One passage does illuminate Lowry's feelings about artificial light and daylight:

> It has been said that Lowry is no colourist, a point of view that may perhaps be related to deliberately restricted palette. On the other hand his pearly or smoky white and the range of his beautiful greys and greens have often been praised. They were all made from the primary colours. It had occurred to me that probably he used these few colours to facilitate painting by artificial light since I supposed they could be manipulated under such conditions with more assurance than a larger number including a variety of primary and secondary colours. This however appears not to have been the origin of this practice that it may indeed have made painting by artificial light more manageable. Lowry painted a great deal at night. It was customary for him to stay up very late and he often worked into the early hours of the morning. He said once he liked working then when he could feel free from the possibility of interruption and nothing could come between him and his painting. He did however always finish his paintings in daylight. Latterly he has sometimes tended to give the impression that he made drawings at night but did not paint much. This idea can only be meant for public consumption for over the years one has been aware of the great amount of painting he had achieved which has necessitated long hours of work after leaving the office.[4]

One thing which Lowry was definitely not was a topographical artist. I have no doubt that his pencil drawings done *in situ* were reliable and accurate and that the full scale drawings of individual houses or office buildings or entire streets, were reliable as reportage of urban life. But there is little evidence that he painted actual cityscapes, whether working from sketches or even photographs. When he confronted a large canvas or board, the first thing he did was to cover it in white and then leave for up to a week to dry and probably then give it another white coat. He might leave it for a further period and would then sketch outlines in pencil or charcoal on the board or canvas with one item leading to another and so on until he had covered the surface with a set of images which he would then paint. But only rarely was the finished painting of a town or city square a work that anyone would recognize as real. In effect he made a composition which interested him and pleased him and which was in no way a topographical record as, say, John Piper might have made. Lowry's cityscapes were in fact mindscapes that spring only partly from his practical observation

Bellevue House, Leaf Square, Salford, 1925, pencil on paper, 24 × 34 cm.

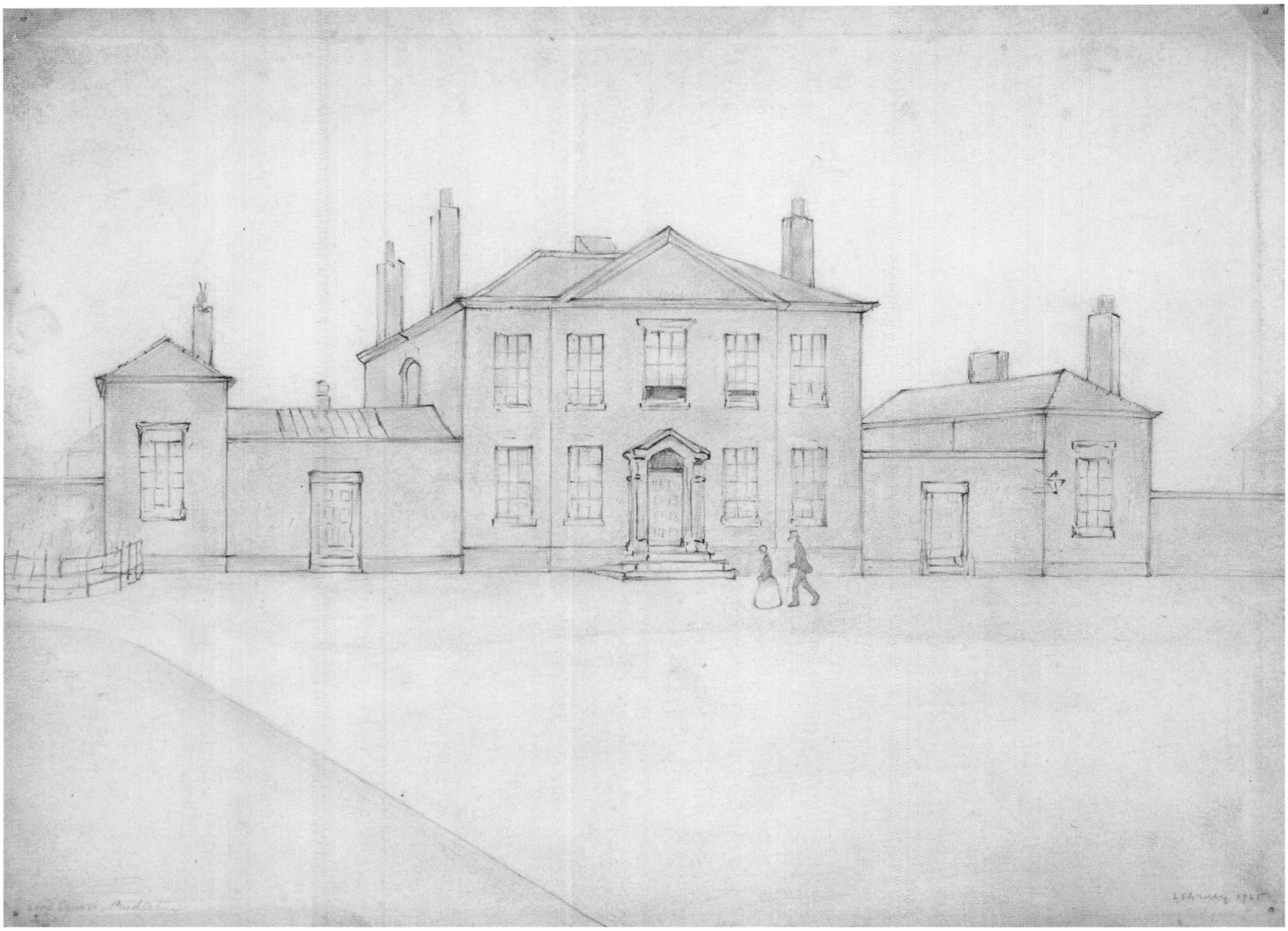

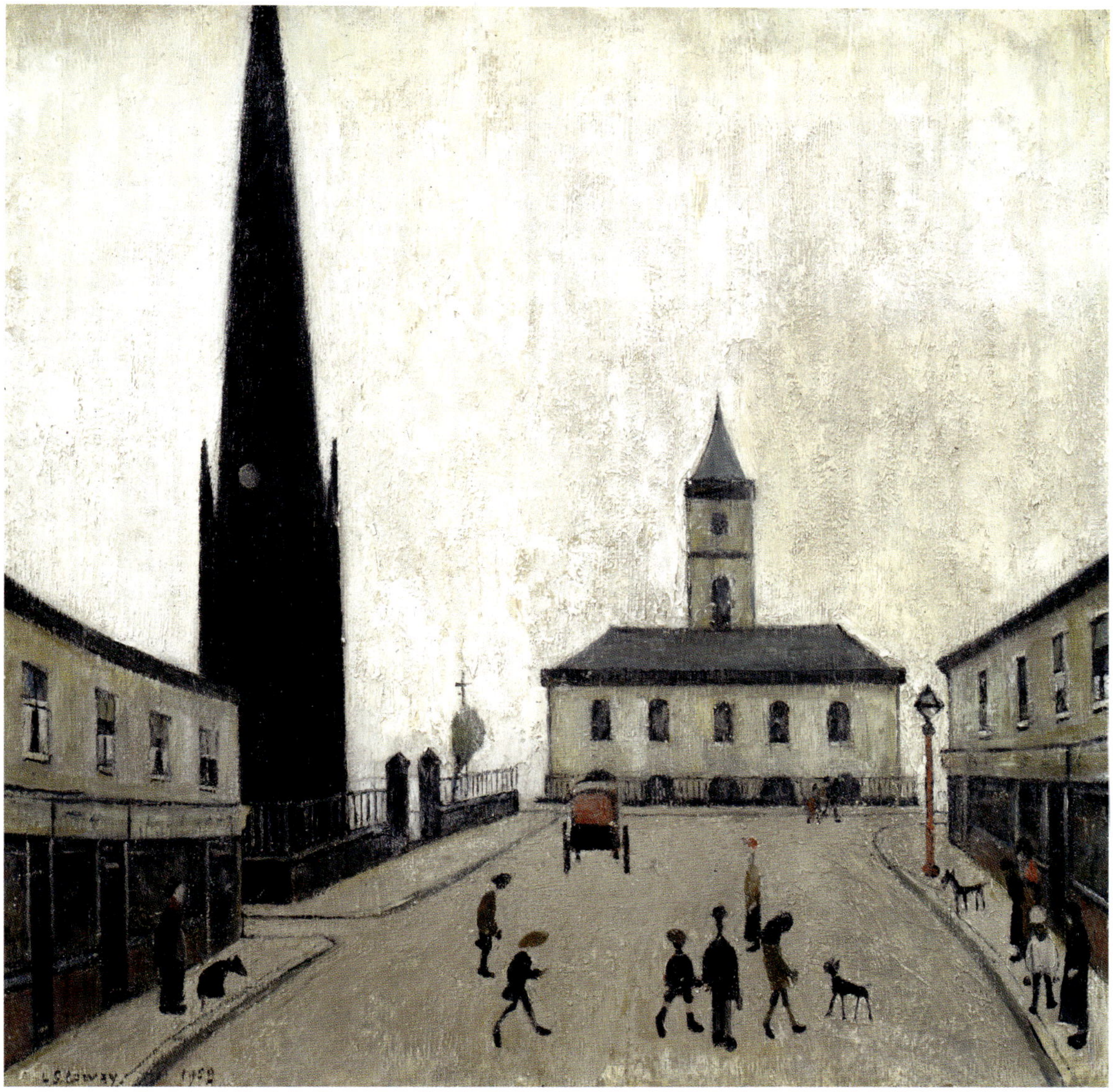

Old Town Hall and St Hilda's Church, Middlesbrough, 1959, oil on canvas, 43.8 × 43.8 cm.

and experience and partly came out of his head, with their own inner logic which was not the logic of the reporter or the photographer or the town planner, but purely the logic of a combination of Lowry's artistic design and the aesthetic beauty he perceived around him in his highly personal spirit of place.

He certainly was not naïve nor a Sunday painter. He was, in his own unique style, a master-craftsman in paint who, in terms of imagery and composition, made the industrial North West's beauty more true and more exciting than any mere reality.

CHAPTER 11

LOWRY AND THE SEA

> *The sea, well I like the sea for its own sake. I'm very fond of the sea … oh yes, I'm very fond of the sea … Well, it comes in, comes in and comes in. There it is, this vast expanse, and I often wonder and often say to friends, I wonder wouldn't it be dreadful … what would happen if the sea suddenly didn't … The tide didn't turn and the sea came on and on and on and on and on. What would it be like? Wouldn't it be wonderful just to see it? Just fancy … on and on and on … didn't stop at all. Went on for ever. Awful isn't it?*[1]
>
> L. S. Lowry

The epigraph above is classic Lowry. Set down in cold print it perfectly expresses for all its faintly rambling, repetitive quality Lowry's ambiguity of feelings for the sea. It is at once beautiful, restful to watch and observe its incessant changing of colour and surface motion and yet simultaneously the source of his doom-laden fantasy about its potential ferocity, something far better known today with instant television pictures of whole countries devastated by floods and tsunamis. Particularly in his later years, during his lengthy love/hate relationship with the North East, the sea brought him much pleasure. At last when he had enough money to stay in a seaside hotel near Newcastle whenever he felt like it, he watched its endless changes and turned even a fierce stormy ocean into a thing of beauty. In this ambivalence there is a direct analogue with his treatment of the worst legacies of the Industrial Revolution in Manchester, Salford and Stockport. There he found beauty among the polluting depredations of the mills and factories, with their never-ending smoke and dirt and the squalor of the cramped, unhygienic little houses that contained the mass of the population. As we know, he transformed what seemed to most people ugliness, meanness and filth into something intrinsically beautiful. The sea, at least on a day when the weather was good, had none of the grim squalor of the city-scapes, only a beauty which he tried again and again to pass on to the viewer.

But while, in the late years, the sea produced for him the apocalyptic vision of eternal destruction set out in the epigraph it was not always so. However difficult his early, mother-dominated life was, there was always, for him and even for her, the joys of modest holidays on the North-West coast in the resort towns like Lytham St Anne's or Grange-over-Sands (but not Blackpool which was vulgar) with their rapacious landladies, the terrible food and beaches on which you could exhaust your legs, when the tide was out, walking barefoot to get to the seemingly distant beginning of the actual sea, the salt-water stinging your eyes and freezing your limbs, leaving physical memories that are today, more than sixty years after those wartime escapes from the big cities, as vivid as any Proustian madeleine.

Detail from *The Sea*, 1963, (p.216).

The Lancashire sea is most clearly captured in Lowry's many paintings of pre-war seascapes full of families at play and the little, multi-coloured yachts that constituted the only "pretty" pictures in Lowry's *œuvre*. At their best they rival Boudin and would not disgrace early Monet and it is no accident that the only painting he did which gained his mother's approval was of *Sailing Boats* (page 97), a painting which, after her death, was treasured by Lowry as the closest thing to his mother's long-sought, but perpetually withheld, recognition that her son was a real artist. It would take a very gifted psychoanalyst to work out the intricacies of Lowry's early fascination with Lytham and his later, long after his mother's death, switch from Lancashire beaches to the far more dramatic Northumbrian coast and resolutely un-pretty pleasures of the sea at Roker.

It is also, I suspect, not mere speculation to say that the sea, wherever he found it, gave him ample opportunity to work with his beloved, and so ingeniously exploited, white paint. More than the industrials, and more than his earth-bound landscapes the views of the sea had one overpowering component which existed on a much smaller – and frequently mostly hidden – aspect, namely an uninterrupted horizon where the preponderant white sky met the edge of the sea. This could, if Lowry wished it so, be another shade of white, its precise colour depending on the state of the water. And, just as his city-scapes were unique, inimitable and quite unlike anything done by other established artists, so his seascapes were also *sui generis*. He was not a follower of Turner and he had more or less nothing in common with the legion of Dutch painters of the sea.

The strength and nature of his marine style was doubtless affected by his love of water in many other forms. The sea was naturally the powerful engine that drove his seascapes but he also turned to rivers, canals, estuaries, lakes, reservoirs, docks, even Manchester City Waterworks, and entire cities built on water such as his challenging portrait of Liverpool, *The Liver Building* (page 209) which he makes as mysterious and as fascinating as a view of Venice by Sickert or Sargent. Painted in 1962, it is dominated by the Liver Building itself, Liverpool's architectural icon long before the city was the designated 2007/2008 Capital of Culture. It looms over the waterfront with its massive bulk, but not obtrusively so, because it is seen dimly, as if it had been painted on a misty day and is virtually without colour, although far from colourless. The colour comes from the activity on the water and in the foreground and is provided by tugs and cargo boats and the bright, small splashes of colour provided by the minuscule prams, children, pedestrians and dogs which point up the vastness of the distant public buildings. Inevitably, and beautifully applied, the predominant colour is the endless varied, sometimes, glowing, sometimes grubby white, containing, as always with Lowry, a rich mixture of delicate tints which show off the painstakingly created "drop" of the white. One is tempted to use the word "futuristic" in connection with this and other comparable paintings; not in the sense of Futurism, the art movement which exploded during Lowry's lifetime but entirely passed him by; but in the sense of a dedicated artist painting in such a way that he knows the picture will not look as he wishes it to look, but will only realize his dream in a near future as it ages between five and ten years or when he is already dead. That

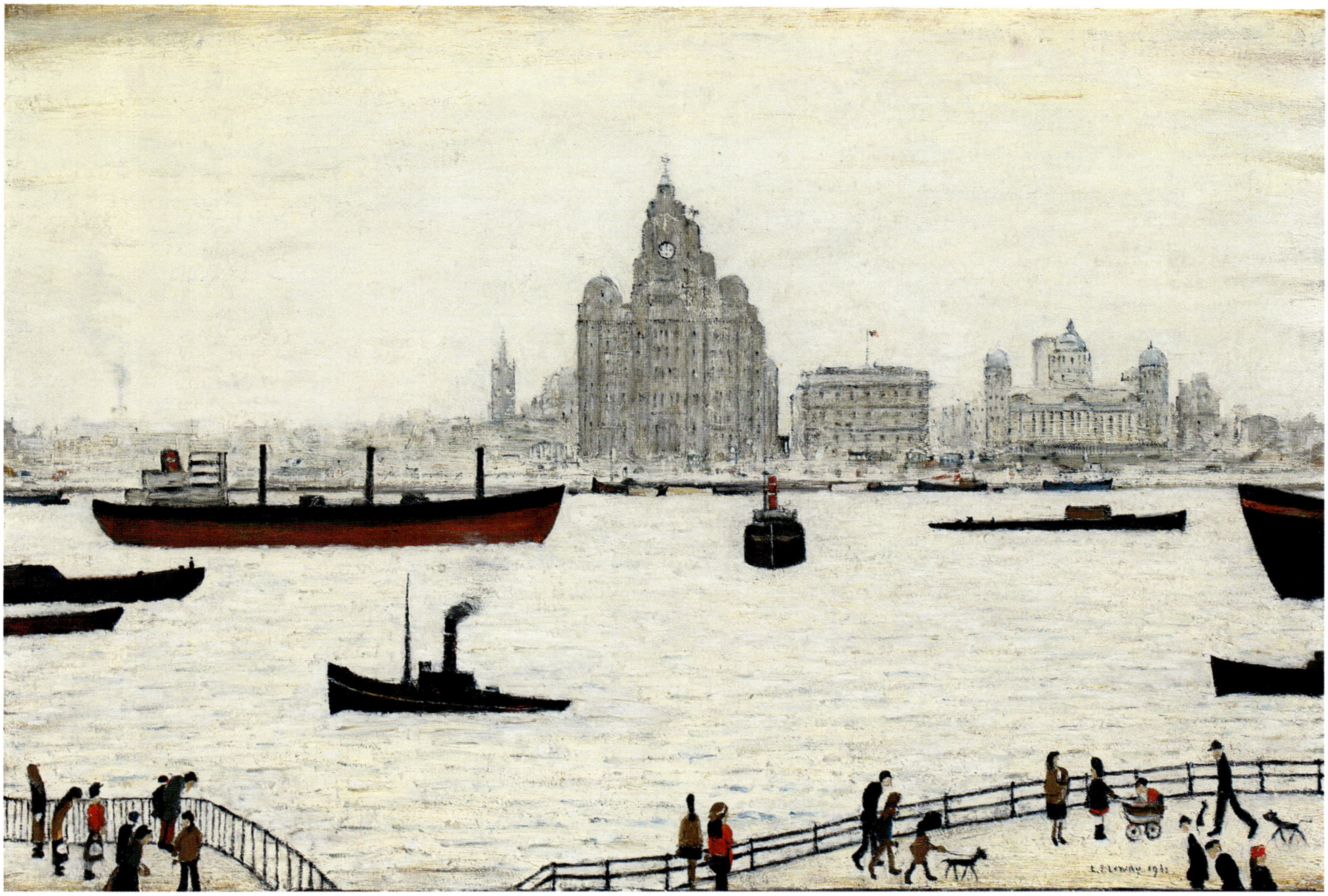

The Liver Building, 1962, oil on canvas, 58.4 × 86.4 cm.

was simultaneously Lowry the grouchy pessimist and Lowry the artist with an eminently practical view of posterity.

In the same Tate Liverpool Lowry exhibition, shown in spring of 2007, which showed *The Liver Building* in public for the first time since 1973, there was one of his classic small pictures, just as memorable in its way as *The Liver Building*. Called *Knott End: Fleetwood Ferry* of 1953, it is oil on board, about six inches high by ten wide, and is a superb miniature example of Lowry's genius. It is a perfect, intimate seascape, the water multi-coloured, rippling with motion. The crowd, as so often, is flawlessly differentiated, not a matchstick in sight, moving with the characteristic flow of those who have just disembarked from the tub-like ferry boat. There was also in the small, but skilfully chosen show, done especially for Liverpudlians to understand their connection with Lowry, a marvellous non-maritime painting which, intentionally or not, was complementary to *The Funeral Party* of

1963 (page 154). Done in 1953 and entitled *City Gentlemen*, it would be pure, idle speculation to assume that they were necessarily Liverpudlian City Gents. Rather, they seem to be universal – or at least Britishly universal – of a well-known type and a type here being sardonically caricatured by a Lowry who clearly had no time for them except as fodder for his satire. There are nine of them in a row and they manage quite immaculately not to interact with each other. They simply display their varied heights, bulks, pompous clothes and briefcases, as if each is wearing the outmoded uniform of some disbanded regiment of faintly shifty poseurs. The fat, the thin, the smoking, glad-hand or ignore their fellows; every one is self-consciously "a character", everyone different. Yet again Lowry reminds

Jetty at Knott End, near Fleetwood, 1957, oil on canvas, 45.7 × 61 cm.

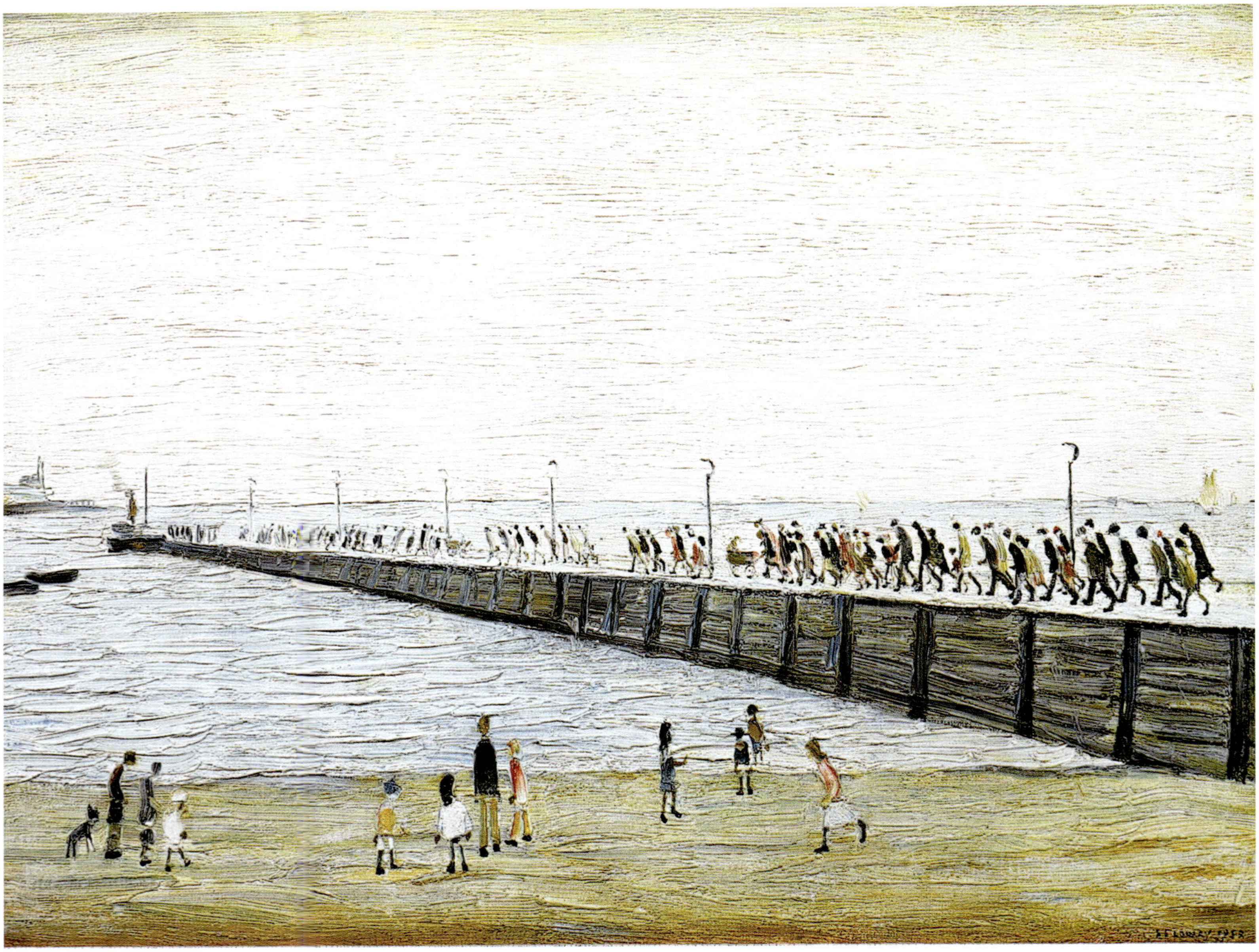

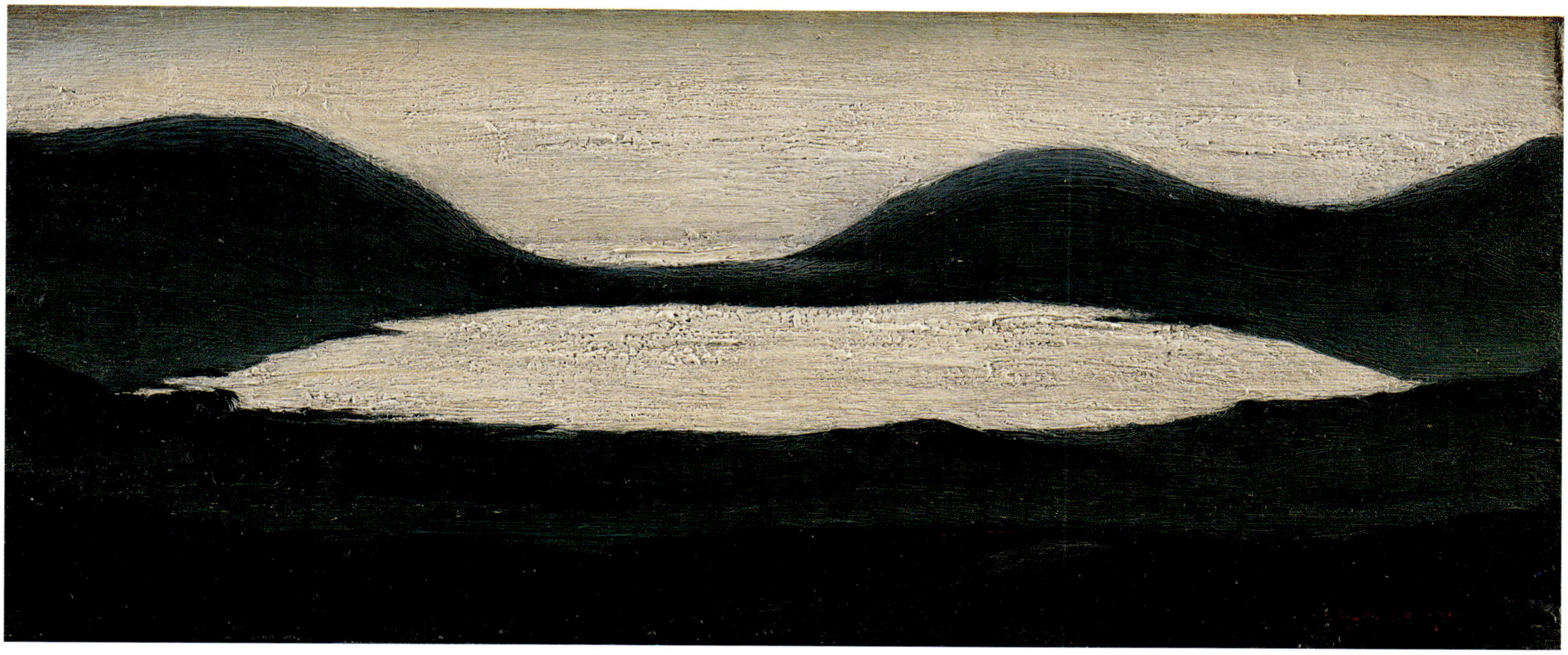

The Lake, 1951, oil on board, 19.1 × 47.3 cm.

one of Daumier at his most cutting and to see this sardonic satire hanging opposite some of his best seascapes is to get an insight into what Lowry *disliked* in direct contrast to what he loved. And, while he famously did not paint shadows, he liked reflexions and there are few reflective surfaces more interesting than water and none more so than absolutely clear water. There is a masterly painting of a boat moored in clear water, where the upper part of the boat is painted upright as far as the waterline and, below the waterline, we are given a precise upside-down mirror image of the upright top half. It is flawlessly executed and one cannot help wondering if Lowry did it so perfectly, and yet so originally, simply to cock a snook at the stuffy R.A.s who called him an amateur because he painted in artificial light and without shadows.

Lowry had a somewhat mixed view about lakes which fascinated him but, in paint, were not always obviously Lowry-like. A painting, such as *The Lake* of 1951 (above) is part study of water and part landscape with the hillside on the upper right recalling the completely breast-like hill he puts into other pictures. Here the breast could also be the buttocks moving left to right into the dip of the waist and then rising again and merging into the torso of a well-shaped woman. There are other paintings of mountain lakes, sometimes showing multiple lakes dominated by his multi-coloured white.

Occasionally Lowry will merge his passions as in *Crime Lake* of 1942 (page 212). This oddly named piece of water, perhaps commemorating some earlier, heinous crime, is near Daisy Nook and is a popular boating lake. It is the complete antithesis of the rather cold, people-less mountain lakes in that it is a densely populated, local pleasure centre, like those in Regent's Park or the Serpentine in London. More than forty boats and countless people

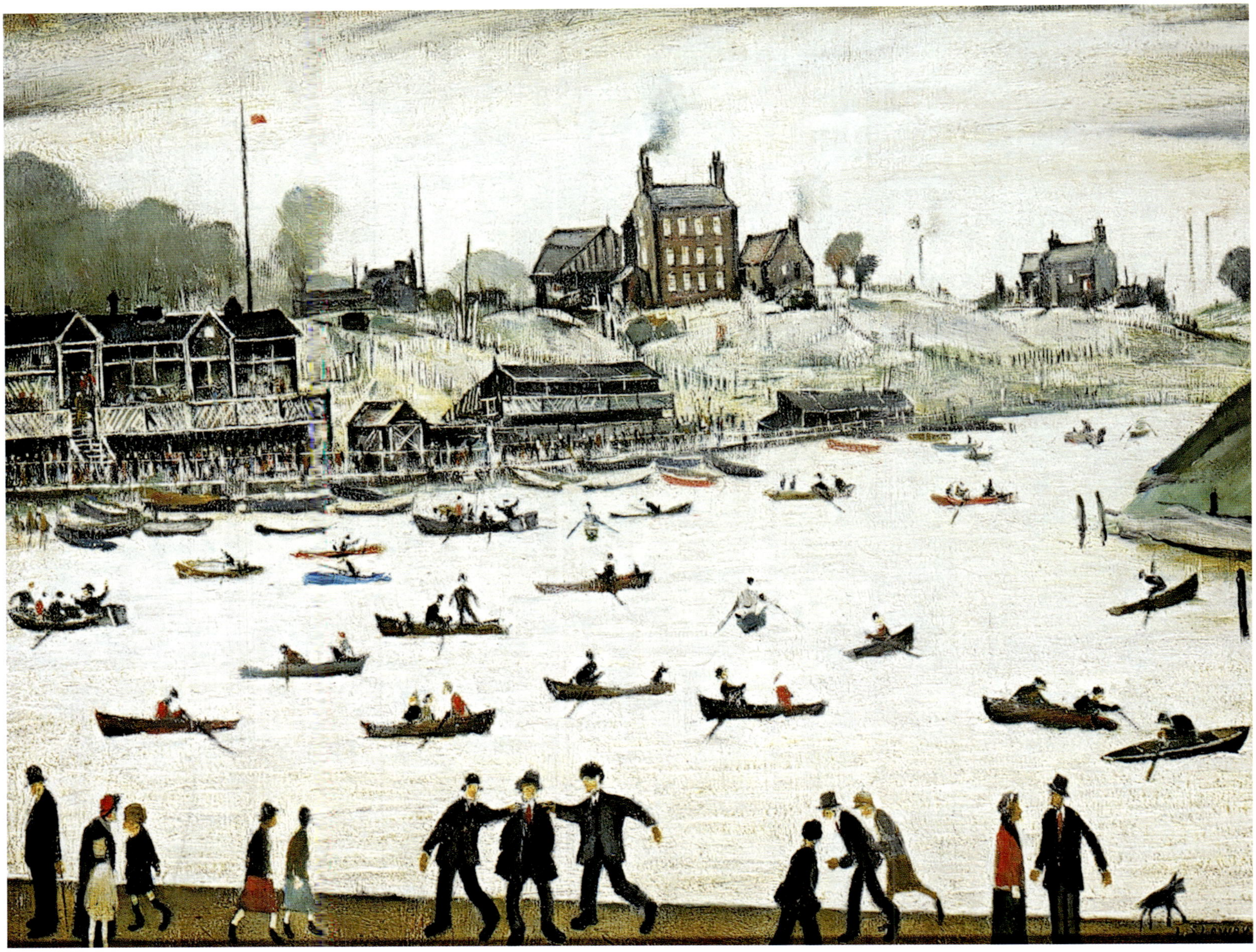

Crime Lake, 1942, oil on canvas, 45.7 × 61 cm.

have taken to the water and there is a lively background of boatyards, shops and some houses. In the foreground there is a small selection of people who include a man being arrested by two plainclothes policemen as Lowry gives us a reference or even a justification for the painting's title.

Crime Lake is an interesting combination of placid water and human bustle, a combination he uses in some of his best paintings of docks in places like Glasgow or South Shields. Yet he can still turn on the gloom, as in *Ship Entering Princess Dock, Glasgow* of 1947 (page 213) which is bereft of any humans and is about as cheerful as the craft bearing the Flying Dutchman. You feel, when you look at this grim work that the ship coming towards you is

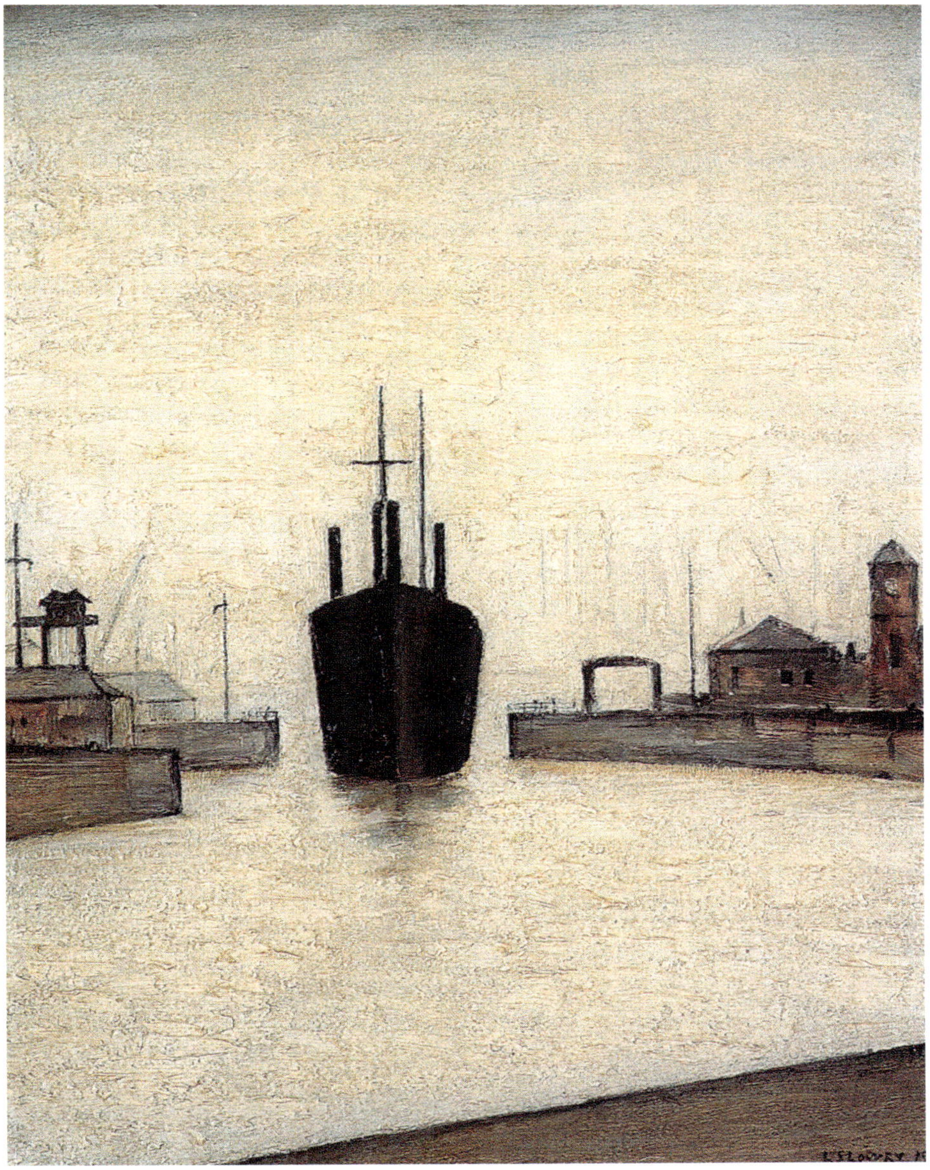

Ship Entering Princess Dock, Glasgow, 1947, oil on canvas, 68.75 × 59.25 cm.

truly doom-laden, that it is going in one direction only and that it won't come back. Charon is its pilot and the painting is as chilling to look at as Böcklin's *The Isle of the Dead.*

Ship Entering Princess Dock, Glasgow is a clear and innocuous title but the picture bears a heavy freight, not so much of doom as of despair, and is one of the few maritime studies by Lowry which is not seen as a source of pleasure. Rather it reminds one in its mood of *The Island*, the painting Howard Jacobson so shrewdly related to Golgotha. That is probably the only Lowry oil painting in which the water is as derelict, if water can be so described, as the building it surrounds and as putrid as the broken-down, skeletal boats on its drab surface are rotten.

As we know, Lowry loves the sea and also fears it and it is interesting that the only other Lowry depiction of water I know of which matches that of *An Island* (page 39) and which

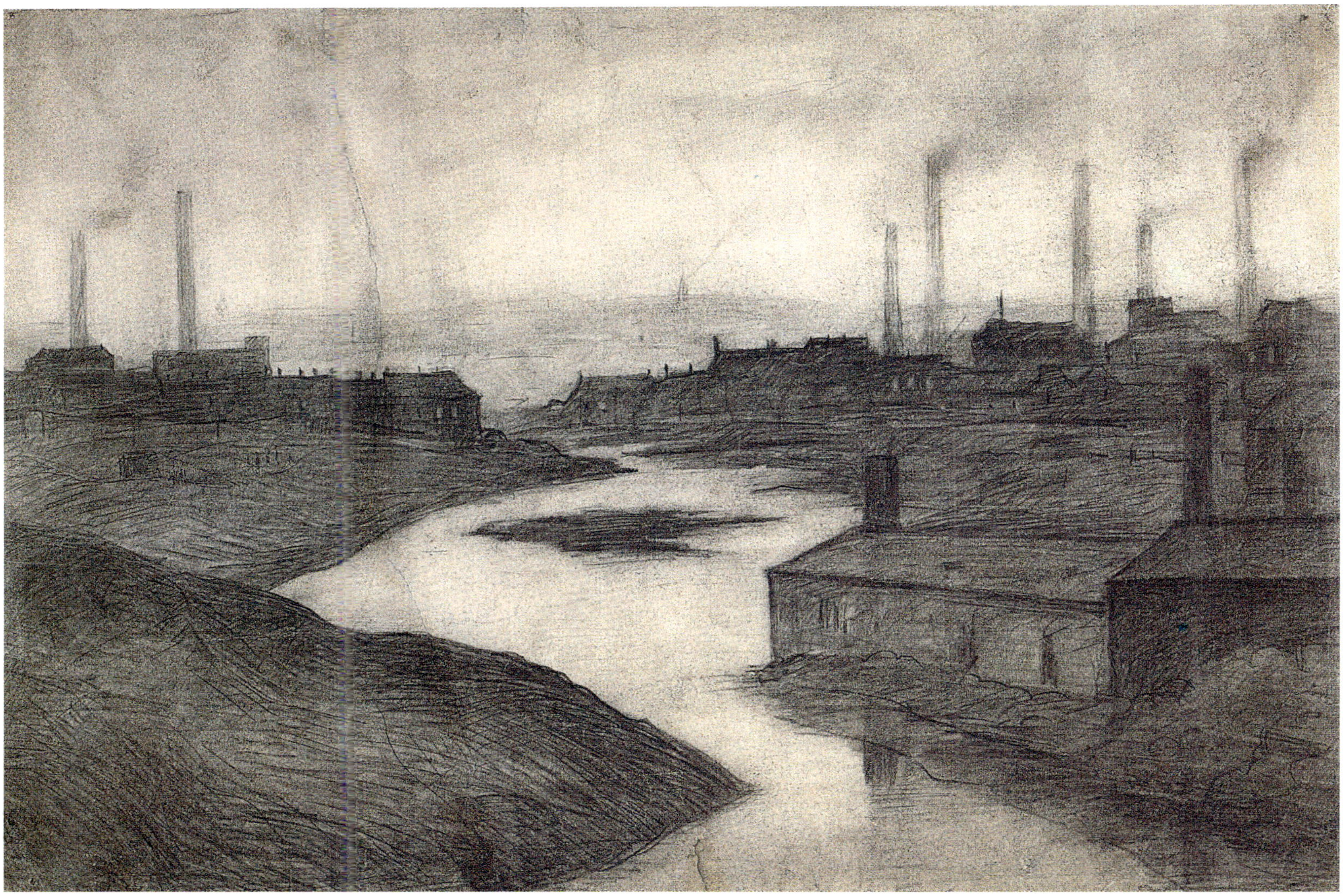

River Irwell at the Adelphi, 1924, pencil on paper, 35.5 × 52.3 cm.

Michael Howard, in his study of Lowry, has juxtaposed with *An Island*, is a fine pencil sketch, done in 1924, called *The River Irwell at the Adelphi* (above). This shows, in almost gruesome detail, the destructiveness of a polluted river in flood, threatening the foundations, and thus the survival, of the industrial buildings on or near the river banks.

But no matter how much Lowry feared the sea he certainly knew how to paint it, how to capture its moods, how to portray its subtle, ever-changing colour scheme. Henry Ford, who made millions when a million dollars was still a gigantic sum is said to have become even wealthier than supposed by marketing his Model T Ford and giving his customers a choice of colour scheme. “You can have any colour you want: so long as it’s black.” Lowry, whose choices of colour were literally limitless, since he could mix his five colours of paint in any way he wanted, used white almost as unsparingly as Ford used black. As has already been observed, his sea pictures enjoyed the luxury of horizons where one white could, and did,

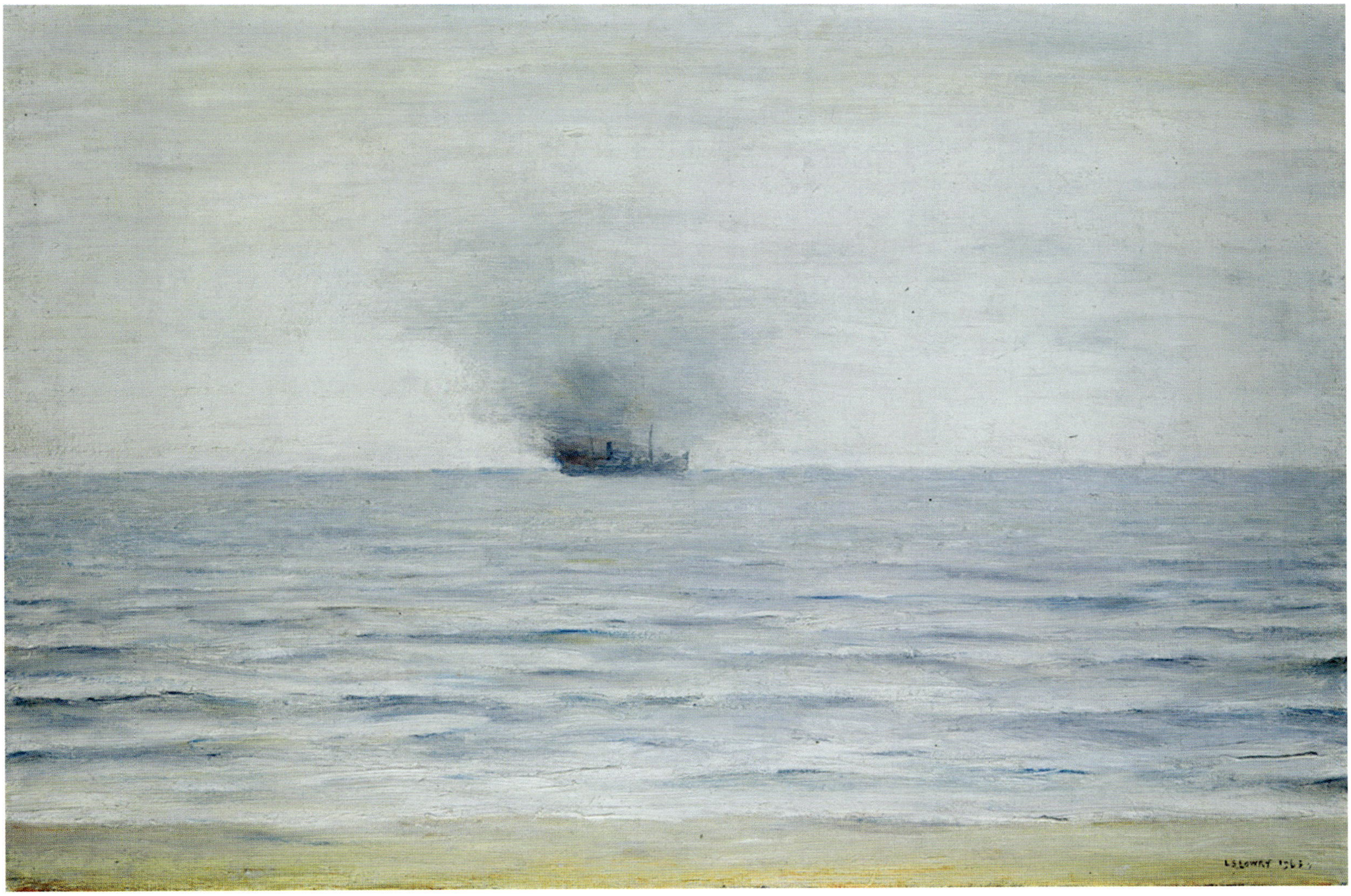

Sea Trials at South Shields, 1963, oil on canvas, 50.8 × 76.2 cm.

meet another so that his white sea and white sky could act as his two palettes rather than a single one, thus giving him two separate colour ranges to work with, two distinct – and distinctive – palettes for a single picture. There is one particular painting which shows this off and which, were it not for a small ship, wreathed in smoke, perched almost centrally on the horizon we would be looking at an abstract painting as rigorous as a de Staël. It is called *Sea Trials at South Shields* (above) and was a relatively late work, done in 1963 when Lowry was 76.

It is interesting because at the bottom there is a yellow strip so that the picture has two significant horizontal lines, in effect an extra horizon and the need for three sets of colours rather than two. The yellow strip is of course the beach at its edge with the sea. The horizon supports a quite small – or, rather, distant – ship partly enveloped in a cloud of smoke which, as it moves towards the sky, is dispersing into what looks like a real cloud. The line of the

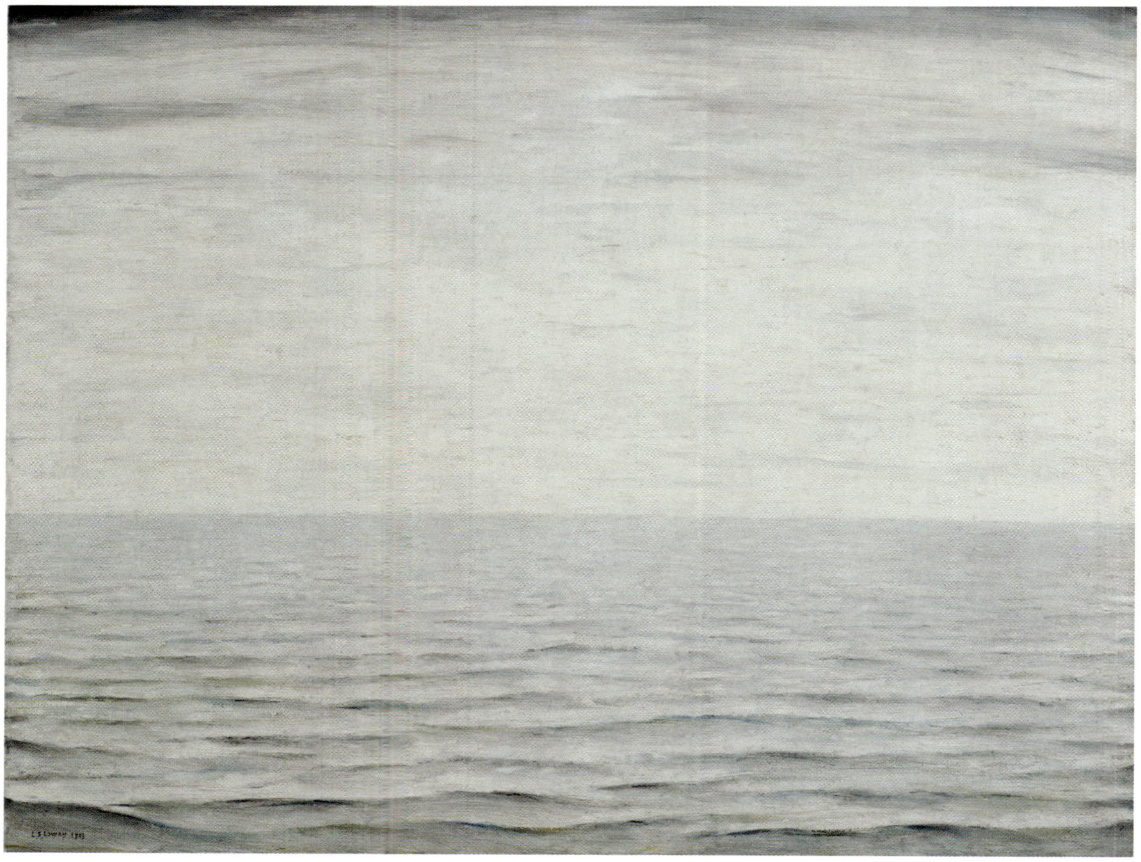

The Sea, 1963, oil on canvas, 76.6 × 102.3 cm.

horizon, often blurred by Lowry so that it is hard to discern the line between land and sky, is here abundantly clear even though Lowry has given us a very blue sea and, in a much paler version, a blue-ish sky.

The sea is not particularly menacing. There are waves but they are – at least for the present – too gentle either to presage or indicate danger, but the vivid blue of the wavelets is underlaid by glimpses of the yellow sand below. The sky is a much paler blue with vestigial reminiscences of the smoke from the ship to add a tinge of grey to the white base. Had it been painted by Whistler it could be called A Symphony in Blue and White.

There are one or two sea pictures which, for all their freedom from the dirt and darkness of the mill scenes, are a kind of maritime substitute for the mill and other industrial scenes of which Lowry had grown tired. *South Shields* of 1962 (page 217) shows a teeming dockyard instead of a teeming mill or factory yard or forecourt. Against a background of heavy muni-cipal dockside buildings there are vast freighters and container ships, one or two rust-buckets and nearly twenty assorted smaller vessels ranging from tugs to privately-owned recreational craft. Sky and sea miss out on the horizon because there is no room for it but both sky and sea have their carefully differentiated white ground and the ships and the onlookers and bystanders provide all the necessary variation of colour. The picture is a breathtaking

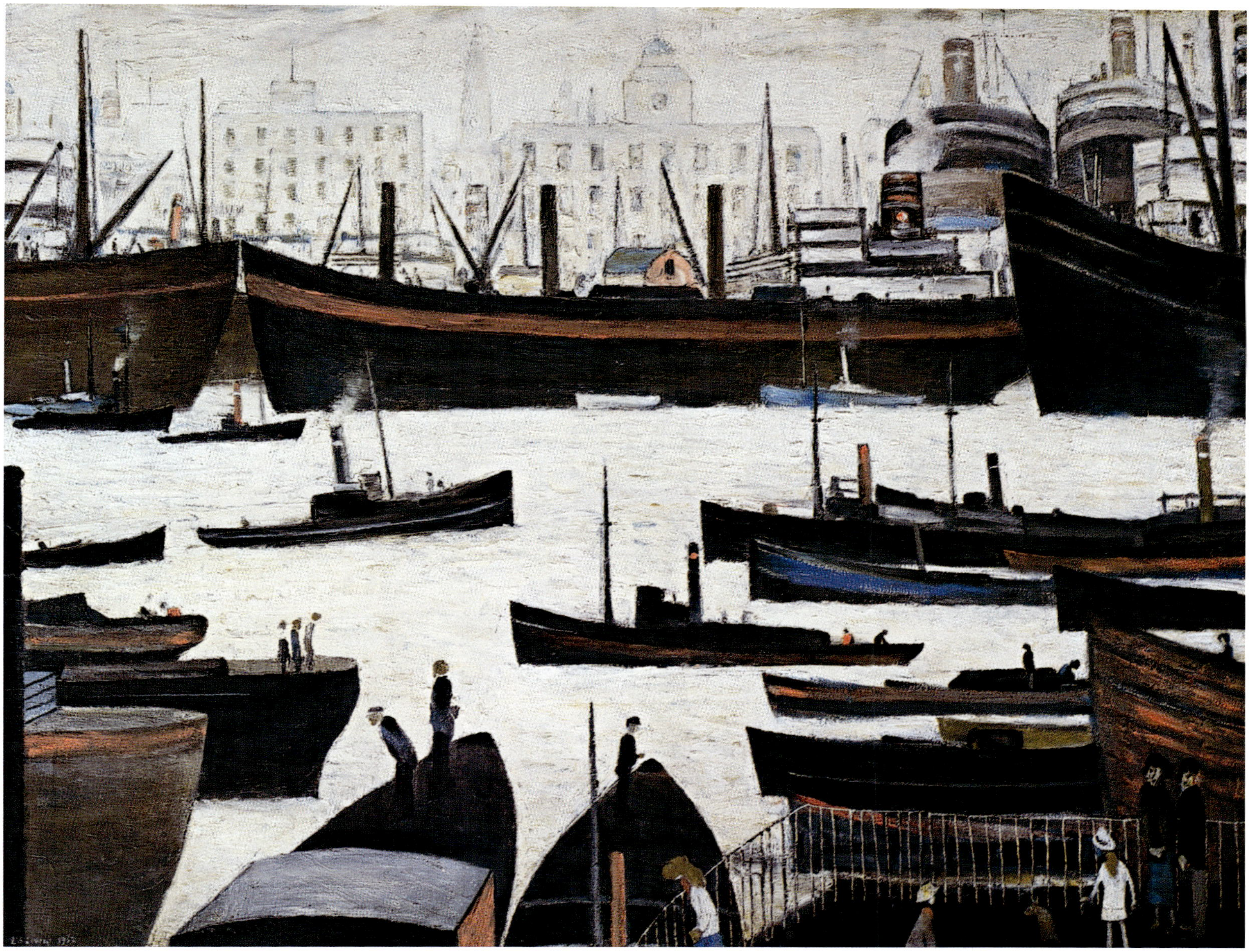

South Shields, 1962, oil on canvas, 76.2 × 101.6 cm.

organizational feat and one can understand why the dealer Andras Kalman preferred it to the more obvious paintings of beaches with little coloured yachts, partly at least because ship building, once the driving engine of North Eastern life was in permanent decline. He has also recalled the attitudes of some of his Manchester gallery's customers who would say "My God! Do you think we want to see pictures of black tugs? Bring us some paintings of the Mediterranean with palm trees and blue seas and bobbing yachts with white sails".[2]

Just as Lowry was a man of mood, so also was he a painter of moods. For all the glib and usually unjustified criticism of his doom and gloom approach, every so often, indeed

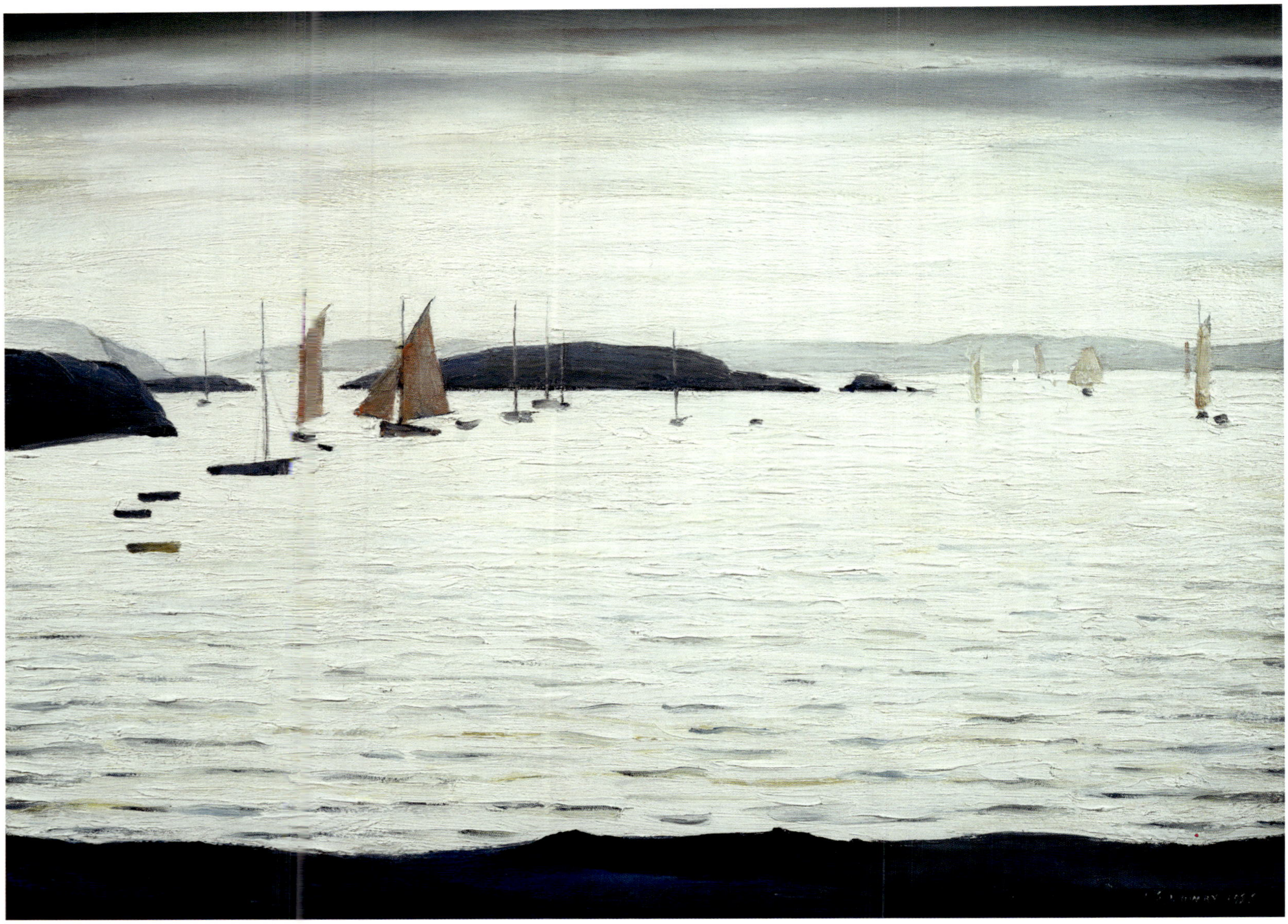

Yachts at Lytham, 1955, oil on canvas, 40.6 × 55.9 cm.

frequently, jollity would break out and painting of good cheer, even happiness, would emerge. This was particularly so in his engagement with the sea. The little yachts craved by Kalman's customers were indeed happy, smiling pictures. Whether his mother really liked them for themselves or whether she merely accepted them because they were not dark, gloomy, and devoted to the activities of the lower orders we cannot ever really know. Nonetheless it was the sea that ensured, at least after his mother died, that cheerfulness could and would break out.

If one looks at *At the Seaside* of 1946 (page 219) one sees the playful side of Lowry's art, perhaps the reliving of some happy childhood excursions to the beach at Lytham or Grange-over-Sands. After all there were, even during the war, occasional hot, sunny days by the

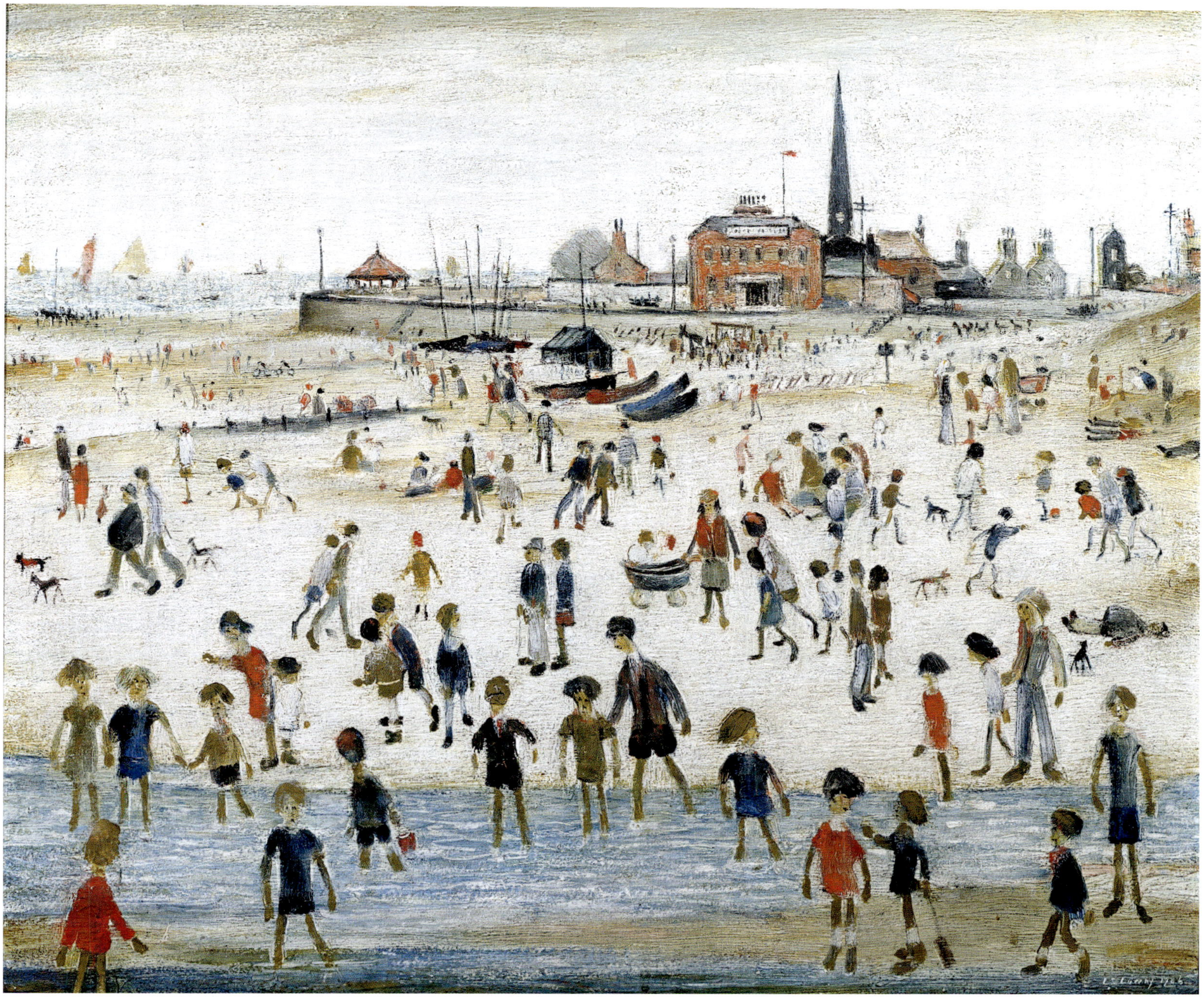

At the Seaside, 1946, oil on canvas, 50.8 × 60.9 cm.

seaside in which children ran about, paddled, maybe actually swam and even the Lowry family might have had a good time. What is especially appealing about *At the Seaside* is that while it could be oozing sentimentality and a lot of cloying nonsense about childhood remembered by Lowry from his Victorian and Edwardian upbringing, there is not an iota of sentimentality to be found. Had there been any of that it would surely not have been bought by the hard-nosed, entirely unsentimental novelist Howard Spring who was its first owner and an early champion of Lowry's work.

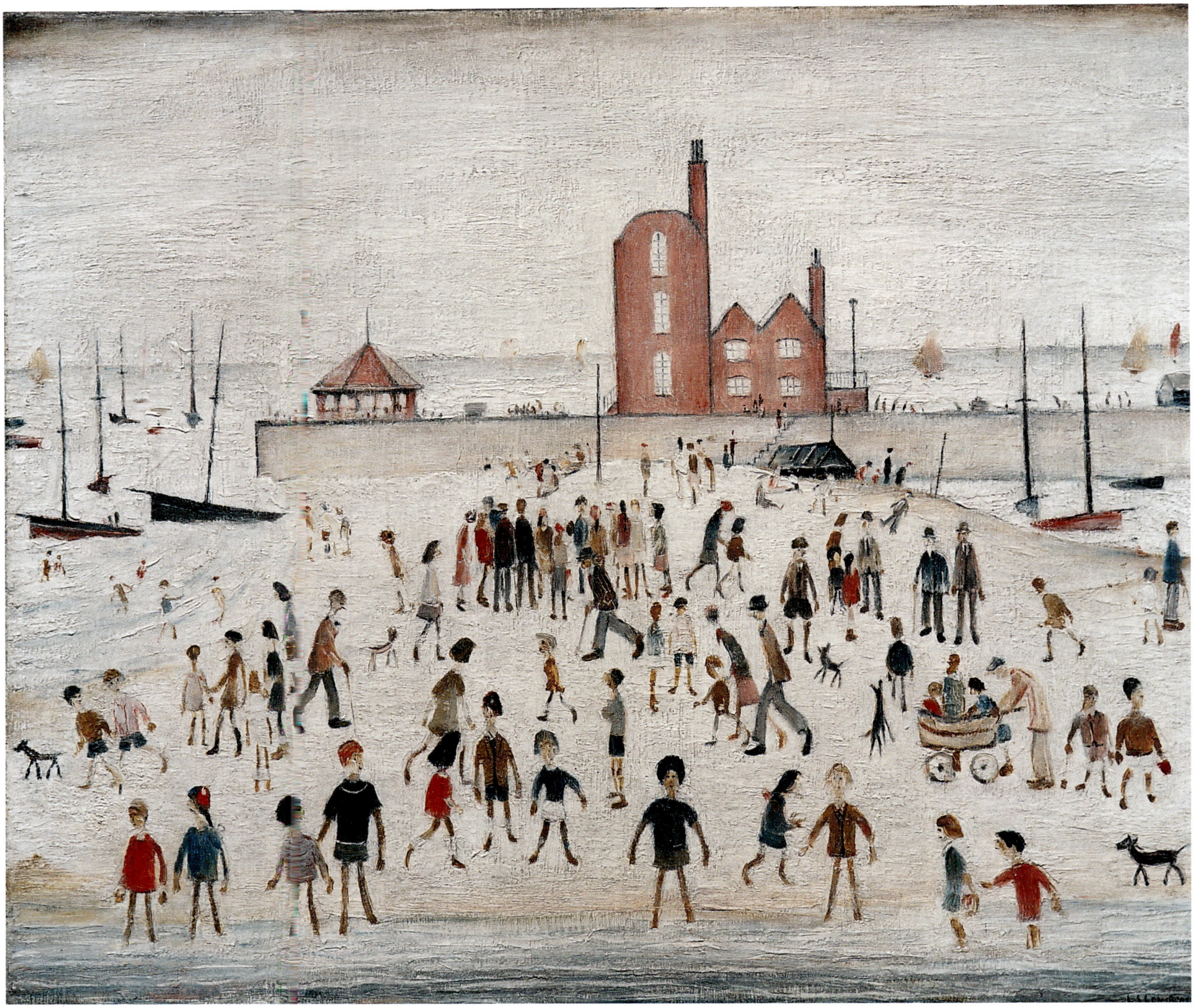

Beach and Promenade, 1948, oil on canvas, 63.5 × 76.2 cm.

Although there are one or two patches of yellowish sand the bulk of the beach is painted in basic Lowry white. The unmistakeable aura of bright, sunlit colours comes from the boats and prams and the clothing of the children. This painting is the reverse of the coin that bears on its other side a painting like *Cripples* done only three years later in 1949.

One of Lowry's finest seaside paintings, possibly the best, is *Beach and Promenade*. Just as there is something faintly incongruous in *At the Seaside* with its black church spire in the background of all that hedonistic pleasure, so, in this picture, (page 220) sticking up behind the sea wall on the far left of the painting there is what appears to be a bandstand, or a shelter for when it is windy, an entirely appropriate ornament to any good Northern beach and sea wall or promenade. But it is hard to know what to make of the huge structure in the centre and behind the promenade or sea wall. One might expect a hotel there but there are not enough windows for that. Try as one will it is hard to see anything other than a factory, albeit a small one. In which case Lowry is taking one of his topographical liberties where he uses real elements of a particular scene and then adds anything else that takes his topographical or architectural fancy, whether from memory of somewhere else or purely imagined.

The beach itself is an odd shape, more or less triangular, with the apex of the triangle pointing towards the terracotta-coloured, and singularly ugly, building. And yet, despite the inherent puzzle Lowry has created, the picture works as a whole. It is, if one recalls Ian McKellen's remarks from the second chapter about the theatrical structure of so many of Lowry's pictures, an immensely theatrical painting. The sea wall and the two buildings form an intriguing and arresting back drop. The triangular beach is pointing backwards with a raked slope. All the action, including some of the boats and all of the large cast are accommodated on the rake of the beach and the straight line of the sea at the front is the fore edge of the stage as all those children face us, the audience.

The colouring of the painting is Lowry at his finest. The bright colours come as usual from the clothing of the people and from the canvas sails of the little boats. The white-based beach is typical of a Northern beach bereft of sunlight, which, presumably, is why all the children are fully clothed, as if the consensus is that it's too cold to run around in bathing costumes. The sky is one of his finest; full of rich blues and pinks as if it were near to dusk. The merging of the different colours of sea and sky at the horizon is worthy of a French Impressionist, as if he was remembering his time with Valette. Although, or perhaps because, it asks questions, this is not only Lowry at his most interesting but also Lowry simultaneously analysing and executing his deep empathy for the sea and the people who use it.

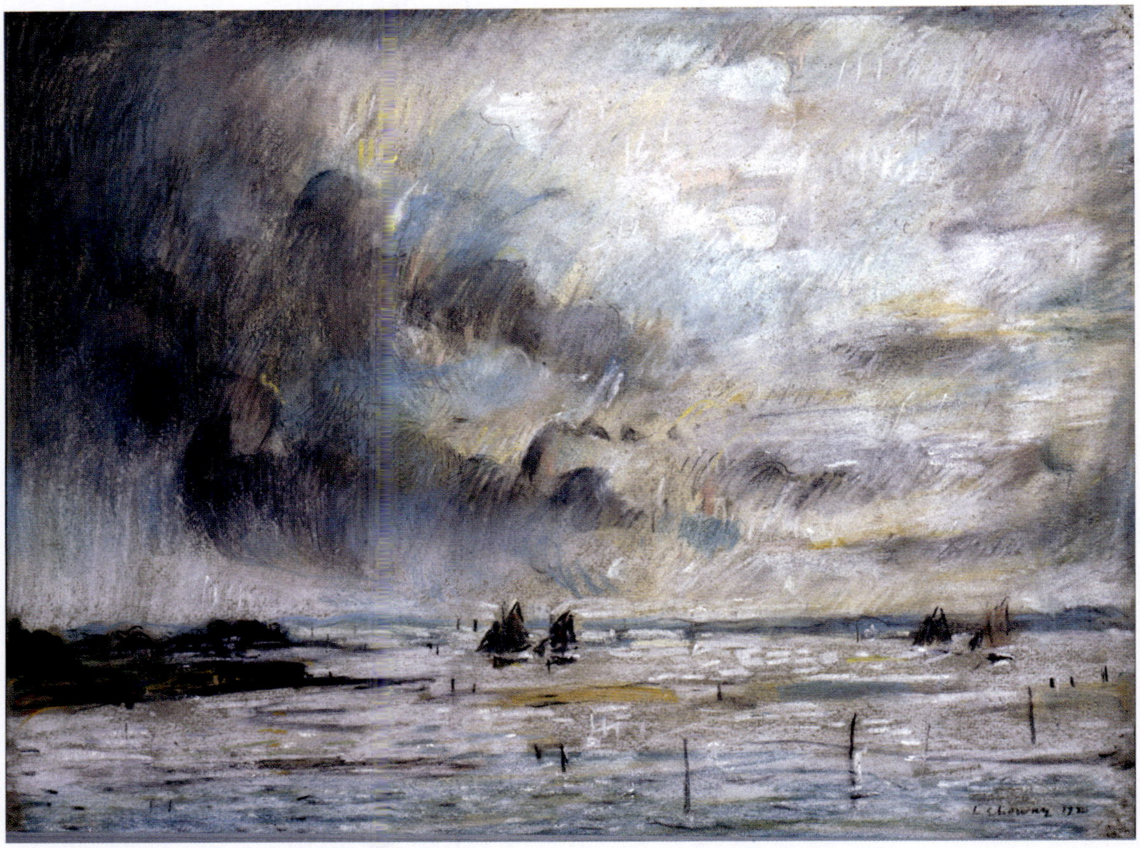

Yachts, Lytham St Anne's, 1920, pastel on paper, 27.9 × 35.6 cm.

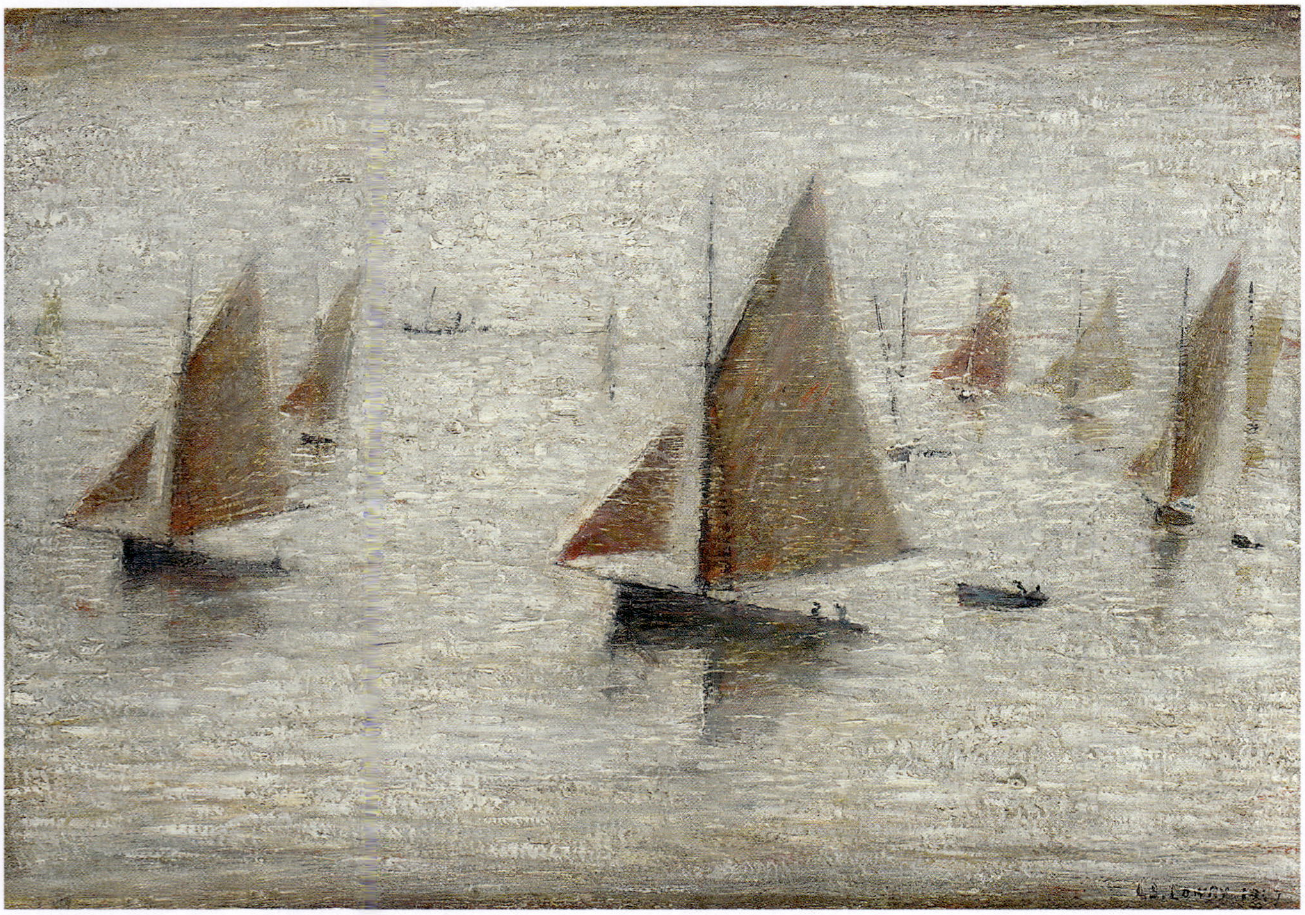

Yachts, 1947, oil on panel, 34.9 × 49.5 cm.

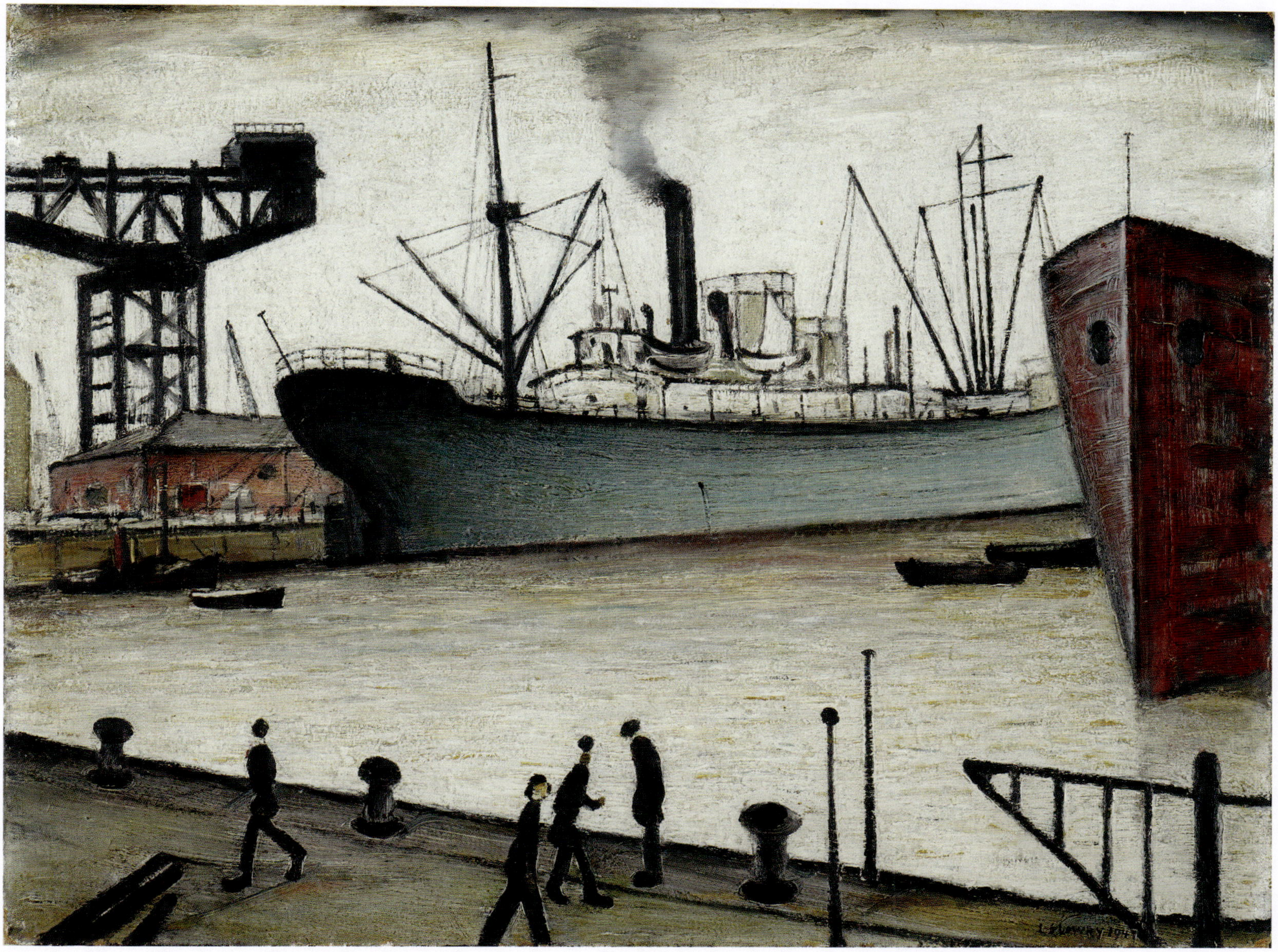

Queen's Dock, Glasgow, 1947,
oil on canvas, 48.5 × 75 cm.

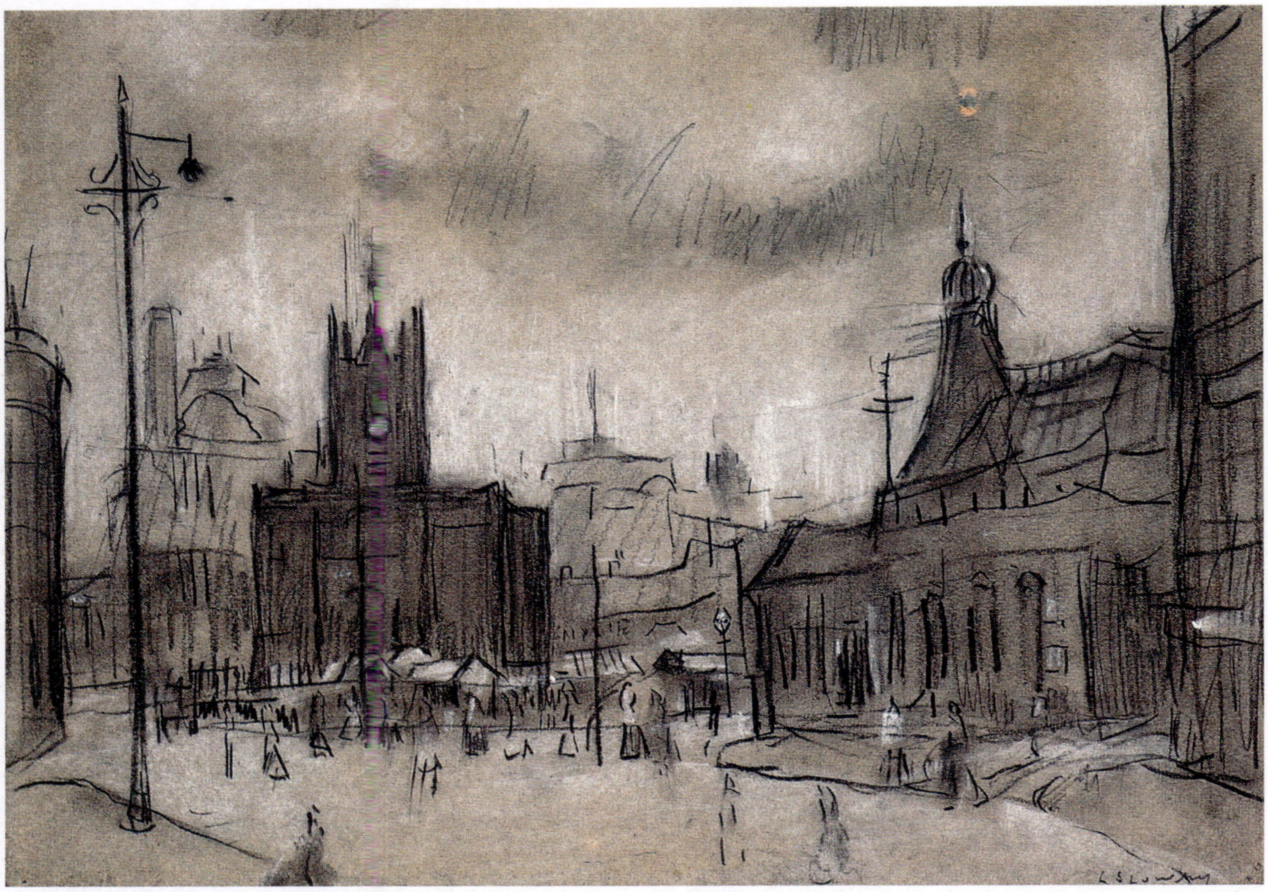

*Flat Iron Market, c.*1925, charcoal, pencil and white chalk on grey paper, 28.3 × 38.3 cm.

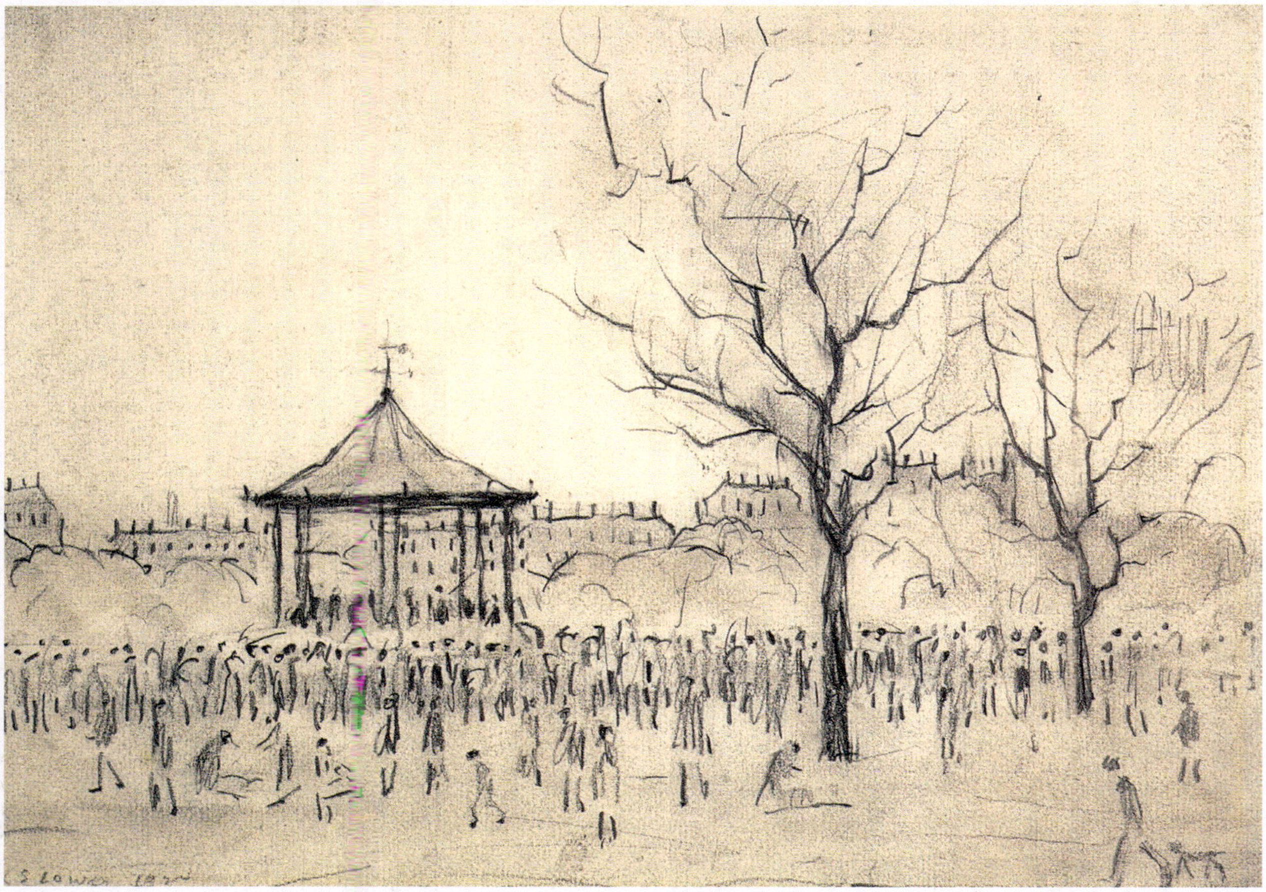

Bandstand, Peel Park, 1925, pencil on paper, 36.7 × 54.6 cm.

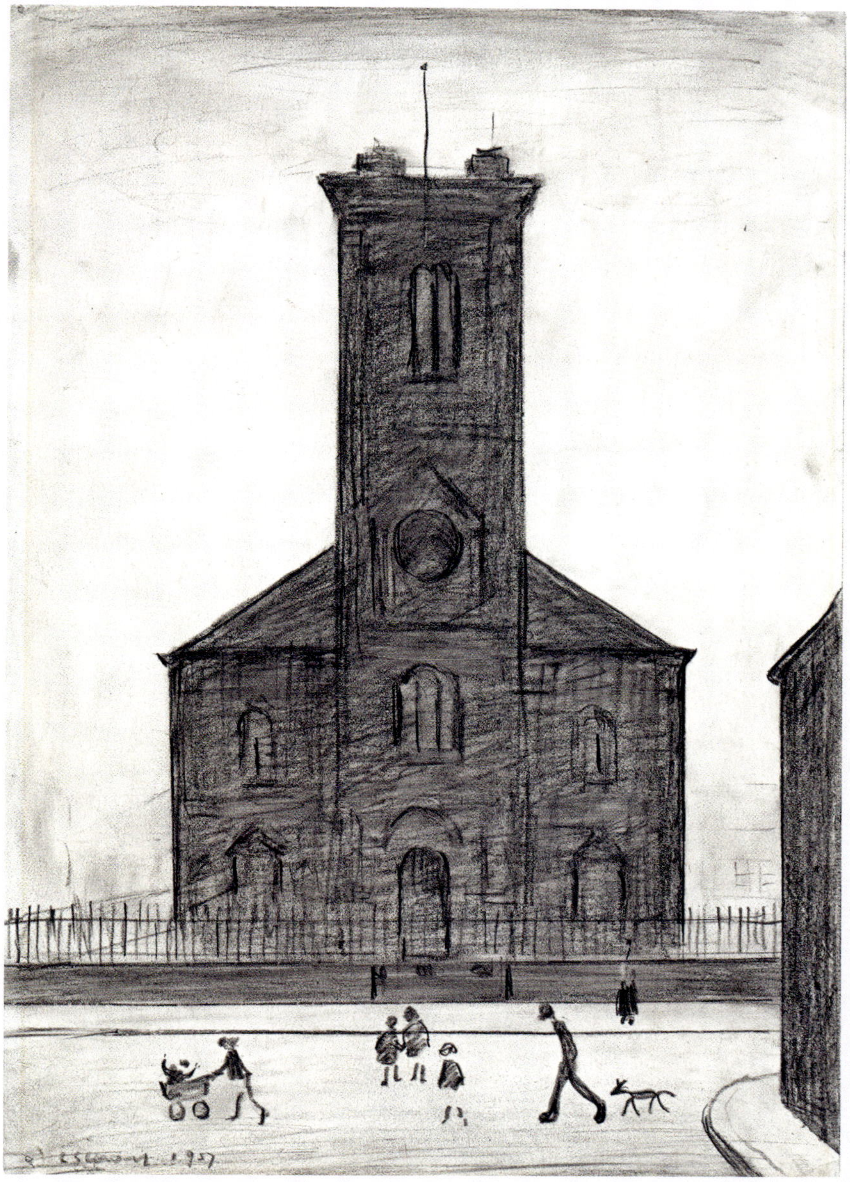

St Stephen's Church, Salford, 1957, pencil on paper, 35 × 24.5 cm.

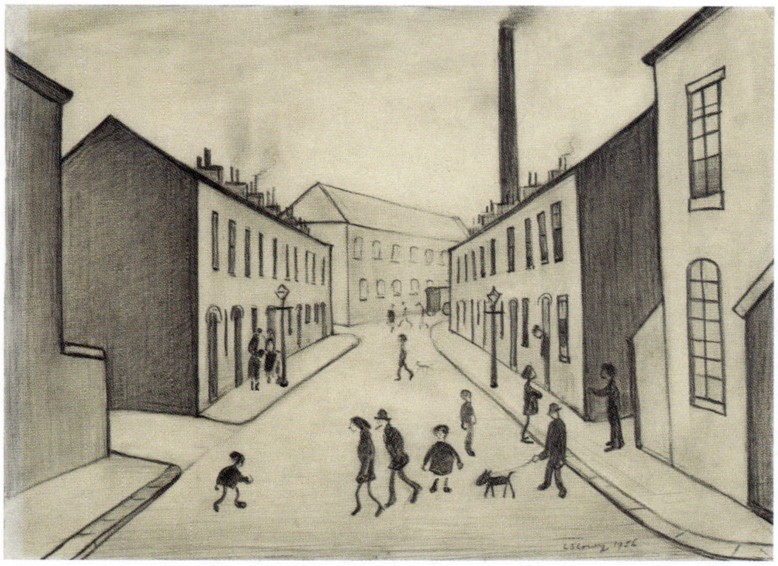

North James Street, Salford, 1956, pencil on paper, 24.4 × 33.7 cm.

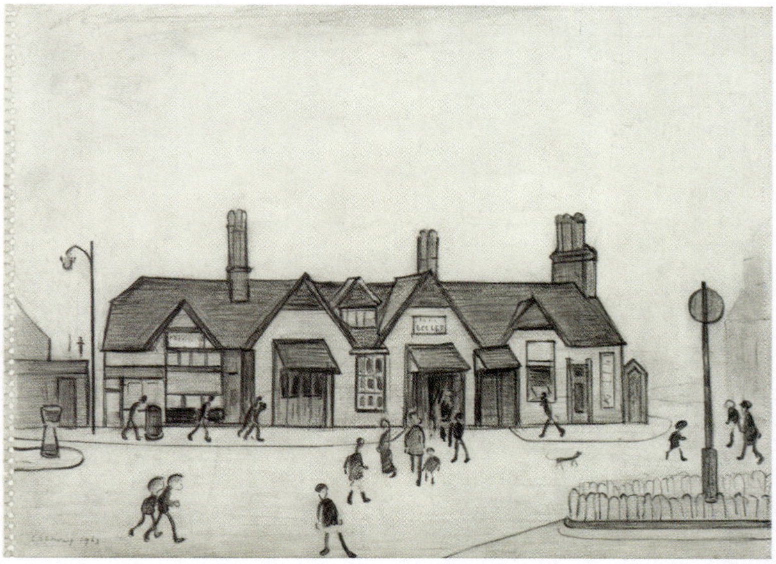

Eccles Railway Station, 1963, pencil on paper, 25.1 × 35.5 cm.

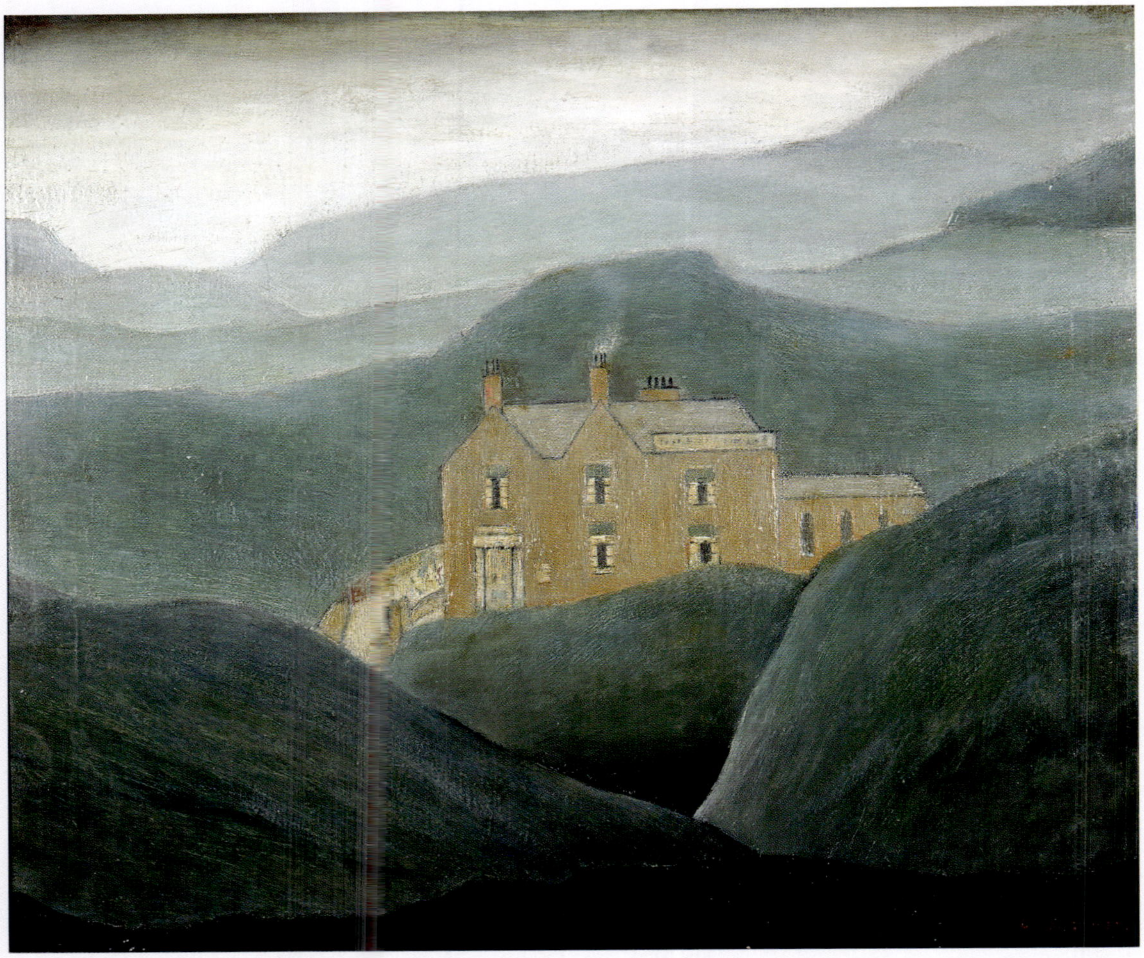

House on the Moor, 1950, oil on canvas, 49 × 59.5 cm.

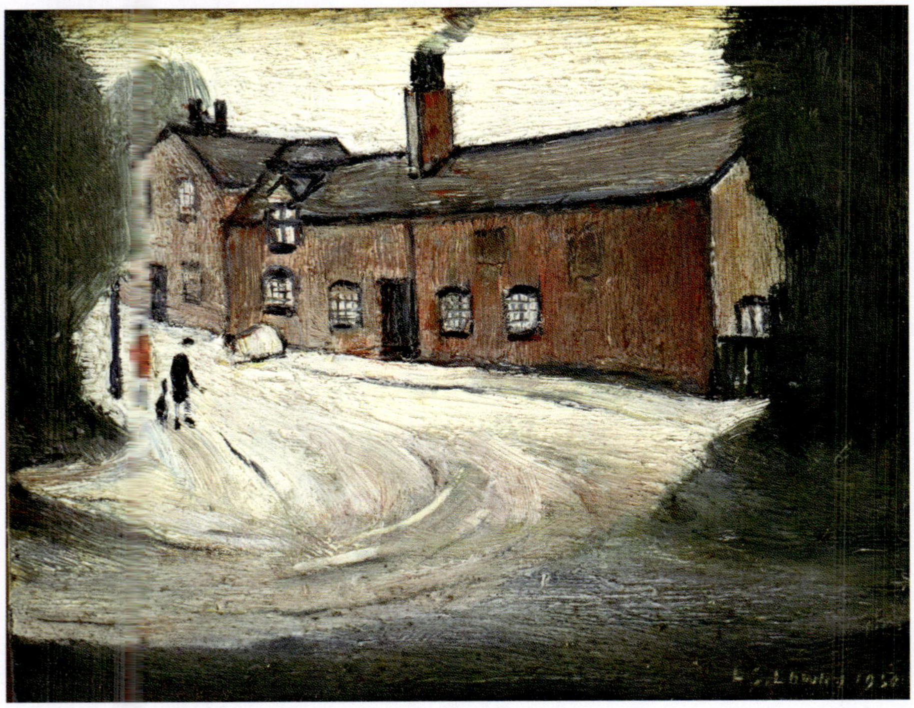

The Mill, Moston, 1950, oil on board, 15.2 × 20.3 cm.

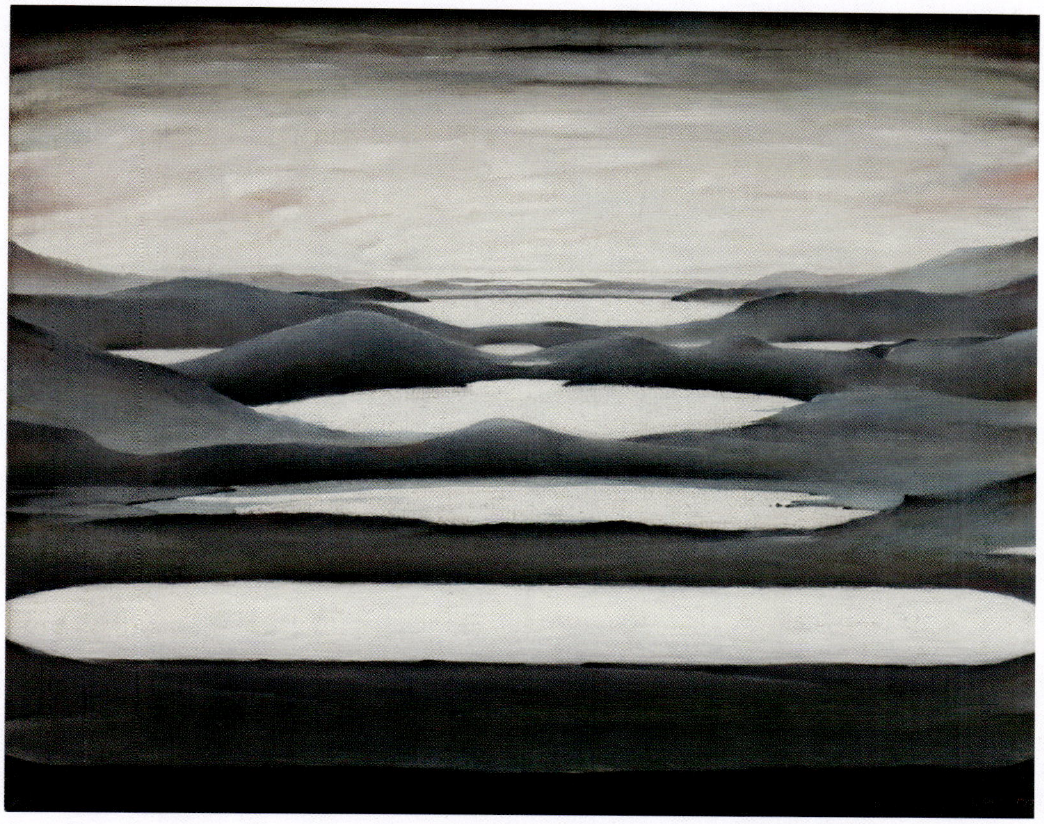

Lake Landscape, 1950, oil on canvas, 71 × 91 cm.

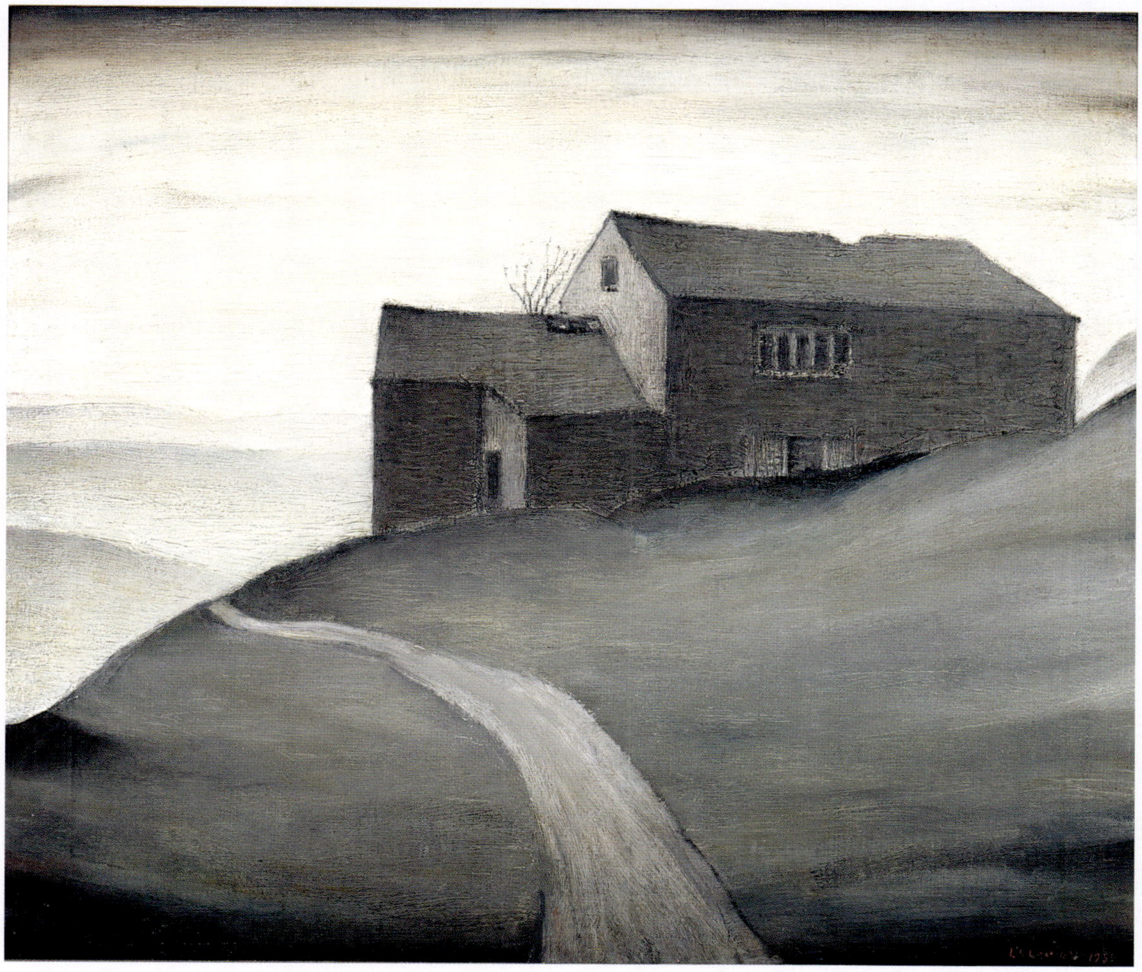

A House on the Moor; Heathcliff's House, 1950, oil on canvas, 50.8 × 61 cm.

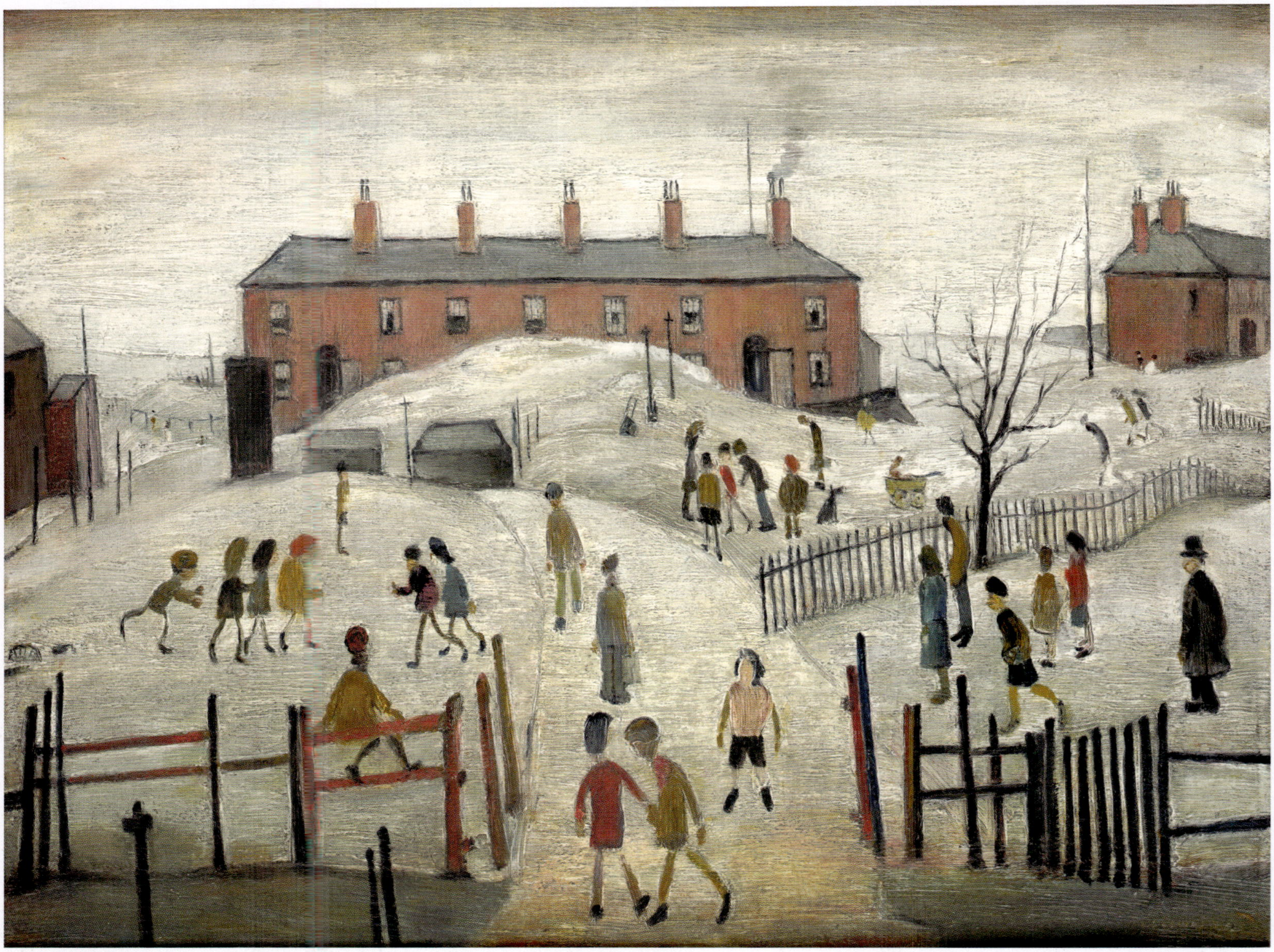

The School Playground, 1951,
oil on canvas, 45 × 60 cm.

Seascape, 1952, oil on canvas,
39.5 × 49.3 cm.

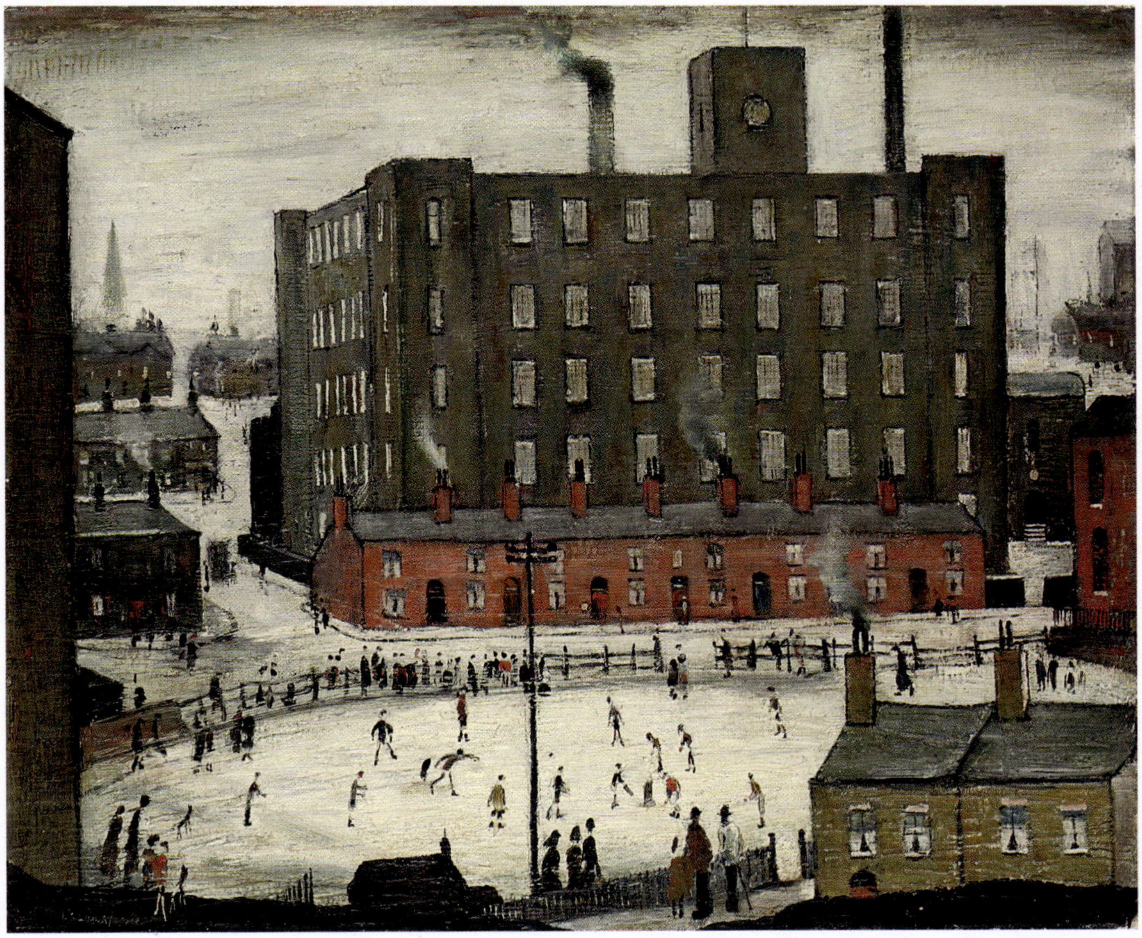

A Cricket Match, 1952, oil on panel,
43.8 × 54 cm.

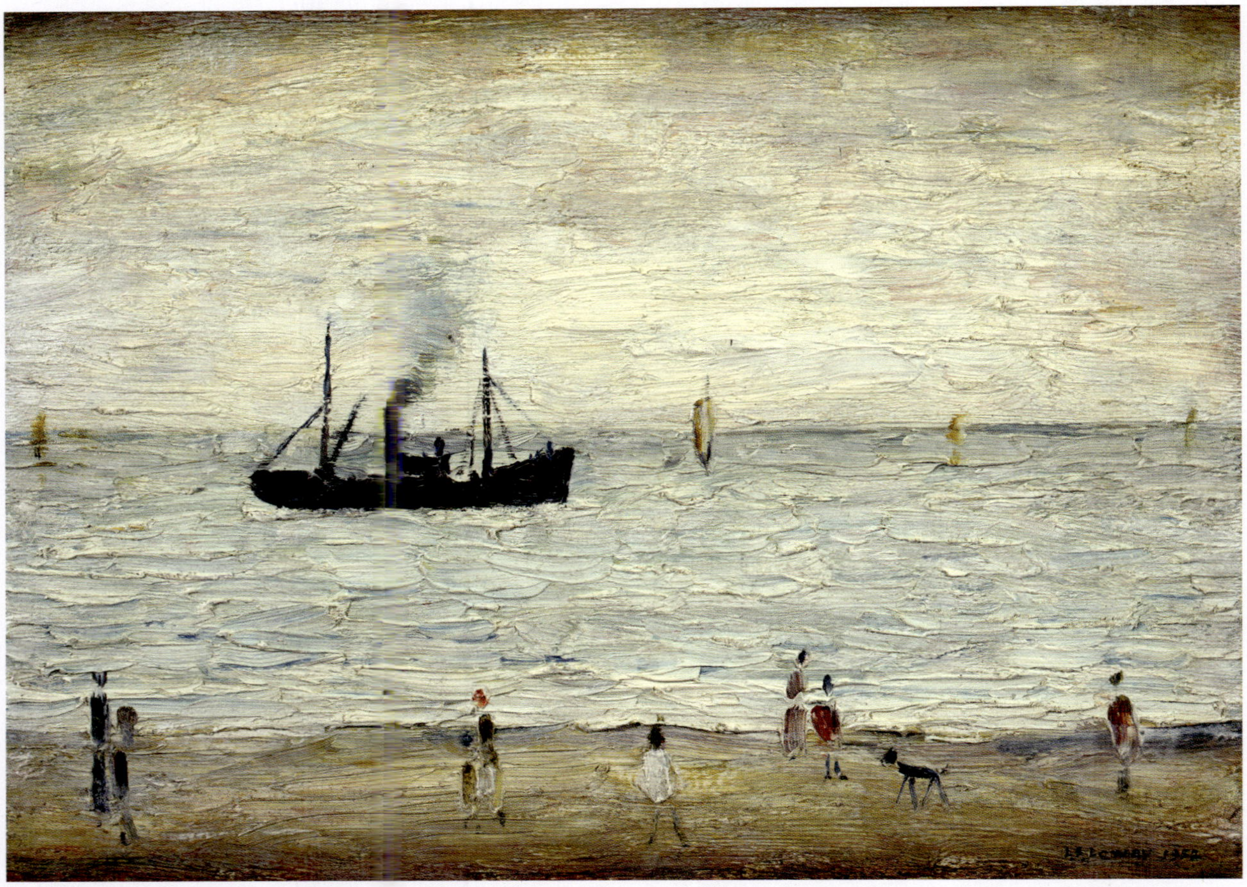

Seascape with Figures, 1952,
oil on panel, 25.4 × 35.6 cm.

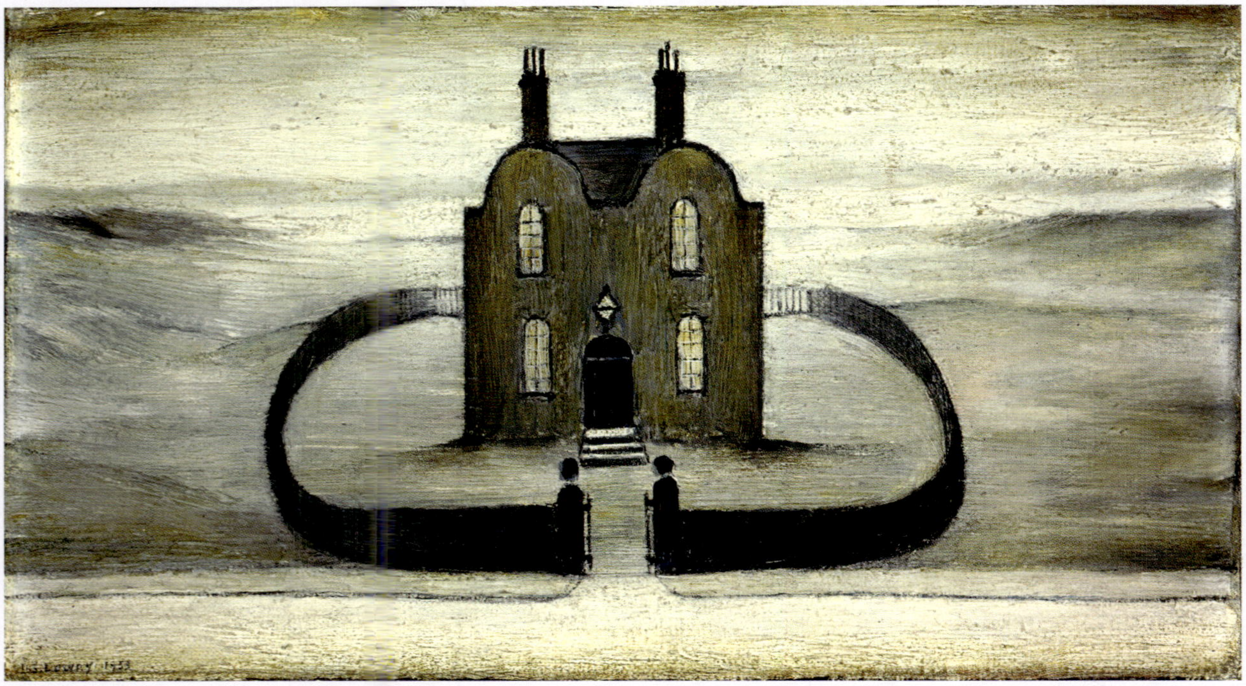

Old House, 1953,
oil on canvas.

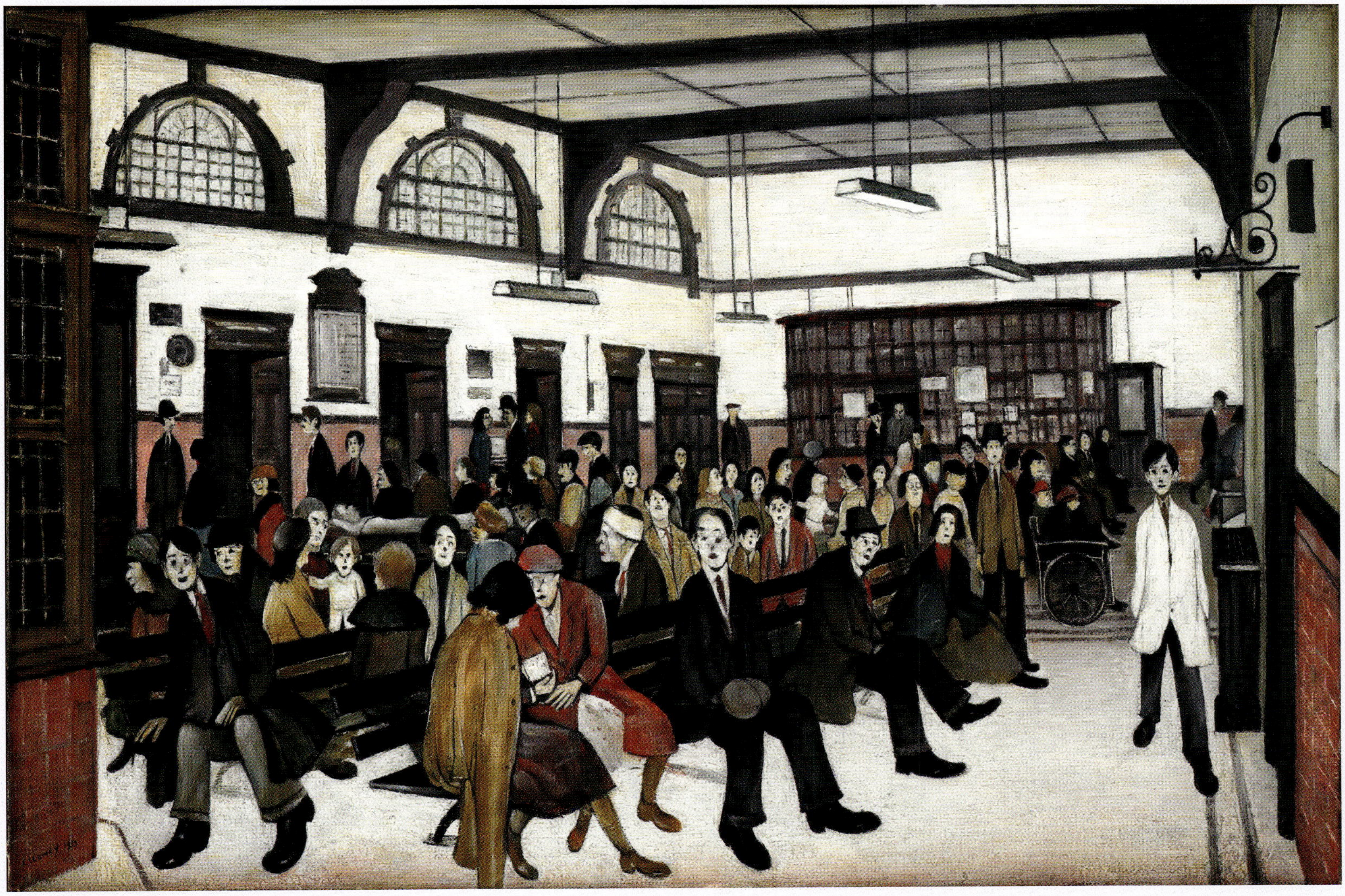

Ancoats Hospital Outpatients Hall,
1952, oil on canvas, 59.3 × 90 cm.

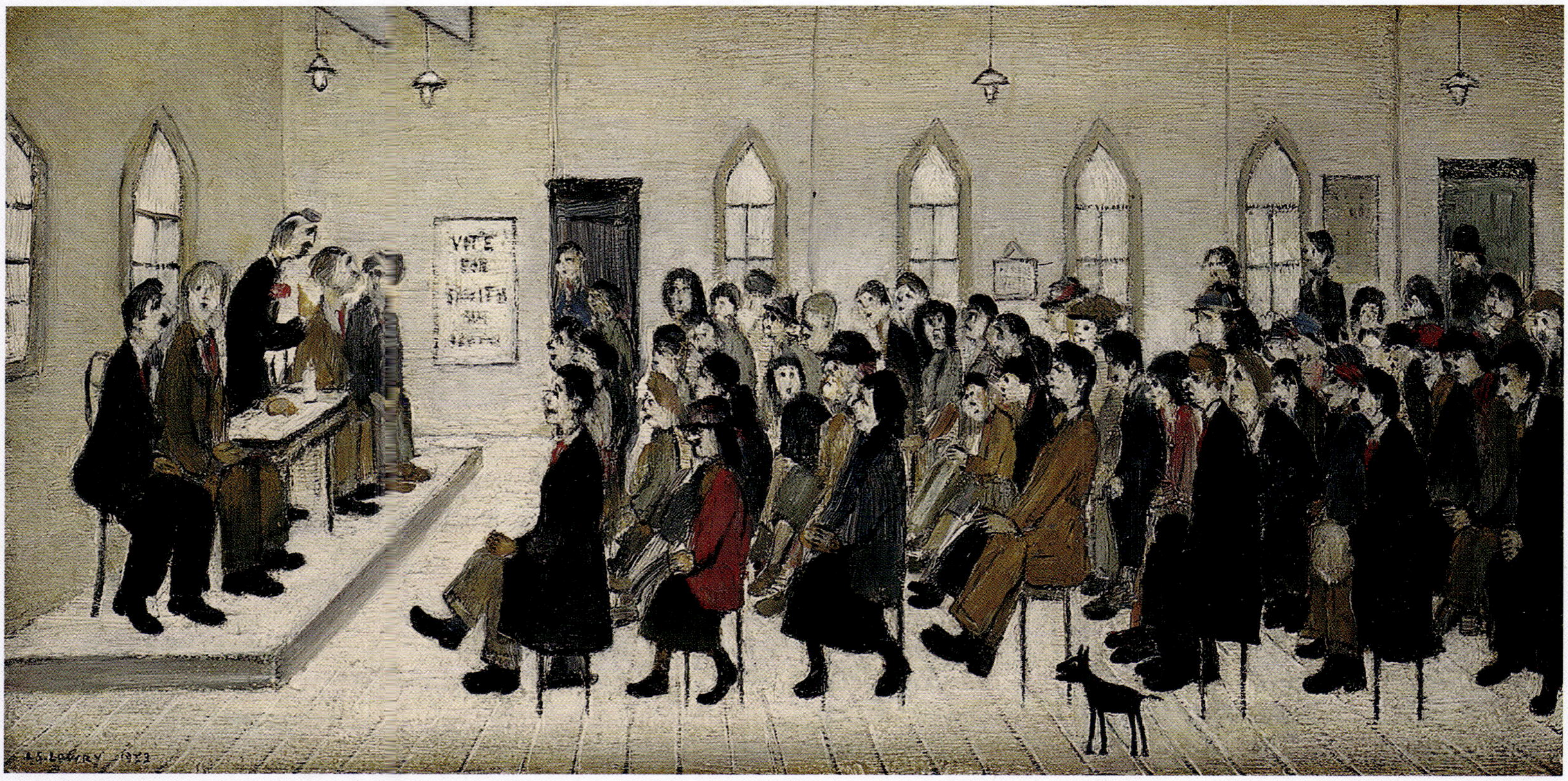

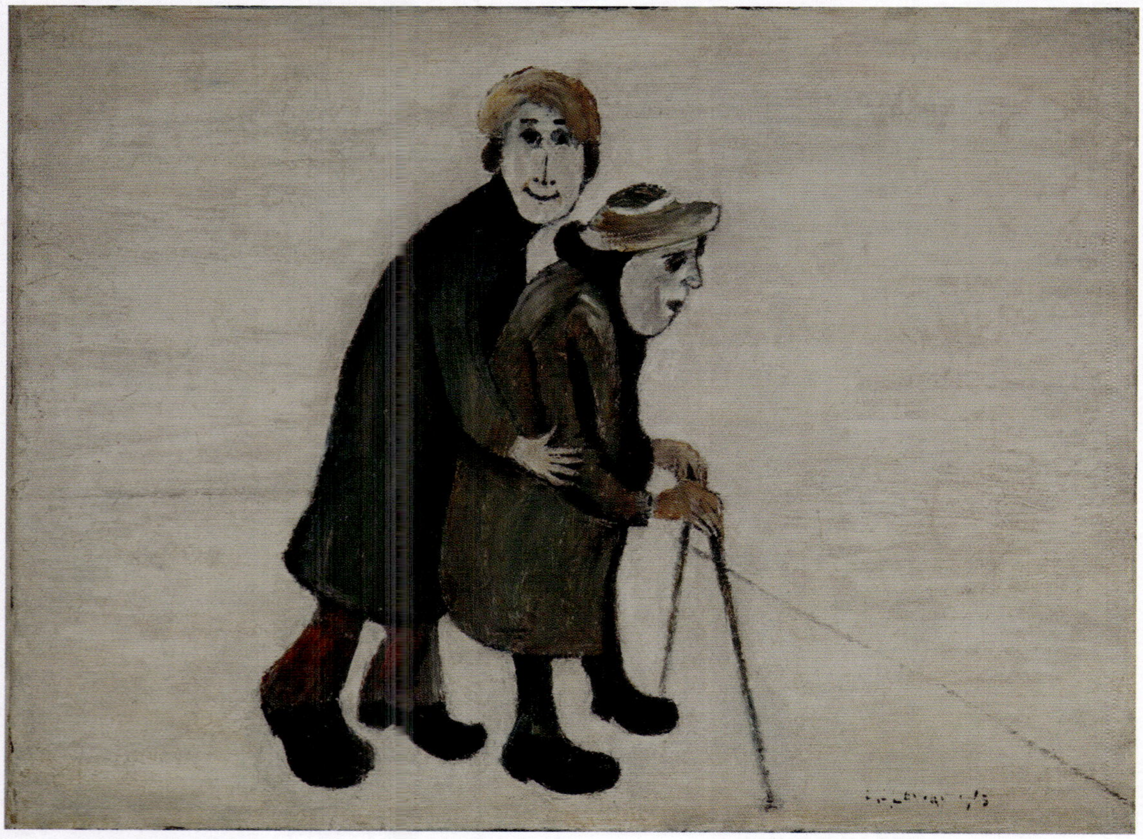

Political Meeting, Ashton-under-Lyne, 1953, oil on canvas, 30.5 × 61 cm.

A Couple Crossing the Road, 1953, oil on canvas, 42.4 × 52.6 cm.

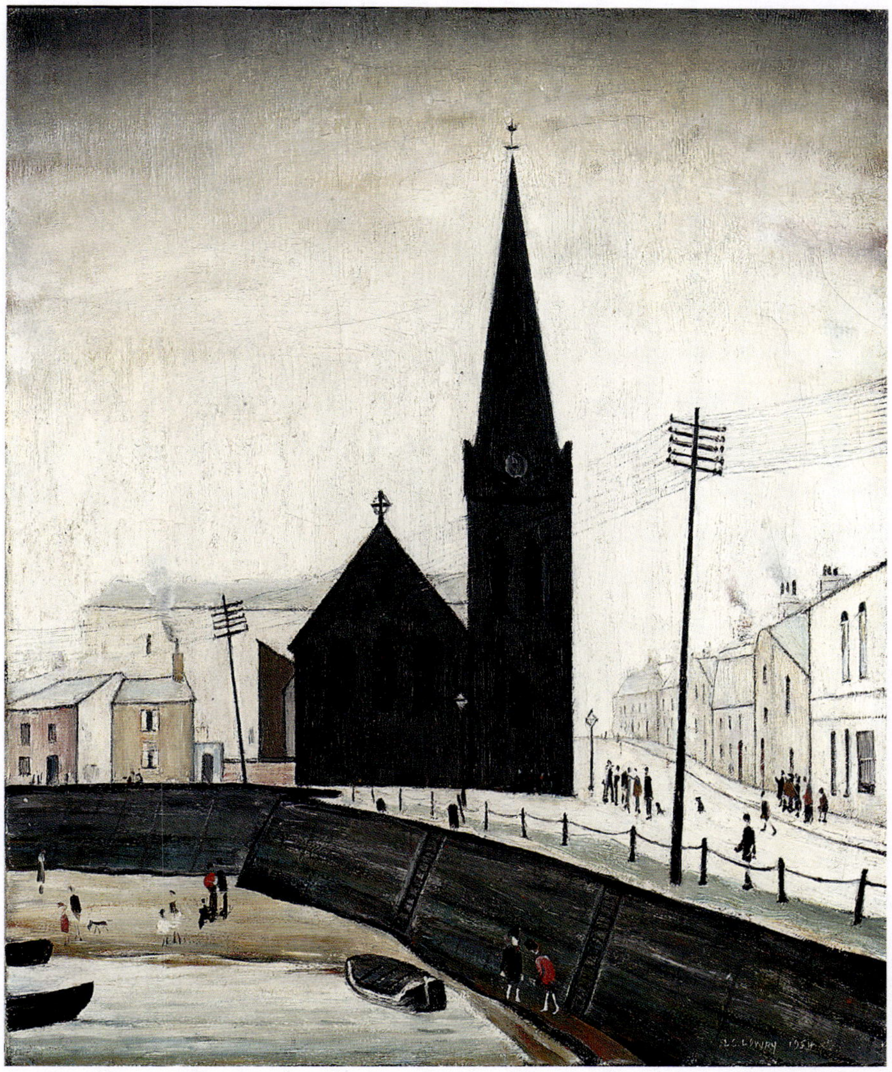

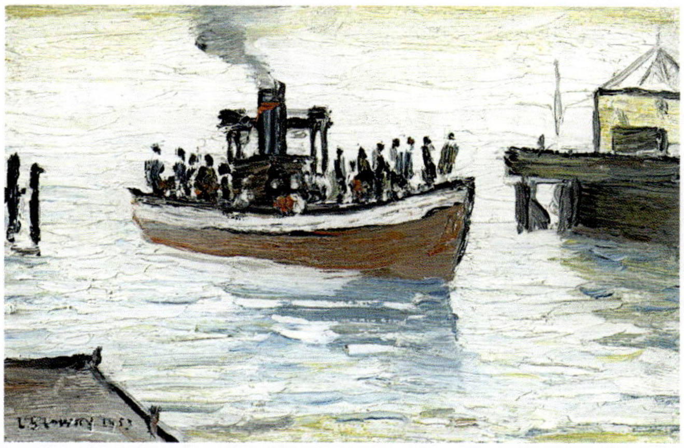

The Ferry, 1953, oil on board,
14 × 21.6 cm.

On The Quay, Maryport, 1954,
oil on canvas, 61 × 50.8 cm.

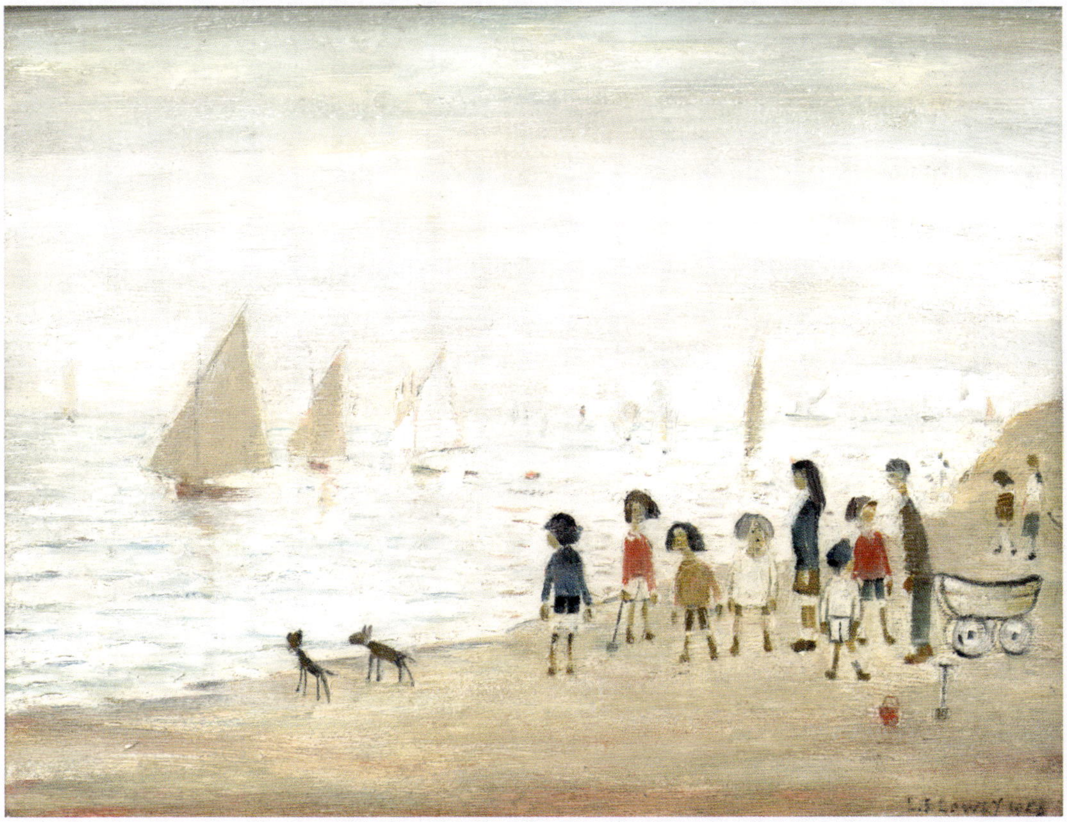

People at the Beach, 1955,
oil on canvas, 30 × 40 cm.

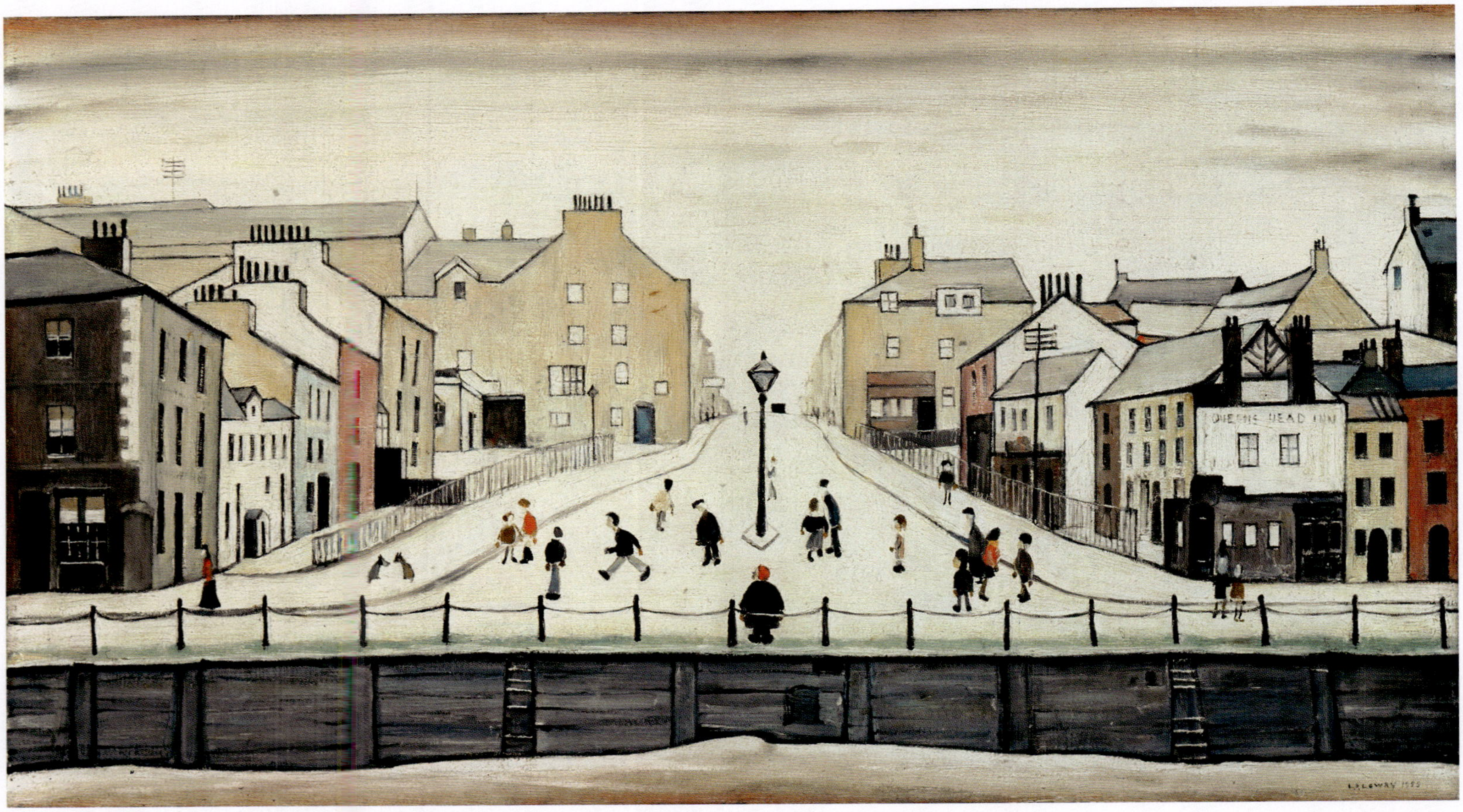

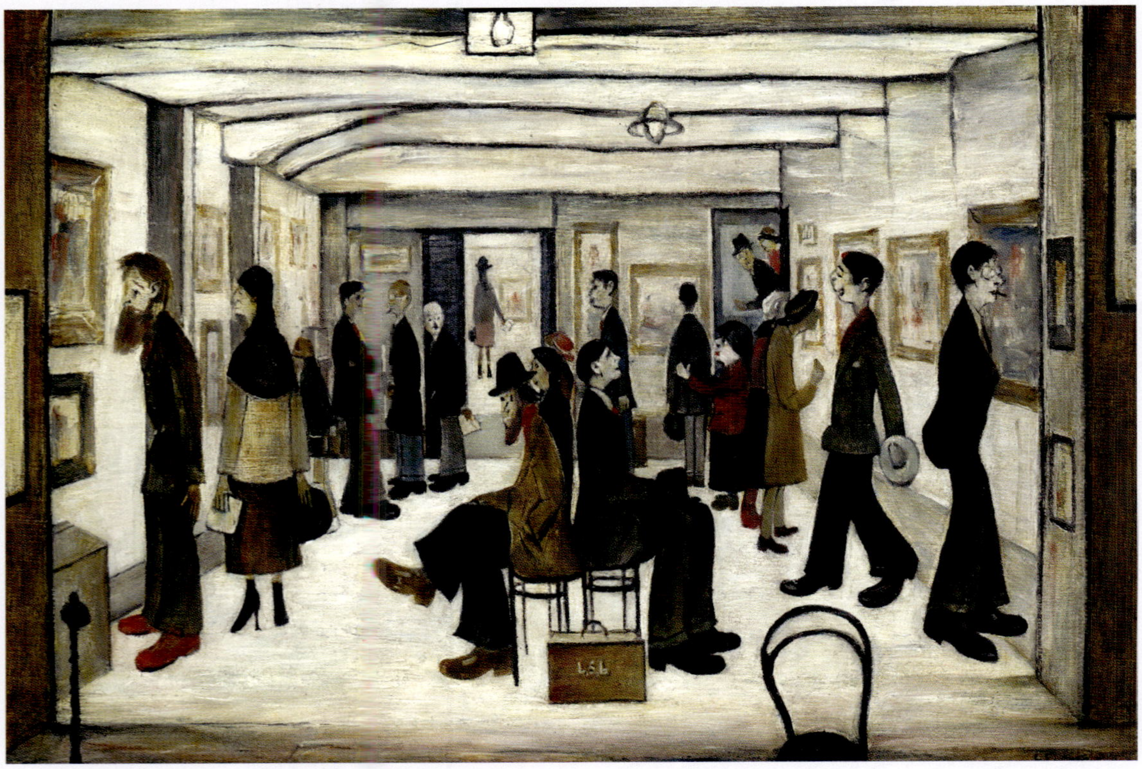

Senhouse Street, Maryport, 1955, oil on canvas, 51 × 91.5 cm.

Private View, Manchester, 1955, oil on canvas, 50.8 × 76.2 cm.

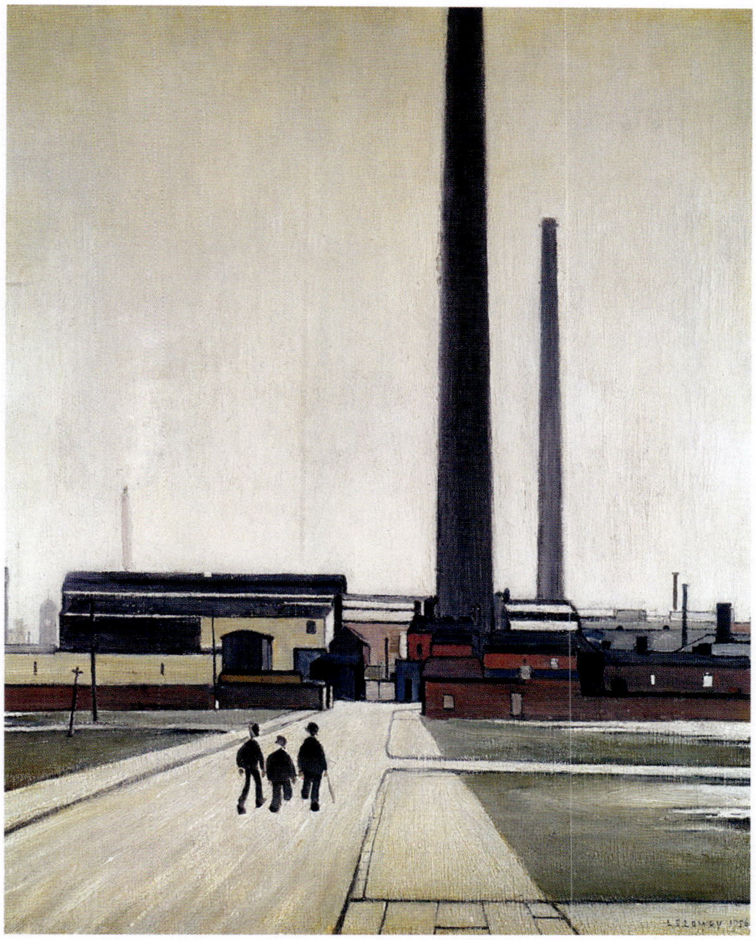

Factory at Widnes, 1956, oil on canvas, 61 × 49.5 cm.

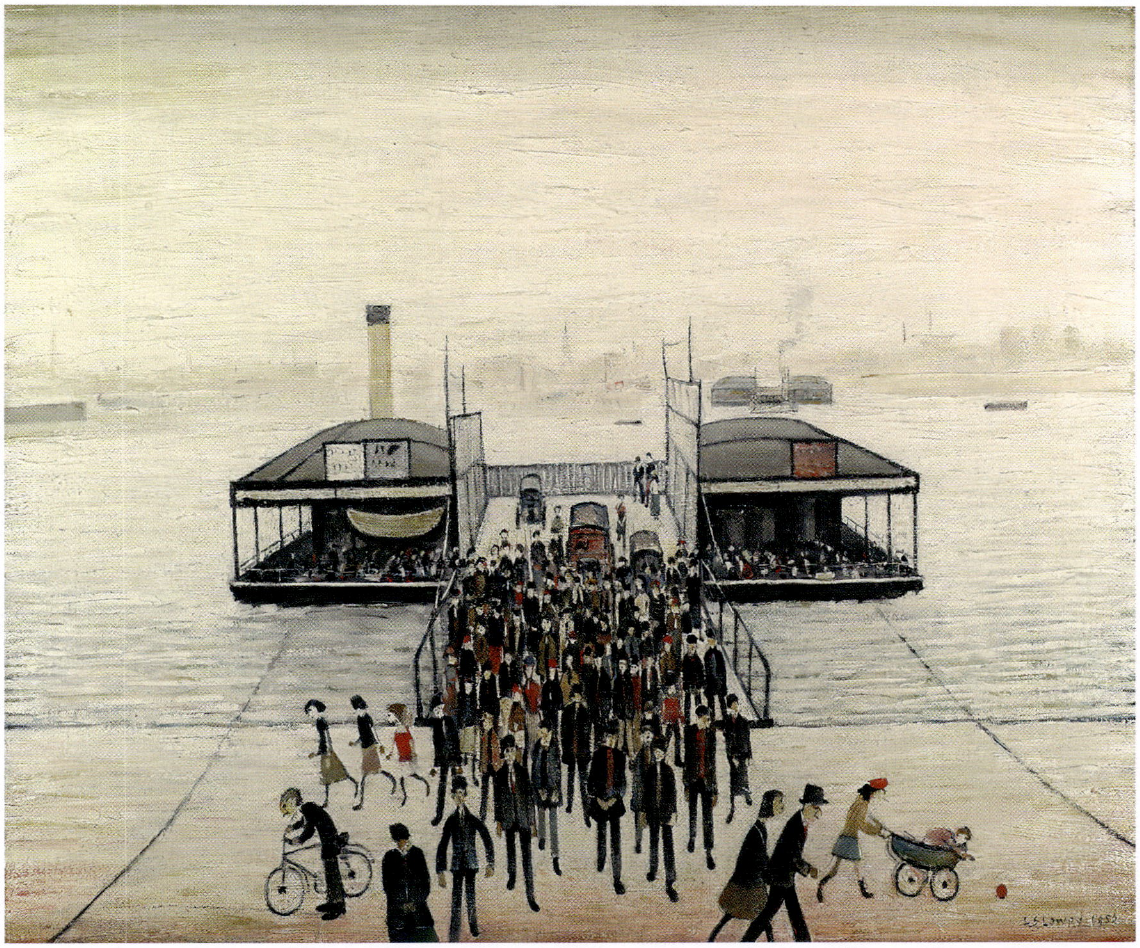

The Floating Bridge, Southampton, 1956, oil on canvas, 55.9 × 64.8 cm.

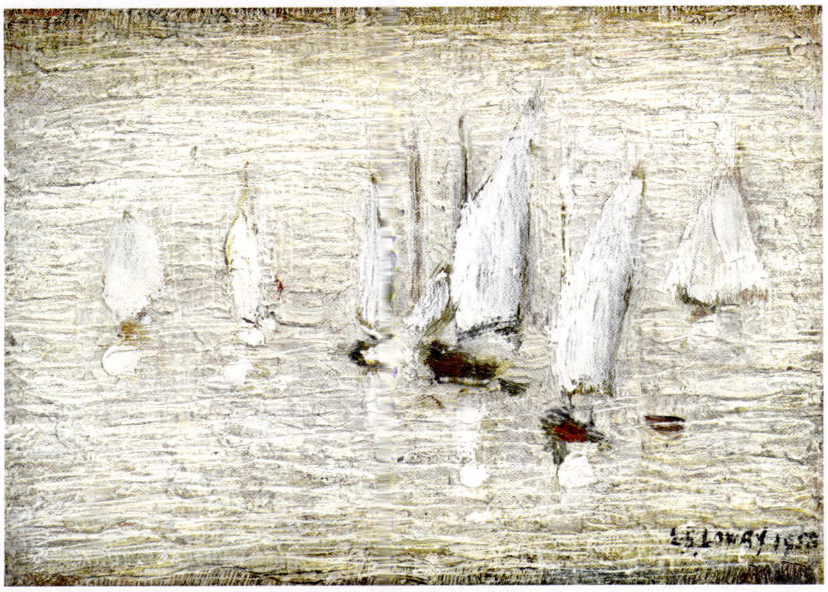

Sailing Ships – on the Fylde Coast, 1956, oil on board, 15.2 × 21.6 cm.

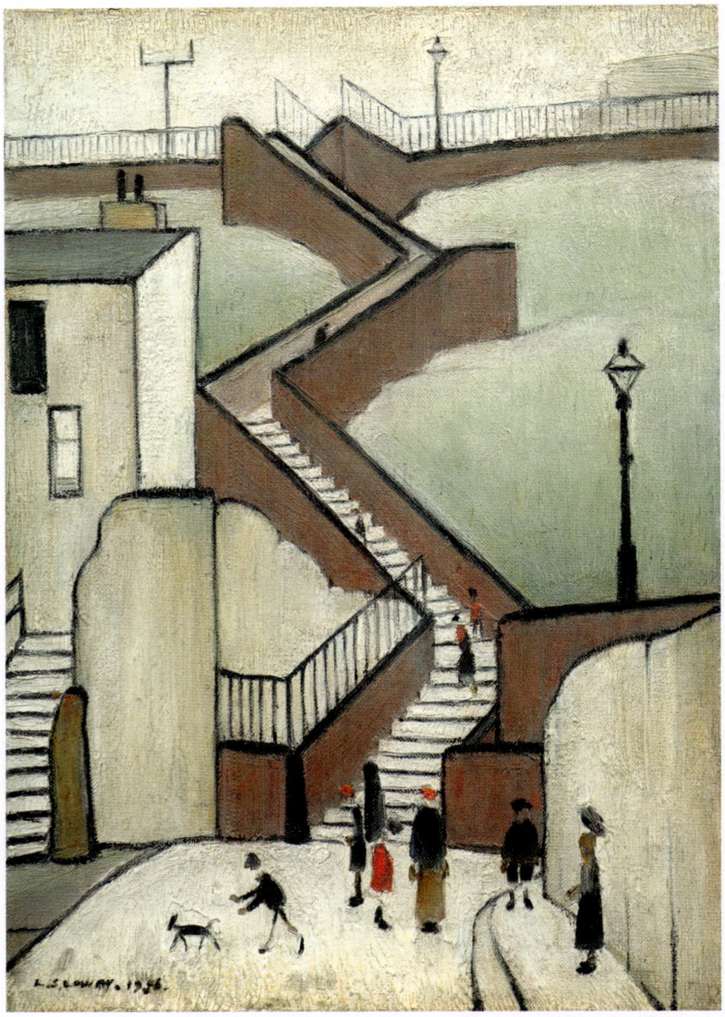

The Steps, 1956, oil on canvas, 35.6 × 25.4 cm.

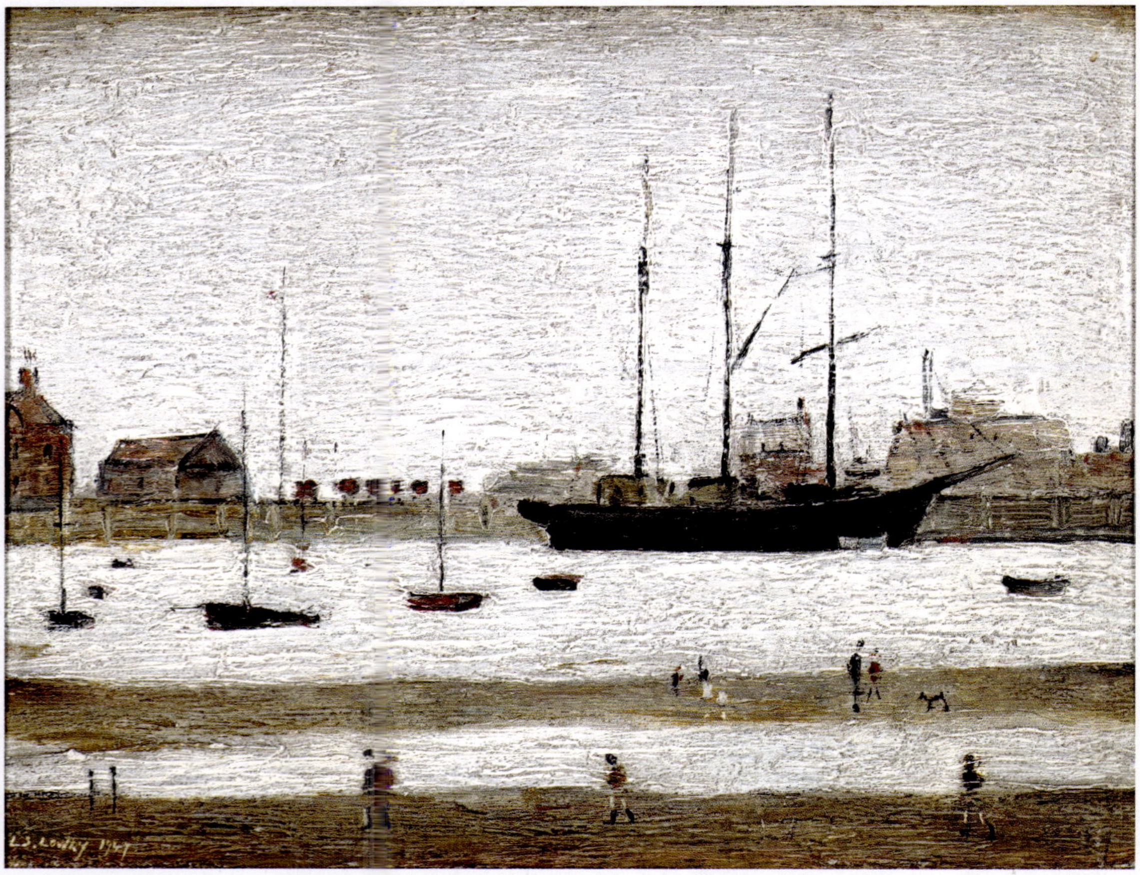

Rhyl Harbour, 1947, oil on panel, 30 × 40 cm.

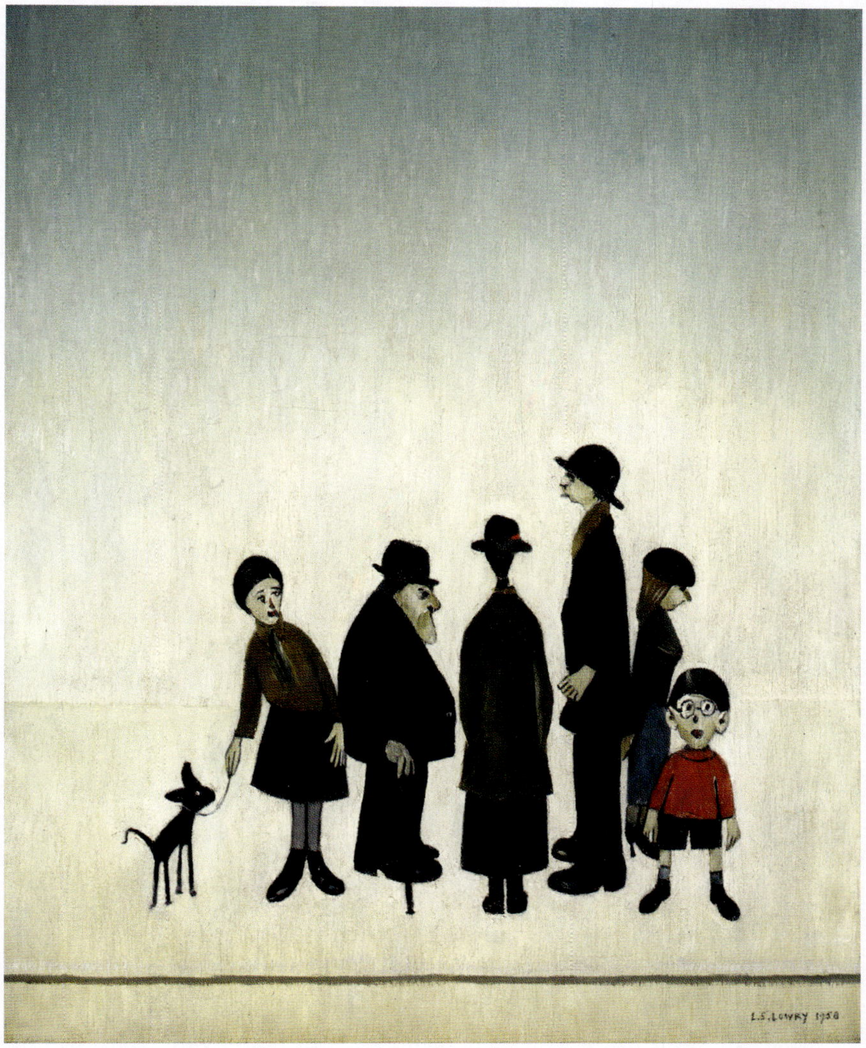

The Family, 1958, oil on canvas, 61 × 50.8 cm.

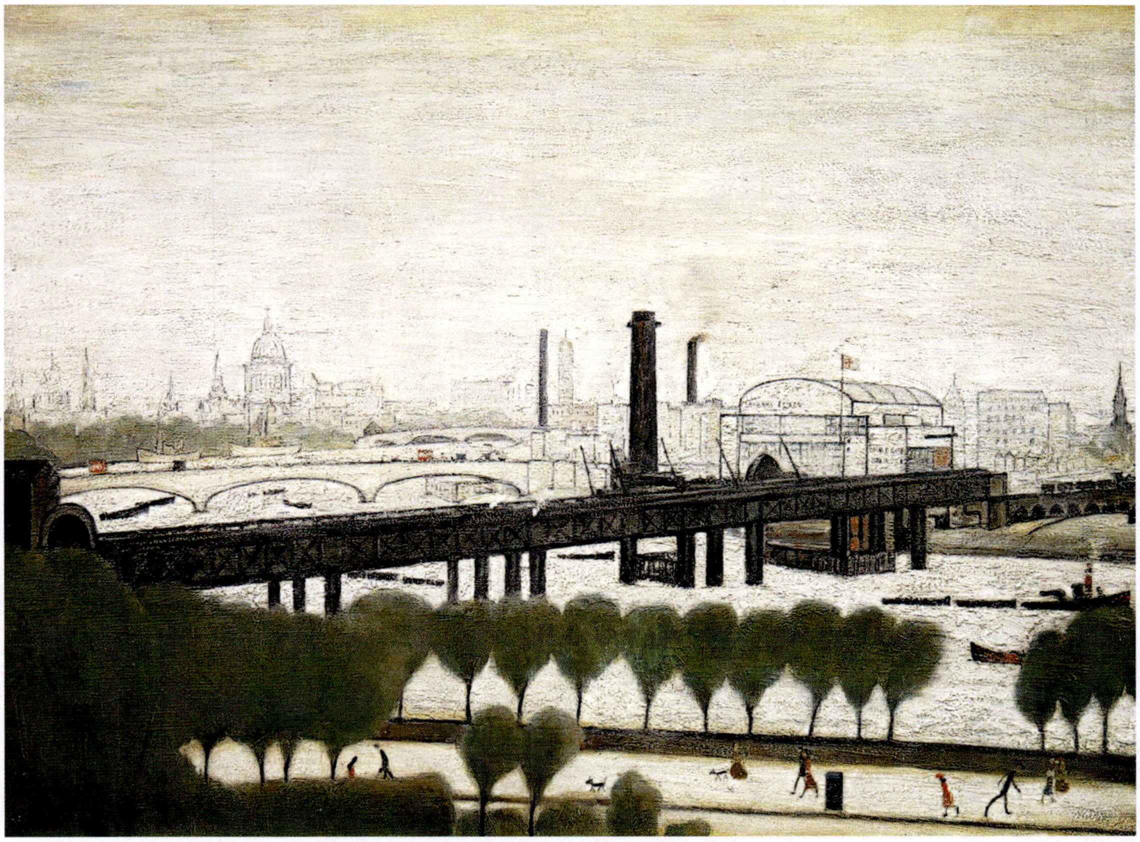

The Thames from Whitehall Court, 1957, oil on canvas, 54.6 × 74.9 cm.

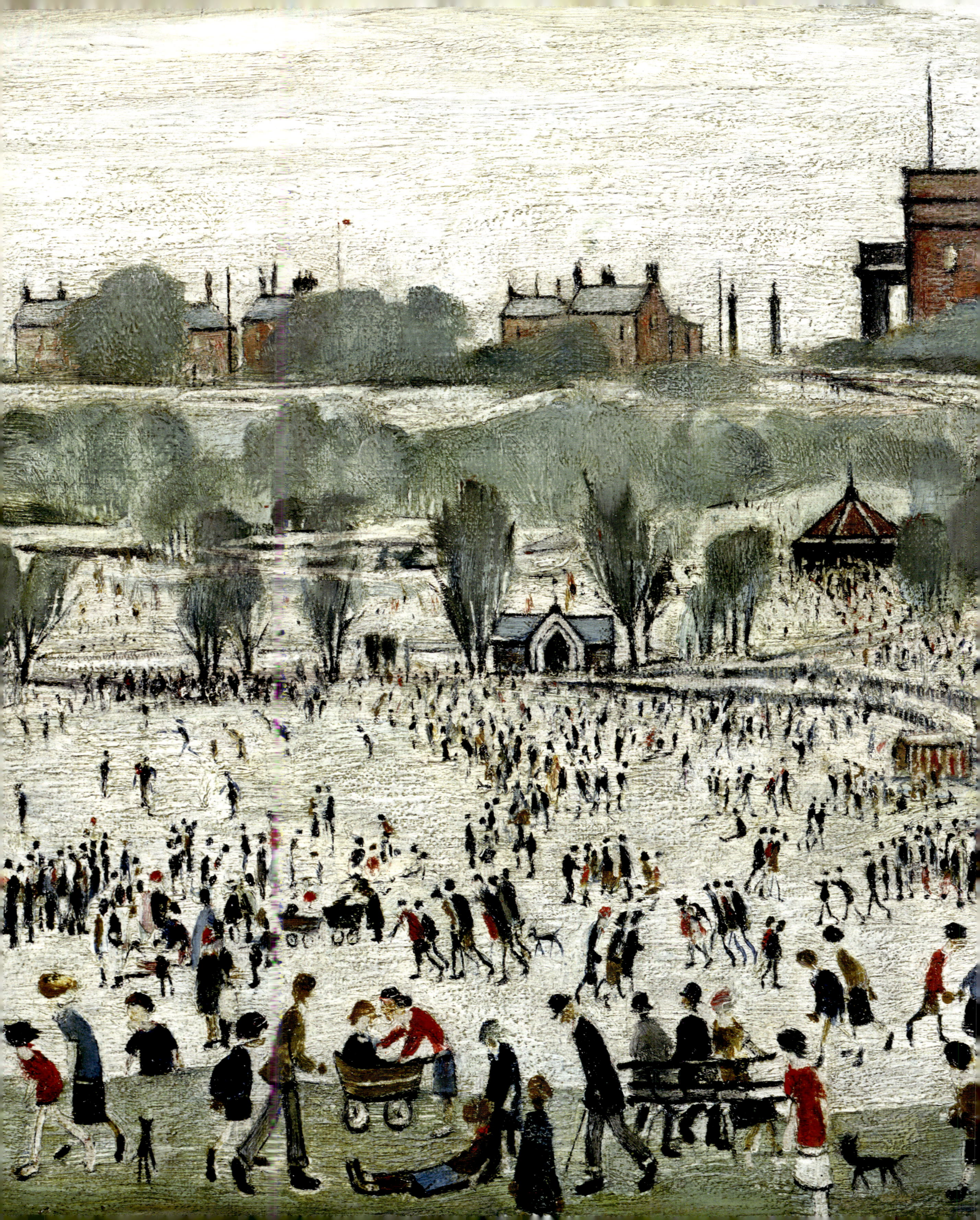

CHAPTER 12

LOWRY AND LANDSCAPE

Steps and things ... I liked doing steps in Ancoats ... in Stockport ... steps anywhere you like, simply because I like steps and the area which they used in what was an industrial area. I did a lot you see. I've never found it interesting to paint pure landscapes. I'm not interested in pure landscape. I've done a few.[1]

L. S. Lowry

The question of Lowry and landscape is not unlike the format of a child's riddle. When is a landscape not a landscape? To which an almost legitimate answer is, when it is by L. S. Lowry. If by landscape we traditionally mean paintings like Cézanne's views of Provence or Constable's rural scenes or even those hybrid paintings by Gainsborough in which the faces and bodies of a couple of languid, not very interesting, aristocrats are posed against an immaculate view of some of the land that they own, then there are very few landscapes by Lowry and those that do exist are as far from being traditional as it is possible to be. Furthermore they rarely even look like "a Lowry" which shouts its identity across a crowded room.

It is in fact almost easier to identify a Lowry landscape by what it does *not* contain rather than by what is included. Lowry's *pure* landscapes have no church spires, no factory chimneys, no belching smoke and, above all, no crowds and hardly any human figures at all. They do, however, tend to include a large amount of white paint. The concept of a traditional English landscape simply did not appeal to him. Thus the celebrated anecdote about his one *plein air* expedition to paint "landscapes" in Cumbria with Sheila Fell. They set up their easels back to back and did not examine each other's work until the day was done. Fell revealed a Cumbrian view and Lowry one of his classic industrial scenes done, as always, from a combination of memory and imagination. In reality Lowry painted many hundreds of landscapes, but they were views of towns, industrial scenes, sea views, pictures of ships and marine activities, vivid renderings of crowded beaches. Some artists raised in grim and grimy urban environments or even in the richer quarters of great cities felt, understandably, drawn to the nearby countryside, if it could be found and visited, and painted what they could not find at home. Others brought up in those circumstances were simply not interested. There are not many Picasso landscapes to be seen and, nearer home, we do not think of mountains and rolling fields when we hear the names of Reynolds, or Wright of Derby or Hogarth. There is no law that says that you have to paint hills and lakes and farms instead of, or in addition to, what you do already paint with such energy and vision.

Lowry clearly had no feeling against landscapes; he simply did not find them as interesting as his more "typical" pictures. Yet, from his juvenilia onwards, he did more than dabble in the genre. Given his respect for his primary artistic mentor, Valette, who was a more than

Detail from *Peel Park, Salford,* 1947, (p.243).

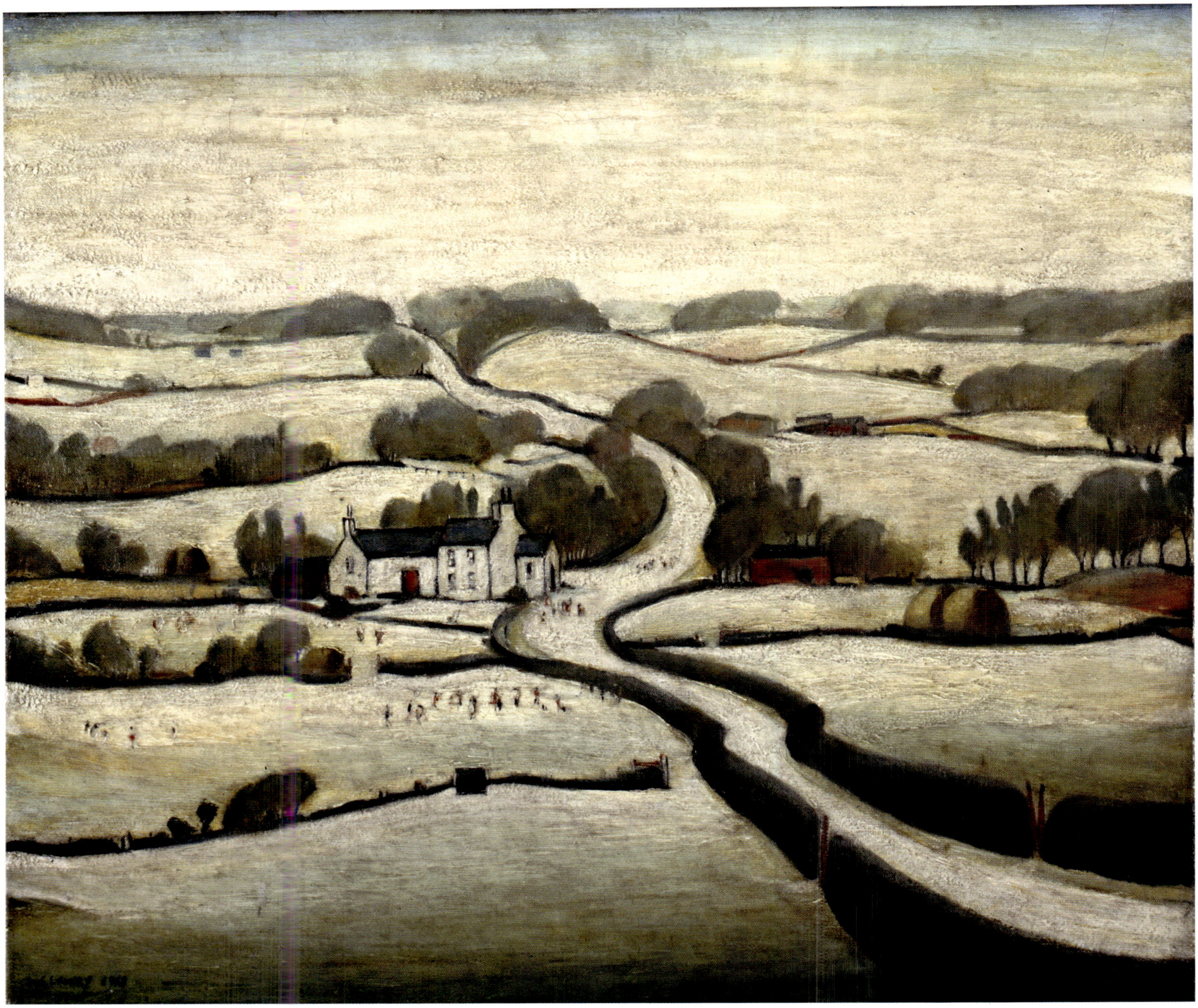

Fylde Landscape, 1958, oil on canvas, 51 × 61 cm.

competent Impressionist and post-Impressionist all rounder, who was, *inter alia*, a serious landscape artist, it would have been surprising if Lowry did not devote at least some of his painterly energy to the *genre* and, as his drawings for *A Cotswold Book* reveal, he was a fine draftsman of the rural scene.

Perhaps the relative lack of appeal of pure landscape was its essential normality, at least in Britain. Lowry was primarily a painter of ugliness which he transformed into beauty and

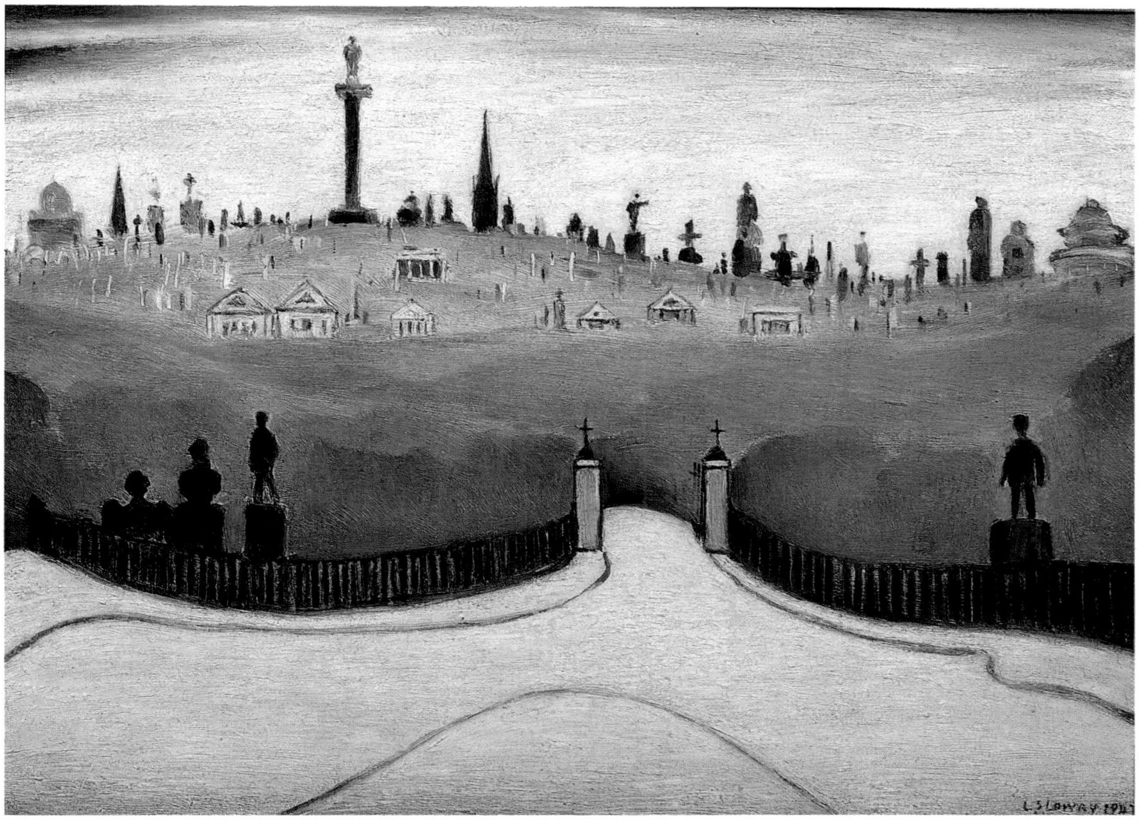

Necropolis, 1947, oil on canvas, 45.7 × 63.5 cm.

of the peculiarities and oddities of the human species that caught his eye; in which case the odder and the freakier the better. Thus one of his most interesting landscapes is his 1947 picture of a Glasgow Cemetery entitled *Necropolis* (above). Sigmund Freud once maintained that there are no jokes and that the bulk of most ironic jokes, about subjects like sex or death, are manifestations of either fear or at least an unhealthy preoccupation with the topic being joked about. In Lowry's case he was certainly in the habit of joking about death and may well, as Michael Howard has suggested in his book, have been fascinated[2] by death; this might well be so, as a grim legacy of his long sojourn with his "bedfast" mother. *Necropolis* is certainly an odd subject for a landscape painting but, in the first place, the land itself *is* fascinating and its associations unavoidable and, secondly, Lowry *has* made a stunning picture of it. The subtleties of his handling of the green surface of the lush parkland in which the corpses are stored is almost the equal of his fundamental treatment of white. The rendering of the differing surfaces as the gentle slopes of the cemetery rise to meet the rows of monuments and statues, (which irresistibly recall the sinister statue of the Commendatore in *Don Giovanni)*, is both apposite and intriguing. The large area of white leading to the gates and the iron fence is, at first glance, too prominent but Lowry disarms this critical viewpoint by the daring use of black lines which call to mind the surface of a rather worn tennis ball in the days when all tennis balls were still white.

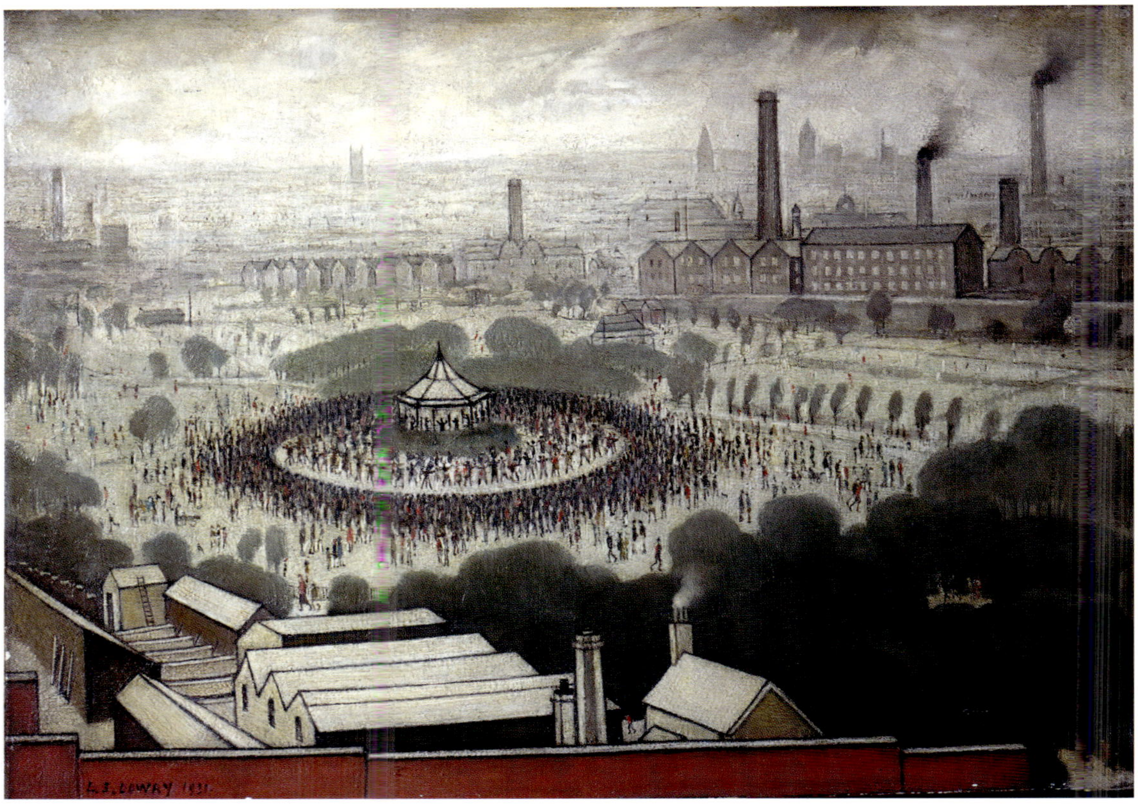

The Bandstand, Peel Park, Salford, 1931, oil on canvas, 43.2 × 62.2 cm.

I suspect that the great height of some of the monuments and statues is somewhat exaggerated but, again, they improve the composition of the painting while reminding us of the towering chimneys and church spires of the cityscapes. Even if one takes some of Lowry's own utterances with a large pinch of salt, it is not entirely surprising that his disavowal of landscape in the epigraph to this chapter should, like the vows of eternal temperance sworn by a chronic alcoholic, be the kind of rule virtually demanding to be broken. There are at least two fine paintings of Lowry's beloved Peel Park in Salford which not only show that Lowry greatly enjoyed doing at least some of his landscapes but that he also seemed to breach his own self-denying ordinance that landscapes will not contain crowds. *Sunday Afternoon* of 1957 is at first glance an industrial since the upper third of this large canvas (114.3 × 152.4 cm.) is a solid panorama of factories, mills and chimneys. The central part of the painting includes crowds too numerously dense to count; yet the view of Peel Park cannot be described as anything other than landscape, whether as it were, true or false. As often noted Lowry was in no way a slavish recorder of what he saw and then painted. Even Peel Park, grand and fascinating as it is, is not quite adequate for Lowry's purposes. Thus he makes the park's entrance much grander than the real one, puts tankers on the River Irwell, and, in his imaginative generosity, at centre right, presents Peel Park with a flourishing but non-existent boating pond.

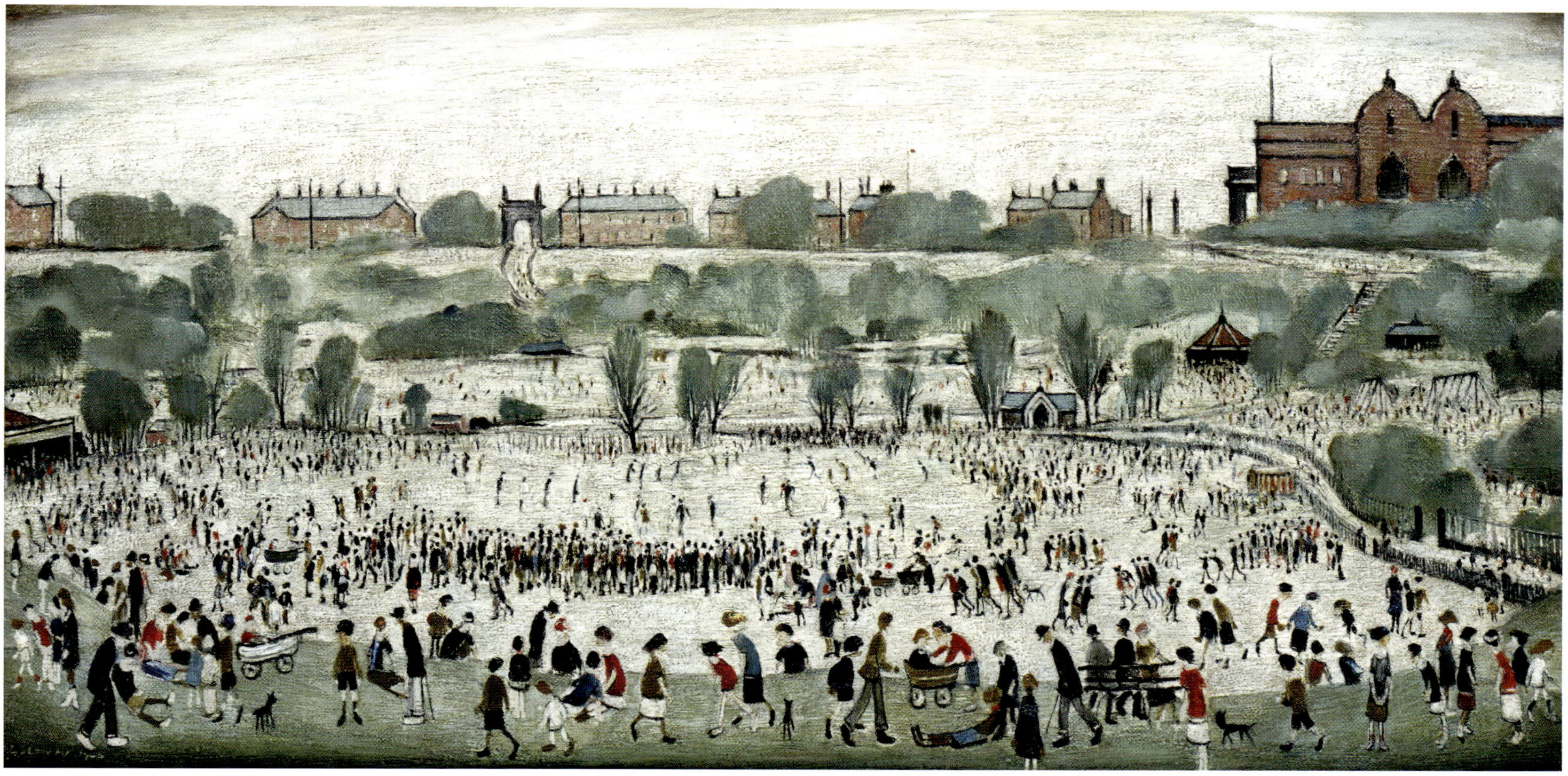

Peel Park, Salford, 1947, oil on canvas, 38.1 × 76.2 cm.

However there is also an almost pure landscape version of Peel Park entitled simply *Peel Park, Salford* of 1944 (above) which is only almost pure in that it does display a substantial, uncountable crowd taking up about forty per cent of the height of the painting and its entire width. It is however a work of considerable beauty and, as in *Necropolis* Lowry has almost as much joy with the range of greens for the grass surface and the healthy trees in leaf as he does with the white.

One could write an entire sub-chapter on Lowry's topographical mendacity or imaginative genius according to one's standpoint, but there is not enough space for it. Instead the reader is referred to an admirable book called *Lowry's City: A Painter and his Locale* by Judith Sandling and Mike Leber, published by the Lowry Press, which analyses and reproduces paintings which are accompanied by photographs of the realities of the truths of the topography. These truths are frequently, and cunningly, adapted and added to by Lowry in his often dazzling skills of composition and organization.

Inevitably there is some sadness involved in reading Sandling and Leber. As so often happens when ugly, failing buildings are erased, whether by war damage or the simple human greed of "developers", so the destroyers lay waste, particularly when *redevelopment* is the goal, to the good buildings, the distinguished architecture which appealed to a landscape painter in the first instance.

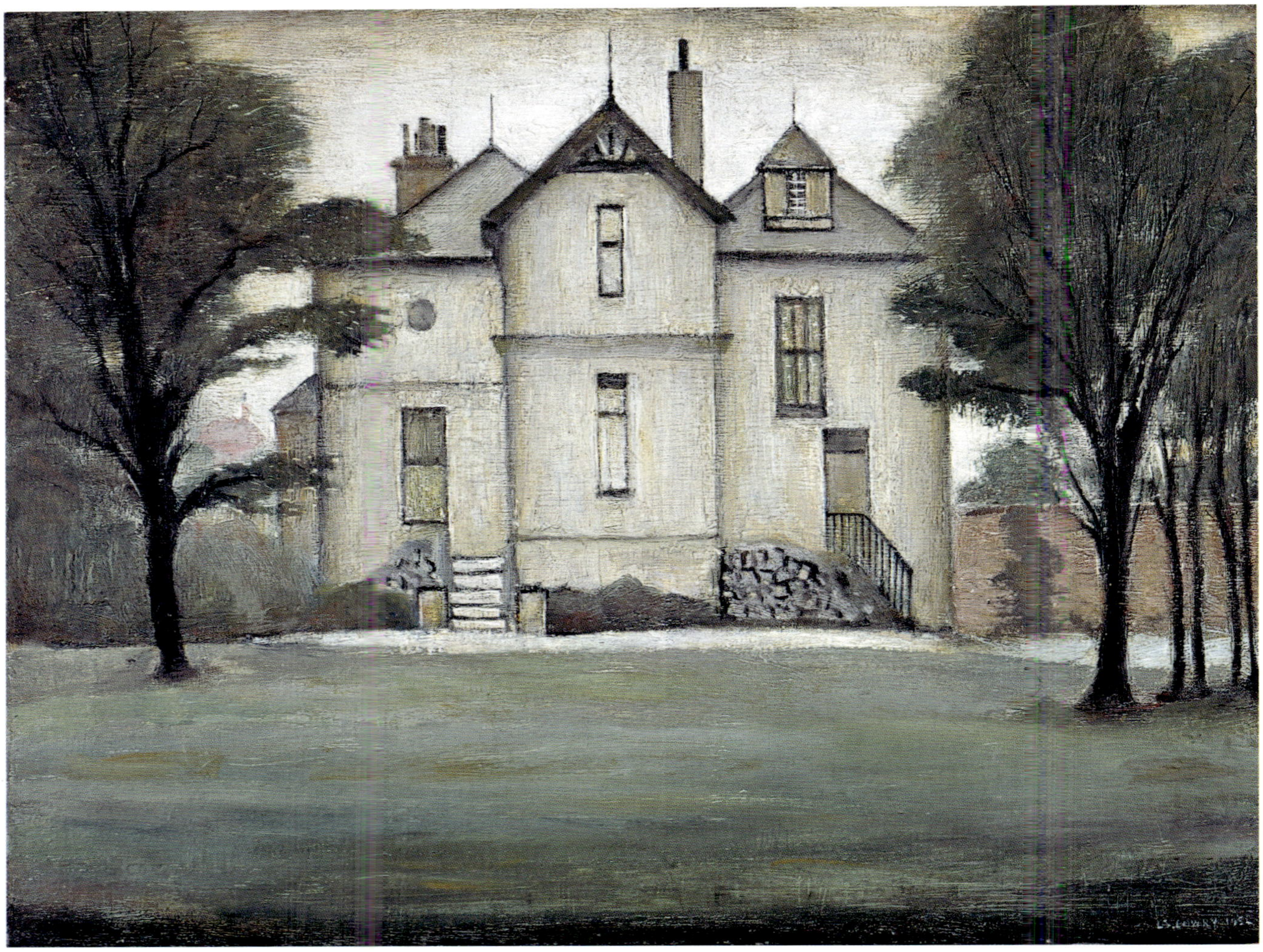

Portrait of a House, 1953, 43.5 × 60 cm.

One does not wholly regret the destruction by bombs, or the site clearances by developers, of grubby slums and tenements; partly because, on the whole, it's good riddance and partly because Lowry often left painted records which are not only aesthetically superior to their models but also a kind of topographical *memento mori*. These now give the viewer intense pleasure; we can also see at least brief glimpses of Lowry's skill as a *recording* landscape painter. I stress the word *recording* because, as we shall see, Lowry's landscapes divide firmly into two categories: the pictures of record and the imagination-aided, if not wholly created, fantasy landscapes.

It is a typical irony that now we can see neither of the originals of the two categories. The imaginary ones cannot be seen precisely because they were imagined and did not exist in the first place; the real ones, built by man were also destroyed by man and therefore exist no longer.

The two most interesting Lowry landscapes of houses are *Portrait of a House* of 1954 (above) and *The Empty House* of 1934 (page 245). *The Empty House* is in a way complemen-

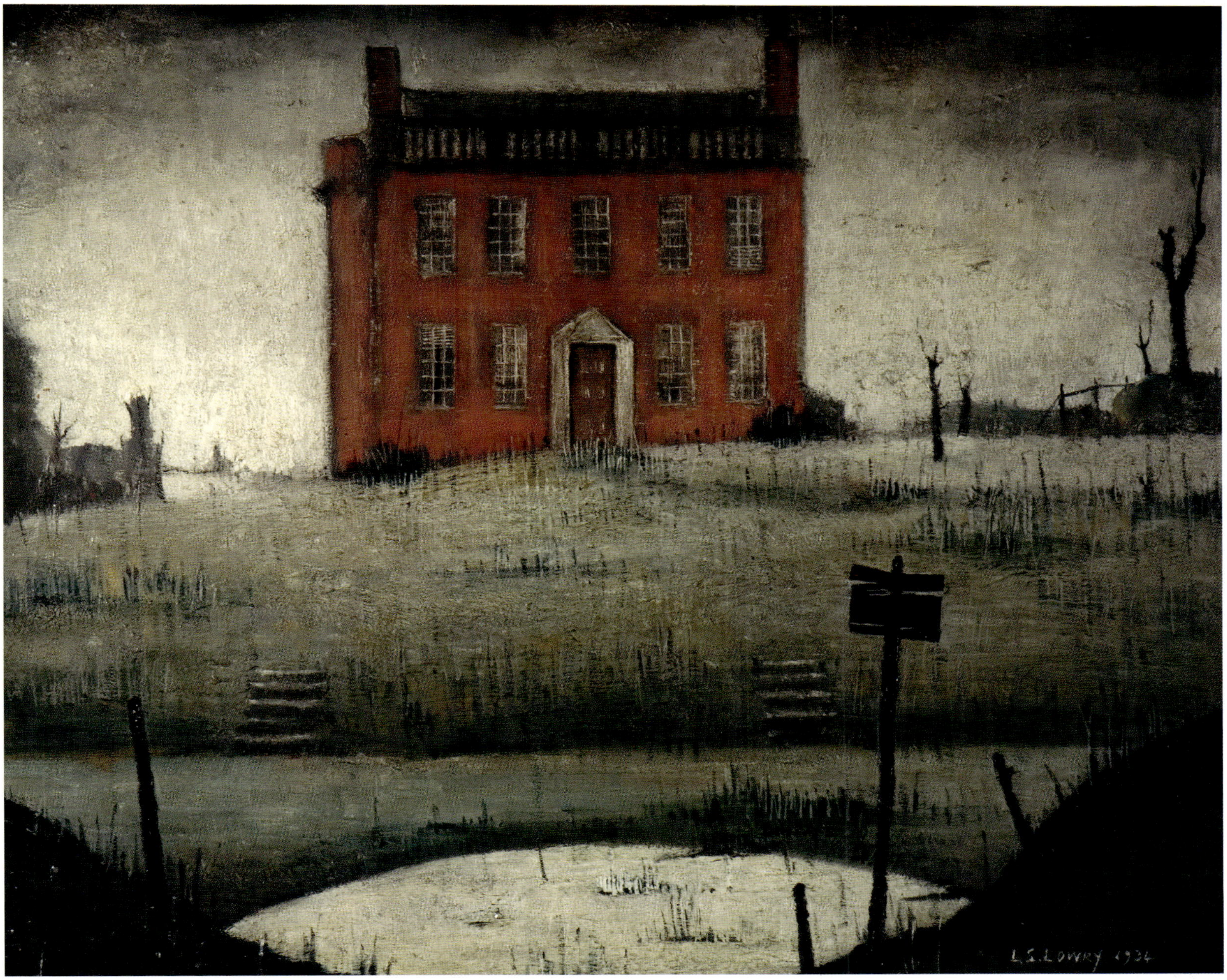

The Empty House, 1934, oil on plywood, 43.2 × 51.3 cm.

tary to that great, depressing, Golgotha-like ruin, *An Island* (page 39) of 1942 which could be categorized as either a very dark landscape indeed or as a war painting. Some critics have suggested that *The Empty House* was a representation of Lowry's emotional state at the time he painted it, (1934). Certainly in 1934 his mother was already long established as a "bed-fast" burden for her son and he had had not a shred of the minor successes that were to come to him around the time she died in 1939.[3] While the ochre, very solid and even imposing house is indeed empty it is not actually a derelict ruin. It might signify depression but hardly emotional collapse or complete breakdown. The land on which it stands, studded with barren, wholly dead trees, with access via some shabby, overgrown steps and long uncut grass playing host to a few non-flowering plants is a far grimmer sight than the house itself, a house manifestly rescuable by a new tenant or owner. All hardly cheerful, but not disastrous either, although it has few external signs that it is a work by Lowry.

Much the same is true of *Portrait of a House* which could pass for the work of any routine academician commissioned by any well-to-do *haut bourgeois* to paint the master's house. Architecturally the house is interesting, doubtless unique for its neighbourhood, and bestowing some distinction upon its owner. The owner at that time was Lowry's friend, the Professor of Bacteriology at Manchester University, the Canadian Hugh Maitland. The house was, called Oaklands in Cheadle Hulme in Cheshire and was doubtless the house in which Maitland and his wife nursed Lowry back to some kind of equilibrium after his nervous collapse following the death of his mother. Perhaps because Lowry allowed himself no liberties of imagination, the rendering of the house is entirely academic and accurate and one can reasonably assume the same of the garden. Yet it is much more obviously a work by L. S. Lowry than *The Empty House* and its subject-matter is ostensibly much more appropriate to Lowry's usual style. *The Empty House* might not have attracted a new tenant or owner and was demolished in the early 1960s. Maitland's house and its extensive grounds were taken over, the house torn down and the site is now "a new housing development".[4] It is salutary that even quite distinguished houses can come and go, yet they continue to be available to posterity in the form of two relatively minor works of art created by a great painter.

It has often been said, with justice, that Lowry was not a *Modern Artist*. Terminology, particularly the vocabulary of criticism, whether of visual art, literature or the performing arts, is as subject to change and fashion as life itself. There is little agreement as to what "Modern" means; it is probably only in the last thirty or so years that it has been necessary to re-invent the word "Contemporary" to distinguish the work of, say, Damien Hirst or Tracy Emin, who are "Contemporary", from, say, Picasso, Matisse, Cézanne, who are "Modern". As we have seen with Lowry, who was precisely of an age that he could have been affected by, and even attracted by, any of the great movements of the last century from Cubism to Futurism to Vorticism, from Neo-Classicism to Neo-Romanticism, all of which reached, and took hold to a greater or lesser extent, in these islands and is dealt in and exhibited in the provinces.

As well as London, Lowry apparently remained either blind to their blandishments or they simply passed him by. He was always, except for his lessons and encouragement from Valette, a cat who walked by himself. The one movement to which he did pay some attention, even some homage, was the Impressionism he inherited from Valette.

Yet Lowry occasionally sprang a surprise. There is a landscape called *Country Lane* of 1914 (page 247) which has been described as influenced by a large Impressionist exhibition held in Manchester in 1909 when Lowry was still a highly impressionable 22-year-old. This picture is an almost unique example of a wholly different style of painting. It has a wide colour range, totally different from the later five-colour limited palette. It is also executed in a heavy impasto style and, one suspects, brushes supplemented by fingers or palette knives. It

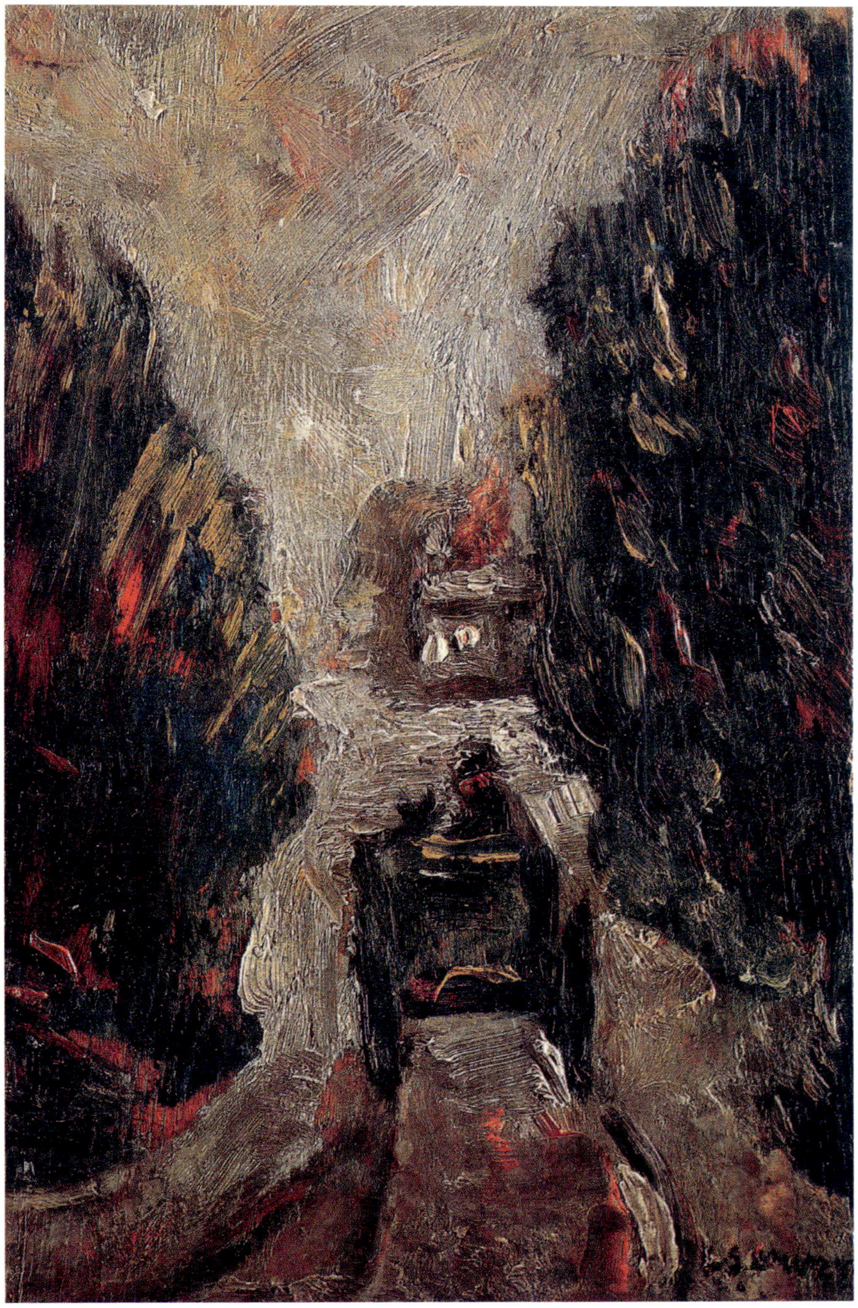

Country Lane, 1914, oil on board, 23.6 × 15.6 cm.

not only does not look like a Lowry, having strong affinities with Chaim Soutine and Jack B. Yeats although, like so many other critical insights, this one is born of typical art historians' hindsight, in that the parallels are there but history provides no actual links between Lowry, Soutine and Yeats, or even Kokoschka. Lowry could well have encountered Kokoschka but certainly not in 1914 when Kokoschka (1886–1980) was fighting and getting wounded in World War I. If they had any knowledge of each other it would have dated from Kokoschka's arrival in England as a refugee after Hitler annexed Austria. Soutine (1894–1943) was also an unknown in England in 1914 outside smart London circles and Jack B. Yeats (1871–1957)

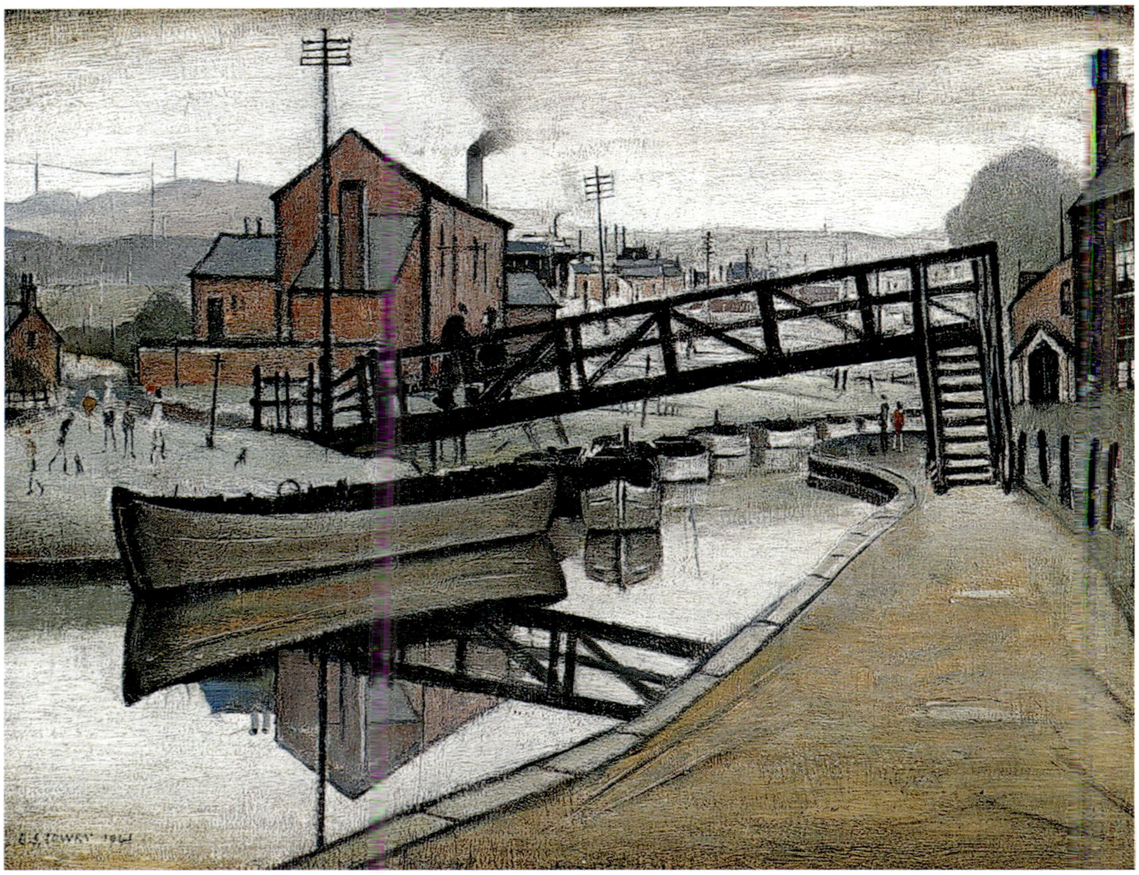

Barges on a Canal, 1941, oil on board, 39.8 × 53.2 cm.

did not develop his thick impasto style until long after 1914. Thus the resemblances are simply one of the odd coincidences in the history of painting for which no rational explanation exists.

As for the so-called Impressionist influence, as it were a bug caught from Valette that does not work either since, if this picture belongs to any movement whatsoever, it is surely Expressionism which fits the bill. In any case it seems as if *Country Lane* is what biologists term a *sport*, something readily identifiable as real but not logically explicable. There were also in the years before World War I some rather dark, heavy, academic landscapes looking not unlike nineteenth-century Dutch paintings and not really interesting, let alone typical of the later Lowry.

In fact the Valette influence, which Lowry freely acknowledged, did leave a vaguely Impressionist stamp on Lowry's mind as some of his sailing boat pictures confirm and which prevailed as late as 1941 when he painted *Barges on a Canal* (above). This is an enchanting landscape, not least because it includes two of Lowry's favourite ingredients, water and boats and could even, at a pinch, be a *plein air* picture in which he, as always, eschews shadows but has great painterly fun with the immaculate reflections in the clear water (naturally painted white) of the two leading barges and the house beyond the bridge.

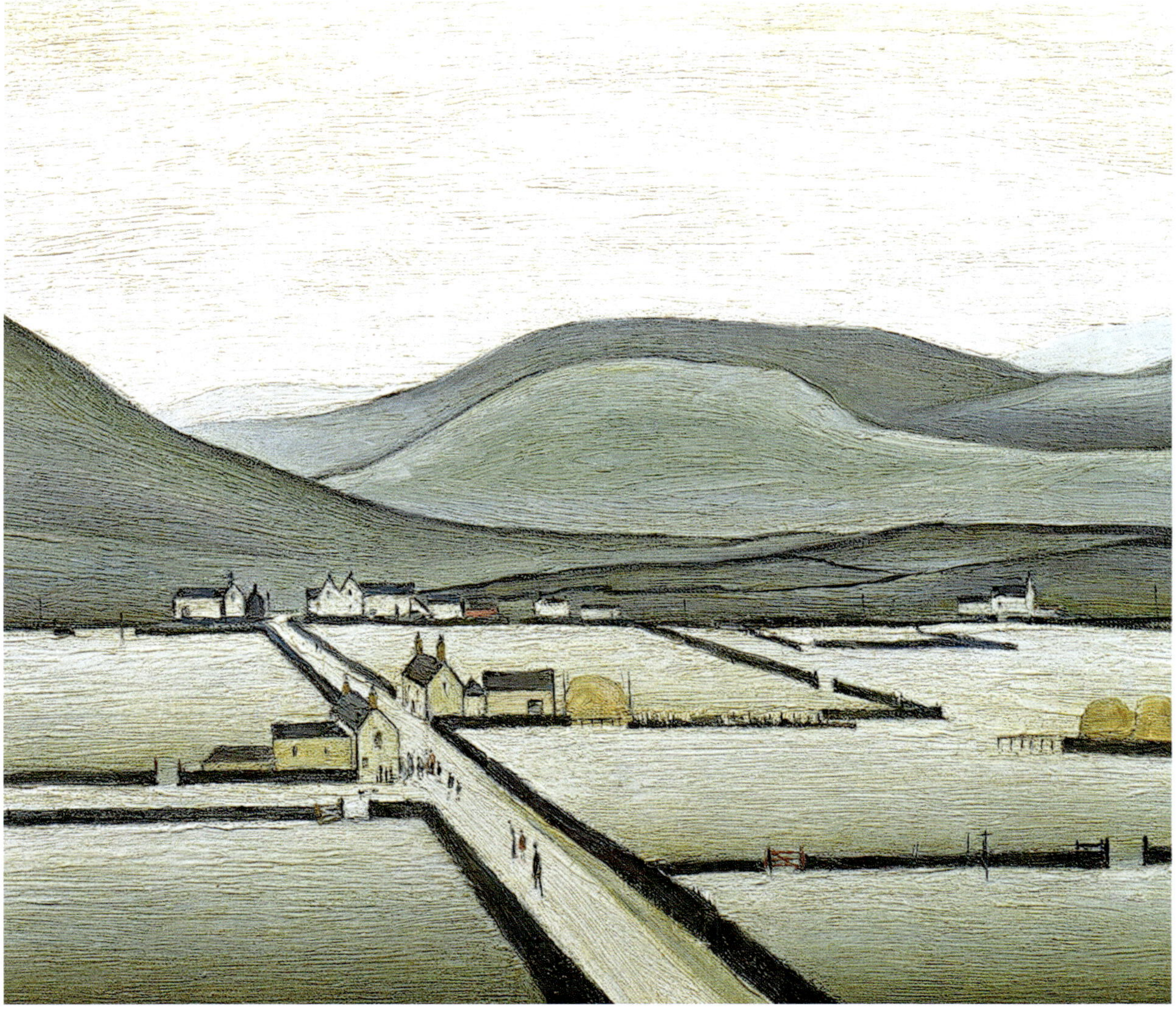

Edge of the Moor, 1952,
oil on canvas, 50.8 × 61 cm.

But, while Lowry's later landscapes, persisting well into the 1950s, were utterly unlike his cityscapes, his "industrials", they had a style of their own. Thus, once you saw what he was doing, they did, at their best, proclaim themselves as readily identifiable Lowrys. *Edge of the Moor* of 1952 (above) and *Fylde* of 1953 (page 250) are among his best rural scenes. *Fylde* is particularly attractive even if – or perhaps because – it is so ambiguous. At first glance it could almost be an abstract picture but it soon reveals itself as an almost limitless stretch of land, all in white with a clear, distant horizon and divided into six fields, three on each side of a road with faint outlines of exiguous pavement. The fields are divided, and enclosed, by black, drystone walls and, while this white world is uninhabited, the overall effect is not, as it might sound, a bleak one. The ambiguity is well expressed by Kalman who points out that Lowry's colour sense, at its eccentric best, gives us a red pole on the left and an "incongruous red gate" on the right. "The rest of it is Lowry's off-white landscape into which you can read a field or snow or whatever you like."[5]

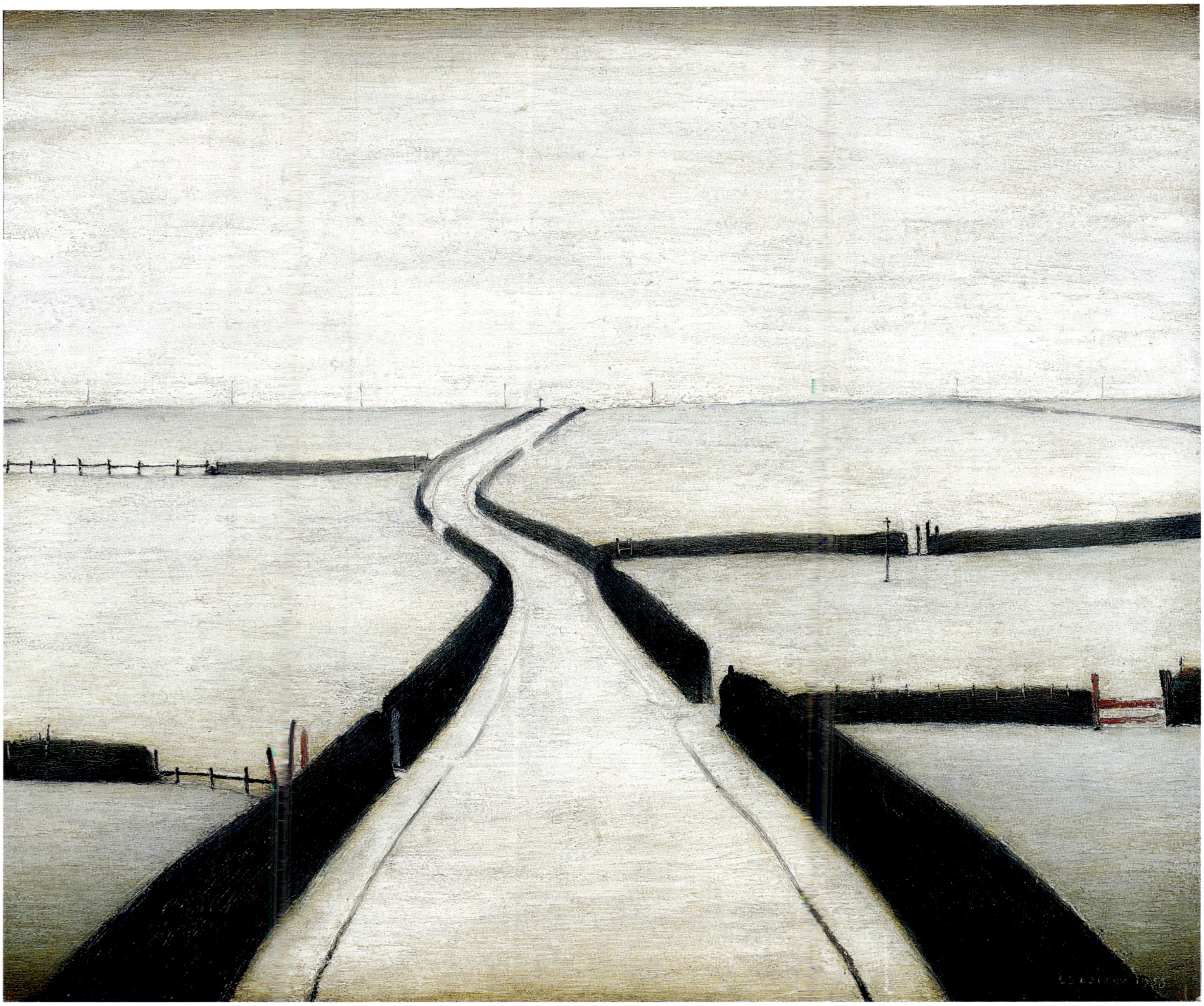

Fylde, 1953, oil on canvas, 48.9 × 59.1 cm.

There is one quite conventional landscape, *A Lancashire Farm* of 1944 (page 251) where the farm, far from being isolated, abuts onto a large private house, with a partial view of other neighbouring houses, street lighting etc. It is as if a village or small town has grown around the farm on the left, with its traditional farm buildings and a couple of carts resting on their rear ends with the empty shafts, devoid of horses, pointing skywards. The buildings and the heap of dead hay and grass turning into compost are dark and dirty but there is a solitary splash of colour, almost dead centre, in the blouse or sweater worn by the woman crossing

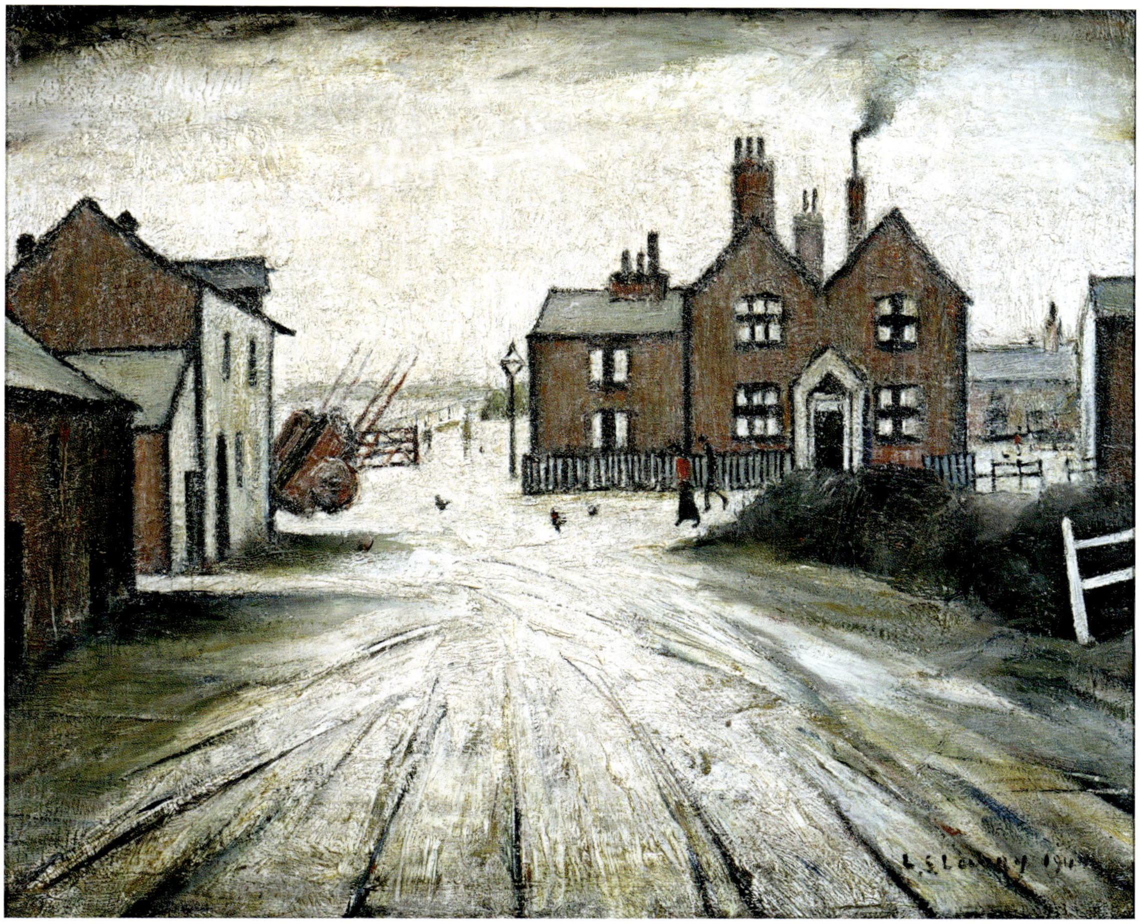

A Lancashire Farm, 1944, oil on canvas, 43.2 × 53.3 cm.

the farmyard. Here the off-white surface *could* in fact be snow or slush, since it is traversed by several criss-crossing cartwheel tracks, and the overall effect is wintry, although not chilling. It is at once a realistic, recording version of a common sight, made beautiful as he makes his mill scenes beautiful, by Lowry's vision mined out of unpromising working environments.

But, for most people who are aware of Lowry's landscapes, that word conjures up the strange mountainous scenery, done predominantly in green with the white reserved for the lake or many lakes that provide horizontal relief from the over-reaching peaks. One of the conventional examples of this type of Lowry landscape is *Welsh Lake* of 1947 (page 252) in which the conventionality is effected by the normal irregularity of mountain surfaces and shapes and the lake with mountains encircling which slope gently down into its shores.

Perhaps the most extreme landscape, the best known and most often reproduced is the *Landmark* done in 1936 (page 253). For obvious reasons it must be reproduced here since to leave it out because it is ubiquitous is the equivalent of not listening to Beethoven's *Fifth Symphony* because it is being played all the time. Basically for all that, there are some subsidiary mountains or hills below the overpowering central peak and, at bottom left, a small white lake. This is a giant projection of a massive female breast, surmounted by an obelisk which does double duty as a freakishly elongated nipple and aureola and as a mere phallic

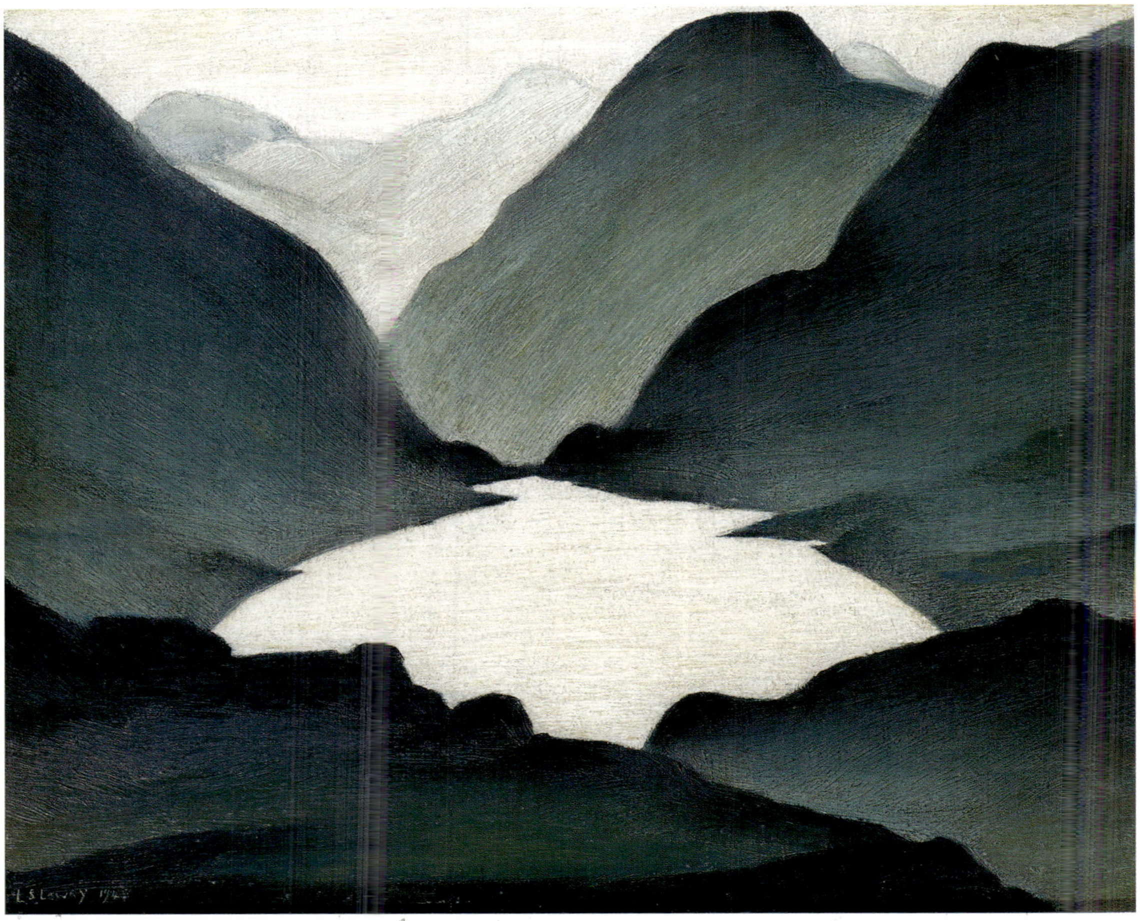

Welsh Lake, 1947, oil on canvas, 40 × 49.5 cm.

symbol, if not a rather slender penis. It is, of course, possible for the immature to snigger and pass on; for the more literally-minded Freudians to smile and say I told you so, but, lifelong student and admirer of Freud that I am, I would rather recall his remark that sometimes a cigar is just a cigar.

That the painting is a work of suppressed eroticism is also wrong. There is nothing suppressed about it. Its meaning is all too obvious and is in a way perfectly respectable. After all the association of mountains and hills of a certain shape with the human breast is a very long one and was not invented by Lowry. One cannot help recalling that Wyoming has a mountain range called The Tetons of which its highest peak is the Grand Teton at over 13,000 feet, making Lowry's little effort a molehill by comparison.

But, Freud and sublimation aside, it is a particularly beautiful painting in composition and in execution. The two lower hills can also pass for parts of two female bodies lying side by side. It is a painting with genuine Surrealist overtones. Kalman believed that it was based on an actual British landscape and that very few of Lowry's paintings were *wholly* invented. Granted that the Lake District was not far away from Salford, Lowry, who was a dedicated traveller in these islands, might have had this imagery triggered off by some real mountain

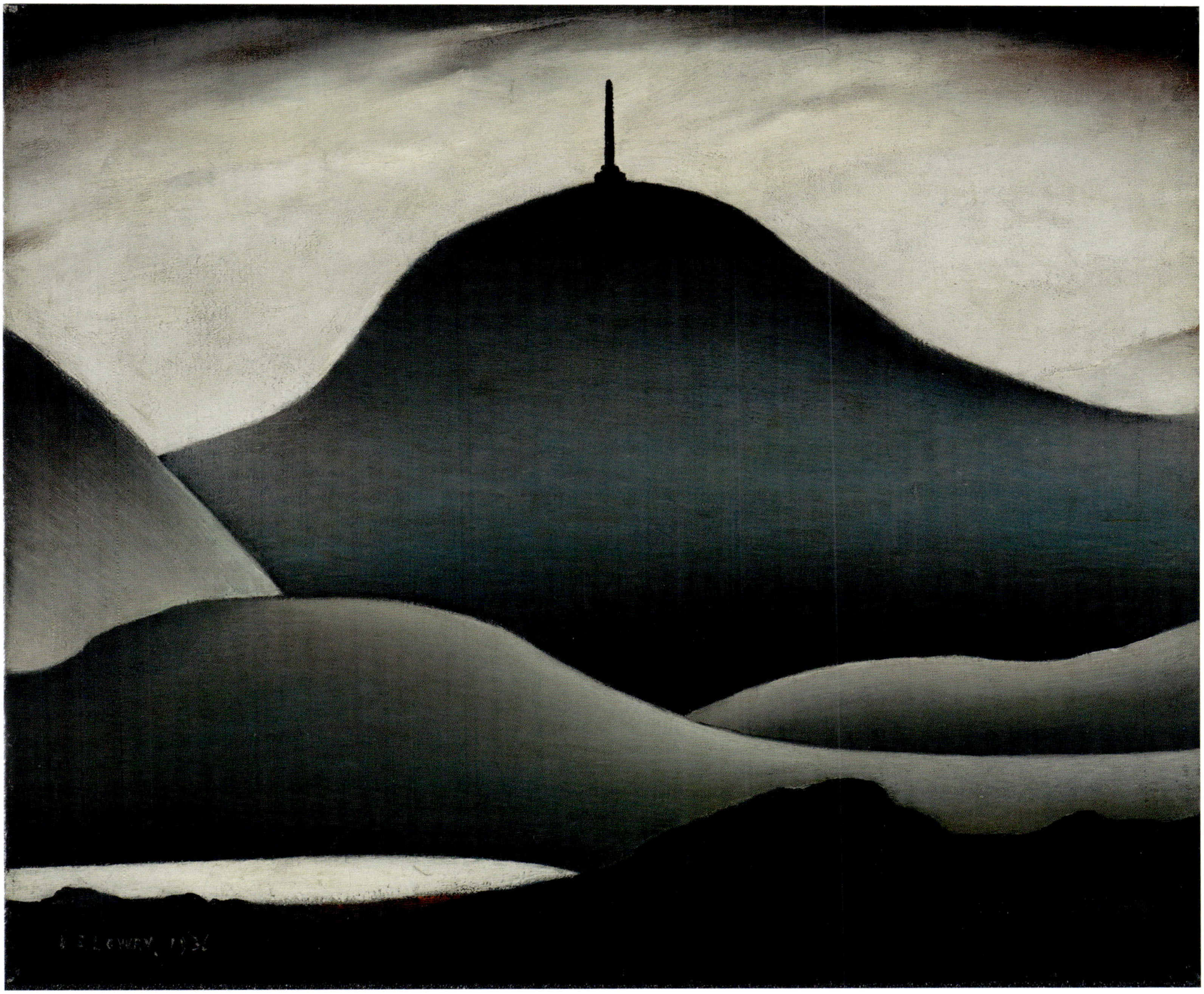

A Landmark, 1936, oil on canvas, 43.4 × 53.6 cm.

scenery but I suspect that is an almost wholly invented scene as most Surrealist compositions are.

It has also been suggested that this painting is a portrait of Lowry's loneliness as well as of sexual desire. That is, bearing in mind that there are no people visible, a possible interpretation if one believes that Lowry was lonely, a judgement that I have always seen as superficial. Solitary yes, lonely or reclusive no. On the evidence of the paintings mentioned in this chapter, had Lowry produced a much larger *proportion* of his *œuvre* in landscape form, I believe he would have been hailed as a master of that *genre* as much as of the industrials.

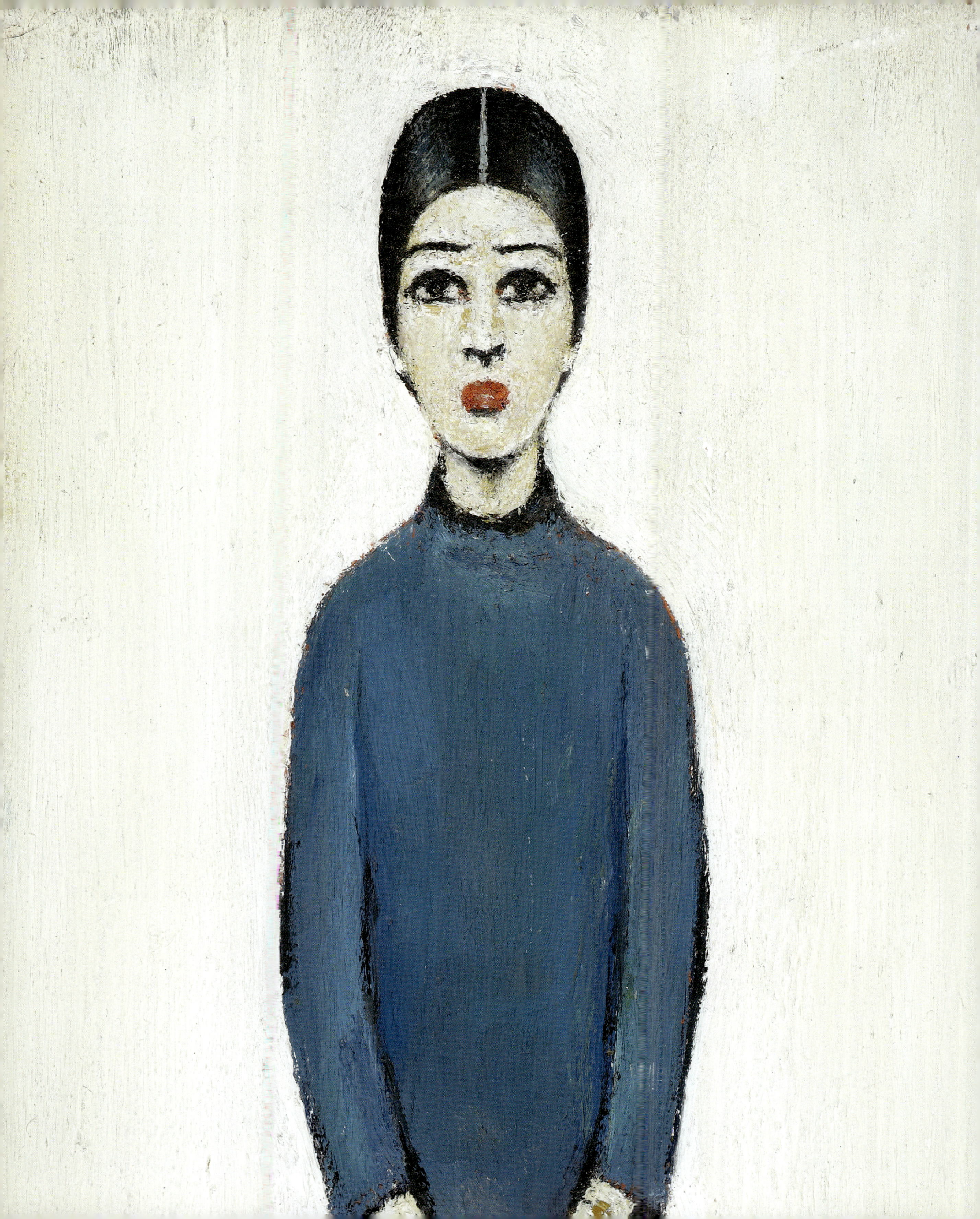

CHAPTER 13

LOWRY AND WOMEN

The Rossetti women are not real women. He used them for something in his mind caused, in my opinion, by the death of his wife. I may be quite wrong there, but significantly they all came after the death of his wife.[1]

L. S. Lowry in conversation with Monty Bloom

In any classical Freudian profile of L. S. Lowry, based upon his life history, not just till adolescence, but deep into his middle age one could be forgiven for assuming him to be homosexual either by nature or by nurture. He was the only child of an apparently loveless marriage with a weak and unsuccessful father whose inadequacies ensured that the family lived a life of shabby genteel poverty and who was the archetypal henpecked husband whom you could easily imagine as the butt of sly humour in a play by Stanley Houghton or any other dramatist of the Manchester School. Add to this a cold, grotesquely snobbish – and hence permanently socially unsatisfied – mother, who was a failed concert pianist reduced to giving piano lessons to keep the family going in posh Victoria Park with a rent they could not afford and you wonder how the young Lowry survived at all. Mrs Lowry possessed Olympic standards of hypochondria and valetudinarianism until her husband died in 1932, whereupon she took permanently to her bed, ('bedfast' was the regional phrase) remaining there until she died, like so many of her type, full of years and complaints, in 1939 aged 83. Lowry was distraught and near breakdown. Even Mrs Lowry's doctor had told Lowry that *his own* health was precarious and that he had to take a break from his nursing duties or collapse himself. Happily, although Lowry was by then fifty-two, he was taken in by loyal friends who, as if he was an orphaned child, clothed and fed him. One should also recall that alongside his efforts to become an artist he had, since his teens, held down a series of jobs from which he had earned a modest living. He had never starved in a garret and had reached a stage when his paintings were being shown and had even begun, at modest prices, to sell. In all that time his mother had never given him a word of encouragement, let alone praise.

Michael Leber has shrewdly observed of Lowry that: "The lack of appreciation for his efforts by his contemporaries could not shake his belief; *more than this, nor could the antipathy of his adored mother*. No matter what the opposition, Lowry held true to his mission.[2]

If my portrayal of Mrs Lowry in this book seems somewhat severe this is in no way personal. When she died in 1939 I could have no personal knowledge of her and the evidence for my implied criticism of her apparent coldness towards the son who worshipped her comes mostly from Rohde's convincing version of her and, in part, from experience of quite a common social type in the English middle-class. Most of us have encountered women who began their adult lives with a modest talent in music or drama or painting, who completed

Detail from *Ann*, (undated), (p.263).

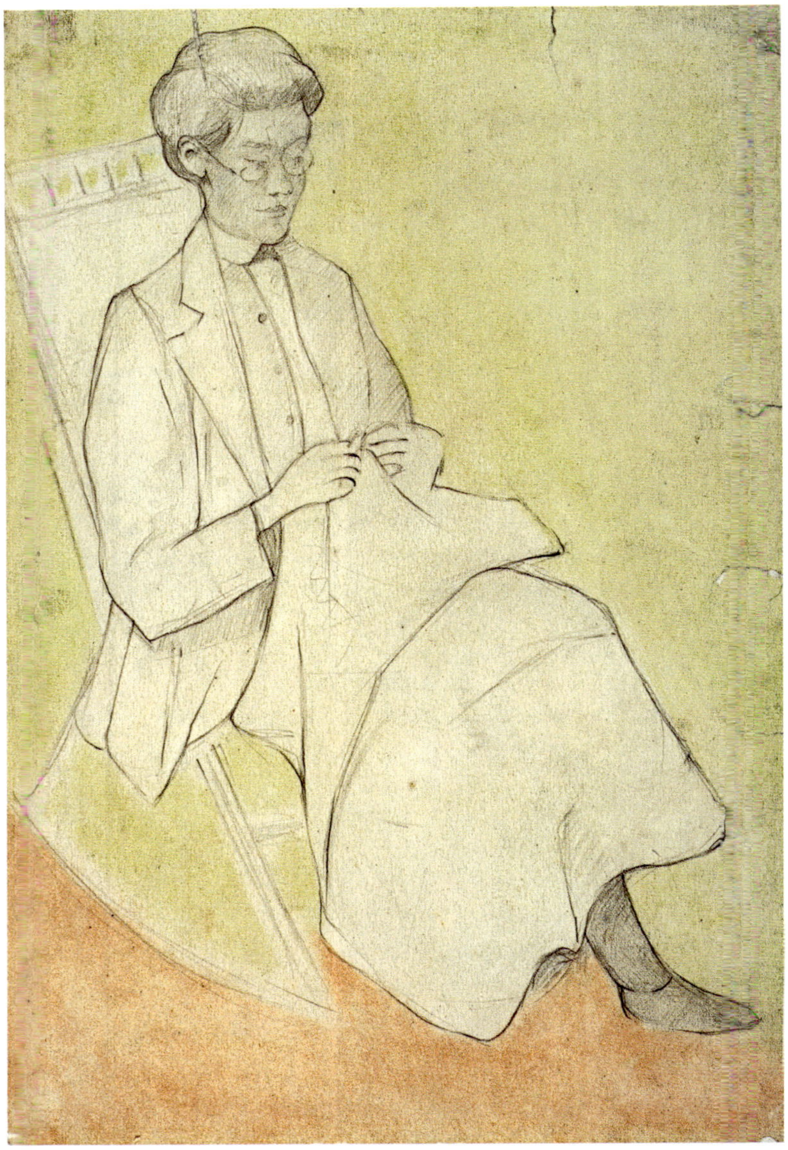

Mother Sewing, 1909, pencil and watercolour on paper, 34.5 × 23.5 cm.

their studies at institutions like RADA or the Royal College of Music or an art school, got nowhere and then settled for a comfortable bourgeois marriage and raised a family to whom – and to their friends – they would frequently confide that she had given up a promising career as a practitioner of one of the arts in order to look after her husband and their offspring. What no one can ever know is whether Mrs Lowry's less than benign emotional neglect of her son's great talent actually constituted a spur to his efforts rather than the discouragement she apparently intended.

Today Manchester has a thriving, entirely open, gay scene but, in those grim inter-war years, there was nothing of that kind. Thus, had Lowry been turned that way by his mother he would doubtless, if he had even had the time, what with rent collecting, studying painting and nursing, have been reduced to cottaging and risking arrest.

Happily, Lowry does not so neatly fall into classic Freudian theory or categorisation in that there is not a shred of evidence that he was homosexually inclined or even, to use a later and briefly voguish descriptive phrase, homosocial. He had many male friendships but these, where the men were married, always included their wives and, as his biographer has made clear, probably the deepest and, for him, the most satisfying relationships were with women.

In an age that has seen the book and the films of Vladimir Nabokov's *Lolita* and the growth of the rich, practising sex tourism on the poor, and with every imaginable perversion available at the touch of a keyboard, it seems almost ill-mannered to point out that Lowry had a series of relationships with teenage girls and women far younger than himself, but so far the most devoted smut-hounds have not come up with the slightest hint of scandal or even impropriety. In fact, if Lowry is to be believed – and there is no evidence to suggest otherwise – he lived and died a virgin. In a remarkable interview with the writer Edwin Mullins entitled "The Lonely Life of L. S. Lowry" for *The Sunday Telegraph* in 1966 Lowry said:

> Had I not been lonely, none of my work would have happened. I should not have done what I've done, or seen the way I saw things. I work because there's nothing else to do. Painting is a marvellous way of passing the time, and very interesting when you get into it. Between 1909 and 1939, when I had my first exhibition, there's really nothing to tell. After about 1909, when we moved house, I lost sight of everybody. I had no close friends at all. I've never been married. I've never had a girl, in fact. And now I'm nearly 80 I think it's too late to start.
>
> There was one girl: at art school. We met in life class for three years; and used the same railway station to go home. It went on like that. When the summer holidays came we'd say 'See you again in October.' I never thought of arranging to see her. And one October she wasn't there, and that was the end of it.
>
> I think I must have been what they call a 'cold fish'. Even now I usually prefer to be by myself. I didn't even notice there was a Great Slump. It didn't come into my curriculum. My mother died in 1939, and I know it sounds ridiculous and sentimental to say but I've never felt much interest in life since then ...[3]

It is possible that Lowry yearned for this girl, but a combination of shyness on his part and the reticence of well brought up young women of the period made any further contact impossible. It is also possible that she was one of Lowry's fantasies of which he had several about which he spoke to his friends, inventing perfectly plausible lives and backgrounds for them as if to convince his audience that he would have married or had affairs if only he'd had the time or if circumstances had been different. On the other hand, he also expressed the view that "a married man lives like a dog and dies like a king; a bachelor lives like a king and dies like a dog".

But his involvements with young women were not all the products of his imagination. There exists a somewhat artless, but entirely convincing, book *The Lowry I Knew* by Doreen Sieja,written by a woman who, as a blonde, buxom teenager went to work at the Pall Mall

Property Company as a clerk just before and during World War II. It gives a neat portrait of routine office life and Lowry's work as rent collector and bookkeeper:

> The Pall Mall office hours were 9.30 am to 5.00 pm, Monday to Friday, and Saturday morning, which we took in turns. The times were a little flexible, we each had our set of books to do and rents to collect from the weekly properties, and so long as this was accomplished no one seemed to mind that Mr Lowry came in around 10.00 am or took a day or so off to go to London on art business. Also he never took a regular holiday time in the summer like the rest of us and was often still there at 5.00 pm when we left. His official capacity was as the company cashier but he collected some rents and his observations in the process often provided him with subjects for his paintings. If he happened to drop a small coin on his rounds, he would not be bothered to pick it up, the local urchins soon realised this so it was no surprise that there was often a straggle of children accompanying him along the streets. He was not at all interested in the business side of our office life, it was definitely a chore to him, but he understood shorthand, bookkeeping and also did some typing. None of it terribly efficiently because he simply was not interested, but everything was done adequately and we all got along splendidly in our personal relationships.
>
> . . . . . .
>
> When Mr Lowry was doing his books he used a pencil, we always knew which was his because it would be well chewed at the end, and he would walk around, looking very harassed, with the pencil between his teeth. He completed the ledgers in ink, sticking his pen viciously into the inkwell and shaking it out behind him so that the surplus ink splattered the wall and floor behind his chair and his fingers because well stained in the process.[4]

They had something more than the usual office friendship and she certainly knew about his travails with his mother:

> His mother was reluctant to be parted from her son for even a brief time until the doctor explained to her that unless he took care she might be left with no son at all; and so Mr Lowry took his first short holiday in years.[5]

They exchanged presents and he took her to concerts. After she married – the witnesses were Lowry and her father – and had a child, Lowry was the family's most regular visitor and once the Siejas left for a better life in Canada they kept up a correspondence but since neither was willing or able to cross or re-cross the Atlantic, never met again.

In so far as Lowry had a meaningful relationship it was with his most significant sitter, other than his mother, a woman called simply Ann, whom he painted often and he also spoke about to his friends with substantial, circumstantial detail as to her profession, her wealth and so on. Thanks to Shelley Rhode's scrupulous detective work, it seems clear that "Ann" did not exist, but probably represented for Lowry an ideal fantasy woman for him to admire and about whom he could expatiate to his friends. Perhaps his ingrained habit of not introducing his many friends to each other was at least partly due to the non-existence

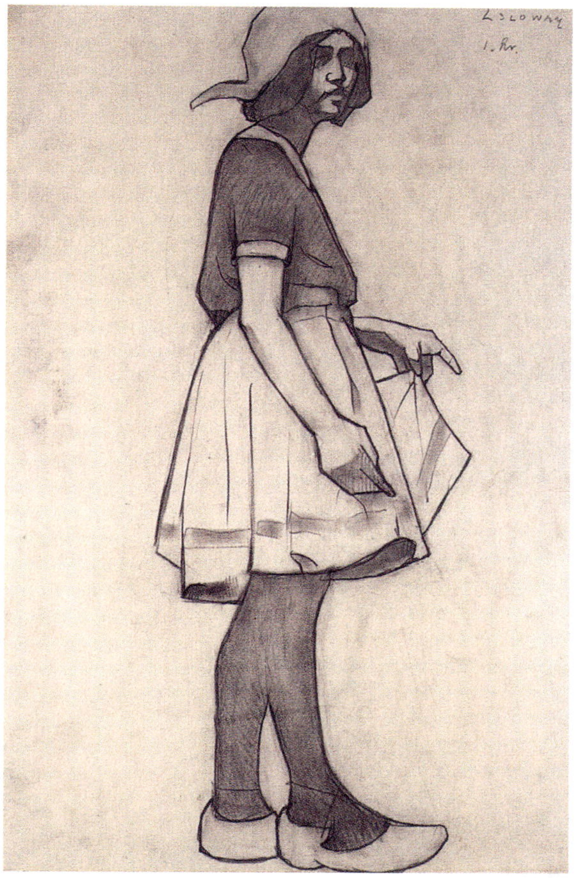

Model in Dutch Costume, c.1917, pencil on paper, 53 × 35.5 cm.

of "Ann", so that he did not have to check which account he had given to x or y and only had to be consistent about her with one person or family at a time.

Sieja's book is particularly interesting in that it appears to corroborate Lowry's relationship with "Ann" and goes into elaborate detail about "Ann's" glittering but brief career as a ballerina and the wealth and sophistication of her family background. "Ann" tried unsuccessfully to get Lowry to visit Italy with her. At one stage:

> Mr Lowry told me that he and Ann had called at our home but got no reply. The electric bell must have been out of order and they did not like to knock too hard in case they woke up the baby, which he felt would be an horrendous thing to do, as once she started to cry there was no shutting her up! This young lady's parents had given her a two-seater Rolls Royce for her twenty-first birthday so I said that I hoped they had parked it outside our front door for the neighbours to see – the kind of remark that Mr Lowry would appreciate. Somehow it seems fate did not want to change the pattern of these people remaining just shadows for me. I know we were home that evening and remembered quite clearly that the weather was quite cold and we were huddled around the living room fire talking to my young cousin who was up from Cambridge.[6]

All this shows how circumstantial and convincing Lowry could be when describing his imaginary relationships to his real friends and one wonders how Sieja could have published this particular in story in 1983, i.e. four years after the first edition of Shelley Rohde's biography had appeared, until one recalls that the Siejas were then living in Canada where a biography of Lowry was unlikely to be noticed widely.

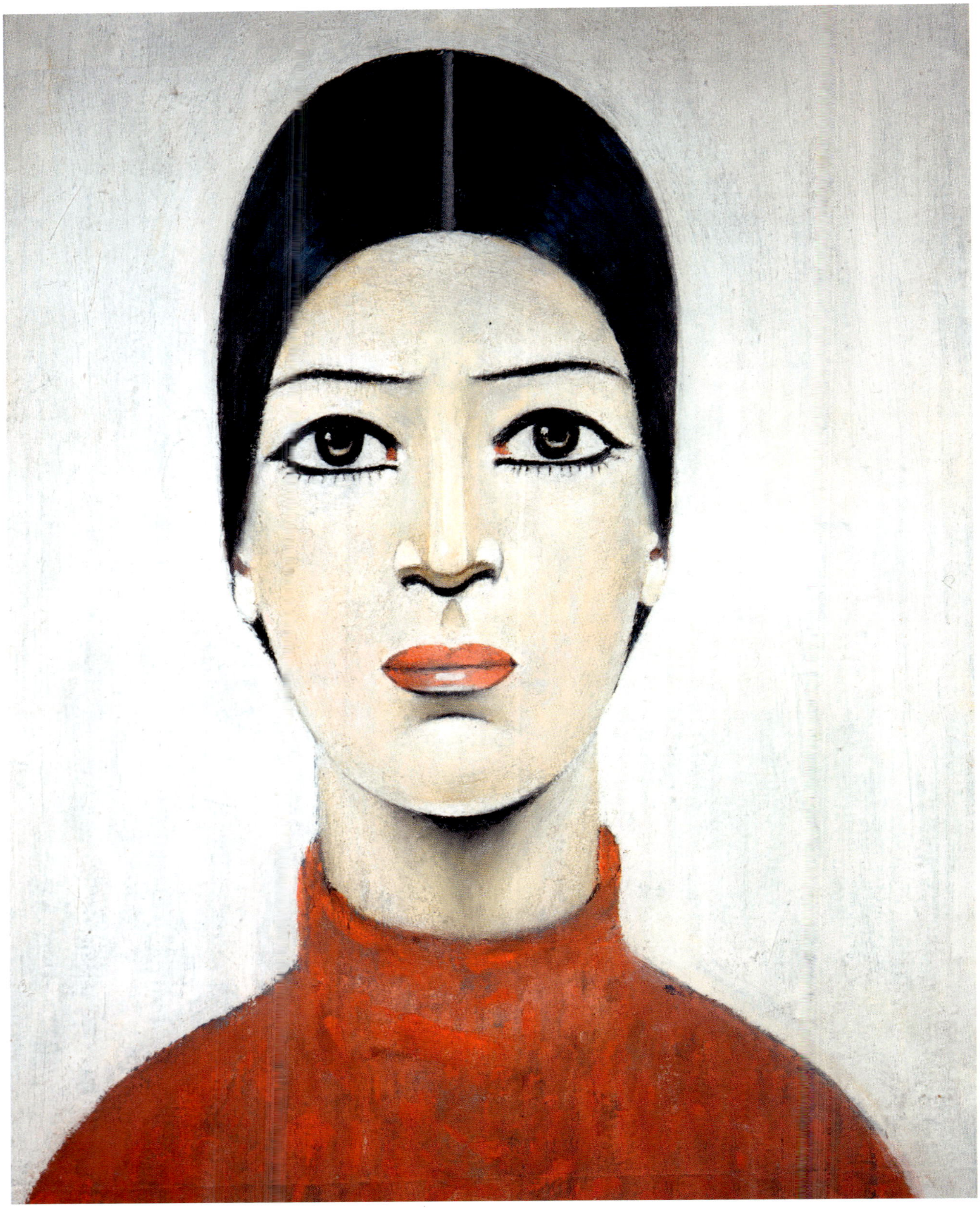

Portrait of Anne, 1957, oil on board, 35.5 × 30.5 cm.

Be that as it may, Rohde's biography is full of information about "Ann" none of which is even second hand, i.e. in Lowry's words to her. It has been garnered only at third hand, i.e. in the form of anecdotal quotations from Lowry's surviving friends when interviewed by Rohde for her book published some three years after his death when witnesses' memories of Lowry were still pretty fresh. Each friend had something different to say about "Ann" which is quite logical since Lowry kept his friends in very separate compartments, hardly ever introduced them to each other and several of them met each other for the first time at his funeral. "Ann" was quite well-off, even rich; she was a first-class tennis player; she drove a Rolls Royce two-seater; she spent a lot of time in Italy; she was a trained ballerina and, having been offered the casting-couch route to the top, she rejected it and gave up dancing; she worked with the poor in Naples. Sometimes she was Ann Hilder; sometimes she had a different surname or none at all. She did not get on well with her parents. She often sat for Lowry who promised to bequeath all of his many portraits of this enigmatic creature to her on his death.

Rohde's suppositions and selection of candidates, all of whom are then analytically knocked down by absence of evidence, or by actual contra-indications, reads like something out of Wilkie Collins or a lesser Victorian novelist. In reality "Ann" is no more identifiable than the Dark Lady of the Sonnets, even if the pursuit is almost as interestingly ambiguous as the perennial Shakespeare problem.

But when it comes to hard facts there is no discernible trace of her. Among the morass of papers in his house at his death there was no letter, not even a postcard from Italy, from her and no mention of her in Lowry's own random jottings, diaries, etc. There was certainly no bequest of any of the many portraits of her. Rohde has quoted a remark Lowry made to the collector Monty Bloom: "The Rossetti women are not real women. They are dreams. He used them for something in his mind, caused in my opinion by the death of his wife."[7]

On another occasion he mentioned that he was well aware that many of the pre-Raphaelite women were fantasy figures. He did not go as far as saying, as one might today, that Rossetti had a strong hair fetish but he certainly realised their unreality just as clearly as he recognised their beauty, studied the paintings so carefully and knowledgeably and, as he grew wealthy bought the best works by them that he could get hold of.

Lowry was nobody's fool yet no one can penetrate his mind sufficiently to establish exactly what he was doing with his repeated depictions of "Ann" other than creating a fantasy construct of his ideal woman. Interestingly enough, given his almost desperate, tortured relationship with his mother who, by withholding love, affection, respect and, above all, encouragement and approval of his work as an artist, could have destroyed both the sanity and the will of a lesser man, there is no resemblance in the many "Ann" images of that mother beyond a certain chilly quality of demeanour.

If one contemplates the most celebrated and frequently reproduced version of "Ann", the oil on board *Portrait of Ann* at the Lowry gallery in Salford (page 260) it is difficult to find any joy, even any pleasure in it. If Ann the woman is a fantasy, i.e. unreal, then it is perhaps appropriate that there is something mask-like in the face.

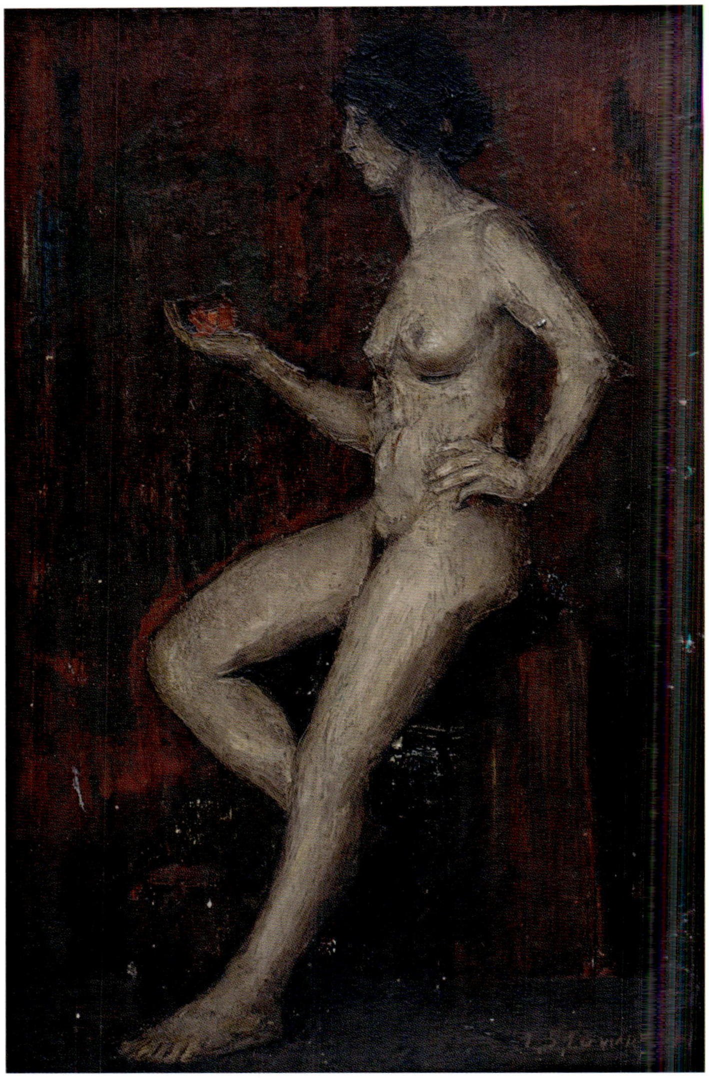

Female Nude, 1912, oil on board, 25.5 × 16.5 cm.

Beauty is often beheld in *Vogue* models or what used to be called Society Beauties as photographed by Baron or Madame Yevonde and was established primarily by a flawless, doubtless carefully made up, perfect symmetry. As to whether that 'beauty' is actually attractive is another and more complex issue. If a beautiful face was to be either attractive or interesting or preferably both, then perfect symmetry has a somewhat deadening effect, one I certainly discern in the mask-like *Portrait of Ann*, 1956. With that fiercely pulled back, glossy hair, she looks like a dancer but she is also altogether too reminiscent of a china doll. She isn't half as interesting or half as sensually attractive as the undated, but probably from the 1920s, pencil drawing *Study of a Nude Woman*. This drawing could be a standard life-class exercise by any gifted artist of the period such as Matthew Smith. Yet it is full of warmth and life and altogether a far more effective study of a female human being than *Portrait of Ann*. There are several other "formal" portraits of Ann which do not add much by way of comprehension of this mysterious figure, but one of them, an undated oil, shows "Ann" standing,

One of the major surprises of my Lowry researches was to find, in a private collection, an oil painting of a nude woman, standing, relaxed and holding in her right hand what looks like an apple or the head of a large flower, done in heavy, almost impasto style and certainly erotic in character. It is in fact an authentic Lowry, undated but probably done in his student days round about 1912. While clearly prentice work, one cannot help wishing there were more of them.

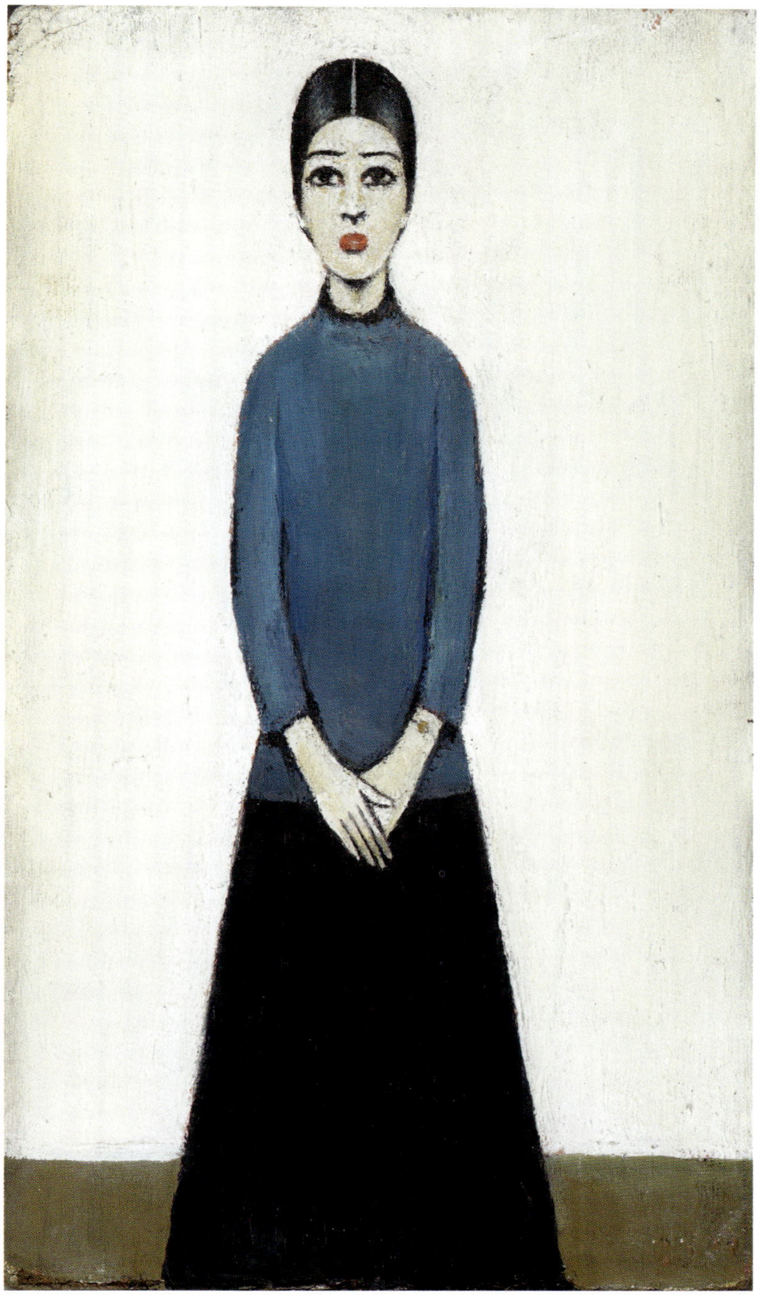

Ann, (undated), oil on board/panel, 47.5 × 34.25 cm.

almost full length wearing a blue sweater and long dark skirt, her hands crossed more or less over her crotch in the classic pose of a dancer at rest, thus perhaps confirming her role as a ballerina (above).

A 1954 oil painting, entitled *Portrait of a Young Girl,* shows a half-length of Ann in profile revealing the long pigtail of her glossy, smooth black hair. *Head of a Girl Wearing a Cloche Hat* (page 264) is interesting in that it is dated 1923, i.e. four decades before the "Ann" paintings described above. The jaw is not as full and heavy as that of *Portrait of a Young Girl* but it is surely, if not of a real woman, then of an imaginary one and, if that is the case, a clear indicator of an ideal, of a fantasy creature who lived only in Lowry's head.

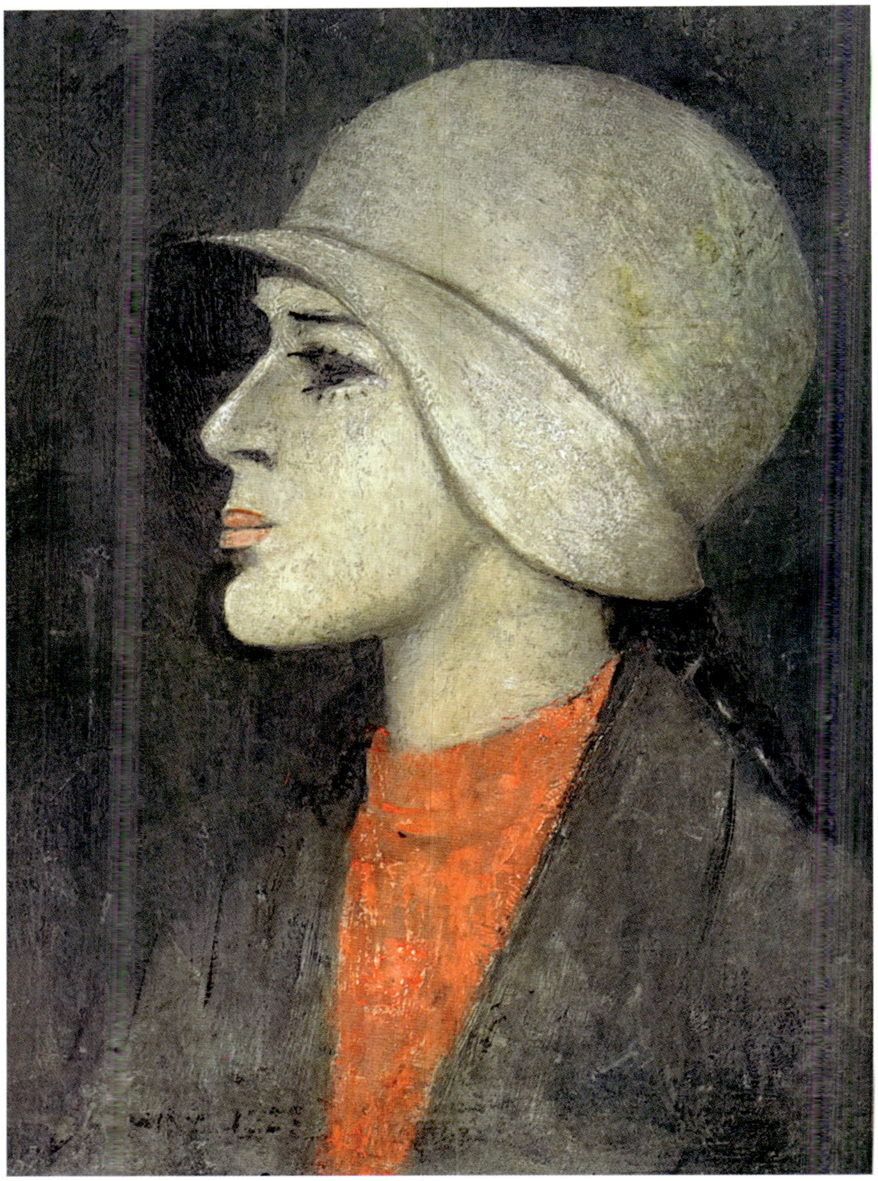

Head of a Girl Wearing a Cloche Hat, 1923, oil on board/panel, 53.2 × 43.5 cm.

This chapter will return later to "Ann" but first one should examine the basic pattern of Lowry's relationships with the very real young women who meant so much to him. It is perhaps worth stressing that, just as he was not homosexual, he was no Charles Dodgson fantasising about female children and producing distinctly erotic photographs of naked little girls any more than Lowry was a Humbert Humbert. In all his relationships with young women they were all, at the beginning at least, in their mid-to-late teens and thus physically mature, i.e. looking like women and not like children. And with each of them there was never a hint of a sexual relationship. Indeed Lowry himself ensured a level of propriety which to those accustomed to late twentieth-century and early twenty-first-century mores can only seem exaggerated, even quaint. He would insist on meeting and knowing the girls' parents, even, in the case of Sheila Fell, making the journey to Aspatria in Cumberland when Fell was a mature and sophisticated twenty-four with a first West End gallery show behind her.

With one girl, whom he took to the annual Christmas pantomime that ran for many weeks – and sometimes even for months – in Manchester, he would ask her to invite a friend, partly to alleviate the vast age gap and partly to act as chaperone. Usually, but not invariably, the link was art.

Perhaps the first significant relationship was with Pat Gerard who was sent along to visit Lowry, clutching her portfolio, when she was only fourteen, by her father, the builder who was making Lowry's Mottram-in-Longdendale house at least liveable. Lowry was captivated by Pat Gerard's liveliness, inspected and respected her paintings and drawings and encouraged her to enter the Manchester School of Art. When she was eighteen she again sought his advice, suggesting that she might try to get into the Slade. Lowry told her that he would write her a reference for the Slade which she could attach to that from the Manchester Art School. She got in, and Lowry thereafter made regular visits to her during her three years in London when he would take her to concerts at the Royal Festival Hall. She became an art teacher in the Cheshire town of Altrincham, married and moved some distance away from Mottram to Knutsford. As she observed, the friendship diminished after that:

> He was not so much upset that I had married, more that I had moved away and could no longer just pop in to see him. On the other hand, he did tire of people; he tired of everyone sooner or later. Each friend had his or her allotted span in Mr Lowry's life and when it was done, he moved on. I don't think anyone was important to him after his Mummy died. I did, at one time, flatter myself that I might have been; but although he enjoyed my company and the fun we had, I don't think any of it really *mattered*. He was fiercely independent.[8]

While her strictures about the duration of his relationships is a fair one, as far as women are concerned, it did not really apply to his male friends and certainly not his friendships with male painters such as James Fitton and David Carr. There were, however, two relationships with women, both triggered by art which fully lasted the course until ended by death.

The first of these is Sheila Fell (born in Aspatria in 1931, died 1979, i.e. three years after Lowry himself). Fell was an immensely gifted painter and a woman of quite bewitching beauty. Lowry was taken by a friend to her first exhibition at the Beaux Arts Gallery and immediately bought two of her large landscapes. That was in November 1955 when Fell was only twenty-three. Subsequently Lowry decided he wanted to meet her and the gallery arranged this early in 1956. Lowry took her to lunch and asked how she was doing financially. Like many young artists, she pretended to be all right but the ever proper Lowry told her that he would like to meet her parents and that he would like to help her in her career. "Would £3 per week be agreeable?" In today's terms that's at least a hundred pounds a week which, if not riches, would certainly make life easier for a tyro painter. Lowry went with

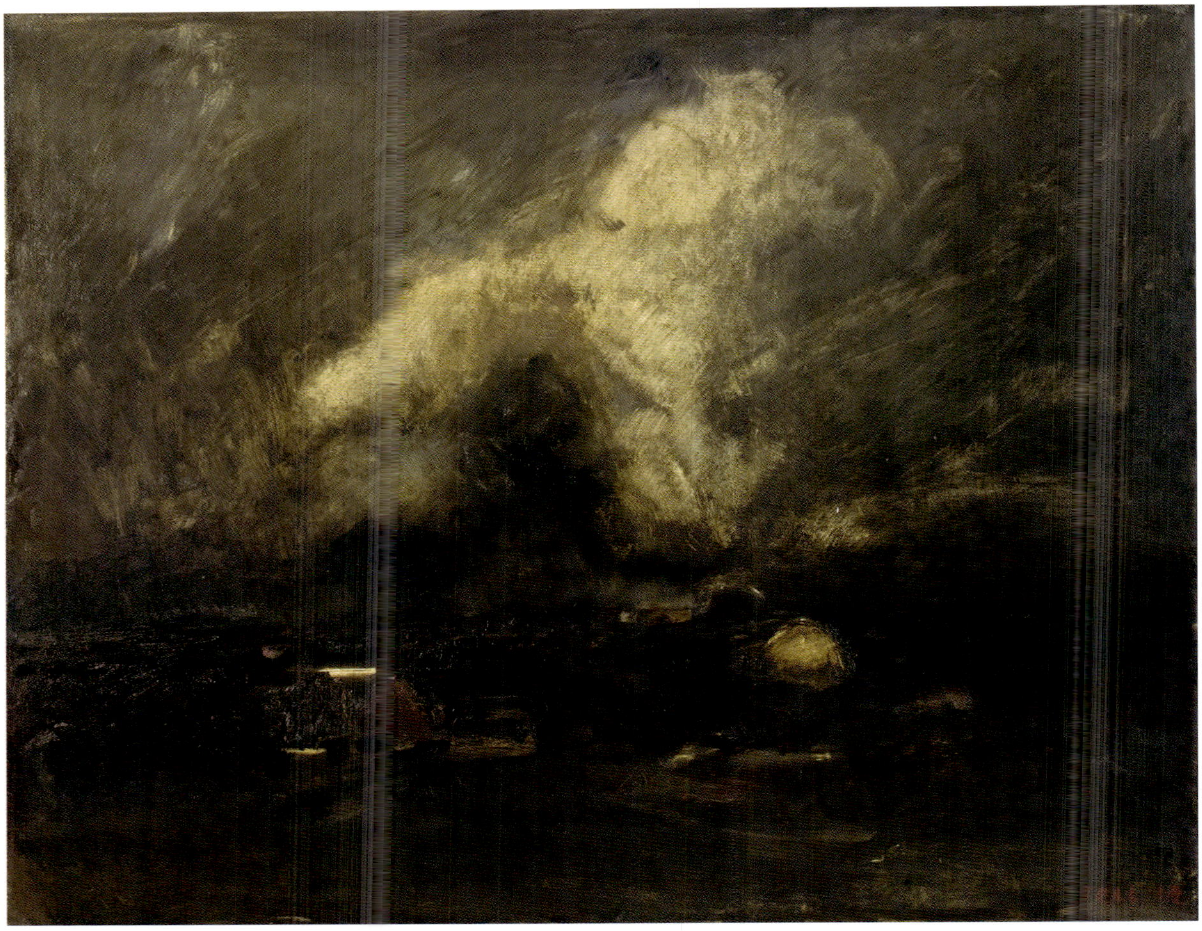

Landscape with a Yellow Cloud, by Sheila Fell, 1962, oil on canvas, 71 × 91.7 cm.

her to her house in Aspatria and they would go off together to paint. It's perhaps worth repeating the wonderful and revealing anecdote that Fell being *plein airiste* produced superb Cumbrian land and seascapes. Lowry being almost exclusively a studio painter might well set up his easel facing the mountain Skiddaw. When, at the end of the day, Fell looked at what Lowry had done she found a classic industrial landscape.[9] Lowry is on record in one art reference book that he thought Fell to be the best English landscape painter of the twentieth century. She was certainly hugely talented and, although made a full R.A. in 1974, died tragically young aged 48. Their admiration was mutual. She wrote of him:

> My admiration of his work was and is enormous; but also of him as a man. As a companion he was marvellously humorous, inquisitive, mischievous as a child and gentle, but he was more than that: he had great shrewdness and understanding. In short, he was unique.[10]

The painting by Fell reproduced above is one of the two bought by Lowry from her *début* show at the Beaux Arts Gallery and now housed, with other works of art acquired during his life by Lowry at the Carlisle Art Gallery.

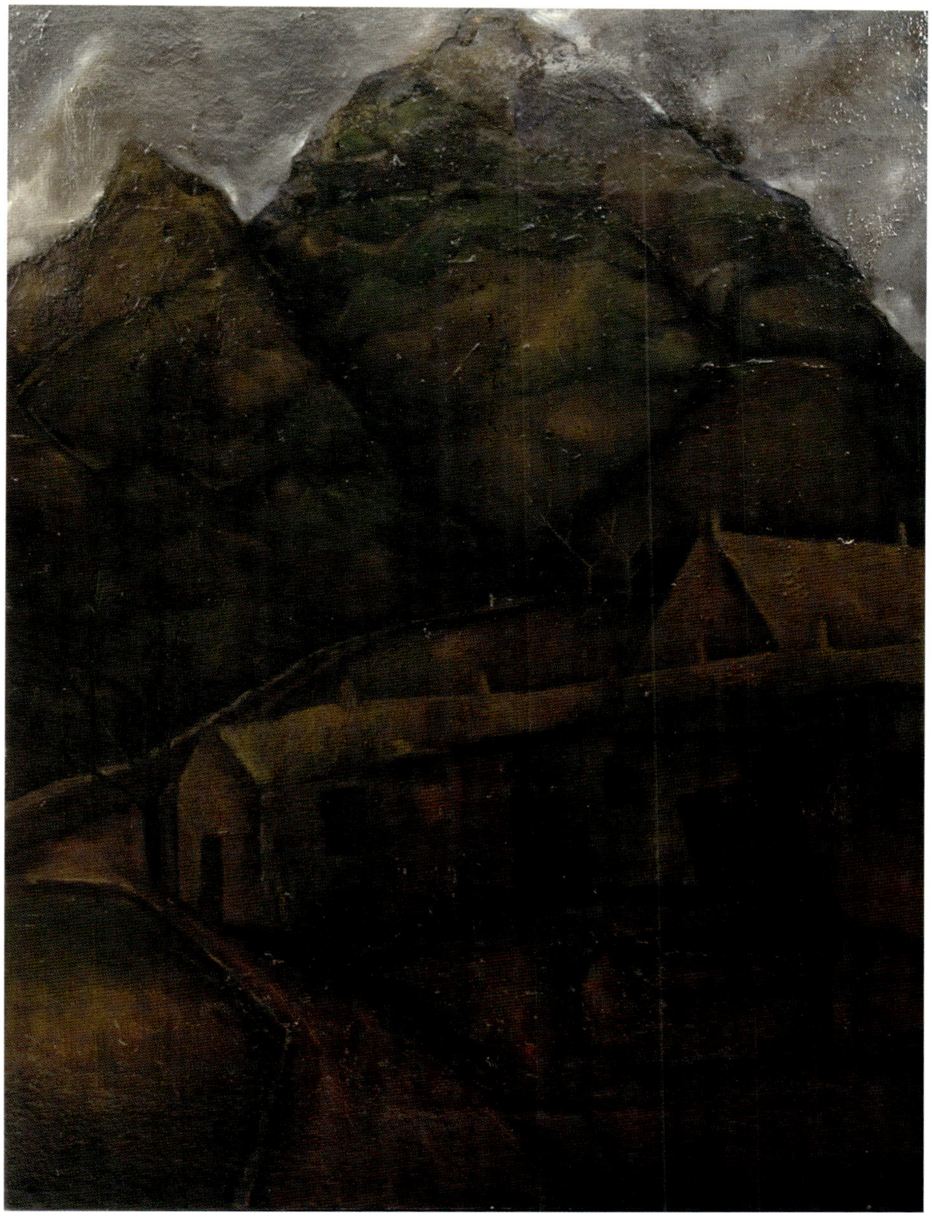

Lake District Farm, by Sheila Fell, *c.*1960, oil on canvas, 91.7 × 71.2 cm.

There is also a theory that in a Fell painting housed at the art gallery in Kendal that it contains a cow painted by Lowry.

The other key relationship between Lowry and a young woman – although the facts related here come from Rohde's biography and from many conversations with the lady in question – reads like a work of fiction but is as far as I can ascertain both accurate and true. In 1957 Lowry received a letter, understandably one of many such, from a girl living in the Lancashire town of Heywood. She wanted advice on how to become an artist. And, furthermore, were they by any chance related? The girl, who was thirteen, signed herself Carol Ann Lowry. Lowry did not answer the letter but stuffed it in the pocket that held other miscellaneous correspondence and old envelopes that he used for sketching when walking or using buses or trams. One day, some months later, he saw a bus with Heywood marked as its destination. He remembered the letter, boarded the bus, found the address, knocked on the door which was opened by Carol, enquired whether Miss Carol Ann Lowry lived there to be assured affirmatively by the child who remembered the letter and ushered him into the living room. There Lowry realised that Carol was alone with a school friend and, proper as ever, established that Carol's mother was out and would return only after 7.00 pm. So he left, saying he would return at that time.

Carol was genuinely interested in art but the actual letter had been dictated by her single parent mother, ambitious and hopefully optimistic about her daughter's future. Alas there was no relationship between L. S. Lowry and this family any more than there was between the painter and Malcolm Lowry. But this did not affect the subsequent relationship between Carol Ann and the artist who soon became known to her family as Uncle Laurie. For reasons that become clear this particular relationship, as far as posterity is concerned, was the most important and, psychologically, the deepest and most interesting of them all and one infinitely more significant than that with the mythical "Ann".

Perhaps the best description of their relationship following the momentous bus ride to Heywood in 1957 comes from Carol Ann Lowry herself:

> … more than my mother, or my father, or anyone. He made me. He moulded me. He fashioned me in his image of Ann and in so doing made me to a great extent like him. I was sufficiently young for him to be able to do it; and sufficiently malleable. I think he recognized that, right from the beginning. Had I been a different sort of person he would not have been able to change me, to make of me what he wished. Looking back, although I was not aware of it at the time, I think I was filling a gap in his life, supplying perhaps his need for a family. Yet ours was never a father and daughter relationship; he was more of a godfather, a fairy godfather who came along with gifts not merely material gifts, but gifts of character and education. He taught me so much and displayed, by example, the virtues of perception, of humility and humour. When he found me I was at an impressionable age and of an impressionable nature; I cannot help but feel it was fate that brought us together, that enabled each of us to fulfil a need in the other.[11]

Lowry was indeed the godfather, the classic benefactor for a lonely, impoverished only child beloved of so many Victorian novels. Lowry made financial arrangements with Mrs Lowry – of which Carol was naturally unaware – and encouraged her self-confessed only skill, that of being able to draw. He paid her fees at the local convent school and arranged for her to have Saturday morning classes at the Rochdale School of Art whose Principal, Leo Solomon, was one of Lowry's carefully compartmentalised friends. As with her predecessors, Carol was taken on outings to Manchester and, as she became older, to London for events that must have been quite overwhelming to a young woman of working class origins such as taking tea at the Royal Academy in the President's Room with Lowry and the then P.R.A. Sir Thomas Monnington.[12]

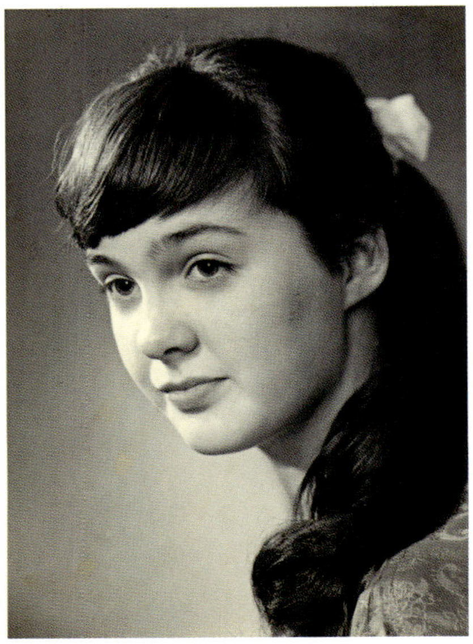

Studio portrait of Carol Ann Lowry (Guttenberg, Manchester) commissioned by L. S. Lowry.

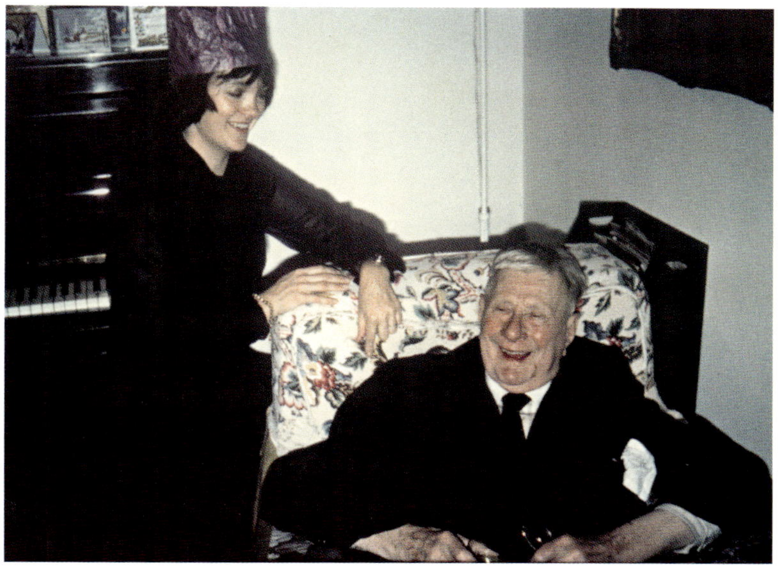

Lowry saw her through her art courses at Hornsey School of Art in London and in Swansea, where she qualified as an art teacher, gave her an allowance and settled a substantial five figure cash sum on her at his bank. She moved to the Isle of Man where she met and, in 1974, married a man called John Spiers. Carol has, with typical common-sensical directness, said of her relationship with Lowry that she did not believe it was more important to him than those with her predecessors:

> I think that I was simply the tag-end of what I, for want of a better description, call the Ann thing. I filled a gap when he needed it and, perhaps, had he lived longer or had he been younger when we met, he would have passed from me to another, younger Ann. I was fortunate, enormously fortunate, that I was the last.[13]

Snapshot of L. S. Lowry and Carol Ann Lowry at her mother's home in the 1970s.

Interestingly enough, although faced with countless opportunities, Lowry never painted or drew her, just as he never painted or drew any of her predecessors. The only young woman he painted and drew was "Ann". Given that Lowry had no close relatives at the time of his death and what he had become to Carol and her mother, it is not all that surprising that Carol should end up as his sole heir and that she inherited all his work, his money, his copyrights (where he had not made them over to patrons or galleries), his collection of works by other artists, and his house. Thus, at a stroke, Carol became a moderately rich woman and acquired a very substantial burden. As anyone who has spent a lifetime working with artists would testify, dealing with artists' widows and children and executors is rarely easy just as an identical testimony could be extracted from the widows and executors. Judging by the sheer volume of loans to other collections, most notably the Lowry Gallery in Salford and Lowry's own collection of paintings and drawings by other artists in Carlisle, Carol Ann Lowry has exercised a devoted and discriminating control over what could so easily have become a mere cash cow. In one way, however, Lowry must have been aware not only of the commercial value of his munificent gift but also of one part of it which, at least, could have been a poisoned chalice.

Some time after the funeral and the reading of the will, Lowry's solicitor asked Carol to meet him at Lowry's bank's vault. There he handed over to her a sealed collection of works by Lowry that had been found in his house but had never before been seen by anyone other than the artist. Carol Ann Lowry, in the presence of the two poker-faced professional men who handed the material over to her was faced with dozens of paintings and drawings, the drawings in particular flawlessly executed, the paintings somewhat looser in style, most done in oil on board and, in several cases, slashed or broken in halves or quarters, sometimes with a quarter or a half missing, of a young woman in varying states of semi-undress or, if fully dressed, then scantily so, but almost invariably in variously severe forms of distress.

At first glance, Carol was frightened that they might have been inspired by her. One or two of the drawings feature her own small, turned-up nose. However, closer and more prolonged inspection revealed similarities with the features of "Ann". Some of the girls were like caricatures of the Dollybirds of the King's Road with the briefest of miniskirts and grotesquely high heels or tottering platform shoes, but the majority of them are like sadistic versions of Hugh Hefner's Playboy Bunny Girls with exaggerated buttocks surmounted by pinched in waists, leading up to moderately sized breasts pushed up by restrictive garments to make them seem big and, transgressing the Hefner code, pushing them so high as to reveal the nipples. Frequently the girls wear exaggeratedly large, high, sharply pointed collars which dig into their throats painfully, thus forcing their heads back into supremely uncomfortable postures.

Now, obviously, hundreds of distinguished artists from the anonymous Greek Vase painters, through the Renaissance to the present day from Lucian Freud to David Hockney, from the heterosexual to the homosexual, have done erotic paintings and drawings which the censorious will always dub pornographic but which take up respected space in our finest museums and galleries and in distinguished private collections. But neither Carol nor the average Lowry fan could be other than surprised by the existence of these works. Are they obscene? Assuming there is a reliable definition of obscenity, probably not. A recent Director of Public Prosecutions, the Prosecution Counsel in the *Lady Chatterley* obscenity trial, was once asked for his criteria for prosecuting obscene magazines and replied that he would sit at his desk with his feet up and look at the magazines brought in by the police. If he had an erection he would prosecute; but that was half a century ago.

The Lowrys, unlike say, some of the erotica produced by Picasso or Schiele which clearly showed penetration or oral congress, do not show any couples actually doing anything. Men are only present in the form of a shadowy arm wielding a weapon, an axe or a sword or a guillotine. What these paintings and drawings are about is the humiliation, subjugation and even torture of women. The clothing they are forced to wear is akin to bondage. The clothes and the postures they enforce range from the uncomfortable to the painful. The girls are, even if the clothes are more Dollybird than bondage victim, not enjoying themselves. This is not *their* sex-play or fantasising. We, the viewers, cannot possibly know what was going through Lowry's mind when he executed these works.

The easy explanation is that they were simply the masturbatory fantasies of a man who remained – or at least claimed to be – a virgin all his life. As we know from the rest of this chapter he was happily and, above all, innocently involved with lots of young and attractive women so that it is hard to believe that any of these very real women inspired these erotic works. Carol is on record in Rohde's biography as follows:

> They are the dream figure – the image of Ann that haunted him more than anyone, more than any one of us, realized. These are the essence of his real, his secret, his private image of Ann, whoever or whatever she was; the one who somewhere, sometime in his life, hurt him dreadfully. Or perhaps it was all of us, each in our own way, who hurt him.[8]

The only other twentieth century artist I can recollect who used women for his art in this way is the German Surrealist Hans Bellmer (1902–1975). He too distorted the female form, but in a much more extreme manner and always for public exhibition and consumption. His statue of a doll in 1935 gave his creature buttocks below her bellybutton, four legs, two arms, two torsos and one head, thus foreshadowing the now notorious infantile, multi-sex-organed juvenile figures by the Chapman Brothers. On the other hand his imagery in photographs and drawings was far more overtly sadistic than Lowry's and there is evidence that he used his partner as his model, making the poor woman suffer being trussed up with cords or even wire. His *Store in a Cool Place* of 1958 (below) shows Ulrica Zürn turned into a large joint of white flesh, tied up as if ready for the oven. Bellmer was sufficiently open about his sadistic cruelty to theorise about it in print:

> To obtain objective evidence [of the reality of the imagination], we will have recourse therefore to the criminal artisan through the most humanly tangible and most beautiful passion, that of removing the wall separating the woman from her image. From the accurate memory we have of a certain photographic document, a man, to transform his victim, had tightly bound her thighs, shoulders and breasts with a criss-cross of tight wire as a precaution, causing her flesh to swell, irregular spherical triangles, lengthening the folds, unsavoury lips, causing an increasing number of breasts never seen before in undisclosable places.[15]

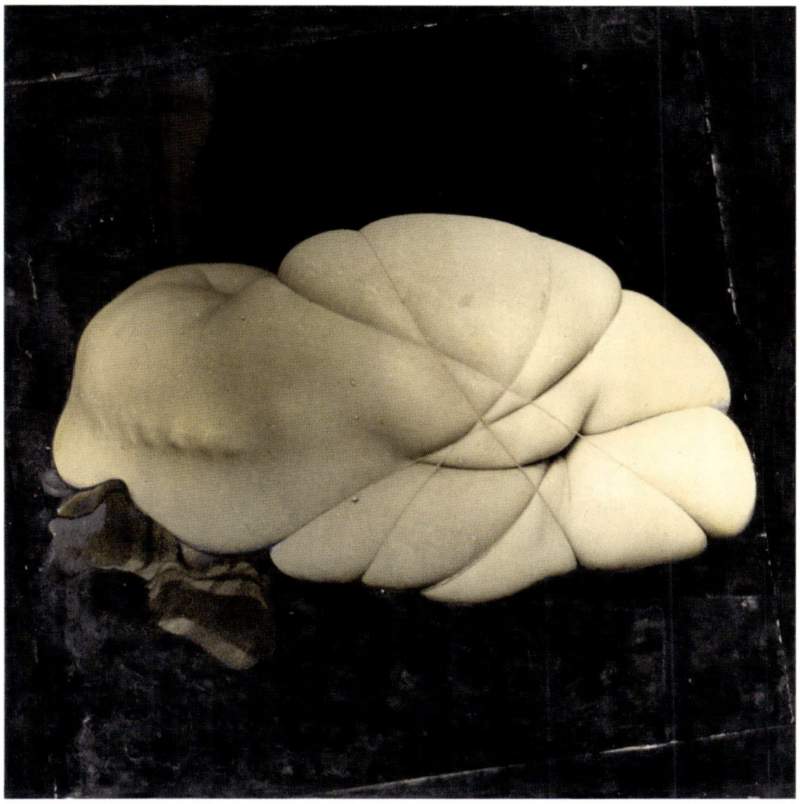

Store In a Cool Place, by Hans Bellmer, 1958, collage of vintage gelatin silver prints and gouache on masonite, 23.4 × 23.9 cm.

I think that with Bellmer what you see is what you get, i.e. nastily exploitative, distinctly and deliberately transgressive, and far beyond, in either intent or execution, these works by Lowry. It is surely interesting that some of the Lowrys were torn up and mutilated by him but equally interesting that he did not destroy them but left them to be found as in the oil painting known as *Mannequin Fragments* (below). Did Lowry tear it up out of shame?; or did he feel it was not good enough as a work of art? In any event it is a striking image, badly executed and reminiscent of Coppélia or the automaton Olympia in Offenbach's *The Tales of Hoffmann*. (Poor Hoffmann, it will be remembered, fell in love with, or in thrall to, four beautiful unattainable women all of whom were at least partly born of fantasy). We can never know to what extent Lowry was in thrall to these late creations or, indeed, to "Ann".

What seems undeniable is that these women were created by Lowry with some cruel, or vengeful, intent. Why else would he have done the drawing known simply as *Girl with Bow*

Mannequin Fragments, (undated), oil on panel.

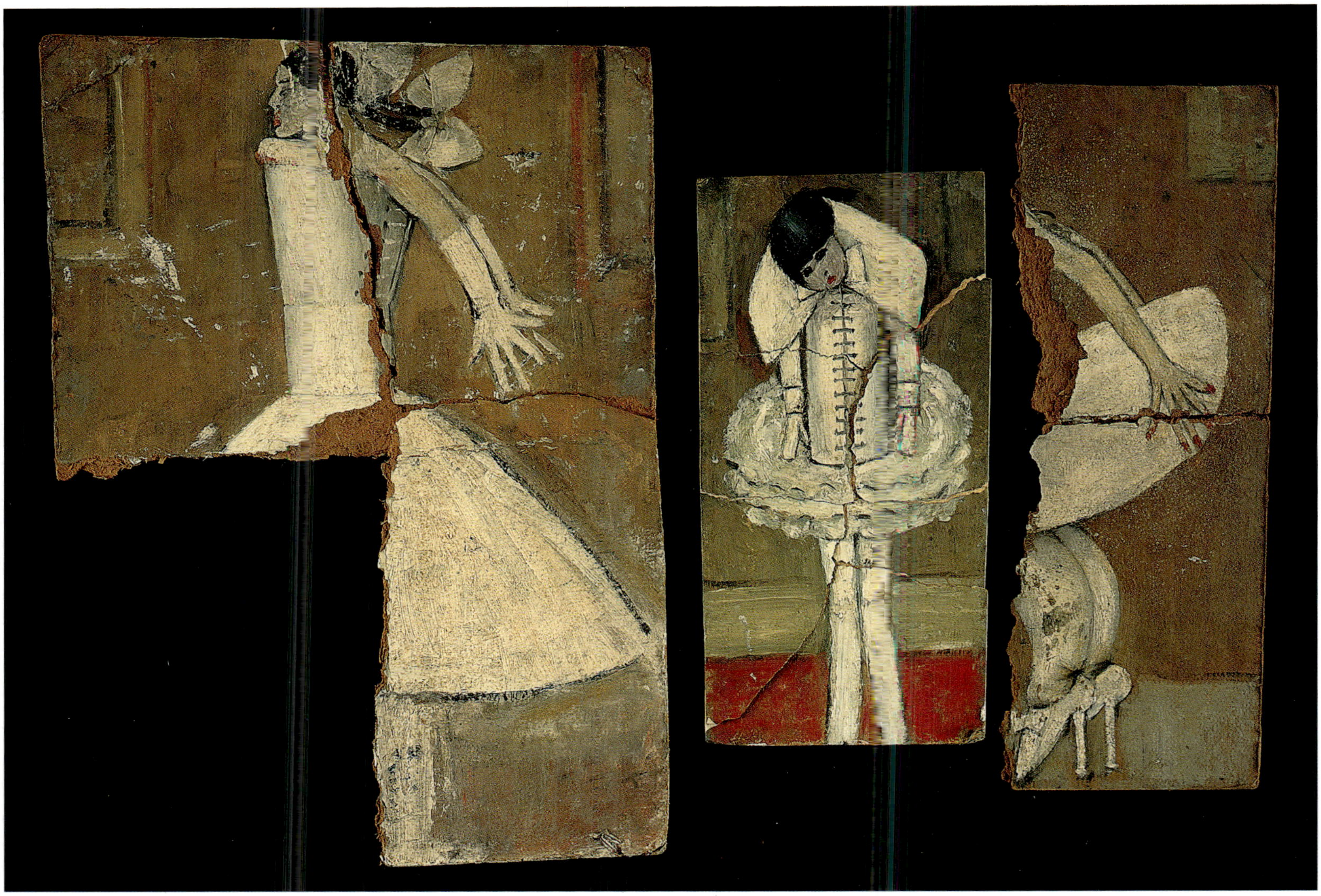

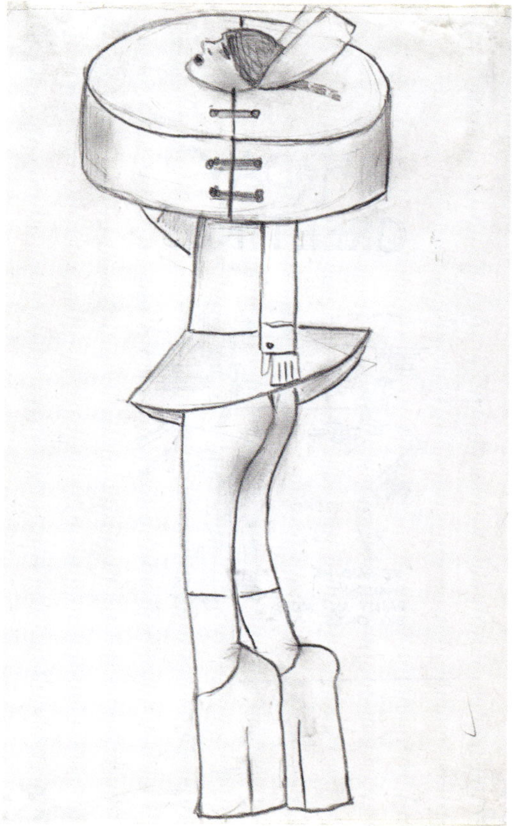

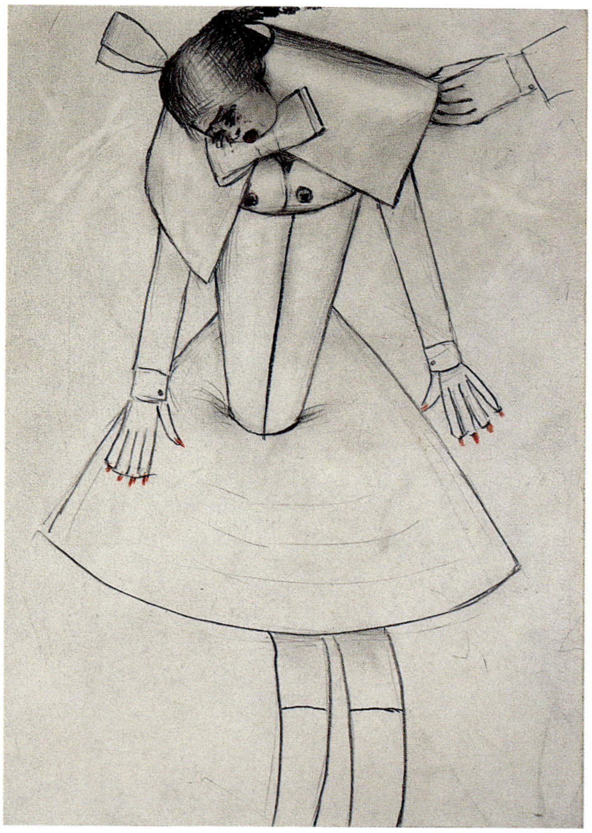

Left: *Girl with Bow*, 1973, pencil on card, 33 × 21.5 cm.

Right: *Girl with Bows*, 1973, pencil and red crayon on paper, 29.8 × 21 cm.

c. 1973? (above left). This was chosen, a little oddly perhaps, as one of four Lowry works in the great exhibition of British art entitled *British Vision: Observation and Imagination in British Art 1750 to 1950* mounted in Ghent in 2007/8.[16] The bow, an almost standard item in most of the drawings, is this time minimal, having been pulled through the collar. The Ghent cataloguer in his note to this work suggests that the collar or ruff is akin to a surgical collar or a garrotte. It is in fact far too large to be a surgical collar and, while the dictionary allows that the deadly Spanish weapon, the garrotte *can* be a collar it is far more usually, since it is used as a highly portable and concealable weapon, simply a wire attached to two small handles so that the impact on the neck is so swift and so deep that the victim can find no adequate defence for it. Surely what Lowry has drawn here is a cangue, a Chinese instrument of punishment where a very heavy collar, akin to a millstone is clamped around the victim or the criminal's neck and left there for several hours or even days to create an intolerable burden on the neck, shoulders and spine, i.e. to cause agony but not, as with a garrotte, designed to kill.

Be that as it may, it is nonetheless a drawing of considerable cruelty and deeply misogynistic in a man who, had a wholly beneficent and massively generous attitude towards young women. Nor is this an isolated work.

In *Girl with Bows* of *c.* 1973 (above right) the girl's breasts are painfully lifted and exposed by the tight sheath dress and a man's hand is adjusting the enormous collar as if he is applying a meat cleaver to the neck. If one looks at these and the other illustrations from this once hidden group of works such as the undated *Mannequin with Bows*, the oil painting *Mannequin and Block* (page 275) and *Untitled*, an undated oil on board it is difficult to see them, any of them, as objects of love whereas the various portraits of "Ann" are much closer to manifestations of love, even of hopeless love, for a creature of fantasy, of the ideal woman who Lowry never had and who, almost certainly, never existed. Even as devoted a sleuth as Shelley Rohde could find no convincing evidence of Ann's existence. The Somerset House records revealed only two possible models: one, of the right period, called Ann Helder was a fair-haired, married woman living in South London who had never met Lowry. The only Ann Hilder, born in the right period and admittedly dark, single and artistic, also denied any personal knowledge of Lowry.[17]

There are in twentieth-century paintings many examples of obsessive sexual relationships between artists and women whether they are muses, mistresses, mere paid models or wives of long standing. Think of Bonnard's multitudinous nude studies of his wife and her equally strong obsession with bathing. Think of the way in which Picasso, perfectly consciously, changed his painting style as he changed his wives or mistresses. Any reasonably acute observer of Picasso can tell at a glance whether a female subject is inspired by Olga Khoklova, Dora Maar, Jacqueline Roque, Marie-Thérèse Walter, etc. As Lowry himself intuited, Rossetti's beauties were at least partially his sexual fantasies. So why should not Lowry have had the pleasure of a fantasy woman who meant so much to him and his art, who represented for him an unattainable but perfect reality?

If one accepts at his own estimation, in his own words, as far as sexual matters are concerned he lived and died a virgin. No one could prove this any more than anyone could disprove it. There is no law, whether Divine or man-made, which compels us to have sex and there are countless people who live without it. One of Freud's most significant followers and protégés, A. A. Brill (1874–1948) who accompanied Freud to America in 1909 and made the first, (not very accurate), translation into English of *The Interpretation of Dreams* in 1913, coined, for those who had no interest in or desire for sexual activity, the rather unkind phrase "Sexual Idiots".

In his Lectures on *Psychoanalytic Psychiatry* he describes both men and women with extreme neurotic conditions which included not only a total lack of sexual experience but also a wholly irrational lack of interest, to the point of actual dislike of the sexual act or even the contemplation of sexual activity. He made it clear that his patients, or those who merely enquired of him or sought his advice without wishing to undergo analysis were, in his opinion, what he termed "Sexual idiots or imbeciles". He also made clear that, attitudes to sex apart, they were intelligent, often successful, members of the professional classes: academics, businessmen and even doctors.[18]

Brill was not an unkind man and was using the language of his trade as practised in the middle of the last century, long before political correctness had so modified plain speaking. He would doubtless have found Lowry and his work fascinating yet would have unhesitatingly

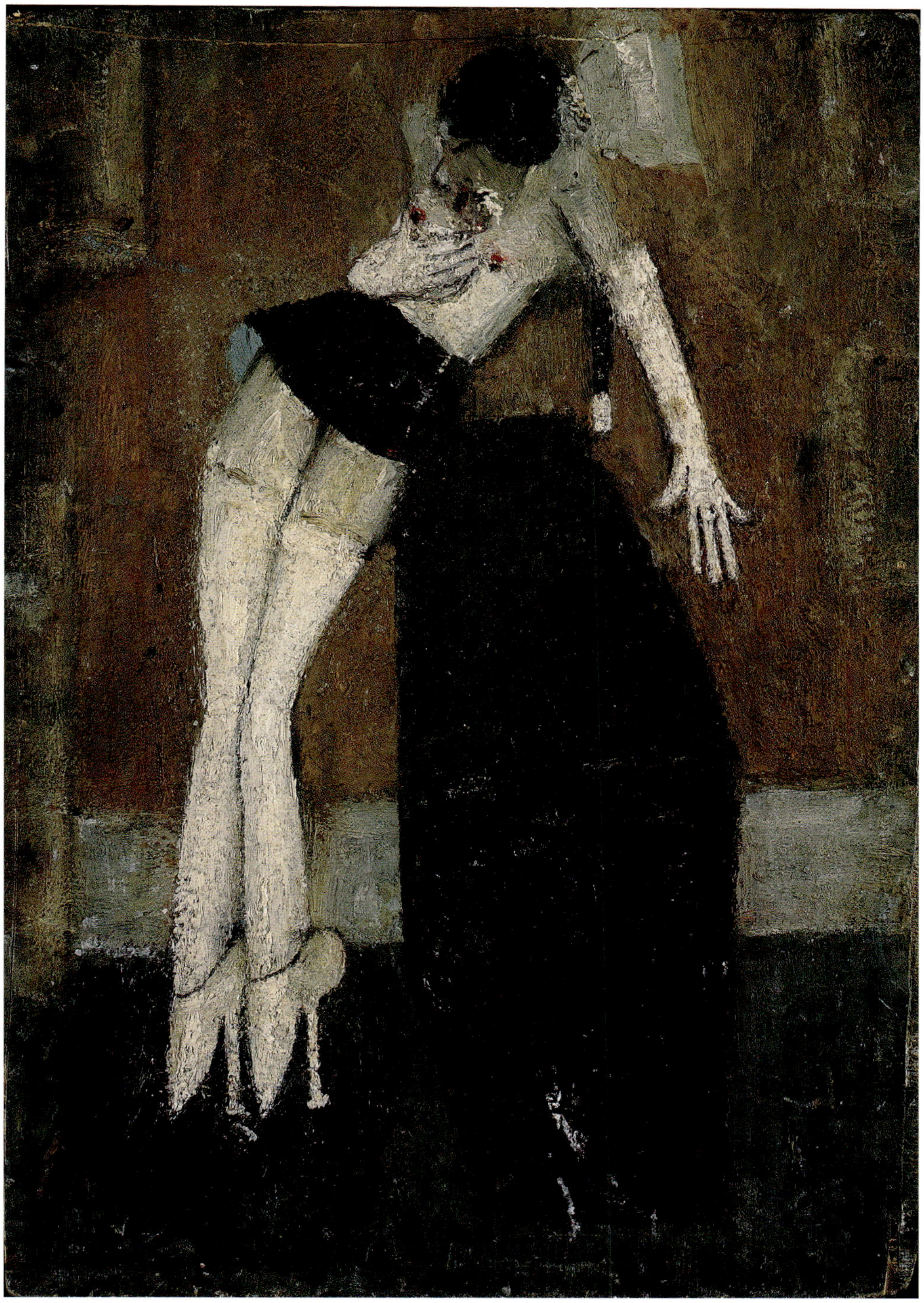

Mannequin and Block,
oil on board, approx 47 × 32 cm.

despatched him to the ranks of "sexual idiot". As one of Freud's most convinced *protégés* he would have made art-critical hay of the hills like breasts and the countless phallic factory chimneys in the industrial paintings. Whether he would have described his conjectures and whether he would have in any way furthered our understanding of Lowry's art is another matter.

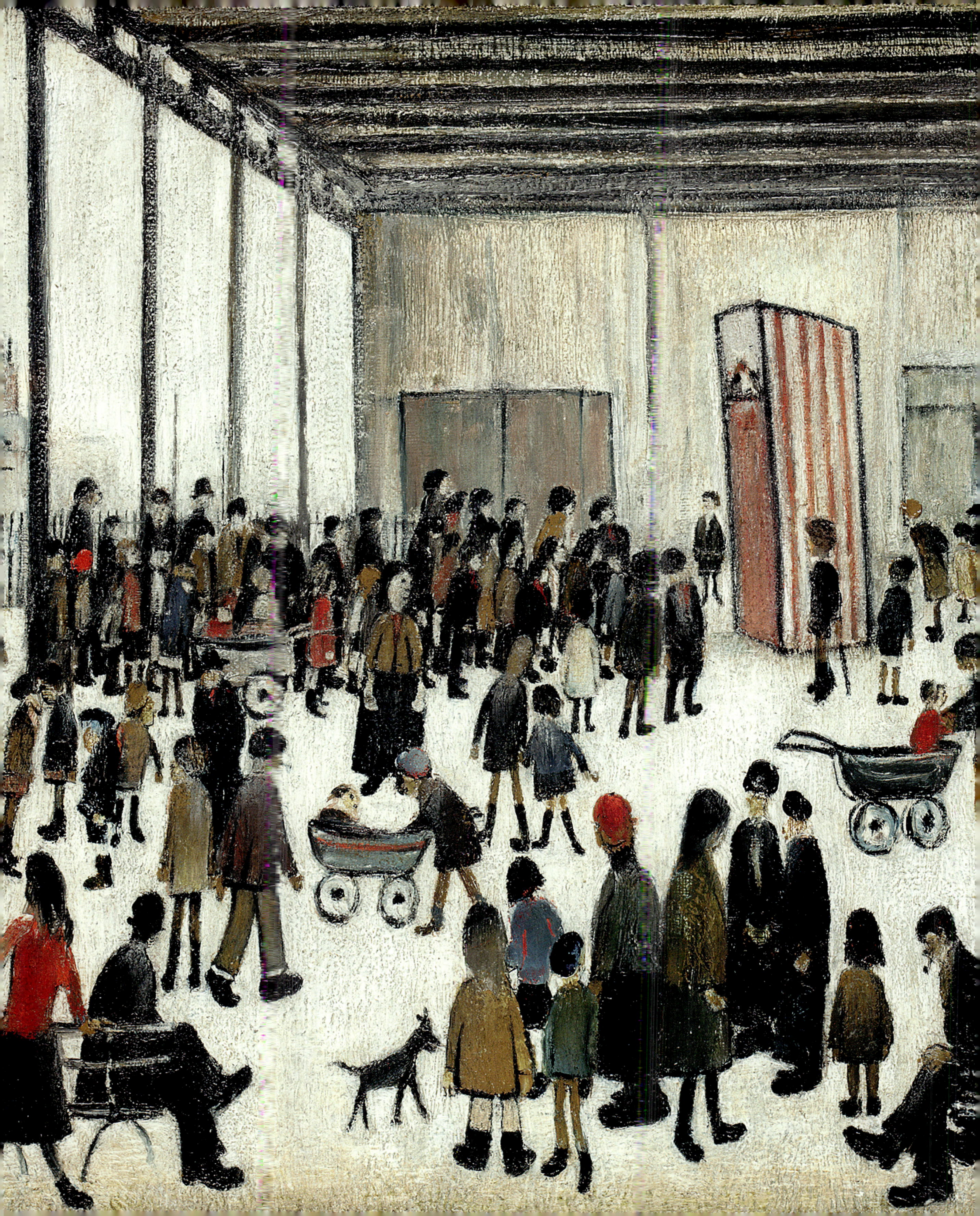

CHAPTER 14

LOWRY AND ASPERGER'S SYNDROME

Not everything that steps out of line, and thus "abnormal" must necessarily be 'inferior'.
Hans Asperger

In 2005 a distinguished professor of psychiatry at Trinity College, Dublin published *The Genesis of Artistic Creativity: Asperger's Syndrome and the Arts*. Michael Fitzgerald put forward a case that numerous highly, and variously, gifted men – only one woman, Simone Weil, was included – suffered the form of Autism known as Asperger's Syndrome. Among the visual artists selected by Fitzgerald was L. S. Lowry. Fitzgerald, understandably and with full acknowledgement, made use of Shelley Rohde's biography as his primary source for thus classifying Lowry and Rohde in turn made use of Fitzgerald's work in her final edition – she died in 2008 – of her biography of Lowry. This was published in 2007 and, for the last version of a much reprinted book, is highly unusual if not actually unique, in being approximately only half the length of the first edition of 1979. This is doubtless due to the fact that author and publisher decided, while reducing the text, to make the book more appealing to an audience in the age of the soundbite by providing lots of colour plates instead of biographical materials. Nonetheless Rohde did find space for a substantial appendix consisting of a dialogue/interview between herself and Fitzgerald on the topic of Lowry's alleged Asperger's Syndrome.

I use the word alleged since I am far from convinced by Fitzgerald's view of Lowry and, where I have a specific knowledge or strong interest in the life and work of some of his other subjects, find myself in strong disagreement with this doubtless widely acknowledged expert on psychiatry. Just as it is almost invariably the case that when one reads a newspaper article about events or works of art where one has had some personal involvement and specific knowledge, one finds a factual error in nearly every paragraph so, having read several other chapters in Fitzgerald's book, I became so wary of some of his other interpretations as to cast serious doubt on his view of Lowry. In his study of Jack B. Yeats he writes:

> Yeats was a tremendous observer, as persons with Asperger's Syndrome oft are. He vividly painted the scenes that were all around him, capturing them in a 'pared down' fashion like the American artist Edward Hopper, who also had Asperger's Syndrome.[1]

I do not know whether Hopper had Asperger's, although he was certainly a very tormented and difficult human being who used to beat his wife. And he certainly captured his greatest subjects in a 'pared down' fashion, one which reduced most of his human figures – apart perhaps from his long suffering wife as nude model – to a stark anonymity. If you think of the people depicted in *Nighthawks* or *Inside a Cinema*, they are immaculately

Detail from *Punch and Judy*, 1943, (p.129).

delineated physical types, observed as types and not as memorable individuals. Yet when Yeats observed people, from the pre-World War I country folk of the West of Ireland and the deliberately chosen "types" of his great series of book illustrations for George A. Birmingham's 1913 book *Irishmen All*, each of these "types" is a rugged individual, full of character, instantly memorable, and, in human terms, a precise antithesis of Hopper's figures. Furthermore, when Yeats developed his later style, with its heavy impasto in which the facial features of his subjects, whether human or equine, are almost sculpted out of the thick paint, these ground-breaking works would surely have been anathematic to the cool, old-masterly precision of Hopper.

At other times Fitzgerald makes one gasp. George Orwell is accused of doing "poorly academically at school" yet Orwell won a Scholarship to Eton, arguably, together with the scholarship exams of Winchester and Manchester Grammar School, the toughest educational tests for that age group in the whole of England.[2] I think that Fitzgerald has abandoned the objectivity of the psychiatrist when dealing with Orwell, since he concentrates on the pejorative reminiscences of his contemporaries to the detriment of testimony from his many friends and supporters and has rather missed the point of his second marriage when he writes:

> He had a bizarre deathbed marriage to a woman named Sonia Brownell, which was highly inappropriate for all concerned.[3]

Of course any deathbed marriage can seem bizarre – for spectators and even for the participants – but inappropriate it was not. Sonia Brownell was at that time the belle of London's literary world, secretary to Cyril Connolly, Editor of *Horizon*, the leading literary magazine of the period. She was a competent translator of French and a woman of spectacular and very English beauty. She was known to the Euston Road School of Painters as the Euston Road Venus. After Orwell's death she had affairs with several painters, writers and philosophers of international rank and for many years she maintained a *salon* crowded with London's leading intellectuals. Be that as it may, Fitzgerald has misread her to the extent of denigrating her a second time in the Rohde interview:

> What do you with your property? You give it to your friend. The one who's there today. You know who did that? George Orwell – he got married on his deathbed and I think all the royalties went to this woman, that was the same kind of thing. She became his heir – a quite inappropriate thing.[4]

In other words Fitzgerald implies that Sonia was simply a somewhat unworthy gold-digger. But what are the facts? Orwell left her an estate probated at less than £10,000, to be precise £9908 14s 11p, which in 1950 was about enough to buy a modest three bedroom house in Kensington. (Lowry's estate was probated in 1976 at £298,459.) Before he died Orwell had paid for a set of insurance policies sufficient to give his adopted son Richard Blair a decent education and his will stipulated that, while Sonia would get all his royalties during *her* lifetime, upon her death the entire literary estate would pass to Richard Blair. While Orwell had become famous before dying, no one could have forecast the prodigious sums earned by the Orwell Estate over the next half-century and still going strong. I have close personal knowledge of Sonia Orwell, as she always called herself.[5] She was probably the most difficult and contumacious woman I have ever had to deal with but, apart from her hospitable *salon*, she lived modestly, and, ironically on a fixed and therefore because of England's rampant inflation, ever-dwindling income doled out to her by George's former accountant. He took over Sonia's financial affairs, handled all of George's subsequently vast royalties and appropriated a large proportion of his earnings, (minus Sonia's allowance), to his own purposes and pockets.

But most of Sonia's difficult and frequently outrageous behaviour was due to her intense worship of George for whose interests and reputation, rather than his royalties, she fought, until cancer killed her, like a bossy tigress.

If the reader of this book feels that this material about Jack B. Yeats and the Orwells is a mere digression I can only plead that if Professor Fitzgerald can get *them* so wrong it must surely cast doubt on what he has to say about Lowry. I should also say that I am no enemy of psychiatry, having, since my undergraduate days, been a devoted student of Freud whose twenty-four volumes of his *Collected Works* are on the shelf below Grove's *Dictionary of Art* in my office. But I do think that those who interpret writers and artists in psychoanalytical terms ought to do so only on the basis of a far deeper knowledge of their works than that displayed by Fitzgerald. One need think only of Freud's interpretations of Ibsen or Leonardo to see how one's perceptions of those two geniuses can be enhanced and illuminated by a mind as original and as well stocked as Freud's.

The trouble with Asperger's Syndrome is that it is hard to define except in the vaguest of terms. The author of *The Complete Guide to Asperger's Syndrome*, Tony Attwood, gives us innumerable different examples of abnormal behaviour – whatever normality is – but in his glossary describes the illness, or the malfunction, only as "An expression of autism located at the milder spectrum of autistic disorders."[6] He also tells us that "Autistic personality disorder" was Asperger's own original definition.[7] Hans Asperger, an Austrian doctor born in 1906, published his views in Vienna in 1938, bravely in the post-Anschluss, Nazi-dominated atmosphere at the time when "mental defectives" were almost as hateful to the Nazis as Jews, communists, homosexuals, gypsies and other *untermenschen*. As he wrote, in part at least to protect some of his young patients from transportation "Not everything that steps out of line, and thus 'abnormal', must necessarily be 'inferior'."[8] Attwood at one stage hypothesises that about one person in 250 has the Syndrome which, if true, represents a significant proportion of the population. (A recent Cambridge University study suggests that there are about 600,000 Britons suffering from either Autism or Asperger's Syndrome.)

Asperger also believed that the psychological disorder was part of a continuum of abilities that *merges into the normal range*, (my italics). It was "a lifelong and stable personality type, and did not observe the disintegration and fragmentation that occurs in schizophrenia".[9]

In other words Asperger's is not as uncommon and not as damaging to the self and others as more extreme forms of aberrant behaviour. As Attwood shows, it can also be allied with special gifts, whether of sensory perception or of artistic creativity. These can be a disadvantage where, for example, phobias concerning particular colours occur.[10] Conversely Attwood points out that:

> There can also be an intense fascination with visual detail, noticing specks on a carpet or blemishes on someone's skin. When the child with Asperger's Syndrome has a natural talent at drawing, and this is combined with the special interest and considerable drawing practice, the result can be works of art that achieve an effect of photographic realism. For example, a young child who has an interest in trains can be precocious in learning to draw railway scenes in perspective, including almost every detail of the locomotive. In contrast, the people in the scene may be drawn at an age-appropriate level of representation.[11]

Perhaps significantly in the case of Lowry, "Some adults with Asperger' Syndrome continue to have a very restricted diet consisting of the same essential ingredients, cooked and presented in the same way, throughout their lives"[12]. Having spent much of my childhood in Lowry country before, during and immediately after World War II I can accept Attwood's statement in its general application, but cannot forebear from remarking that in the working class and at best impoverished white-collar circles in which I moved, that's how the vast majority of the industrial North West of England ate anyway, either willy nilly or from choice and, from my present day observation, it's still how many of them like to eat when transported direct from Manchester to the Costa del Sol or the stag nights in Prague or Amsterdam.

Ironically, although Fitzgerald does not mention this aspect, it's the one part of Asperger's Syndrome that *does* apply very clearly to Lowry, as the deep focus on his finicky eating habits exercised by Tilly Marshall in her occasionally ambiguously hostile account of Lowry's personal habits shows.[13] When Fitzgerald is confronted by Rohde[14] with the painting called *Cripples* he sees it as an artistic work and also a fundamentally implausible, unreal picture. Rohde explains that Lowry's friend and fellow painter David Carr had challenged Lowry's veracity in that particular picture, whereupon Lowry counterchallenged Carr and they went off together to look for crippled, maimed or otherwise odd-looking people and Carr admitted defeat after Lowry had got the total observed on their excursion into three figures. Fitzgerald then pounces on Lowry's conduct as definitely autistic, comparing it with the child-like practice of counting how many Jaguar cars had been seen in the course of a particular journey, which in turn is part of Autism/Asperger's tendency to be heavily into mathematics and numeracy. Well of course, that kind of thing is childlike, even nerdy or geeky, as is the practice of train spotting beyond one's schooldays. But surely there is a simpler explanation for Lowry's cripple counting. One need only look at his work to see that he wasn't into counting or numeracy as such. He was merely feeding his obsession with the oddity of humanity. He found it funny and recorded it whenever he observed it as being odd or funny or even a little bit mad. Not that he particularly had it in for the halt and the lame. When he painted their oddities, their deviations from the norm, he did it with irony, with sympathy and even with compassion. There was neither contempt nor cruelty. In fact, in so far as he made use of these, as it were involuntary subjects he could be – and was – much more satirical in intent when he painted "normal" people such as a group of businessmen in suits and ties.

When it comes to Lowry's later, erotic works Fitzgerald observes "The last thing that comes to mind is eroticism ... I suppose the bow [of the woman's dress] could be slightly coquettish, even sexual if you are looking for that kind of thing ..."[15] As I deal fully, and separately, with the erotic works in Chapter 13 I shall leave that subject at this point.

Suffice to say that I cannot find in either Fitzgerald's Lowry chapter in his book or in the Shelley Rohde interview any decisive proof that Lowry manifested Asperger's Syndrome, if he had it at all, in either his art or his life. There were certain characteristics listed as common in Asperger's patients by Attwood which were categorically absent from Lowry's personality, namely difficulty with reading and problems with numeracy (Asperger's sufferers can also be highly gifted mathematically). Lowry was an avid reader of classic literature and fond of quoting from Montaigne and La Rochefoucauld, not authors to have made much of an impression on backward readers. He was also, like many a Northerner before and after him, very shrewd about figures particularly when it came to his hatred of the Inland Revenue and his ability to spot instantly, and then take appropriate remedies, any attempt to short-change him.

That he was eccentric and odd is indisputable but, apart from his celibacy (see Chapter 13, LOWRY AND WOMEN) he was as normal as any other North-Western Englishman of his time, place and class. He had, considering his abbreviated schooling, his domestic background, the appalling restrictions and obligations of having to cope with his valetudinarian mother until he was deep into middle-age, a fresh, engaging, outgoing personality. He would act the curmudgeon when he felt like it but that was mostly a self-protective act reserved for offensive would be patrons or critics. That he chose to live so frugally even when commercially successful, did not conceal his great generosity or his capacity for friendship. In his life, as in his art, he was not only his own man but also one who brought pleasure to all who valued and understood him.

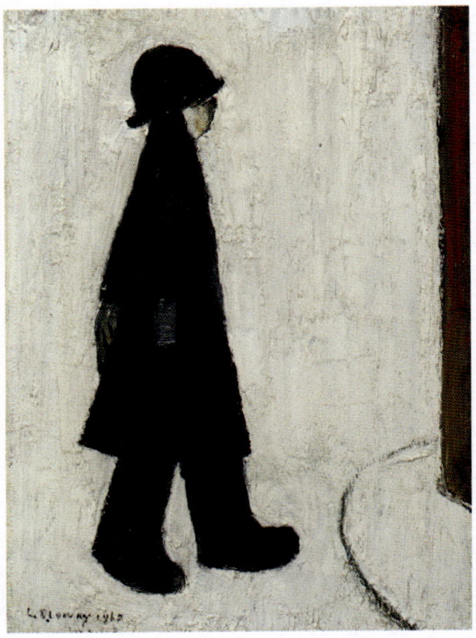

A Man Walking, 1960, oil on board, 23.5 × 17.1 cm.

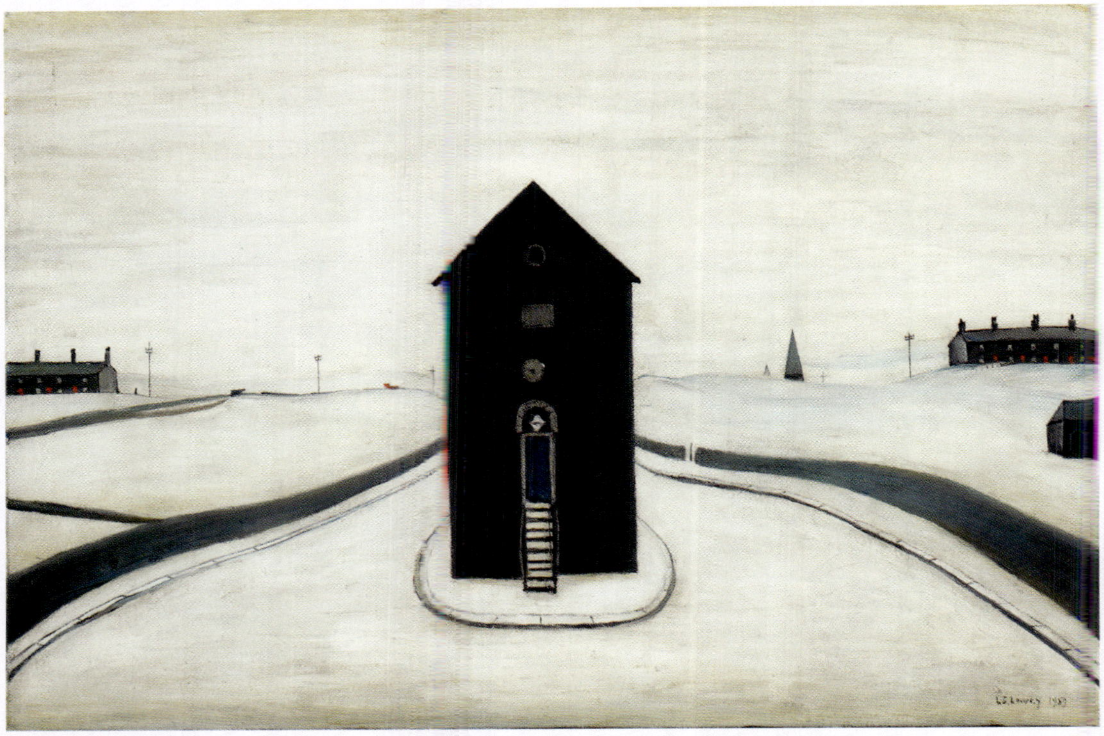

The Toll House on the Moor, 1959, oil on canvas, 61 × 50.8 cm.

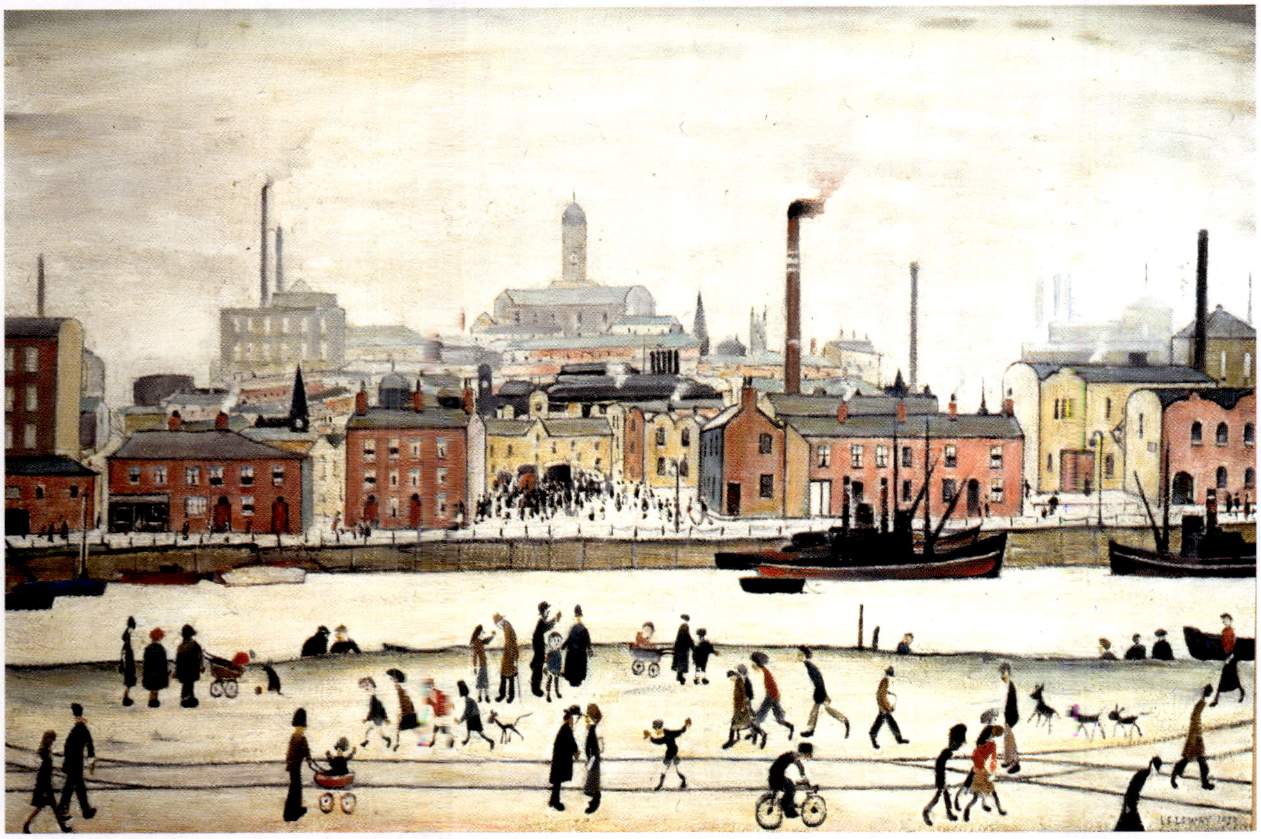

Northern River Scene, 1959, oil on canvas, 50.8 × 76.2 cm.

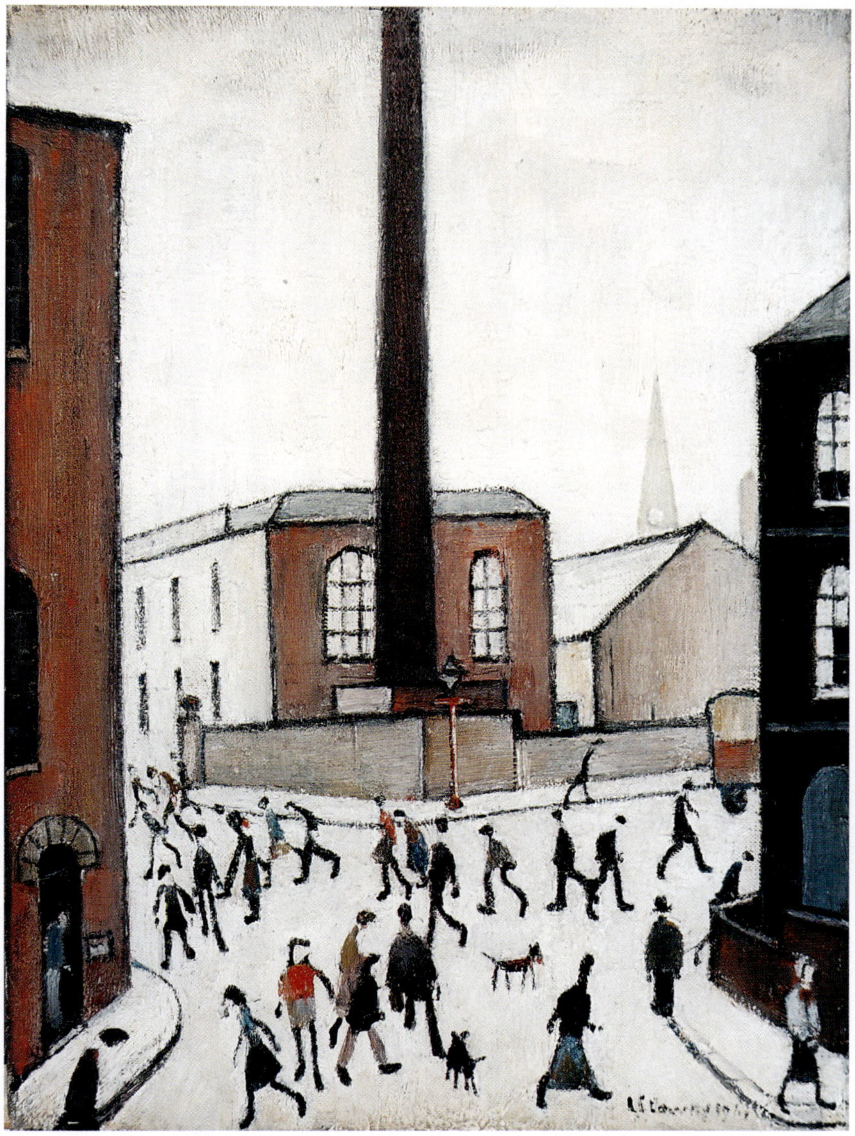

City Scene, 1949, oil on canvas,
36 × 25.5 cm.

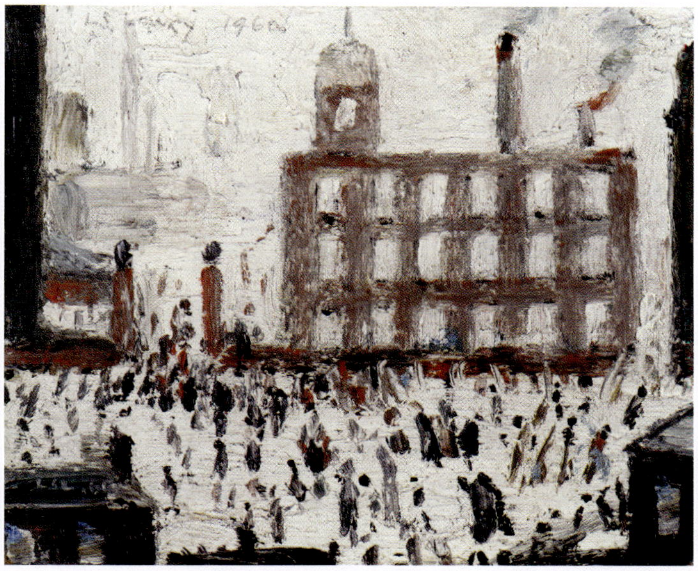

Factory Scene, 1960, oil on board,
11.4 × 14 cm.

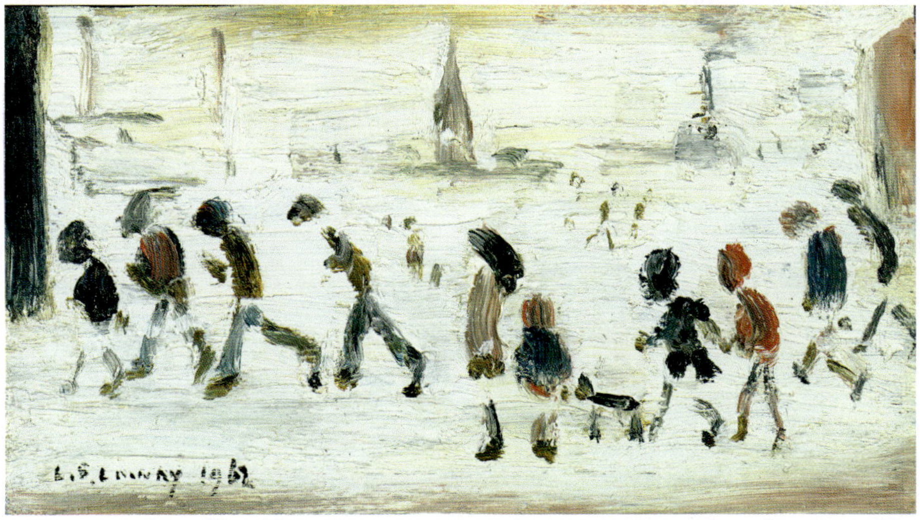

Children Playing in the Street, 1962,
oil on panel, 13.3 × 22.9 cm.

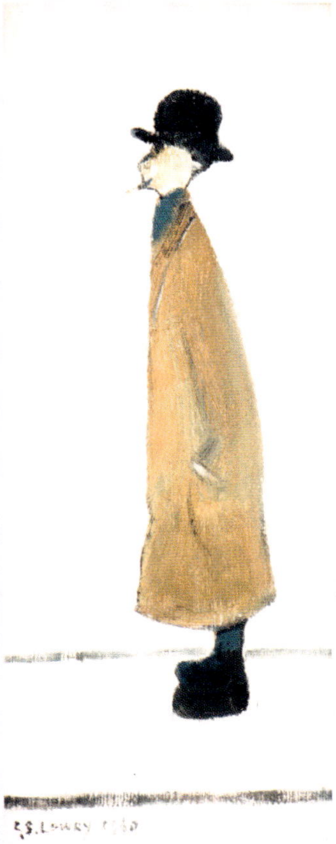

Gentleman Looking at Something, 1960,
oil on board/panel, 24.5 × 10 cm.

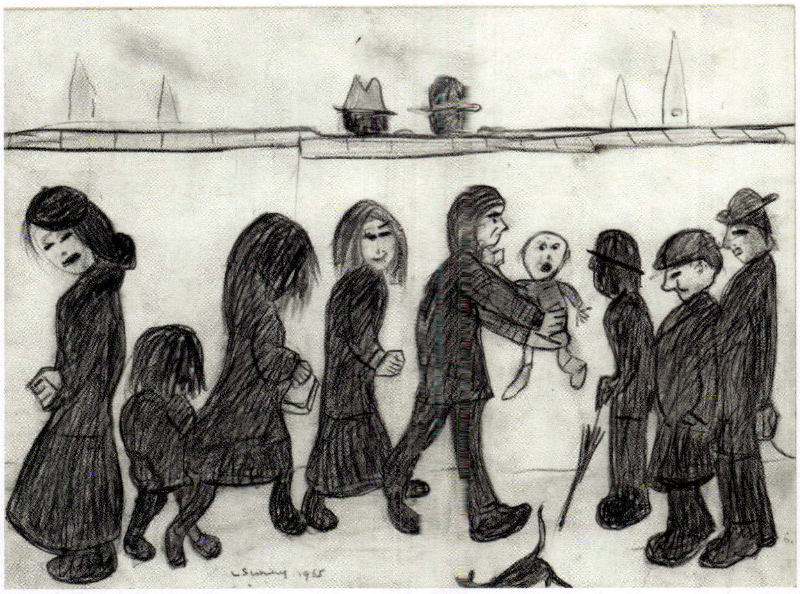

Man Holding a Child, 1965, pencil on paper.

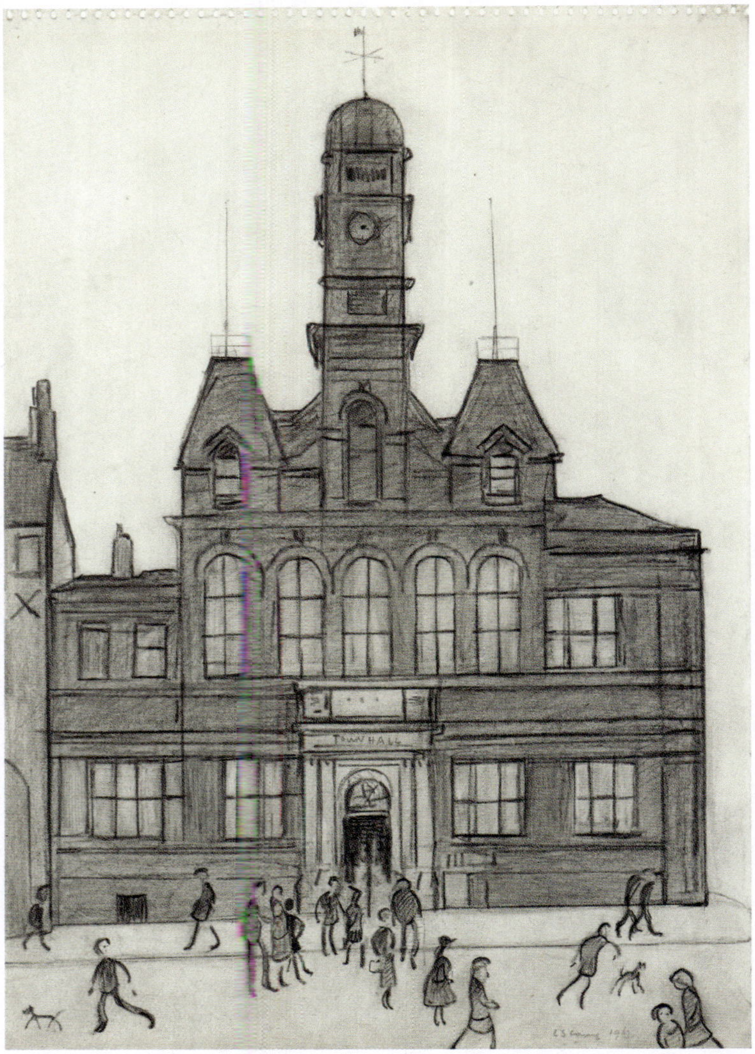

Eccles Town Hall, 1963, pencil on paper, 34.3 × 24.8 cm.

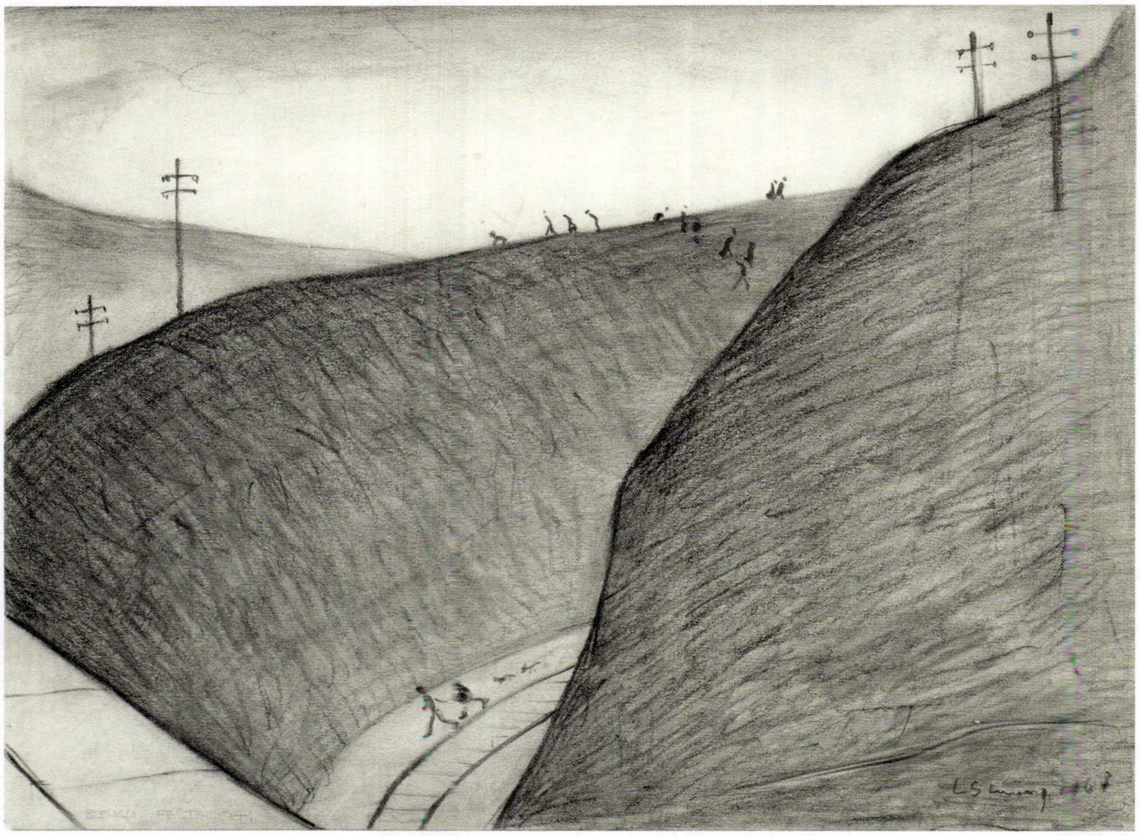

Untitled – Blaenau Festiniog, 1963, pencil on paper, 24.8 × 34 cm.

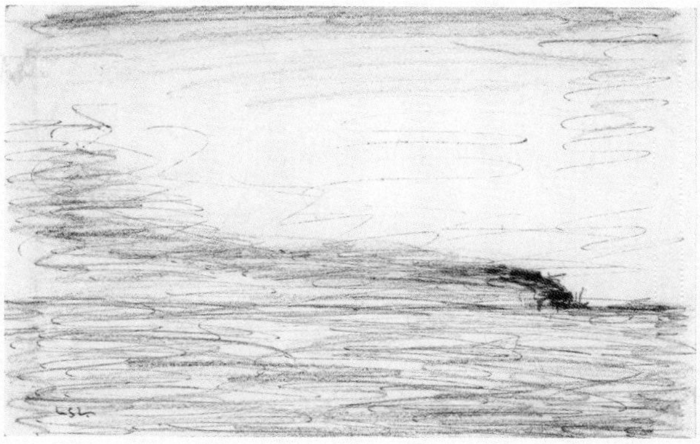

Sea Trials off South Shields, c.1965, pencil on paper.

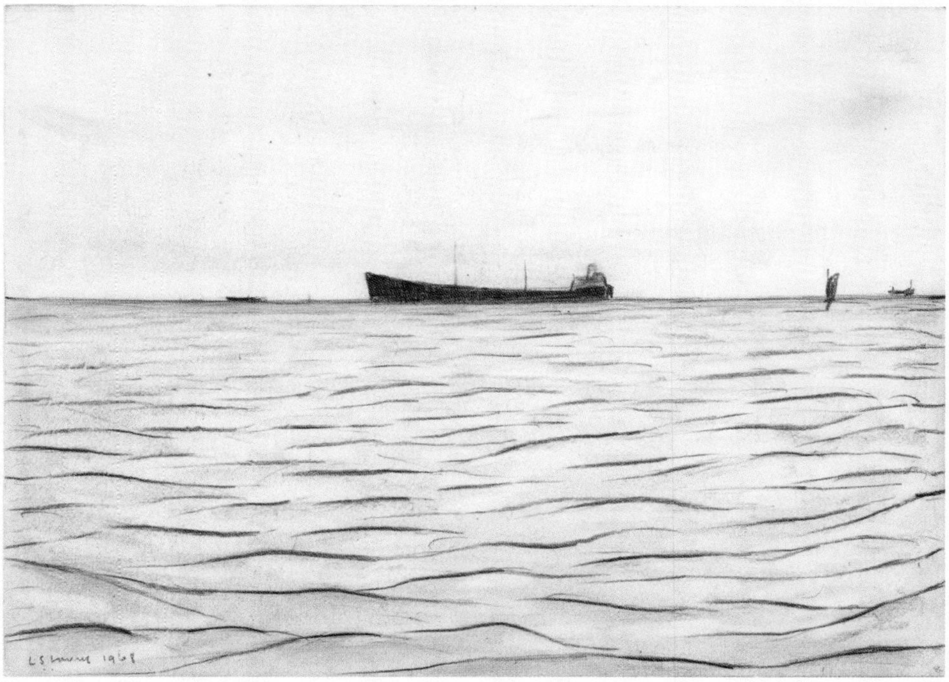

Tanker at Sea, 1968, pencil on paper.

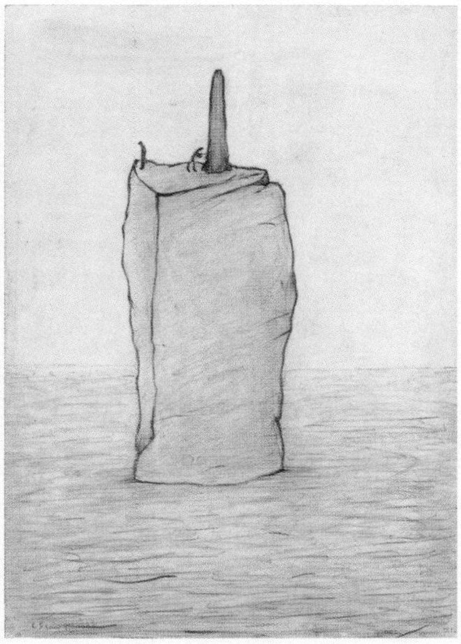

Figures on a Rock, 1968, pencil on paper.

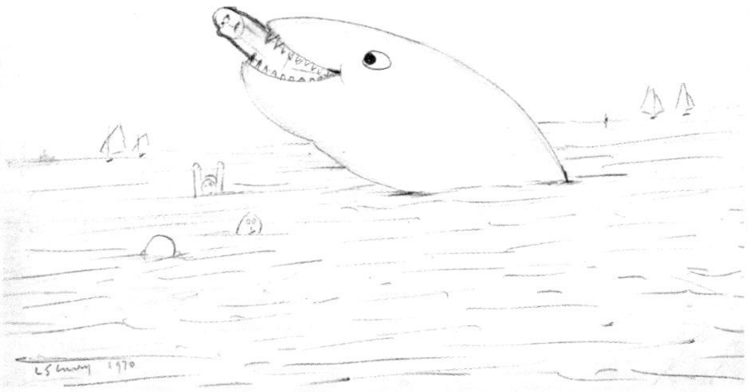

The Shark, 1970, pencil on paper.

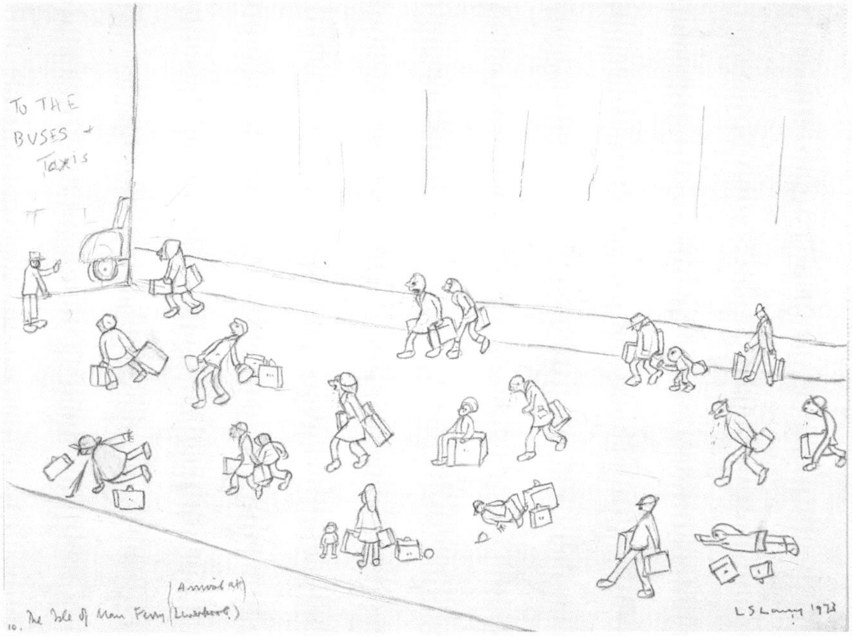

The Isle of Man Ferry, Arrival at Liverpool, 1973, pencil on paper, 26 × 35 cm.

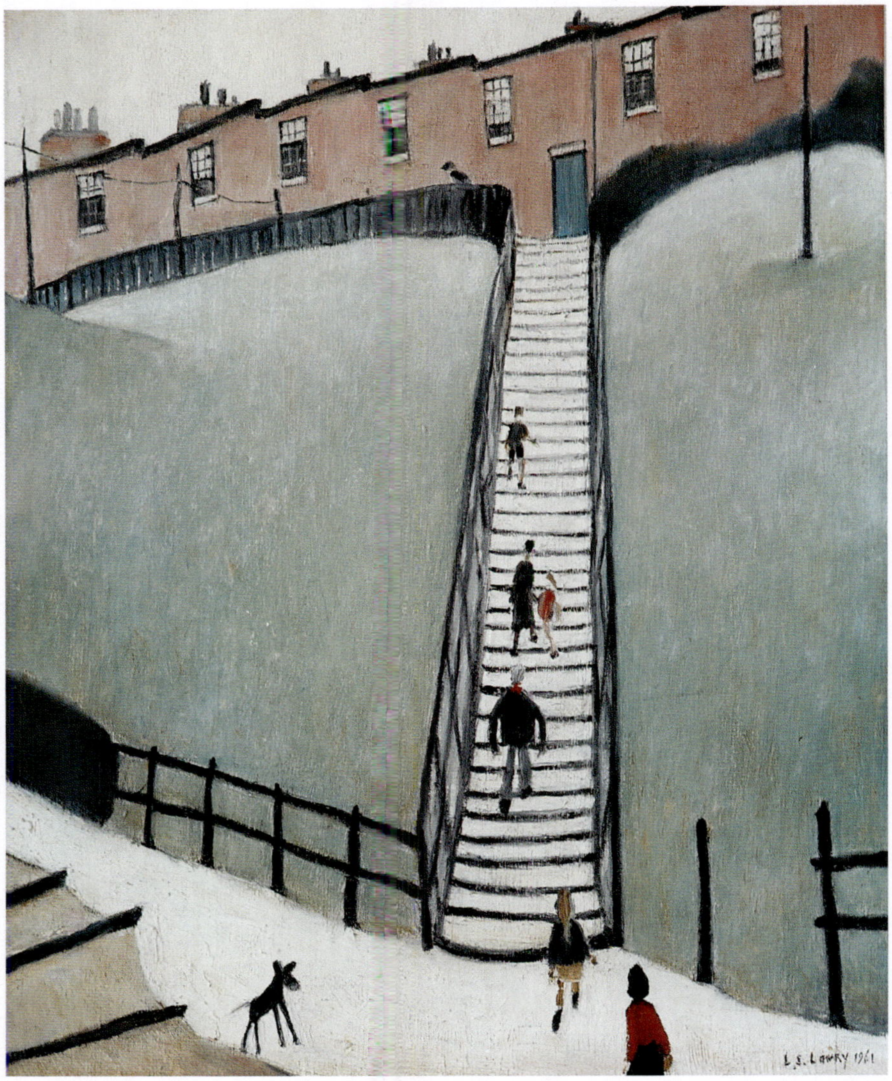

The Old Terrace Steps, 1961, oil on canvas, 59.5 × 49.5 cm.

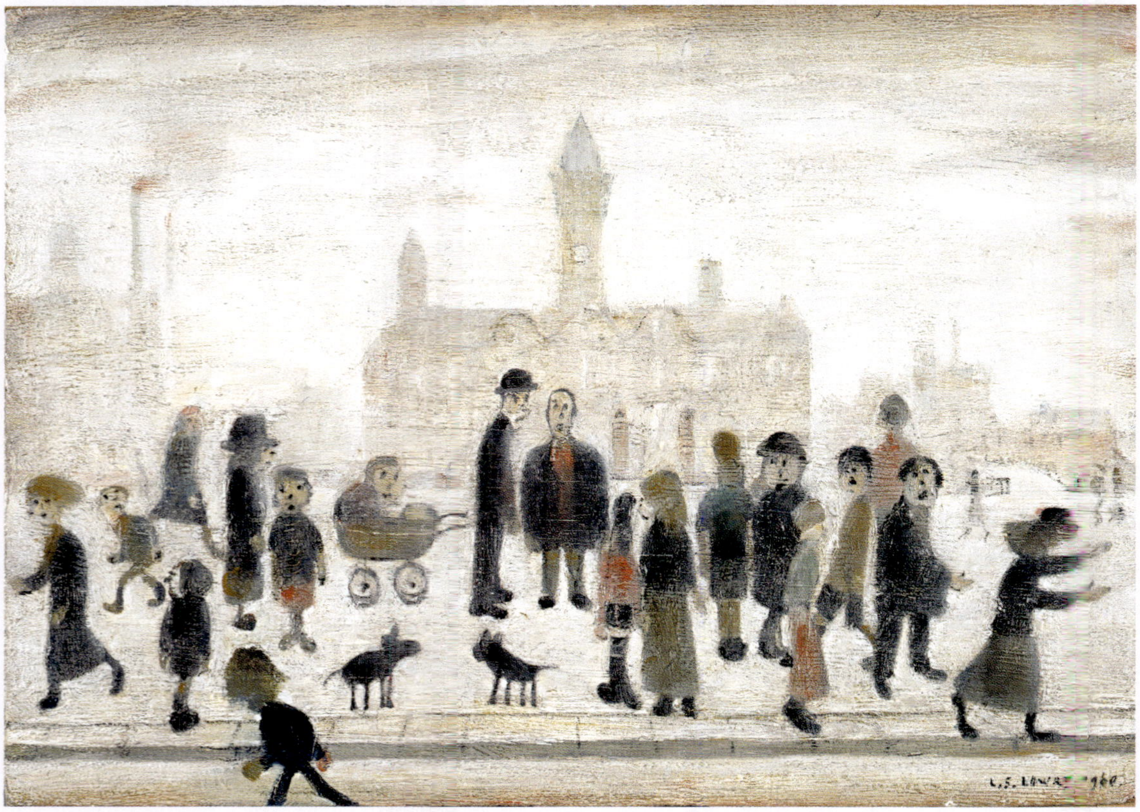

Hyde Town Hall, 1960, oil on board/ panel, 41.5 × 54.5 cm.

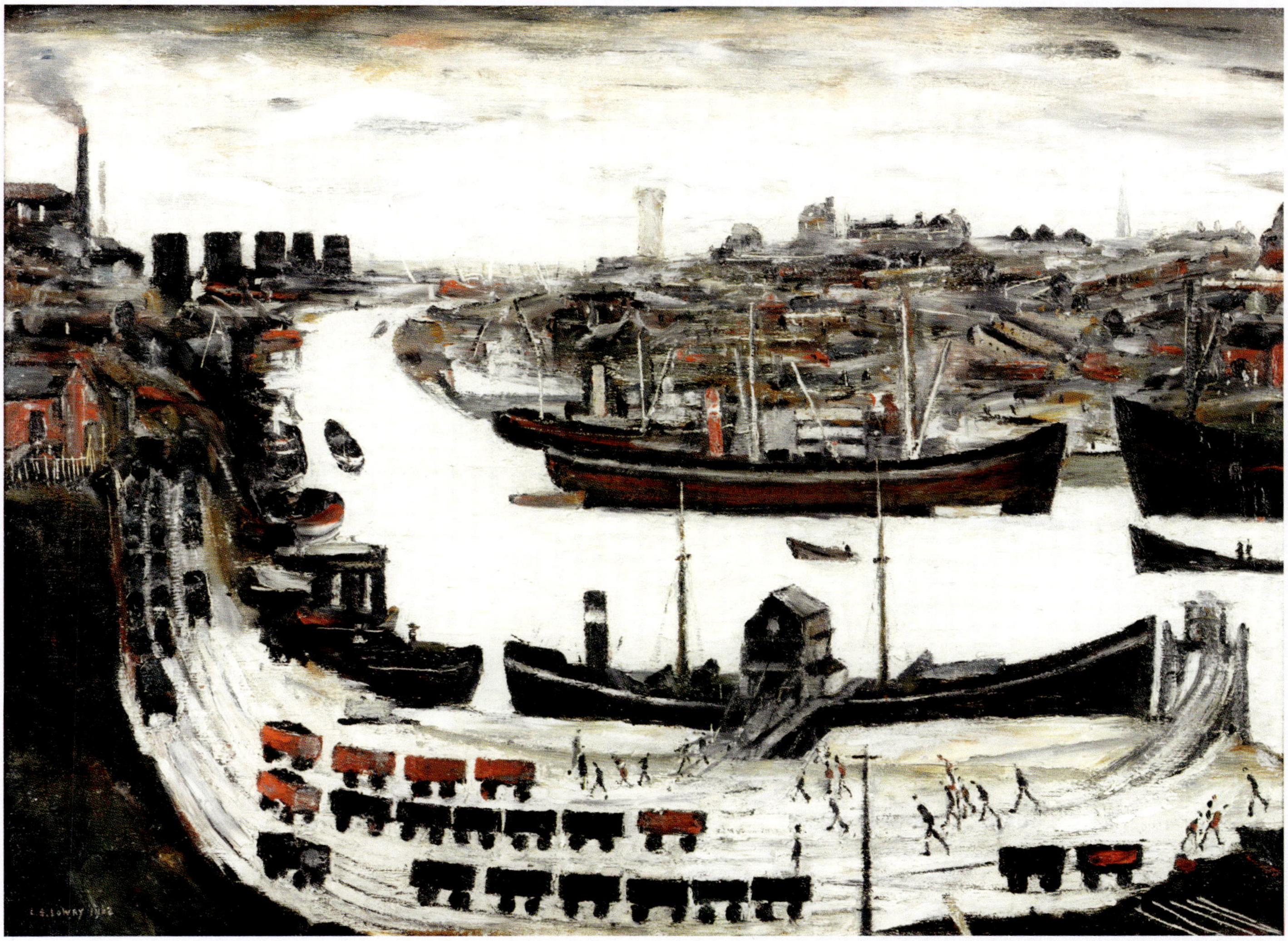

Dockside, Sunderland, 1962,
oil on canvas, 56 × 76 cm.

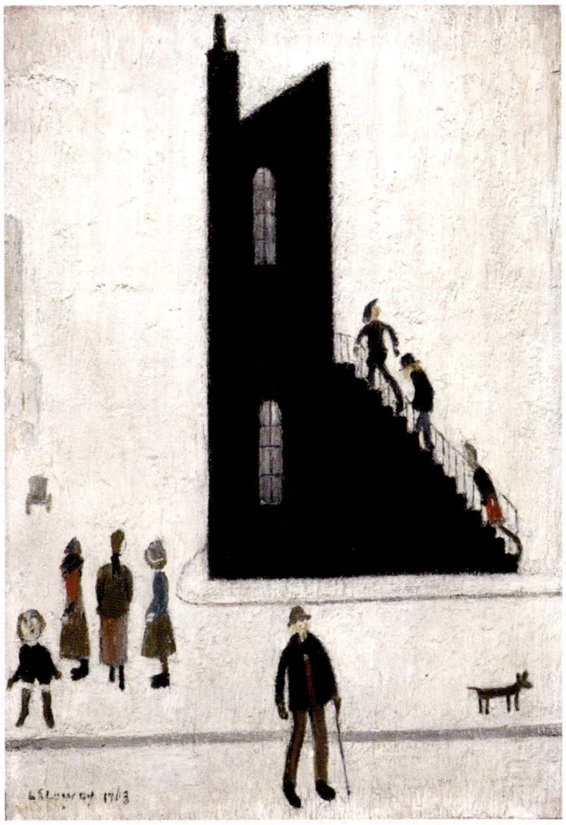

A House, 1963, oil on panel,
43 × 30.5 cm.

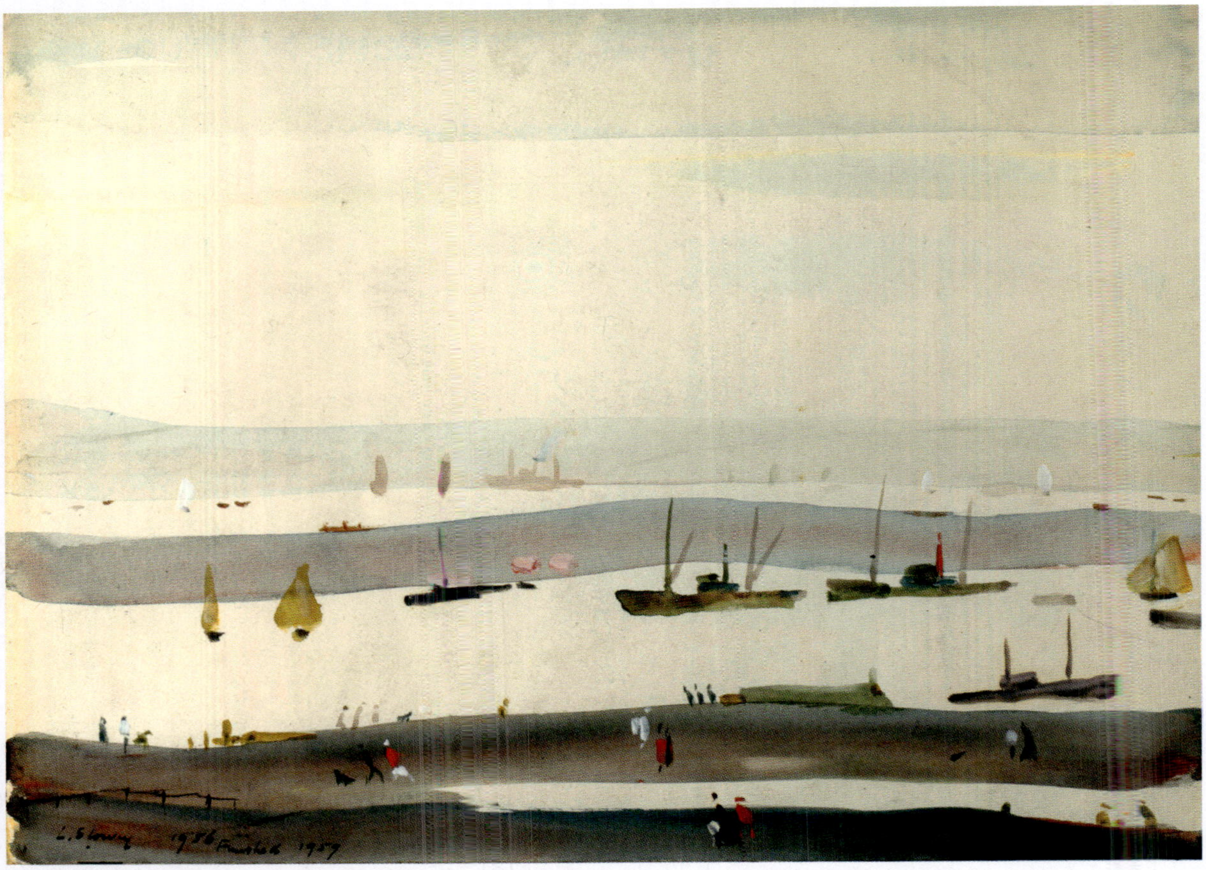

The Estuary, 1959, watercolour on paper, 24 × 34.2 cm.

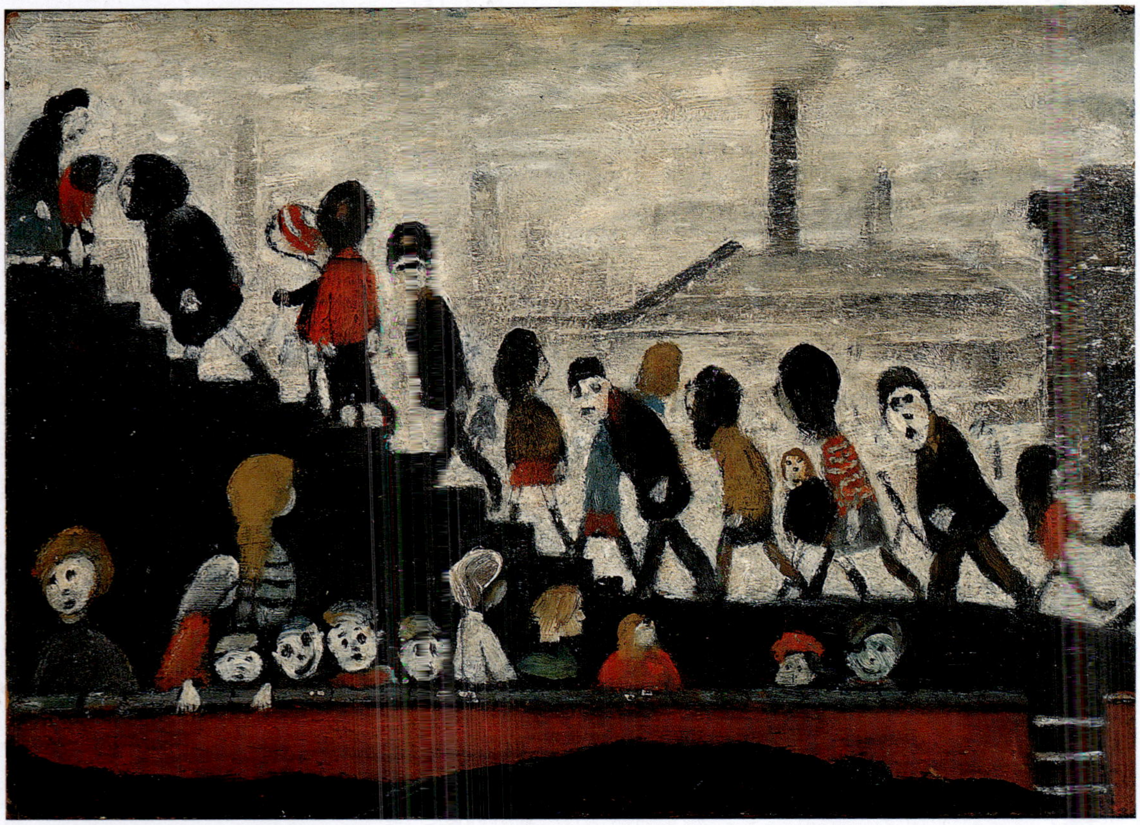

Children on the Steps, (undated), oil on board, 25.2 × 35.5 cm.

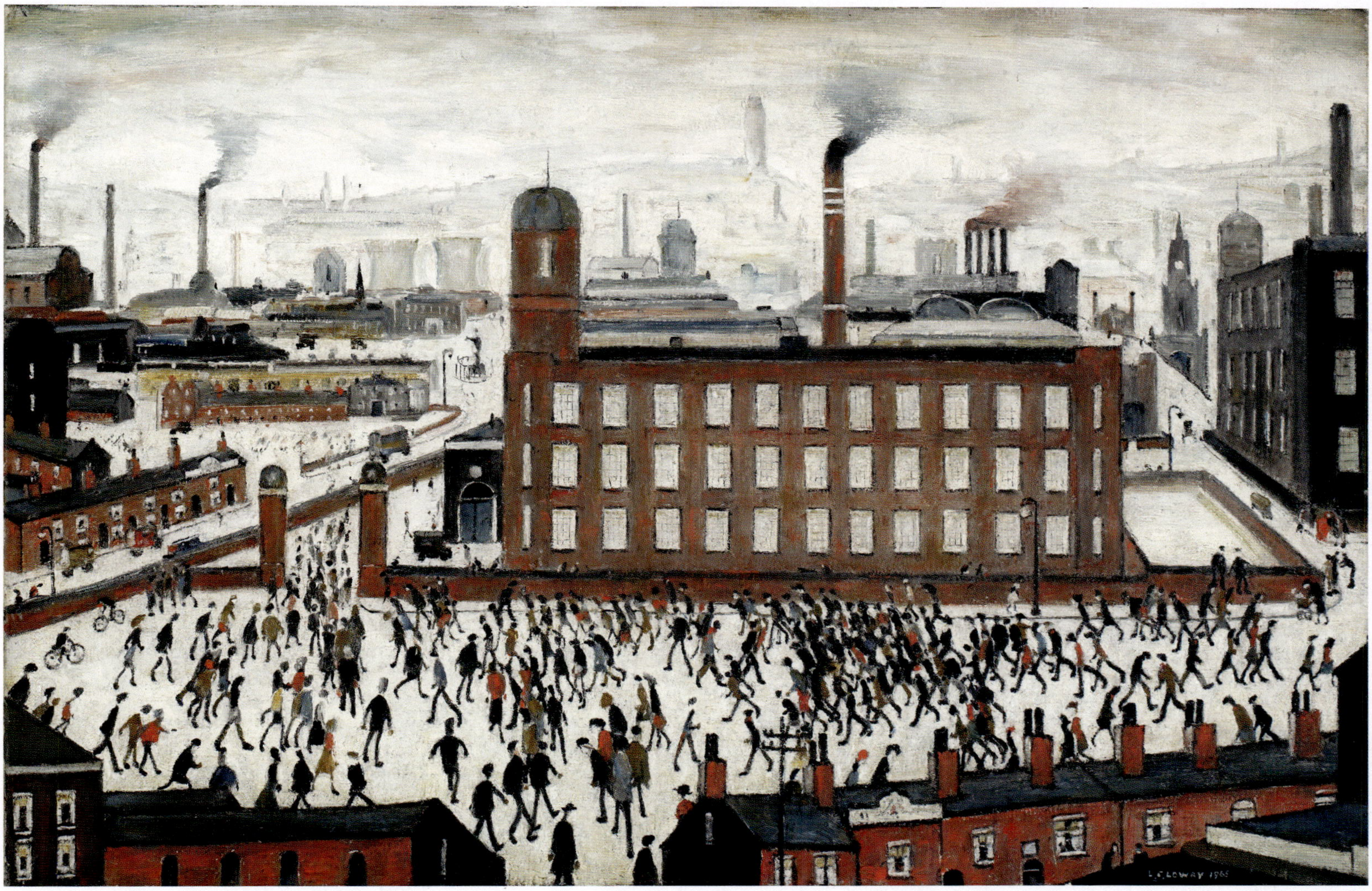

Industrial Scene, 1965, oil on canvas, 56 × 86.3 cm.

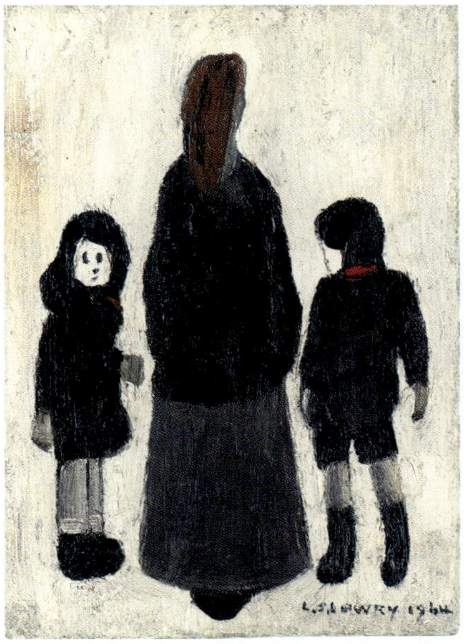

Mother and Children, 1964, oil on board, 17.8 × 12.7 cm.

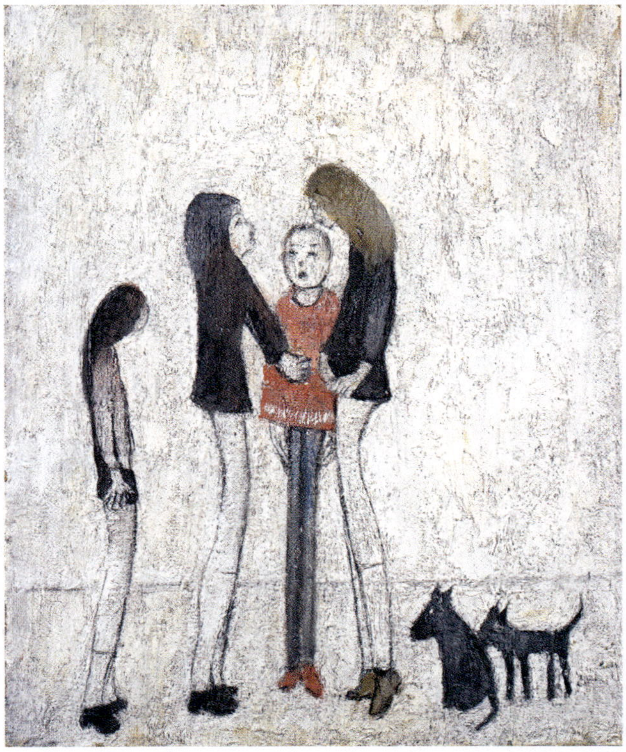

Teenagers, 1965, oil on board, 25.5 × 21.5 cm.

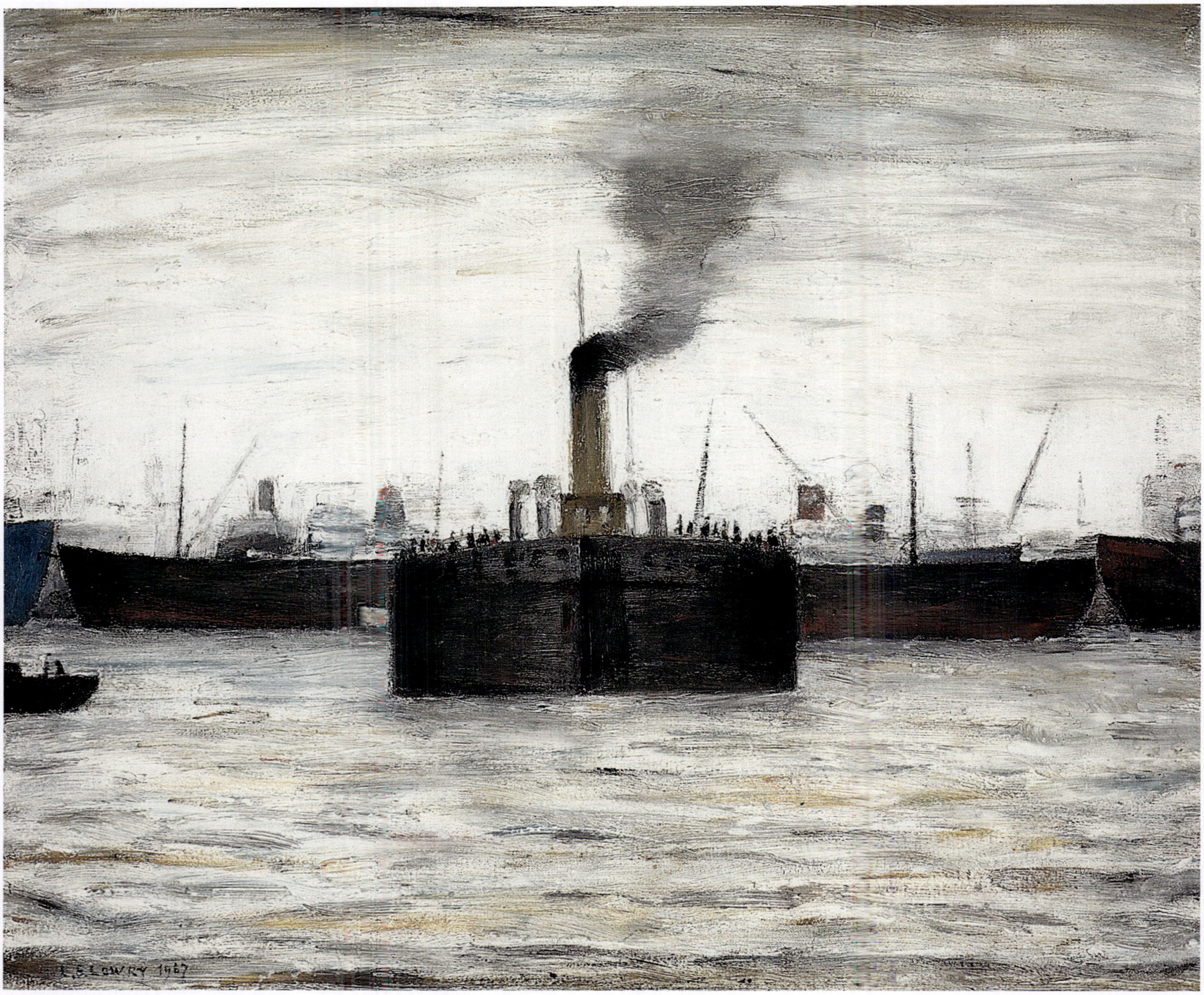

The Ferry, South Shields, 1967,
oil on canvas, 49.5 × 59.5 cm.

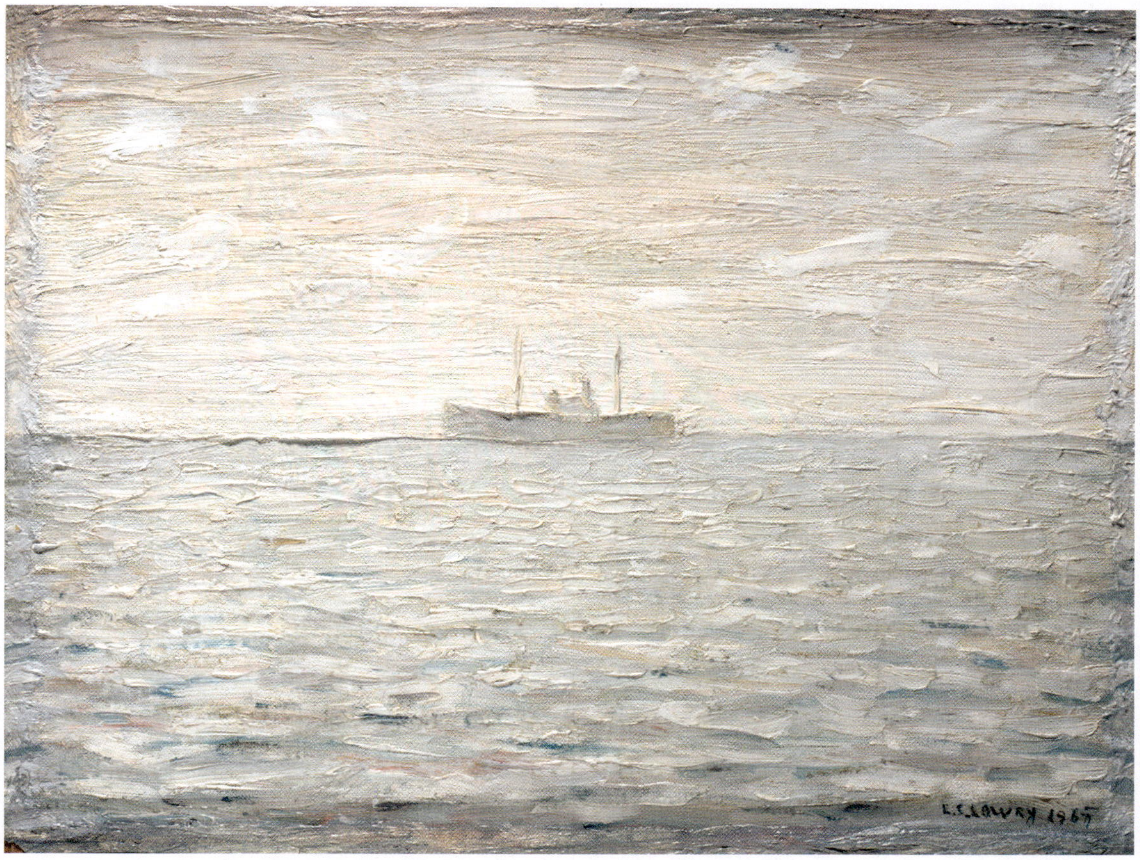

Waiting for the Tide, 1965,
oil on board/panel, 43 × 54 cm.

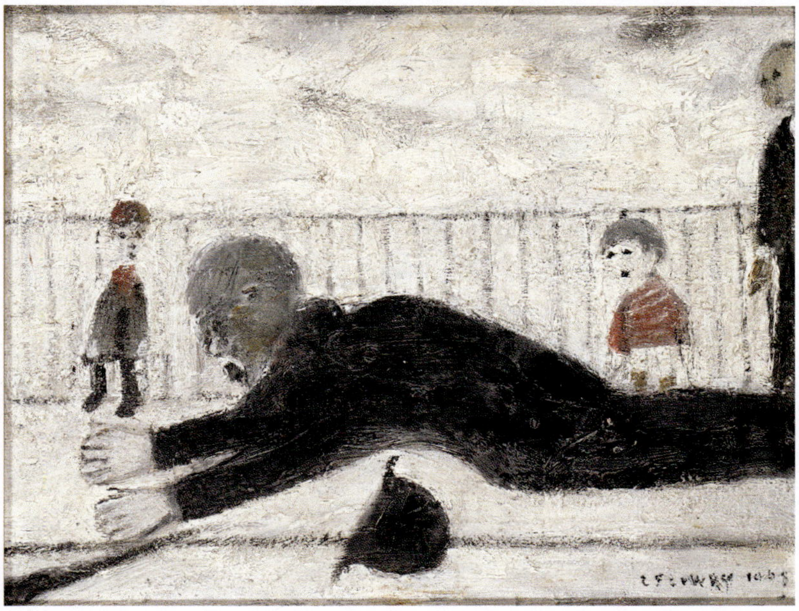

Man Falling Over, 1968, oil on board,
20.5 × 26.5 cm.

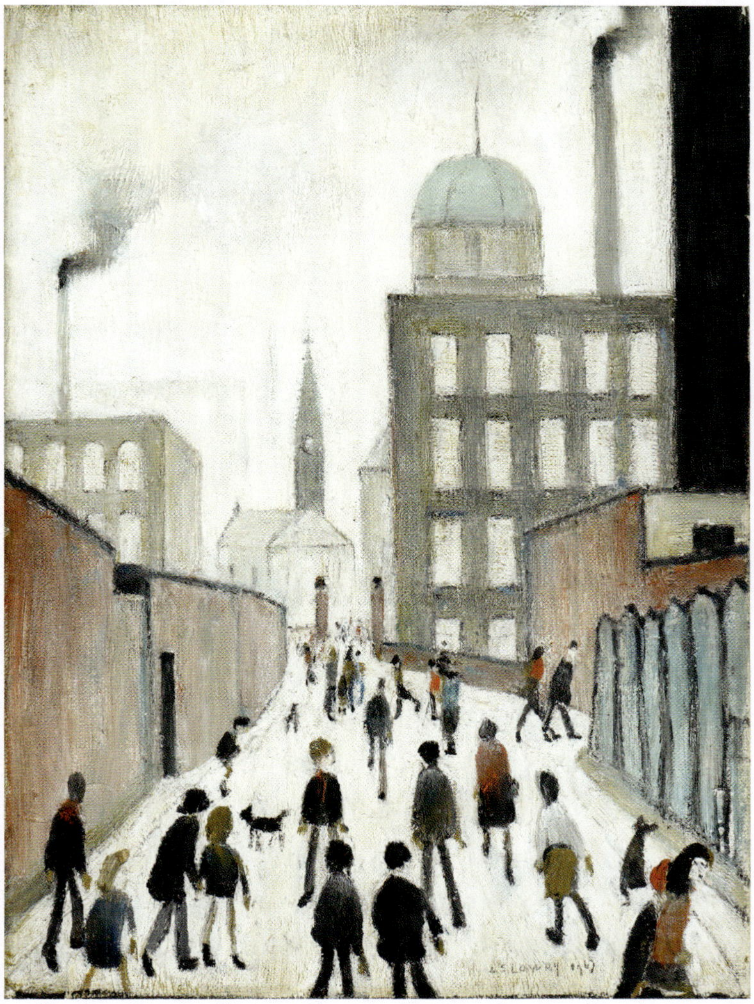

Mrs Swindell's Picture, 1967,
oil on canvas, 39.5 × 29.5 cm.

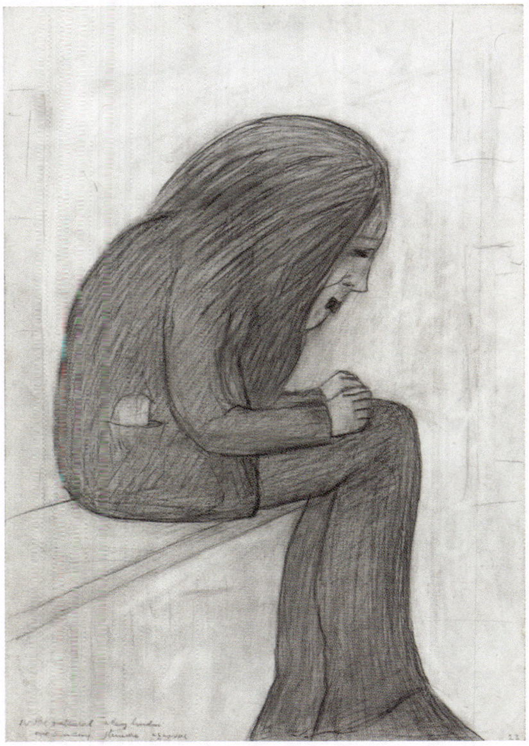

In The National Gallery One Sunday Afternoon, (undated), pencil on paper, 42 × 29.5 cm.

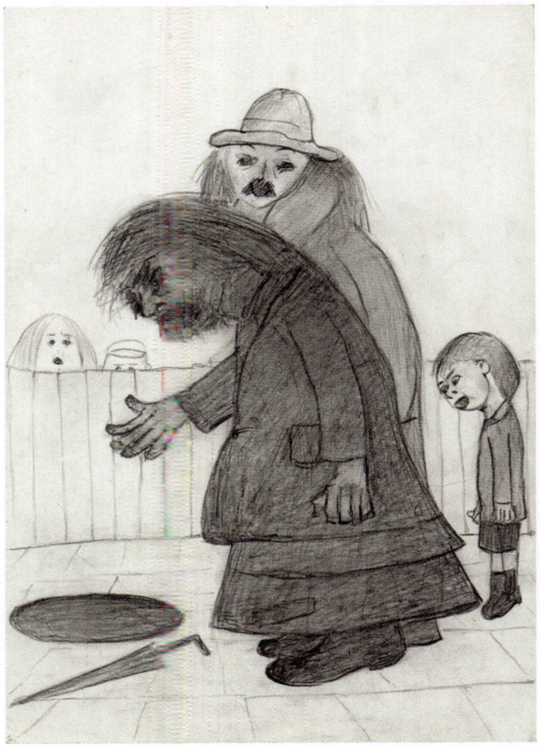

Untitled – Man Falling down a Hole, (undated), pencil on paper, 41 × 29 cm.

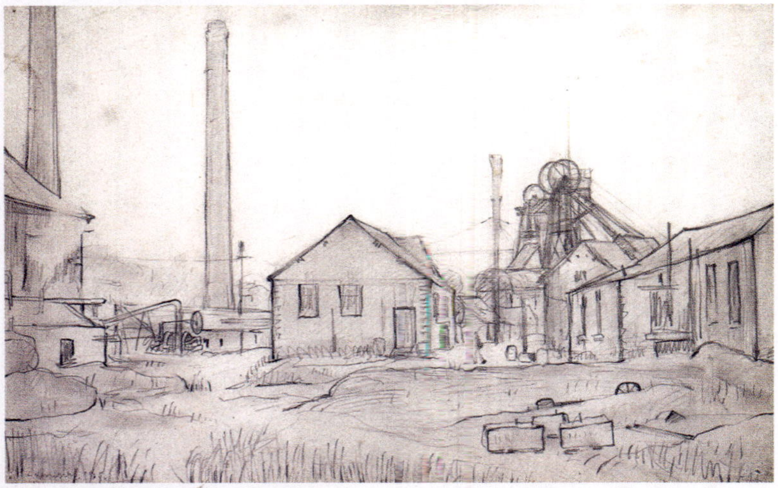

Pit Head Scene, Wet Earth Colliery, 1925, pencil on paper.

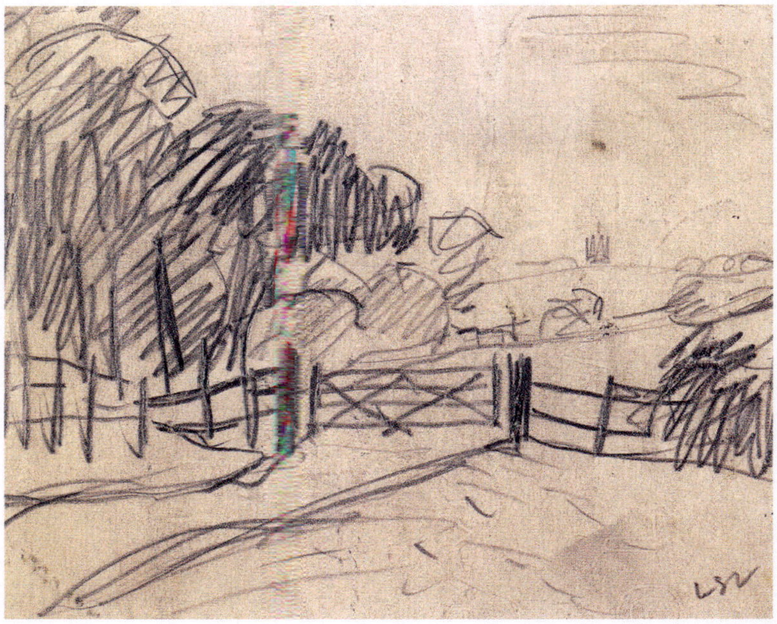

View from Morton Moss, (undated), pencil on paper.

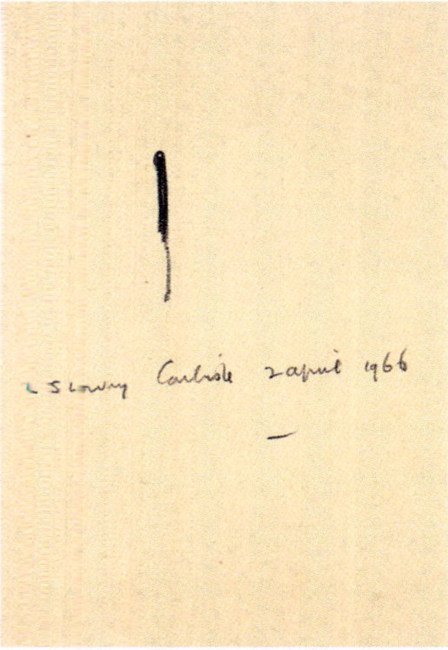

Minimal Drawing of Girl, Carlisle, 1966.

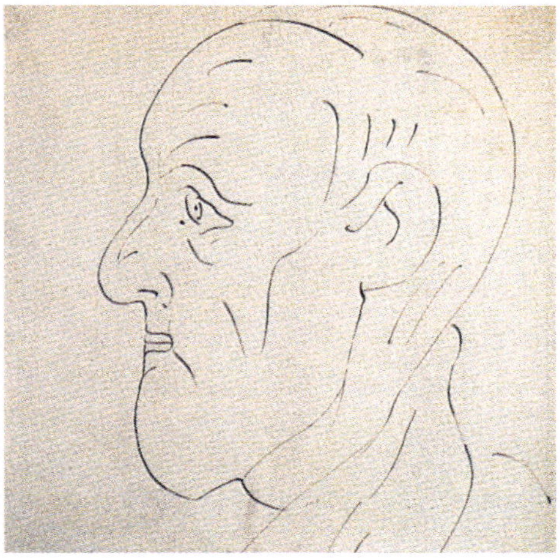

Head of a Man, (undated).

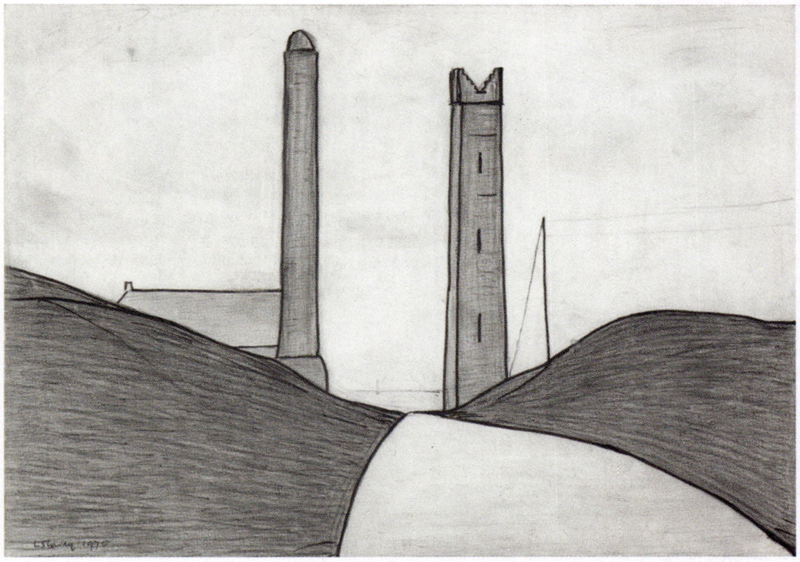

Near Drogheda, 1970, pencil on paper.

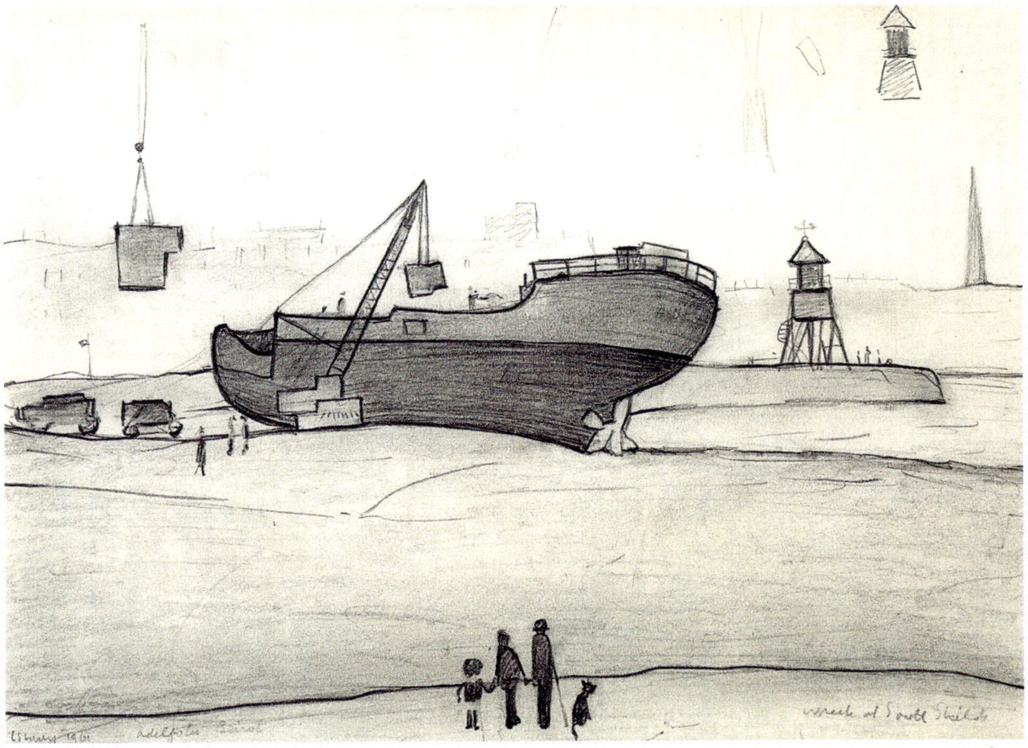

Wreck at South Shields,
1961, pencil on paper.

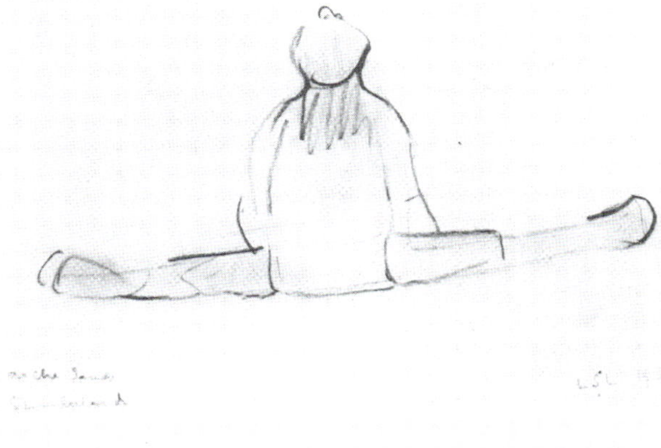

On the Sands, Sunderland,
1966, pencil on paper.

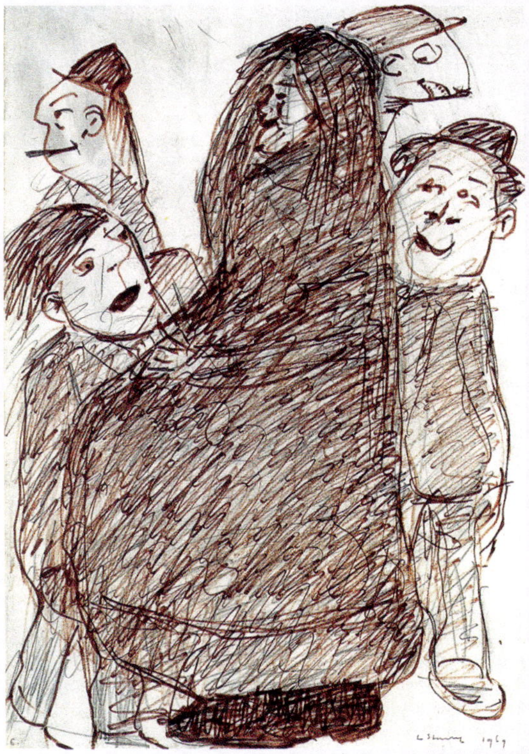

Woman in Black, 1969,
pencil and pen and ink on paper.

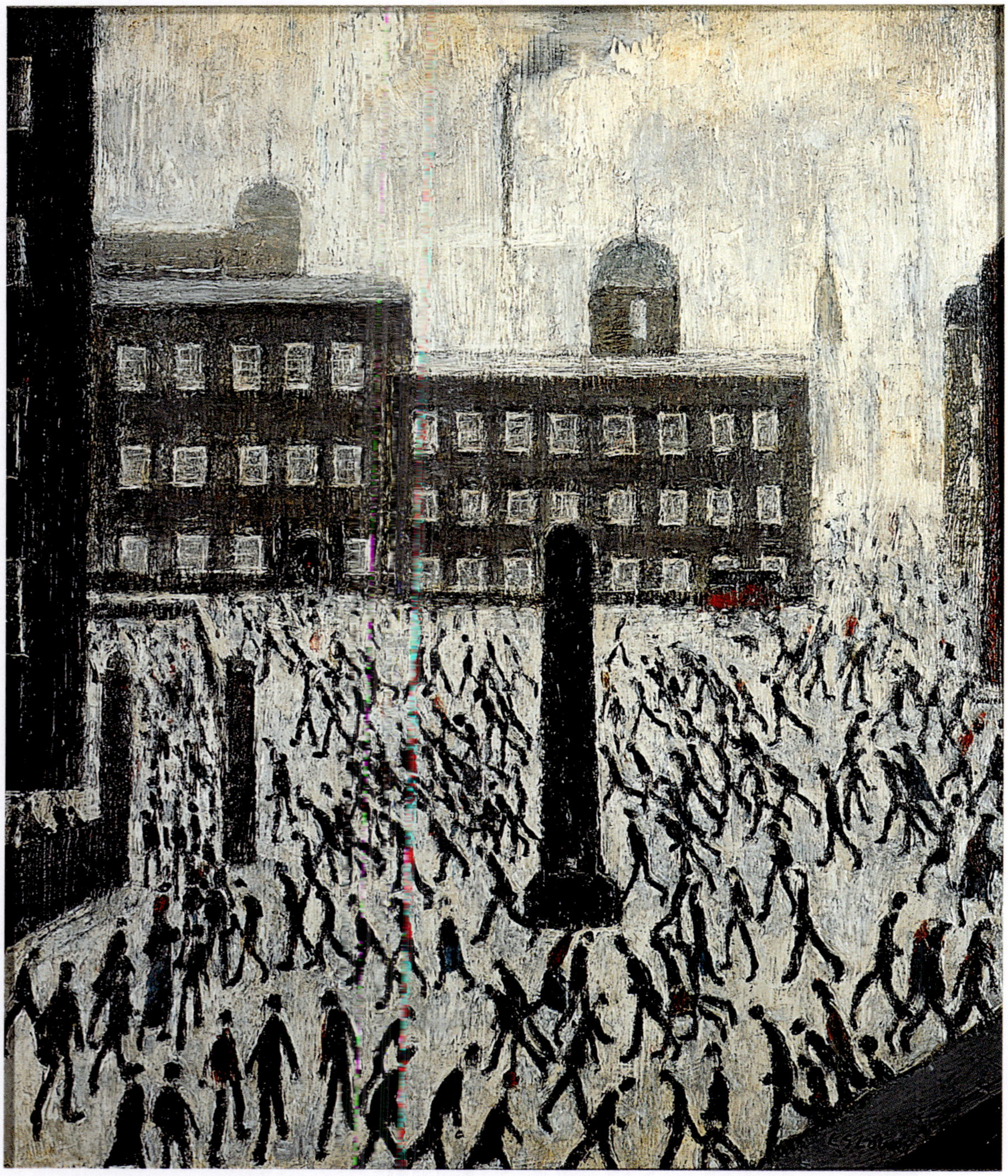

Industrial Scene with Monument, 1972, oil on board/panel, 46.5 × 43 cm.

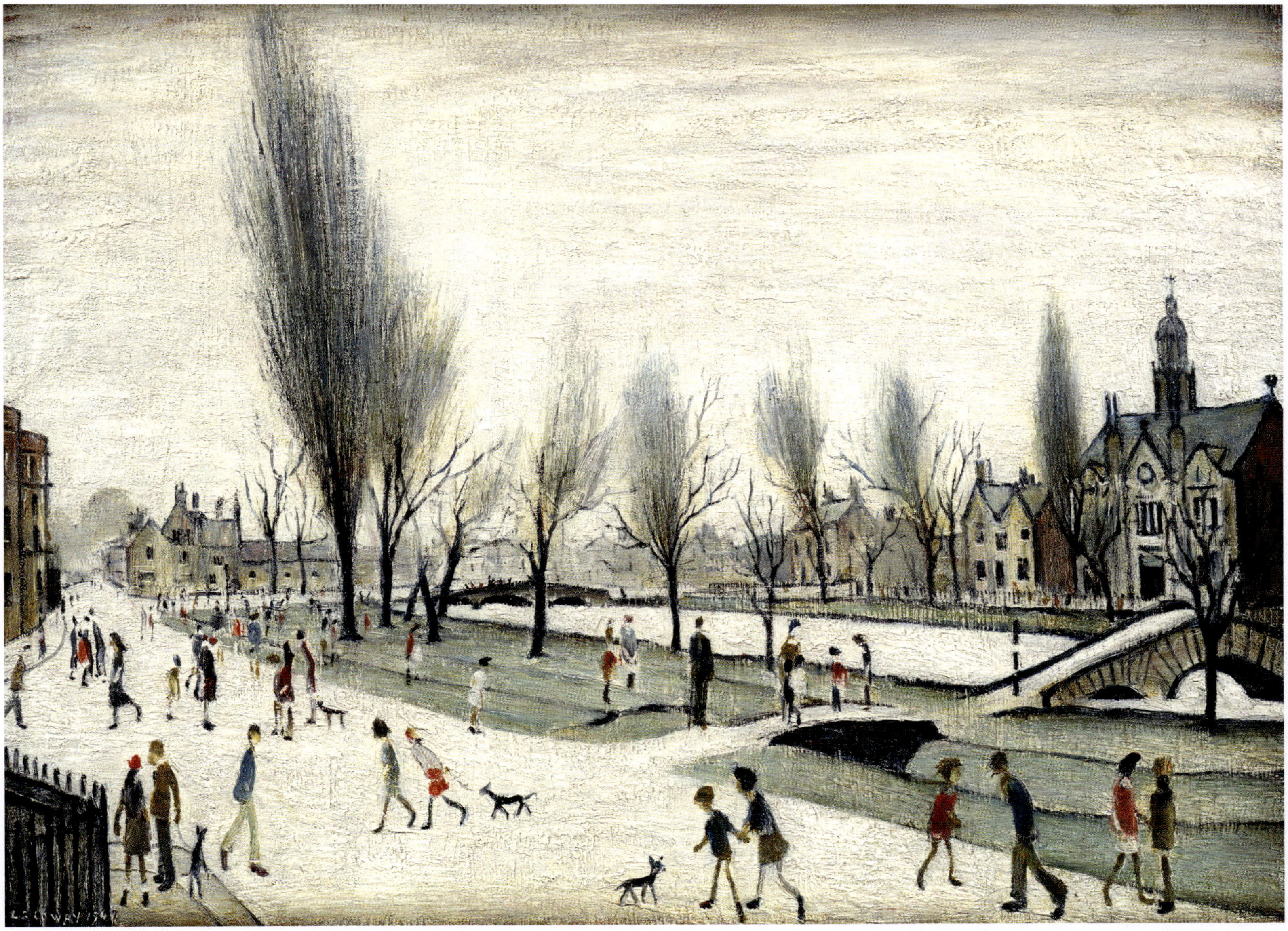

Bourton-on-the-Water, 1957,
oil on canvas, 45.7 × 61 cm.

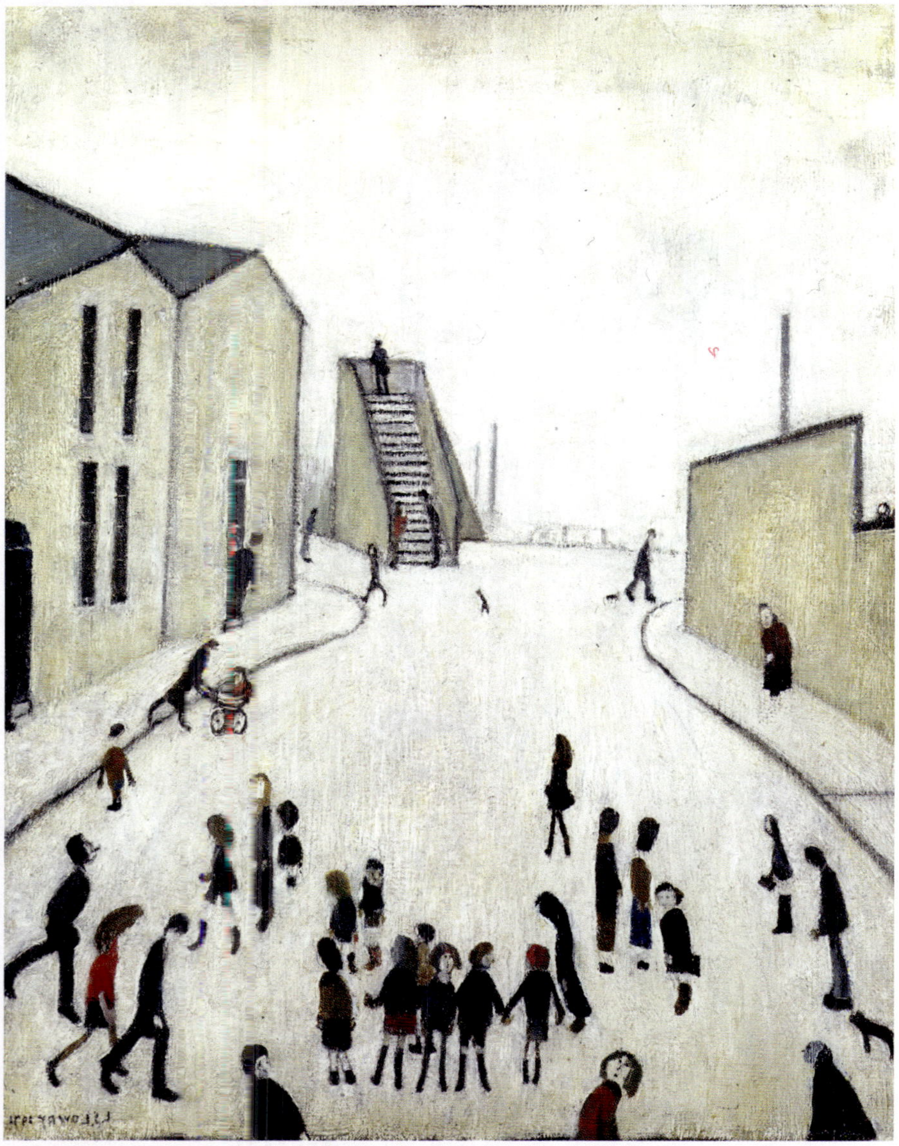

A Footbridge, Stockport Steps, 1971, oil on canvas, 49.5 × 39.5 cm.

Stormy Sea, 1968, oil on board, 37.5 × 71.25 cm.

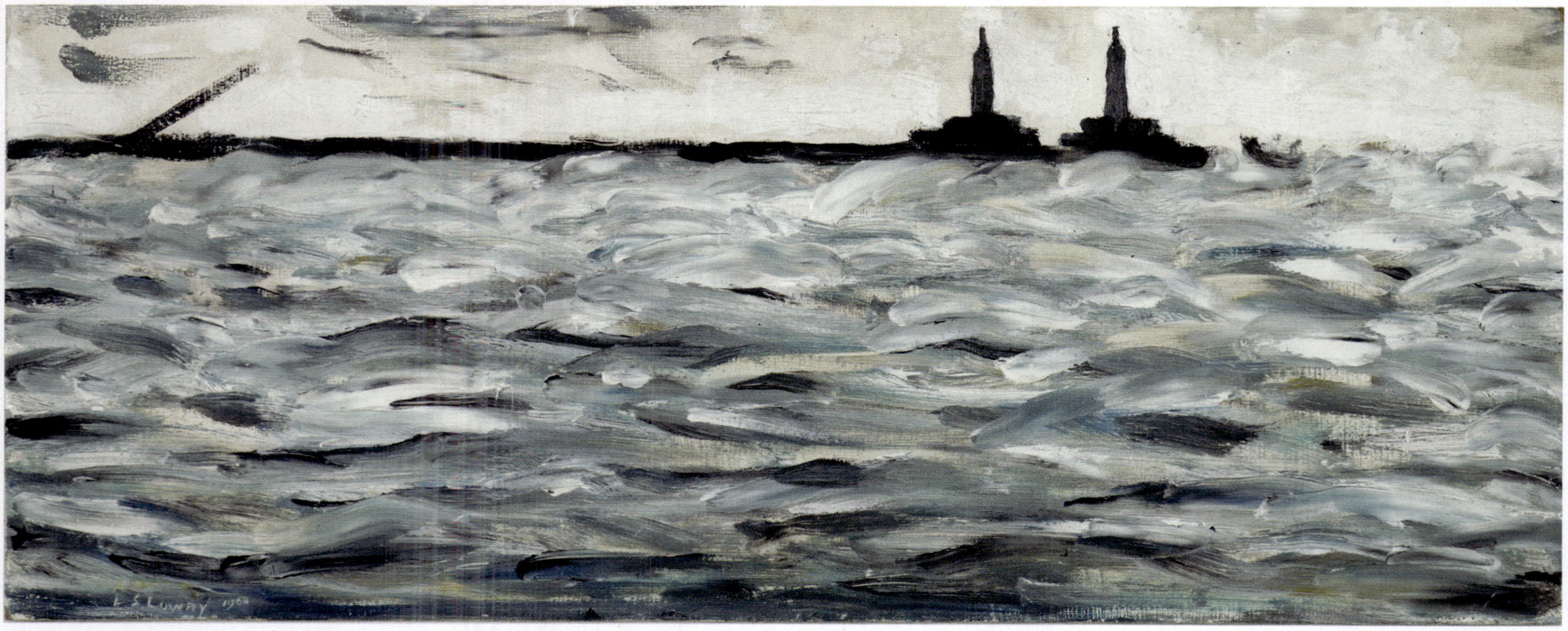

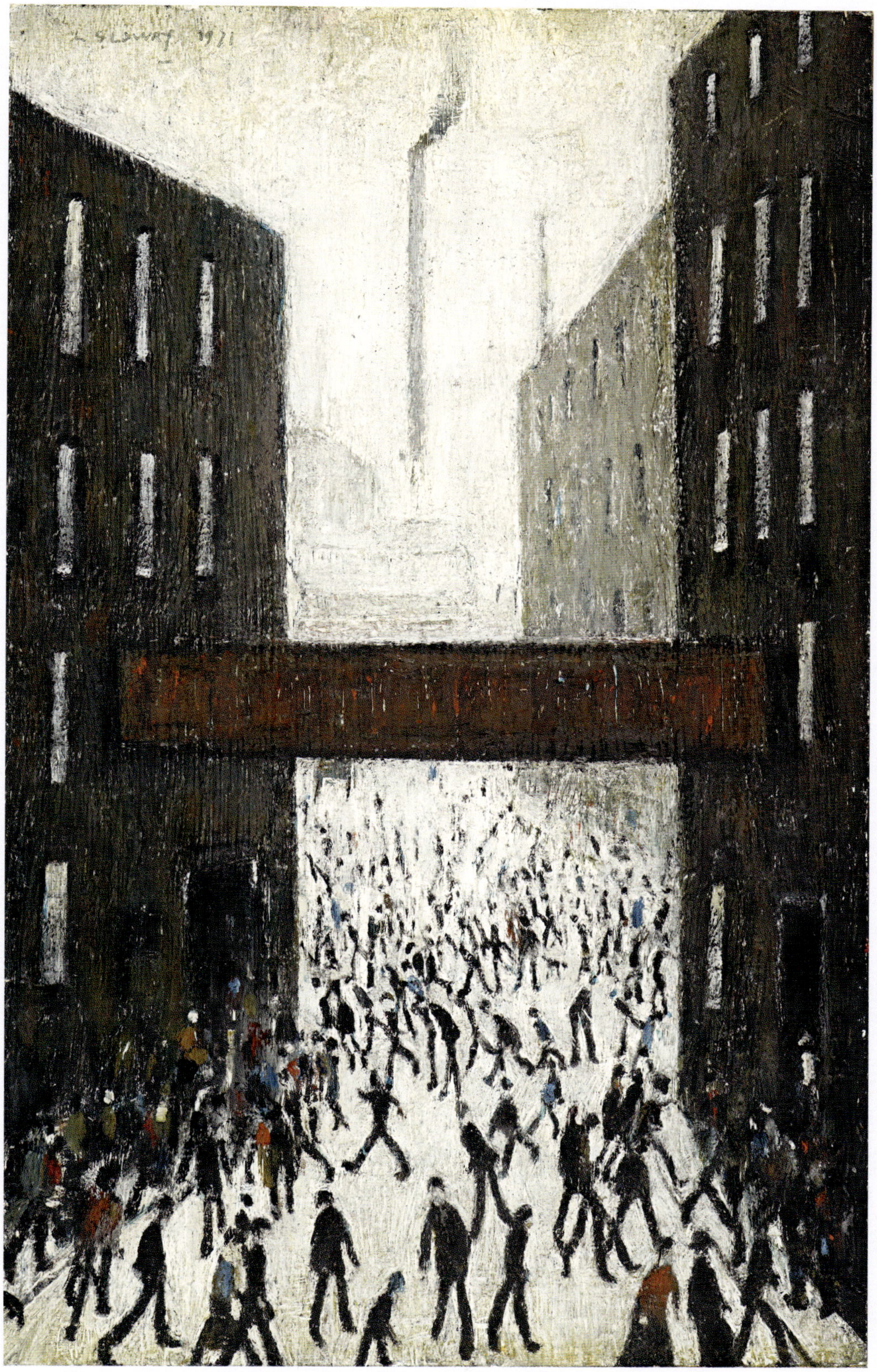

Mill Scene, 1971, oil on panel, 50.5 × 39 cm.

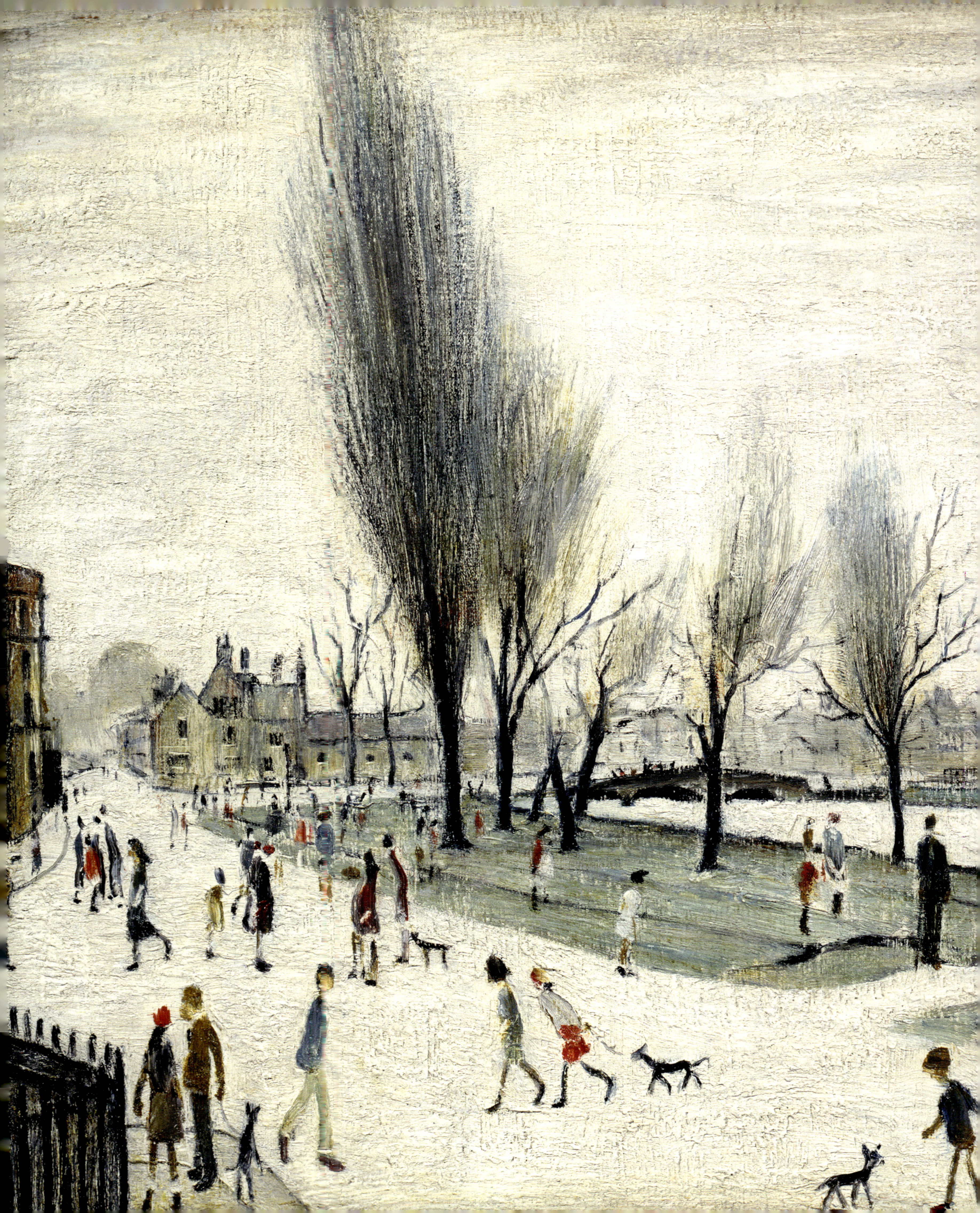

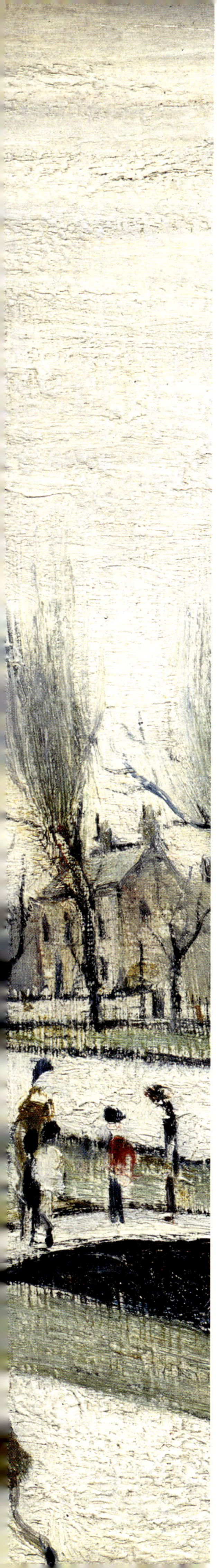

Detail of *Bourton-on-the-Water*, (p.295).

CHAPTER 15

EPILOGUE

The only reality is fiction.

Carlos Fuentes

On Thursday 12 February, 1976 Lowry was expecting an evening visit from his friend Philip Robertson to his Mottram-in-Longdendale house and had a bad fall, leaving him conscious but helpless. Rescued by Robertson's arrival and his housekeeper, Lowry became a reluctant patient in Glossop Hospital where he died, aged 87, on 23 February, 1976 of pneumonia after a stroke.

His funeral, which he had frequently stated would be attended by only two people, attracted a crowd of two hundred and nine months after his death the Royal Academy drew substantial queues to his retrospective; an exhibition whose numerical success was equalled, up to that time, only by the Turner show two years earlier. The Probate value of his Estate was £298,459, about £8 million at the time of publication of this book; which is still a relatively modest amount for an artist whose best paintings now sell for millions of pounds.

The deathbeds of the great have always had a deep fascination for the general public as for the families and friends of the deceased and Shelley Rohde has supplied useful information about Lowry's last visitors and their conversations which could as well be true as *ben trovato*.

Having known Lowry over several years and his work for nearly six decades I have an understandable curiosity about his departure. I have long trusted in the great Mexican novelist and essayist Carlos Fuentes's dictum about reality and fiction, which merely states that novelists can often be as, if not more, truthful and reliable than historians or biographers. The finest account of the beginning of the end of L. S. Lowry was written by Paul Driver who, like me, spent his formative years in Manchester and Salford and published this vivid account of Lowry's fall in his 1996 book *Manchester Pieces*.[1] Because of his empathy with his subject the chapter is in its entirety:

From *Manchester Pieces* by Paul Driver

Chastity

final monologue of an old painter

There is more to life than exams.

– L.S. Lowry

Yet he had what might least be expected of such a man, a talent for life.

– Frank Kermode in *The Listener*

WAIT!

I'm coming, Mr Morris! DON'T GO! Oh Mr Morris.

Oh! Oh!

It's no use! Not a bit.

Mr Morris! Come back, don't go, I've slipped!

Biscuits!

No use at all. Well, I'm stuck here. Little Laurie's done for now.

*

Slept so badly last night.

That fiendish dream, I still feel it. About dealers. Horrible. Couldn't paint it. Or could I? A little pencil sketch . . . some sharks? No. Can't do any of that at all now. It's over. This time really over.

Damn this house! So cold and damp. I just can't move me flippin' knees. And these ridiculous biscuits dropping through the letter box. Kit-Kats!

Well, that's just like Mr Morris, the old rogue.

If only Mr Shaw had stayed a little longer. He had to go home to his family and his tea, of course.

Where's *my* family? No one. Never. My mother died.

Oh mother!

Nobody. Just a garden fence around me. And what a garden! Never been out *there*!

Never liked this house. Cold, damp, ugly. Rooms too small. Station two miles away, taxi three. If I fling m'pocket-book at the door it'll make a bit of noise. And this mucky plate.

No use. Aren't folk at the bus-stop?

ANYONE THERE?

No use. Let's try the leather slippers.

ANY-one there?

It's what I always say. The unmarried man lives like a king but dies like a dog. Oh why won't me knees budge? M'legs are like jelly.

Mother, poor old mother, poor little Laurie needs you. A heap on the floor, it's come to that. A big clumsy good-for-nothing heap on the hall floor. And your clocks ticking away, mother, after all these years. Your Tompion.

Mother.

Why did you have to die so soon, before it started? The success, mother. I'm famous. I'm an RA. They've put me on a postage stamp. Twice refused a knighthood, what do you say to that? Could have been a Companion of Honour!

But I went on being a tramp. Well, you'd gone.

If only I could shift meself to that telephone. A few feet and I could be flat on m'back where I'd want to be, on the old armchair with me feet in the fire.

Damn these clocks.

Tick, tick, tick, tick. Stop!

I'm fed up with it all. I'm just SICK of it all!

*

Uh?

How I could have nodded off in this fix? At least I didn't have that dream again. But why've I just dreamt of old Bernard Taylor?

Bernard Taylor. Bernard Taylor. Good old *Manchester Guardian*. Good to me. He was right of course. No one's ever been righter. My industrial scenes were too dark, that was the problem. You couldn't see the figures against the background. I laid on all the flake-white just to show him, but he was quite right.

Who else has caught the milky Manchester light, sir? Who has caught the colour of the smog? The damp-charged afternoon? The mean streets? Not Valette. Lowry.

Yes, I've put the industrial scene on the map.

I did my experiment. Six years waiting to see how the white went down. Like making whisky! And how it *did*, a lovely creamy grey-white. Perfect! Even me father thought that was interesting. Paintings won't be at their best till after I'm dead! Well, they won't have to wait long now!

In Pendlebury they laughed at me for thirty years . . .

That posh lady who drove up to m'door here and sent her lackey asking me for a painting, only it had to be one of me *good* ones.

I only do bad ones, I said. Ha, ha!

But I drew the life for twelve years. That's the foundation of it all.

Matchstick men! Hmph! Not matchstick figures, my word sir! They're a *shorthand*. Do they think I couldn't do realistic figures perfectly well if I wanted to? They're not caricatures! People look like that. I've set eyes on them all.

They're figures in motion. Scurrying about. Not so easy.

But I'm stuck here. Where's m'wallet, I'll try flingin' that.

Dreadful companions, clocks!

*

Oh my God, my God! I'm fed up with this. *Fed. Up.*

I'm dying. Won't be long now, really won't, this time.

Why doesn't anyone come? I've so many friends. Or do I mean so few?

Never had a girl, that's all passed me by.

Must remember to tip out those *Playboy* magazines.

And those drawings of Ann. Very peculiar. Why do I do them? Must be going potty.

Nothing's ever *happened* to me. Not till now at any rate.

Shouldn't have built a life round parents. They die. Station Road, Chorley Road, here, retirement. Had a life to get through and I've got through it. Bothering nobody.

Bothering everybody! Bit of an old pest, I suppose. An *inconvenient* object. Yes. Not a very nice man. Well, humanity's the lowest form of animal life, I always say. I'm dying like a dog.

S'pose I could try for one of these biscuits.

*

No one. NOBODY.

Where *are* they? I get a telephone against my will and I can't even get to it. A nice surprise Mrs Swindles'll have in the morning!

What a life it's been! What a plod! The loneliness. Life.

What are we *doing* it for?

I don't blame rent collection. Plodding the streets, visiting the tenants, all the funny people, I got them into pictures sooner or later, nothing wasted.

What did I feel for them?

Loved them for the shapes they made. Loved their caps and shawls and clogs and bowler hats.

Love the pattern the crowd makes when there's been an accident or something. No sentiment in my pictures, sir!

People are like automatons. You watch them eating or running for a bus, it's so funny! They think they can do as they please. But they can't. They're not free, no one is. No more am I.

Pinned to the floorboards! Walking-sticks and trilbies for company. Toppled canvasses. Chocolate biscuits.

Well I may as well have one. Bit of comfort. As good as religion. Crinkly silver foil lying on the floor like my life.

Never had time for sentimentality.

They've all gone away from me. Maud, Kathleen, Doreen, Pat, Carol Ann. They never understood. Only Ann, fascinating Ann, always faithful Ann. With the gorgeous black stuff round the eyes.

And *she* doesn't even exist. But *I've* cut off from them. Always kept apart, kept my friends apart. Always covering up.

Had to! Those Royal Academy people would have been delighted. 'He's just a Sunday painter, we always knew!' They all wanted to write me off. A primitive. But I'm not, y'know! I use simple materials but I'm not a simple man.

Manchester Academy people were even worse! Now they come knocking at me door. But Mr Rayner's dying, he blurted it right out this afternoon! Mr Shaw didn't know what to say and I said nothing.

I'm demising too.

*

Tick, tick, tick. Mother speaking in all these clocks telling different times.

Never could have married.

Couldn't leave you, bedfast all those years. You had me fast, mother! And I nearly went out of my mind. I couldn't go with anyone after all that. All I could do was paint. Painting got me through. Wonderful way of getting rid of the time.

Now it's me who's floorfast!

Had to stick to that vision. I'd seen all that beauty! I'd not have seen it if I hadn't been lonely.

Twenty years painting the streets of Salford. Wandering streets, day in, day out, like one of the queer folk m'self.

But I loved some of those places almost better than anywhere. The old terrace steps. The footbridge in Ancoats.

You never understood, mother. You'd never even look through your bedroom curtains.

I painted the yachts you said you'd like me to. Lytham St Anne's. And I painted your bedroom, your deathbed. So silent.

Trapped in your world for ever, because of the beauty of the industrial scene, which you wouldn t even look at.

The embarrassment of it all, mother!

*

Dear me, a mouse! And another. My housemates! Come and have a bit of chocolate! Must have been nesting in that old *Financial Times*.

Champion little mice. Quite tame, aren't you? Great breeders. Perhaps you like the smell of old paint?

You've all been nibblin' this stair carpet for years, nothing left of it.

Come and nibble at me, Mr Mouse, I feel like a lump of old cheese.

I could do with just a sip of nice cold tomato soup.

That would be a comfort.

Must be eight now, at least. Pity these clocks are all wrong. Even m'watch has stopped. May as well chuck it at the door.

ANYONE THERE?

No one's coming.

Fiendish February weather. They've all hurried home for their teas. Well, what else is there?

And I've scared the mice off too.

This is *not* what the Iron Duke meant by 'masterly inactivity'.

Can't even put the music on to while away the hours.

*

How did I ever do it, any of it?

Couldn't do it now. It's all over. Not even a tiny sketch now. Too much like hard work. Even the thought of starting makes me feel sick.

Rum business, this art.

Folk always coming here wanting something from me, something for nothing. 'Have you a drawing? Give an opinion on this! Will you sign that?' Nobody asked me to paint, and now everybody's asking me to. And always more industrial landscapes. Well, I've no time for them.

I prefer the solitary figures, they go deeper. Even if no one else thinks so. Excepting the Marshalls of course. And Mr Bloom. But he sold his in the end.

Change my will? Leave my paintings to rot in a museum cellar? Not on your life!

But dear me, I've enjoyed fiddling with m'pencil in my time. Fiddled away thousands of hours. Rubbing with me fingers, night after night, nudging the line, getting the tension in it. With a drawing you can show the tension between people. Painting's different.

Never could paint shadows. So I let it be artificial. Won't use a medium or a glaze.

Never knew what I was going to do with the empty canvas. Knew I'd get something on it by the end of the day, or the night more like. Things just cropped up. Like a dream. A vision.

Getting the balance right, I'm good at that, dear me yes. *Was* good at it. The composition. That's my forte.

Marvellous way of passing the time! Middle of the night, the world's absolutely quiet, *Lucia* on the gramophone, same aria over and over, crackle crackle scratch. I love monotony as well as music.

Not *this* monotony.

Anyone THERE?

Nobody comes when I want them. Only the wind off Saddleworth Moor. Damn that draught!

*

The sun never shines in my pictures. And no one's cheerful. They're all too busy fighting the battle of life. Never happy unless they're drunk. *Father Going Home!*

I've never touched a drop. Didn't dare. Saw what it could do.

All grotesque, my characters – misfits, cripples. Split my sides laughing at them.

But I *do* feel sorry for them. They've had a shock from life. It was too much for them. Whatever they tried to do it baffled them.

And what do I know about warmth and love? *Sex?*

I know about cripples and wasteland and empty houses. Bare boards. Cobwebs. Biscuit wrappers!

People think I'm a cold fish.

But I got the humour in! *The Same Girl Coming Back. Figure of a Girl with the Least Effort.*

All my characters are really me, my mood.

Me the man with red eyes, the man lying on the wall in summer. Me the lost ones on the park bench, the woman with the beard, the cripple on the trolley, the hump-backed girl. Me Ann even.

Me the dog with five legs. Me the dark lonely churches and collieries and houses and ships. All me. My ghosts.

I couldn't be any other way. I couldn't go away from mother and father. Couldn't be sociable. What if I didn't have the talent! I had to find it. I'm a very simple man.

But I'd seen all that beauty of dereliction.

*

A knock? Or am I dreaming? I'm dozing.

Oh I'm going to die.

Why, mother, have I never had the experience? The common experience of humanity!

I've always done just what I wanted to do.

So many nevers! Never been abroad. Never been in a plane. Never driven a car. Never smoked. Never taken *drugs*, my goodness. Not like the young people these days!

But Rossetti took his chloral!

Rossetti's dream women. Proserpine. *His* Ann. Wonderful artist! And they say he couldn't draw!

For me the kissing never began and now I'm utterly clapped out.

There *is* someone out there.

Probably a Moors Murderer!

No. I'm alone in this cold world. With cold macs and trilbies and packing cases. And Mr and Mrs Mouse.

I've lived too long.

It can't all be waste, *can* it? Suffering wherever you turn. I don't understand a thing!

Who'll tell me what it's all about?

There *must* be something after.

*

The cold waves, coming in towards you, nearer and nearer. What if they didn't stop one day but just kept on coming? That *would* be the end of it all.

I must go back to Sunderland and see the sea.

So vast. Generally I'll put nothing on the sea when I paint it. A tiny boat, if I must.

I'll take a taxi. Mrs Marshall will be good to me. Lots and lots of cream and nuts for Little Laurie.

I'm not a bad old chap. Everyone takes me in.

*

Uh?

What's that!

Another dream. Nasty. Stockport viaduct, train half off the side, shrieks . . . sharks . . . monsters . . . people falling into the air . . .

Last of my accident scenes!

Legs are stone cold. Can't shift at all.

This won't do, sir, won't do at all!

Seven walking-sticks in the stand and couldn't walk to save his life! Man Lying on the Floor, that's my story sir, and I'm sticking to it. Someone should do a painting of *me*. House on the Moor. They'd better hurry!

Lonely grey stone house and big round hills like titties. Moors Murderers lurking in the hills. Put in a plume of chimney smoke, if you must.

Lovely Ann inside the house with the black stuff round her big eyes and her hair tied up tight and lots of lipstick on her little red lips.

Lovely Ann in the front bedroom with her long red nails and a great big bow tight tight round her neck. Lovely Ann's in a straitjacket.

Lovely Ann's growing a beard . . .

Oh mother, I'm running out of time!

I don't want to die!

Drifted about for a lifetime and now I'm in a straitjacket. I'm practically in my coffin.

Mother! Since you died the world's been very much too big for me.

Is that too silly sentimental?

*

Come here Mr Mouse, I'll tell you something. I can't *stand* Rembrandt. Loathe him! Too big. Can't get hold of him. He's like life! Frightening. Now take Boudin's beach scenes. Small-scale, but I can get hold of *him*.

What is this greatness anyway? Will *I* live?

What about *my* beach scenes? My fairgrounds. My best work maybe? *Daisy Nook*. Mottram. Peel Park. Piccadilly Gardens. Panoramas. *Bargoed*. *Ebbw Vale*. Sheer joy of space.

Will it all last?

I'm waiting . . .

It must be long past nine. Past ten.

Space, space, space, give me space! That's what it's all about! Pure space. *Daisy Nook*. Space of the imagination. Not the grotesques.

Space that *isn't* me. *Not* my ghosts.

Space opening out.

Light.

Uh?

What's that knocking?

Who's there? Wait! WAIT!

I'm on the FLOOR!

It's you!

Of course, Thursday night! But you don't sound like yourself, Mr Robertson. You don't have a key?

What took you so long anyway?

Well, thank God you've come!

Now I can rest easy.

I believe that Driver's ironic, cool detachment has delivered an affectionate re-creation, a verbal portrait, a character sketch in miniature of a larger than life character, essentially true to the man and artist I knew. That Lowry was, by all conventional standards, an odd man is self-evident. But so were William Blake and Stanley Spencer and their very different styles of painting and their reputations have burgeoned. So it is with Lowry, like Blake and Spencer again, a unique English eccentric whose popularity should not obscure or deny his genius.

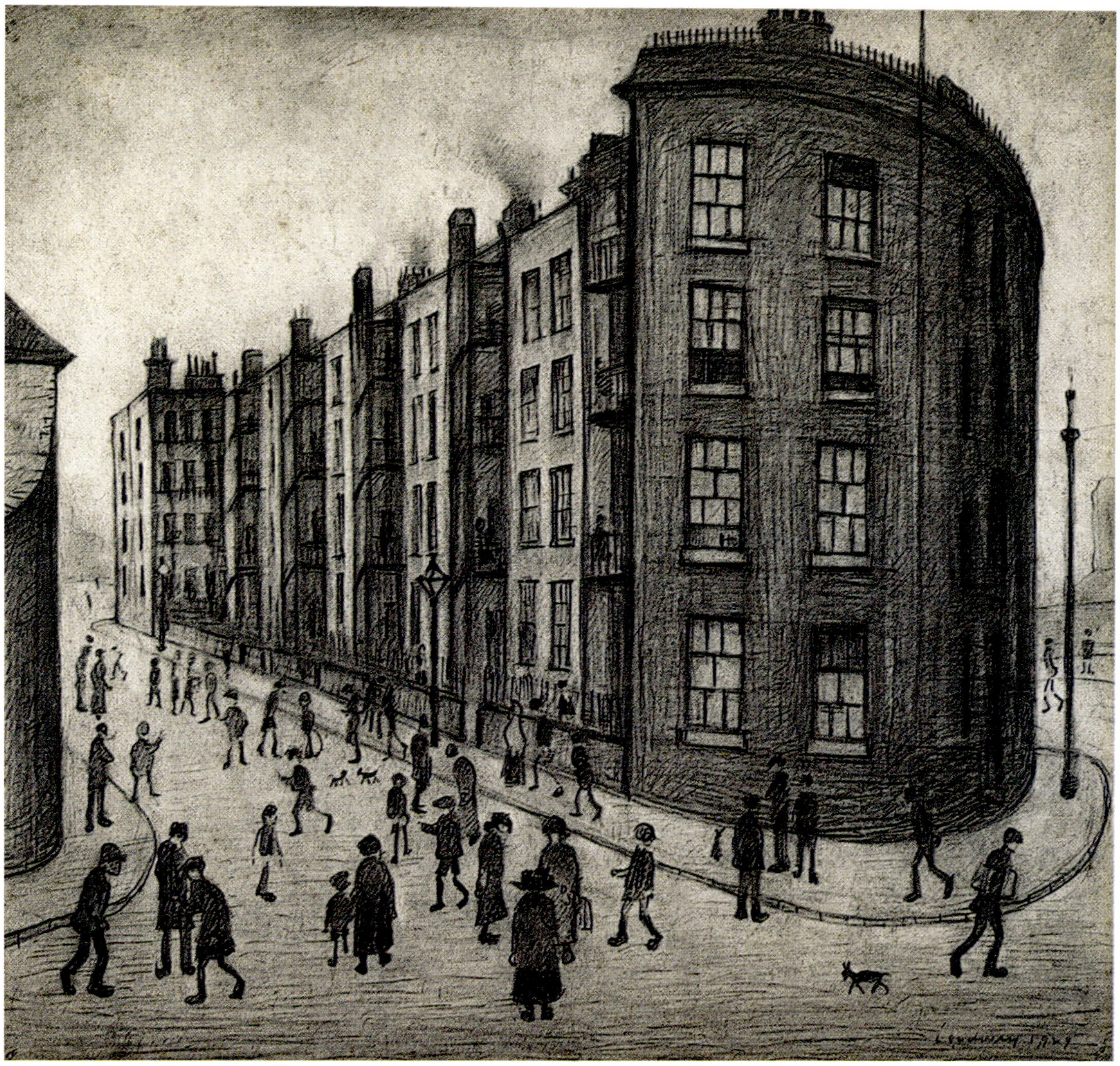

Dwellings, Ordsall Lane, Salford (also called *Oldfield Road Dwellings*), 1927, pencil on paper, 41.2 × 43.2 cm., (see oil painting on p.105).

NOTES

CHAPTER ONE: LOWRY IN PERSON

1. An art documentary film made by John Read in 1957 entitled 'L. S. Lowry'. There is an archive copy of this film at the Lowry in Salford.
2. Stanley Houghton (1881–1913), the best playwright of the so-called Manchester School of Writers had his major success with the social realist drama *Hindle Wakes*, first performed in 1912 and a mainstay repertory play thereafter for most of the twentieth century. It deals with the "elicit romance" between a poor mill girl and the caddish son of the mill owner and its aftermath when the mill girl proves more honourable and stronger in character than the mill owner and his family.

CHAPTER TWO: LOWRY IN PERSPECTIVE

1. John Rothenstein, *Modern English Painters*, Volume 2, Arrow Books, 1962, page 35.
2. John Rothenstein, *op. cit.*, page 39.
3. John Rothenstein, *op. cit.*, pages 40–41.
4. Walter Greenwood, *Love on the Dole*, Vintage Classics, page 11.
5. Howard Jacobson in a public debate on Lowry at Queen Elizabeth Hall, London, on February 1st 2009.
6. Walter Greenwood, *op. cit.*, page 12.
7. Walter Greenwood, *op. cit.*, page 20.
8. Walter Greenwood, *op. cit.*
9. Walter Greenwood, *op. cit.*, page 24.
10. Walter Greenwood, *op. cit.*, pages 53–54.
11. Walter Greenwood, *op. cit.*, page 86.
12. Terry Eagleton, *The Gatekeeper*, Penguin, 2001, pages 48–49.
13. Terry Eagleton, *op.cit.*, page 54.
14. Terry Eagleton, *op. cit.*, page 46.
15. Terry Eagleton, *op.cit.*, page 54.
16. Shelley Rohde, *A Private View of L. S. Lowry*, Collins, London, pages 178–179.
17. Martin Esslin, *The Theatre of the Absurd*, 3rd Edition, Methuen, 2006.
18. Luigi Pirandello, *Six Characters in Search of an Author and other plays*, translated and edited by Mark Muza, Penguin Books, 1995, page 29.
19. Luigi Pirandello, *op. cit.*
20. Luigi Pirandello, *op. cit.*

CHAPTER THREE: BEGINNINGS

1. Epigraph, Howard Jacobson, L. S. Lowry lecture, Salford, 25 March, 2007.
2. Rohde, *op. cit.*, pages 65–66.
3. Rohde, *op. cit.*, pages 72–73.
4. Cécilia Lyon, *Adolphe Valette*, Lyon, Phillimore & Co Ltd, Chichester, 2006.
5. Cécilia Lyon, *op. cit.*, pages 82–85.
6. Cécilia Lyon, *op. cit.*, pages 92–93.
7. Cécilia Lyon, *op. cit.*, page 116.
8. Cécilia Lyon, *op. cit.*, page 116.
9. Rohde, *op. cit.*, page 128.
10. Rohde, *op. cit.*, page 142.

CHAPTER FOUR: THE ROAD TO SUCCESS

1. L. S. Lowry in conversation with Maurice Collis in *The Discovery of Lowry*, Alex Reid and Lefevre Ltd, London, 1951.
2. Collis, *op. cit.*, page 18.
3. Rothenstein, *op. cit.*, page 38.
4. Collis, *op. cit.*, page 20.
5. Rothenstein, *op. cit.*, page 23.
6. Collis, *op. cit.*
7. Rhode, *op. cit.*, page 99.
8. Rhode, *op. cit.*, page 101–102.
9. *The Manchester Guardian*, 31st October 1921.
10. Harold Timperley, *A Cotswold Book*, Jonathan Cape, 1931.
11. Rhode, *op. cit.*, page 116.
12. Rhode, *op. cit.*, page 124.
13. Berger, *op. cit.*, page 100.
14. George Orwell, *The Road to Wigan Pier*, Victor Gollancz, 1937, quoted in Berger, *op. cit.*, p 100.

CHAPTER FIVE: LOWRY ESTABLISHED

1. Andrew Lambirth, Lambirth and Kalman, *op. cit.*, page 9.
2. Rohde, *op. cit.*, page 140.
3. Rohde, *op. cit.*, page 139.
4. Rohde, *op. cit.*, page 140.
5. Judy Sandling and Mike Leber, *Lowry's City: A Painter and his Locale*, Lowry Press, Salford, 2000.
6. Julian Spalding, *L. S. Lowry*, Phaidon. 1979, page 3.
7. L. S. Lowry, quoted in *Mr Lowry at Home*, published by Manchester City Art Galleries, (no date).
8. Rohde, *op. cit.*, page 142.
9. Rohde, *op. cit.*, page 144.
10. Kalman/Lambirth, *op. cit.*, page 76.
11. Kalman/Lambirth, *op. cit.*, page 93.
12. Rohde, *op. cit.*, page 224.
13. Rohde, *op. cit.*, page 226.

CHAPTER SIX: ENTER MONTY BLOOM

1. Epigraph, Julian Spalding, *op. cit.*, page 13.
2. Rohde, *op. cit.*, page 233.
3. Lambirth/Kalman, *op. cit.*, page 114.
4. Rohde, *op. cit.*, page 234.
5. Lambirth/Kalman, *op. cit.*, page 41.
6. Rohde, *op. cit.*, pages 239.
7. Rohde, *op. cit.*, page 240.
8. Rohde, *op. cit.*, page 240–1.
9. Rohde, *op. cit.*, page 240.
10. Rohde, *op. cit.*, page 241.
11. Rohde, *op. cit.*, pages 240–1.
12. Rohde, *op. cit.*, page 244.
13. Rohde, *op. cit.*, page 245.
14. Rohde, *op. cit.*, page 244–5.
15. Rohde, *op. cit.*, page 246.
16. Rohde, *op. cit.*, page 246.
17. Rohde, *op. cit.*, pages 246–7.
18. Rohde, *op. cit.*, page 252.
19. Lambirth/Kalman, *op. cit.*, page 68.
20. Rohde, *op. cit.*, page 241–2.
21. Lambirth/Kalman, *op. cit.*, page 132.

CHAPTER SEVEN: AN INTERLUDE: LOWRY AND DAVID CARR

1. Epigraph: David Carr, from a letter to his mother quoted in Bryan Robertson and Ronald Alley's *David Carr: The Discovery of an Artist*, Quartet Books, 1987.
2. Rohde, *op. cit.*, pp 210–11.
3. Gwynneth Reynolds and Diana Grace, *Benton End Remembered*, Unicorn Press, 2002.
4. Rohde, *op. cit.*, pages 210–11.
5. Robertson and Alley, *op. cit.*, page 9.
6. Robertson and Alley, *op. cit.*, page 25.
7. Robertson and Alley, *op. cit.*, page 29.
8. Rohde, *op. cit.*, page 232–3.

CHAPTER EIGHT: LOWRY AND CROWDS

1. Epigraph, Alberto Moravia, *The Conformist*. Two of the thoughts of Marcello Clerici the young Fascist who is the principal protagonist of Alberto Moravia's novel about Italian Fascism in the 1930s and 1940s. *The Conformist* published by Steerforth Press, Hanover, New Hampshire, in a translation by Tami Calliope 1999. The Italian edition was first published in 1951 by Bompiani. The first quotation is on pages 74–75, the second on pages 85–86.
2. Alberto Moravia, *The Conformist*.
3. Rohde, *op. cit.*, pages 62–63.
4. Howard Jacobson, Lowry lecture at Salford, 25 March, 2007.
5. Sir Kenneth Clark, Essay *A Tribute to L. S. Lowry*. From the catalogue of an exhibition at The Monk's Hall Gallery, Eccles, 1964.
6. David Riesman, Nathan Glazer and Reuel Denney, *The Conformist*, Yale University Press, 2001, page XXVIII.
7. David Riesman, Nathan Glazer and Reuel Denney, *op. cit.*, page 126.
8. Elias Canetti, *Crowds and Power*, translated by Carol Stewart. First published in England 1962 by Victor Gollancz. This extract taken from the American edition published by Farrar, Straus and Giroux, New York. Pages 171–2.
9. Elias Canetti, *op. cit.*, page 16.
10. Elias Canetti, *op. cit.*, pages 15–16.
11. Elias Canetti, *op. cit.*, page 19.
12. Journal of the Royal Society of Medicine. Article on *The Fever Van* by L. S. Lowry by J. H. Sarginson and Lucy Guppy. Issue April 2003.
13. John Berger, *Lowry and the Industrial North*. First published in *New Society* in 1966 and reprinted in *About Looking*, Bloomsbury, 2009, pages 97–98.
14. John Berger, *op. cit.*, page 99.
15. David Riesman, Nathan Glazer and Reuel Denney, *op. cit.*, page 146.
16. John Berger, *op. cit.*
17. Correspondence in May 2009 from Edwin Mullins to the author.
18. Correspondence in May 2009 from Edwin Mullins to the author.

CHAPTER NINE: LOWRY AND ABROAD

1. Epigraph, Howard Jacobson, from text of Howard Jacobson's Lowry Lecture, Salford, 25 March, 2007.
2. Conversation with L.S. Lowry and Edwin Mullins in the *Sunday Telegraph* in 1966.

CHAPTER TEN: LOWRY'S TECHNIQUE

1. Shakespeare, Chorus, Act 5 of *Henry V*.
2. Edwin Bowes, *Painting and Lowry. Coming from the Mill: A Reconstruction*.
3. Mervyn Levy, *The Paintings of Lowry*, quoted in Bowes, *op. cit.*, page 11.
4. Kalman/Lambirth, *op. cit.*, page 113.

CHAPTER ELEVEN: LOWRY AND THE SEA

1. L. S. Lowry, from an interview with the author in September 1966.
2. Kalman/Lambirth, *op. cit.*, pages 144–145.

CHAPTER TWELVE: LOWRY AND LANDSCAPE

1. Epigraph, L. S. Lowry, from an interview with Hugh Maitland, quoted in Sandling and Leber, *op. cit.*, page 60.
2. Howard, *op. cit.*, page 216.
3. Sandling and Leber, *op. cit.*
4. Sandling and Leber, *op. cit.*
5. Kalman/Lambirth, *op. cit.*

CHAPTER THIRTEEN: LOWRY AND WOMEN

1. A quotation from the 1956 Granada TV programme about Lowry made by Leslie Woodhead.
2. Sandling and Leber, *op. cit.*
3. Edwin Mullins interview with L.S. Lowry for the *Sunday Telegraph*, 1966.
4. Sieja, Doreen, *The Lowry I Knew*, pages 19–20.
5. Sieja, *ibid.*, pages 27–28.
6. Sieja, *ibid.*, pages 73–74.
7. Shelley Rohde, *L. S. Lowry: A Life*, Haus Books, London, 2007, page 149.
8. Rohde, *op. cit.*, page 171.
9. Rohde, *op. cit.*, page 179.
10. Rohde, *op. cit.*, page 179.
11. Rohde, *op. cit.*, pages 188–9.
12. Rohde, *op. cit.*, page 190.
13. Rohde, *op. cit.*, page 194.
14. Rohde, *op. cit.*, page 196.
15. From *Petite Anatomie de l'inconscient physique ou l'Anatomie de l'Image*, translated by Sue Rose, quoted in *Surrealism: Desire Unbound*, edited by Jennifer Mundy, Tate Publishing, London, 2001. [Reproduced as Fig. 159 *Store in a Cool Place* 1958. Source is page 167 of the Tate Surrealism Catalogue of 2001. The work is apparently owned by Ubu Gallery, New York and Gallerie Berinson, Berlin]
16. *British Vision: Observation and Imagination in British Art 1750 to 1950*, mounted in Ghent in 2007/8 published by Mercator Fonds, page 169.
17. Rohde, *op. cit.*
18. Brill, A. A., *Lectures on Psychoanalytic Psychiatry*, John Lehmann, London, 1948, pages 53, 79, 98.

CHAPTER FOURTEEN: LOWRY AND ASPERGER'S SYNDROME

1. Fitzgerald, *op. cit.*, page 215.
2. Fitzgerald, *op. cit.*, page 15.
3. Fitzgerald, *op. cit.*, page 19.
4. Rohde, revised edition of 2007, pages 236–237.
5. Before turning to art history I was a publisher and, from 1971 to 1984 was head of Secker & Warburg which published all of Orwell's work as well as Bernard Crick's pioneering – and still the best available – biography of Orwell. Those who require further details concerning Sonia Orwell should read the admirable brief biography of her, *The Girl from the Fiction Department: A Portrait of Sonia Orwell* by Hilary Spurling, Hamish Hamilton, London, 2002.
6. Tony Attwood, *The Complete Guide to Asperger's Syndrome*, Jessica Kingsley Publishers, London and Philadelphia, 2008, page 348.
7. *ibid.*, page 348.
8. *ibid.*, page 11.
9. *ibid.*, page 13.
10. *ibid.*, page 284.
11. *ibid.*, page 285.
12. *ibid.*, page 284.
13. Tilly Marshall, *Life with Lowry*, Hutchinson, London, 1981.
14. Rohde, *op. cit.*, page 237.
15. Rohde, *op. cit.*, page 239.

EPILOGUE

1. Paul Driver, *Manchester Pieces*, Picador, 1996, pages 187–198.

BIBLIOGRAPHY

Alley, Ronald and Robertson, Bryan, *David Carr: The Discovery of an Artist*, Quartet Books 1987.

Andrews, Allen, *The Life of L. S. Lowry*, Jupiter Books (London) Ltd, 1977.

Attwood, Tony, *The Complete Guide to Asperger's Syndrome*, Jessica Kingsley Publishers, 2007.

Barber, Noel, Lowry chapter from *Conversations with Painters,* Collins, 1964.

Berger, John, *About Looking,* Bloomsbury Publishing, 2009.

Bowes, Edwin, *Painting a Lowry: Coming from the Mill, a Reconstruction*, The Lowry Press, 2002.

Brill, A. A., *Lectures on Psychoanalytic Psychiatry*, John Lehmann, 1948.

Canetti, Elias, *Crowds and Power*, translated by Carol Stewart, Victor Gollancz, 1962.

Collis, Maurice, 'The Discovery of L. S. Lowry', Alex Reid and Lefevre Ltd, 1951.

Donn, Henry, *The Illustrated Limited Editions of L. S. Lowry*, This book bears neither a date nor a publisher's imprint and was presumably printed and published by the author. As no other comparable work exists it has perforce to serve as a catalogue raisonnée of Lowry's graphic output. Given the amount of fraudulent advertising in the newspaper colour magazines in the 1960s and 1970s and the number of ill-informed, innocent citizens who parted with their money for what were advertised as 'genuine original artist's prints numbered and signed by the artist' people should recall the immortal warning *caveat emptor:* these so-called 'prints' were in fact mere commercially produced *reproductions* which had never been near an etching press or a proper lithographic stone. Anyone who is offered a 'genuine Lowry print' should keep his wallet firmly closed and seek advice from a reputable dealer or auctioneer.

Eagleton, Terry, *The Gatekeeper: A Memoir* Penguin, 2001.

Fitzgerald, Michael, *The Genius of Artistic Creativity: Asperger's Syndrome and the Arts*, Jessica Kingsley Publishers, 2005.

Greenwood, Walter, *Love on the Dole*, Vintage, 1993.

Kalman, Andras and Lambirth, Andrew, *L. S. Lowry: Conversation Pieces,* Chaucer Press, 2003.

Howard, Michael, *Lowry: A Visionary Artist*, Lowry Press, 2000.

Lambirth, Andrew, *The Loneliness of Lowry*. This is the catalogue of the Lowry exhibition at the Abbott Hall Art Gallery, Kendal in 2010 for which Lambirth has written an admirable introduction.

Leber, Michael and Sandling, Judith, *L. S. Lowry*, Phaidon Press, 1987. This book was published in the year of Lowry's centenary and contains Edwin Mullins's acute appreciation of the artist originally written for the *Sunday Telegraph*, 1965.

Levy, Mervyn, *The Drawings of L. S. Lowry, Public and Private*, Jupiter Books, 1976.

Levy, Mervyn, *L. S. Lowry R.A. 1887–1976*. Levy contributes the introductory essay on Lowry in the Catalogue of the Royal Academy posthumous retrospective tribute exhibition. Royal Academy Publications, 1976.

Lyon, Cécilia, *Adolphe Valette*, Phillimore & Co. Ltd., Chichester, 2006.

Malcolm, Janet, *Reading Chekhov: A Critical Journey*, Granta Books, 2001.

Marshall, Tilly, *Life with Lowry*, Hutchinson 1981.

Moravia, Alberto, *The Conformist,* translated by Tarni Calliope, Zoland Books, New Hampshire, U.S.A. 1991.

Mullins, Edwin, 'L. S. Lowry'. Being the introductory essay for the Catalogue of the Arts Council Lowry Retrospective Exhibition of 1966–7, shown at the Tate Gallery, London, Sunderland Art Gallery, City Art Gallery, Bristol and the Whitworth Art Gallery in Manchester.

Pirandello, Luigi, *Six Characters in Search of an Author and Other Plays*, translated by Mark Musa, Penguin 1995.

Read, John, 'Artist into Film', being an essay on the making of Read's BBC Television film about Lowry published in *The Studio*, volume CLV, No. 780 in March 1958, 'L. S. Lowry: an Unclassifiable Genius'.

Reynolds, Gwynneth and Grace, Diana (Editors), *Benton End Remembered: Cedric Morris, Arthur Lett-Haines and the East Anglian School of Painting and Drawing*, Unicorn Press, 2002.

Riesman, David and Glazer, Nathan and Denney, Reuel, *The Lonely Crowd*, Yale University Press, 2001.

Rohde, Shelley, *A Private View of L. S. Lowry*, Collins, 1979, revised and fully illustrated edition with title *L. S. Lowry: A Life*, Haus Books, 2007.

Rosenthal, T. G., article in *Studio International*, November, 1966.

Rosenthal, T. G., essay in *Daily Telegraph*, 4 March, 2000.

Rothenstein, John, *Modern British Painters,* two volumes, Arrow Books, 1962.

Sandling, Judith and Leber, Mike, *Lowry's City: A Painter and his Locale,* The Lowry Press, 2000.

Sieja, Doreen, *The Lowry I Knew,* Jupiter Books (London) Ltd, 1983.

Spalding, Julian, *Lowry*, Phaidon Press, 1979.

Timperley, H. W., *A Cotswold Book,* illustrated with drawings by L. S. Lowry, Jonathan Cape, 1931.

ACKNOWLEDGEMENTS

First and foremost I must state my gratitude to Carol Ann Lowry, not a relative, but surely the most devoted of the artist's champions and the guiding spirit of the Estate of L. S. Lowry. She was kind enough to allow me to write this book, was generous in her hospitality and a fount of information and above all refrained from authorial interference. Would that all artists' estates were so professional and objective.

Having, of late, lost much of the mobility and tenacity of youth, I am particularly indebted to Zelie Walker. She has a first class honours degree in art history, a budding and busy career at Christies's and also, for the last three years, was my research assistant and, with amazing and unfussy skill, regularly obtained and found for me the unobtainable and the unfindable. That she is my god-daughter makes her professional company all the more enjoyable.

Part of the account of my meetings with Lowry appeared in *The Daily Telegraph* of 4 March 2000 and I am particularly grateful to Paul Driver for allowing me to reproduce in toto his luminous essay *Chastity* as the epilogue to this book. I have read virtually everything written about Lowry and this imagined account both reads like the truth and is the best piece of prose about him.

My special thanks go to those who read the manuscript in draft and made many useful suggestions: Paul Driver, Andrew Lambirth, Edwin Mullins, Professor Frances Spalding CBE, and Zelie Walker.

Without the patient and invaluable provision of electronic archival material and free access to the store rooms of The Lowry in Salford the sheer mechanics of researching the book would have been impossible, for which I thank Claire Stewart, Curator of The Lowry.

Others who made my task both easier and more enjoyable include Dame Joan Bakewell, Nicola Bion, Dr Dora Black, Chris Bowler, David Brierley CBE, Dr Robert Carr, Rex Cowan, Melva Crowell, Jonathan Horwich, Linda Knights, Dr Samantha Lackey, Sandra Martin, Primrose Hill Books, David Scrace, Michael Simpson, Hugh and Amanda Tempest-Radford and the many staff members of galleries, dealers, museums and art libraries, without whose daily labours this, and the majority of art books, would never get written.

Lastly my thanks and love to my wife and children who saw me through a long period of serious illness without too much delay in the writing and prevented me from becoming a completely grumpy old man.

PICTURE CREDITS

The publisher would like to thank the following organizations below for permission to reproduce their material. Any errors or omissions are entirely unintentional and the publisher will, if informed, make amendments in future editions of this book.

Aberdeen Art Gallery & Museum: 248

Anthony Crickmay/V&A Images/Victoria and Albert Museum: 53

The Arts Council Collection/South Bank Centre: 127

Bridgeman Art Library/Birmingham Museum and Art Gallery: 22

Christies Images Ltd: 60, 73*t*, 75, 80*t*, 90, 120, 129, 151, 152, 175, 188*t*, 192t, 209, 222*t*, 226*b*, 229*b*, 230*b*, 232*t*, 234*t*, 240, 276, 287*b*, 296*t*

Collection: Christchurch Art Gallery Te Puna o Waiwhetu, New Zealand: 235*t*

Crane Kalman Gallery: 149*r*, 150, 169, 215, 219, 241, 250, 251, 252

© Crown copyright: UK Government Art Collection: 134

© The Estate of L. S. Lowry: 70, 72*t*, 72*b*, 78*b*, 79*tl*, 79*tr*, 79*br*, 81*b*, 95, 97, 113, 124*tl*, 125*b*, 130, 137, 147, 153*l*, 153*r*, 155*l*, 155*r*, 191*br*, 195*t*, 196, 202, 206, 213, 216, 223, 225*br*, 244, 247, 254, 256, 263, 264, 269, 273*l*, 273*r*, 282*tl*, 284*tl*, 284*tr*, 284*b*, 285*mr*, 285*br*, 286*b*, 289*br*, 291*t*, 291*bl*, 292*tl*, 292*tr*, 293*tr*, 294, 296*b*, 297

The Fitzwilliam Museum, University of Cambridge: 45, 82, 99

Richard Green Gallery, London: 33, 55, 76, 77, 80*b*, 110, 126, 166, 173, 179, 194, 205, 218, 230*t*, 233*tr*, 234*b*, 236*tl*, 236*tr*, 237*t*, 238, 243, 282*tr*, 283*tr*, 283*bl*, 295, 298

Guttenberg/The Estate of L. S. Lowry: 268

© The Lowry Collection, Salford: 6, 41, 52, 56, 58, 63, 67, 71, 73*b*, 74, 78*tl*, 78*tr*, 100, 101, 115, 121*b*, 122, 124*tr*, 124*b*, 125*t*, 125*ml*, 125*mr*, 154, 158, 181, 184, 191*tl*, 191*tr*, 191*bl*, 200*l*, 200*r*, 204, 211, 214, 224*t*, 224*b*, 225*t*, 225*bl*, 226*t*, 229*t*, 253, 259, 260, 272*l*, 272*m*, 272*r*, 275, 285*tl*, 285*tr*, 285*bl*, 288*t*, 292*mr*, 292*bl*, 292*br*, 293*tl*, 293*mr*, 293*bl*, 293*br*

Gordon Macgregor/The PCF, London: 98

Manchester Art Gallery: 39, 49, 64, 65*l*, 65*r*, 66*l*, 68, 81*t*, 94, 116, 118, 119, 121*t*, 182, 188*b*, 190*t*, 190*b*

Roy Miles Fine Paintings/Bridgeman Art Library: 87

The Museum of Modern Art, New York/Scala, Florence: 186

Nottingham Castle Museum and Art Gallery: 51

Courtesy of The Potteries Museum and Art Gallery, Stoke-on Trent: 245

Private Collection: 2, 34, 44, 66*r*, 79*bl*, 112, 144, 149*l*, 156, 162, 163, 201, 210, 212, 217, 220, 227*b*, 249, 262, 283*tl*, 283*br*, 286*t*, 288*b*

Private Collection/Photo © Christie's Images/ Bridgeman Art Library: 233*tl*, 235*b*, 282*b*, 289*bl*, 290

Private Collection/Courtesy of Halcyon Gallery, London: 10, 189, 228, 233*b*

Private Collection and courtesy of Sotheby's: 43, 46, 128, 171, 192*b*, 193, 222*b*, 236*b*, 237*b*, 291*br*

Going to the Match is owned by the Professional Footballers' Association with reproduction rights kindly granted by the Lowry Estate: 133

F. W. Schmidt/Private Collection: 114

State Art Collection, Art Gallery of Western Australia: 123

Tom Stuttard, © Salford City Council: 141

Sunderland Museum & Winter Gardens, Tyne & Wear Archives & Museums: 287*t*

Tate, London, 2010: 85, 102, 105, 108, 109, 146, 305

On loan to Tullie House Museum & Art Gallery, Carlisle: 266, 267

Ubu Gallery, New York & Galerie Berinson, Berlin: 271

Walker Art Gallery, Liverpool, National Museums of Liverpool: 177

Whitworth Art Gallery, University of Manchester: 227*t*, 231, 232*b*, 289*t*

York Museums Trust (York Art Gallery): 242

A SELECT LIST OF PAINTINGS BY L. S. LOWRY IN PUBLIC COLLECTIONS (August 2010)

Measurements are given in centimetres, height before width.

ABERDEEN

Aberdeen Art Gallery and Museums

Barges on a Canal, 1941, oil on board, 39.8 × 53.2

Derelict Building, 1941, oil on canvas, 43.3 × 53.2

BELFAST

Ulster Museum

Street Scene, 1947, oil on canvas, 51.2 × 41.2

BEXHILL

Bexhill Museum

Old Windmill, Bexhill, 1960, oil on canvas, 60 × 50

BIRMINGHAM

Birmingham Museum and Art Gallery

An Industrial Town, 1944, oil on canvas, 45.8 × 60.9

In the Park, 1940, oil on canvas (no dimensions available)

BRADFORD

Cartwright Hall Art Gallery

Industrial Landscape, Ashton-under-Lyne, 1952, oil on canvas, 115 × 152.5

CAMBRIDGE

The Fitzwilliam Museum

After the Wedding, 1939, oil on canvas, 53.3 × 43.5 cm

The Procession, 1938, oil on canvas, 46 × 61

Kettle's Yard (a department of the University of Cambridge)

Mountain Lake, 1943, oil on board, 21 × 38

CARDIFF

National Museum of Wales

Men Fishing, 1966, oil on board, 26 × 35

Old Salford Street Scene, 1922, oil on board, 23.8 × 12

The Doctor's Visit, (undated), oil on board, 37 × 47.7

COVENTRY

The Herbert Art Gallery

Ebbw Vale, 1960, oil on canvas, 114 × 152

DERBY

Derby Museums and Art Gallery

Houses near a Mill, 1941, oil on canvas, 50.8 × 40.7

EDINBURGH

Scottish National Gallery of Modern Art, Edinburgh

Canal and Factories, 1955, oil on canvas, 61 × 76.3

Royal Scottish Academy

Hawker's Cart, 1929, oil on board, 114.3 × 101.6

GLASGOW

Kelvingrove Art Gallery and Museum

A Village Square, 1943, oil on canvas, 45.7 × 61

Cranes and Ships – Glasgow Docks, 1947, oil on canvas, 46.3 × 56.5

River Scene, 1942, oil on plywood, 45.5 × 63.4

Seascape, 1950, oil on canvas, 63.5 × 76.2 cm

VE Day, 1945, oil on canvas, 76.6 × 102

HUDDERSFIELD

Huddersfield Art Gallery

Huddersfield, 1965, oil on canvas, 59.5 × 75

The Level Crossing, Burton-on-Trent, 1961, oil on canvas, 54 × 75

KIRKCALDY

Kirkcaldy Museum and Art Gallery

An Old Street, 1937, oil on panel, 51.5 × 35.5

LEAMINGTON SPA

Leamington Spa Art Gallery and Museum

The Mission Room, 1937, oil on board, 36.8 × 50.8

LEEDS

Leeds City Art Gallery

Industrial Landscape: The Canal, 1945, oil on canvas, 60.9 × 76.2

LEICESTER

Leicestershire Museums, Art Galleries & Records Service

Industrial Landscape: River Scene, 1950, oil on canvas, 110.2 × 148.3

LINCOLN

The Usher Gallery

Britain at Play, 1943, oil on Canvas, 45.7 × 61

Lincoln, 1950, oil on canvas, 19.5 × 23.5

View of a Town, 1936, oil on canvas, 40.6 × 50.8

LIVERPOOL

Walker Art Gallery

The Fever Van, 1935, oil on canvas, 43.1 × 53.3

LONDON

Arts Council Collection, Hayward Gallery

July, the Seaside, 1943, oil on canvas, 66.6 × 92.7

Seascape, 1965, oil on panel, 26.7 × 77.8

The Park, 1946, oil on canvas, 38 × 80

Woman Riding on a Tractor, 1961, oil on canvas, 35.5 × 25.3

Government Art Collection

Grantley Hall, near Ripon, 1952, oil on canvas, 51 × 76.5

Lancashire Fair, Good Friday, Daisy Nook, 1946, oil on canvas, 72 × 92

The Procession passing the Queen Victoria Memorial, Coronation, 1953, oil on canvas, 50 × 63

Imperial War Museum

Going to Work, 1943, oil on canvas, 45.8 × 61

National Maritime Museum

Greenwich Reach towards Deptford Power Station, 1959, oil on canvas, 51 × 76

Royal Academy of Arts

Station Approach, 1962, oil on canvas, 40.7 × 50.9

Woman with a Shopping Bag, 1959, oil on board, 40 × 12.1

Science Museum

A Manufacturing Town, 1922, oil on panel, 64.5 × 74.5

Tate Britain

A Young Man, 1955, oil on canvas, 51 × 60.5

Coming Out of School, 1927, oil on plywood, 34.7 × 53.9

Dwellings, Ordsall Lane, Salford, 1927, oil on plywood, 43.2 × 53.3

Hillside in Wales, 1962, oil on canvas, 76.2 × 101.6

Industrial Landscape, 1955, oil on canvas, 114.3 × 152.4

The Old House, Grove Street, Salford, 1948, oil on canvas, 45.7 × 61 cm

The Pond, 1950, oil on canvas, 114.3x × 152.4

MANCHESTER

Manchester Art Gallery

An Accident, 1926, oil on panel, 36.3 × 61

An Island, 1942, oil on canvas, 45.6 × 60.9

An Organ Grinder, 1934, oil on canvas, 53.3 × 39.4

Coming Home from the Mill, 1928, oil on panel, 43 × 53.3

Industrial Landscape, 1955, gouache and watercolour on paper, 26.8 × 37.9

Laying a Foundation Stone, 1936, oil on canvas, 45.7 × 61

Piccadilly Gardens, 1954, oil on canvas, 76.2 × 101.6

St Augustine's Church, Manchester, 1945, oil on canvas, 46 × 61.3

St John's Church, Manchester, 1938, oil on board, 31 × 30.3

Street in Pendlebury, 1948, oil on canvas, 61 × 46

Waiting for the Shop to Open, 1943, oil on canvas, 43.3 × 53.3

The Whitworth Art Gallery

A Couple Crossing the Road, 1953, oil on canvas, 42.4 × 52.6

Ancoats Hospital Outpatients' Hall, 1952, oil on canvas, 59.3 × 90

Industrial Scene, 1965, oil on canvas, 56 × 86.3

In a Park, 1963, oil on canvas, 76.5 × 101.9

Lake Landscape, 1950, oil on canvas, 71 × 91.5

MIDDLESBROUGH

Middlesbrough Institute of Modern Art

The Old Town Hall and St Hilda's Church, Middlesbrough, 1959, oil on canvas, 41 × 31

NEWCASTLE-UPON-TYNE

The Laing Art Gallery

Old Chapel, Newcastle-upon-Tyne, 1965, oil on canvas, 60.8 × 45.7

River Scene or Industrial Scene, 1935, oil on plywood, 37.5 × 51.4

NEWPORT, Gwent

Newport Museum and Art Gallery, South Wales

Francis Street, Salford, 1957, oil on canvas, 40 × 50.5

NORWICH

Norwich Castle Museum and Art Gallery

Landscape with Farm Buildings, 1954, oil on canvas board, 40.4 × 50.2

NOTTINGHAM

Nottingham Castle Museum and Art Gallery

The Arrest, 1927, oil on canvas, 53.3 × 43.2

Industrial Panorama, 1953, oil on canvas, 58.4 × 81.3

OLDHAM

Gallery, Oldham

The Procession, 1927, oil on canvas, 39.5 × 59

PRESTON

Harris Museum and Art Gallery

Millworkers, 1948, oil on canvas, 50.8 × 41.2

ROCHDALE

Touchstones Rochdale Art Gallery

Our Town, 1943, oil on canvas, 43 × 62

RUGBY

Rugby Art Gallery and Museum

Monday Morning, 1946, oil on panel, 50.8 × 26.7

SALFORD

The Lowry

Still Life, *c.*1906, oil on canvas, 23.5 × 33.5

Arden's Farm, Swinton, *c.*1909, oil on board/panel, 17.5 × 25.5

Clifton Junction – Morning, 1910, oil on board/panel, 20.2 × 34.8

Clifton Junction – Evening, 1910, oil on board/panel, 19 × 35.5

Portrait of the Artist's Father, 1910, oil on canvas, 41 × 31

Portrait of the Artist's Mother, 1912, oil on canvas, 46.1 × 35.9

Portrait of a Boy, *c.*1913–1914, oil on board/panel, 37.3 × 26.4

Head of a Bald Man, *c.*1913–1914, oil on panel/board, 37.3 × 26.4

The Lake, 1937, oil on canvas, 43.4 × 53.5

House on the Moor, 1950, oil on canvas, 49 × 59.5

Country Lane, 1914, oil on board/panel, 23.6 × 15.6

Frank Jopling Fletcher, 1919, oil on canvas, 48.7 × 38.7

A Doctor's Waiting Room, *c.*1920, oil on board/panel, 27.3 × 40.9

Woman in a Chair, 1921 and 1956, oil on board/panel, 41.8 × 34

Regent Street, Lytham, 1922, oil on board/panel, 25.6 × 35.6

Swinton Moss, 1922, oil on board/panel, 14 × 19.5

Self Portrait, 1925, oil on board/panel, 57.2 × 47.2

Peel Park, Salford, 1927, oil on board/panel, 35.5 × 50.5

Bandstand, Peel Park, 1928, oil on board/panel, 29.2 × 39.2

Coming from the Mill, 1930, oil on canvas, 42 × 52

A Landmark, 1936, oil on canvas, 43.4 × 53.6

Head of a Man, 1938, oil on canvas, 50.7 × 41

Market Scene, Northern Town, 1939, oil on canvas, 45.7 × 61.1

The Bedroom, Pendlebury, 1940, oil on canvas, 35.8 × 51.2

Blitzed Site, 1942, oil on canvas, 23.5 × 33.4

An Old Farm, 1943, oil on board/panel, 28.5 × 37.9

Level Crossing, 1946, oil on canvas, 46.1 × 56.1

The Cripples, 1949, oil on canvas, 76 × 101.5

The Lake, 1951, oil on board/panel, 19.1 × 47.3

Landscape in Cumberland, 1951, oil on board/panel, 15.9 × 58.7

The Funeral Party, 1953, oil on canvas, 76.1 × 102

Seascape, 1952, oil on canvas, 39.5 × 49.3

Portrait of Ann, 1957, oil on board/panel, 35.5 × 30.5

Man Lying on a Wall, 1957, oil on canvas, 40.7 × 50.9

Gentleman Looking at Something, 1960, oil on board/panel, 24.5 × 10

St Mary's Church, Swinton, 1960, oil on canvas, 22 × 14.5

Head of a Boy, *c.*1960, oil on board/panel, 21.5 × 21

Two People, 1962, oil on board/panel, 29.5 × 24.5

The Sea, 1963, oil on canvas, 76.6 × 102.3

Mill Scene, 1965, oil on canvas, 49.5 × 59.5

Bargoed, 1965, oil on canvas, 122.2 × 151.7

Tanker, *c.*1965, oil on board/panel, 25.3 × 35.5

A Beggar, *c.*1965, oil on board/panel, 19 × 11.5

A Ship, *c.*1965, oil on board/panel, 11.50 × 19

People with Dogs, *c.*1965, oil on board/panel, 18 × 13

Group of People, 1959, 19 August, watercolour on paper, 35.6 × 25.5

Going to Work, 1959, watercolour on paper, 27 × 38.5

Landscape with House, 1952, watercolour on paper, 23 × 34

The Estuary, 1956–9, watercolour on paper, 24 × 34.2

Yachts, 1959, watercolour on paper, 26 × 36.2

Four Figures, *c.*1965, oil on board/panel, 19 × 15.2

Teenagers, *c.*1965, oil on board/panel, 25.5 × 21.5

Woman with a Handbag, *c.*1969, oil on board/panel, 16.7 × 11.9

Waiting for the Tide, South Shields, 1967, oil on canvas, 15.1 × 30.5

A Street Scene (St Simon's Church), 1928, oil on board/panel, 43.8 × 38

A Fight, *c.*1935, oil on canvas, 53.2 × 39.5

Discord, 1943, oil on board/panel, 42.5 × 52.5

Industrial Landscape, 1953, oil on canvas, 45 × 60

Pit Tragedy (recto); *Head* (verso), 1919, oil on canvas, 39 × 49

Portrait of a House, 1953, oil on canvas, 43.5 × 60

Flowers in a Window, 1956, oil on canvas, 50.8 × 61

Landscape, *c.*1912, oil on canvas, 33.5 × 23.5

Street in Cwm, South Wales, 1960, oil on canvas, 46 × 25.5

Fishing Boats at Lytham, 1915, pastel and pencil on paper, 40.7 × 49.5

Lancashire Street, 1951, oil on board/panel, 22.2 × 27.9

Beach Scene, Lancashire, 1945, oil on canvas, 45.8 × 61

Family Group, 1940, oil on board/panel, 33 × 38.2

Two Men on a Park Bench, 1964, oil on canvas, 40.7 × 50.8

Children Playing, 1959, oil on wood panel, 12.5 × 17

Going to Work, 1967, oil on canvas, 30.5 × 25.4

Three Children, (undated), oil on board, 17.8 × 12.7

People Talking, 1930, oil on canvas, 43.8 × 54

The Waterloo Dock, Liverpool, 1962, oil on canvas, 58.4 × 81.3

A Court, Manchester, 1964, oil on canvas, 40.6 × 30.5

Girl with Red Scarf and Trousers, 1967, oil on canvas, 25.4 × 20.3

Group of People, 1959, oil on board/panel/wood panel, 16.5 × 15.2

Girl Walking, *c.*1965, oil on board/panel/wood panel, 19.7 × 6.5

Gentleman Looking at Something, 1963, oil on canvas, 24 × 20

Figures with a Cat, 1967, oil on board, 35.5 × 25.4

A Group of Figures, (undated), oil on board/canvas, 35.5 × 25.4

A Church, 1966, oil on wood panel, 35.5 × 26

Lancashire Lane, 1946, oil on canvas, 26 × 36.2

People Talking, (undated), oil on board/panel and wood panel, 16.5 × 14.5

Ebbw Vale Steel Works, 1962, oil on canvas, 50.8 × 61

Bargoed, 1964, oil on woodboard, 121.5 × 153.5

Bolton, 1960, oil on canvas, 22 × 30

Salford Street Scene, 1928, oil on board/panel, 41.9 × 30.5

The Clown, 1961, oil on woodboard, 45.7 × 35.6

Man Looking Through a Hole in the Fence, (undated), oil on canvas, 45.7 × 35.6

Sudden Illness, 1920, oil on board/panel/woodboard, 9.34 × 17.5

Woman with a Beard, 1957, oil on canvas, 59 × 49

Girl with a Red Hat on a Promenade, 1966, oil on board/panel, 45.5 × 61

Two Dogs, 1960, oil on woodboard, 25.5 × 20.3

Tennis Player, 1927, oil on board/panel/woodboard, 24.2 × 12.1

Northern Hospital, 1926, oil on board/panel/woodboard, 43.2 × 53.2

Portrait of Ann, 1959, oil on board/panel, 53 × 43

Mannequin with Figure Behind, 1960s, oil on board/panel, 47 × 32.2

Mannequin Fragments, (undated), oil on panel

Mannequin Fragments, (undated), oil on panel

Mannequin and Block, 1973, oil on board, 47 × 32

Portrait of Girl, (undated), oil on board

Head of a Girl Wearing a Cloche Hat, 1923, oil on board

Portrait of a Young Girl, 1954, oil on board

Ann in a Blue Jumper, (undated), oil on board

Woman on Hands and Knees, 1960, oil on board/panel, 15 × 15

Lady Explaining, 1935–1965, oil on board/panel, 33 × 23.2

Portrait of Ann, 1956, oil on board, 15 × 13

Portrait of Ann, 1959, oil on board/panel, 17 × 14.5

Portrait of Ann, 1957, oil on board/panel, 35.5 × 30.5

Works on loan to The Lowry from the Lowry Estate

Portrait of Ann, 1957, oil on canvas

Portrait of Ann in Red Jumper, (undated), oil on canvas, 34.5 × 24

Portrait of Ann (with Plait and Black Jumper), 1954, oil on board/panel, 36 × 25.5

Ann, (undated), oil on board/panel, 47.5 × 34.25

Portrait of Girl with Short White Socks, 1960, oil on board/panel, 32.5 × 28.75

Two Heads, (undated), oil on board/panel, 29 × 28.5

Girl Seen from the Front, (undated), oil on canvas, 78 × 68

Untitled (Houses and Fencing) (recto); *Untitled (Factories)* (verso), (undated), pastel on paper, 26 × 35.7

Girl Seen from the Back, 1964, oil on canvas, 77.5 × 68

Portrait of Ann, 1957, oil on canvas

Girl in Cloche Hat, 1927, oil on board/panel, 53.25 × 43.5

Portrait of Ann in Red Jumper, (undated), oil on canvas, 34.5 × 24

Head of a Boy, 1962, oil on canvas, 67 × 57.75

Portrait of Ann (with Plait and Black Jumper), 1954, oil on board/panel, 36 × 26.5

Portrait of a Man, (undated), oil on board/panel, 47.5 × 37.5

Mill Scene, 1971, oil, 50.5 × 39

Grey Sea, 1970, oil on board/panel, 35.5 × 50

Landscape – Lytham St Anne's, (undated), oil on canvas, 27.5 × 32

Man with Bowler Hat, (undated), oil on canvas, 52.25 × 31

Lady with Red Hat, 1960, oil on board panel, 29.25 × 17.5

The Haunt, 1969, oil on board/panel, 32 × 29

Man with Trilby Hat, (undated), oil on board/panel, 31.25 × 19.25

Portrait of a Wren, (undated), oil on canvas, 46.5 × 39

Ann, (undated), oil on panel/board, 47.5 × 34.25

Portrait of Male Model, 1908?, oil on canvas, 44.25 × 34.25

Portrait of Girl with Short White Socks, 1960, oil on board/panel, 32.5 × 28.75

The Spire, 1960, oil on board/panel, 88 × 67.5

Group of Figures, (undated), oil on board/panel, 39.25 × 34

Man in a Trilby, 1960, oil on board/panel, 74.75 × 64.75

SHEFFIELD

The Graves Art Gallery

Meeting Point, 1965, oil on canvas, 30 × 20

Street Scene (recto); *Portrait of a Firewatcher* (verso), 1925, oil on panel, 40.7 × 50.1

SOUTHAMPTON

Southampton City Art Gallery

The Canal Bridge, 1949, oil on canvas, 71 × 91.2

The Floating Bridge, Southampton, 1956, oil on canvas, 50.8 × 76.3

SOUTHPORT

The Atkinson Art Gallery

Street Scene, 1935, oil on canvas, 43 × 53

STOCKPORT

Stockport Art Gallery

A Street in Stockport: Crowther Street, 1930, oil on board, 51.5 × 41.3

STOKE-ON-TRENT

The Potteries Museum and Art Gallery

Empty House, 1934, oil on plywood, 43.2 × 51.3

SUNDERLAND

Sunderland Museum and Winter Gardens

Dockside, Sunderland, 1962, oil on canvas, 56 × 76

The Sea at Sunderland, 1965, oil on canvas, 21 × 26.5

River Wear at Sunderland, 1961, oil on board, 51 × 60

SWINDON

Swindon Museum and Art Gallery

Winter in Pendlebury, 1943, oil on panel, 44 × 24

WAKEFIELD

Wakefield Art Gallery

The Toll Booth, Glasgow, 1947, oil on paper, 55 × 45.5

YORK

York Museums Trust (York Art Gallery)

Clifford's Tower, York, 1953, oil on canvas, 35.6 × 50.8

The Bandstand, Peel Park, Salford, 1931, oil on canvas, 43.2 × 62.2

AUSTRALIA

PERTH

Art Gallery of Western Australia

The Rival Candidates, 1942, oil on canvas, 45.8 × 61.0

NEW ZEALAND

CHRISTCHURCH

Christchurch Art Gallery

Factory at Widnes, 1956, oil on canvas, 61 × 50.5

USA

NEW YORK

Museum of Modern Art

Ships Near Cumberland Coast, 1963, oil on board, 30.1 × 48.7

MILWAUKEE

Milwaukee Art Museum

Landscape, 1943, oil on canvas, 30 × 60

INDEX

Figures in *italic* refer to picture captions.